OneStream Financial Close Handbook

Ryan Connors, Kelly Darren,
Jessica McAlpine, Michael Malandra,
Michael Queeney

Published in 2022 by OneStream Press.

ISBN: 978-1-8382528-4-7

 OneStream Press is an imprint of Play Technologies (England) Limited. 6 Woodside, Churnet View Road, Oakamoor, ST10 3AE, United Kingdom.

www.OneStreamPress.com

Disclaimer

While the advice and information in this book is believed to be true and accurate at the date of publication, OneStream Press, the author, and OneStream Software LLC do not guarantee the accuracy, adequacy, or completeness of any information, and are not responsible for any errors or omissions or the results obtained from the use of such information.

OneStream Press, the author, and OneStream Software LLC make no warranty, express or implied, with respect to the material contained herein, and hereby disclaim any liability to any party for any loss, damage, or disruption caused by errors or omissions, whether such errors or omissions result from negligence, accident, or any other cause.

Note: Any Files provided for Exercises in this OneStream Press Book are for the use of Customers and Partners in an On-Premise environment and are not supported by the OneStream Support Team.

About the Authors

Ryan Connors is a Senior Delivery Manager on the OneStream Partner Enablement team. He joined OneStream in 2018 and has 10 years of experience with CPM technology. Ryan currently resides in Hingham, Massachusetts, with his wife Alyson and son Cooper.

To my father, Jimmy. Thank you for always supporting me. Your memory will live on forever.

Kelly Darren is the Global Domain Director for the Financial Close process at OneStream Software. She is a CPA and CSSBB and has worked in industry within Shared Service departments, responsible for improving close processes within organizations. Specializing in this area, she moved into accounting software, working for BlackLine Systems. She subsequently worked for a consulting firm implementing SAP BPC, focusing on consolidation, before joining OneStream in 2018.

I would like to thank OneStream for allowing me to be an integral contributor in this space and to my husband, Michael Darren, who has always been my rock and encouragement to go beyond my dreams.

Jessica McAlpine is a CPA and the Group Product Director for Financial Close and Consolidations at OneStream Software. In her role, she leads the product strategy for the close and consolidations domain. Prior to joining OneStream in 2019, she spent seven years as an Administrator for an early adoption customer, and was a member of the team that implemented consolidations, planning, and tax provision. Jessica has also worked in external and internal audit.

I'd like to thank my boys, Brian, my husband, and Grayson and Cooper, my kiddos, for all your love and support. And my mom, Lynn, and sister, Amy, for showing me that we women can do anything we put our minds to.

Michael Malandra was employee #56 at OneStream and has over 20 years of experience in Financial Consolidations and Reporting, Account Reconciliations, Variance Analysis, Planning and Forecasting, and Cost Benefit Analysis. In 2015, when joining OneStream, he became one of four OneStream architects in the Services organization. He then joined Direct Analytics in 2020, where he has continued architecting multiple OneStream applications.

Thanking everyone who has impacted my journey would become a book unto itself, so I will start with the most important person, my lovely and wonderful wife, Margaux. I cannot thank you enough for all the support you have shown me over the years, from leaving your highly successful career in New York City and following me to Arizona, back to New Jersey, and finally to Pittsburgh. To my three beautiful children: Makayla, Michael, and Matthew; to my partner in crime, Mike Queeney; to all my OneStream colleagues (you know who you are); and finally (in no particular order) – Lauren K, Todd A, Peter F, Steve M, Terry S, Eric D, Jerri M, Jon G, Eric O, Chul S, Debra O, Dawn W, Christine K, Jenn S, and of course Tom and Bob – Thank You!

Mike Queeney is a Managing Partner at Direct Analytics and has been a partner with OneStream since their founding. Mike has worked in CPM for over 20 years, implementing integrations, models and solutions for his clients. After moving on from the Oracle/Hyperion suite, Mike has fully committed to the OneStream model of CPM and works diligently to give clients the best-in-class service that accompanies OneStream software.

It has been a long career in this business, so it would be hard to mention everyone, but I would like to thank Hemsha, Greg, Nan, Terry, Lauren, and my partner in Onestream, Mike Malandra, for listening to me rant while getting this project completed. It has been a fantastic experience. I am humbled to have been able to work with so many talented people in my career and during the writing of this book.

Technical Reviewers

Jason Ruge has been a leader in the software industry for over 25 years, focusing on delivering product excellence in his roles within Software Quality Assurance. His acute attention to technical details and passion for quality has led him to be involved as Technical Editor on multiple publications across several industries, most recently being OneStream Financial Close. He is one of the original members of the OneStream MarketPlace Engineering team, leading and guiding the organization through scale and delivery for all OneStream Solutions. He leans heavily on his faith to lead with deep compassion, honesty, and integrity to be a role model and mentor to his peers and extended teams.

This professional dedication goes to the following: Mike Phipps – your partnership and willingness to figure things out together as we got rolling in MarketPlace Engineering has been such a great experience. We helped each other along the way and, without even realizing it, helped shape the foundation of excellence we have all come to expect from the MarketPlace Engineering organization. Adam Romatz – your superior technical knowledge matched with your humble leadership style has put you in rare air in my career. Your desire to care about the 1 Pixel changes with me and yet also help lead the technical revolution within MarketPlace Engineering will have a very broad-reaching impact for many years to come. Jessica McAlpine – sharing this OneStream journey with you has been a highlight of my entire career. I am so proud of your growth and accomplishments and look forward to seeing you continue to flourish in your OneStream career. Your trust and collaboration have been very special to me, and I wouldn't trade them for anything. Shawn Stalker – when we first met in March 2018, you laid out a vision for the OneStream MarketPlace that convinced me to join OneStream. Thank you for your trust and partnership to help accomplish everything we have so far, and I am sure the best is yet to come.

Shawn Stalker joined OneStream in 2013 and serves as the Vice President of MarketPlace Development. Shawn has worked in the Corporate Performance Management (CPM) area for over 20 years, maintaining, implementing, and supporting consolidation and financial systems. He has worked on products including Oracle Hyperion Enterprise, Oracle Hyperion Essbase, Oracle Hyperion Financial Management and OutlookSoft before joining UpStream Software in 2006, where he helped to build their development and QA teams. He worked at UpStream through acquisitions by Hyperion and then Oracle prior to joining OneStream, where he helped start the QA and MarketPlace teams.

For my Wife… Always.

Errata

Despite best efforts, mistakes can sometimes creep into books. If you spot a mistake, please feel free to email us at **errata@OneStreamPress.com** (with the book title in the subject line).

The errata page for this book is hosted at **www.OneStreamPress.com/FinancialClose**

Table of Contents

Chapter 3: Implementing Account Reconciliations 79

Chapter 4: Using Account Reconciliations 113

Chapter 5: Transaction Matching Overview 183

Chapter 6: Transaction Matching Administration 187

1

Account Reconciliations Overview

Account Reconciliations are a key step to the financial close process. At its most basic, an Account Reconciliation can be defined as:

The ability to substantiate an account balance using independent means to validate the accuracy of transaction inflows and outflows to ensure that the ending balance is what it should be.

Reconciliations have been a part of business from the beginning of time. Validating balances and transactions is part of daily operations. For example, if you sell a glass of lemonade for $1, it is easy to ensure that you receive the $1 at the time of the transaction. However, if the lemonade stand is open and happens to be set up on a running path with hundreds of runners stopping for lemonade, now the flow of transactions becomes very rapid. The exchange of product for money is happening at a pace that is very difficult to keep track of. What does the lemonade stand owner do at the end of the day? They reconcile the cash in the till to the glasses of lemonade sold, to ensure that all the cash was received, aka an Account Reconciliation.

Expand that example to today's world with global organizations that employ thousands of employees, transacting in many currencies, purchasing significant materials, selling a multitude of products, and it starts to become complicated and difficult to manage. How do we ensure the financial balances are complete and accurate? How do we make sure errors are not being made that have a material financial impact? How do we fend off theft or fraud? One way that organizations mitigate these potential issues is by performing Account Reconciliations.

Reconciliation Process

When performing Reconciliations, it is typically part of the organization's month-end close process and is performed within the General Accounting and Shared Service departments. As mentioned, companies may choose to perform Reconciliations to mitigate risk, but they may also prepare Reconciliations to facilitate audit requests, statutory obligations, or the more prevalent requirement of Sarbanes-Oxley. The Reconciliation process is defined into three key areas:

1. Preparation
2. Review and sign-off
3. Monitoring

Preparation

Preparing the Reconciliation is the process of analyzing the ending General Ledger balance at a point in time. Account Reconciliations are performed typically on Balance Sheet Accounts but can be done on any Account that is significant to the organization. The Reconciliation preparation for most organizations is a very manual process of gathering information, setting up workpapers, and then performing the analysis. Unfortunately, although the most important step is the analysis, Preparers spend significant time on the former.

The different types of Reconciliations that a User will prepare are broken down into the following categories:

- Cash – Bank, Investments, etc.
- Customer-Related – Account Receivables, Deferred Revenue, etc.

- Vendor-Related – Accounts Payables, Accruals, etc.
- Business Operations – Inventory, Fixed Assets, Intercompany, etc.

How the User analyzes the Account depends on the types of transactions flowing through it. Customer receivables are confirmed through analysis of the subledger, while Cash Accounts are mainly substantiated utilizing bank information. Reserve Accounts, meanwhile, are validated through calculation. Whatever the method, a good Reconciliation will include the General Ledger balance, detailed explanations, and all the analysis and support needed to substantiate the balance to within a threshold set by the organization's accounting policies.

Review and Approve

Once a Reconciliation is prepared, the User must sign-off on the workpapers. In addition, every Reconciliation typically requires a review and approval process to validate the Preparer's work. Depending on the importance of the Account, it may require multiple Approvers to reduce risk. For all roles, the sign-off process is the User attesting that they performed their responsibilities regarding the Reconciliation process in accordance with the organization's policies.

Monitoring

Monitoring is the overarching control process to ensure that everything is being done as expected. This process helps to inform management of any identified issues or risks.

Monitoring includes:

- Ensuring all Reconciliations have been completed within the due date set.
- Sign-offs have been completed by the required roles.
- Newly-created General Ledger Accounts have been included in the Reconciliation process and properly assigned to End-Users to complete and review.
- Adjustments identified in the process have been escalated or corrected.

Manual Reconciliation Process

The process, as defined above, is typically manual in most organizations. Reconciliations are prepared in Excel in varying file formats, and the files are saved to shared folders or printed – depending on the requirements – with an overall Administrator tracking the process to ensure all the work has been done. Although the manual process has worked for many years, as companies grow and become more global with multiple financial systems, it is very difficult to ensure the accuracy, completeness, and validity of the work performed.

The typical issues we see prevalent in a manual process today are:

- Ensuring the General Ledger balances are accurate and up-to-date.
- All required Reconciliations for a specific period have been prepared.
- Any past due Reconciliations are identified.
- New Accounts are properly included in the process.
- Reconciliation explanations fully validate the General Ledger balances within the threshold set.
- Proper support has been attached.
- Identified open items that need correction are highlighted.
- Open items are properly aged.

In addition, a manual process is tedious from an approval perspective. Gathering Reconciliation approvals manually can be done in many ways. In some organizations, the Preparer would print the Reconciliation and walk it around for physical signatures. Others would leverage emails to document approvals. We have also seen Users copying a signature image into the Excel file, which requires someone opening the file to ensure sign-off. All of these methods are very time-consuming and prone to error.

Automating with OneStream

Moving your process to OneStream, and using the Financial Close solution, not only eliminates the concerns identified above, but also results in a more streamlined, automated solution, delivering the four key pillars of a good Reconciliation process:

1. Visibility
2. Standardization
3. Efficiency
4. Control

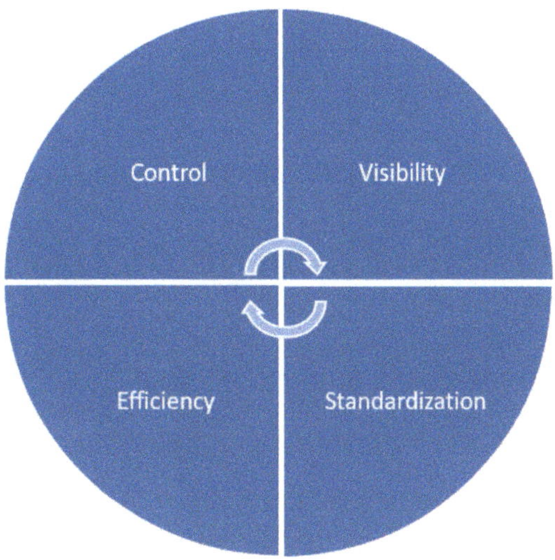

Figure 1.1

The following sub-sections highlight a few of the items that the solution delivers, relating to each of the key pillars.

Visibility

- Global repository for all Reconciliations and related support.
- Delivered Dashboards and scorecards to monitor the organization's process for complete governance.
- Detail item classification; aging and reporting to escalate potential issues and risk.
- The ability to drill down from the consolidated financial statement balance to the underlying Reconciliations, to better understand the financial statement line item.

Standardization

- A Reconciliation template library with the ability to associate specific templates to specific Accounts to ensure standardization across the organization.
- The User Interface is consistent – regardless of the Reconciliation – for ease of preparation, review, and audit.

- The ability to assign risk, due dates, and frequencies to ensure Reconciliations are performed consistently.
- Item Type classifications are used to categorize open items across the organization.
- Rejection Reason Codes are employed to help identify why Reconciliations are sent back to the User.

Efficiency

- Leverages the trial balance loaded for Actuals to populate the two key processes – Consolidations and Reconciliations – ensuring that they are both in sync.
- Automatically creates the Reconciliation for the User, and populates it into the proper period based on the frequency set.
- Electronic Workflow routes the Reconciliation to the appropriate Users based on the number of required approvals, with email alerts if desired.
- An Auto Reconciliation process that systematically prepare or fully approve Reconciliations that meet specific rules, thus eliminating manual intervention.
- Identifies and creates Reconciliations for new Accounts created in the underlying General Ledger.

Control

- Balances are automatically updated with new trial balance loads, ensuring the Reconciliation is up-to-date.
- The segregation of duties is enforced, preventing Users from preparing and approving their own work.
- Thresholds are set to ensure Reconciliations are not prepared if not fully explained to within the threshold set.
- Reports are available to monitor the process and confirm Reconciliations are done within the due date set.
- Corrections are identified and aggregated to determine if there are any material corrections that need to be addressed.

Next Level of Excellence

Utilizing OneStream's Account Reconciliation Solution elevates the overall process. However, the OneStream application offers *additional* value that many may not be aware of, including:

1. Single Solution
2. Data Integration
3. Financial Intelligence
4. Reporting

We will discuss each of these areas at a high level, but more detail on each topic can be obtained in the OneStream Foundation Handbook.

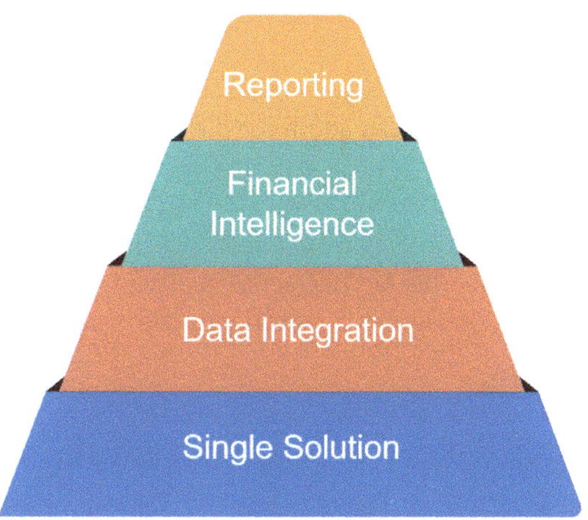

Figure 1.2

Single Solution

One of the difficult issues facing financial processes today is the many systems that are involved. Data is consistently moving around organizations and being replicated in multiple tools to support different processes. The trial balance alone is used to satisfy consolidations, financial and management reporting, Reconciliations, forecasting, budgeting, and tax provision calculations, to name but a few! If each of these processes is in separate software, imagine the time it takes to load the data, validate that it matches the source, and ensure it is kept up to date when changes are made. The time and effort are exhausting, not to mention the costs and risks associated with supporting disparate systems. Now, focusing on Reconciliations, how do we ensure that the balances used in the Reconciliation process are truly the balances used for financial reporting? Do I have to reconcile my Reconciliations? If using a point solution or Excel, the answer is YES! However, when utilizing OneStream, this multiple system loading and reconciling is resolved.

At the base of the pyramid in Figure 1.2 is the single solution. Having a single solution to maintain and control all your critical processes is, by far, one of the most beneficial aspects of the OneStream application. The system leverages the single trial balance load to populate all the processes identified above. Not only does this mean we are all utilizing the same data, but as the underlying data changes, all processes properly reflect the updated information and are kept in sync.

In addition, a single solution reduces our technical footprint. Instead of maintaining multiple solutions, which Users need to access and be trained on, there will be a single solution for maintenance.

Data Integration

Gathering data is an important step in the process. Reconciliations not only require General Ledger balances, but you may also need journal entries, subledgers, third-party reports, bank transactions, and more to perform your work. Collecting the data can be time-consuming, difficult to extract, and require manual manipulation, depending on the data format.

For OneStream, data integration is a foundational process and a core competency of the Platform. Being able to bring in data from any source system, either through flat files or direct connects, and enriching the data using Transformation Rules, significantly reduces the amount of work for the User. Eliminating manual manipulation will also ensure the data is processed consistently each time it is received, and reduces errors. In addition, OneStream does not require a specific file format, so you do not need to change the layout of your file extracts.

Data integration also supports bringing in data at varying levels. Instead of just bringing in subledger or third-party balances, the system can bring in the detail and aggregate the information, allowing you to view a balance with drill down capabilities. Also, if using direct connect to bring in the data, you can set up drill back to the source to query information as needed.

Financial Intelligence

Financial intelligence is the ability to aggregate, calculate, translate, and create logic in the process. Inherent in the application, the Account Reconciliation solution can leverage the existing financial intelligence of OneStream to enhance a User's Reconciliation experience. They can use the dimensionality of the application to create more detailed Reconciliations or the hierarchies to report Reconciliation performance at varying levels. Business logic can also be created to write Completion Rules or Certification Rules beyond what is already delivered. Financial intelligence does not exist in other point solutions and is a significant differentiator when utilizing OneStream.

Reporting

Reporting is important to managing the process. As you will see later in this book, the Account Reconciliation solution delivers standard Dashboards and Reports. However, each organization typically has different metrics they use to monitor the process. Unlike other solutions that result in Users extracting the data to other software to produce the needed reporting, OneStream has robust reporting capabilities *within* the application, meaning you can create any Report needed.

The reporting capabilities within OneStream also allow Users to create and surface any information from the system. We can combine data from different processes like Consolidation, Reconciliations, and Forecasting, to present better reporting and analysis. If the data is in the system, you will be able to report on it.

Also, Reports built within OneStream can be exported, printed, or emailed. The system also allows for scheduled reporting, which will automatically email or save Reports on a scheduled basis using the **Parcel Service** capabilities.

Let's Go

Now, let's begin our detailed discussion of the Account Reconciliation solution. In the next three chapters, we will: 1. Walk through the administration process and how to set up the solution, 2. Share implementation best practices, and 3. Finish with the User's experience. It is an exciting journey you are embarking on, and we know you will soon see the many benefits of using OneStream for your Account Reconciliation process!

2

Account Reconciliations Administration

The administration of Account Reconciliations first requires you – as an Implementor or Administrator – to understand the components of the solution. Once you have read this chapter, you should be able to properly identify which parts of the solution will need to be configured to meet your business needs. It is important that you read this chapter in its entirety prior to implementing the solution. After you have implemented the solution, this chapter will help you understand how to maintain your solution going forward.

Solution administration first starts with the initial solution settings. From there, we will move to Security, the Administration page, and finally the Audit page.

Settings

The Settings page is the first step you will take in establishing your Account Reconciliation application. Within this page, you will create the initial configuration for the entire application. As this page is used to set up your application, only OneStream Administrators or Account Reconciliation Global Administrators (also referred to as Reconciliation Administrators) may access this page. This security access is configured in Global Options, discussed in this section.

There are six different sections within settings, including:

- Global Setup
- Control Lists
- Templates
- Access Control
- Certifications
- Uninstall

Global Setup

These settings are applied across the entire solution and include options related to our Account Reconciliation environment, User Interface, and the defaults for your Reconciliation attributes.

Global Options

Security Role (Manage Reconciliation Setup)

Anyone assigned to this OneStream User Group is considered an Account Reconciliation Super-User and is also referred to as an Account Reconciliations Global Administrator, meaning they have access to all aspects of the Account Reconciliation application.

Once a group is assigned, initially by a OneStream Administrator, anyone within the group will have the ability to configure all aspects of Account Reconciliations as well as the ability to prepare, approve, comment, or view any Reconciliation.

The only role that supersedes the Reconciliation Administrator is the OneStream System Administrator, and as such, any OneStream Administrator can perform all the actions within Account Reconciliations that a Reconciliation Administrator can perform. As this group's rights encompass all aspects of Account Reconciliations' configuration, the default group assigned upon install is Administrators.

To change the group assigned, select a system Security Group from the drop-down and then click Save at the bottom of the page. To create a group to be used, go to the System tab, select Security, and then Create Group. Note that this action requires membership in the ManageSystemSecurityGroups role. The steps for group creation and assignment apply to all security roles.

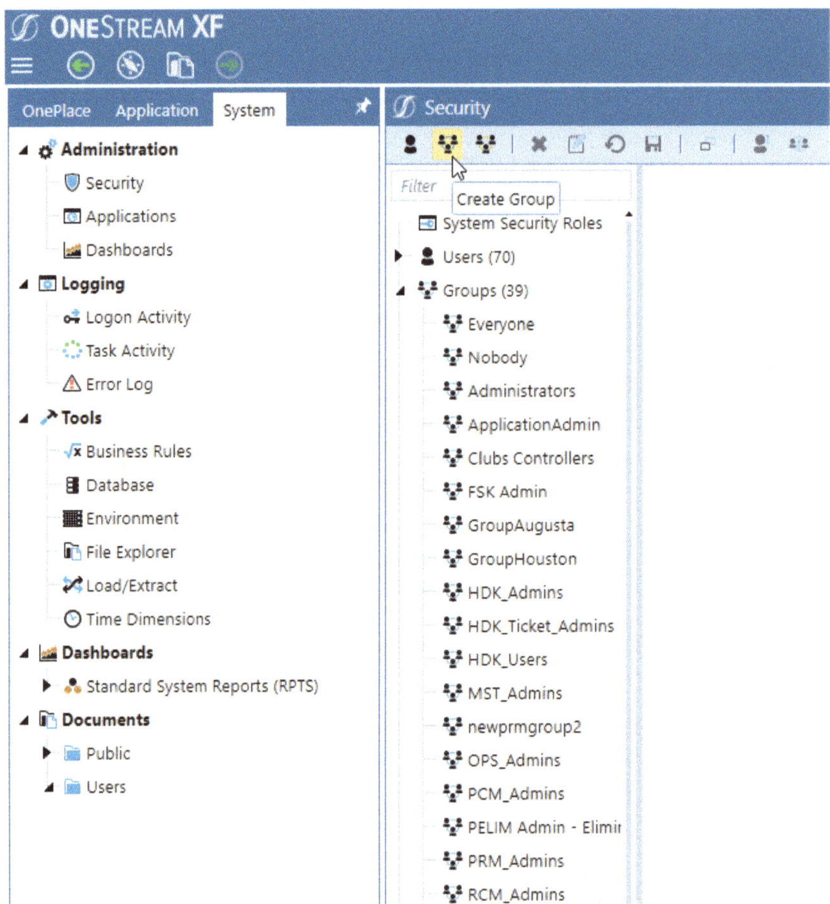

Figure 2.1

Security Role (Reconciliation View Only)

Members of this OneStream User Group can see all Reconciliations within the application, regardless of preparation state, but cannot make any changes to Reconciliations, including adding detail items, making comments, adding attachments, etc. Typically, customers use this role for either internal auditors or upper-level management.

Security Role (Auditor)

Members of this OneStream User Group can only see Reconciliations that are fully complete, meaning they have either been prepared and all levels of approval have been completed, or they have been fully Approved via AutoRec Rules. This role is used whenever you want your auditors to only see Reconciliations that are complete and thus ready for external review. For example, your company may keep Reconciliations In Process while balances are still changing. In such instances, the use of this role would be recommended.

All Reconciliations Require R-Doc

Reconciliation support that relates to the entire Reconciliation balance is referred to as **R-Doc**, where the R stands for Reconciliation. For example, a bank statement that ties to the subledger would be an R-Doc since it supports the balance in its entirety, and is a statement that is known to be readily available in concurrence with the Reconciliation process.

In instances where it is known that such support is available for all your Reconciliations, set this setting to True. However, note that there are other types of support that can also be provided for Reconciliations, such as **I-Docs**, which relate to each individual detail line item of support. As such, the use of this setting may not be advisable for many companies as – when enabled – all Reconciliations that are not completed via AutoRec will require an R-Doc to be attached. The implications of requiring supporting documentation to be added to each Reconciliation could be quite time-consuming, especially when you consider your low risk and low balance Accounts. Accordingly, really think about whether this setting is truly necessary before enabling this feature.

Enable Mass Actions

Within the **Reconciliation Grid** is the ability to select and perform an action on multiple Reconciliations by checking the box to the far left. This functionality is included for situations where customers have large volumes of Reconciliations and do not want to go through every single Reconciliation and then click a separate icon to perform an action on that Reconciliation.

Let's walk through an example of when mass actions would be useful.

Anna is an accountant responsible for all accrual accounts at her company. In order to get ahead of her close work, she begins providing supporting detail for her 50 subledger Accounts as soon as initial balances are available. By day two, Anna has all balances supported, and her unexplained amounts are within the thresholds. However, due to the complex nature of the accrual Accounts, last-minute entries and adjustments are frequent and balances may change, therefore requiring Anna to continue her work. At a certain point, balances are final, and Anna knows her Reconciliations are complete. Anna doesn't want to go into each Reconciliation and select the Prepare icon; rather, she would like to select all of her Reconciliations and press Prepare once. In this instance, enabling mass actions would be utilized.

The actions that may be taken are divided into two User types: Preparer and Approver. By default, enable mass actions for Preparer and Approver are set to False. By setting either Preparer or Approver to True, the User type set to True may set multiple Reconciliations to the same state type at once. For Preparers, the actions available are prepare or recall; for Approvers, the actions available are approve, unapprove, or reject.

Transaction Matching Integration

The Transaction Matching solution may be used to create detail item support for your Reconciliations. The process to set up mapping, detail item creation, etc., is discussed later in this book, but as an overview, support from Transaction Matching may either be pushed from a Match Set to the corresponding Reconciliations, or pulled into a Reconciliation from a Match Set. To bring about this integration, select Enable, and the page will then display Enabled (Upon Save). Once you have selected Save at the bottom, the integration will be enabled.

> **Note:** It is important to observe that once enabled, integration may not be reversed, so be sure you want to utilize this functionality before setting up this feature.

Process Reconciliations on Complete Workflow

Running Process updates the Reconciliation balances from the Actual Workflow for the given period. Setting this to True will initiate a process for Reconciliations within the Workflow before marking a Workflow as complete.

Upon running Process – which in this instance would be upon completing the Workflow – the system will check to see if any balances have been changed and, if they have, the status of the Reconciliations will change from Approved to Balance Changed, thus indicating that additional work needs to be performed and preventing the Workflow from being completed. This setting helps ensure that, at the time of Workflow completion, all balances that have been reconciled are accurate and tie to the reported financial statements.

Source Scenario

Account Reconciliation queries this Scenario's Stage or Import balances to populate period balances. Most often, customers will use their Actual Scenario as the source, as these are also the balances used to create the consolidated financial statements. While consolidated financials will look at the Target Accounts, or the Chart of Accounts maintained in the OneStream Account Dimension, Account Reconciliations pull in the Source Account balances. The **Source Accounts** are the trial balance or GL Chart of Accounts maintained in the ERP, which are then transformed into the OneStream Accounts upon validation of Actuals. The method by which OneStream derives the Inventory of Reconciliations is discussed further within the Definition section.

Reconciliation Scenario

When setting up this Scenario, ensure it is separate from your Source Scenario which, as recommended above, would be Actual. Within this book, we will be using an example Reconciliation Scenario called Actual AR. It is recommended that the Reconciliation Scenario mirror the Source Scenario but be assigned a different Type, such as Model, so that a different Workflow can be assigned to Account Reconciliations. In this way, locking the Actuals Workflow will not affect locking Account Reconciliations, and vice versa.

Figure 2.2 is an example setup of a Reconciliation Scenario.

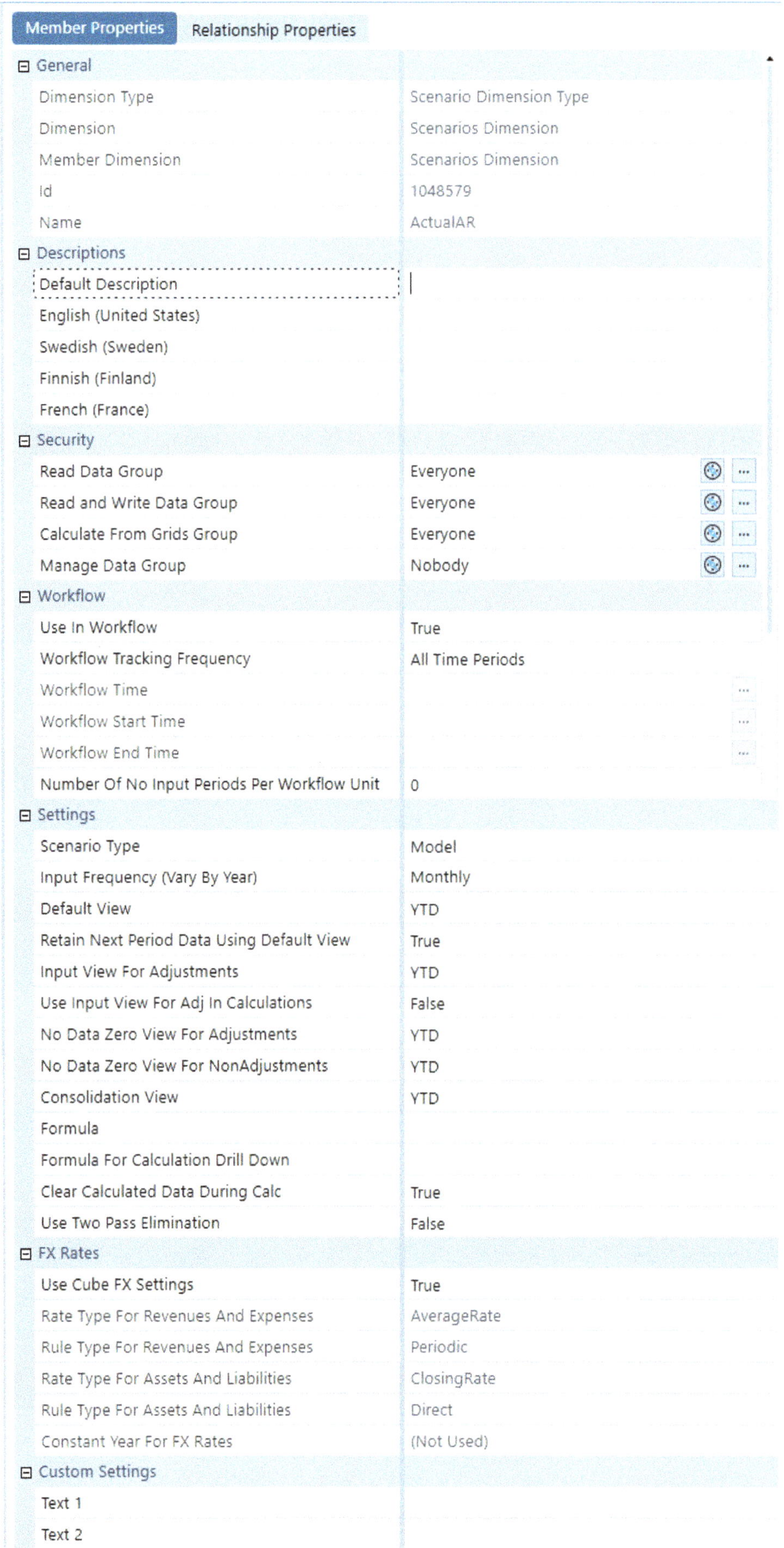
Member Properties
Relationship Properties
General
Dimension Type
Scenario Dimension Type
Dimension
Scenarios Dimension
Member Dimension
Scenarios Dimension
Id
1048579
Name
ActualAR
Descriptions
Default Description
English (United States)
Swedish (Sweden)
Finnish (Finland)
French (France)
Security
Read Data Group
Everyone
Read and Write Data Group
Everyone
Calculate From Grids Group
Everyone
Manage Data Group
Nobody
Workflow
Use In Workflow
True
Workflow Tracking Frequency
All Time Periods
Workflow Time
Workflow Start Time
Workflow End Time
Number Of No Input Periods Per Workflow Unit
0
Settings
Scenario Type
Model
Input Frequency (Vary By Year)
Monthly
Default View
YTD
Retain Next Period Data Using Default View
True
Input View For Adjustments
YTD
Use Input View For Adj In Calculations
False
No Data Zero View For Adjustments
YTD
No Data Zero View For NonAdjustments
YTD
Consolidation View
YTD
Formula
Formula For Calculation Drill Down
Clear Calculated Data During Calc
True
Use Two Pass Elimination
False
FX Rates
Use Cube FX Settings
True
Rate Type For Revenues And Expenses
AverageRate
Rule Type For Revenues And Expenses
Periodic
Rate Type For Assets And Liabilities
ClosingRate
Rule Type For Assets And Liabilities
Direct
Constant Year For FX Rates
(Not Used)
Custom Settings
Text 1
Text 2

Figure 2.2

Reconciliation Account Dimension

This is a drop-down filter that contains all Account Dimensions within the Application. To configure, select the Account Dimension that contains the Accounts to be reconciled. Throughout this book, we will be reconciling the `CorpAccounts` Dimension.

Reconciliation Account Member Filter

Enter an Account-based Member Filter used to query a list of accounts to reconcile. For example:

```
A#[Balance Sheet].Base, A#1000, A#2000.Base
```

If Extensible dimensionality is being used on the Accounts Dimension in this application, this Member Filter must be adjusted to query Accounts differently across each Cube. This is because an Account could be a Base Member in one Account Dimension and a Parent in another. Here is an example of this syntax:

```
A#[Balance Sheet].Base.Options(Cube=[GolfStream],
ScenarioType=Actual),A#[Balance Sheet].Base.Options(Cube=[Houston],
ScenarioType=Actual)
```

Auto Creation Reconciliation Definition

If set to True, when an Administrator clicks Discover on the Definition page within the Reconciliation Administration, a Reconciliation Definition is added for any Account in the **Account List** that does not yet have one. Upon creation, the definition will be set to the default setup, discussed later, but can be updated at any time.

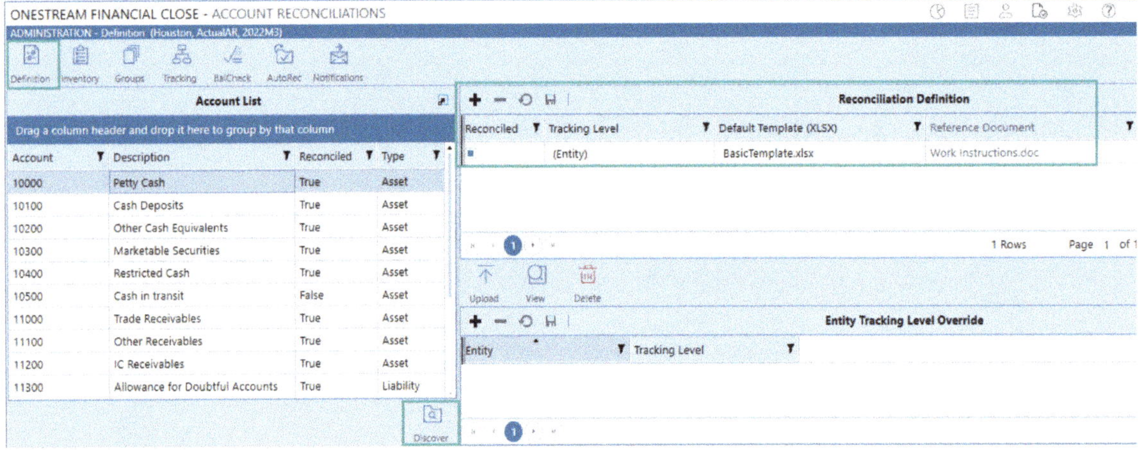

Figure 2.3

Email Connection

This is the named emailed connection used for notification emails. The name of the connections in this drop list derives from the initial server configuration.

To set up an email connection, find the **OneStream Server Configuration Utility** and run it as an Administrator.

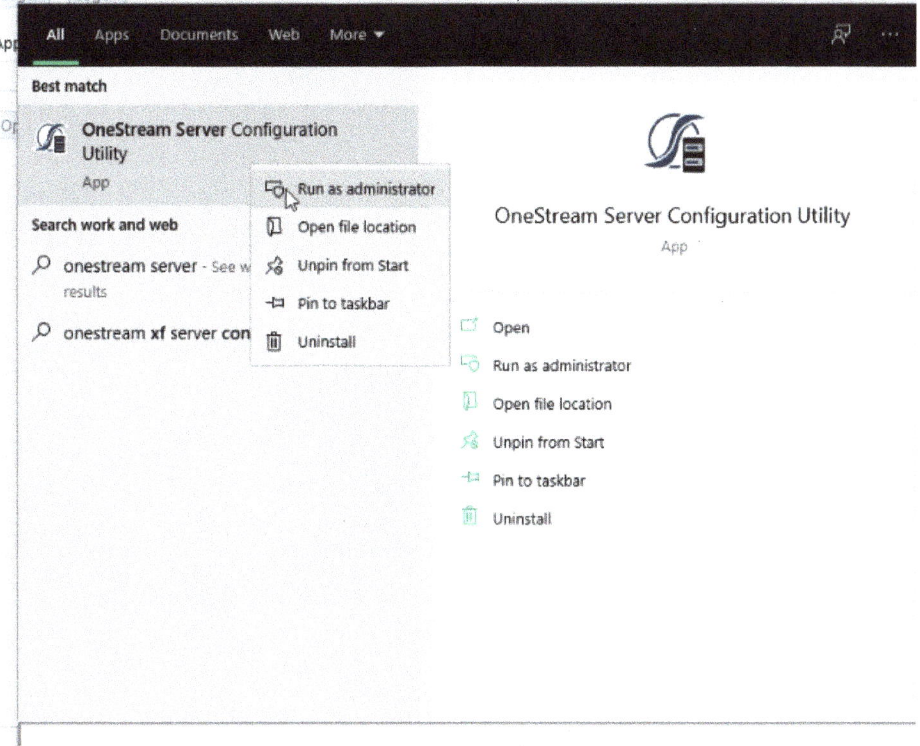

Figure 2.4

Next, select File, and then Open Application Server Configuration File.

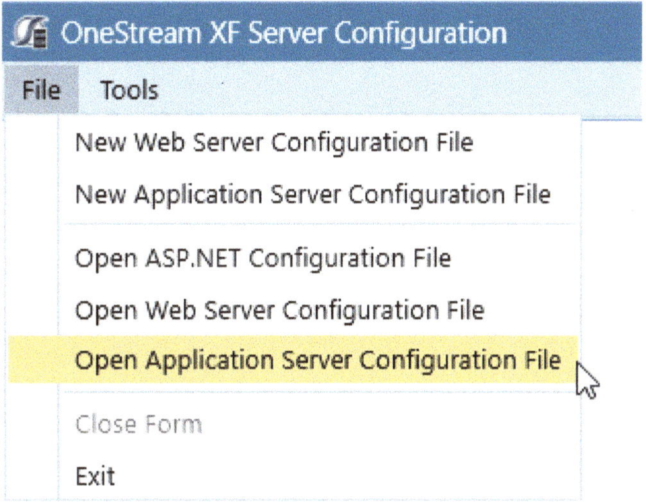

Figure 2.5

Then, open your application configuration file.

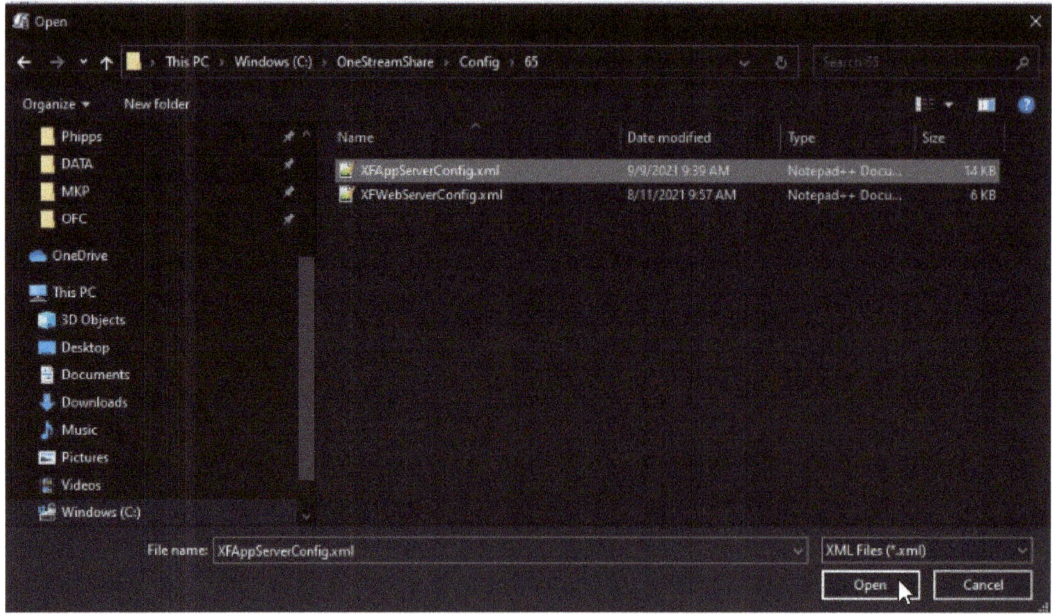

Figure 2.6

Under Databases, click on the ellipsis to edit the Database Server connections.

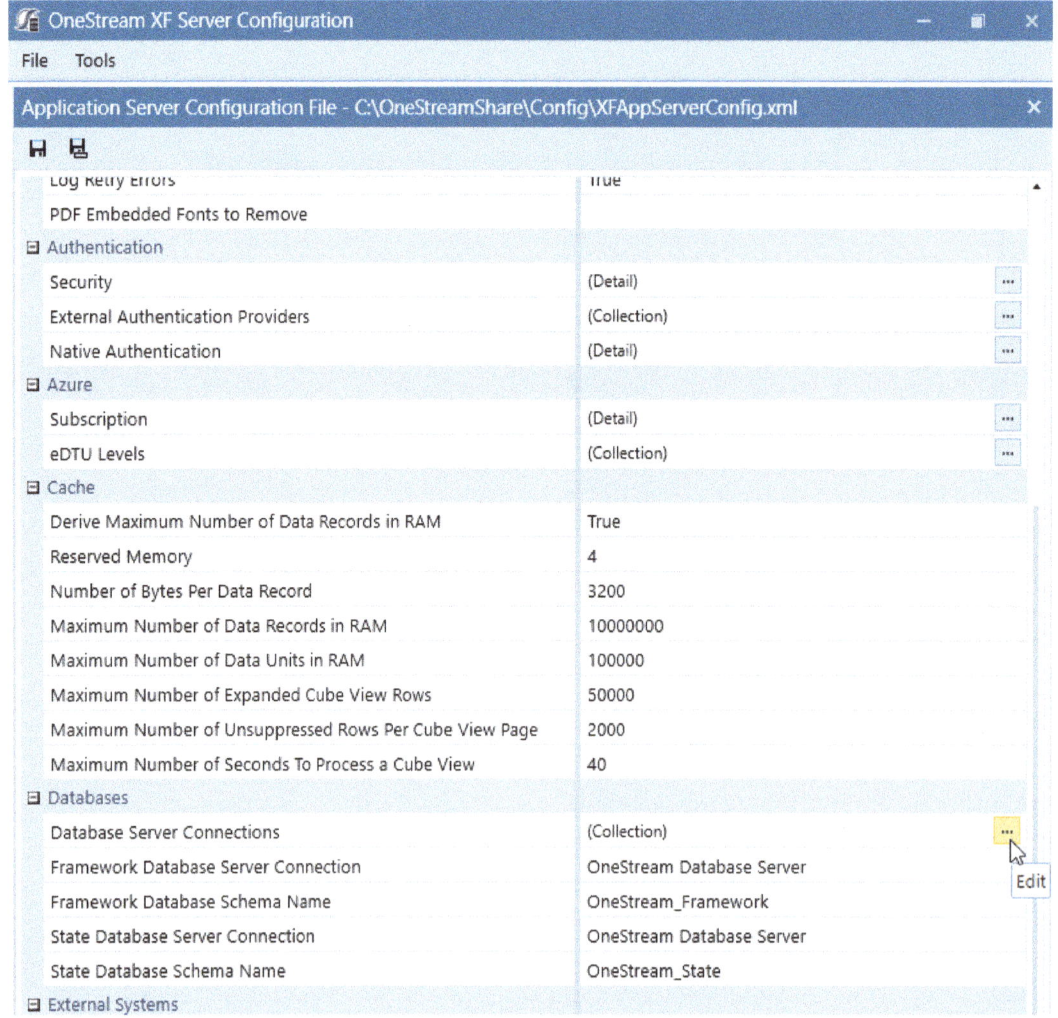

Figure 2.7

Add and name your Database Server connection.

> **Note:** The Database Provider Type must be *email* to appear in the settings drop-down, and a **connection string** must be provided. The name of the connection created will appear in the drop-down; in the Figure 2.8 example, it is OneStreamEmail.

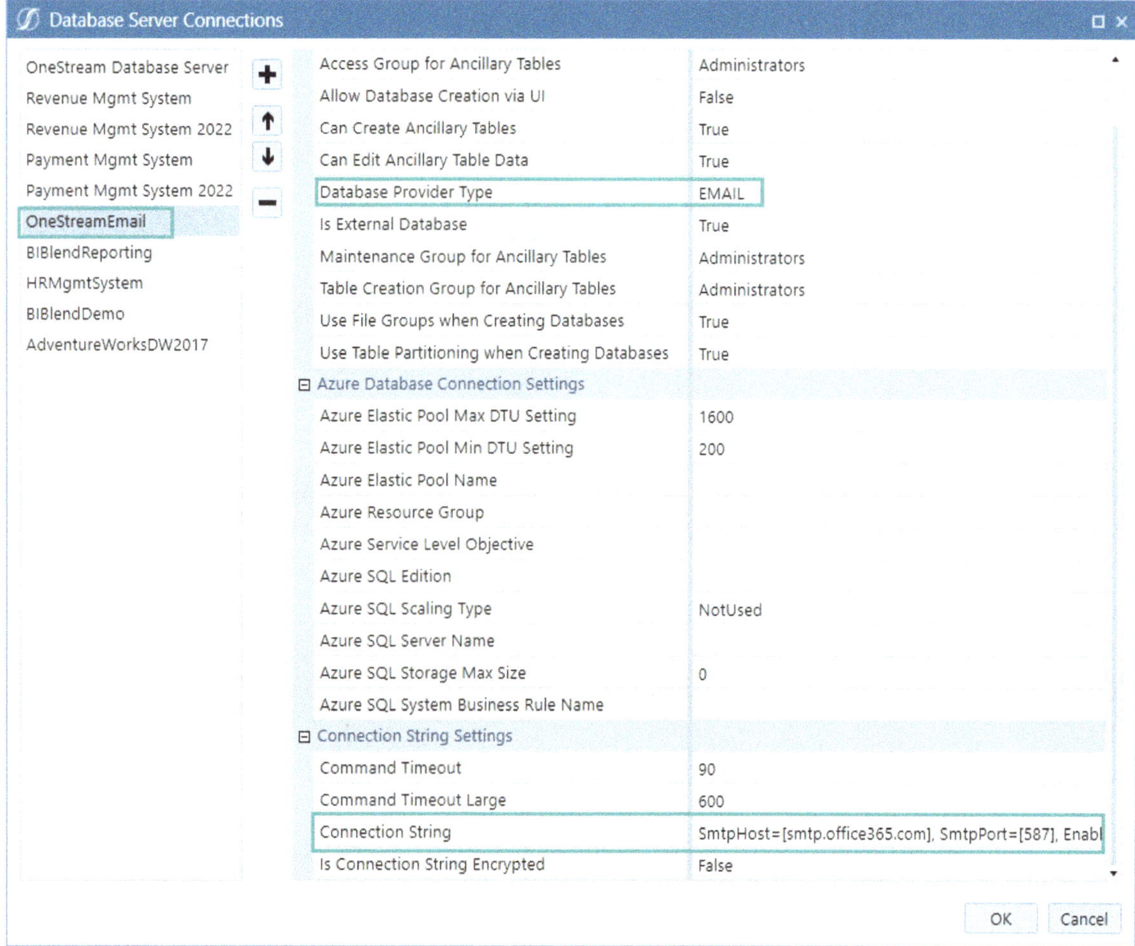

Figure 2.8

Reconciliation Definition Email Notification Types

By default, these email notifications are set to False, but when set to True the following emails are sent to all Reconciliation Administrators (those set to manage Reconciliation setup):

- **New OneStream Accounts:** A new Account is added to the Account List with the Definition page after running Discovery.
- **New Reconciliations Discovered:** A new Reconciliation is added to the Reconciliation Inventory after running Discovery.
- **Balance Changed:** A Reconciliation balance was changed after it was marked Complete or set to In Process.

Multi-Currency Reconciliations

The impact of multi-currency is discussed throughout this book. Enabling multi-currency allows you to have a **currency type** set at the Source Account level (GL Account). The Account currency type for each Reconciliation item is an attribute maintained within the Reconciliation Inventory. This differs from the Local currency (maintained on the Entity Dimension) and Reporting currency (maintained at the Cube level). Therefore, each Reconciliation may have a different Account currency.

Reconciliations with a common Target Entity will have the same Local currency, as this currency is held on the Entity, and all Reconciliations within an application will have a single Reporting currency, as Account Reconciliations reference a single Cube.

In addition, for Reconciliations where multi-currency is enabled, Account, Local, and Reporting Currencies all display in the Account Reconciliations Grid, as shown below. Note that the Reconciliation within the grid, in Figure 2.9 for Target Entity `Frankfurt`, is a multi-currency Reconciliation and thus has an Account currency balance; the second, `Houston Heights`, is single and therefore does not have an Account currency balance.

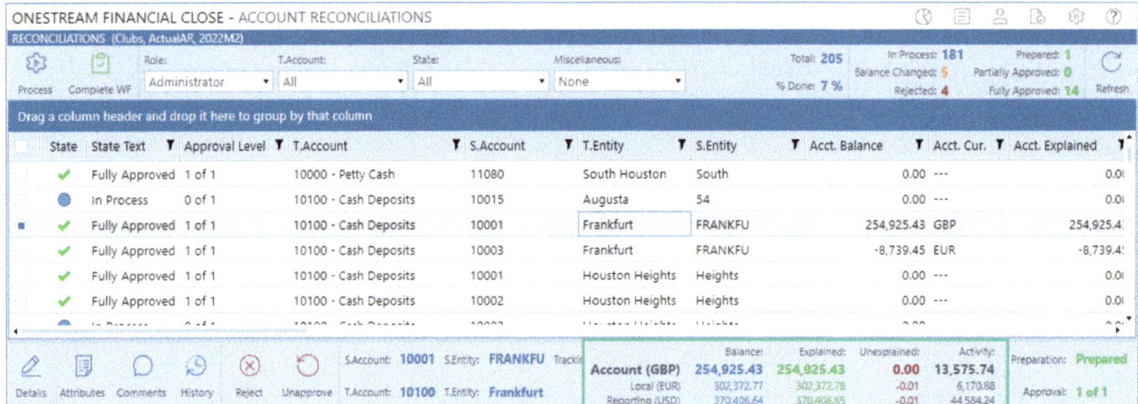

Figure 2.9

To enable multi-currency, select Enable on the Global Options page, and the page will then display Enabled (Upon Save). Once you have selected Save, at the bottom, the integration will be enabled.

> **Note:** Once enabled, this integration may not be reversed, so be sure you want to utilize this functionality before setting up this feature.

FX Rate Type

Single-Currency Solutions

The FX rate type that is being used to calculate the Reconciliation balances on specific Reports. Examples include `ClosingRate` or `AverageRate`. If this is not populated, no translated values are available in Reports. This must be set even if multi-currency is enabled because some Reconciliations within the Reconciliation Inventory may remain single-currency.

Multi-Currency Solutions

The FX rate type that is being used to translate Reconciliation balances from Local currency to Account currency and from Local currency to Reporting currency. Translation from one currency level to another only occurs if the Account and/or Reporting balances are not loaded into Stage. Local currency is the Base-level currency and is the level that is reconciled for single-currency applications. Therefore, Local balances are required for multi-currency Reconciliations. This is also the rate type that is used to translate detail items from the detail currency type to the Account.

FX Reporting Currency

Single-Currency Solutions

The currency type used as the target currency for Reports that translate values. If this is not populated, no translated values will be available on these Reports. For solutions where multi-currency is enabled, but not all Reconciliations are multi-currency (such as the `Houston Heights` and `Frankfurt` example above), this is the rate type that would be used to translate the Local currency to the Reporting currency for reporting purposes. As `Houston Heights` is a single-currency Reconciliation, the following options appear once the Report icon is selected at the bottom of the page.

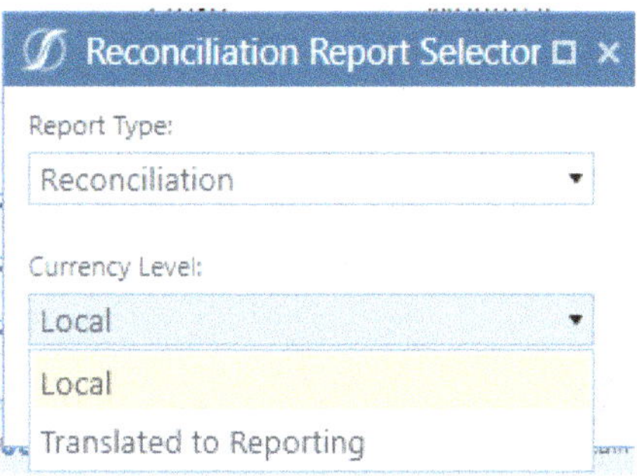

Figure 2.10

After selecting Translated to Reporting, the following Report will run using the direct Translation.

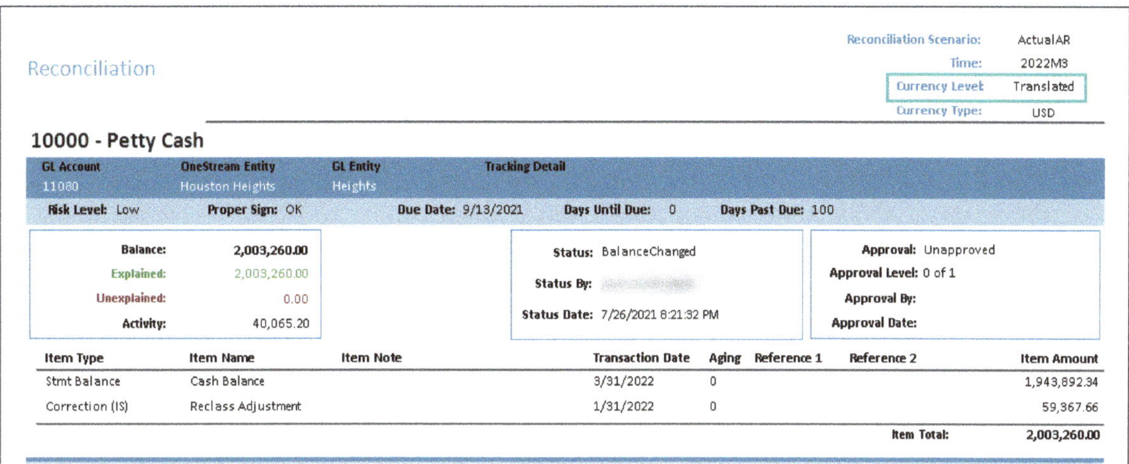

Figure 2.11

A note on Translation for single-currency Reconciliations. Account Reconciliations provides a translated value in certain Reports for the convenience and analysis of the Administrator or End-User. This translated value is not stored but is calculated based on settings in Global Options as the Report is being processed. This is a simple Translation being run that assumes a Calculation similar to the *direct* Translation Method of multiplying what is expected to be a Year-to-Date value by the FX rate type specified in Global Options; however, these are not the same Translation algorithms being processed, and no custom Translation Methods (i.e., Business Rules) are supported. These Reports note that they are translated by listing this FX Reporting currency in the right-side of the Report's header section.

Since `Frankfurt` is multi-currency, the Reporting currency has already been calculated within the Reconciliation and it, therefore, has the following available Reports.

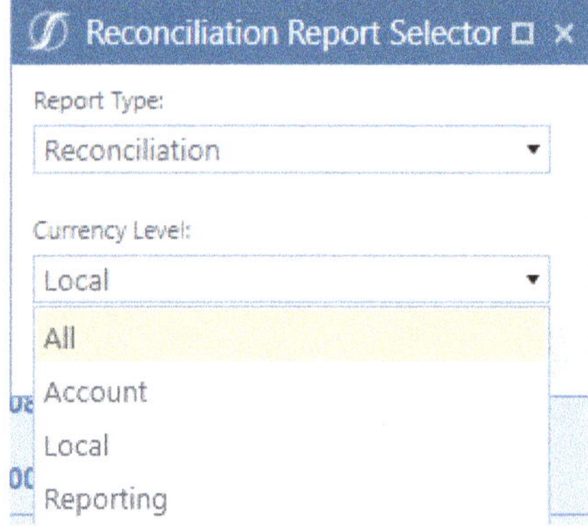

Figure 2.12

Frankfurt's Reporting Currency Report shows a Currency Level of Reporting instead of Translated.

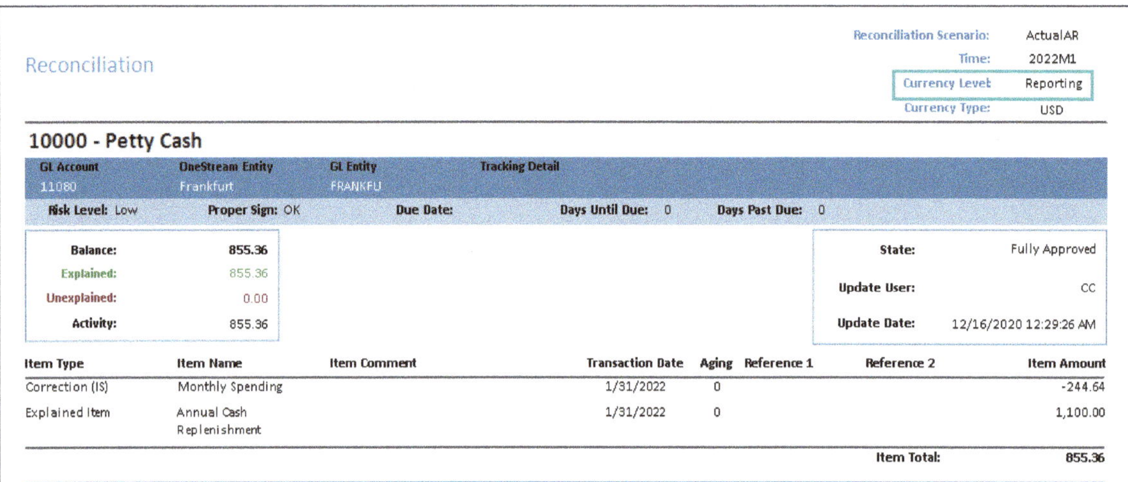

Figure 2.13

Audit Files Use Target Name Only

This controls the naming convention for audit package files. When set to True, audit files that are created will only use the Target Account and Entity in the file name. When set to False, the audit files are created with the Source and Target Account and Entity in the file name. The default is set to Not Selected, (False). The check box should be selected if there is the possibility of the file name length exceeding the Windows limit of 260 characters. If the file name exceeds 260 characters, the audit package file will not be generated. Windows 10 does enable Users to change the 260-character limit by changing the Windows Group Policy.

Global Defaults

Global defaults are used upon the initial creation of a Reconciliation when the Discover process is run.

Default Reconciliation Definition

If the Auto Create Reconciliation Definition Global Option is set to True, these are the default properties that will be assigned to all new Reconciliations created during the Discover process within the Definition page. There are three default properties that can be configured:

- **Reconciled** – The default is set to True, which indicates that the Reconciliation must be completed.

- **Tracking Level** – This is a drop-down list that is derived from the Tracking page within Administration. The level selected will determine the granularity of the Reconciliation. By default, OneStream provides a tracking level of Entity, which means Reconciliations will be discovered for instances where Source and Target Entities are different and when Source and Target Accounts are different. For example, in the screenshot below, there are six Target Accounts that came into the Import step: `10001`, `10002`, `10003`, `10004`, `11234`, and `11238` (item 1) from two different Source Entities: `Heights` and `South` (item 2). The total balance for these Accounts is $87,906,473.35, which would appear as a single line of cash on the consolidated financials for the Parent company `Houston`.

		2			1	Source Intersections
Amount (Raw)	SourceID	HoustonEntiti	Time	View	HoustonAcco	Label
27,459,481.56	Trial Balance & Hea	Heights	(Current)	YTD	10001	Cash - Operating Chase
41,189,222.34	Trial Balance & Hea	South	(Current)	YTD	10001	Cash - Operating Chase
3,548,475.73	Trial Balance & Hea	Heights	(Current)	YTD	10002	Cash - Operating Wells Fargo
5,322,713.59	Trial Balance & Hea	South	(Current)	YTD	10002	Cash - Operating Wells Fargo
-452,548.18	Trial Balance & Hea	Heights	(Current)	YTD	10003	Cash Disbursements - Chase Bank
-678,822.27	Trial Balance & Hea	South	(Current)	YTD	10003	Cash Disbursements - Chase Bank
-56,328.10	Trial Balance & Hea	Heights	(Current)	YTD	10004	Cash Disbursements - Wells Fargo
-84,492.15	Trial Balance & Hea	South	(Current)	YTD	10004	Cash Disbursements - Wells Fargo
6,997,935.56	Trial Balance & Hea	South	(Current)	YTD	11234	Deposits
4,665,290.37	Trial Balance & Hea	Heights	(Current)	YTD	11234	Deposits
-2,673.06	Trial Balance & Hea	South	(Current)	YTD	11238	Deposits on Trade Receivables
-1,782.04	Trial Balance & Hea	Heights	(Current)	YTD	11238	Deposits on Trade Receivables

Figure 2.14

You can see, after transformation, how the Source Accounts have all transformed to the Account `10100`, which is maintained in the Account Dimension. The Entities have also been transformed to the Target Entities – `Houston Heights` and `South Houston` – but the total of the amounts is still the same, $87,906,473.35.

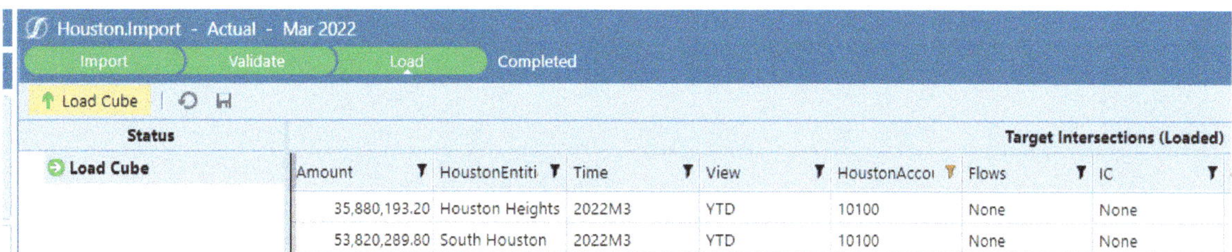

Houston.Import - Actual - Mar 2022

Import | Validate | Load | Completed

Load Cube

Status	Target Intersections (Loaded)					
Load Cube						
Amount	HoustonEntiti	Time	View	HoustonAcco	Flows	IC
35,880,193.20	Houston Heights	2022M3	YTD	10100	None	None
53,820,289.80	South Houston	2022M3	YTD	10100	None	None

Figure 2.15

While the Actual balances have aggregated into a single balance sheet Account, there have been 12 different Reconciliations created within Account Reconciliations, since there are two different Entities and six different Source Accounts.

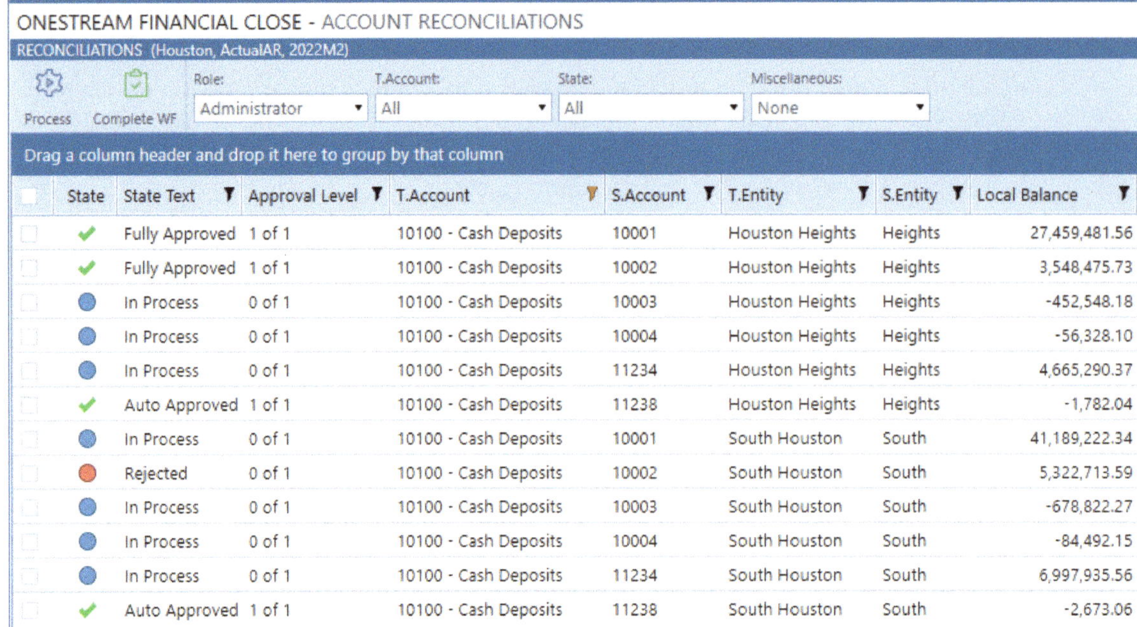

State	State Text	Approval Level	T.Account	S.Account	T.Entity	S.Entity	Local Balance
✔	Fully Approved	1 of 1	10100 - Cash Deposits	10001	Houston Heights	Heights	27,459,481.56
✔	Fully Approved	1 of 1	10100 - Cash Deposits	10002	Houston Heights	Heights	3,548,475.73
●	In Process	0 of 1	10100 - Cash Deposits	10003	Houston Heights	Heights	-452,548.18
●	In Process	0 of 1	10100 - Cash Deposits	10004	Houston Heights	Heights	-56,328.10
●	In Process	0 of 1	10100 - Cash Deposits	11234	Houston Heights	Heights	4,665,290.37
✔	Auto Approved	1 of 1	10100 - Cash Deposits	11238	Houston Heights	Heights	-1,782.04
●	In Process	0 of 1	10100 - Cash Deposits	10001	South Houston	South	41,189,222.34
●	Rejected	0 of 1	10100 - Cash Deposits	10002	South Houston	South	5,322,713.59
●	In Process	0 of 1	10100 - Cash Deposits	10003	South Houston	South	-678,822.27
●	In Process	0 of 1	10100 - Cash Deposits	10004	South Houston	South	-84,492.15
●	In Process	0 of 1	10100 - Cash Deposits	11234	South Houston	South	6,997,935.56
✔	Auto Approved	1 of 1	10100 - Cash Deposits	11238	South Houston	South	-2,673.06

Figure 2.16

The tracking level can get even more granular to include IC, Flow, and UDs, if those items vary on your import and you wish to reconcile at that level. An example of this would be to reconcile at the cost center level by utilizing a UD.

- **Default Template** – this is a drop-down list of templates that are maintained on the Templates page of Settings.

Default Reconciliation Attributes

The default primary Preparers and Approvers discovered are set here. Information on security roles and actions are discussed within Security.

Default Reconciliation Time-Based Attributes

The default attributes for all new Reconciliation Inventory items discovered are set here. Information on each attribute – including definitions, how they are populated, etc. – are discussed within the Reconciliation Inventory section.

Control Lists

Control Lists are used to populate certain parameter-driven, selectable drop-downs, and various Reports throughout the solution. OneStream provides default items within each list to get you started with your configuration process, but these lists can be updated as necessary by your company.

Item Types

When a Preparer creates a detail item to support the Reconciliation balance, they can select an Item Type from a drop-down list. This control list is what is used to populate the drop-down.

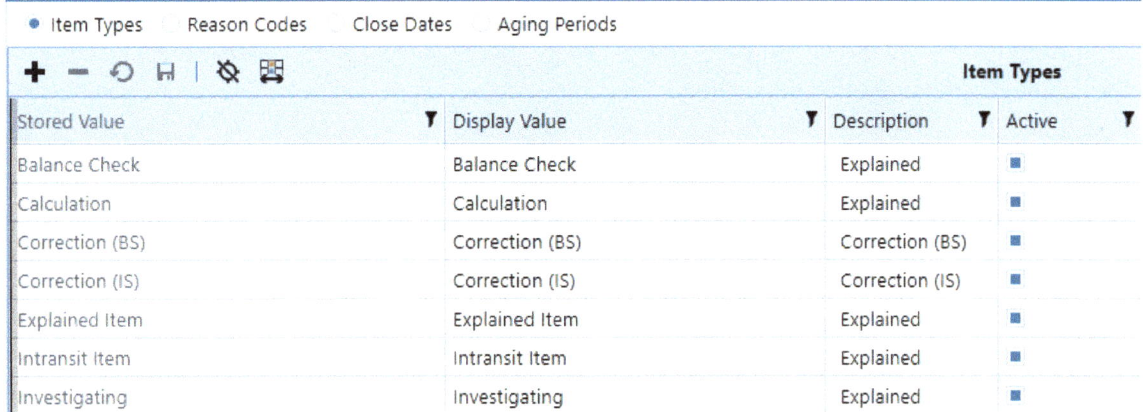

Stored Value	Display Value	Description	Active
Balance Check	Balance Check	Explained	■
Calculation	Calculation	Explained	■
Correction (BS)	Correction (BS)	Correction (BS)	■
Correction (IS)	Correction (IS)	Correction (IS)	■
Explained Item	Explained Item	Explained	■
Intransit Item	Intransit Item	Explained	■
Investigating	Investigating	Explained	■

Figure 2.17

Stored Value

This is the text that is written to the Account Reconciliation tables when an item is added. The End-User will not see this value.

Display Value

Item Type text that is displayed to Preparers once they create a detail item.

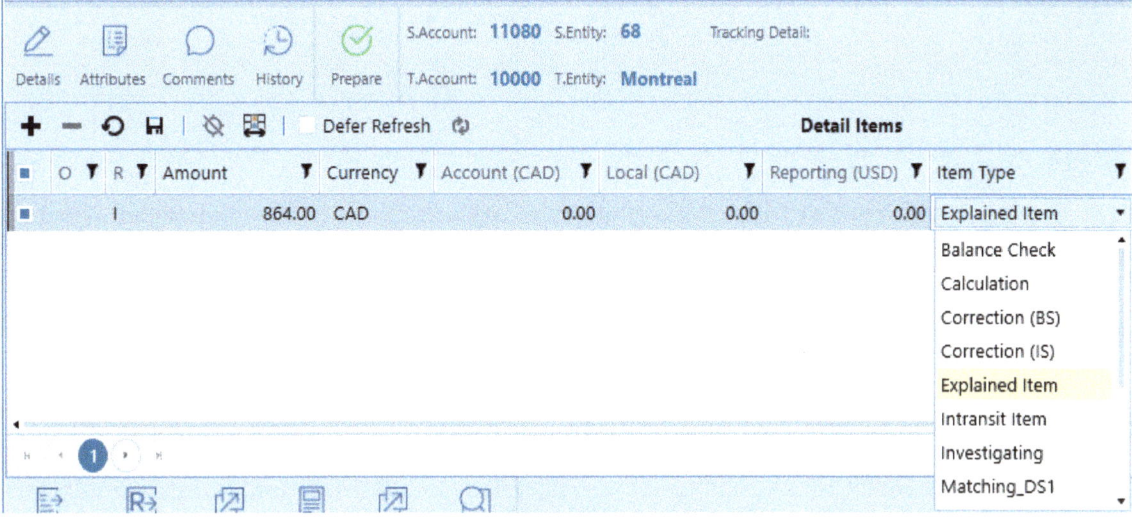

Figure 2.18

Description

The type of item added to a Reconciliation. This drop-down list is prepopulated to include:

- **Correction (BS)** and **Correction (IS)** – These items indicate an issue with the current balance in the GL and require a correction. Additional reporting is available, based on this item class.
- **Explained** – Used when a balance is being properly explained and supported (e.g., no correction is required).
- **Statement** – This should be used in instances where an external statement is used to support the detail item, such as a bank statement.

These descriptions are not used within the out-of-the-box Account Reconciliation solution but can be utilized for custom dashboarding (if desired by your company) to help classify and quantify the items that have been created for a period.

Active

By default, this is set to True. Note that an Item Type cannot be deleted. As such, if you do not want one of the Item Types (that was previously included in the control list) to display to End-Users, set the status to False.

Reason Codes

When an Approver clicks Reject or Unapprove, they are prompted to select a Reason Code from the drop-down list and provide optional Reason Text. The drop-down list is edited within this Control List.

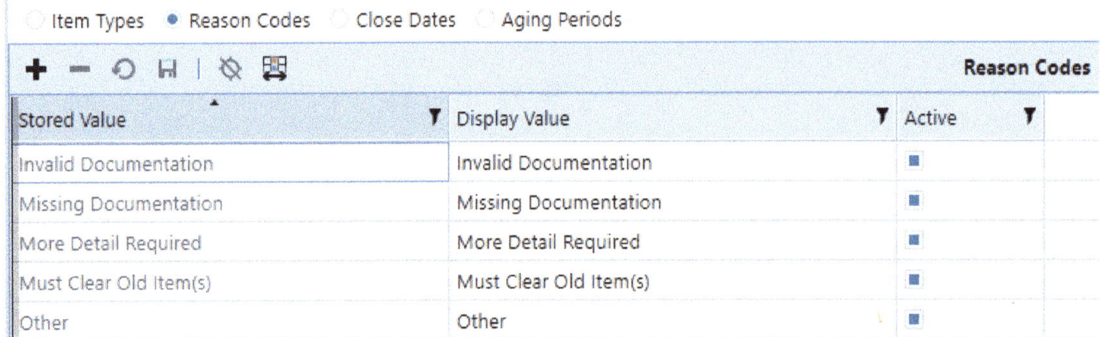

Figure 2.19

Stored Value

This is the text that is written to the Account Reconciliation tables when an item is added. The End User will not see this value.

Display Value

Reason Code text that displays to Approvers once they reject or unapprove a Reconciliation.

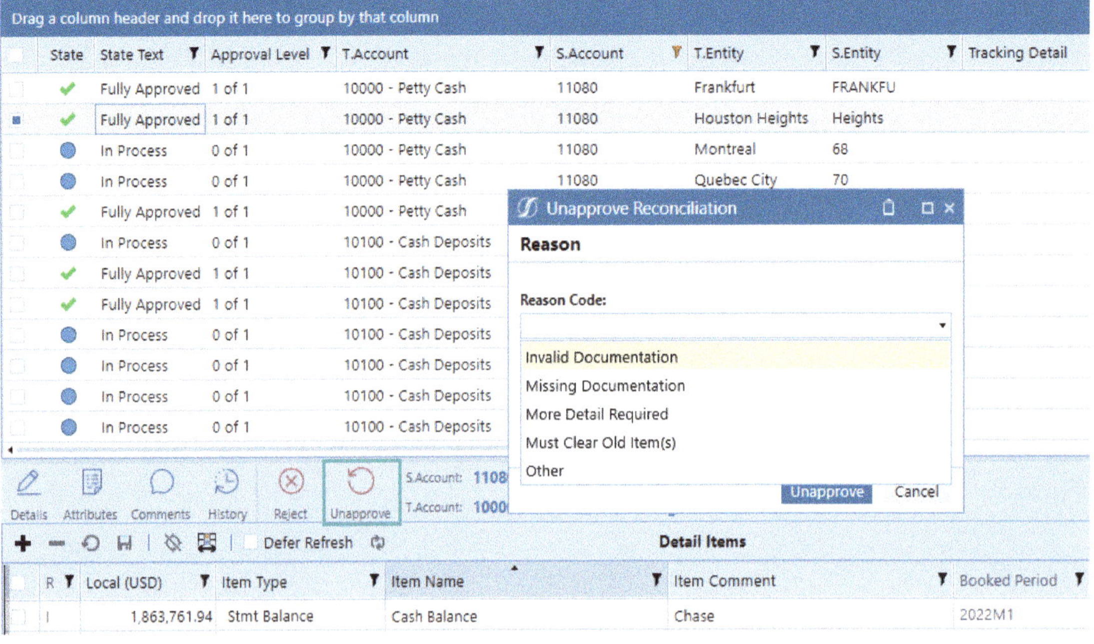

Figure 2.20

Active

By default, this is set to True. If set to False, the Approver will not see the Reason Code. However, Reason Codes *can* be deleted, so it may be best to delete the Reason Code if it is not being used – for maintenance purposes.

Close Dates

Close Dates set a specific date and time for a Workflow time period. For example, if you are preparing M1 Reconciliations and are on a standard monthly calendar, you are performing your January Reconciliations. However, your close process may start *before* January 31, or it may start on the last day of the month, but the date falls on a weekend. Use this setting to customize the actual start date of close for each period. This date will then be used to calculate if Reconciliations are past due, regardless of a User's location.

> **Note:** Close dates must be set for every Workflow time period; if they are not, the date shown on the Reconciliations page is 1900/01/01.

WF Time

The Workflow time period. Click the + button to add one record for each Workflow time period related to the Source Scenario, or Actual for our examples.

The list of Workflow time periods is for the currently-selected Workflow year, plus the following year. This includes all frequencies of time (half-years, quarters, months, and weeks, if applicable) for this application. Choose a time period relevant to the **input frequency** of both the Source Scenario and Reconciliation Scenario involved in Account Reconciliations. The input frequency properties of each Scenario (for example, monthly) must match. It is also important to note that if your company plans to utilize Transaction Matching to support Account Reconciliations, which will be discussed later, the input frequency for matching must also match Source and Reconciliation. Most customers will, therefore, typically perform Reconciliations on a monthly basis.

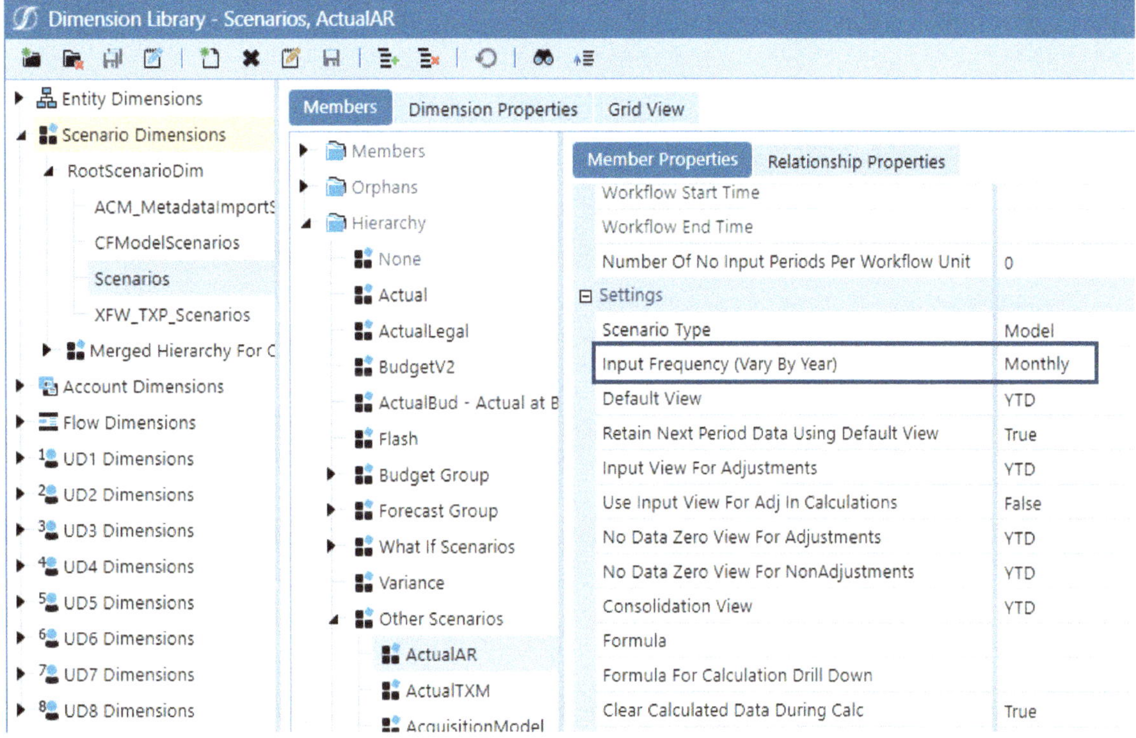

Figure 2.21

Close Date Local (Day 0)

Using the date picker, or by typing in the date, select the date when the financial close starts for the Workflow time period. This will be your day 0 for close, so – in Figure 2.22, below – day 1 of the March close would be April 1; day 2 would be April 2; and so on.

These days of close are what are used to determine when a Reconciliation is due, based on the **Approver Workday Due** attribute set in the Reconciliation Inventory.

> **Note:** Account Reconciliations does not take weekends or holidays into account, so the workday due would need to be changed in the example of day 2 (April 2), falling on a weekend. In this instance, Reconciliations due on day 2 of close (which is April 4, based on the calendar) would be set as due on workday 4, for Account Reconciliation purposes.

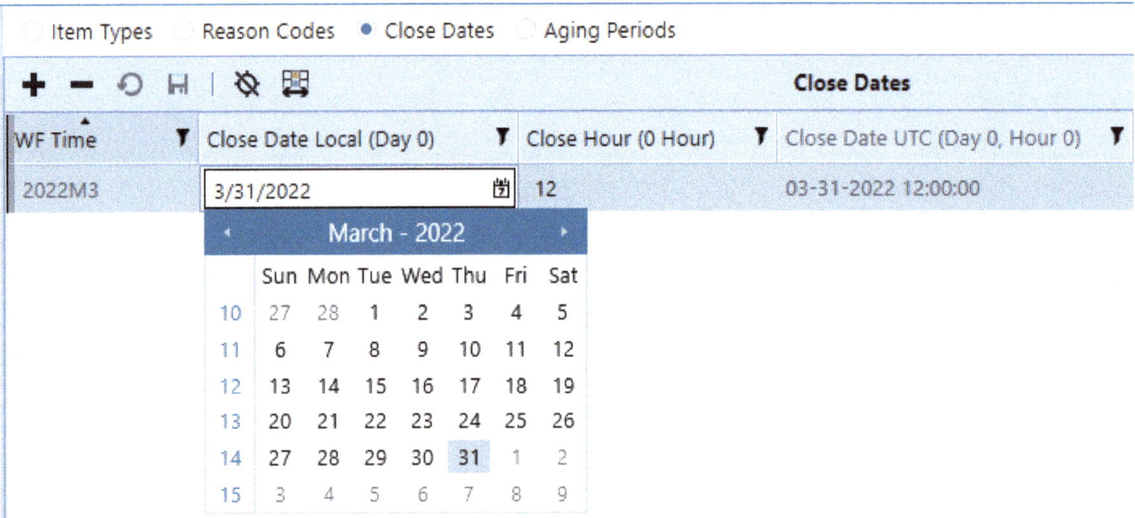

Figure 2.22

Close Hour (0 Hour)

Set to the hour of day the close will start for local time. For example, if close starts at 5:00PM, set this to 17. Local time is determined by the time zone where your OneStream Server is located. Due date Calculations do not take close hour into account.

Close Date UTC (Day 0, Hour 0)

The column is calculated upon Save. The close date local (Day 0) is converted to the UTC (Coordinated Universal Time, aka GMT/Greenwich Mean Time) equivalent for the purposes of comparing the current local time for when a Reconciliation Inventory item is due.

The close date setting is used to calculate when Reconciliations are due. Let's walk through an example of when a Reconciliation would be marked as upcoming and past due.

Assume a Reconciliation is assigned an Approver workday due of 0 on the Reconciliation Inventory. The Approver due date that will appear in the Reconciliation Grid will be 3/31/22. Using the close date from Figure 2.22, the Reconciliation would show due in 0 days, on March 31, and on April 1 the Reconciliation would move to due in 0, and past due 1.

Aging Periods

Upon saving a detail item, the aging is calculated by taking the last day of the Workflow period less the transaction date. These periods are used to group detail item aging into aging buckets, which can be later utilized to determine actionable items, including potential write-offs. The default period start dates are:

- 0: 0 to 30 days
- 31: 31 to 60 days
- 61: 61 to 90 days
- 91: 91+ days

You can add periods to this, and edit current period starts. For example, if a period start of 121 were added, a new bucket of 91 to 120 would be created, and the last bucket would be 121+.

If you were reconciling March balances, or in M3 (in Figure 2.22), and created a detail item with a transaction date of 3/15/22, the aging that would appear for the detail item would be 16, or 31 less 15. That aging of 16 would fall into the bucket between 0-30 on the aging analysis. If the detail item was carried forward into the next period, the aging would recalculate for the period and would appear as 46 (16 from the prior period plus 30 days in April). When looking at the aging analysis for April, the item would now appear in the 31-60 bucket in the aging analysis, but will still appear in the 0-30 bucket in March.

Templates

The Control List stores the templates that get assigned to Reconciliations through the Global Defaults (upon initial creation) or within the Reconciliation Definitions (if a different template to the Global Default template is necessary, the template must be updated). Account Reconciliations comes with a few example templates. You can use these templates as a starting point for your organization as you create custom templates and upload them to this Control List. If you do modify existing templates, make sure you change the name of the template upon upload. Otherwise, the template that you customized with the same naming convention utilized by OneStream will be replaced following any upgrades.

Within the Templates page, there are a few actions at the bottom.

- **Upload:** Select this icon to add a new Excel template to the solution.
- **View:** Select this icon to open a read-only copy of the selected template.
- **Delete:** Select this icon to delete the selected template. Note that the template may only be deleted if it is not currently assigned to a Reconciliation.
- **Replace**: To change the template assigned to any existing Reconciliation Definition, select the original template from the drop-down list and then select New Template from the drop-down and click the Replace icon. This replacement will occur on all Reconciliations where the original template was assigned in the Reconciliation Definition.

When viewing the basic template that comes with Account Reconciliations, there are substitution variables replaced with values from the Reconciliation being processed. Figure 2.23 shows the design view.

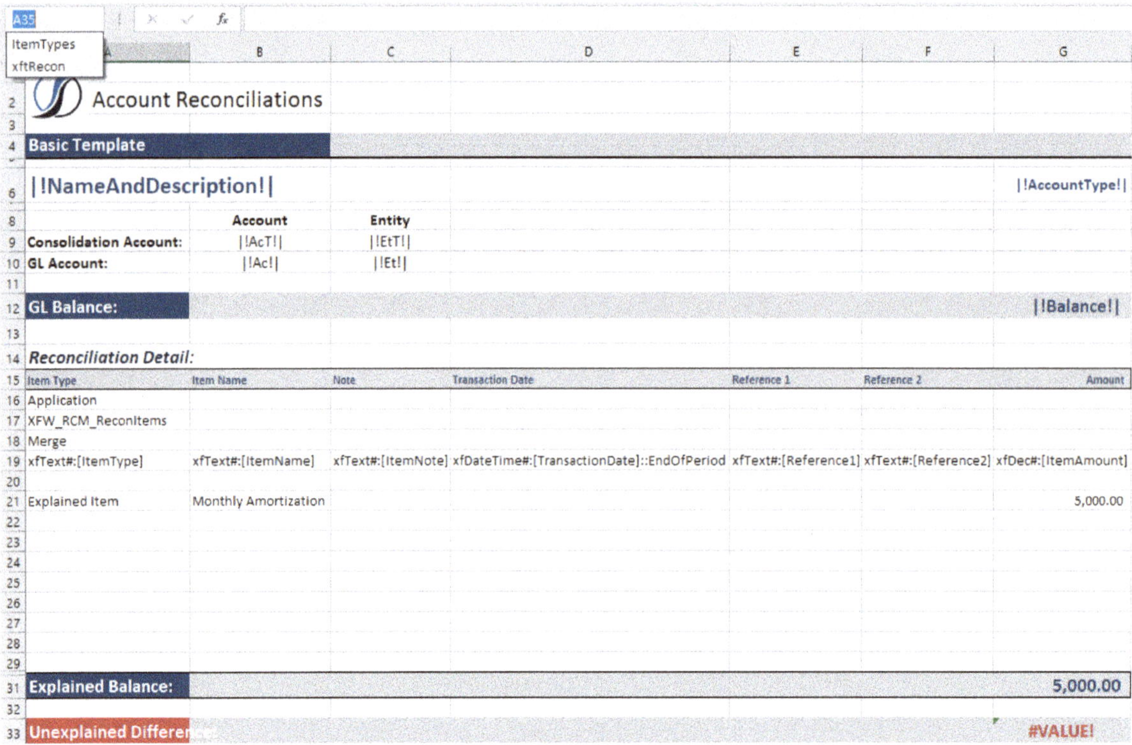

Figure 2.23

If the basic template was assigned to a Reconciliation Definition and the template was then opened within a Reconciliation Workspace, the substitution variables would be replaced with the Reconciliation information at runtime, as shown in Figure 2.24.

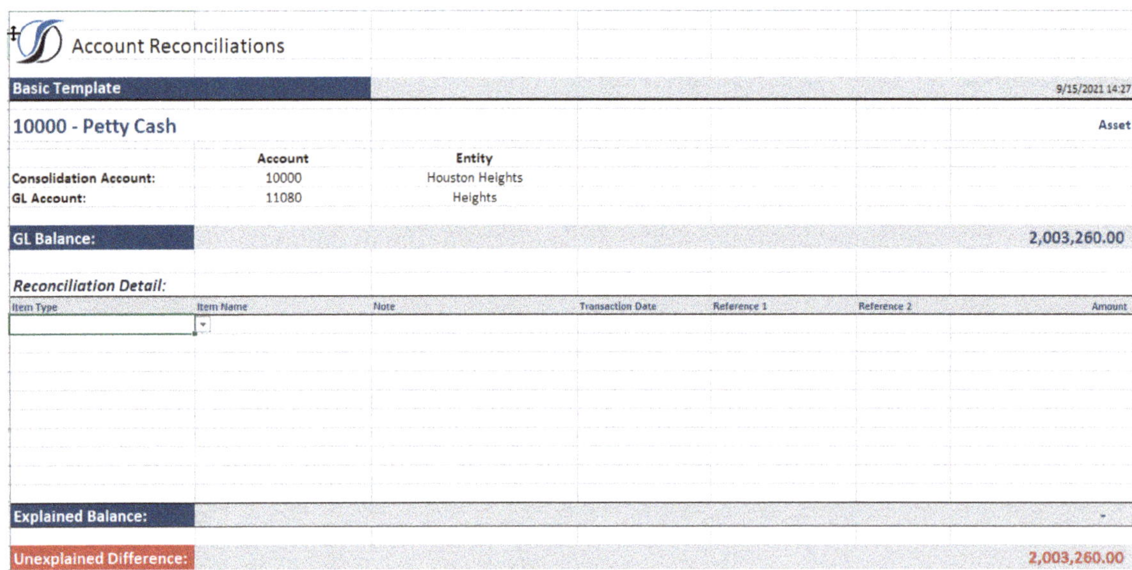

Figure 2.24

> **Note:** Item Type is a drop-down list. This is a data validation list that is populated from the Item Types tab. Make sure you update the list to include all Item Types you have set up in your Item Types control list.

Figure 2.25 shows how this appears as a multi-currency S-Doc template, with `MultiPeriodTemplate.xlsx` being the example template provided. Note that the named range of xftRecon is selected, and rows 16-20 are unhidden but are normally hidden. This named range would need to be extended if additional rows are needed for import. The top-left cell of such a named range must be the cell with the word Application in it, and the bottom-right cell of the range should be the last column of the last row to be imported. It is acceptable to include additional empty rows in this range. OneStream can read in multiple xft-named ranges on one or more sheets of the same Excel workbook. Save this file in Excel xlsx format.

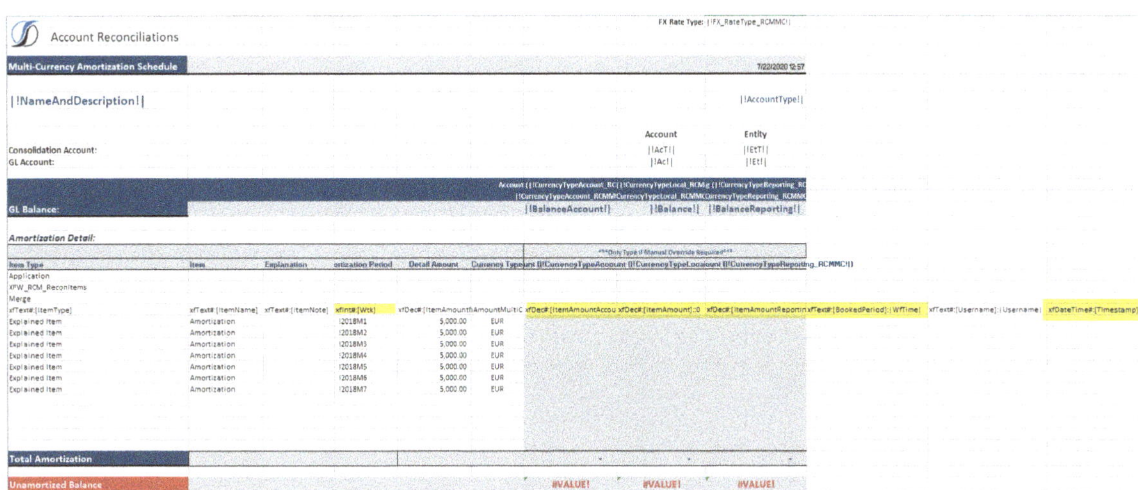

Figure 2.25

A few hidden column tokens of note:

- **Wtk:** Workflow Time Key – These OneStream time periods contain an exclamation point as the first character (for example, !2018M1). This helps OneStream look up the time key for this period and store that value in the database upon import. Include as many rows as periods of data are necessary, even if spanning years.
- **Item Amounts (multi-currency solutions):** These columns are automatically translated within the template. The template is pulling FX rates for the period in order to translate the detail amount balances. The translated amounts are for display purposes only, because Translation of the detail amounts takes place upon import into OneStream. Further, only current period balances will be translated on the template.
- **BookedPeriod:** The |WFTime| substitution variable is used, which means that every row being imported will be booked to the same WF period that was processed at the time.
- **TimeStamp:** The date and time this template was imported, which will be the same for each time period.
- **AgingDays:** The calculated days aged for the detail item upon template upload.

Templates that support multiple currencies are included for solutions that have multi-currency enabled. In the multi-currency basic template and multi-currency multi-period template, columns are included to allow for detail amount, detail currency type, Account balance, and Reporting balance.

For single-currency Reconciliations, only Local balances are loaded, and as such, if a Reconciliation is set to single-currency, the templates that do not include multi-currency functionality must be used. The currency type for each currency level appears within the template and FX rates are automatically pulled in order to show the conversion that will occur on import.

> **Note:** OneStream still utilizes Translation functionality within the system to translate detail amounts.

The translated balances of Account, Local, and Reporting for the detail items are for informational purposes only. However, if an override is necessary for any of the levels, OneStream accepts the overridden amount upon upload of the template (if overrides are permitted on the Reconciliation). To identify balances that were overridden within the template, amounts overridden display bold, and the override alert appears on the face of the Reconciliation.

For multi-period templates, informational translated balances only display for the current month because future rates are not available at the time of template creation.

Access Control

Access Control is part of the security setup within Account Reconciliations. This is discussed in detail in the Security section of this chapter.

Certifications

Certifications are utilized within Account Reconciliations, similar to how they are utilized within the Workflow process. However, instead of seeing the statements at the time of Workflow completion, Preparers have the ability to view the certifications at the time of each Reconciliation preparation, and Approvers can view the certifications at the time of each Reconciliation approval. Like Workflow certifications, these are customizable text and can be modified to meet your company's requirements.

Role

Select the User role that will see the certification upon action (either preparation or approval). Note that Approver certifications are present to *all* Approvers regardless of Approval level.

Message

Input the text you would like presented to either the Preparer or Approver when preparing or approving Reconciliations, respectively.

Active

By default, this is set to True. If set to False, the certification will not be displayed. Certifications can be deleted, though, so it may be best to delete the certification if it is not being used – for maintenance purposes.

Comment Required

This indicates that a Preparer or Approver must also add a comment – in addition to reviewing the certification – at the time of preparation or approval. If set to False, comments are not required but can be added if the Preparer or Approver chooses. All comments are displayed on the Comments page found within the Reconciliation header.

Time Stamp & User ID

The date and time the certification settings were created or modified, and the ID of the User who made the changes.

Figure 2.26 shows the dialog presented to Users upon Preparation or Approval of Reconciliations, how to view the certifications, and where comments are inputted.

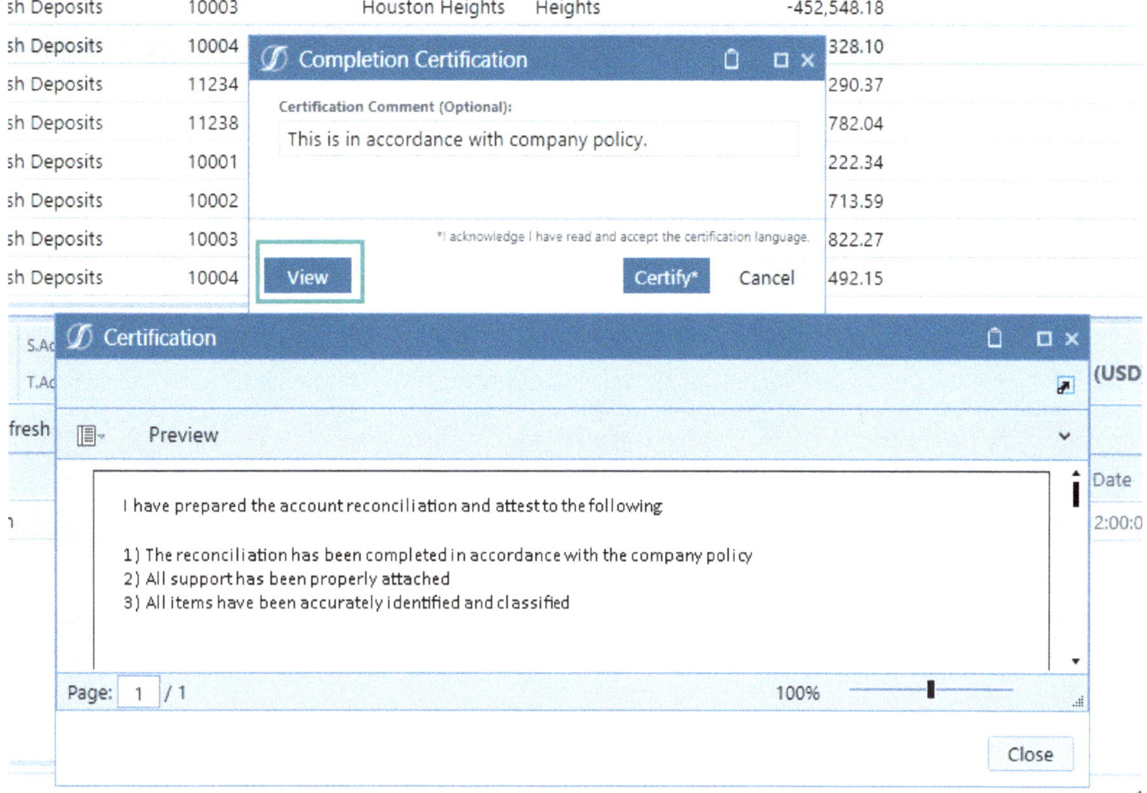

Figure 2.26

Uninstall

The Uninstall page allows you to uninstall either the User Interface or all solutions within OneStream Financial Close, which would include Account Reconciliations and Transaction Matching. If uninstall is performed as part of an upgrade, any modifications that were made to standard solution contents are removed.

Uninstall UI – OneStream Financial Close

Removes all solutions within OneStream Financial Close, including all Dashboards and Business Rules but leaves the databases and related tables. Performing this step is encouraged for most upgrades as Dashboards are often modified within the solutions. However, it is important to note that when this is done, the Workspace Dashboard Name for every Workflow Profile must be reassigned.

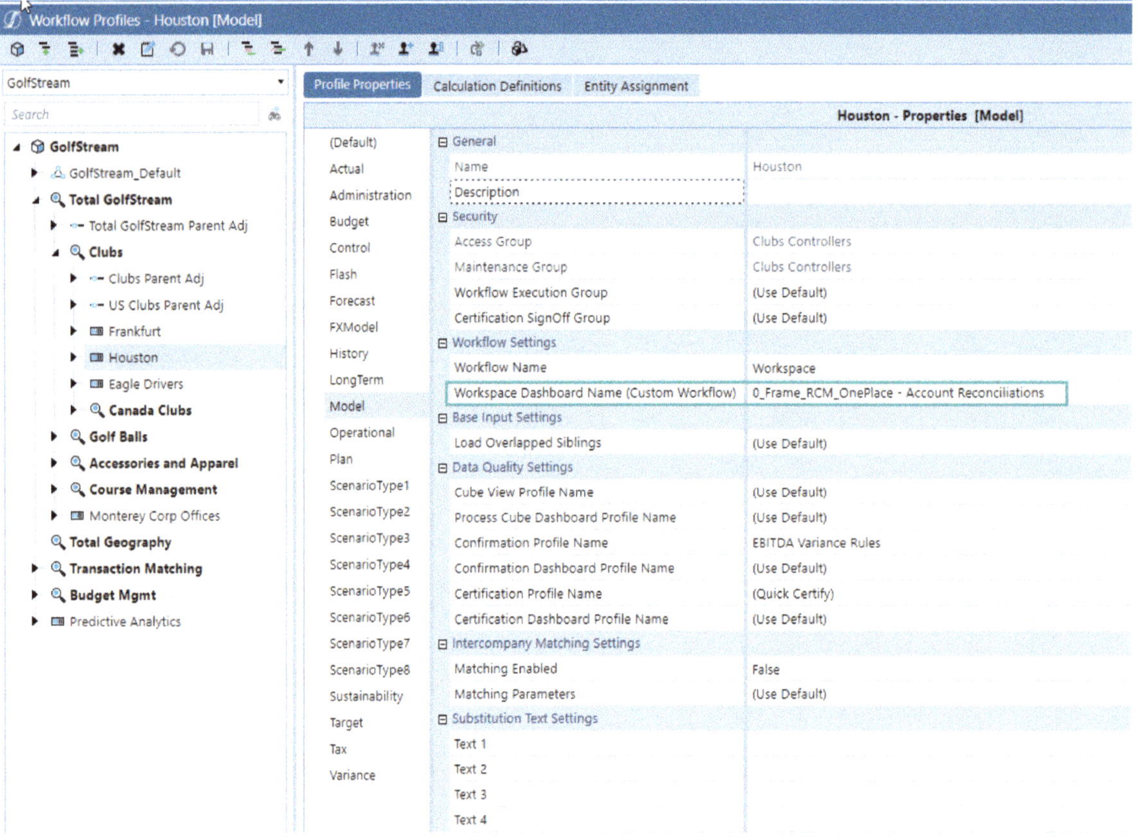

Figure 2.27

Uninstall Full

Removes all related data tables, all data, all solutions' Dashboards, and all Business Rules. Select this option to completely remove the solutions.

> **Note:** This option is irreversible and is therefore not recommended.

This option should be utilized only if your company has determined they will not be using any of the OneStream Financial Close solutions, or if the release notes for the version being installed state that the upgrade is *so significant in its changes to the data tables* that this method is required.

Settings Summary

The initial settings – covered above – help define the entire 'shell' of your Account Reconciliations solution. Now that you've defined your overall framework, let's dive into the nitty gritty with Security!

* * *

Security

Security within Account Reconciliations is configured in a few different places. As an overview, Users may take action on Reconciliations at any role equal to, or below, the role they are assigned, as long as they have not already taken action on the Reconciliation – in order to support segregation of duties.

For example, if User Lynn is assigned as the Primary Approver 1, she may either prepare OR approve at Level 1, but she may not do both, and she cannot approve at Levels 2-4.

In turn, assume Brian is the primary assigned Approver 1 within the Reconciliation Inventory, and Amy is the primary assigned Approver 2 within the Reconciliation Inventory. As such, there are two levels of approval required, and assume there is no Access Group assigned.

Brian is out on vacation for the period, so Amy Approves the Reconciliation on his behalf as a Level 1 Approver. To complete the Reconciliation, there are multiple options:

1. An Administrator can perform the Level 2 Approval. This would be the recommended approach – in this instance – as the primary Approver 1, Brian, is only temporarily unable to perform his duties, and therefore no additional administration would need to be performed on the attributes.
2. The Reconciliation may be Recalled or Rejected. Once this is done and the Reconciliation is sent back to an In Process state:
   a. The Administrator can change the number of approvals required to one for the current period.
   b. An Administrator may add an Access Group for the current period so that someone can perform the Level 2 Approval as a backup.
   c. An Administrator can change the attributes so that Amy is Approver 1, and assign someone else as Approver 2.

The table in Figure 2.28 outlines the various roles, what platform system security roles may be assigned to the role, where the role is configured, and the actions the role may take (assuming no prior action was taken).

Role	Assignable System Security Roles	Configuration	Actions
Viewer	Users and Groups	Access Control	• Can only see the data and activity for Reconciliations
Commenter	Users and Groups	Access Control	• Preform all Viewer actions • Can add, delete, or edit their own comments when Reconciliation is In Process or Prepared • Can add comments once a Reconciliation is Fully Approved (not delete or edit)
Preparer	Users	Reconciliation Inventory	• Perform all Commenter actions • See all assigned Reconciliations, regardless of role, within the Reconciliation Workspace • Filter Reconciliations within the Reconciliation Workspace using the Primary Preparer filter to

Role	Assignable System Security Roles	Configuration	Actions
			see Reconciliations where they are the Primary Preparer • Filter Reconciliations within the Reconciliation Workspace using Preparers or Approvers filter to see Reconciliations where they are the Backup or Primary Preparer • Create detail items • Attach supporting I-Doc, R-Doc, S-Doc, and T-Doc • Run Process, which will pull balances from Stage for all Reconciliations to which they are assigned • Perform preparation duties by clicking the Prepare button • Receive Rejected, Approved, Unapproved, Comment, or Balance Change notifications if they are assigned to the Reconciliation (see notifications section for more detail) • Recall Prepared Reconciliations (Reconciliation without any approval), putting them back to an In Process state
Backup Preparer	Users and Groups	Access Control	• All actions a Primary Preparer may perform except filter Reconciliations within the Reconciliation Workspace using the Primary Preparer filter to see Reconciliations where they are the Primary Preparer • Receive Rejected, Approved, Unapproved, Comment, or Balance Change notifications if notify is set to True on the Access Control setup (see notifications section for more detail)
Approver 1	Users	Reconciliation Inventory	• Preform all Primary Preparer actions • Filter Reconciliations within the Reconciliation

Role	Assignable System Security Roles	Configuration	Actions
			Workspace using the Primary Approver filter to see Reconciliations where they are the Primary Approver • Filter Reconciliations within the Reconciliation Workspace using Preparers or Approvers filter to see Reconciliations where they are the Backup or Primary Approver • Recall Reconciliations (Reconciliation without any approval), putting them back to an In Process state • Reject Prepared Reconciliations (Reconciliation without any approval), putting them back to an In Process state. Rejecting Reconciliations requires providing a Reason Code. • Reject Auto Prepared Reconciliations • Receive Completed or Comment notifications if set to True on the Global Options • Unapprove Reconciliations that are at a Level 1 approval (cannot unapprove above their level), sending the Reconciliation back to a Prepared state.
Backup Approver 1	Users and Groups	Access Control	• All actions a Primary Approver 1 may perform except filter Reconciliations within the Reconciliation Workspace using the Primary Approver filter to see Reconciliations where they are the Primary Approver • Receive Completed or Comment notifications if notify is set to True on the Access Control setup
Approver 2	Users	Reconciliation Inventory	• Perform all actions as Primary Approver 1, including prepare and perform Level 1 approval

Role	Assignable System Security Roles	Configuration	Actions
			• Perform Level 2 approval if they have not prepared or performed Level 1 approval • Unapprove Level 2 approval, sending the Reconciliation back to status of Partially Approved (if previously Fully Approved because only two Approvals were required), and approval of Approved Level 1 of X (either 2, 3, or 4)
Backup Approver 2	Users and Groups	Access Control	• All actions a Primary Approver 2 may perform except filter Reconciliations within the Reconciliation Workspace using the Primary Approver filter to see Reconciliations where they are the Primary Approver • Receive Completed or Comment notifications if notify is set to True on the Access Control setup
Approver 3	Users	Reconciliation Inventory	• Perform all actions as Primary Approver 2, including prepare and perform Level 1 & 2 Approvals • Perform Level 3 approval if they have not prepared or performed Level 1 or Level 2 approval • Unapprove Level 3 approval, sending the Reconciliation back to Status of Partially Approved (if previously Fully Approved because only three approvals were required), and approval of Approved Level 2 of X (either 3 or 4)
Backup Approver 3	Users and Groups	Access Control	• All actions a Primary Approver 3 may perform except filter Reconciliations within the Reconciliation Workspace using the Primary Approver filter to see Reconciliations where they are the Primary Approver

Role	Assignable System Security Roles	Configuration	Actions
			• Receive Completed or Comment notifications if set to True on the Global Options and if notify is set to True on the Access Control setup
Approver 4	Users	Reconciliation Inventory	• Perform all action as Primary Approver 3, including prepare and perform Level 1-3 Approvals • Perform Level 4 approval if they have not prepared or performed Level 1-3 approval • Unapprove Level 4 approval, sending the Reconciliation back to Status of Partially Approved and approval of Approved Level 3 of 4
Backup Approver 4	Users and Groups	Access Control	• All actions a Primary Approver 4 may perform except filter Reconciliations within the Reconciliation Workspace using the Primary Approver filter to see Reconciliations where they are the Primary Approver • Receive Completed or Comment notifications if notify is set to True on the Access Control setup
Local Admin	Users and Groups	Access Control	• Navigate to the Reconciliation Administration page • View Reconciliation Inventory items where the Access Group attribute is set to an Access Group where they are Local Admin • Edit Reconciliation attributes for Inventory items where they are the Local Admin • Edit Access Groups, including assignment and members, to assigned Reconciliations, within the Reconciliation Inventory page

Role	Assignable System Security Roles	Configuration	Actions
			• View and edit Reconciliation Inventory attributes to Account Groups they manage • Process Reconciliations for Base-level Workflow Profiles
Account Reconciliation Admin	Users	Global Options	• Navigate to the Reconciliations Settings page and modify and configure all Reconciliation Settings • View all pages within the Administration (Definition, Inventory, Tracking, Bal Check, AutoRec) and modify and configure all settings • Run Discover • View all Reconciliation Inventory items and can edit all attributes • Can view all Reconciliations in the Reconciliation Grid • Unapprove or reject Fully Approved Reconciliations • Create, modify, and delete members of the Access Groups • Assign Local Admins to Access Groups • Process Reconciliations for Parent-level Workflow Profiles • Unapprove Auto Approved Reconciliations • Complete a Reconciliation WF once all underlying Reconciliations are Fully Approved
OneStream System Admin	Users	System Security	• Perform all actions as Reconciliation Admin • Assign Account Reconciliation Admin

Figure 2.28

Figure 2.29 shows the Workflow a Reconciliation may go through and the various states it may take. The diagram shows only three levels of approval, but (again) a Reconciliation may have up to four levels. For reference, AG refers to Access Group members or back-up roles.

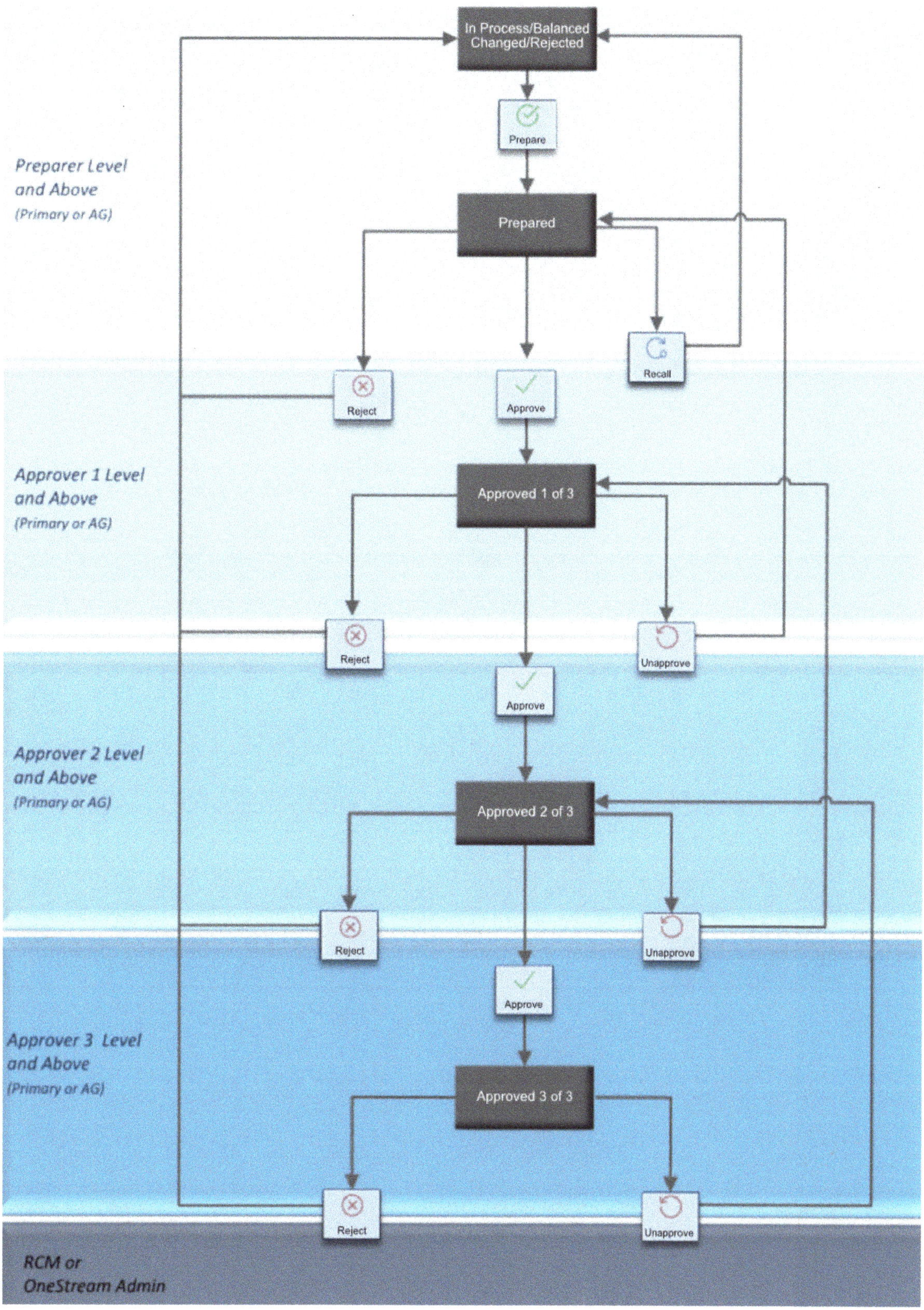

Figure 2.29

Figure 2.30 shows the actions each role type may take for a Reconciliation that is In Process.

Reconciliation State- In Process										
			Assigned Role							
			Auditor	Viewer	Commenter	Primary Preparer/ AG Preparer	Primary Approvers 1-4/ AG Approvers 1-4	Local Admin	Account Reconciliation Admin	OS Admin
Capability	View	View Rec		✓	✓	✓	✓	✓	✓	✓
	Comment	Add Comment on Rec (can't edit or delete)			✓	✓	✓		✓	✓
	Preparation	Prepare Rec				✓	✓		✓	✓
		Recall Rec								
	Approval	Approve Rec								
		Reject Rec								
		Unapprove Rec								
	Administration	Edit Rec Attributes						✓	✓	✓

Figure 2.30

Figure 2.31 shows the actions each role type may take for a Reconciliation that is Prepared.

Reconciliation State - Fully Approved ✓										
			Assigned Role							
			Auditor	Viewer	Commenter	Primary Preparer/ AG Preparer	Primary Approvers 1-4/ AG Approvers 1-4	Local Admin	Account Reconciliation Admin	OS Admin
Capability	View	View Rec	✓	✓	✓	✓	✓	✓	✓	✓
	Comment	Add Comment on Rec (can't edit or delete)	✓		✓		✓		✓	✓
	Preparation	Prepare Rec								
		Recall Rec								
	Approval	Approve Rec								
		Reject Rec					✓		✓	✓
		Unapprove Rec					✓		✓	✓
	Administration	Edit Rec Attributes								

Figure 2.31

Figure 2.32 shows the actions each role type may take for a Reconciliation that is Fully Approved.

Reconciliation State - Fully Approved ✓										
			Assigned Role							
			Auditor	Viewer	Commenter	Primary Preparer/ AG Preparer	Primary Approvers 1-4/ AG Approvers 1-4	Local Admin	Account Reconciliation Admin	OS Admin
Capability	View	View Rec	✓	✓	✓	✓	✓	✓	✓	✓
	Comment	Add Comment on Rec (can't edit or delete)	✓		✓		✓		✓	✓
	Preparation	Prepare Rec								
		Recall Rec								
	Approval	Approve Rec								
		Reject Rec					✓		✓	✓
		Unapprove Rec					✓		✓	✓
	Administration	Edit Rec Attributes								

Figure 2.32

Primary Preparer and Approvers

Primary Preparers and Approvers are assigned at the Reconciliation level on the Reconciliation Inventory, on the Administration page, using a drop-down that includes all Security Users within the Platform.

The assignment of primary roles was done to prevent the creation of Access Groups for each Reconciliation. The intention behind this design is that primaries would be assigned, and then minimal Access Groups would be created to be utilized as backup roles. Utilizing the assignment of primary roles will assist in your solution's performance since the system will not have to loop through each Access Group to determine if you have the proper credentials. Instead, it will look directly to the Reconciliation Table.

Access Groups

Again, Access Groups are intended to be used for backup roles. To create an Access Group:

1. Navigate to the Access Control page within Settings.
2. Select + to create a new group.
3. Name the Access Group. This name is what will appear in the drop-down of available Access Groups in the Reconciliation Inventory. Note this name cannot be changed upon Save.
4. Add a description for the Access Group. This description will not appear in the solution but is for your reference. Save the Access Group.
5. Once the Access Group is created, you can assign either Security Users or Security Groups. To add a new User, select +.
6. Select a User from the drop-down.
7. Assign a role to that User. This will be a backup role in instances where the Primary is not available to perform their duties. If you would like this User to receive email notifications, set the Notify box to True.
8. To assign Security Groups to perform backup duties, navigate to the bottom-right and select +.

9. Select a Security Group from the drop-down. In the example, in Figure 2.33, RCM_Commenters was selected, meaning any time a User was added or removed from the RCM_Commenters Platform Security Group, the change would also be reflected in their access to Account Reconciliations. This has been added to reduce the maintenance of Security Groups in instances where a customer decides to utilize Groups that were already created in the platform.
10. Assign a role to the Security Group.

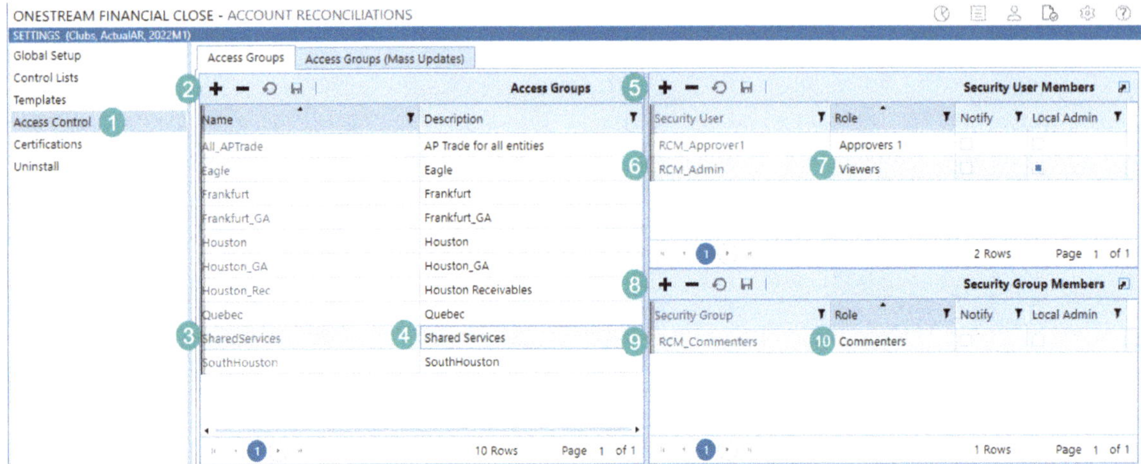

Figure 2.33

Access Groups (Mass Updates)

The Security User Members and Security Groups Members grids show all Access Groups that were created on the Access Group page – and their members – to easily edit multiple Access Groups at once without having to manually click through each Access Group. For example, in Figure 2.34, all Users are shown for the two Access Groups that I have set up within my system, HoustonAG and SharedServices, and I can add Users or Groups to either of these Access Groups. I can also edit the roles for either Access Group.

> **Note:** When changes are made, the lines do not turn yellow, as is typical on other areas of the platform where edits are made to indicate a save is needed. Rather, the Save button is black instead of light gray. Make sure you save all changes before navigating away from this page.

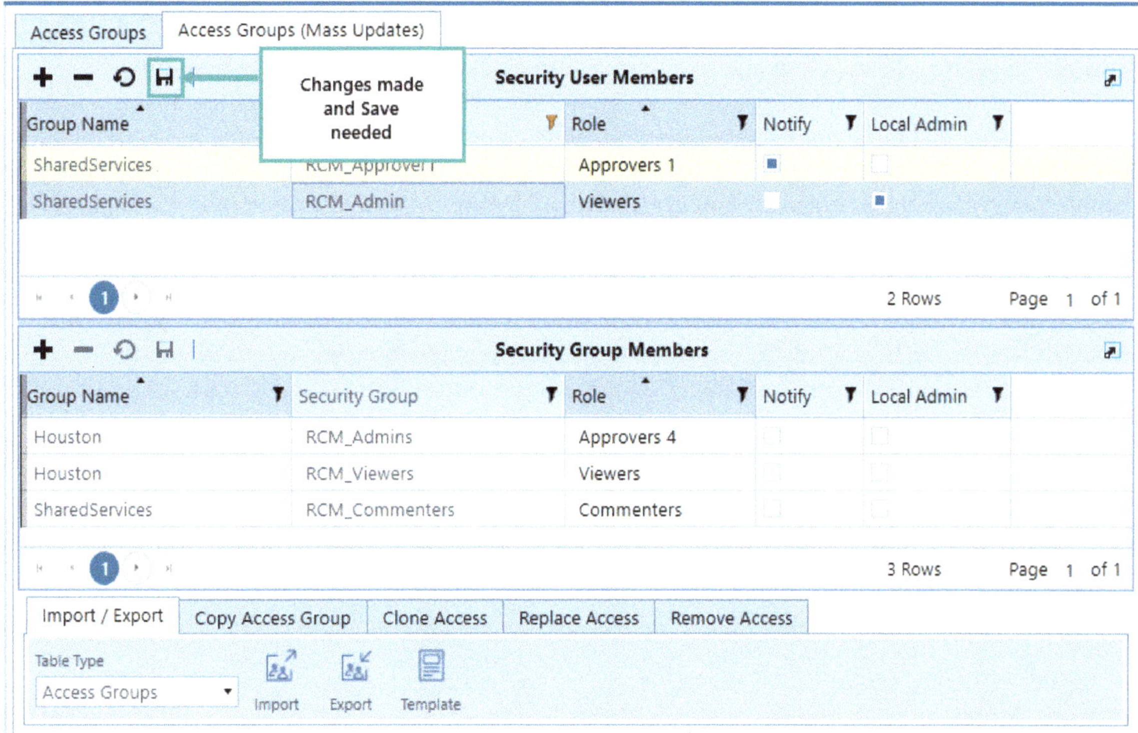

Figure 2.34

Import/Export

This option allows the ability to first export the Access Group information into an Excel template. From there, the preset Excel range can be edited to make changes to Access Group settings. Information is provided at the top of the exported Excel template on how to edit the Access Group information. Once you have completed editing, you may then import changes directly into the solution. This is useful when first setting up Access Groups or making mass updates to existing Access Groups.

Copy Group Access

Utilize this feature when you would like to use an Access Group already created as a starting point for future groups. For example, you may know Jenna will always be a backup Preparer, Chelsea will always be a backup Approver 1, and Amanda will be backup Approver 2. In this instance, you could create an Access Group with those members and role assignments, and utilize it as your framework for creating additional Access Groups.

Select an Access Group from the drop-down and enter the name of the new (Target) Access Group to be created and then click Copy. The new Access Group will then appear on the Access Group screen along with the Users and User roles; you can now easily add one-off members to each Access Group as necessary.

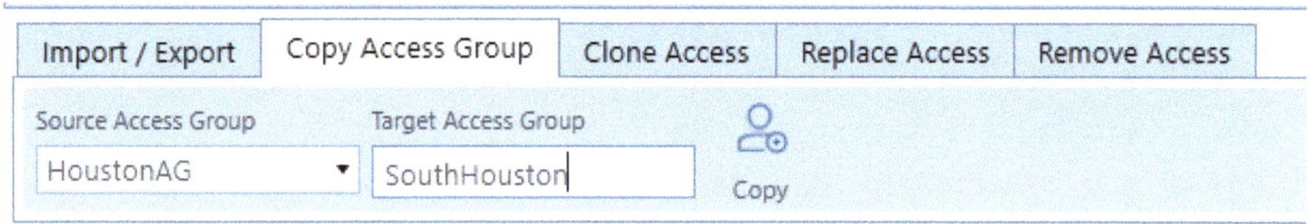

Figure 2.35

Clone Access

Utilize this feature when you would like to mirror the access of Users or Groups already set up within the Access Groups. For example, if a new employee – Katie – started to assist Jenna in her Preparer back-up duties, you would select User Jenna from the drop-down as the Source and then select Katie as the Target. Upon selecting Clone, Katie would appear in all Access Groups that Jenna was previously assigned to (along with Jenna), and both would have the role of Preparer. The same applies for a Security Group.

Select a Source User or Source Group as the model User/Group and a Target User or Target Group, and then click Clone. The Target User/Group is added into every Access Group that the Source User/Group is in. If the Target User/Group was previously in an Access Group that the Source User/Group is *not* in, the Target User/Group is removed from that Access Group. The Target User and Source User will have the same access.

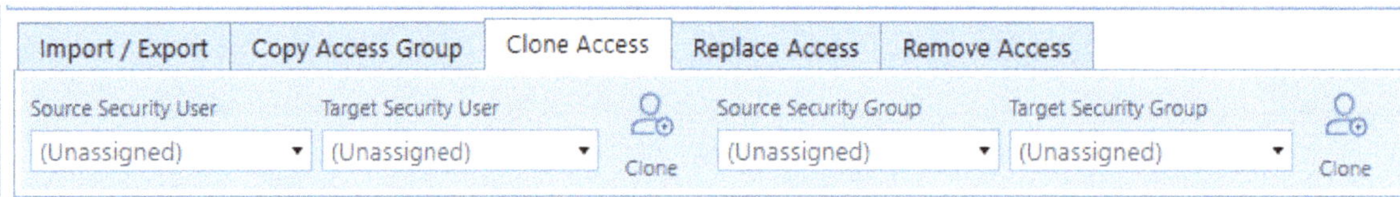

Figure 2.36

Replace Access

Utilize this feature when you want to remove previously established access and replace it with a different User or Group. For example, using the same example as above, let's assume Jenna has moved departments and Katie is completely taking over her role. In this instance, I would want to remove all of Jenna's access and replace her with Katie.

Select a Source User or Source Group who will be replaced in every Access Group with the Target User or Target Group upon clicking Replace. Note that filtering between the Clone and Replace tabs will not refresh your drop-down selections, so make sure your selections are correct before selecting Replace.

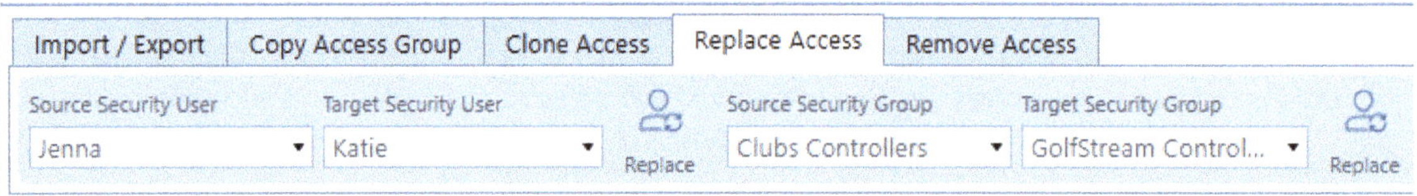

Figure 2.37

Remove Access

This will remove the User or Group from every Access Group upon selecting Remove. Again, note that the Source selections will hold from the other tabs, so be sure to review that you have the correct User or Group selected prior to clicking Remove.

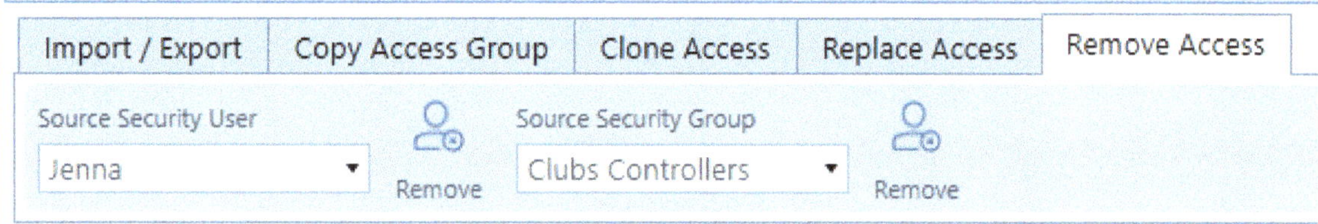

Figure 2.38

Security Summary

Security is the second phase of administration because it is where you establish which Users have the ability to make changes to Reconciliation attributes (Local Admins), which Users can see which Reconciliations, and which Users can take action on Reconciliations.

With Security in the bag, let's take a look at Administration.

* * *

Administration

Account Reconciliation Administration contains pages to define your Reconciliations, configure your Reconciliation attributes within the Inventory, configure Account Groups, create tracking levels, create Balance Check levels, create AutoRec Rules, and create notification methods. Administration relates to the entire Account Reconciliation application. This area can only be accessed by Account Reconciliation Administrators and OneStream Administrators.

Definition

The Reconciliation Definition page is the first step in creating the Reconciliation Inventory. Within this page, you will:

- **Perform the Discover process** – which finds the Accounts to be reconciled, based on the filter you established in Global Options.
- **Assign default Definitions** – which are set at the T.Account, or OneStream Account Dimension level.
- **Assign Tracking Level Overrides** – which are used if tracking levels vary by Entity.

Discover

Upon first opening this page, the Account List will appear empty. A Reconciliation Administrator can click Discover and, upon initial discovery, the system will create the Account List by first looking to the Account Member Filter that was set within the Global Options.

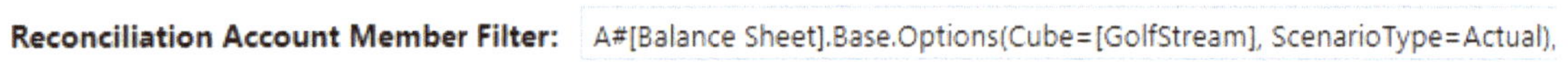

Reconciliation Account Member Filter: A#[Balance Sheet].Base.Options(Cube=[GolfStream], ScenarioType=Actual),

Figure 2.39

If the Account is within the Member Filter, the Account will be added to the Account List. In addition, OneStream looks to Stage at this point to see if a balance exists for the Account. If a balance does exist, the Reconciled column is set to True.

Upon populating the Account List, the Discover process will also automatically assign the default Reconciliation Definition of Entity, which is the lowest tracking level that includes only Account and Entity. If you wish to have a different tracking level assigned, be sure to assign it to the Global Defaults prior to clicking Discover. From there, the system then loops through the Stage data again and reads balances for the current and future Workflow periods to see if anything exists in Source to determine where Reconciliations exist for the different tracking level instances.

For example, in M1 there may be five Source Accounts imported to the Source Stage for the Petty Cash Target Account, and two Source Entities – Houston and South Houston. However, Houston and South Houston may only have balances in two of the Source Accounts. In this instance, four Reconciliations would be added to the Reconciliation Inventory in M1. Moving into M2 during Discover, both Entities' imported balances for all five Source Accounts – six additional Reconciliations – would be added to the Reconciliation Inventory that were not created in M1, for a total of ten Reconciliations.

Discover then assigns all default Reconciliation attributes to the Reconciliation Inventory, which are configured in Global Defaults. Note that this is for the initial creation of the Reconciliation Inventory, or for any new Inventory items discovered in the prior period, (in the example above, this would be the four created in M1 and the six created in M2). If the Reconciliation was added in a prior period, and attributes were assigned, the attributes would pull from the prior period for future periods.

For example, in M1, as established, four Reconciliations were added to the Reconciliation Inventory and the default attributes were assigned. After initial attribute assignment, either the Local Admin (for Reconciliations where they are assigned) or the Reconciliation Administrator can make updates to the attributes. Note, in Figure 2.40, the default attribute that was assigned on creation was a Risk Level of Low.

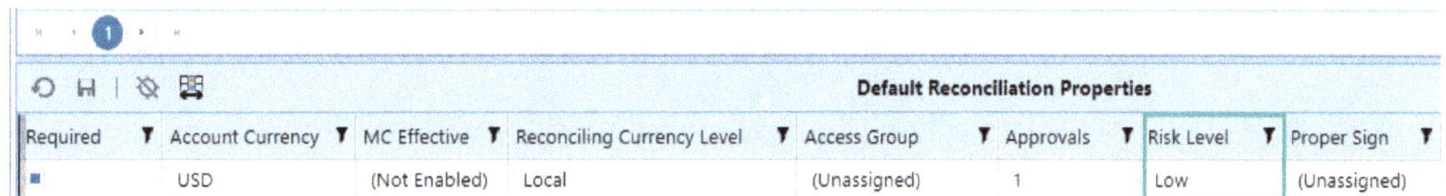
Default Reconciliation Properties

Required	Account Currency	MC Effective	Reconciling Currency Level	Access Group	Approvals	Risk Level	Proper Sign
■	USD	(Not Enabled)	Local	(Unassigned)	1	Low	(Unassigned)

Figure 2.40

However, in M1, the Administrator has changed the Risk to Medium for the four Reconciliations.

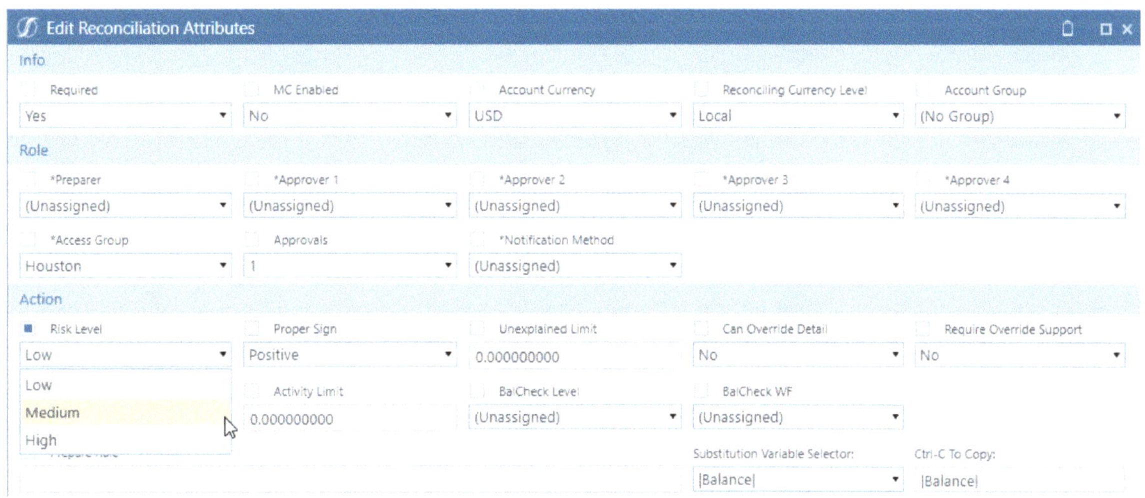

Figure 2.41

Upon clicking Discover, the attributes assigned to the new Accounts will be the default of Low, and the Reconciliations created and updated in M1 will have the attributes assigned in M1 pulled forward (Risk Level of Medium), as shown in Figure 2.42.

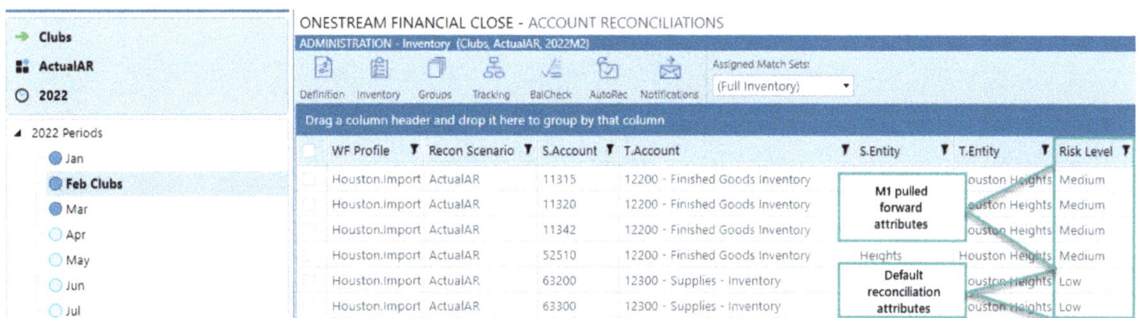

Figure 2.42

Once the discovery has been run for a period, all attributes are created. Therefore, if you were to make changes to attributes in M1 after discovery was run in M2, the M1 changes made after discovery in M2 would *not* be reflected in M2. Additionally, any attribute changes made in future periods will not be reflected in prior periods. In this way, the Reconciliation Inventory attributes are time-based.

Click the Task Activity icon to show the results of the discovery process and how many new Reconciliation Inventory items were discovered. You can either have the Reconciliation

Administrator manually run the discovery process, or a OneStream Administrator could utilize the Task Scheduler within the platform to automate this step.

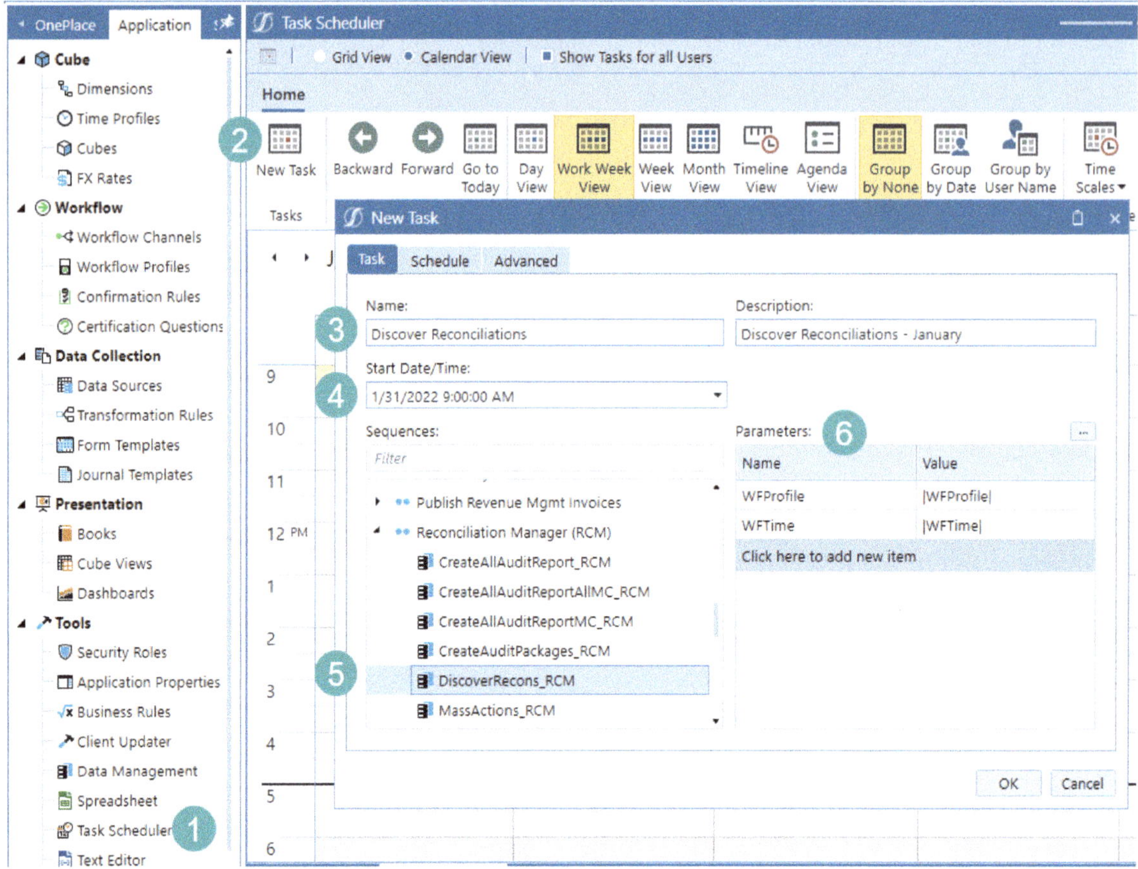

Figure 2.43

1. Go to Application – Task Scheduler
2. Select New Task
3. Add a Name and Description
4. Set the Date and Time you would like discovery to occur
5. Locate and select the DiscoverRecons_RCM sequence under Reconciliation Manager (RCM)
6. Assign the Parameters – will default to parameter settings
    a. |WF Profile| - Name of the Workflow Profile
    b. |WFTime| - Workflow time period
7. Click OK

Account List

OneStream will auto populate the: 1. Account (number), 2. Description, 3. Reconciled (which is not part of the Member property and therefore auto set to True), and 4. Type based on the settings within the Account.

Figure 2.44 shows the Petty Cash Account properties in the Account Dimension, and Figure 2.45 shows the properties established upon discovery for the Petty Cash Account. Note that the properties are the same in both.

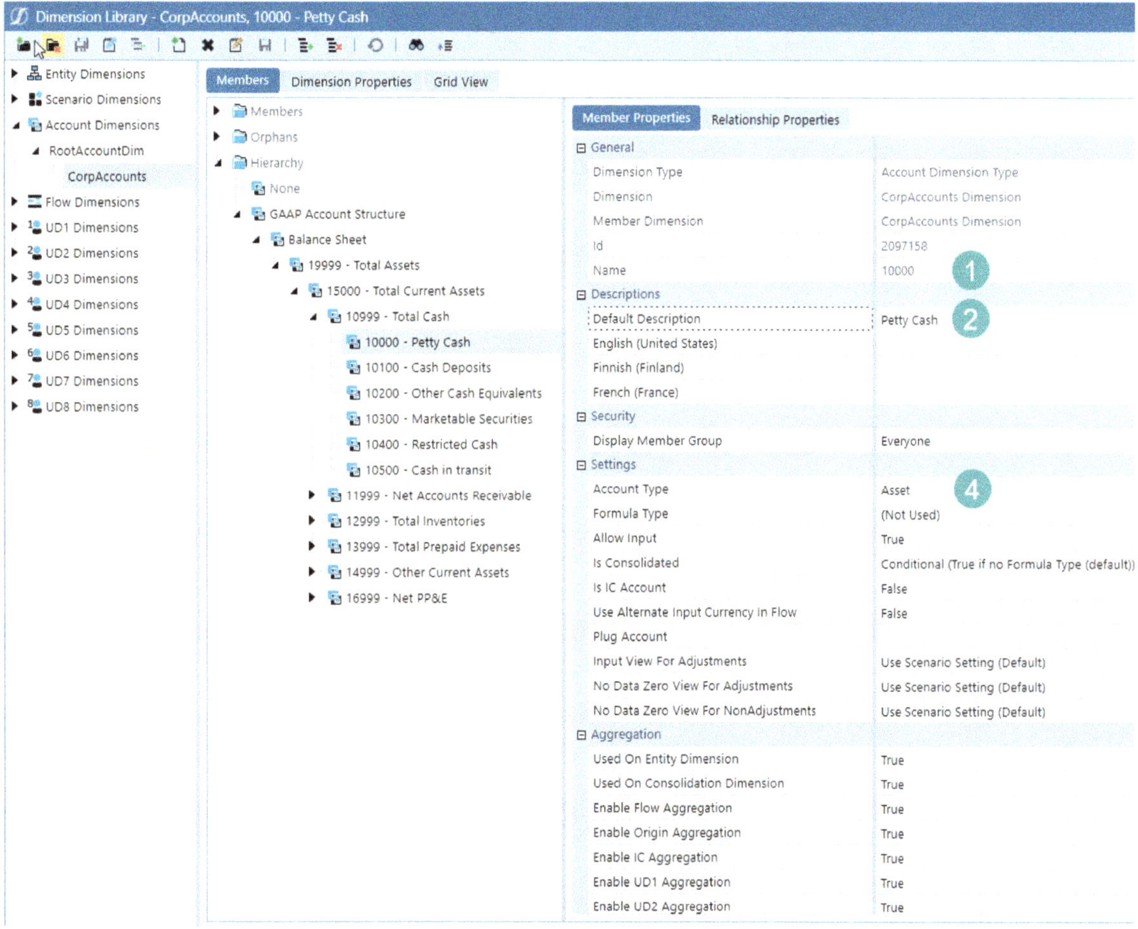

Figure 2.44

The only item that is not a property in the Account Dimension is 3. Reconciled, which is just used for Account Reconciliations. None of the properties can be changed in the Account List grid.

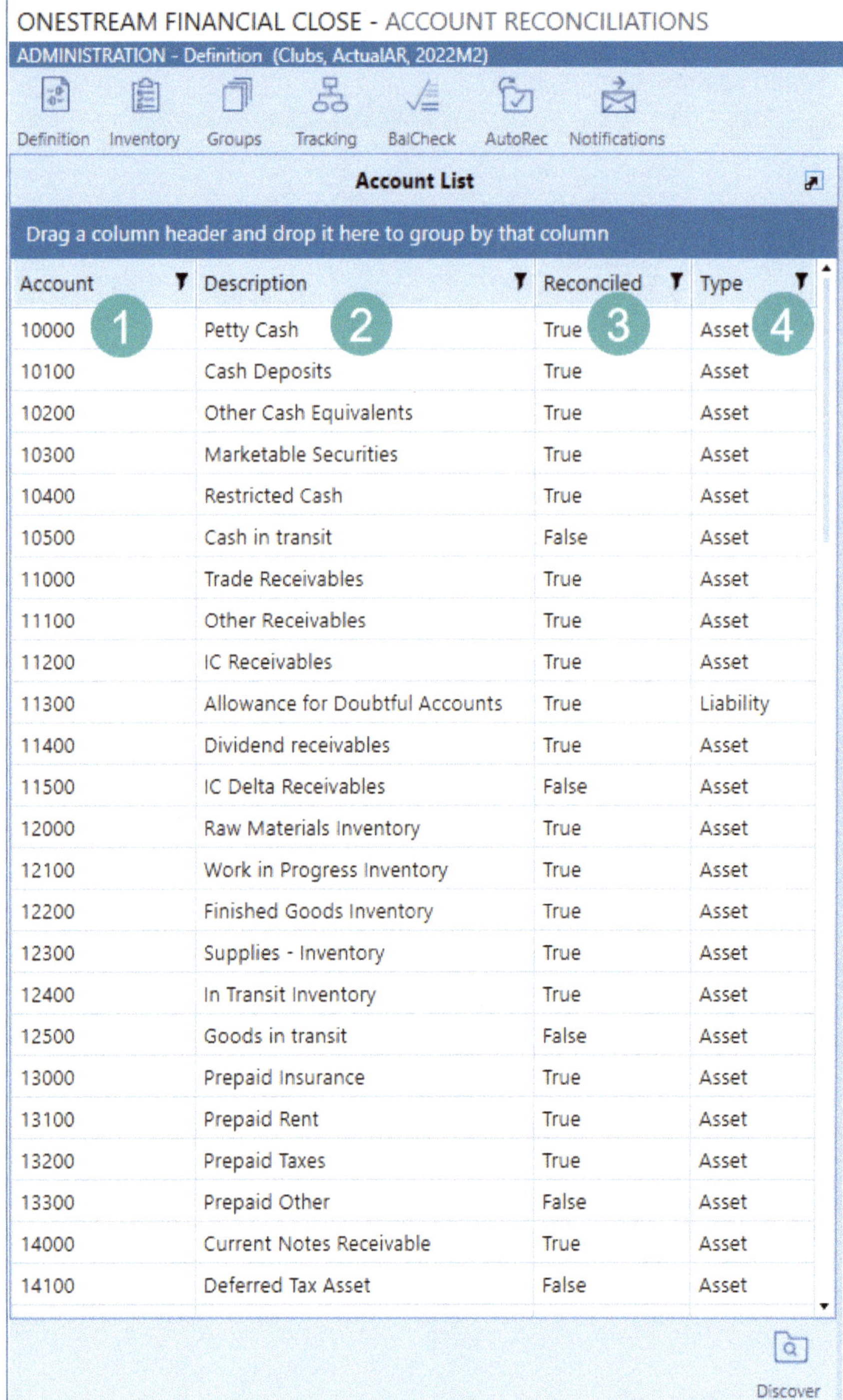

Account	Description	Reconciled	Type
10000	Petty Cash	True	Asset
10100	Cash Deposits	True	Asset
10200	Other Cash Equivalents	True	Asset
10300	Marketable Securities	True	Asset
10400	Restricted Cash	True	Asset
10500	Cash in transit	False	Asset
11000	Trade Receivables	True	Asset
11100	Other Receivables	True	Asset
11200	IC Receivables	True	Asset
11300	Allowance for Doubtful Accounts	True	Liability
11400	Dividend receivables	True	Asset
11500	IC Delta Receivables	False	Asset
12000	Raw Materials Inventory	True	Asset
12100	Work in Progress Inventory	True	Asset
12200	Finished Goods Inventory	True	Asset
12300	Supplies - Inventory	True	Asset
12400	In Transit Inventory	True	Asset
12500	Goods in transit	False	Asset
13000	Prepaid Insurance	True	Asset
13100	Prepaid Rent	True	Asset
13200	Prepaid Taxes	True	Asset
13300	Prepaid Other	False	Asset
14000	Current Notes Receivable	True	Asset
14100	Deferred Tax Asset	False	Asset

Figure 2.45

Reconciliation Definition

While each Account will have default Reconciliation properties assigned upon initial discovery, it is possible to alter the properties for each Account at any point.

Within the Reconciliation Definition, you can add (upload), view, and delete reference documents to each Account. These reference documents are your company's internally-created documents that you would like your End-Users to be able to reference during the time of Reconciliation preparation. For example, you may want to include a set of instructions on how the Reconciliation is to be prepared, a list of required supporting documentation, etc.

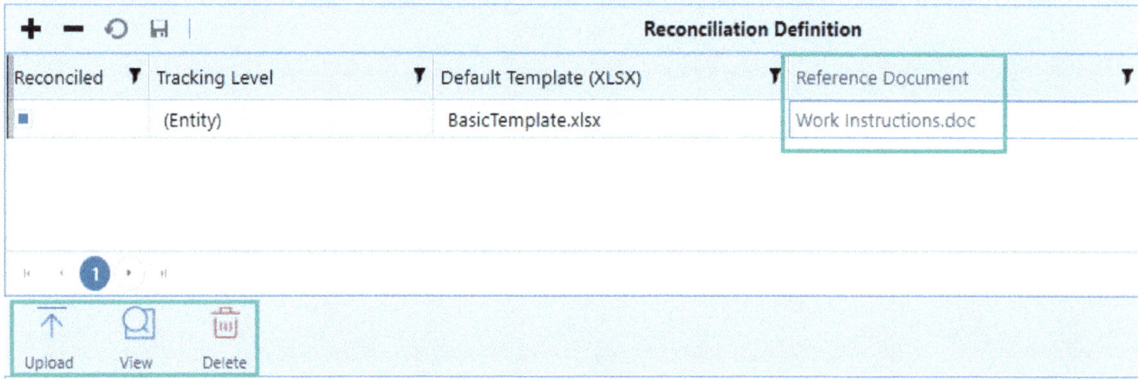

Figure 2.46

Entity Tracking Level Override

There are times when an Account needs to be tracked in the Reconciliation Inventory at a level that is an exception for certain Entities, beyond the setting for that Account in general (as set in the Reconciliation Definition).

In these cases, click + to add an exception per Entity that requires one for this Reconciliation Definition.

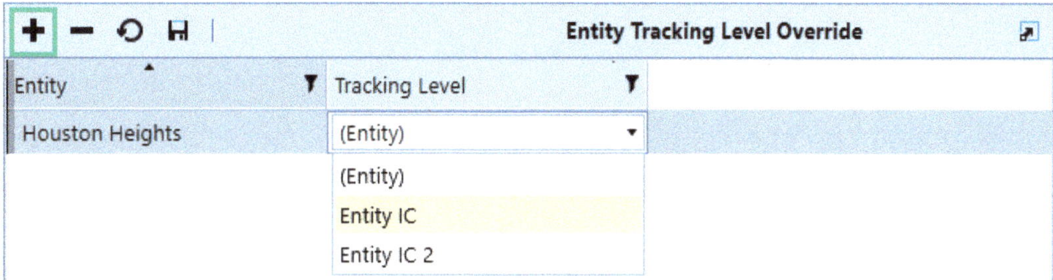

Figure 2.47

For instance, Account 10000 has a tracking level of (Entity), which means by Entity and Account. But for that same Account and Entity – Houston Heights – we may need to track this Account by Entity, Account, and IC. In this instance, a new tracking level would be created on the Tracking page; Entity Houston Heights would be selected from the drop-down, and the new tracking level – Entity IC – would be assigned.

Inventory

The Reconciliation Inventory is a Grid View and is the complete list of all Reconciliations that were created in the current or prior periods when the discovery process was run, as discussed in the Definition section. The Reconciliations displayed within the Inventory will be based on the Workflow Profile selected. As such, to see the complete listing, ensure you are at the top Parent Workflow Profile. Additionally, only a Reconciliation Administrator can view the complete Inventory; Local Administrators will only see Reconciliations where they are assigned as Local Administrator within the Access Group.

Filters

All attributes within the Reconciliation Inventory can be filtered by utilizing the filter icon on the right of the column header. Using this filter, you can select multiple items, select all, or show only certain values, based on your own needs.

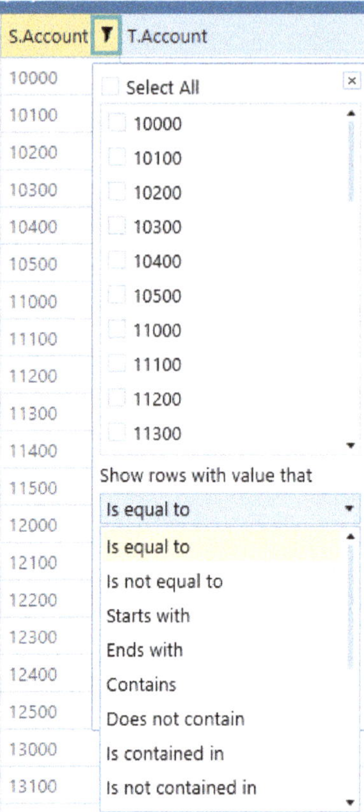

Figure 2.48

The **Assigned Match Set filter** has also been added to the top of the Inventory to filter important information that is not an attribute within the Inventory.

Assigned Match Sets

This filter is only applicable for solutions where **Transaction Matching Integration** is enabled and is utilized to easily identify Reconciliations that have Match Sets assigned for detail item creation. The assignment of Match Sets will be discussed in the Inventory Actions section. The drop-down will contain the following:

- **(Full Inventory)** – Complete list of Reconciliation Inventory without any filtering related to Match Sets.
- **(All)** – All Reconciliations where one or more Match Sets have been assigned.
- **(None)** – Reconciliations that do not have a Match Set assigned.
- **Match Set Name** – This drop-down will contain all Match Sets that are set up within the **Transaction Matching Global Settings – Match Sets**. Select a Match Set to view Reconciliations that have Match Set assigned.

Attributes

Administrators can configure and update the attributes for a Reconciliation if the Reconciliation has not been Prepared in the current Workflow Period. If the Reconciliation has been prepared, it must be placed back into an In Process state to update attributes. This is to ensure that attributes for a period are accurately reflected in the Inventory and are the same as the attributes required at the time of Reconciliation preparation. Except for those noted, all attributes are WF time-based.

Attributes that have (Multi-Currency Enabled) added to the header will only appear if this setting has been set to True within the Global Settings. The Reconciliation Inventory grid comes with all attributes showing by default.

To change the order of column headers, or to hide any columns that are not utilized by your company, (S. UDs, for example), right-click on any cell in the grid, and select Column Settings (Figure 2.49). From there, move columns to the left that you would like hidden and move columns up or down in the list of Visible Columns for ordering preferences (Figure 2.50) and select OK to Save.

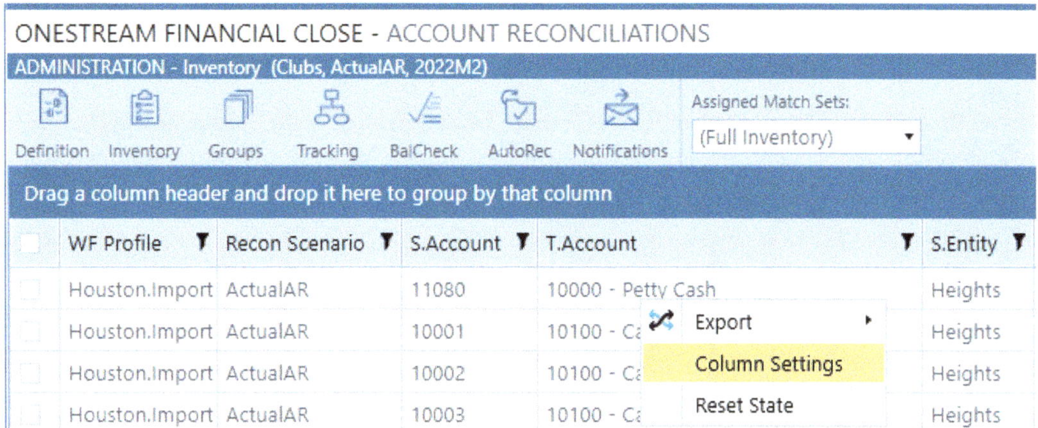

Figure 2.49

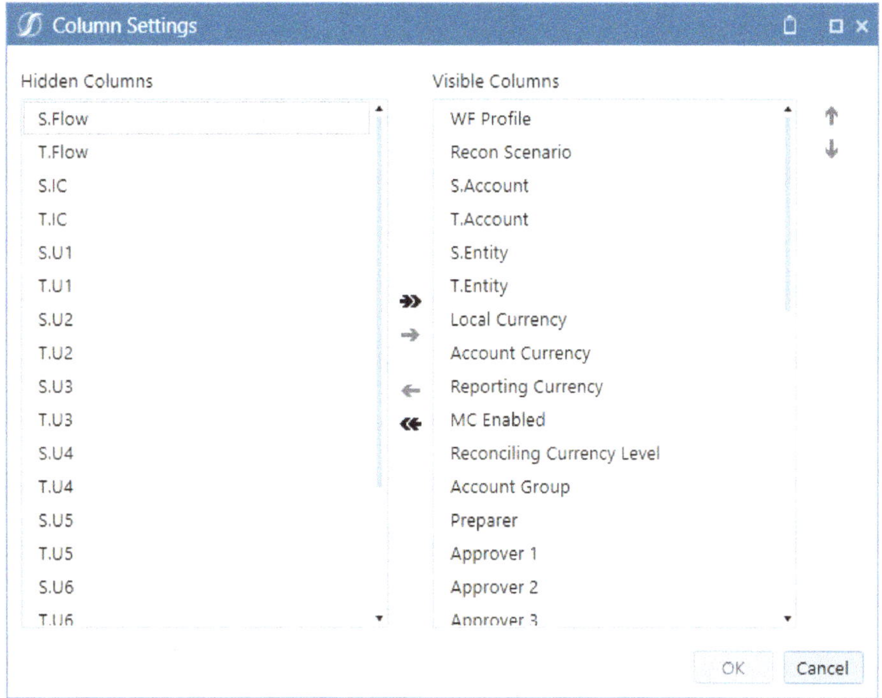

Figure 2.50

WF Profile

This is the Workflow Profile where the Reconciliation was discovered for the Source Account and is a Base Input Child Import Workflow Profile. In other words, this is where the data was imported into Stage for the Reconciliation. In order to perform any action on a Reconciliation, a User must have access to this Import Workflow Profile, as this is where the balances originate.

Recon Scenario

This will default to the Reconciliation Scenario set in Global Options.

S. Account

Source Account. This will be your ERP or GL Account and is the Account that is originally imported into OneStream prior to any Transformation Rules. Source Accounts are derived from that Workflow Profile's Transformation Rules (Figure 2.51) and are based on the imported Source Values (Figure 2.52). This attribute cannot be changed.

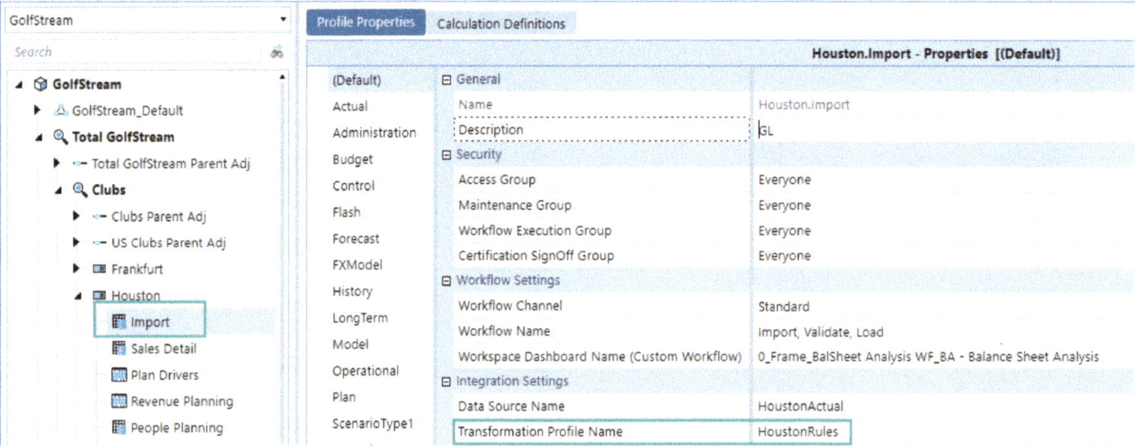

Figure 2.51

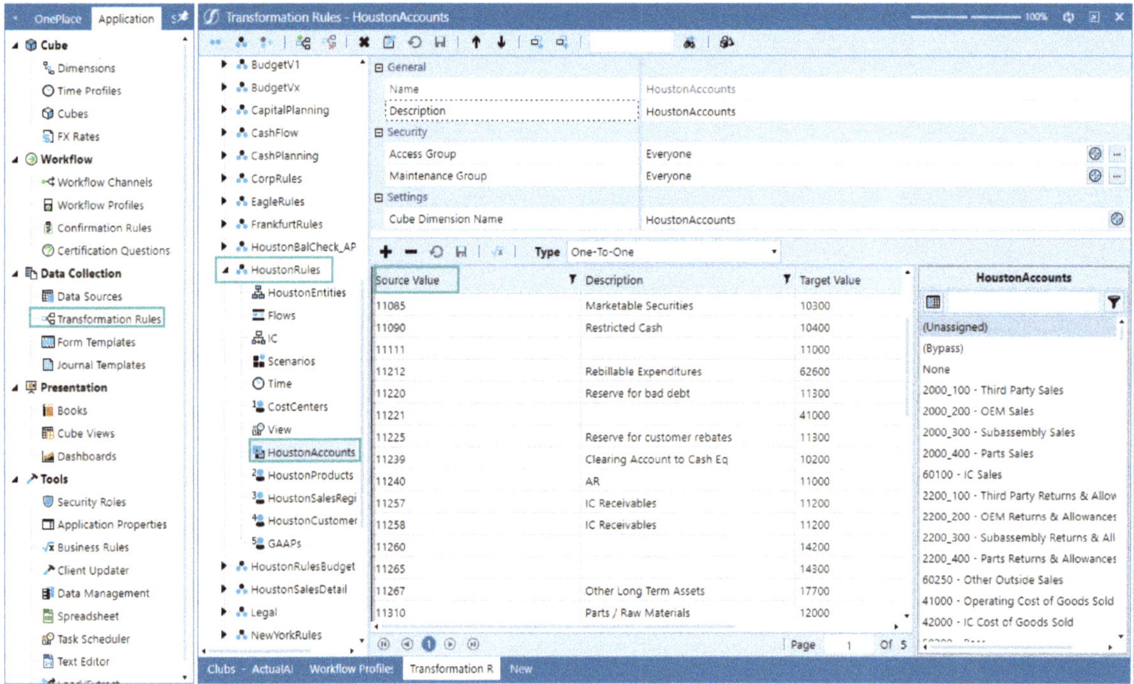

Figure 2.52

T. Account

Target Account for the Cube. This list of Accounts is populated by the Account Dimension for the Cube. This attribute cannot be changed.

S. Entity

Source Entity. This will be your ERP or GL Entity and is the Entity that is originally imported into OneStream prior to any Transformation Rules. Source Entities are derived from that Workflow Profile's Transformation Rules and are based on the Source Values that are imported, in the same way Source Accounts are used. This attribute cannot be changed.

T. Entity

Target Entity for the Cube. This list of Entities is populated by the Entity Dimension for the Cube. This attribute cannot be changed.

S. Flow

Source Flow from Stage. This attribute cannot be changed.

T. Flow

Target Flow for the Cube. The list of Flows is populated by the Flow Dimension for the Cube. This attribute cannot be changed.

S. IC

Source Intercompany from Stage. This attribute cannot be changed.

T. IC

Target Intercompany for the Cube. The IC list is populated by the IC Dimension for the Cube. This attribute cannot be changed.

S. U1 – U8

Source User Dimensions from Stage. The Source UDs are derived from that Workflow Profile's Transformation Rules and are based on the Source Values that are imported, in the same way Source Accounts are used. This attribute cannot be changed.

T. U1 – U8

Target User Dimensions for the Cube. This list of UDs is populated by the specific UD Dimension (UD1-8) for the Cube. This attribute cannot be changed.

Currency (Single-Currency) or Local Currency (Multi-Currency Enabled)

Currency type for the Local-level balance. It is not editable within Account Reconciliations as it is maintained within the Entity Dimension.

Account Currency (Multi-Currency Enabled)

Currency type for the Account-level balance. This will be a drop-down of all currency types within the currency filter in Application Properties. The default currency type will be set to Local and will therefore be the T. Entity's currency type. This may be changed by selecting a different currency from the drop-down.

The currency type may be changed after a multi-currency Reconciliation has been completed. The currency type labels will change for all periods, including previously completed Reconciliations, which may have been completed using the original currency type. If having historical Reconciliation balances translated to the updated currency type is desired, prior periods must be unlocked and Reconciliations reprocessed if the Account currency type is modified.

Reporting Currency (Multi-Currency Enabled)

Currency type for the Reporting-level balance. This is not editable as it is derived from the Cube currency. Only a single reporting currency is allowed per Cube.

MC Enabled (Multi-Currency Enabled)

This is a check box that, by default, is set to False, meaning the Reconciliation will be a single-currency Reconciliation, only the Local balance will be used, and no Translation will occur. If set to True, the Reconciliation will show three currency levels on the Reconciliation header: Account, Local, and Reporting.

This setting provides the ability to have single-currency Reconciliations and multi-currency Reconciliations within the same Account Reconciliation instance. Multi-currency Calculations, including Translation, will not occur in periods where this setting is False. As the attribute is time-based, you may have a single-currency Reconciliation in the first period, multi-currency in the second, and then go back to single-currency in the third, and appropriate Translation would occur for only the periods required.

Determining whether multi-currency is useful for your organization is an important consideration to take into account during implementation. While Account currency may not be used/required, being able to see reporting within the Reconciliations page may be helpful. In this instance, where only two currency levels exist (e.g., Local and Reporting), it is recommended that multi-currency be enabled, the Account currency default set to Local, and the MC Enabled be set to True for each Reconciliation.

Reconciling Currency Level (Multi-Currency Enabled)

This determines the currency level – either Account, Local, or Reporting – to be used for the Reconciliation. The default is Local, as this is the level that was previously reconciled prior to multi-currency enablement. This reconciling level applies to the Unexplained Limit, Prepare Rules, AutoRec, Balance Change, and Balance Checks. For example, if the Unexplained Limit for a Reconciliation is set to 0, the reconciling currency level is set to Account, and the Unexplained Limit is 0 for the Account level but 100 for the Local, then the Reconciliation could be prepared. However, if the reconciling currency is set to Local in the example above, the Reconciliation could not be prepared.

The reconciling currency level is easily identified as it is the level in larger, bold font.

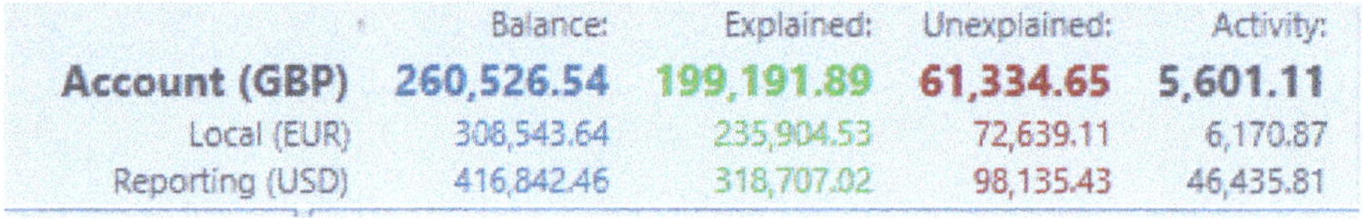

	Balance:	Explained:	Unexplained:	Activity:
Account (GBP)	**260,526.54**	**199,191.89**	**61,334.65**	**5,601.11**
Local (EUR)	308,543.64	235,904.53	72,639.11	6,170.87
Reporting (USD)	416,842.46	318,707.02	98,135.43	46,435.81

Figure 2.53

Account Group

A drop-down list of all Account Groups created by the Account Reconciliation Administrator. If an Account Group is selected for the Reconciliation, the Reconciliation will become part of the Account Group upon Save. If set to (No Group) the Reconciliation is reconciled individually. If the User is a Local Admin, the list of Account Groups is limited to only those they manage. The Local Admin can change the assignment of a Reconciliation Inventory item to a different Account Group, but once assigned, they are unable to set as (No Group).

Preparer (Not Time-Based)

This is the Primary Preparer for the Reconciliation. The drop-down list contains all enabled Users within the Platform system security. In order to minimize Access Groups created, and for the auditability of role assignments, it is encouraged to have a Primary Preparer assigned. However, if a Preparer is assigned in the Access Group assigned to the Reconciliation, this is not required.

Unlike other attributes, Preparer, Approver 1-4, and Access Groups are not time-based. This is so that if a role changes, the new User has the ability to utilize prior Reconciliations for reference, and so that people removed from roles no longer have the ability to take action on Reconciliations.

Approver 1 – 4 (Not Time-Based)

These are the Primary Approvers, Levels 1-4, for the Reconciliation. The drop-down list contains all enabled Users within the platform system security. In order to minimize Access Groups created and for the auditability of role assignments, it is encouraged to have a Primary Approver assigned. However, if an Approver is assigned in the Access Group assigned to the Reconciliation, this is not required.

At least one Approver must be set up for each Reconciliation, and the number of Approvers assigned must align with the number of approvals required. Once a User is assigned to a primary role, they cannot be assigned to another primary role. For example, if Grayson is the Preparer assigned on the Reconciliation Inventory, he cannot be assigned as the Approver 1 as well, in order to enforce segregation of duties. Further, if no Primary Approver 1 was assigned on the Inventory, at least one would need to be assigned within the Access Group assigned to the Reconciliation.

Access Group (Not Time-Based)

If desired, assign Access Groups created within the **Access Control** in Settings. As discussed previously, this is where you will assign Viewer, Commenter, and Local Admin roles, in addition to any backup Preparer or Approver roles. Again, Preparers and Approvers do not need to be included in an Access Group if a Primary has been assigned. However, it is always helpful to have these backups assigned in case of absence. Additionally, a User can be assigned as a Primary role and can still be a backup role within the Access Group. However, upon performing any action on the Reconciliation, the User will not be able to perform further action on the same Reconciliation.

Let's walk through an example of when a Primary may also be assigned as a backup. Assume the Preparer, Grayson (discussed above), works in the Shared Services Department and is primarily responsible for Accounts Payable Reconciliations. As such, he is assigned as the Primary Preparer on the Reconciliation Inventory for all AP Reconciliations. His co-worker, Cooper, also works in Shared Services and is primarily responsible for Accounts Receivable Reconciliations. As such, he is assigned as the Primary Preparer on the Reconciliation Inventory for all AR Reconciliations. However, in the case of absence, Grayson can prepare Cooper's Reconciliations, and vice versa. In this instance, we would create an Access Group called Shared Services, add both Grayson and Cooper as Preparers within the Group, and assign that Access Group to all the AP and AR Reconciliations.

Approvals

Use this drop-down to select the number of approvals (1 through 4) that are required for the Reconciliation. Ensure that the number of Approvers assigned to the Reconciliation aligns with the number of approvals required.

Risk Level

Choose from High, Medium, or Low risk for this attribute. As with other time-based attributes, you may want to frequently change this attribute to help identify when more review needs to be done on a Reconciliation. For example, an Account may have no activity due to initial start-up in the first few months, so it is set to low risk. However, the balance of the Account may increase, requiring you to increase the risk. This attribute is often also used when compiling AutoRec and Prepare Rules.

Proper Sign

The choices in the drop-down are Unassigned, Positive, or Negative. Assign what sign the value should come in for the Reconciliation. For example, if your liabilities come in as negative, assign Negative for all your liabilities. If a balance comes in that is not the proper sign, based on this configuration, you can easily filter that balance out within the Reconciliation Workspace, discussed later.

Unexplained Limit

This will set whether a Reconciliation can be prepared if the explained value is within a certain absolute value threshold. By default, a Reconciliation is not prepared unless the balance is explained to the penny. If the Unexplained Limit is set to 1000 and the Currency is USD, then the Reconciliation can be prepared if the difference is explained within $1000 USD.

Prepare Rule

These are custom rules that create restrictions on when a Preparer can mark the Reconciliation as Prepared. Rules created here will override the Unexplained Limit.

Example 1:

```
|Balance| < 1000
```

Example 2:

```
|BalanceAccount| < 1000
```

Example 3: This logic will set a global unexplained limit based on currency by retrieving the closing FX rate for the individual Reconciliation's currency relative to USD.

```
|UnexplainedBalance| < XFBR
MyCustomBusinessRule,UnexplainedLimitHelper,Currency=|Currency|,
Time=|Wtk|)
```

AutoRec Rule

This is a drop-down list populated from the list of rules created within the AutoRec page. The default is set to (Unassigned), meaning the Reconciliation does not have an AutoRec Rule applied. See the AutoRec section for more information on how to create and maintain these rules.

A second item, (Legacy), will exist in all solutions which first checks the balance to see if it is zero and, if so, will automatically reconcile that Reconciliation. Otherwise, it checks the activity in this Reconciliation since the last period and compares it to the absolute value of the Activity Limit.

Activity Limit

If an AutoRec Rule is created that has Activity selected, the rule will check the activity (differences in balance) in this Reconciliation since the last period and compare it to the absolute value of the activity value calculated. For instance, if the balance was explained last month at $1000, the new balance is $100, and the Activity Limit is $500 – this Reconciliation would not automatically reconcile. This column is only used in instances where an AutoRec Rule is assigned, and that rule contains an Activity component.

BalCheck WF Profile

Reconciliations that are supported using alternate source data files are considered **Balance Check Reconciliations**. For example, you could bring in your detailed Accounts Receivable Register from your AR software to support the GL balance. Assigning a Workflow Profile Import will make the Reconciliation a Balance Check type. When data is loaded into this BalCheck WF Profile, Account Reconciliations will pull the balances from the BalCheck WF Profile – based on the BalCheck Level assigned – and create a B-Type detail item for the Reconciliation. If the balance pulled ties to the Reconciliation balance, the Reconciliation would automatically reconcile.

To create a BalCheck Import to be included in the drop-down:

1. Create an Import step under the WF Profile.
2. Select the Model Scenario.
3. Set the Profile Active to True. (Make sure this is True for the Scenario referenced in the Global Settings for Reconciliation Scenario, or Model in our example, as OneStream only looks to that Scenario to populate the drop-down.)
4. Select the Data Source Name.

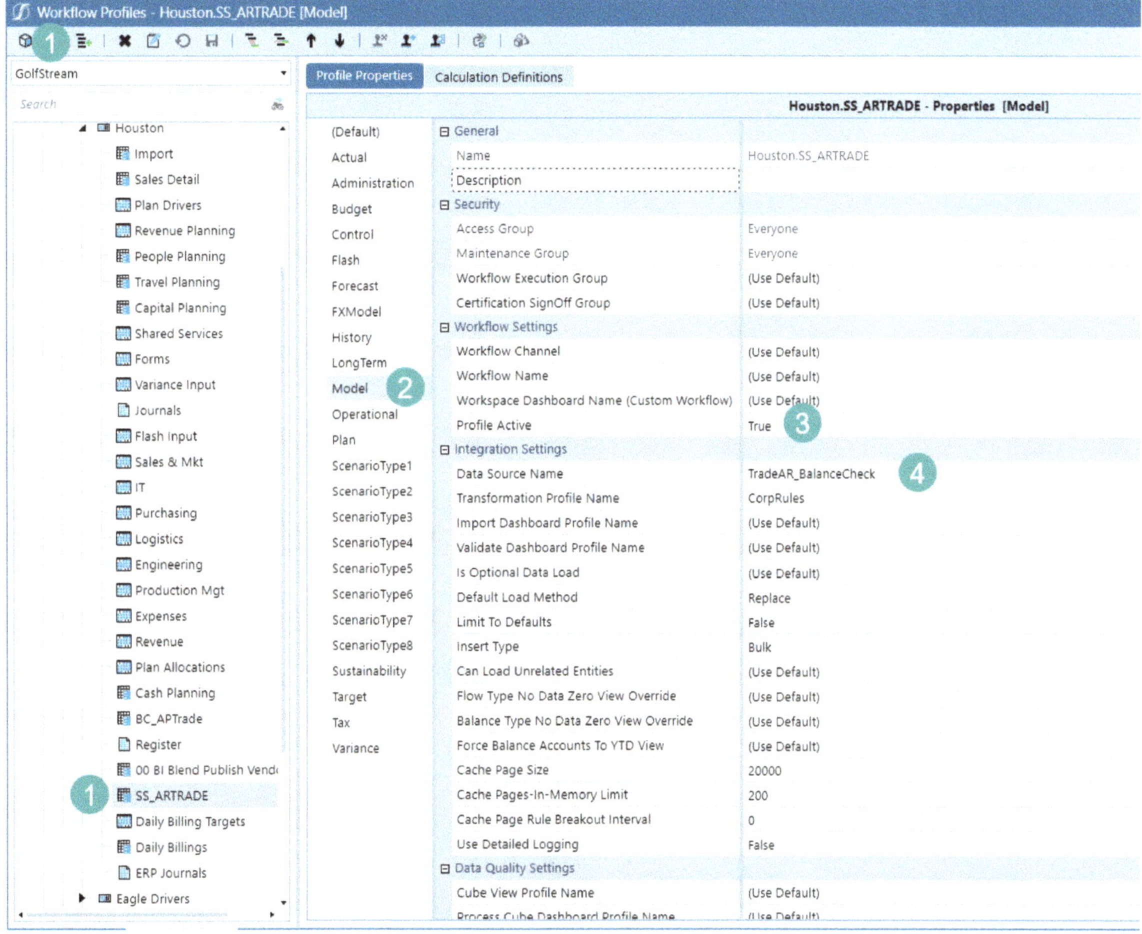

Figure 2.54

Multi-Currency Solutions

Loading in detail amounts, detail currency types, Account level, and Reporting level balances requires identifying the columns related to these items within the Data Source.

> **Note:** Detail amount represents the transaction amount, which could be in a currency type that is different to any Reconciliation currency level, and is different to what is loaded for single-currency solutions since they just load Local currency balances.

Detail amounts, Account amounts, and Reporting amounts need to be set to the data type of Attribute Value, and Detail currency needs to be set to the data type of Attribute. Local amounts must exist for BalCheck to properly translate and calculate; if null, values will not translate. As such, ensure null values are replaced with zeros.

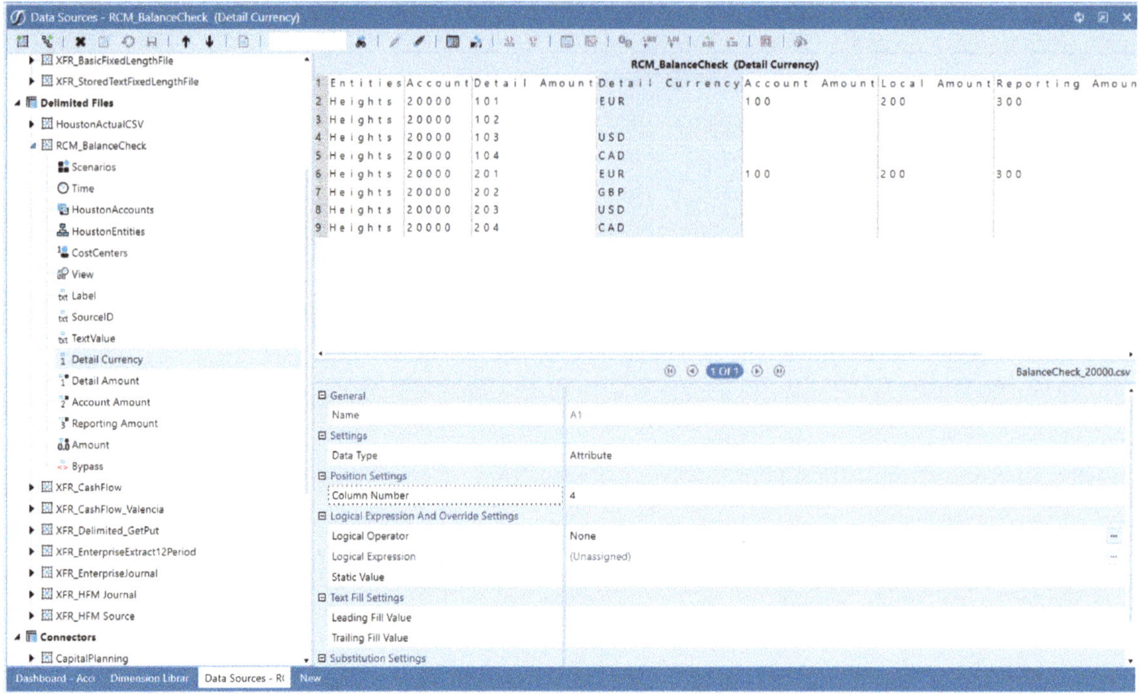

Figure 2.55

BalCheck Level

This is a drop-down list populated from the list of levels created within the BalCheck page. The default is set to (Unassigned), meaning the Reconciliation does not use Balance Check. In order to ensure the balances being pulled from the support are aligned within the Reconciliation, Balance Check-level granularity must match that of the tracking level. Therefore, if the Reconciliation's tracking level includes UD1, the Balance Check that supports that Reconciliation should also include UD1.

Allow Override (Multi-Currency Enabled)

When set to True, the ability exists to override translated Account, Local, and Reporting amounts for detail items. If FX rates exist for the current period, upon Save (creation) of a detail item, OneStream will automatically translate the Account, Local, and Reporting amounts. If Allow Override is enabled, the ability exists to manually input amounts for any of the currency levels. If only one level is overridden, the other translated balances will remain. Similarly, if FX rates have not been entered for the current period and a level is overridden, the override balance will appear and the amounts to be translated will appear as zero. Amounts that are overridden will hold, period over period, if a detail item is pulled forward.

When an amount is overridden using zero, OneStream automatically retranslates the amount using the rates in the FX rates table. If showing a zero balance for a currency level is required, a new detail item must be created with a detail amount of zero, and enter the opposite balance for the currency level that needs to be set to zero (i.e., offset balance).

Override Support Required (Multi-Currency Enabled)

When set to True, supporting documentation – either an I-Doc or R-Doc – is required for all detail items with translated amounts that were manually overridden. Note that an S-Doc will also satisfy this requirement.

Preparer Workday Due

Type in any integer value, negative or positive, to indicate which close day the Reconciliation must be prepared by. OneStream will look to the close date for the Workflow period and, based on that date and the Preparer workday due, will calculate the calendar date that the Reconciliation must be prepared by. Note that Account Reconciliation does not take holidays or weekends into account when calculating the calendar date due. As such, make sure you take these dates into account for each period and note that workdays due may vary from period to period. For example, assume day 1 of close for October is *Friday, October 1*, as shown in Figure 2.56. In accounting terms, it is assumed that day 2 would be *Monday, October 4*; however, for purposes of workday assignments, you would select workday due of 4 – four days – after day 0 (*September 30*).

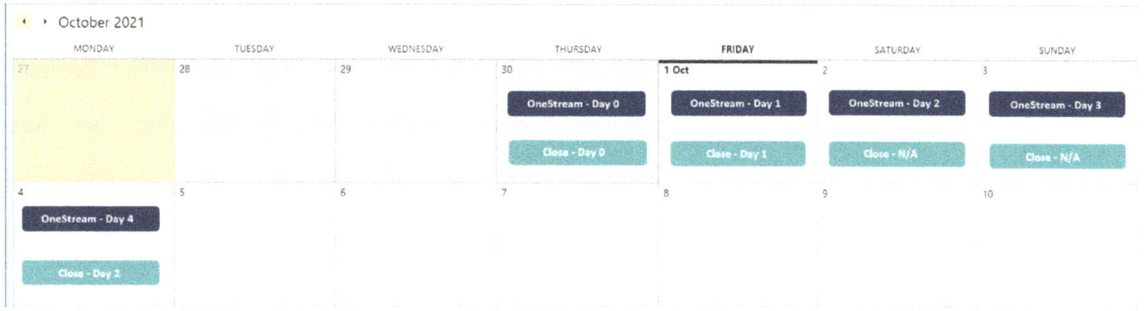

Figure 2.56

Approver Workday Due

Type in any integer value, negative or positive, to indicate which close day the Reconciliation must be fully approved by. OneStream will look to the close date for the Workflow period and, based on that date and the Approver workday due, will calculate the calendar date that the Reconciliation must be fully approved by. This date is also used to determine how many days until the Reconciliation is due and when it is past due.

Frequency

This is a text input field that determines how often the completion of this Reconciliation Definition is required. The default is 1-12, which indicates months 1-12. This can be 3,6,9,12 if quarterly is required, or enter another type of frequency expression.

Template

The template assigned will default to what is set for the Target Account in the Reconciliation Definition. The template assigned can be changed to any templates stored within the Reconciliation Templates under Settings.

Notification Method (Not Time-Based)

This is a drop-down list populated from the list of methods created within the Notifications page. The default is set to (Unassigned), meaning the Reconciliation does not have a notification method applied. See the Notifications section for more information on how to create and maintain these methods.

Required

By default, this is set to True. If the Reconciliation is no longer required to be completed, set this to False. Once a Reconciliation has been prepared, it cannot be deleted from the Inventory, regardless of which Workflow period you are in for audit purposes. As such, all Reconciliations that are not required are displayed at the end of the Reconciliation Inventory by default.

Update User

The User who last updated an attribute for the Reconciliation.

Update Time

The date and time an attribute was last updated for the Reconciliation.

Discovery User

The User who ran the discovery process that created the Reconciliation.

Discovery Time

The date and time a Reconciliation was first discovered, or an Account Group was created.

Inventory Actions

The icons at the bottom of the Reconciliation Inventory allow you to make updates and changes to the Inventory. To view the icons at the bottom, click on any Reconciliation within the Inventory grid.

Edit

To edit any of the Reconciliation attributes, select the checkbox on the far left of the Inventory and then click the Edit icon. To edit all Reconciliations within the Inventory at once, select the checkbox at the top.

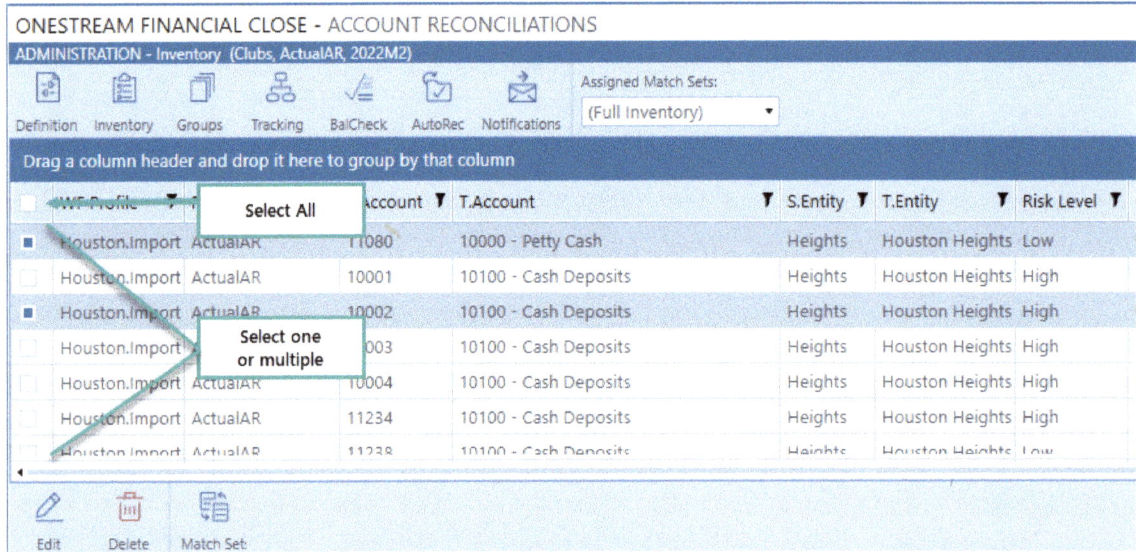

Figure 2.57

Upon clicking Edit, a dialog will appear with all Inventory attributes. If a single Reconciliation is selected, the attributes defined for that Reconciliation will be displayed. If multiple Reconciliations are being edited at once, the attributes for the first Reconciliation selected will be displayed.

To edit an attribute, select the checkbox next to the attribute, such as Access Group, shown in the example in Figure 2.58. Depending on the attribute type being edited, there will be either a drop-down or a text box input.

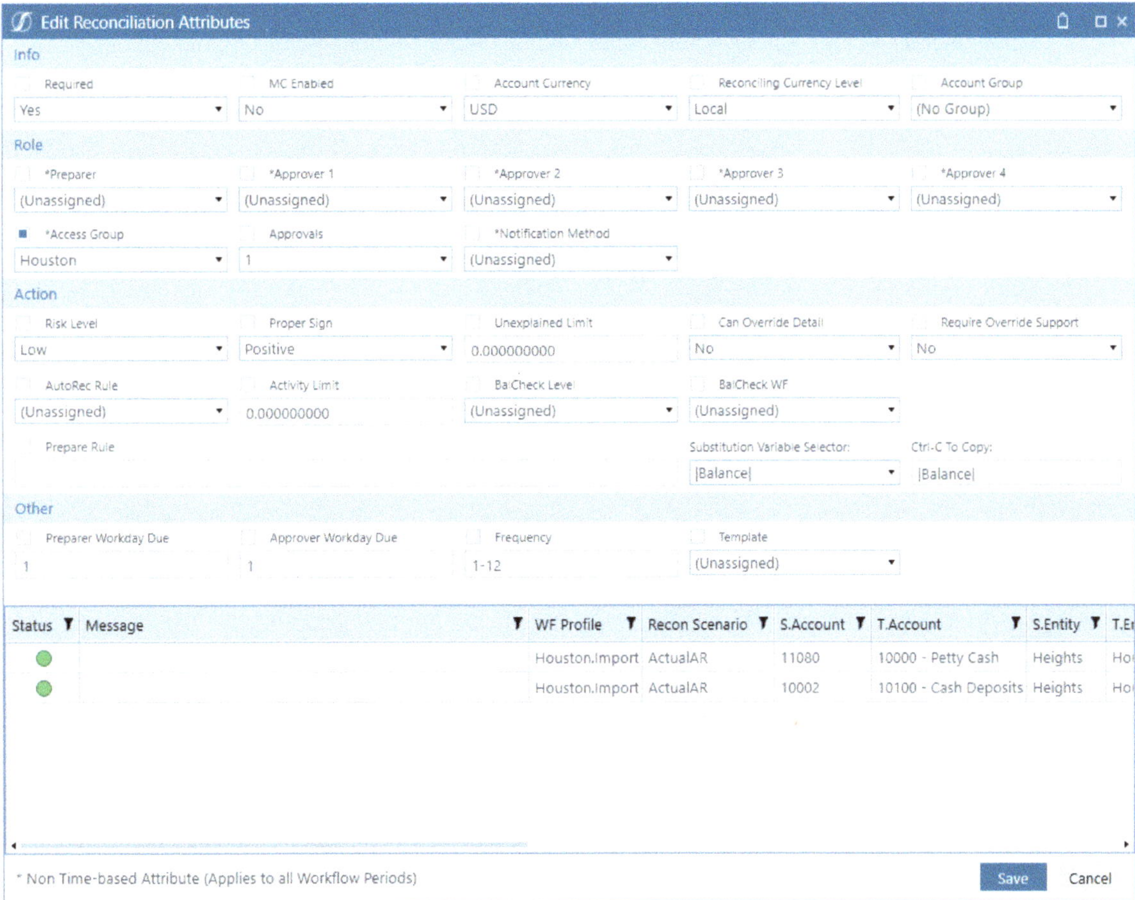

Figure 2.58

The check box selection is designed to ensure that changes being made are intentional and to ensure only attributes needing to be changed are appropriately updated. Otherwise, all Reconciliations that are selected would have their attributes changed to mirror the first Reconciliation selected (the default display).

The grid at the bottom of the dialog lists all Reconciliations that are being edited. If the status is a green circle and the Message column is blank, the Reconciliation has not yet been prepared for the period and the attribute that has been selected will be updated for the Reconciliation, as shown in Figure 2.58. If the status is locked, the Message column states Reconciliation has been prepared for the period, as shown in Figure 2.59. As the Reconciliation has been prepared for the period, the attribute that has been selected will not be updated for the Reconciliation.

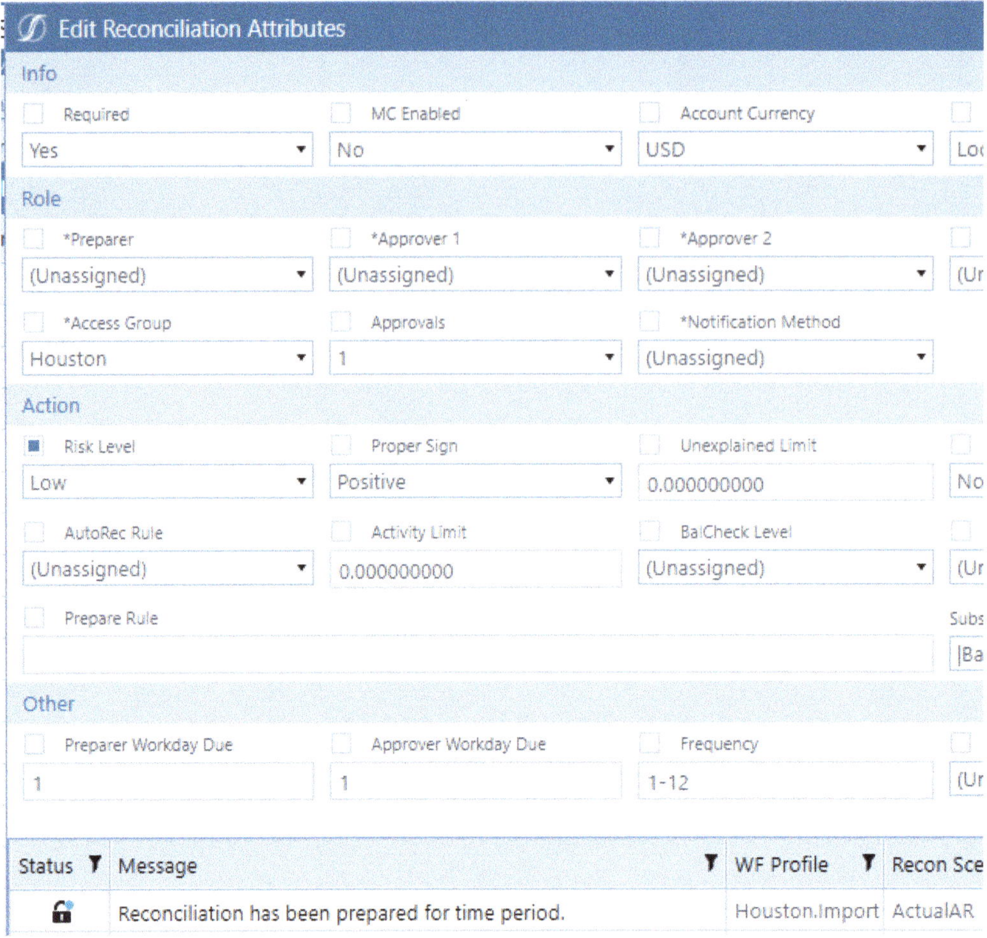

Figure 2.59

Delete

To delete a Reconciliation from the Inventory, select the checkbox on the far left of the Inventory and then click the Delete icon. A Reconciliation may not be deleted if it has been prepared in any period.

Export

While the edit dialog is very User-friendly and allows an Administrator to easily visualize changes being made on the fly, it may not be ideal for an initial implementation. As a reminder, upon initial discovery, all Reconciliations will have the same default attributes, which is often not accurate for most customers, and attributes need to be edited en masse.

For implementations, utilization of the Export feature allows consultants to export the entire Reconciliation Inventory as a CSV file that is opened in Excel. In order to import the changes made in Excel, a **named range** must be added to the file starting with the letters `xft`, covering appropriate rows starting with the cell with the word Application in the top-left cell. This file should then be saved in Excel `xlsx` format.

Import

Once the updates have been made and the file is saved in the appropriate format, click the Import icon, which will open a file explorer dialog. Select the Excel or CSV created to merge changes. It is necessary for the User to close this file before importing it. This button is not accessible by Local Admins.

Template

When you click the Template icon, a pre-filled Excel Template for the loading of Account Groups will open. Note that some field entries (such as WF Profile, Recon Scenario) must start with `!`

because the import process replaces those text values with a long numeric key. This button is not accessible by Local Admins.

Access

Selecting this icon will open a dialog to update the Access Group Members, both Users and Groups, for the Reconciliation that is selected. Note that because Access Groups assigned to Reconciliations could vary rec to rec, you can only select one Reconciliation at a time for this icon to appear.

Match Sets

This icon will only appear when **Transaction Matching Integration** is enabled in Global Options. Once integration is enabled, select this icon to assign one or many Match Sets to the Reconciliation.

If you assign multiple Match Sets, when in Account Reconciliations, and you pull detail information from Transaction Matching to create detail items, a drop-down will appear to select the Match Set from which you would like to create detail items. Once you select the Match Set from the drop-down, all transactions related to that Reconciliation, based on the mapping set up in Transaction Matching, will appear as available to create detail items. This means that transactions from all Match Sets assigned – that have mapping aligned with the Reconciliation tracking level – will be available to create detail items.

Details on how to create the detail items from Transaction Matching are discussed in more detail in Chapter 6. Creating detail items from Match Sets cannot be assigned to Account Groups at this time.

Groups

Account Groups provide the ability to combine multiple individual Reconciliations into a single item to be reconciled. This allows you to have fewer Reconciliations to prepare but still allows you to see the granularity of the Child Reconciliation balances, thereby providing the means to identify possible misstatements at the source level.

An example of when an Account Group may be used would be if you have multiple Source Accounts all rolling up to the same Target Account.

> **Note:** Remember, your Source Accounts are your GL Accounts, and your Target Accounts are your Financial Statement Accounts, or those held in the OneStream Account Dimension.

You may want to look at your cash balance in total, not at each source/GL level. In this instance, an Account Group would help your organization. Additionally, you may want to look at the Cash Account in total – after Translation – since you have a global organization with different Local currencies. In this instance, you can utilize OneStream's Translation capabilities to take those Account and/or Local balances and translate up to the Reporting currency level. When an Account Group is being reconciled, the experience of performing a Reconciliation is the same as at a Child Rec level, in terms of adding attachments and comments, preparing, and approving, etc. This is discussed more in Chapter 4.

To create an Account Group, select the Create icon in the middle of the Groups page. Within the Create Group dialog, you must provide an Account Group name and assign the following attributes within the Info section:

Workflow Profile: This is the Workflow Profile where this Account Group will be shown for reconciling. This can be either a Review level or Base Input Import-level Workflow Profile.

T.Account: Target Account in the Cube. This will help filter results and guide the drill down process.

S.Account (Display Name): Source Account. This is a text field box that is to be defined by you. Use the display name to notify the User as to what type of Account Group this will be.

T.Entity: Target Entity in the Cube. Specify an Entity; the Entities to which this Account Group are applied, however, are more related to the Source Accounts from the Reconciliation Inventory. Depending on the Reconciliation Inventory items added to this Account Group, there could be many Target Entities. This will help filter results and guide the drill down process.

S.Entity (Display Name): Source Entity. This is a text field box that is to be defined by you. Use the display name to the User to reflect what Type of Entity this will be. The Entities seen when preparing Reconciliations are those related to the Workflow Profile.

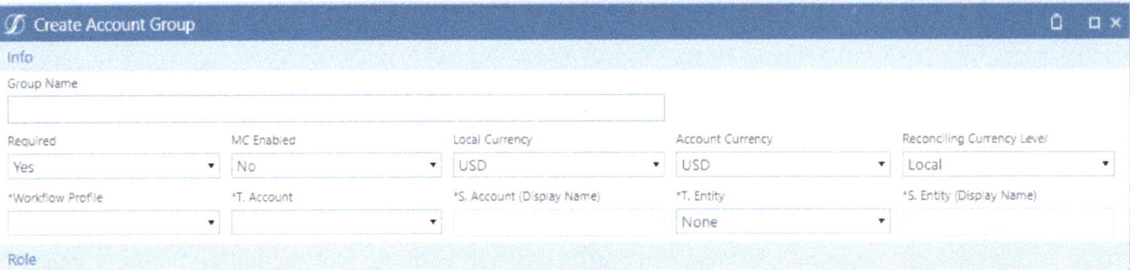

Figure 2.60

> **Note:** All Info attributes that must be assigned to an Account Group have an asterisk in front of the title. These attributes must be assigned because they are not part of the default Reconciliation properties and are assigned only to Account Groups. Additionally, these attributes are not time-based, meaning if they are edited, the change will be reflected in all time periods. Figure 2.60 shows the area of the Create Group dialog that contains the attributes that are assigned only to Account Groups.

Single-Currency Solutions

Account Groups should be created for the same Local currency type since, by an Account Group's nature, the untranslated source data will be aggregated together for analysis. Again, this is because single-currency applications do not translate balances. For example, if there is a person who reconciles all the Fixed Asset Accounts, first create an Account Group for each Local currency type to be reconciled, and then add Accounts with the same Local currency type to each of these Groups from the Reconciliation Inventory.

Multi-Currency Solutions

Account Groups may be created using any currencies included in **Application Properties** and maintained in the FX Rates grid. The Account Group will be a single Reconciliation for the translated aggregate of the Source Account, Local, and Reporting currencies. For example, if a company reconciles all Intercompany Accounts at a consolidated level and the Local currencies are different, a multi-currency Account Group may be created to reconcile the related Accounts in a single, consolidated currency. First, each currency level is translated to the Account Group currency and then aggregated. When creating a new multi-currency Account Group, both Account and Local currency must be selected for the Group for multi-currency enablement. After the Account and Local currencies are selected, multi-currency Account Groups are reconciled the same as single-currency, in that detail items are used to support the aggregate balance of all Child Reconciliations.

Once an Account Group has been created, you can assign that Group to individual Reconciliations within the Inventory. When an Account Group is assigned to a Reconciliation, the attributes of the Account Group are assigned to the individual Reconciliation, as shown in the message of the Edit dialog in Figure 2.61.

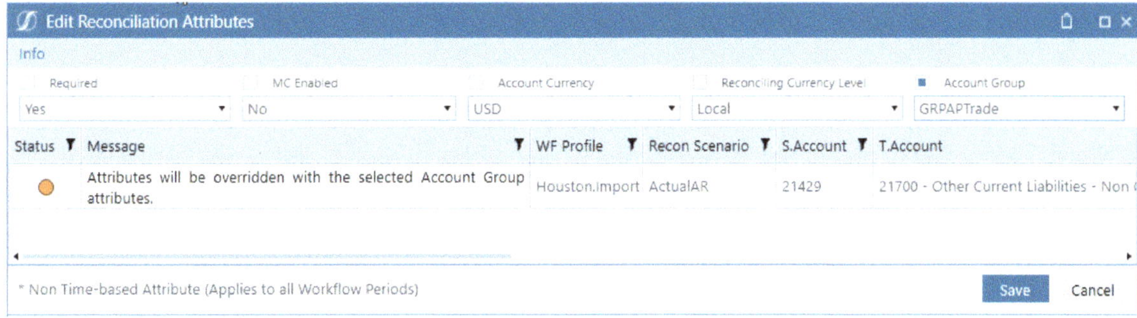

Figure 2.61

Changes to Account Groups

Attributes of Account Groups and Child Memberships within Account Groups can change over time. Below are the effects of this:

- If a Reconciliation that was previously reconciled individually is added as a Child of an Account Group, the individual Reconciliation Inventory item can be reviewed in historical periods with its previous balance.
- If a Child Reconciliation is removed from an Account Group, it will retrieve its balance and the state of the Reconciliation will be Balance Changed.
- If the Children that compose the Account Group change over time, the total balance for the Group previously stored for a WF Period will not change in historical periods if the Account Group Reconciliation was Approved, even if Process is executed again in that period. The Approved balance is essentially locked. If Process is executed again against an Account Group whose members have changed, and the Reconciliation for the Group is not Approved, the balance will change for the Group based on current Child Memberships.
- If a new Account Group is created and existing Reconciliations that have a history are added as Children, the Account Group will not have any historical activity in prior months as the Account Group did not exist.
- If an Account Group has all of its Children removed, it is recommended to have the Account Group be auto reconciled because – from that point forward – the balance for the Group will be zero. If the Account Group that now has no Children had Child Reconciliations that were reconciled individually in the past, it is advised to clear the required attribute for the Account Group in order for the individual historical Reconciliations to be audited. Note that in previous periods, where the Account Group Reconciliation was fully Approved, the balance and membership will remain for audit purposes.
- When a new Account Group is created after prior periods have been processed, it would show a state of In Process.
- Process Warning: When a Reconciliation is removed from an Account Group, a Process will need to be done by an Account Reconciliations Administrator or Application Administrator at the review-level Workflow Profile to ensure that all Account Groups and Reconciliation balances are updated. When this occurs, a warning icon will appear next to the Process button on the Workflow page. This warning icon will be removed for Users after an Administrator processes the Reconciliations and the Workflow page is refreshed.

A Child Reconciliation will inherit the attributes of the Account Group when added to the Group. For example, if a single Reconciliation had a risk ranking of high and was then added to an Account Group with a low risk ranking, the risk ranking of the individual, or Child Reconciliation, would be low upon save. The exceptions to this rule are those attributes that are set at the time of Account Group creation and discussed above (WF Profile, S. Account, T. Account, S. Entity, and T. Entity) and Account and Local currency. The two currencies are not inherited for multi-currency purposes. These attributes, which are specific to individual Child Reconciliations, are easily identified within the grid at the bottom of the page as they have a blue background, as shown in Figure 2.62.

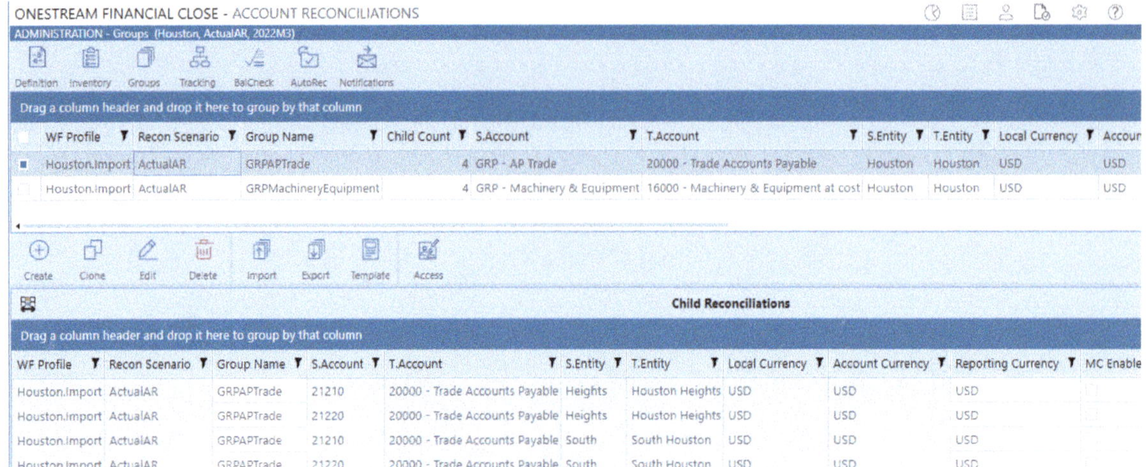

Figure 2.62

> **Note:** It is the Account Group's attributes that are referenced within OneStream for Reconciliation purposes, but for audit purposes – and to allow for consistency – these attributes are aligned. Additionally, if an individual Reconciliation is removed from an Account Group, the attributes it had while part of the Account Group will remain at the time of removal. Therefore, in our example above, the Reconciliation's risk level would remain low upon removal; it would not revert to high.

Like single Reconciliations, Account Groups may be edited, deleted, imported, and exported. These actions are discussed in the Inventory Actions section. One item to note is that a Group may not be deleted if an individual Reconciliation is assigned. The number of individual Reconciliations assigned is noted in the Child Count column within the top grid.

Additionally, you may clone an Account Group. This action will replicate all attributes of the original Account Group selected. Upon selecting the icon, the Create Account Group dialog will appear with all attributes assigned. From there, you will need to give the Group a name and you may change any attributes necessary.

> **Note:** Cloning will not assign the Children to the clone, as they are already assigned to the original Account Group, and each individual Reconciliation may only be assigned to one Account Group. To assign the Child Reconciliations, you must now go to the Inventory page and edit the Reconciliations to be added.

Tracking

This page is used to create the granularity of the Reconciliations. By default, OneStream provides a tracking level of Entity, which means Reconciliations will be discovered for instances where the Source and Target Entity are different, and when Source and Target Accounts are different. An example of this default was explained in the Global Defaults section of Settings. When creating tracking levels, Entity and Account will always be part of the tracking level; therefore, the first column – Entity Active – cannot be set to False. You can take the granularity beyond Entity and Account by creating a new tracking level and selecting the Dimensions you would like to have Reconciliations to be split out by, if that Dimension is also included in your import. The more Dimensions you include will result in more Reconciliations. For example, your Accrued Payroll may be broken out by Cost Center, which you have set as your UD4. In this instance, you would create a new tracking level, click UD4 to True, and save the new tracking level, called `Entity Cost Center` in Figure 2.63.

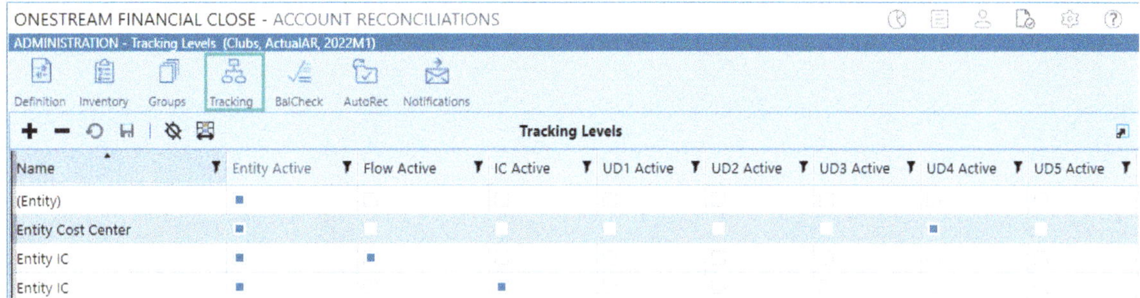

Figure 2.63

Next, assign this tracking level to the Payroll Accrual Account on the Definition page, as shown in Figure 2.64. Upon discovery, the Payroll Accrual Account would then be broken out by Entity, Account, and UD4 (Cost Center). As the tracking levels will be applied upon discovery, it is important to add the additional tracking levels, outside of the Entity default, *prior* to running discovery. Once a Reconciliation has been discovered and added to the Inventory, it cannot be deleted if it has previously been prepared. So, in this example, had we not added the Entity Cost Center tracking level to the Accrued Payroll Account, the Account would have only been broken out by Entity and Account on initial creation. If the Entity Cost Center was later assigned, you would see the original Reconciliations broken out by only Entity and Account and then see Reconciliations broken out by Entity, Account, AND Cost Center.

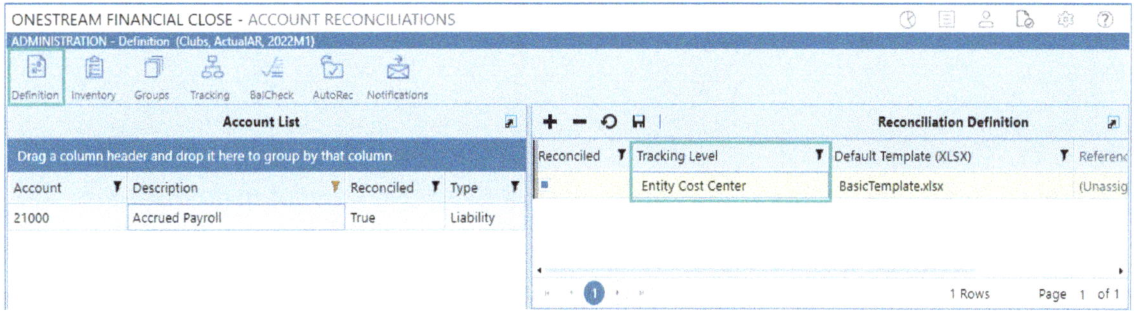

Figure 2.64

Balance Check

The Balance Check page is used to create the level of Balance Check granularity, similar to how we create tracking level granularity on the Tracking page. Here, you can create Balance Check levels that will populate the drop-down list on the Reconciliation Inventory for BalCheck Level. Balance Check levels can be created for any single Dimension or combination of Dimensions. This allows balances being pulled from a single source file to be split to the corresponding Reconciliations at the same granularity of detail as is provided within tracking levels. Therefore, to ensure the balances being pulled from the support are aligned within the Reconciliation, Balance Check-level granularity must match that of the tracking level.

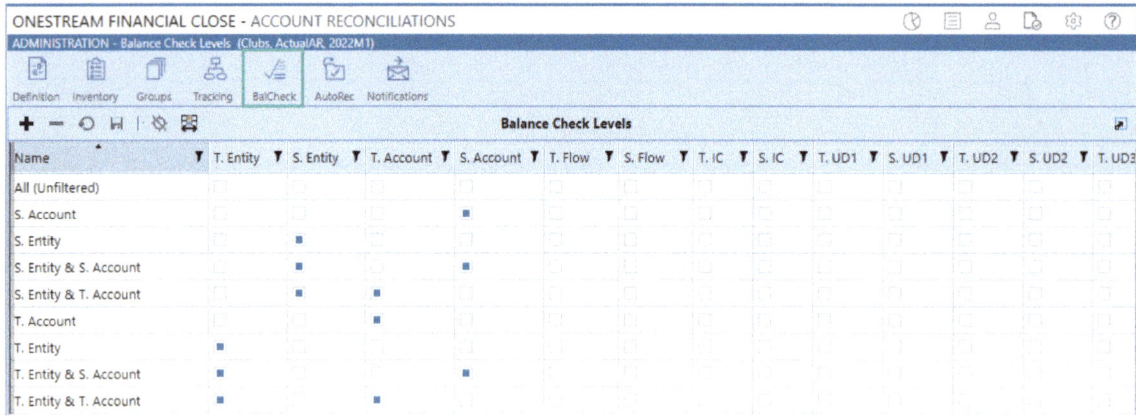

Figure 2.65

There are several types of Balance Check levels that are prepopulated within the solution:

All Entities & Accounts: As long as the assigned Transformation Rules pass their test, then there is included functionality to pull the Balance Check figure into the Reconciliation as an explanation.

T.Entity: Works by filtering the Balance Check items loaded to the Stage to just the values that match the Target Entity of the selected Reconciliation that references the Balance Check Workflow Stage data.

S.Entity: Works by filtering the Balance Check items loaded to the Stage to just the values that match the Source Entity of the selected Reconciliation that references the Balance Check Workflow Stage data.

T.Account: Works by filtering the Balance Check items loaded to the Stage to just the values that match the Target Account of the selected Reconciliation that references the Balance Check Workflow Stage data.

S.Account: Works by filtering the Balance Check items loaded to the Stage to just the values that match the Source Account of the selected Reconciliation that references the Balance Check Workflow Stage data.

T.Entity & T.Account: Works by filtering the Balance Check items loaded to the Stage to just the values that match the combination of Target Entity and Target Account of the selected Reconciliation that references the Balance Check Workflow Stage data.

S.Entity & S.Account: Works by filtering the Balance Check items loaded to the Stage to just the values that match the combination of Source Entity and Source Account of the selected Reconciliation that references the Balance Check Workflow Stage data.

T.Entity & S.Account: Works by filtering the Balance Check items loaded to the Stage to just the values that match the combination of Target Entity and Source Account of the selected Reconciliation that references the Balance Check Workflow Stage data.

AutoRec

The AutoRec page is used to create custom rules to automatically reconcile Reconciliations, based on criteria created by you. Here, you can create and maintain a rule in a single place that can be applied to multiple Reconciliations. Changes to any part of a rule's expression, support types allowed, etc., can be made to the rule, and those changes will apply to all Reconciliations where the rule is assigned.

The page is accessible by Reconciliation Global Administrators and OneStream Administrators. Rules can be created to either automatically prepare a Reconciliation or fully approve a Reconciliation, meaning no other action is necessary. For all checkboxes related to detail item support types, if the box is selected, a Reconciliation will be permitted to auto reconcile if that Item Type exists. Zero Balance, Activity, and Expression are criteria that *must* be met to allow for

Automatic Reconciliation. If Zero Balance and Activity are both selected, both criteria must be satisfied in order to automatically reconcile.

> **Note:** It is recommended not to change the name of the rule once it has been used. This is because the information on the history of the Reconciliation will show the rule name at the time the rule was applied. If the name has changed, it may be hard to determine which rule was applied.

Prepare Only

Set this column to True if you want the Reconciliation to only go to an Auto Prepared state, meaning that approval is required for the Reconciliation. Often, customers will utilize this feature for Reconciliations that only need to be reviewed on a quarterly basis. For example, if you have low risk accounts that are Auto Approved, and no review is performed in M1 and M2, you could set a rule to where this checkbox is not selected for those periods. However, in M3, you could create a rule where Auto Preparer Only is set to True, apply the new rule on the Reconciliation Inventory, and – upon Process – the Reconciliation will only Auto Prepare. In this instance, an Approver would need to approve the Reconciliation for it to go to a Fully Approved state.

B-Items

B-Items are Balance Check items, so if this box is selected and a B-Item is provided to support the Reconciliation (and other criteria are met), the Reconciliation will automatically reconcile. Bank statement balances are an example of a frequently used B-Item, so let's use a bank statement as an example. To create an AutoRec Rule that will fully approve the Reconciliation:

1. Click + to add a new line.
2. Name the rule.
3. Set the B-Items column to True.
4. Add an Expression to qualify when the Reconciliation can AutoRec.

In the Balance Check Only Rule, in Figure 2.66, if the Unexplained Balance is greater than -1 and the Unexplained Balance is less than 1 (meaning if the balance is between 1 and -1), the Reconciliation will automatically reconcile and will show a state of Auto Approved, meaning no further action is necessary. Note that the B-Item box is checked in this rule, meaning the Reconciliation would auto complete if a B-Item existed; however, the B-Item is not required.

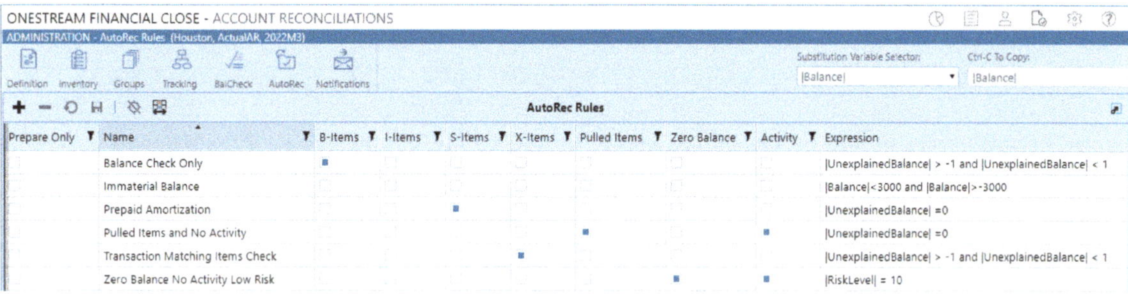

Figure 2.66

I-Items

Again, this column relates to detail item support; therefore, if this column is selected, a Reconciliation will be able to AutoRec if an item individually created in the current period exists.

Walking through our Balance Check example, let's assume we used a bank statement to support our cash Reconciliation and the B-Item does not agree with the Reconciliation balance. In that instance, the Preparer would need to create an I-Item to explain the variance. If the I-Item column were selected, after the Preparer added the I-Item and Process was run, the Reconciliation would go to Auto Approved. Would you want the Reconciliation to go to the state and not have the

Reconciliation reviewed and approved? Probably not, since manual intervention occurred on the Reconciliation. For that reason, you would not check the I-Item column in this instance. However, let's say the Reconciliation balance is immaterial, less than $100, and is low risk. In this instance, you could create a rule where I-Items are allowed and create an Expression, as shown in the example in Figure 2.67. In this example, the Reconciliation will be Auto Approved after an I-Item is added and Process is run, if the Balance is less than $100.

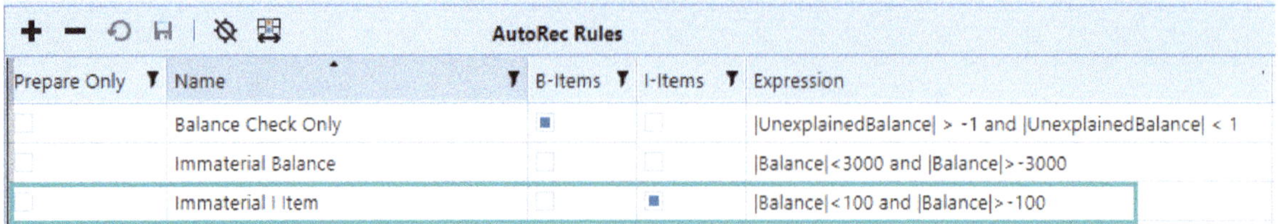

AutoRec Rules

Prepare Only	Name	B-Items	I-Items	Expression
☐	Balance Check Only	■	☐	|UnexplainedBalance| > -1 and |UnexplainedBalance| < 1
☐	Immaterial Balance	☐	☐	|Balance|<3000 and |Balance|>-3000
☐	Immaterial I Item	☐	■	|Balance|<100 and |Balance|>-100

Figure 2.67

S-Items

If selected, a Reconciliation will be able to AutoRec if multi-period templates or S-Items are used to support the reconciling currency balance. The booked period for the S-Item must be prior to the current Workflow period. If the S-Item was created in the current Workflow period, AutoRec functionality will be prohibited.

An example of an S-Item would be an amortization template for a fixed asset. When the amortization support is initially created, and used to support a Reconciliation, the Reconciliation would not AutoRec. However, in future periods, if the amortization support is pulled forward and ties to the Reconciliation balance, the Reconciliation will move to an Auto Approved state upon Process.

X-Items

X-Items are items that are created from Transaction Matching. These items can be either pushed from Transaction Matching, or pulled from Account Reconciliations. If this column is set to True, and the X-Item support ties to the reconciling currency balance for the Reconciliation, the Reconciliation will move to an Auto Approved state upon Process.

Pulled Items

This relates to all detail items pulled from prior periods. If this is selected, any item pulled from a prior period will allow the Reconciliation to AutoRec. For example, assume in M1 that you create an I-Item to support the balance within the Unexplained Limit. In M2, the balance for the Reconciliation does not change and you pull forward the I-Item created in M1. After pulling the item forward, and running Process, the state will move to Fully Approved, as the balance is now fully supported.

Zero Balance

If selected, the Reconciliation will automatically reconcile if the balance for the period is zero.

Activity

If selected, the Reconciliation will automatically reconcile if the reconciling currency has not changed or if the activity for the reconciling currency is within the activity limit threshold established in the Reconciliation Inventory.

Expression

This is a text box that allows for User-defined text. Rule logic can include any item from the **Substitution Variable Selector**, so utilize this drop-down to facilitate expression creation.

OneStream uses an ADO.NET data table-calculated column to interpret expressions, so there is no OneStream parser logic involved. Choices from the Substitution Variable Selector can be used to make these more dynamic. The expression evaluator supports the following operators and more:

- l And, Not, In, Between, Like, Null, Or, Trim
- Open bracket '(' and close bracket ')'
- <=, >=, <>, =
- + (addition)
- - (subtraction)
- * (multiplication)
- / (division)
- % (modulus)
- Conditional 'if'
- Substring

Example:

```
|BalanceChange| > 1000 And |BalanceLocal| = 0
```

XFBR String Business Rules can also be used to determine the expression to be placed here at run time.

Remember, when creating expressions, that they must be aligned with the reconciling currency level. Also, when creating expressions – `|Balance|`, `|UnexplainedLimit|`, `|Currency|` – all apply to the Local currency level.

AutoRec Rules cannot be run for Account Groups until FX rates have been entered for the period. This is because the source currencies need to translate to the Account Group currencies before Reconciliation.

Notifications

The Notifications page is used to create custom notification methods that can then be applied to a Reconciliation. Creating multiple notification methods and assigning them to individual Reconciliations allows you to get very granular with your notifications.

Maybe you really want Users to be aware Reconciliation state that is high risk, such as a certain accrual. In that case, you can have notifications sent whenever the state is changed (as shown in the Accruals example in Figure 2.68), but maybe you're not as concerned about the state of your Petty Cash Account. In this instance, you could keep the notification method to unassigned for that Reconciliation and no notifications would be sent. In this way, you can limit the number of emails your Users receive to those which are the most important for your company. By default, the solution comes with a predefined method of **All Notifications** which sends out all notification types to all Users and User groups.

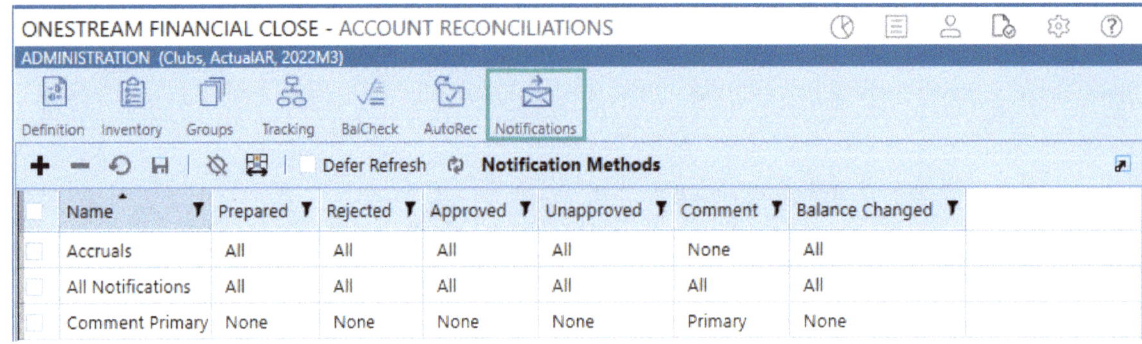

Figure 2.68

Within this page, first add a line to create a notification method, then name the method. From there, you will select which notifications will be sent for that method and who will receive the notifications.

All: All Users and Security Groups assigned to the Reconciliation, whether assigned as a primary role or as a backup via the Access Group, will receive the applicable notification. Note that Access Group members must have Notify set to True to receive notifications (Figure 2.69).

None: The notification will not be sent to any Users.

Primary: Only the Primary Preparer or Approver(s) will receive the applicable notification.

Access Group: Only members of the Access Group will receive the applicable notification. Additionally, only those members within the Access Group that have Notify set to True will receive the notification. For example, in Figure 2.69, Approver 2 would receive notifications sent to Approvers, but Approver 1 would not.

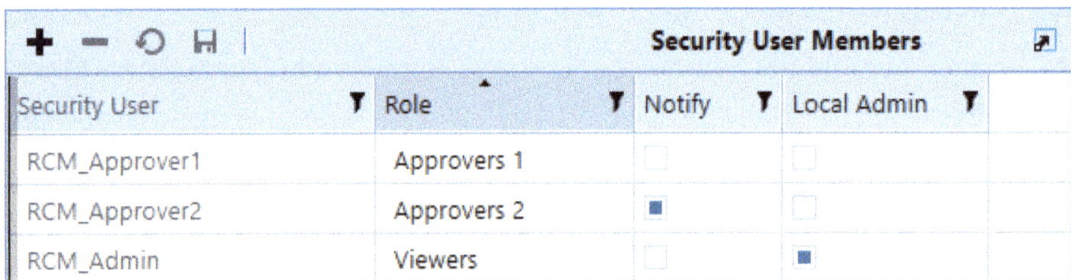

Figure 2.69

State Email Notification Types

This section describes which role receives the notification, and the purpose of the notification. Note that for each notification type, you may select if the Primary, Access Group back-up User, or both roles receive the notification, depending on selection within the column.

Prepared: Upon preparation of a Reconciliation, either by a User or by the system (Auto Prepared), an email is sent to the Approver(s) 1 to notify them that approval is now required.

Rejected: An email is sent to the Preparer(s) to notify them of rejection, thus putting the Reconciliation to an In Process state that needs to be prepared.

Approved: An email is sent to the next level Approver(s), notifying them that their approval is now actionable. For example, if the Reconciliation was Approved by Approver 1, Approver 2 would receive notification.

Unapproved: An email is sent to the level below to notify that the Reconciliation has been moved down in approval. For example, if the Reconciliation was previously Approved by Approver 1 and Approver 2 Unapproved, the state would move from Approved 1 of 2 to Prepared. Approver 1 would receive an email notifying them they have to act on the Reconciliation.

Comment: An email is sent to the Preparer(s) and Approver(s) to notify them that comments have been made.

Balance Changed: An email is sent to the Preparer to notify them that the balance of the Reconciliation has been changed, thus putting the state back to In Process, requiring the Reconciliation to be prepared again.

The following business case walks through when each email would be sent if the All Notifications method were applied to a Reconciliation:

- On day two, Mike has prepared all four of his assigned Reconciliations and provided detail item support within the unexplained threshold. As such, he marks them as Prepared. Upon this state change, Mike's next level of approval – Adam (Approver 1) – will receive a Prepared notification for each Reconciliation to notify him those Reconciliations (where he is the Approver) are prepared.
- Adam, Approver 1, reviews the four Reconciliations and notices Mike forgot to provide supporting documentation, or an R-Doc, for one Reconciliation.
    - Adam approves three Reconciliations, moving them to a Partially Approved state.
        - Jason, the next level of approval, receives an Approved notification for the three Approved Reconciliations. Jason approves two of the Reconciliations, moving them to Fully Approved, and unapproves the third moving it to Prepared.
        - Adam receives an Unapproved notification. He reviews again and approves the Reconciliation.
        - Jason receives an Approved notification and approves the third Reconciliation moving it to a Fully Approved state.
    - Adam rejects the Reconciliation without support.
        - Mike receives a Rejected notification letting him know the Reconciliation has been Rejected and, therefore, there is more work to perform at the preparation level. Mike adds the appropriate supporting documentation and makes a comment on the Reconciliation, notifying Adam, "Appropriate documentation has been added and agrees to GL balance."
        - All three Users receive a Comment notification.
        - Adam approves the fourth Reconciliation, moving it to Partially Approved, and Jason receives an Approved notification.
        - Jason approves the Reconciliation and moves it to a Fully Approved state.
    - On day three, a late adjustment is made on one of Mike's GL Accounts and a new trial balance is loaded into Actuals. Upon running Process, the balances for one of Mike's previously Fully Approved Reconciliations has now changed and the Reconciliation's state has moved to Balance Changed. Mike will receive an email, such as the one shown in Figure 2.70, to notify him that the Reconciliation must be prepared again, as the balance is no longer supported. Once prepared, the notifications will follow the same path as outlined above.

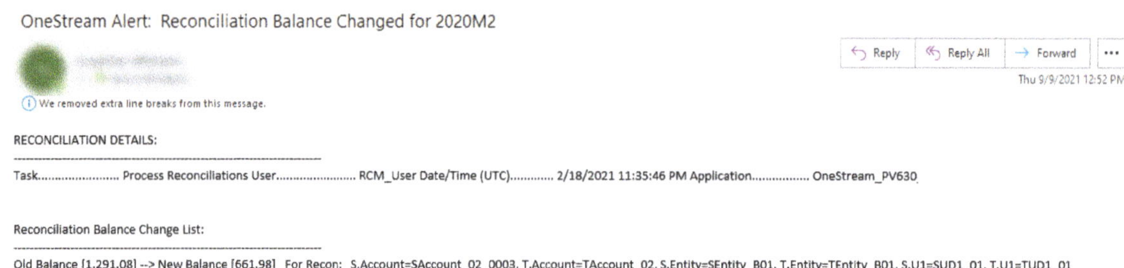
OneStream Alert: Reconciliation Balance Changed for 2020M2

Reply | Reply All | Forward | ...

Thu 9/9/2021 12:52 PM

We removed extra line breaks from this message.

RECONCILIATION DETAILS:

Task...................... Process Reconciliations User...................... RCM_User Date/Time (UTC)............ 2/18/2021 11:35:46 PM Application................ OneStream_PV630

Reconciliation Balance Change List:

Old Balance [1,291.08] --> New Balance [661.98] For Recon: S.Account=SAccount_02_0003, T.Account=TAccount_02, S.Entity=SEntity_B01, T.Entity=TEntity_B01, S.U1=SUD1_01, T.U1=TUD1_01

Figure 2.70

Administration Summary

As you can see, there is a ton of potential granularity within the Administration page, and it enables you to configure the solution to meet your company's many needs. If you want to update these attributes every period, go for it! If not, that's fine as well. The true intent is to allow the solution to meet your needs.

With Administration out of the way, let's move onto the final section of this chapter: Audit.

* * *

Audit

The Account Reconciliation Audit page contains three different audit logs that show changes that were made to Reconciliation attributes. The page was created to provide Administrators with transparency into what Reconciliation attributes changed, plus *who* and *when* the change was made.

To view a Report, first select which type of Report to view: 1. Security Roles, 2. Time-based Attributes, or 3. Account Groups. Next, select the start and end date to define the time range for when you would like to see changes. This period will default to the last seven days if no time range is selected. Finally, if reviewing the Time-based Attribute log, select the WF period to which the change was applied. All Reports can be exported for further analysis and review, or perhaps to provide to your auditor, by right-clicking on any cell and selecting Export.

Time-Based Attributes

This Report will show changes made to the following Reconciliation attributes:

1. Required
2. MC Enabled
3. Account Currency
4. Reconciling Currency Level
5. Account Group
6. Approvals
7. Risk Level
8. Proper Sign
9. Unexplained Limit
10. Prepare Rule
11. AutoRec Rule
12. Activity Limit
13. BalCheck Level
14. BalCheck WF Profile
15. Allow Override
16. Override Support Required
17. Preparer Workday Due
18. Approver Workday Due
19. Frequency
20. Template

All columns within the Report can be filtered, if desired. Additionally, you may hide columns that do not relate to your company – such as tracking detail – by right-clicking on any cell, and selecting Column Settings.

Time Stamp: Shows date and time (UTC) the attribute was changed.

WF Period: The WF period for which the change was applicable.

User: The User that made the change.

T. Account, S.Account, T. Entity, and S. Entity, Tracking Detail: Reconciliation Definition to identify which Reconciliation was modified.

Attribute: Identifies which attributes were changed.

Original: Attribute value before the change was made.

Update: Attribute value after the modification.

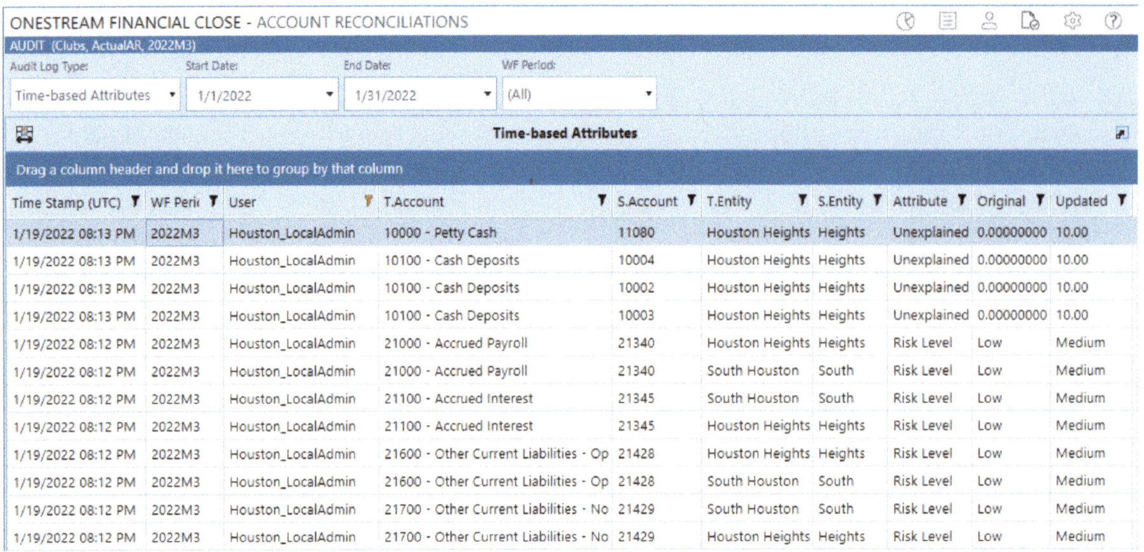

ONESTREAM FINANCIAL CLOSE - ACCOUNT RECONCILIATIONS

AUDIT (Clubs, ActualAR, 2022M3)

Audit Log Type: Time-based Attributes | Start Date: 1/1/2022 | End Date: 1/31/2022 | WF Period: (All)

Time-based Attributes

Drag a column header and drop it here to group by that column

Time Stamp (UTC)	WF Peri	User	T.Account	S.Account	T.Entity	S.Entity	Attribute	Original	Updated
1/19/2022 08:13 PM	2022M3	Houston_LocalAdmin	10000 - Petty Cash	11080	Houston Heights	Heights	Unexplained	0.00000000	10.00
1/19/2022 08:13 PM	2022M3	Houston_LocalAdmin	10100 - Cash Deposits	10004	Houston Heights	Heights	Unexplained	0.00000000	10.00
1/19/2022 08:13 PM	2022M3	Houston_LocalAdmin	10100 - Cash Deposits	10002	Houston Heights	Heights	Unexplained	0.00000000	10.00
1/19/2022 08:13 PM	2022M3	Houston_LocalAdmin	10100 - Cash Deposits	10003	Houston Heights	Heights	Unexplained	0.00000000	10.00
1/19/2022 08:12 PM	2022M3	Houston_LocalAdmin	21000 - Accrued Payroll	21340	Houston Heights	Heights	Risk Level	Low	Medium
1/19/2022 08:12 PM	2022M3	Houston_LocalAdmin	21000 - Accrued Payroll	21340	South Houston	South	Risk Level	Low	Medium
1/19/2022 08:12 PM	2022M3	Houston_LocalAdmin	21100 - Accrued Interest	21345	South Houston	South	Risk Level	Low	Medium
1/19/2022 08:12 PM	2022M3	Houston_LocalAdmin	21100 - Accrued Interest	21345	Houston Heights	Heights	Risk Level	Low	Medium
1/19/2022 08:12 PM	2022M3	Houston_LocalAdmin	21600 - Other Current Liabilities - Op	21428	Houston Heights	Heights	Risk Level	Low	Medium
1/19/2022 08:12 PM	2022M3	Houston_LocalAdmin	21600 - Other Current Liabilities - Op	21428	South Houston	South	Risk Level	Low	Medium
1/19/2022 08:12 PM	2022M3	Houston_LocalAdmin	21700 - Other Current Liabilities - No	21429	South Houston	South	Risk Level	Low	Medium
1/19/2022 08:12 PM	2022M3	Houston_LocalAdmin	21700 - Other Current Liabilities - No	21429	Houston Heights	Heights	Risk Level	Low	Medium

Figure 2.71

Security Roles

This Report is for security attributes that are not time-based. This means that if the security is changed, the applicable change will show for *all* time periods. As discussed previously, this is because if a User takes over a Reconciliation role, they need to be able to view all past Reconciliation activity. Additionally, if a User is removed from having access to a Reconciliation, they should no longer be able to view the Reconciliation, even though they have prepared it in the past.

This Report will show changes made to the following Reconciliation attributes:

1. Preparer
2. Approver 1
3. Approver 2
4. Approver 3
5. Approver 4
6. Access Group

> **Note:** This is the assignment of the Access Group. This does not show you changes made to the Access Group membership.

The columns for this Report are the same, except Attribute is titled Security Role/Access Group instead. Additionally, the WF Profile column has been removed as the change is reflected in all time periods.

Time Stamp (UTC)	User	T.Account	S.Account	T.Entity	S.Entity	Security Role/Access Group	Original	Updated
1/17/2022 12:03 AM	Houston_LocalAdmin	10000 - Petty Cash	11080	Houston Heights	Heights	Access Group	Houston_GA	Houston
1/17/2022 12:03 AM	Houston_LocalAdmin	10100 - Cash Deposits	10001	Houston Heights	Heights	Access Group	Houston_GA	Houston
1/17/2022 12:03 AM	Houston_LocalAdmin	10100 - Cash Deposits	10002	Houston Heights	Heights	Access Group	Houston_GA	Houston
1/17/2022 12:03 AM	Houston_LocalAdmin	10100 - Cash Deposits	10003	Houston Heights	Heights	Access Group	Houston_GA	Houston
1/17/2022 12:03 AM	Houston_LocalAdmin	10100 - Cash Deposits	11238	Houston Heights	Heights	Access Group	Houston_GA	Houston
1/17/2022 12:03 AM	Houston_LocalAdmin	11300 - Allowance for Doubtful Accounts	11220	Houston Heights	Heights	Access Group	Houston_GA	Houston
1/17/2022 12:03 AM	Houston_LocalAdmin	12300 - Supplies - Inventory	63200	Houston Heights	Heights	Access Group	Houston_GA	Houston
1/17/2022 12:03 AM	Houston_LocalAdmin	13000 - Prepaid Insurance	11420	Houston Heights	Heights	Access Group	Houston_GA	Houston

Figure 2.72

Account Groups

This Report is for Account Group attributes that can be defined only at the Account Group level and are not time-based. This means that if the attribute changed, the applicable change would show for all time periods. As discussed previously, these are the attributes that are assigned at the time of Account Group Creation and include:

1. T. Account
2. S. Account
3. T. Entity
4. S. Entity
5. WF Profile
6. Local Currency
7. Account Currency
8. BalCheck WF Profile

As the definitions for Account Groups are not set at the time of creation, and can be changed, these columns are not included in this page but, rather, are included in the attributes that can be shown to have changes (items 1-4 above). Figure 2.73 shows all the columns included in the Account Groups Audit Log.

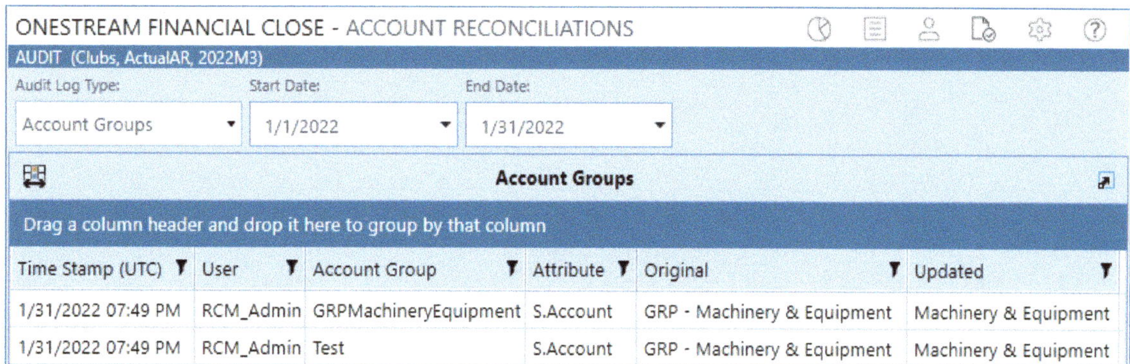

Time Stamp (UTC)	User	Account Group	Attribute	Original	Updated
1/31/2022 07:49 PM	RCM_Admin	GRPMachineryEquipment	S.Account	GRP - Machinery & Equipment	Machinery & Equipment
1/31/2022 07:49 PM	RCM_Admin	Test	S.Account	GRP - Machinery & Equipment	Machinery & Equipment

Figure 2.73

Audit Summary

The Audit page came about following requests from a number of customers, and we were genuinely excited to deliver this feature. It will help to streamline your audit processes and offer the transparency you need in the Reconciliation process.

* * *

Conclusion

In this chapter, we have learned about the components that are used to configure your Account Reconciliation solution. Additionally, we have provided examples of how Reconciliations are discovered and how their attributes are defined. With the knowledge gained here, you are now ready to move on to implementing the solution in your development environment, which will be discussed in the next chapter.

3

Account Reconciliations Implementation

Understanding Account Reconciliation Projects

In the fall of 2016, I was asked by Peter Fugere to implement a new OneStream MarketPlace solution called **Reconciliation Control Manager**, or RCM for short. Eventually, the solution's name was officially changed to **Account Reconciliations**. This solution was combined with Transaction Matching to become OneStream Financial Close, the MarketPlace solution that exists today.

Although the look and feel of the solution has changed, the core functionality has not. When data is imported into OneStream and loaded to Financial Reporting, Account Reconciliations can leverage that Stage data to create Reconciliations that help a company to identify and correct any errors before internal or external auditors review the financial information.

The Concept of Project Phases

When discussing the phases of a project, we are not referring to a phased rollout. In other words, this does not mean that Corporate will go live on Account Reconciliations first, followed by North America, Central America, South America, and Europe. When we discuss the phases of an Account Reconciliation project, we are referring to the entire project itself. This is then broken down into groups of activities that will help the Project Team manage the implementation. These phases are meant to be a group of tasks that need to be completed for the project to proceed smoothly. Typically, companies will need to move activities from phase to phase because the activity will not be completed while the Users are available for the project. The goal is to complete all the tasks in each phase before any project downtime.

An Account Reconciliation project can be run like any other Consolidation or Planning project. The technical complexity may be less involved than the aforementioned projects, but the timeline can be longer. An Account Reconciliation project needs to be more flexible because Users may not be entirely dedicated to the project and have other responsibilities. In other words, Users have a day job that will take priority. Sometimes, this priority means Users are available only 50% of the month; sometimes, Users are available only 25% or 10% of the month. It is very important to schedule tasks according to Users' availability. After all, for a successful implementation, Users are your partners in all OneStream projects.

> **Note**: Account Reconciliation Users typically have close-related tasks to complete in a very specific timeframe. User Acceptance Testing (UAT) should then be completed before Users become unavailable for the project – usually between month-end closes. If UAT cannot be completed in a quarter-end month like March, then UAT should be pushed out to April. This may also cause you to move UAT from Phase 2 to Phase 3.

By assuming your End-User will have other obligations, your Account Reconciliation project may have some downtime while those Users are completing their month-end close tasks. Breaking the project into four distinct phases is the best way to ensure that we can get the most out of the Project Team while they are available for the project.

The phases will change slightly, depending on whether a Consolidation project has been (or will be) completed. This is because the Account Reconciliations MarketPlace Solution configuration is dependent on the items that would have been built for a Consolidation project.

> **Note:** Due to Sarbanes-Oxley rules, Account Reconciliations is a tremendous risk control that can be easily configured for any company using OneStream. Consolidation and Account Reconciliation projects both leverage Dimensions, Time profiles, Cubes, FX rates, Workflow Profiles, data sources, and Transformation Rules, and these are just the basic objects. More advanced items – such as Business Rules, Task Scheduler, and Data Management Processes – can also be leveraged.

If a Consolidation project has not been completed, the Account Reconciliation project will be broken down into four phases in this manner:

- Phase One:
    - Discovery
    - Pre-Project Planning
    - Requirements and Design Session
        - General Application Build Activities
        - Project Team/Key Stakeholders Introduction
        - Timeline
        - Project Management
        - Scope Discussion
    - Key Stakeholders sign-off on Configuration Settings
    - Design Document Created
    - Review Design and Client Sign-off
- Phase Two
    - Build Tasks
    - Key Stakeholders sign-off on Build and User Acceptance Testing (UAT)
    - UAT
    - Key Stakeholders sign-off on UAT
- Phase Three
    - User Training
    - Parallel(s)
- Phase Four
    - Key Stakeholders sign-off Go-Live
    - Go-Live

If a Consolidation project has been (or will be) completed, the milestones for the Account Reconciliation project will be broken down into four phases in this manner:

- Phase One
    - Discovery
    - Pre-Project Planning
    - Requirements and Design Session
        - Project Team/Key Stakeholders Introduction
        - Timeline
        - Project Management

        - Scope Discussion
    - Key Stakeholders sign-off on Configuration Settings
    - Design Document Created
    - Review Design and Client Sign-off
- Phase Two
    - Build Tasks
    - Key Stakeholders sign-off on Build and UAT
    - User Acceptance Testing
    - Key Stakeholders sign-off on UAT
- Phase Three
    - User Training
    - Parallel(s)
- Phase Four
    - Key Stakeholders sign-off Go-Live
    - Go-Live

Phase One

Phase One is the most important to the project because this is where the client will help define the Account Reconciliation configuration. When a Consolidation project has been (or will be) completed, then the metadata Dimensions leveraged in Account Reconciliations will already be defined.

If this is the first OneStream project, then it is important to clearly define if the metadata Dimensions you have created will be leveraged for a Consolidation project. Whenever possible, build the metadata in such a way that it *can* be leveraged in a Consolidation project; this will avoid any rework in the future and will make it easier to keep the Account Reconciliation configuration intact.

The objective of this phase is to define the remaining project phases and to provide the client with the ability to leverage the work for later projects. We do not want to limit future projects if possible. There are times when a Consolidation project will include more User-defined Dimensions than an Account Reconciliations project. For example, a client may want departments or products in a User-defined Dimension to create financial statements or help report on balances. However, these departments or products are not needed for Account Reconciliations. If you can easily identify User-defined Dimensions, then build them into metadata. This gives you the flexibility to add these Dimensions into Account Reconciliations if needed.

It is important to understand that Entities and Balance Sheet Accounts should be the same for both projects. It is okay if Entities and Accounts need to be added, but if OneStream Entities or Accounts need to be changed later for a Consolidation project, then that may add new Reconciliations to the Account Reconciliation Inventory.

Phase Two

Phase Two encompasses the main configuration of the Account Reconciliations solution (the build steps), User testing, and sign-off from the client. As previously mentioned, UAT can be moved from Phase two to Phase three, depending on the availability of Users. It is important to have the build completed in one phase. Whenever possible, it is recommended to add time to a phase, as opposed to breaking up the build steps.

Phase Three

The third phase consists of User training and a delayed parallel of the client's current Account Reconciliation process. Typically, try to schedule three delayed parallels that consist of only a handful of Accounts; this can always be reduced later. The main objective of the parallels is to have the Users repeat the User training on Reconciliations that have already been completed using the client's existing process. The repetition of the process will help Users become self-sufficient; in turn, leveraging work that has already been completed will help shorten the learning curve.

Phase Four

Phase four consists of discussions with the client and meetings to review the project and address any remaining questions before a go-live sign-off. Once the client is live, it is important to support the new Account Reconciliation Administrator(s).

Case Study – Implement Account Reconciliations for GolfStream

Congratulations! Your company has just signed a statement of work with GolfStream to implement Account Reconciliations, with the intent of configuring Transaction Matching in the future. We will use the steps outlined in the following sections to configure Account Reconciliations for GolfStream.

Before getting started, create a dedicated folder for GolfStream. Under that folder, create another folder called `PMO`. This will help you organize your project.

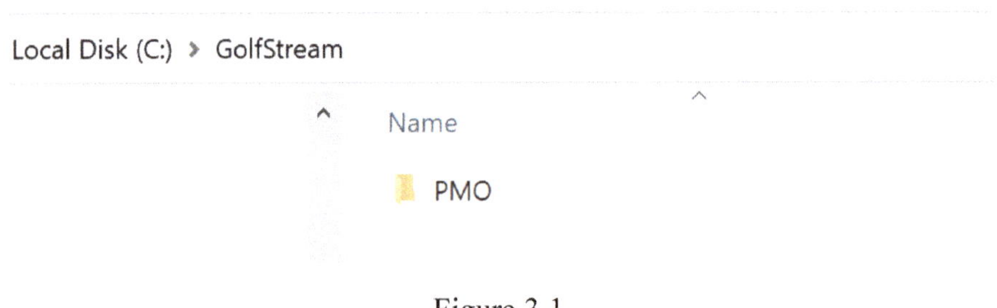

Figure 3.1

Phase One

Think of these phases as building blocks, and Phase One is the cornerstone of the entire project. Having the project detailed in this manner will help to ensure it is easy to track and manage.

Discovery

If possible, talk to the client before any requirements are discussed. Every Account Reconciliation project has the same framework, so there are questions that can be clarified before any meetings are scheduled. In the Discovery step of Phase One, we are trying to define items that do not change from client to client. For example, every client should be able to provide how many Reconciliations are being completed on a monthly, quarterly, and yearly basis. Every client should know which Users will prepare Reconciliations, and which will approve, comment, and view.

Although every Account Reconciliation project has the same framework, there are circumstances unique to every client. Send the client questions regarding their current Account Reconciliation process before meeting with them. This will help keep your meetings on point, and both you and your client will be prepared for the requirements discussion. Any pre-planning you can do will help in the long run. Always keep the end of the project in mind as you review these questions. The objective of the Discovery step is to plan prior to the project start.

Questionnaire

A key tool that can be leveraged in the Discovery stage is a questionnaire that can be sent to the client prior to requirements and design meetings. These questions are typically general in nature, focusing on the client's current Reconciliation process, and will help you get an understanding of the type of project the client needs.

This will also help the design and requirements meeting move along smoothly. It's always better to be prepared! There are a few sample questions in Appendix 1.

Current Reconciliation Process

It is important to understand if the client has a current Reconciliation process or not. In a situation where the client does not have a Reconciliation process, then the concept itself is new. There should be more time spent on training and educating not only for Users, but the Project Team themselves. The *adoption* of Account Reconciliations in OneStream should always be a key success factor. The best way to ensure there is adoption is through education and training. Understanding this is important when creating an estimate of hours for the statement of work.

If a client has a Reconciliation process, then you should understand how complex it is. Some clients use software, spreadsheets, or sometimes a combination of both. Build all training, videos, and documentation with the client's *current* process in mind. The documentation should help a client seamlessly transition from one process to the Account Reconciliation solution in OneStream.

This discussion should provide a listing of current Reconciliations, current Reconciliation Users and their roles (Preparers and Approvers), and examples of data sources.

Requirements and Design Sessions

The requirements and design sessions should be collaborative. Although the client may have a good idea of what they want, they will still be looking for informed suggestions. Either way, always be prepared! One way to do this is to have Account Reconciliations already configured in GolfStream with examples readily available. If GolfStream is not an option, a presentation with screenshots is your best alternative.

Application Metadata Review

Regardless of whether this is the first OneStream project or not, reviewing the client's metadata is mandatory. Understanding the source data will help you understand how the Reconciliations will work in OneStream. For simplicity, we will use the application metadata from the OneStream GolfStream application.

Dimensions

If the Account Reconciliations MarketPlace solution is the first project, you will need to create Dimensions. Entities, Scenarios, and Accounts are required for Account Reconciliations. These new metadata Members will need to be attached to a Cube, and a Reporting currency will need to be selected. Workflows, data sources, and Transformation Rules will also need to be created. The Flow and User-defined Dimensions can provide more detail to the Account Reconciliations and can also be leveraged for a Consolidation project. If the client would like more detail in the Reconciliation, User-defined fields are the best option.

If a Consolidation project has been or will be completed, then discuss the detail needed in the Account Reconciliation configuration. The Flow and User-defined Dimensions give the client the ability to create detailed Reconciliations.

> **Note:** The Account Reconciliation Inventory is based on the Source Accounts mapped to Target Accounts through Transformation Rules.

The following figure shows the Account Dimension used in the GolfStream Cube that will also be leveraged to configure the Account Reconciliation MarketPlace solution.

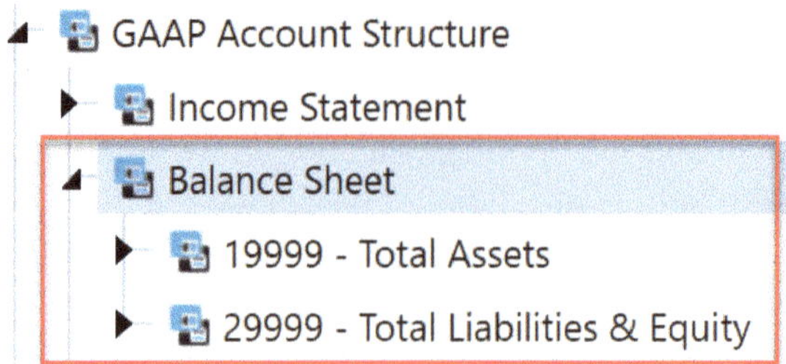

Figure 3.2

Workflow

The Workflow will be the User access point for OneStream. You will have to bind Account Reconciliations to a review or a Base Input Workflow. If these objects have already been built, then understanding the existing security is very important. You will have to incorporate Account Reconciliations security into the application and not change the security that already exists. Users will need to be in the Access Groups attached to the import Workflows that control the data flow.

> **Note:** *Issue* - a User has the proper security for the Account Reconciliation Workflow, is added to the Access Groups attached to the proper Reconciliations, but still does not see any Reconciliations.
>
> *Solution* - The User also needs access to the appropriate import Workflow.

Figure 3.3 shows the Houston Base Input Workflow to which Account Reconciliations is bound.

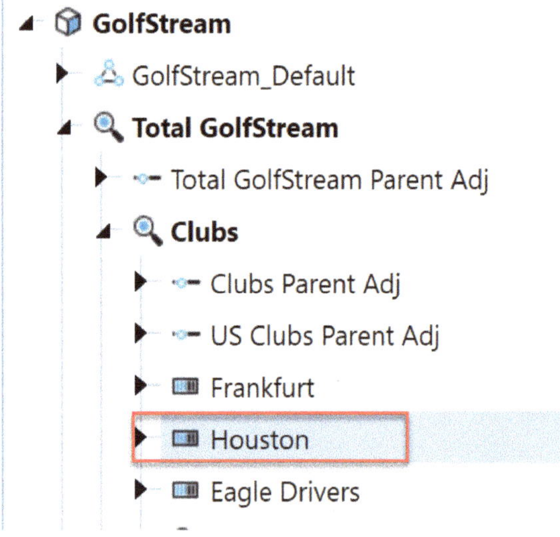

Figure 3.3

The Access Group WF_Houston gives Users the ability to see the Account Reconciliations Dashboard. (The Scenario Type named Model is used for Account Reconciliations in this discussion.)

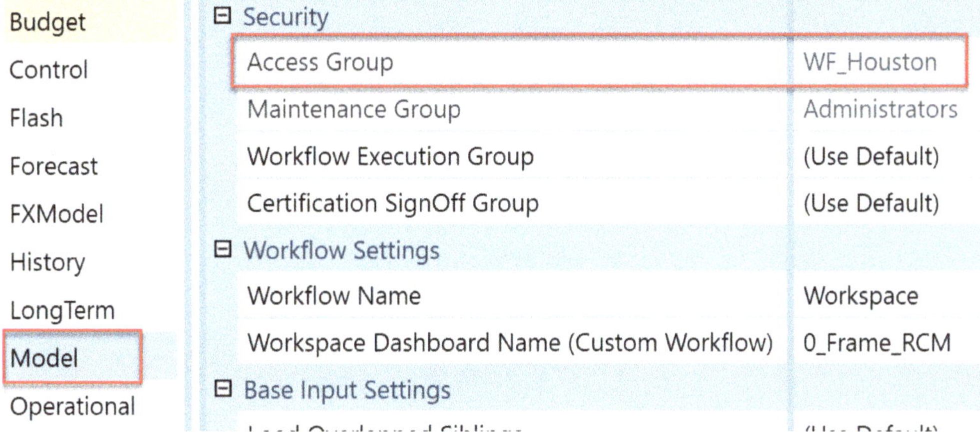

Figure 3.4

Despite this, the User does not see any Reconciliations.

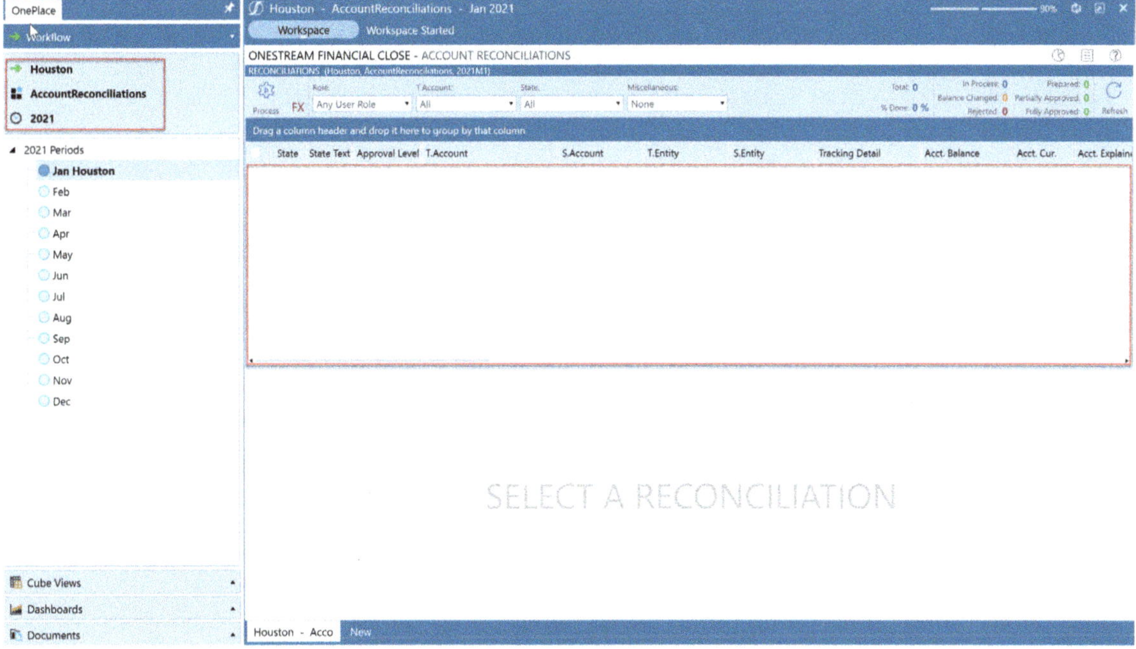

Figure 3.5

The User needs access to the Workflow where the *Actual* data is imported.

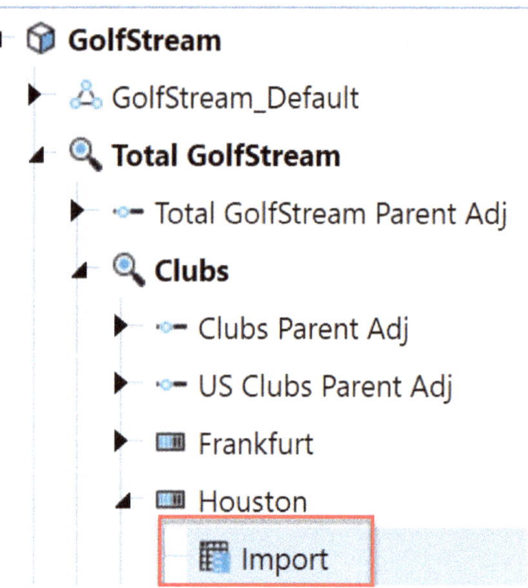

Figure 3.6

Add the proper Workflow Security Group to the Access Group Member.

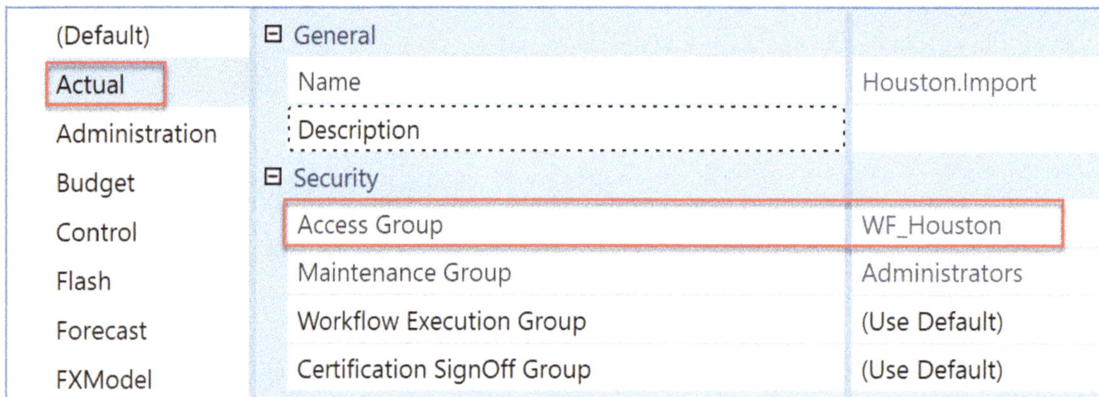

Figure 3.7

The User can now see the Reconciliations.

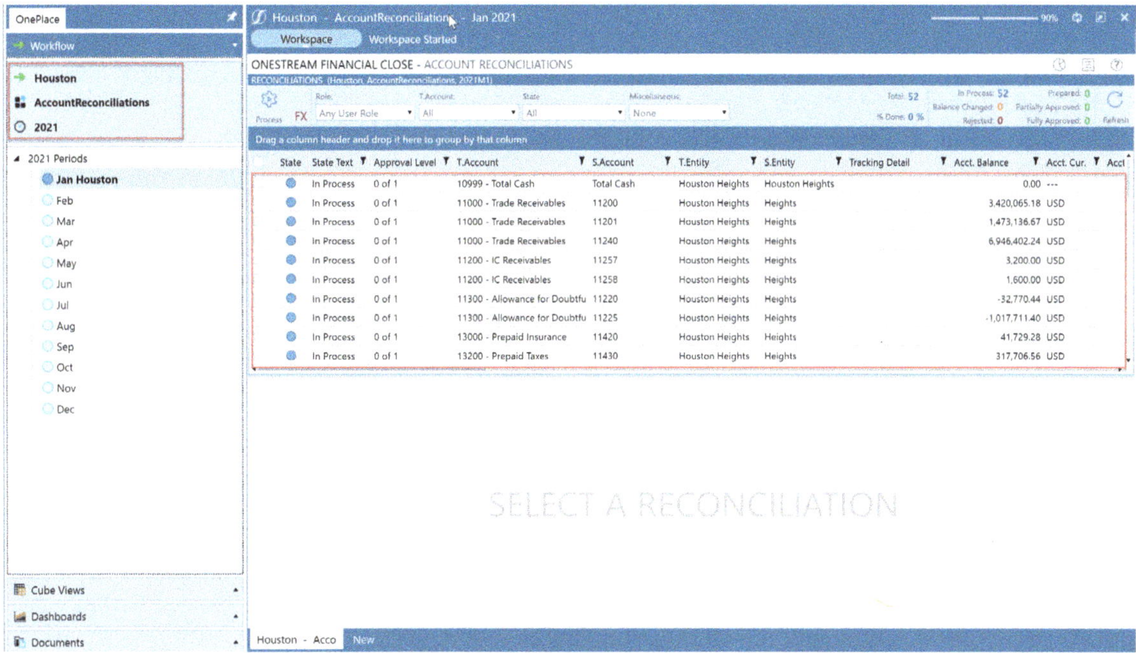

Figure 3.8

Project Team Introduction

Learn *who* the client believes is important for the Project Team. Get an understanding of what each person's job entails and how their normal duties are impacted by the project. Is this person in IT or a User? Will this person be the one who makes or follows decisions?

Many times, a project will be progressing until the Users start UAT and you receive unpleasant feedback. Always be prepared for criticism from the Users. Learning a new process is not always easy, so be patient and over-communicate when meeting with Users. Have support from the Project Team before UAT begins. One way to do this is to make sure all communication is clear and concise throughout the project and includes *everyone* involved.

Timeline

Have a timeline created before the project starts, based on the information collected from the client during Discovery. This sets the expectation of *when* you will need Users to be available and will help the client plan that availability.

Creating the timeline before meeting with the Project Team will also give the client time to prepare for the project. Changing the timeline for unforeseen activities will naturally impact the deadline. By tracking and addressing these issues, you will gain more insight into a client's process that – in turn – will lead to better outcomes. Solving these issues in OneStream is more than possible; more often, it is very possible! This demonstrates your willingness to be a 'partner' with the client and not just a run-of-the-mill Consultant.

Project Management

Managing the Account Reconciliations project is the key to a successful implementation. Talk about how the client would like to manage the project when discussing the timeline. A project manager should have been identified when the Project Team was discussed. Sometimes these tasks are added to an existing Project Team member and the client already has standard project management documentation. In these situations, leverage the format of existing Status and Budget Update Reports. Regardless of the client's preference, send a Weekly Status and Budget Report, and schedule weekly meetings to discuss these documents and the project with the Project Team.

Scope Discussion

It is extremely important to have a detailed and extensive scope discussion with the client. Make sure expectations are expressed and *documented.* By this point in the meetings, try to have a grasp of how the client is structured. You will need answers to each of these questions:

- What divisions/Entities/geographies are included in the Reconciliation population?
- Is the client reconciling the Balance Sheet and/or Income Statement (typically, only Balance Sheet Accounts are included in the Account Reconciliation population)?
- Will there be any subledger Reconciliations?
    - If so, how will the subledger information be loaded into OneStream?
- Discuss special Account classifications that might be needed. What does the client want to do with high, medium, and low-risk Accounts? Find out if there is a need for advanced rules. This will be important because complex rules can add time to the build.
- What is the cycle time for Account Reconciliations? What is the expected cycle time once the new process is live?
- Review the existing reporting, and discuss reporting requirements.
- Define the training and rollout timelines.
- Balance Check integrations?
- Multiple currencies?

OneStream Account Reconciliations Overview

Many clients have seen demonstrations, but typically the last demo the Project Team attended was at least a few months (or maybe even years) prior to the start of this project. If possible, schedule a OneStream Account Reconciliations demonstration or – at the very least – walk through a few Reconciliation examples in the client's copy of GolfStream.

Review Design

Creating a **design document** to track all the configuration settings is very important. Schedule a meeting with the Project Team and walk through these settings, making sure all questions are answered. It may be helpful to show some examples again from GolfStream so the client can visualize the result of the decisions they are making.

Case Study – Implement Account Reconciliations for GolfStream

In Phase One, we will want to define as many settings as possible before starting to configure them. Remember that the first time the settings are configured, those settings are applied to *all* the Base-level Reconciliations. These settings need to be defined so that the client can see the results of their setting choices. Once the client is satisfied with the default settings, then they can decide to change the configuration on an individual Base Reconciliation basis.

Once the Inventory is created using the default settings, then the Account Group can also be created and applied to the individual Reconciliations. This will reduce the number of Reconciliations that Users will have to reconcile.

All the tasks are listed in the appendix, but the following tasks are related to Phase One only.

Phase	Task
1	**Requirements and Global Design**
1	Discovery and Requirements Sessions
1	Reconciliation Inventory Overview - Basic Configuration
1	Review inventory with team
1	Client Analysis of Inventory (assign Preparers and Approvers)
1	Design
1	Design Sessions
1	Design Document Draft Completed
1	Design Document Acceptance/Sign-off
1	Key Stakeholders Signoff

Figure 3.9

The company, GolfStream, makes golf-related products all over the world. Specifically, they sell golf clubs, balls, apparel, accessories, and electronics. For this project, the CFO would like to configure Account Reconciliations for GolfStream's Houston division.

Houston is made up of two Entities: Houston Heights and South Houston. Houston's close process is run by one analyst and one manager – Houston Analyst 1 and Houston Manager 1 – respectively. During this project, GolfStream needs to add an Administrator for just Account Reconciliations, three additional analysts, and three additional managers to help with the Reconciliations.

Documentation is the focus of Phase One. A project plan can be created using only the go-live date. In GolfStream's case, the CFO would like to start using Account Reconciliations for the September close in October. Working backward from 10/01, we can create our milestones in this manner:

Milestone	Completed By	Phase
Design and Requirement Sessions	**06/18/22**	1
Key Stakeholders sign-off on configuration settings	**06/18/22**	1
Design Document Completed	**07/02/22**	1
Design Document Acceptance/Sign-off	**07/16/22**	1
Build Completed	**07/30/22**	2
User Acceptance Training	**08/27/22**	2
Key Stakeholders sign-off on UAT	**08/27/22**	2
Migrate (Build) to Production	**09/03/22**	3
End User Training	**09/17/22**	3
Parallel 1 Sign-off	**09/21/22**	3
Parallel 2 Sign-off	**09/22/22**	3
Parallel 3 Sign-off	**09/23/22**	3
Key Stakeholders sign-off on Go-Live	**09/24/22**	4
Go-live	**10/01/22**	4
Support	**10/29/22**	4

Figure 3.10

When creating project milestones, and as discussed previously, it is important to consider when the Users will be available to prepare and approve Reconciliations. Users do not have many deadlines in the first two weeks of each month because of their availability. However, members of the Project Team will need to make decisions and be involved in meetings.

Once the timeline has been created, schedule Design and Requirement sessions with the client. These sessions can be broken into two-hour blocks if being onsite for multiple days is not possible.

Account Reconciliations Discovery Agenda

Agenda

- Project Team Definition and Introduction (limit to core Account Recon team)
- Implementation Methodology (PowerPoint)
- Define Milestone Dates
    - Discovery and Requirements Sessions (Month/Day/Year)
    - Design Document Acceptance/Sign-off (Month/Day/Year)
    - Client Analysis of Basic Inventory (assign Preparers and Approvers) (Month/Day/Year)
    - Basic configuration sign-off (Month/Day/Year)
    - Security Sign-off (Users and who approves/prepares each Reconciliation) (Month/Day/Year)
    - Reconciliation Settings Sign-off (Month/Day/Year)
    - Build Sign-off (Month/Day/Year)
    - User Acceptance Testing Sign-off (Month/Day/Year)
    - Complete Conducting User Training Sign-off (Month/Day/Year)
    - Parallel 1 Sign-off (Define Months to Reconcile) (Month/Day/Year)
    - Parallel 2 Sign-off (Define Months to Reconcile) (Month/Day/Year)
    - Parallel 3 Sign-off (Define Months to Reconcile) (Month/Day/Year)
    - Operations Finance Go/No-Go Decision (Month/Day/Year)
    - Go Live (Month/Day/Year)
- Break
- Current State Reconciliation process (client describes the current process)
    - Please provide examples if possible
    - Divisions/Entities/Geography included in the Reconciliation population
    - Assets/Liabilities/Equities
    - Standard Reconciliations (typical Reconciliations)
    - Subledger vs. GL Reconciliations
    - Discuss Special Account classifications/Risk level/Advanced Rules
    - Cycle Time
    - Reporting Requirements
- PMO
    - Schedule status meetings
    - Discuss progress reports (what is required)
    - Schedule follow up meetings
- Q&A

Getting access to the client's system is very important. Have the client *specifically* detail which Entities and Accounts are needed for the configuration. Create Cube Views and export them to Excel so the client can start defining which Accounts and Entities will be included in the Account Reconciliations project.

In this case study, we are only concentrating on Houston Entities and the entire Balance Sheet. Total Cash will be grouped by OneStream Entity (Houston Heights Total Cash, South Houston Total Cash, etc.). Inventories will be grouped at the Total GolfStream level.

	Description	Workflow	WF Security
Total GolfStream	Total GolfStream		
Clubs	Clubs		
North America Clubs	North America Clubs		
Canada Clubs	Canada Clubs		
Montreal	Montreal		
Quebec	Quebec		
US Clubs	US Clubs		
Agusta	Agusta		
Carlsbad	Carlsbad		
Houston	Houston	Houston	WF_Houston_Access
Houston Heights	Houston Heights	Houston.GLImport	WF_Houston_Access
South Houston	South Houston	Houston.GLImport	WF_Houston_Access
Europe	Europe		

Figure 3.11

Accounts	Description	Acc Type	Group?	Entity
10000	Petty Cash	Asset	Yes	
10100	Cash Deposits	Asset	Yes	
10200	Other Cash Equivalents	Asset	Yes	
10300	Marketable Securities	Asset	Yes	
10400	Restricted Cash	Asset	Yes	
10999	Total Cash	Asset	Yes	By Base Entity
11000	Trade Receivables	Asset	No	
11100	Other Receivables	Asset	No	
11200	IC Receivables	Asset	No	
11300	Allowance for Doubtful Accounts	Liability	No	
11999	Net Accounts Receivable	Asset		
12000	Raw Materials Inventory	Asset	Yes	
12100	Work in Progress Inventory	Asset	Yes	
12200	Finished Goods Inventory	Asset	Yes	
12300	Supplies - Inventory	Asset	Yes	
12400	In Transit Inventory	Asset	Yes	
12999	Total Inventories	Asset	Yes	Total Company
13000	Prepaid Insurance	Asset	No	
13100	Prepaid Rent	Asset	No	
13200	Prepaid Taxes	Asset	No	
13300	Prepaid Other	Asset	No	
13999	Total Prepaid Expenses	Asset		

Figure 3.12

Understanding the client's security design is also very important. As per the previous example, Users will need access to the import Workflows that are used to import data. Review the existing security, and plan on how to layer in the Account Reconciliations Security Groups.

> **Note:** Creating a security matrix is very helpful in this process. It will be easier to identify any issues that security may cause when Users attempt to prepare and approve Reconciliations.

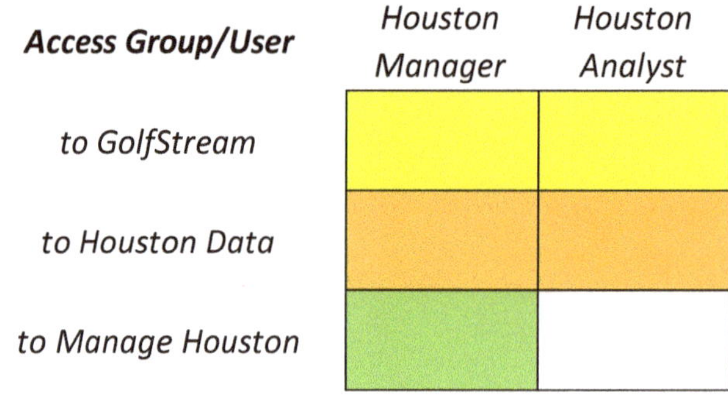

Access Group/User
Houston Manager
Houston Analyst
to GolfStream
to Houston Data
to Manage Houston

Figure 3.13

Review the existing Scenarios and identify unused Scenario Types. Choose one unused Scenario Type to be assigned to the new Account Reconciliations destination Scenario. In this case, we are using the Model Scenario Type for the new AccountReconciliations Scenario.

Name	ScenarioType
None	Actual
Flash	Flash
Actual	Actual
PreservedActual	Actual
ActualBud	Actual
BudgetDrivers	Budget
Budget Group	Actual
BudgetV1	Budget
BudgetV2	Budget
BudgetV3	Budget
Budget	Budget

Figure 3.14

Scenario Type	Actual	Model	Operational	Plan	Sustainability
Scenario:	Actual	AccountReconciliations		Plan	
	PreservedActual				
	ActualBud				
	Budget Group				
	CapEx Group				

Figure 3.15

You will need to create new Security Groups for the Users of Account Reconciliations and build the Account Reconciliations with the current security design in mind. The Users will need access to the Actual Import Workflows, the new Account Reconciliations Scenario, and the ancillary tables.

The configuration settings can be set based on the information provided by the client already. Any settings not provided by the client can be turned on so that the clients see the result.

Run Discover once the Accounts are defined. You can use OneStream Parent Accounts in the Member Filter; since none of the GL Accounts are mapped to OneStream Parent Accounts, there will not be any Reconciliations in the Inventory for those OneStream Parent Accounts, only the Child Accounts of the selected Parent.

Create Account Groups based on the information provided to you by the client. These can be created manually or through the **Group Update Template** provided in the solution. Once the groups are created, add the individual Account Reconciliations to the newly-created Account Group on the Inventory page. The last step is to run the Process button on the Reconciliation page. The number of Reconciliations will be reduced when this process has been completed.

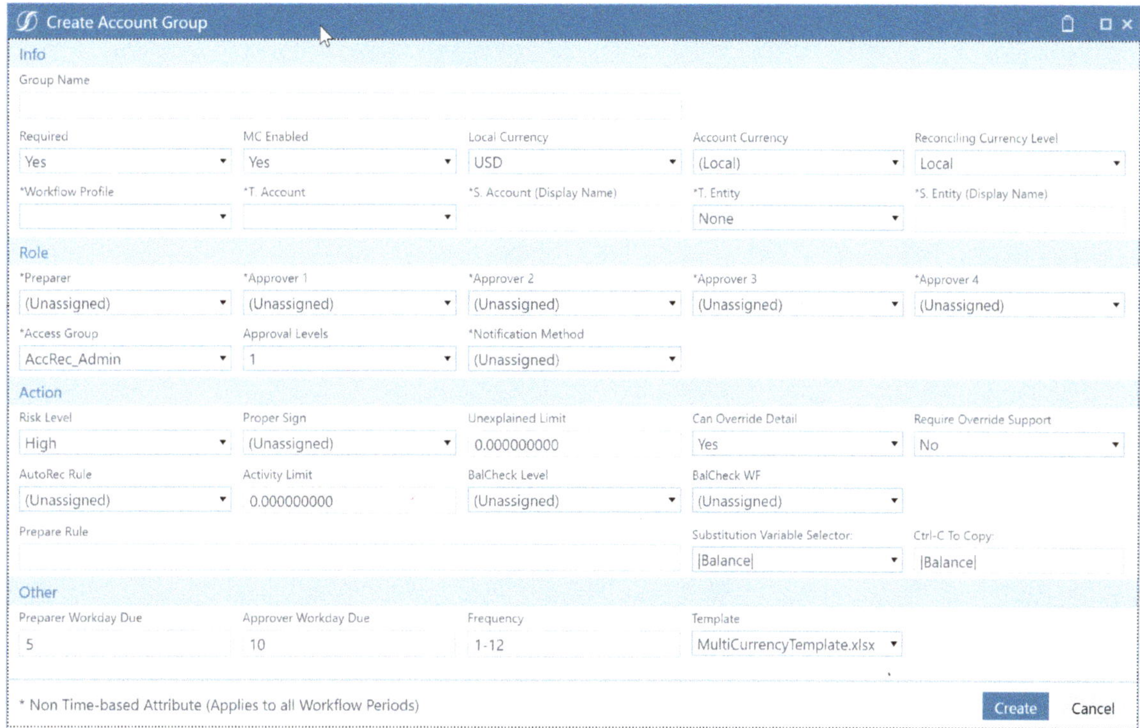

Figure 3.16

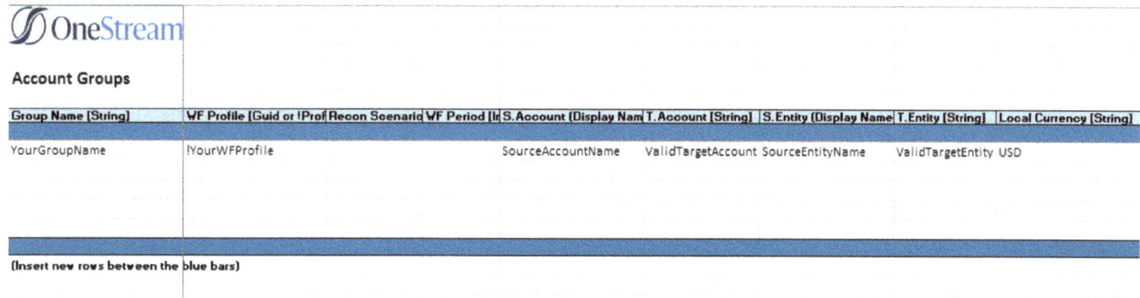

Figure 3.17

Once the Groups have been created and populated, the client can review the Inventory and generate the Users, plus roles that should be assigned to each User. This can be done by logging into OneStream and reviewing the Reconciliations, providing an existing list of which User is responsible for each Account by Entity, or by downloading the Inventory to a CSV file and filtering on the group column.

In this example, the client is downloading the Reconciliations from the Reconciliation page itself.

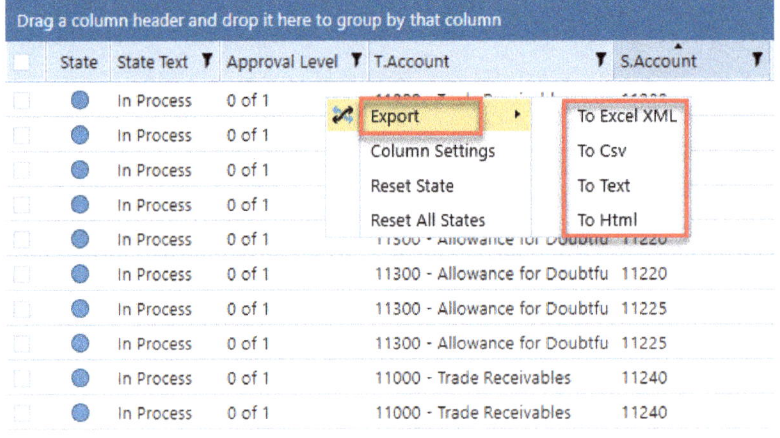

Figure 3.18

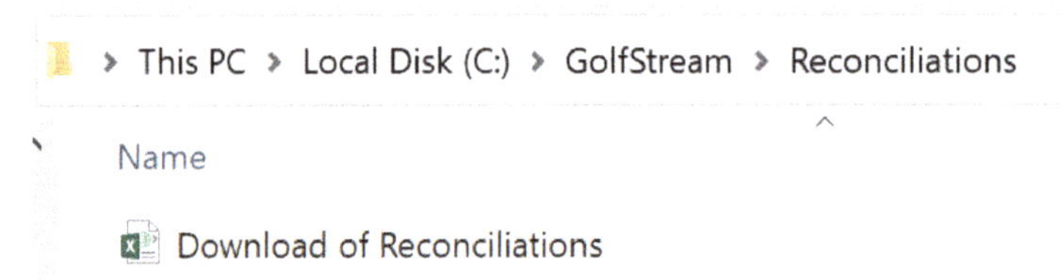

Figure 3.19

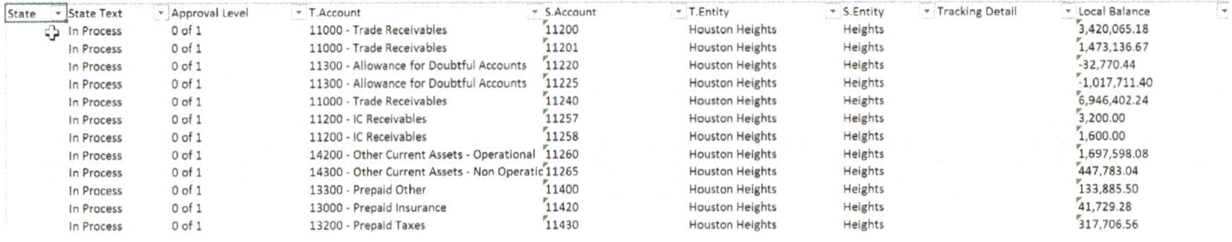

State	State Text	Approval Level	T.Account	S.Account	T.Entity	S.Entity	Tracking Detail	Local Balance
	In Process	0 of 1	11000 - Trade Receivables	11200	Houston Heights	Heights		3,420,065.18
	In Process	0 of 1	11000 - Trade Receivables	11201	Houston Heights	Heights		1,473,136.67
	In Process	0 of 1	11300 - Allowance for Doubtful Accounts	11220	Houston Heights	Heights		-32,770.44
	In Process	0 of 1	11300 - Allowance for Doubtful Accounts	11225	Houston Heights	Heights		-1,017,711.40
	In Process	0 of 1	11000 - Trade Receivables	11240	Houston Heights	Heights		6,946,402.24
	In Process	0 of 1	11200 - IC Receivables	11257	Houston Heights	Heights		3,200.00
	In Process	0 of 1	11200 - IC Receivables	11258	Houston Heights	Heights		1,600.00
	In Process	0 of 1	14200 - Other Current Assets - Operational	11260	Houston Heights	Heights		1,697,598.08
	In Process	0 of 1	14300 - Other Current Assets - Non Operatic	11265	Houston Heights	Heights		447,783.04
	In Process	0 of 1	13300 - Prepaid Other	11400	Houston Heights	Heights		133,885.50
	In Process	0 of 1	13000 - Prepaid Insurance	11420	Houston Heights	Heights		41,729.28
	In Process	0 of 1	13200 - Prepaid Taxes	11430	Houston Heights	Heights		317,706.56

Figure 3.20

In this next example, though, the client is downloading the Reconciliations from the Inventory page. The Inventory page can only be accessed by Users that have Administration rights.

Figure 3.21

From the Administration page, navigate to the Inventory page.

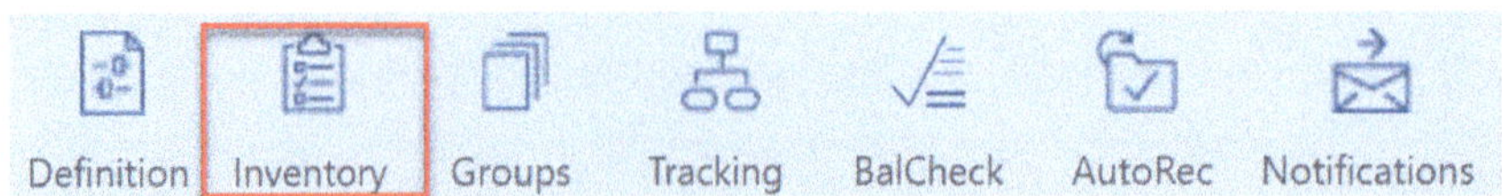

Figure 3.22

Reconciliations can now be exported by clicking on the Export icon.

Figure 3.23

It is important to remember to filter this file on Account Reconciliations that are *not* part of an Account Group.

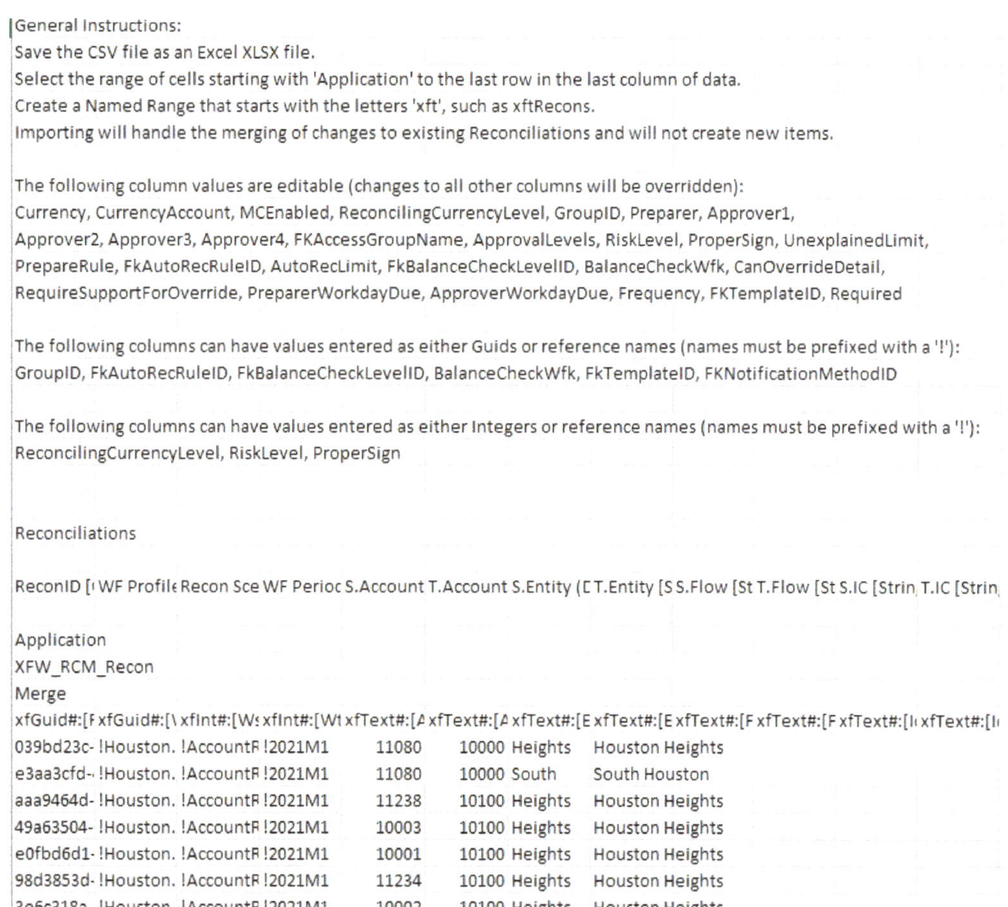

General Instructions:
Save the CSV file as an Excel XLSX file.
Select the range of cells starting with 'Application' to the last row in the last column of data.
Create a Named Range that starts with the letters 'xft', such as xftRecons.
Importing will handle the merging of changes to existing Reconciliations and will not create new items.

The following column values are editable (changes to all other columns will be overridden):
Currency, CurrencyAccount, MCEnabled, ReconcilingCurrencyLevel, GroupID, Preparer, Approver1,
Approver2, Approver3, Approver4, FKAccessGroupName, ApprovalLevels, RiskLevel, ProperSign, UnexplainedLimit,
PrepareRule, FkAutoRecRuleID, AutoRecLimit, FkBalanceCheckLevelID, BalanceCheckWfk, CanOverrideDetail,
RequireSupportForOverride, PreparerWorkdayDue, ApproverWorkdayDue, Frequency, FKTemplateID, Required

The following columns can have values entered as either Guids or reference names (names must be prefixed with a '!'):
GroupID, FkAutoRecRuleID, FkBalanceCheckLevelID, BalanceCheckWfk, FkTemplateID, FKNotificationMethodID

The following columns can have values entered as either Integers or reference names (names must be prefixed with a '!'):
ReconcilingCurrencyLevel, RiskLevel, ProperSign

Reconciliations

ReconID [	WF Profile	Recon Sce	WF Perioc	S.Account	T.Account	S.Entity (E	T.Entity [S	S.Flow [St	T.Flow [St	S.IC [Strin	T.IC [Strin
Application											
XFW_RCM_Recon											
Merge											
xfGuid#:[F	xfGuid#:[\	xfInt#:[W	xfInt#:[W	xfText#:[A	xfText#:[A	xfText#:[E	xfText#:[E	xfText#:[F	xfText#:[F	xfText#:[I	xfText#:[I
039bd23c-	!Houston.	!AccountR	!2021M1	11080	10000	Heights	Houston Heights				
e3aa3cfd-	!Houston.	!AccountR	!2021M1	11080	10000	South	South Houston				
aaa9464d-	!Houston.	!AccountR	!2021M1	11238	10100	Heights	Houston Heights				
49a63504-	!Houston.	!AccountR	!2021M1	10003	10100	Heights	Houston Heights				
e0fbd6d1-	!Houston.	!AccountR	!2021M1	10001	10100	Heights	Houston Heights				
98d3853d-	!Houston.	!AccountR	!2021M1	11234	10100	Heights	Houston Heights				
3e6c318a-	!Houston.	!AccountR	!2021M1	10002	10100	Heights	Houston Heights				

Figure 3.24

Next, the client needs to focus on the Account Reconciliations that *are* part of an Account Group. To extract the Account Groups, have the client follow these steps. From the Administration page, select the Groups icon.

Figure 3.25

Select the Export button and a CSV file will open on your desktop.

Figure 3.26

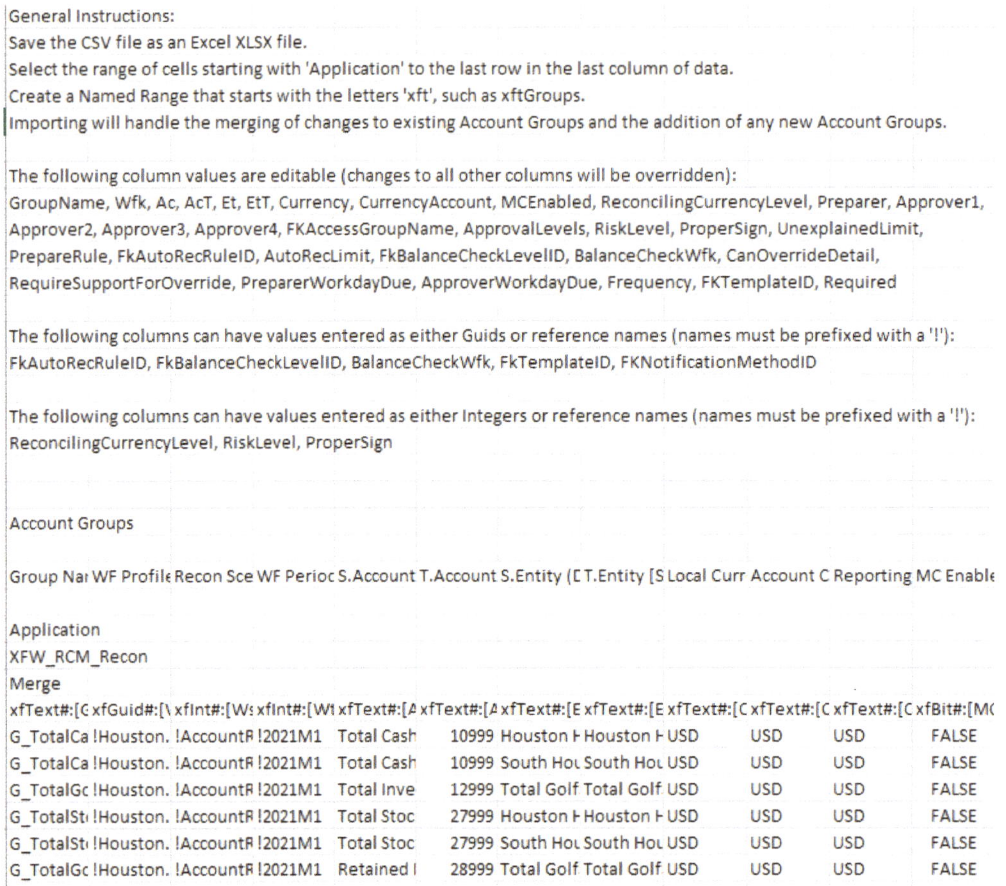

General Instructions:
Save the CSV file as an Excel XLSX file.
Select the range of cells starting with 'Application' to the last row in the last column of data.
Create a Named Range that starts with the letters 'xft', such as xftGroups.
Importing will handle the merging of changes to existing Account Groups and the addition of any new Account Groups.

The following column values are editable (changes to all other columns will be overridden):
GroupName, Wfk, Ac, AcT, Et, EtT, Currency, CurrencyAccount, MCEnabled, ReconcilingCurrencyLevel, Preparer, Approver1, Approver2, Approver3, Approver4, FKAccessGroupName, ApprovalLevels, RiskLevel, ProperSign, UnexplainedLimit, PrepareRule, FkAutoRecRuleID, AutoRecLimit, FkBalanceCheckLevelID, BalanceCheckWfk, CanOverrideDetail, RequireSupportForOverride, PreparerWorkdayDue, ApproverWorkdayDue, Frequency, FKTemplateID, Required

The following columns can have values entered as either Guids or reference names (names must be prefixed with a '!'):
FkAutoRecRuleID, FkBalanceCheckLevelID, BalanceCheckWfk, FkTemplateID, FKNotificationMethodID

The following columns can have values entered as either Integers or reference names (names must be prefixed with a '!'):
ReconcilingCurrencyLevel, RiskLevel, ProperSign

Account Groups

Group Nai	WF Profile	Recon Sce	WF Perioc	S.Account	T.Account	S.Entity (E	T.Entity [S	Local Curr	Account C	Reporting	MC Enable
Application											
XFW_RCM_Recon											
Merge											
xfText#:[G	xfGuid#:[\	xfInt#:[Ws	xfInt#:[Wt	xfText#:[A	xfText#:[A	xfText#:[E	xfText#:[E	xfText#:[C	xfText#:[C	xfText#:[C	xfBit#:[MC
G_TotalCa	!Houston.	!AccountR	!2021M1	Total Cash	10999	Houston H	Houston H	USD	USD	USD	FALSE
G_TotalCa	!Houston.	!AccountR	!2021M1	Total Cash	10999	South Hou	South Hou	USD	USD	USD	FALSE
G_TotalGc	!Houston.	!AccountR	!2021M1	Total Inve	12999	Total Golf	Total Golf	USD	USD	USD	FALSE
G_TotalSt	!Houston.	!AccountR	!2021M1	Total Stoc	27999	Houston H	Houston H	USD	USD	USD	FALSE
G_TotalSt	!Houston.	!AccountR	!2021M1	Total Stoc	27999	South Hou	South Hou	USD	USD	USD	FALSE
G_TotalGc	!Houston.	!AccountR	!2021M1	Retained I	28999	Total Golf	Total Golf	USD	USD	USD	FALSE

Figure 3.27

Once the client returns the files with User roles included, you can organize them in a way that will help create Security Groups. These Security Groups can be created on the System tab and then assigned to the Access Groups, which are then assigned to the Account Reconciliations.

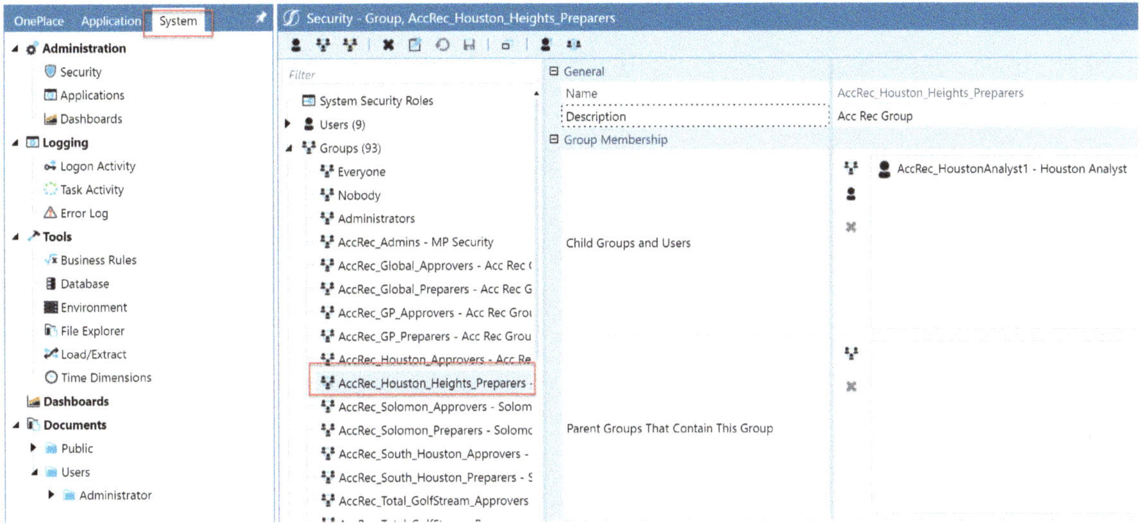

Figure 3.28

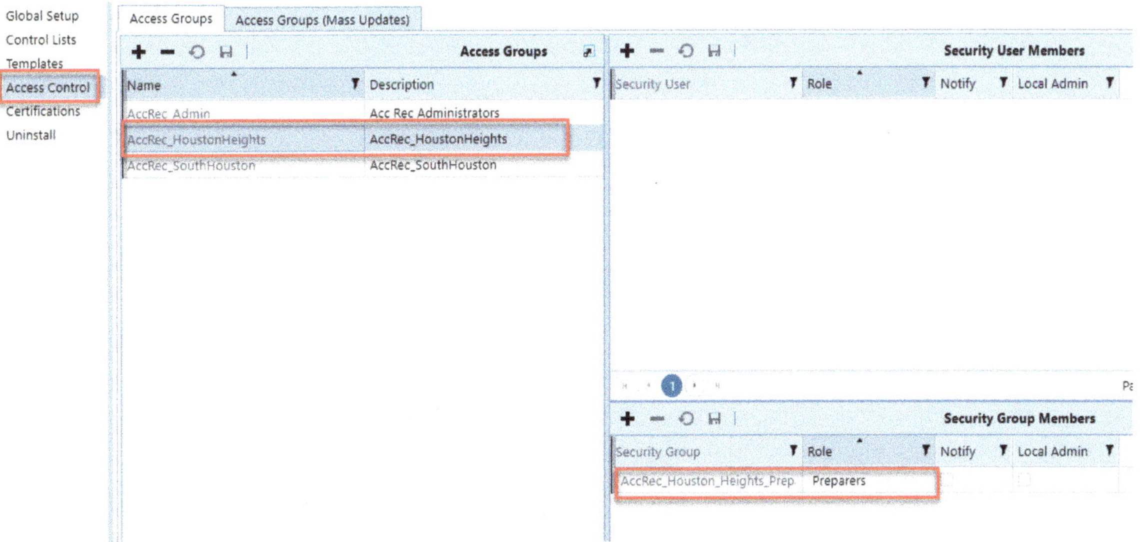

Figure 3.29

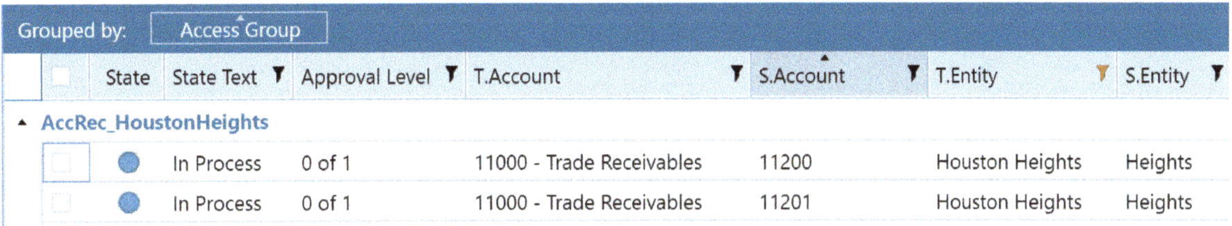

	State	State Text	Approval Level	T.Account	S.Account	T.Entity	S.Entity
AccRec_HoustonHeights							
		In Process	0 of 1	11000 - Trade Receivables	11200	Houston Heights	Heights
		In Process	0 of 1	11000 - Trade Receivables	11201	Houston Heights	Heights

Figure 3.30

Alternatively, you can go directly to the Access Control page and create the security there. The difference is that – in this second option – the User is added to the Access Control group, whereas in the first example, a System Security Group is added to the Access Control Group.

Both options work, but creating Security Groups on the Security tab will provide more flexibility to the client.

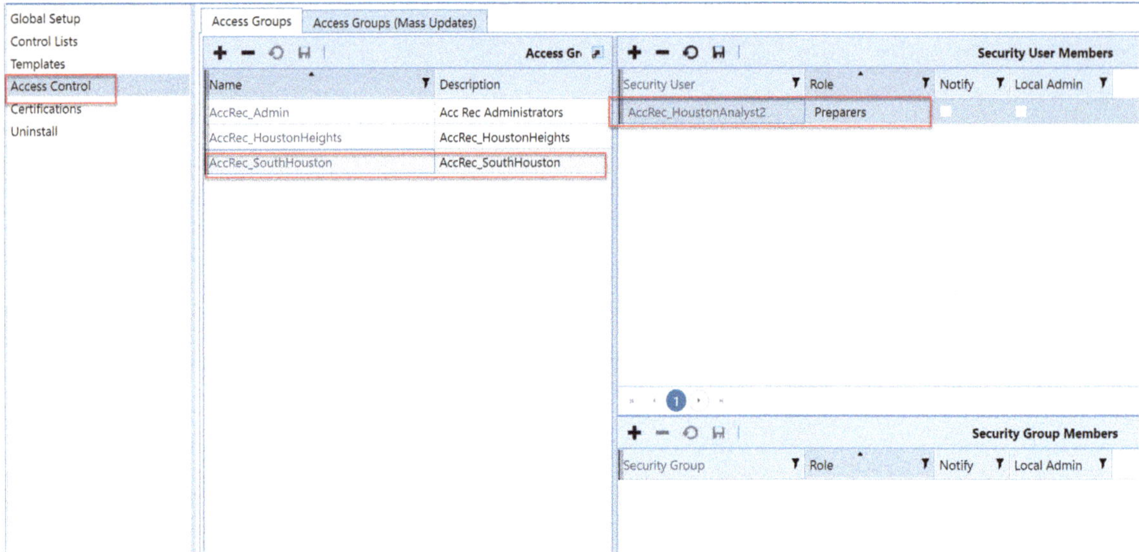

Figure 3.31

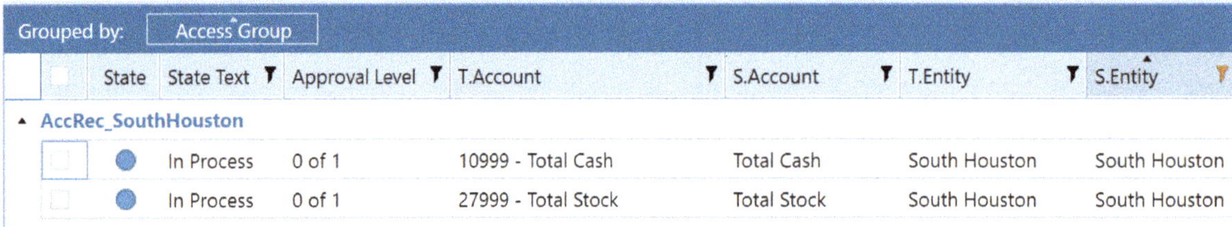

Grouped by: Access Group

	State	State Text	Approval Level	T.Account	S.Account	T.Entity	S.Entity
AccRec_SouthHouston							
	●	In Process	0 of 1	10999 - Total Cash	Total Cash	South Houston	South Houston
	●	In Process	0 of 1	27999 - Total Stock	Total Stock	South Houston	South Houston

Figure 3.32

Create a design document that the client can use to review the configuration of the solution, along with Account Groups and security. The design document is very important because it also covers the timeline and the scope of the project. It is also important to review the document with the client to make sure everything is understood.

After reviewing the Users, make sure they all have valid OneStream IDs. *Never* delete an old OneStream User ID because the audit logs will be impacted. Instead, set the Is Enabled setting to False for User IDs that no longer use OneStream.

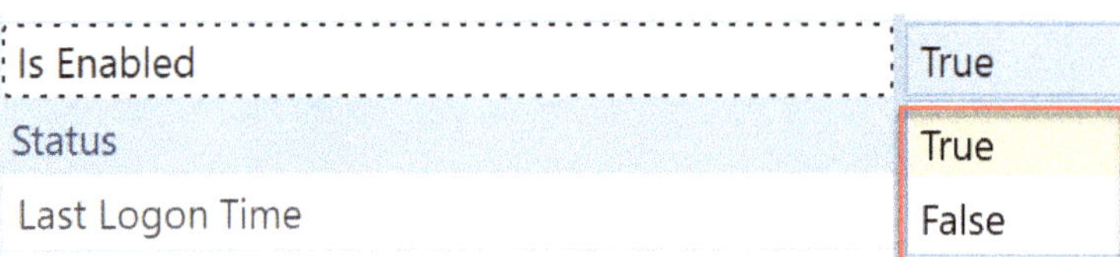

Figure 3.33

Send the completed design document to the client and have the client send any feedback or comments. This should be an iterative process. Once all the client's questions and concerns are addressed in the design document, they will be able to sign and approve the document. This will facilitate a smoother build phase and will help with any scope discussions that may arise.

Phase Two

If Phase One is the cornerstone of the project, then Phase Two is the structure itself. The Global Options are set, and the solution is configured to the client's specifications. The client will be able to see how their data is being used in the solution, and will not have to rely on examples from

GolfStream. This phase is also the time to adjust the configuration and address any issues that may arise.

Configuration

Configuring **Global Options** and **Global Defaults** is the core of the build. You will have a workable Inventory once the Discover process is completed, but it is better to spend time on all the settings *before* running Discover. Remember the adage "measure twice and cut once." Review the settings twice and run Discover once!

Discover has run on default settings, and there is an Inventory showing in Account Reconciliations. A default Base-level Reconciliation is a combination of a Stage (GL) Account and a OneStream Entity. You now need to go back to the Global Defaults and add UD1 as a tracking level, expanding the Reconciliation Definition to include the UD1 along with the Stage (GL) Account and a OneStream Entity. This will result in doubling the Inventory, at the very least. If each Reconciliation has more than one UD1, then each line of data will be added to the Inventory.

Avoid the temptation to jump right in and start configuring Global Options and Global Defaults. There are a few things that need to be created before the configuration starts. For the Global Options tab, create the Security Groups that will be used in Security Roles selections.

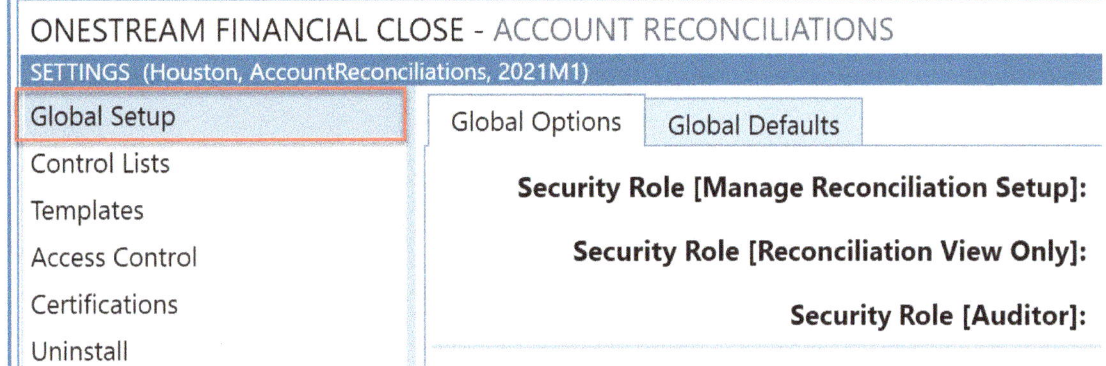

Figure 3.34

Next, create a new Scenario under Dimensions (using an unused Scenario Type; see "Source Scenario" in the previous chapter) that will be used for Reconciliation source selection.

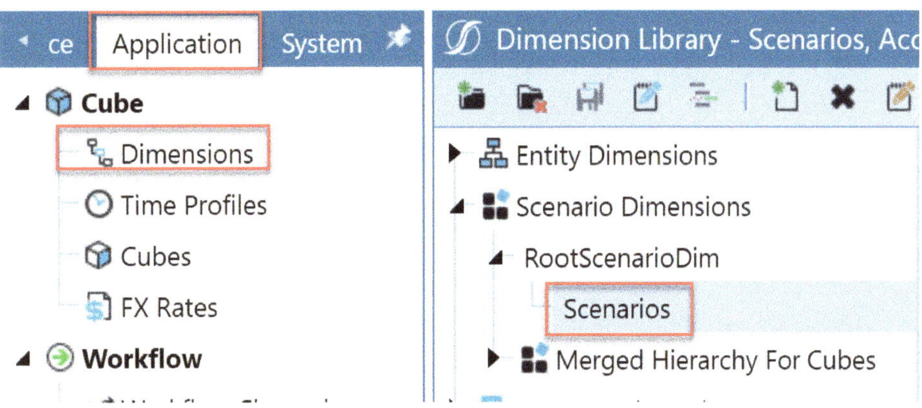

Figure 3.35

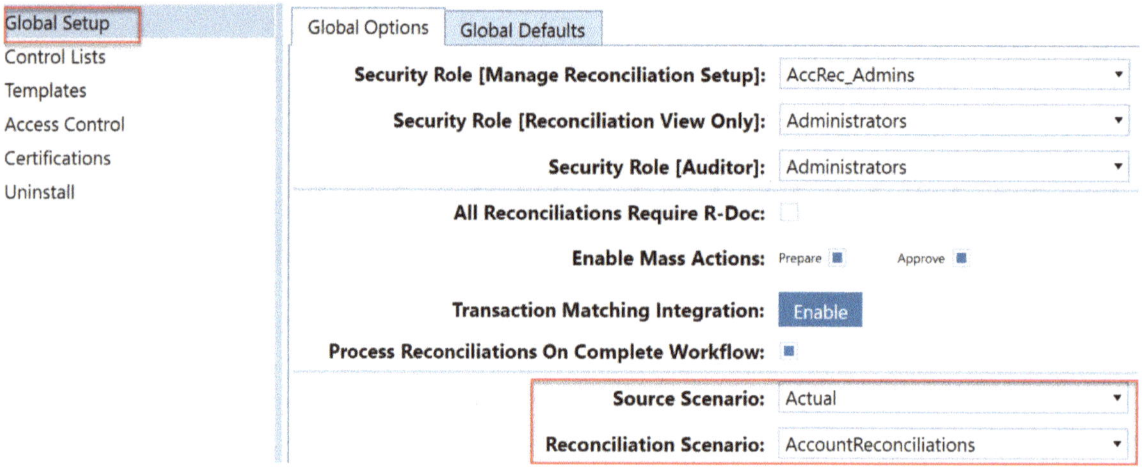

Figure 3.36

An email connection can also be set up prior to configuring Account Reconciliations.

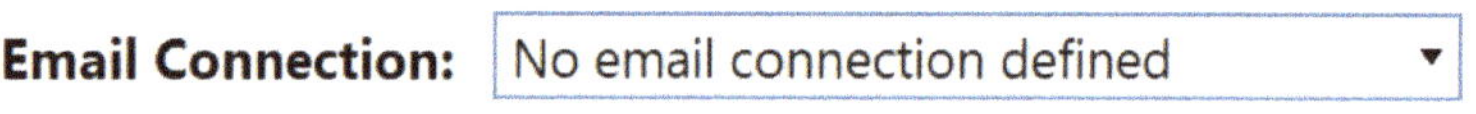

Figure 3.37

On the Global Defaults tab, create a new tracking level if the default (Entity) is not detailed enough.

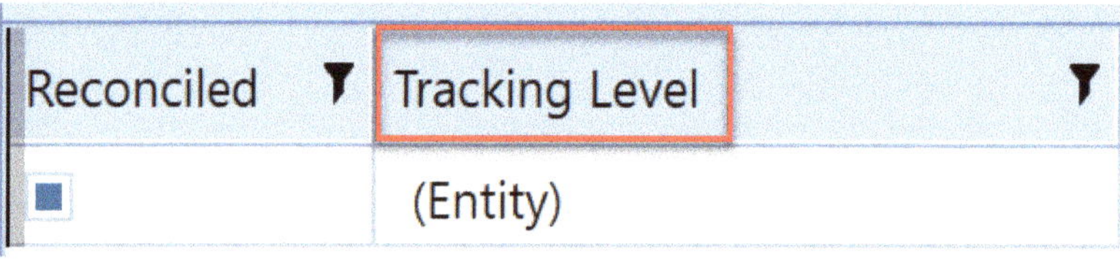

Figure 3.38

Create a Security Group under Access Control that will give the Account Reconciliation Administrator a way to track new Reconciliations. When new Reconciliations are discovered, the `RCM_Admin` access control group will be assigned to them. The Users in this group will be able to view the Reconciliations and – through a process that will be created in the project – the responsible person can ensure that proper responsibility is assigned.

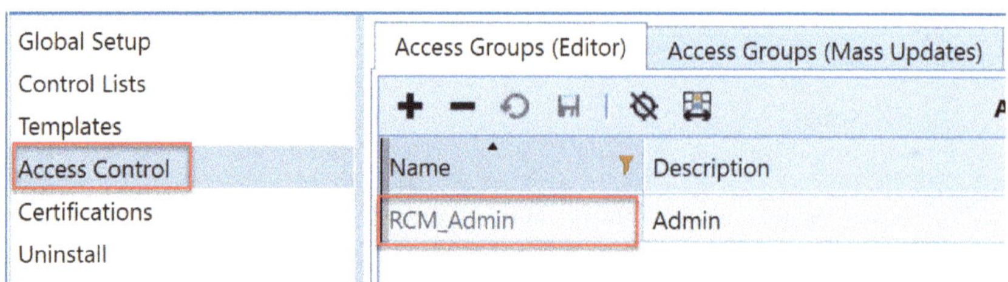

Figure 3.39

Default Reconciliation Properties

Figure 3.40

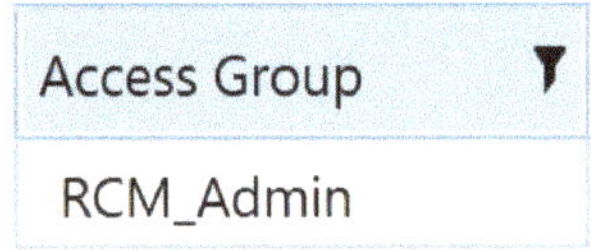

Access Group
RCM_Admin

Figure 3.41

Consider tasks that are configured outside of Account Reconciliations, which impact the solution.

These might include:

- Integrations for Balance Check Reconciliations.
- Non-Stage data that needs to be incorporated into the Account Reconciliation Inventory (Journals and Forms).
- New Accounts (Stage and OneStream).

Settings

The remaining settings can be updated after Discover has been processed. However, it is important to have these settings defined and updated *before* User Acceptance Testing.

- Control Lists are Item Types, Reason Codes, Close Dates, and Aging Periods. Item Types will impact Preparers; Reason Codes will impact Approvers; Close Dates will impact the detail of the Reconciliation; and the Aging Periods will impact the transaction detail of the Reconciliation.
- Access Control will give Users the ability to prepare, approve, view, or comment on each Reconciliation. Access Control groups create the security for each Reconciliation. It is important to define security early in the project so that Users can validate the settings. Users will need to interact with all their Reconciliations during training or User Acceptance Testing.
- Certifications are available for the Preparer and Approver roles.

Automation

Automation is not an Account Reconciliation setting, but it is a major feature of OneStream. The Discover and Process steps can be automated by creating a Data Management sequence for each function and adding these new tasks to the **scheduler** feature in OneStream. Both of these processes need to run any time close-related data is loaded into OneStream.

Build Sign-off

Review the Account Reconciliations MarketPlace solution with the Project Team when the build is complete. This needs to be a milestone in your project timeline. Give yourself enough time to demonstrate the entire configuration to the team in an interactive session that should last 60 to 120 minutes. Enlist several End/Power Users to help with the demonstration. Have one User assigned to each role to give the Project Team different views of the solution. Log in as sample Users if you don't have access to Users.

> **Note:** This meeting is key and will energize the team and create momentum when going into User Acceptance Testing.

User Acceptance Testing

User Acceptance Testing is critical in any project, so it cannot be underestimated. This can easily be moved to Phase Three if needed. The primary objective is to have Users perform Reconciliations and give feedback to the Project Team on anything that needs to be improved or corrected. Some issues can be solved with more education, but other issues may require updates to the configuration. All issues should have a resolution date before User training, and all issues need to be resolved before going live.

Case Study – Implement Account Reconciliations for GolfStream

In Phase Two, we want to configure Account Reconciliations with the settings established in Phase One. The difference between the preliminary configuration and the Phase Two configuration is that the client has validated the settings. There should be no change at this point without a scope change discussion with the client. Phase Two can be divided into two sections:

1. Build
2. User Acceptance Testing (UAT)

Phase	Task
2	**Build**
2	Global Setup
2	Global Options
2	Build and Test Email connection
2	Account Rec Settings
2	Tracking Levels
2	Basic Template
2	Security Group
2	Approvals
2	Workday Due
2	Proper Sign
2	Frequency
2	Unexplained Limit
2	Complete Rule
2	Can AutoRec
2	AutoRec Limit
2	Standard Recs
2	Balance Check Recs and New Import Profiles
2	Control Lists
2	Control Lists - Item Types and Reason Codes
2	Define Close Dates
2	Templates
2	Access Control
2	Security Design
2	Security Matrix Build
2	Security Build
2	Certifications
2	Definitions
2	Specialized Reconciliation Definitions
2	Reference Documents
2	Entity Tracking Level Overrides
2	Inventory
2	Review settings
2	Create Account Groups
2	Assign Reconciliations to Account Groups
2	Assign access groups to Reconciliations
2	Workflows
2	Assign Dashboards to Workflows
2	Advanced Rules
2	Complete Build
2	Solution Signoff

Figure 3.42

The build should be primarily completed but update any configuration settings based on the client's feedback. Be aware that some changes will increase the Account Reconciliation Inventory. For example, if you are required to add a new tracking level for UD1 Members, this will increase the Inventory by the number of Base UD1 Members. If UD1 has 10 Base Members and the new tracking level is applied to three Account definitions, then the Inventory can potentially increase by 30 new Reconciliations.

The number of new Reconciliations will be dependent on how many Entity/Account/UD1 intersections have data. In this situation, the original Account Reconciliations need to have their Required status changed to False.

Although the configuration settings are a major part of the build, there are other important aspects that should not be overlooked. Creating and uploading reference documentation, templates, the User Acceptance Testing, and an Administration document should also be done in Phase 2.

Phase	Task
2	UAT
2	Security Validation
2	Prepare Reconciliations for 1 Month
2	Use Templates on selected Reconciliations
2	Approve Reconciliations for 1 Month
2	Security Validation
2	Prepare Reconciliations for 1 Month
2	Use Templates on selected Reconciliations
2	Approve Reconciliations for 1 Month
2	UAT Signoff
2/3	Migrate to Production

Figure 3.43

Schedule UAT as soon as you can, so there is time to train the Users and capture any feedback that they may have. Leave yourself time to incorporate this feedback so the Users can run through the UAT steps again. This will help the client see the changes in the configuration before User training.

Leverage UAT training documentation for User Training/Quick Start guides. This will save valuable time that can be spent supporting the client during this stressful time in the project.

Once UAT has been completed, and sign-off has been obtained, install Account Reconciliations in the production environment, and migrate the development artifacts. Once the settings have been configured, run Discover, add Account Groups and Access Groups, then finally update the newly-created Inventory so it matches the settings in development. The last step is to Process the Reconciliations for the first month of User Training.

Phase Three

In this phase, the client will lead the way once User training has been completed. Allow for sessions of 120 minutes to accommodate any questions or issues that may arise. There is still time to make changes to individual Reconciliations, but be aware of downstream impacts these changes may have on the remaining time in Phases 3 and 4.

User Training

Know your audience! Creating training documentation that is too complicated will confuse Users and they will have a bad experience with OneStream. One way to avoid this is by understanding Users before the training documents have been created. There is time in the first two phases to understand if these particular Users are new to OneStream or if they have had other interactions with the software. If this is the first time a User has logged into OneStream, then add some steps on how to get into the system. It may sound like common sense, but it will only frustrate Users if they cannot complete this simple first stage.

Delayed Parallels

The User should select the more complicated Reconciliations during the delayed parallels. Once they have completed the first month, they can validate the Reconciliation against what was completed in the client's former process. The User can then go to the next time the Reconciliation needs to be completed and pull line items and support through to the current month. Encourage questions from Users and make yourself available to them, so they feel comfortable with the process before going live.

Case Study – Implement Account Reconciliations for GolfStream

In Phase Three, we want to start delivering the solution to the User audience.

Phase	Task
3	**Training**
3	Security Validation
3	Prepare Reconciliations for 1 Month
3	Use Templates on selected Reconciliations
3	Approve Reconciliations for 1 Month
3	Security Validation
3	Prepare Reconciliations for 1 Month
3	Use Templates on selected Reconciliations
3	Approve Reconciliations for 1 Month
3	Security Validation
3	Prepare Reconciliations for 1 Month
3	Use Templates on selected Reconciliations
3	Approve Reconciliations for 1 Month
3	Training Signoff

Figure 3.44

Schedule training sessions with the client. Keep the sessions to two hours and allow for follow-up sessions with Users. Once the security setup is completed, you can create more detailed test scripts. For example, in our case study, Houston Analyst 1 is responsible for all the Houston Heights Reconciliations as a Preparer. You can create a sign-off script asking the User to attest to the fact that they can access the specific list of Accounts. This would become the **Security Validation** for the training and can be used for the delayed parallels.

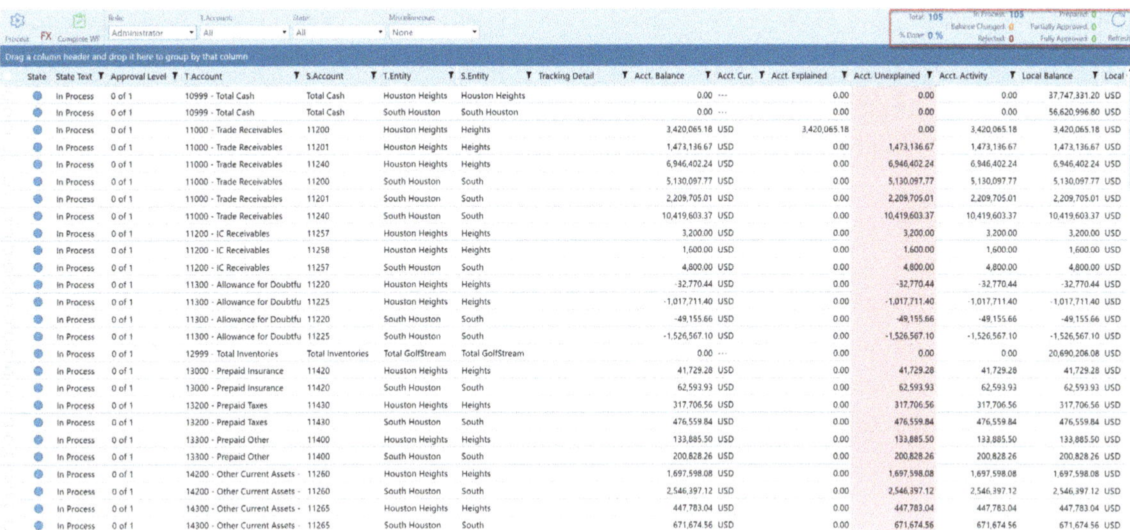

State	State Text	Approval Level	T.Account	S.Account	T.Entity	S.Entity	Tracking Detail	Acct. Balance	Acct. Cur.	Acct. Explained	Acct. Unexplained	Acct. Activity	Local Balance	Local
	In Process	0 of 1	10999 - Total Cash	Total Cash	Houston Heights	Houston Heights		0.00	---	0.00	0.00	0.00	37,747,331.20	USD
	In Process	0 of 1	10999 - Total Cash	Total Cash	South Houston	South Houston		0.00	---	0.00	0.00	0.00	56,620,996.80	USD
	In Process	0 of 1	11000 - Trade Receivables	11200	Houston Heights	Heights		3,420,065.18	USD	3,420,065.18	0.00	3,420,065.18	3,420,065.18	USD
	In Process	0 of 1	11000 - Trade Receivables	11201	Houston Heights	Heights		1,473,136.67	USD	0.00	1,473,136.67	1,473,136.67	1,473,136.67	USD
	In Process	0 of 1	11000 - Trade Receivables	11240	Houston Heights	Heights		6,946,402.24	USD	0.00	6,946,402.24	6,946,402.24	6,946,402.24	USD
	In Process	0 of 1	11000 - Trade Receivables	11200	South Houston	South		5,130,097.77	USD	0.00	5,130,097.77	5,130,097.77	5,130,097.77	USD
	In Process	0 of 1	11000 - Trade Receivables	11201	South Houston	South		2,209,705.01	USD	0.00	2,209,705.01	2,209,705.01	2,209,705.01	USD
	In Process	0 of 1	11000 - Trade Receivables	11240	South Houston	South		10,419,603.37	USD	0.00	10,419,603.37	10,419,603.37	10,419,603.37	USD
	In Process	0 of 1	11200 - IC Receivables	11257	Houston Heights	Heights		3,200.00	USD	0.00	3,200.00	3,200.00	3,200.00	USD
	In Process	0 of 1	11200 - IC Receivables	11258	Houston Heights	Heights		1,600.00	USD	0.00	1,600.00	1,600.00	1,600.00	USD
	In Process	0 of 1	11200 - IC Receivables	11257	South Houston	South		4,800.00	USD	0.00	4,800.00	4,800.00	4,800.00	USD
	In Process	0 of 1	11300 - Allowance for Doubtfu	11220	Houston Heights	Heights		-32,770.44	USD	0.00	-32,770.44	-32,770.44	-32,770.44	USD
	In Process	0 of 1	11300 - Allowance for Doubtfu	11225	Houston Heights	Heights		-1,017,711.40	USD	0.00	-1,017,711.40	-1,017,711.40	-1,017,711.40	USD
	In Process	0 of 1	11300 - Allowance for Doubtfu	11220	South Houston	South		-49,155.66	USD	0.00	-49,155.66	-49,155.66	-49,155.66	USD
	In Process	0 of 1	11300 - Allowance for Doubtfu	11225	South Houston	South		-1,526,567.10	USD	0.00	-1,526,567.10	-1,526,567.10	-1,526,567.10	USD
	In Process	0 of 1	12999 - Total Inventories	Total Inventories	Total GolfStream	Total GolfStream		0.00	---	0.00	0.00	0.00	20,690,206.08	USD
	In Process	0 of 1	13000 - Prepaid Insurance	11420	Houston Heights	Heights		41,729.28	USD	0.00	41,729.28	41,729.28	41,729.28	USD
	In Process	0 of 1	13000 - Prepaid Insurance	11420	South Houston	South		62,593.93	USD	0.00	62,593.93	62,593.93	62,593.93	USD
	In Process	0 of 1	13200 - Prepaid Taxes	11430	Houston Heights	Heights		317,706.56	USD	0.00	317,706.56	317,706.56	317,706.56	USD
	In Process	0 of 1	13200 - Prepaid Taxes	11430	South Houston	South		476,559.84	USD	0.00	476,559.84	476,559.84	476,559.84	USD
	In Process	0 of 1	13300 - Prepaid Other	11400	Houston Heights	Heights		133,885.50	USD	0.00	133,885.50	133,885.50	133,885.50	USD
	In Process	0 of 1	13300 - Prepaid Other	11400	South Houston	South		200,828.26	USD	0.00	200,828.26	200,828.26	200,828.26	USD
	In Process	0 of 1	14200 - Other Current Assets -	11260	Houston Heights	Heights		1,697,598.08	USD	0.00	1,697,598.08	1,697,598.08	1,697,598.08	USD
	In Process	0 of 1	14200 - Other Current Assets -	11260	South Houston	South		2,546,397.12	USD	0.00	2,546,397.12	2,546,397.12	2,546,397.12	USD
	In Process	0 of 1	14300 - Other Current Assets -	11265	Houston Heights	Heights		447,783.04	USD	0.00	447,783.04	447,783.04	447,783.04	USD
	In Process	0 of 1	14300 - Other Current Assets -	11265	South Houston	South		671,674.56	USD	0.00	671,674.56	671,674.56	671,674.56	USD

Figure 3.45

Send the training and quick start guides to Users and upload them to OneStream. Take advantage of OneStream's file system and create folders so Users can access the training documentation.

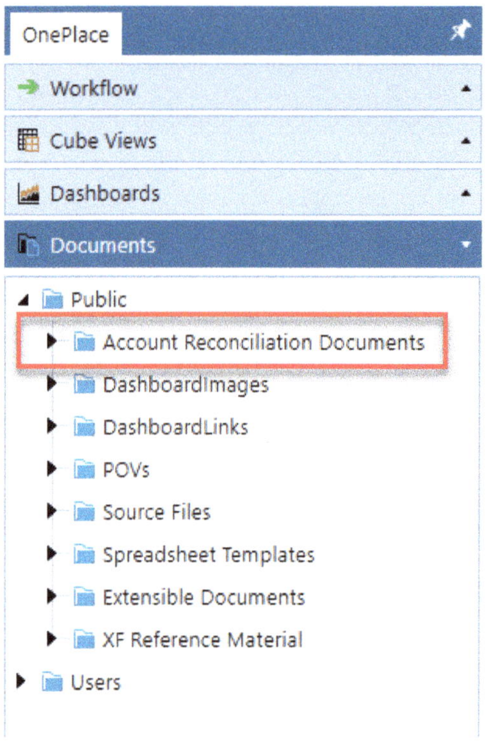

Figure 3.46

Phase	Task
3	**Parallel**
3	Security Validation
3	Prepare Reconciliations for 1 Month
3	Use Templates on selected Reconciliations
3	Approve Reconciliations for 1 Month
3	Parallel 1 Signoff
3	Security Validation
3	Prepare Reconciliations for 1 Month
3	Use Templates on selected Reconciliations
3	Approve Reconciliations for 1 Month
3	Parallel 2 Signoff
3	Security Validation
3	Prepare Reconciliations for 1 Month
3	Use Templates on selected Reconciliations
3	Approve Reconciliations for 1 Month
3	Parallel 3 Signoff

Figure 3.47

Schedule parallels once the documentation has been completed. Reiterate to Users that the objectives of these sessions are to:

- Have Users validate security – Users should review all the Reconciliations they have access to, and verify that they should see these Reconciliations.

- Have Users learn how to prepare Reconciliations, attach supporting documentation, pull items and documents forward, and use templates.
- Have Users learn how to approve Reconciliations, review supporting documentation, create audit files, and add comments.
- Have Users learn how to view and comment on Reconciliations.
- Capture User feedback – this is very important because it will give the client a list of objectives for a follow-up project or – if the issue is small – it will help improve the project by incorporating ideas from Users.
- If feedback is incorporated into the current scope, then the User should re-test the issue before going live.

Phase Four

The final phase of the project should be brief and painless. Review all the decisions and issues to date with the Project Team and finalize a go-live date. All issues should have been resolved by this point, but it's important to review them *one last time* with the Project Team.

Go Live

Congratulations! This is the moment that you and your client have been working towards! Going live with OneStream Account Reconciliations is a very exciting time. Take a deep breath and celebrate the fact that you have helped your client expand their OneStream footprint, and you have participated in the *Art of the Possible*!

Post-Go Live Support

It's always important to support the client after the project is live. One approach is to schedule a touch-base meeting every day for the first live week and decrease the frequency every week post-go-live. By the end of the first go-live close, the client should be self-sufficient on Account Reconciliations.

Case Study – Implement Account Reconciliations for GolfStream

In Phase Four, we are preparing for take-off! This should be a time for celebration. You and your client have gone through a MarketPlace solution implementation with a successful result.

4	**Deployment**
4	Key Stakeholders sign-off on Go-Live
4	Communication to Field on Go-Live Instructions
4	Go-Live
4	**Post Go Live support**

Figure 3.48

Schedule a meeting with the key stakeholders to discuss the overall project. You can discuss what worked well and what didn't. Were the measures of success met? At this meeting, the decision to go live should be agreed to.

The client should be able to communicate to Users and management that the project was a success and that Account Reconciliations will be managed in OneStream.

Once the client is live, provide support for Users for the first month. This will help the client adapt the solution fully, and all the hard work done on the project will be validated!

Conclusion

OneStream's Account Reconciliation MarketPlace solution is unlike any other product in the market and creating a structured manner to configure the solution is a critical success factor. Over the years, the solution has changed but my approach has stayed the same. Treat the configuration process like any other project and you will be successful!

Chapter Appendix

Questionnaire Example

1. What is the overall timeline?
   An example timeline would be:

    a. Kick-off at the end of January
    b. Design sign-off by the end of February
    c. UAT at the end of March
    d. Parallel 1 at the end of April
    e. Parallel 2 in mid-May
    f. Go live in June

   The GolfStream timeline:

    a. Kick-off the week of 06/18/22
    b. Design sign-off the week of 07/16/22
    c. UAT at the end of August
    d. Parallels 1, 2, and 3 at the end of September
    e. Go live in October

2. Are there any current or future projects scheduled that will impact GL Accounts or Accounts that are submitted into OneStream?

    Account Reconciliations will use GL and OneStream Accounts to create the Reconciliation Inventory. There will be an impact on Account Reconciliations if the Base-level OneStream Accounts change.

    GolfStream: No.

3. Will OneStream-only data need to be included in the Reconciliations (e.g., Form or Journal data)?

    This data will need to be moved from the Cube to Stage, so it is included in the Account Reconciliation Inventory.

    GolfStream: No.

4. How many Users reconcile Accounts today?

    All Users will need a OneStream ID/license.

    GolfStream: 10 No new licenses will be needed.

5. Estimate the number of expected Reconciliations and who will Prepare and Approve each Reconciliation?

   Account Reconciliations has the following User roles:

   ***Preparer** – Can see assigned Reconciliations and perform preparation duties through clicking the Prepare button.*

   ***Approver 1 through Approver 4** – Choose up to ten levels of Approvers. There must be a User assigned to at least as many Approver levels as there are Approvals on the Reconciliation that this Access Group is assigned to. So, if the Reconciliation has Approvals set at 3, there must be at least a User assigned to the related Access Group at Preparer, Approval 1, Approval 2 and Approval 3 in order to be able to prepare, and ultimately approve, the Reconciliation.*

   ***Commenter** – Optional. This User can see the data and activity but can only make Comments related to this Reconciliation.*

Viewer *– Optional. This User can see the data and activity but cannot make Comments related to this Reconciliation.*

6. Will any Accounts be grouped?

   Grouping Reconciliations will reduce the overall number of Reconciliations that need to be completed in a month. There are many ways to group Accounts, but Accounts can be mainly grouped by Entity, Account, or across currencies.

   GolfStream: Yes.

7. How many currencies are reconciled?

   GolfStream: Four, but only USD for this project.

8. Are there any non-Balance Sheet Account Reconciliations?

   Typically, only Balance Sheet Accounts are reconciled.

   GolfStream: No.

9. How many levels of approval will most Reconciliations need?

   There can be up to four levels of approval for each Reconciliation.

10. What Risk Levels will be needed? (Low/Medium/High)

11. When are Reconciliations due for Preparers?

12. When are Reconciliations due for Approvers?

13. How often will the Reconciliation need to be performed? (i.e., What is the frequency? Monthly, quarterly, yearly?)

14. Are there any unexplained limits other than zero? (ex. 0.00 = all Reconciliations have to be done to the penny).

15. What dollar amount would be used to auto reconcile Accounts?

16. Are there any Reconciliations that need special rules (e.g., auto reconcile if the balance changes by less than 3%, then prepare or approve the Reconciliation)?

17. Will any subledger data need to be reconciled?

18. Will each subledger feed equal one Reconciliation, many Reconciliations? How many Entities are in the subledger feed?

Milestone Examples

Milestone	Completed By	Phase
Design and Requirement Sessions	TBD	1
Key Stakeholders sign-off on configuration settings	TBD	1
Design Document Completed	TBD	1
Design Document Acceptance/Sign-off	TBD	1
Build Completed	TBD	2
User Acceptance Training	TBD	2
Key Stakeholders sign-off on UAT	TBD	2
Migrate (Build) to Production	TBD	3
End User Training	TBD	3
Parallel 1 Sign-off	TBD	3
Parallel 2 Sign-off	TBD	3
Parallel 3 Sign-off	TBD	3
Key Stakeholders sign-off on Go-Live	TBD	4
Go-live	TBD	4
Support	TBD	4

Figure 3.49

Detailed Tasks

Phase	Task
1	**Requirements and Global Design**
1	Discovery and Requirements Sessions
1	Reconciliation Inventory Overview - Basic Configuration
1	Review inventory with team
1	Client Analysis of Inventory (assign Preparers and Approvers)
1	Design
1	Design Sessions
1	Design Document Draft Completed
1	Design Document Acceptance/Sign-off
1	Key Stakeholders Signoff
2	**Build**
2	Global Setup
2	Global Options
2	Build and Test Email connection
2	Account Rec Settings
2	Tracking Levels
2	Basic Template
2	Security Group
2	Approvals
2	Workday Due
2	Proper Sign
2	Frequency
2	Unexplained Limit
2	Complete Rule
2	Can AutoRec
2	AutoRec Limit
2	Standard Recs
2	Balance Check Recs and New Import Profiles
2	Control Lists
2	Control Lists - Item Types and Reason Codes
2	Define Close Dates
2	Templates
2	Access Control
2	Security Design
2	Security Matrix Build
2	Security Build
2	Certifications
2	Definitions
2	Specialized Reconciliation Definitions
2	Reference Documents
2	Entity Tracking Level Overrides
2	Inventory
2	Review settings
2	Create Account Groups
2	Assign Reconciliations to Account Groups
2	Assign access groups to Reconciliations
2	Workflows
2	Assign Dashboards to Workflows
2	Advanced Rules
2	Complete Build
2	Solution Signoff
2	**UAT**
2	Security Validation
2	Prepare Reconciliations for 1 Month
2	Use Templates on selected Reconciliations
2	Approve Reconciliations for 1 Month
2	Security Validation
2	Prepare Reconciliations for 1 Month
2	Use Templates on selected Reconciliations
2	Approve Reconciliations for 1 Month
2	UAT Signoff
2/3	Migrate to Production
3	**Training**
3	Security Validation
3	Prepare Reconciliations for 1 Month
3	Use Templates on selected Reconciliations
3	Approve Reconciliations for 1 Month
3	Security Validation
3	Prepare Reconciliations for 1 Month
3	Use Templates on selected Reconciliations
3	Approve Reconciliations for 1 Month
3	Security Validation
3	Prepare Reconciliations for 1 Month
3	Use Templates on selected Reconciliations
3	Approve Reconciliations for 1 Month
3	Training Signoff
3	**Parallel**
3	Security Validation
3	Prepare Reconciliations for 1 Month
3	Use Templates on selected Reconciliations
3	Approve Reconciliations for 1 Month
3	Parallel 1 Signoff
3	Security Validation
3	Prepare Reconciliations for 1 Month
3	Use Templates on selected Reconciliations
3	Approve Reconciliations for 1 Month
3	Parallel 2 Signoff
3	Security Validation
3	Prepare Reconciliations for 1 Month
3	Use Templates on selected Reconciliations
3	Approve Reconciliations for 1 Month
3	Parallel 3 Signoff
4	**Deployment**
4	Key Stakeholders sign-off on Go-Live
4	Communication to Field on Go-Live Instructions
4	Go-Live
4	**Post Go Live support**

Figure 3.50

4

Using Account Reconciliations

As I write this chapter, I am reminded of my days working within the General Accounting department. I spent a lot of time preparing and approving reconciliations. Back then, the process was completely manual; I would prepare the Reconciliation in Excel, print my file and all the supporting documentation, obtain physical signatures, and then store the information in a binder for historical purposes. If, within this process, there was a change of any kind (account balance updated, Approver changes, or spelling errors), I had to update the Reconciliation and start the process again.

Painful, to say the least.

As my career progressed, technology advanced and software was developed to automate the account reconciliation process. I have used many of the different point solutions in the market and, although good solutions, they did not fully support the entire process. I still performed many activities external to the solution, and was required to leverage other software packages to compensate for missing processes and reporting.

It was not until I started at OneStream that I found a platform that truly supports the end-to-end process. OneStream takes an organization from the trial balance to daily financial signaling to Account Reconciliations and, finally, to financial statements ensuring financial integrity throughout the process. Without a doubt, OneStream is the leader in the record-to-report space.

In the following chapter, we will walk through the Account Reconciliation Solution from the End User's perspective. We will be discussing how you navigate the system to prepare a Reconciliation, the sign-off and approval process, and the overall reporting and monitoring capabilities. In addition to walking through the different roles and responsibilities, we will also talk about the best practices in preparing a Reconciliation.

Reconciliation Workflow

The process starts by navigating to the Reconciliation Workflow.

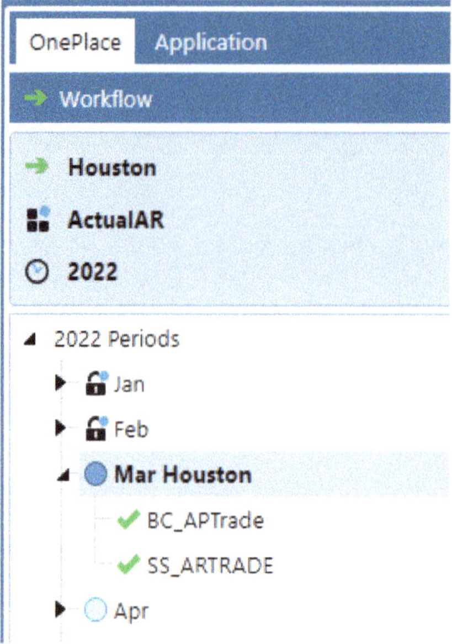

Figure 4.1

Depending on your implementation, you can either have a single Reconciliation Workflow or multiple Workflows that segregate the process by Entities, Business Units, etc. The setup of the Workflow is done by the Administrator and is discussed in detail in Chapter 2. In this section, we will be talking about how you can leverage the Workflow to perform your work.

The Reconciliation Workflow is used to access the **Reconciliation Workspace** for a specific period. You access the Reconciliations and all related reporting for the period selected within the Reconciliation Workspace. Based on how long the organization has used the Account Reconciliation Solution, you can access historical Reconciliations by navigating to the specific period within the Workflow.

The Workflow can also be leveraged to add supporting data to the Reconciliation process like subledgers or third-party information. The loading of data can be automated to populate the Reconciliation with the ability to drill down to the detail within the Workflow or drill back to the source system if utilizing the **Direct Connect** process. We refer to this process as **Balance Check**. You will learn more about Balance Check functionality later in this chapter.

Workspace

The Reconciliation Workspace is linked to the Workflow and all Users will leverage the Workspace to perform their responsibilities.

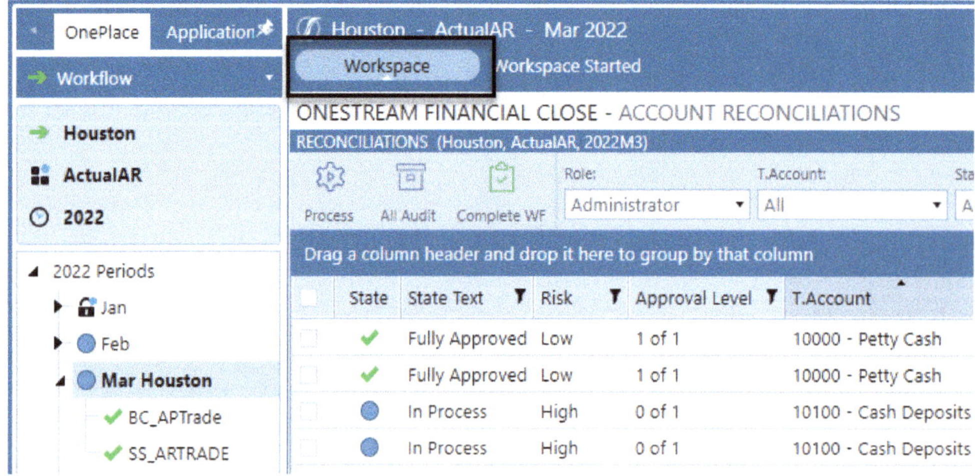

Figure 4.2

The Workspace defaults to the Reconciliations page, although the solution also contains pages for Analysis and Reporting, Administration, Audit, Settings, and Help. You can navigate to the other pages by utilizing the navigation icons in the top-right corner. The icons that are visible to you will depend on your security.

Within this chapter, we will walk through the Reconciliations and Analysis and Reporting pages. The Administration, Audit, and Settings pages were defined in detail in Chapter 2.

Navigation Icons

The navigation icons allow you to move between the different pages of the solution.

Figure 4.3

The icons available are dependent on the User's security and are described in Figure 4.4 below.

Icon	Description	Roles	Definition
	Analysis and Reporting Page	All Roles	Navigates to the solution-delivered reporting.
	Reconciliations Page	All Roles	Navigates to the Reconciliations Grid and Detailed Reconciliation View. Solution defaults to this page.
	Administration Page	Local and System Admins	Navigates to the Reconciliation Definition, Inventory, Groups, Tracking, BalCheck, AutoRec, and Notifications for attribute maintenance.
	Audit Page	Local and System Admins	Navigates to the Audit Page, where the system reports the changes made to Security Roles, Attributes and Account Groups.
	Settings Page	System Admins	Navigates to the Global Settings, Control List, Templates, Access Control, and Certifications.
	Help Page	All Roles	Navigates to the Help page.

Figure 4.4

Reconciliations Page

The Reconciliations page is the default when navigating to the Reconciliation Workspace because it is the page where the Users spend most of their time. This page is used differently by each User, depending on their role and responsibilities. For management, we tend to see Users employ the grid to monitor the Reconciliation process and view specific Reconciliations as needed. Preparers and Approvers will use the Reconciliations page to navigate and perform their work, review, and sign-off. Often, we see Auditors leverage this page to perform their required audit testing.

The Reconciliations page is a treasure trove of information and capabilities. The page can be broken up into three key areas:

1. Header
2. Reconciliation Grid
3. Reconciliation Details

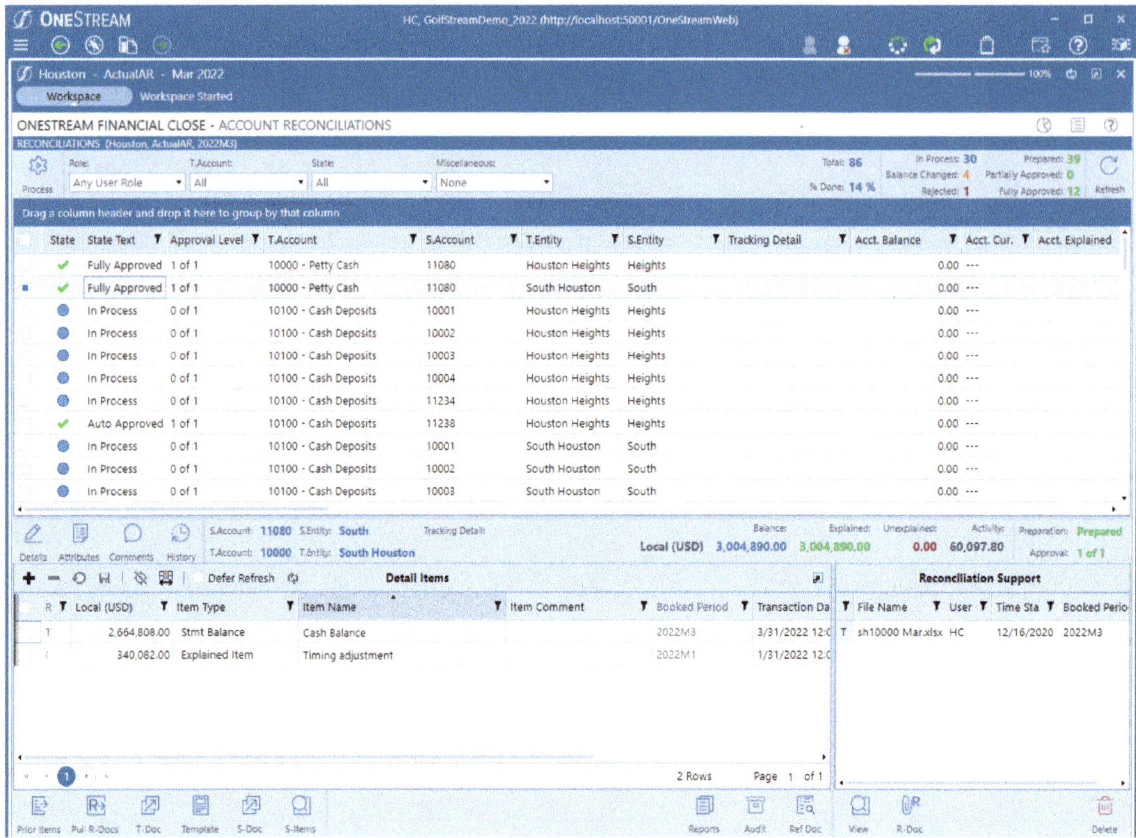

Figure 4.5

Header

The header section contains the Process icon, the top grid filters, and the status bar.

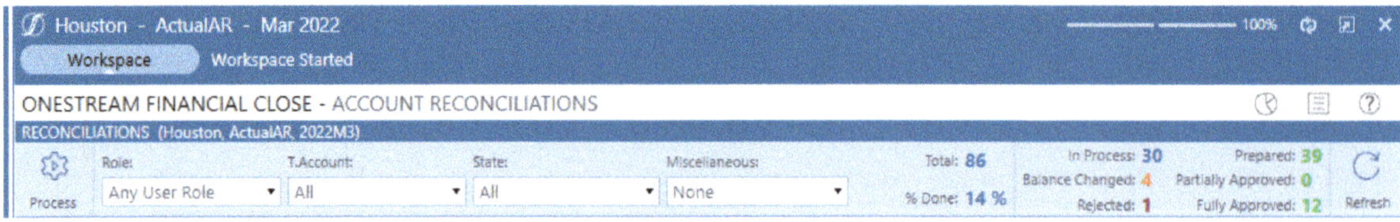

Figure 4.6

Process Icon

The Process icon is used to update the Reconciliations, which includes:

1. Creating the initial Reconciliation for the period.
2. Updating the Reconciliation balances for new trial balances or supporting data.
3. Updating certain attribute changes such as Account Groups.

4. Applying the AutoRec Rules for the given period.

Figure 4.7

Although typically run by the Administrator to update all Reconciliations for the specific Workflow, Preparers and Approvers can also run the process. If run by the Preparer or Approver, only the Reconciliations associated with these Users will be updated.

Top Grid Filters

The top grid filters are focused around four key areas that Users tend to view: Role, T.Account, State, and my new favorite Miscellaneous.

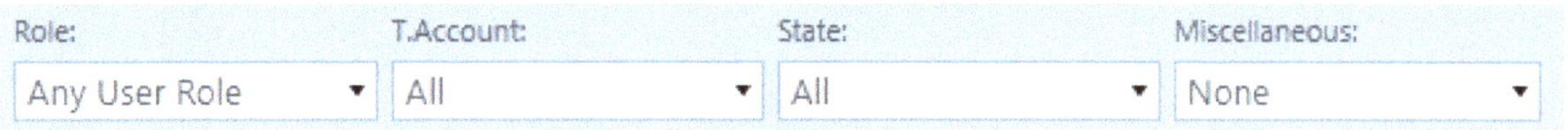

Figure 4.8

These filters are applied to the grid and narrow down the Reconciliations presented, based on the selections made. The available filters, and the selections in the drop-downs, are dependent on your security. Also, when leveraging top filters, the statistics will update in the status bar for the subset of Reconciliations. Let us walk through *when* and *why* you would use each filter.

Role

The Role filter allows you to narrow down the Reconciliations in the grid based on your assigned roles. As a User, I may be a Preparer on some Reconciliations and an Approver on others. Because I hold multiple responsibilities within the Reconciliation process, being able to retrieve Reconciliations based on a specific role or multiple roles allows me to be more efficient and targeted in my work. The different role options are defined in the table below.

Role Filter	Definition
Any User Role	Displays all Reconciliations where the User has an assigned role. This is the default selection for Users unless you are a System Administrator or Auditor.
Primary Preparer	Displays all Reconciliations where the User is assigned as Primary Preparer.
Primary Approver	Displays all Reconciliations where the User is assigned as a Primary Approver 1, 2, 3 or 4.
Primary Preparer/Approver	Displays all Reconciliations where the User is either assigned as Primary Preparer or Primary Approver 1, 2, 3 or 4.
AG Preparer	Displays all Reconciliations where the User is assigned as Preparer within the respective Access Group.
AG Approver	Displays all Reconciliations where the User is assigned Approver 1, 2, 3 or 4 within the respective Access Group.

Role Filter	Definition
AG Preparer/Approver	Displays all Reconciliations where the User is assigned Preparer or Approver 1, 2, 3 or 4 within the respective Access Groups.
Any Preparer/Approver	Displays all Reconciliations where the User is assigned as Primary Preparer, Primary Approver 1, 2, 3 or 4, Preparer within the Access Group, or Approver 1, 2, 3 or 4 within the Access Group.
Viewer	Displays all Reconciliations where the User is assigned the Viewer role within the Access Group.
Commenter	Displays all Reconciliations where the User is assigned the Commenter role within the Access Group.
Administrator	Displays all Reconciliations. This selection is only available for System Administrators and is the default when navigating to the Reconciliations page.
Auditor	Displays all Reconciliations that are in the Fully Approved state. If a User has Auditor security, the filter will default to this role and no additional options will be available.

Figure 4.9

Some things to note about the Auditor role. It is not expected that a User would have an action role (Preparer, Approver, Commenter, etc.) and the Auditor role. If you have multiple roles in the Reconciliation process – including Auditor – the Auditor role will prevail and prevent you from accessing Reconciliations that are not in the Fully Approved state. On the contrary, it is not expected that an Administrator would also be an Auditor. Therefore, if you are assigned as an Administrator and Auditor, the Administrator role will prevail and you will have access to all Reconciliations. Below is the Auditor view for reference.

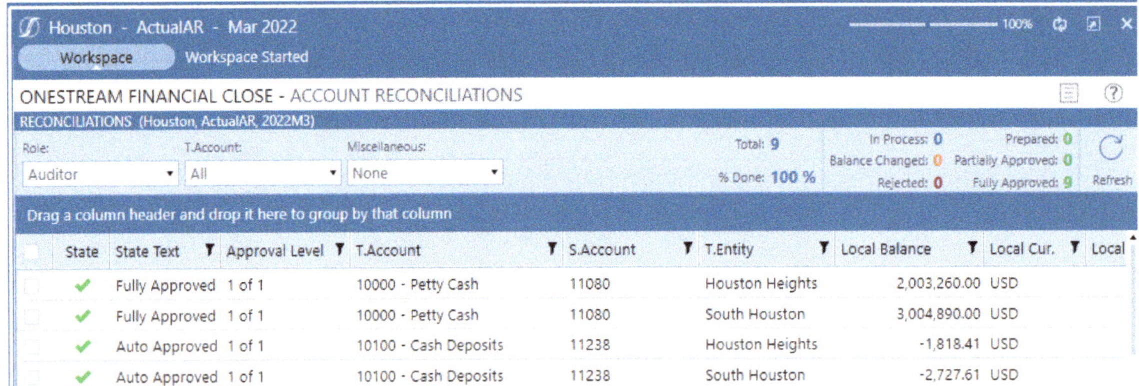

Figure 4.10

T.Account

T.Account stands for Target Account. Target Accounts represent the OneStream Accounts that ERP Source Accounts are mapped to upon data import. The mapping process aligns the Reconciliations to the financial statements. The ability to filter by T.Account allows you to see all the Reconciliations that roll into a particular financial statement line and manage the process accordingly. The T.Account filter will be limited, based on your security. You will only have access to the T.Accounts that contain your respective Reconciliations.

State

The State filter will narrow the grid based on the Reconciliation state. This filter has multi-select capabilities allowing you to view multiple states in a single search. For example, before I work on In Process Reconciliations, I may want to focus on my Rejected Reconciliations first – to quickly clear my Approver's comments and then focus on my Balance Changed Reconciliations that may only need minor updates. This allows me to really target my work.

The different states are defined below.

State	Definition
All	Retrieves all Reconciliations regardless of the state.
In Process	Reconciliation has been created, but the Preparer has not yet marked it Prepared.
Rejected	Reconciliation was Prepared but subsequently Rejected by an Approver
Prepared	Reconciliation has been Prepared but not yet Approved at any of the approval levels.
Auto Prepared	Reconciliation that has been Prepared through the AutoRec process, requiring a manual approval, and not yet Approved.
Partially Approved	Reconciliation that has been Prepared and Approved by some of the Approvers but not yet Approved through all required approval levels.
Fully Approved	Reconciliation that is Prepared and Approved through all required approval levels.
Auto Approved	Reconciliation that is Prepared and fully Approved via the AutoRec process.
Balance Changed	Reconciliation has been created from a trial balance load; and a new, updated balance has been loaded that is different from the original balance. Regardless of the state of the Reconciliation, it will be updated to Balance Changed and moved back to the Preparer's Workflow to be reviewed/updated.

Figure 4.11

Miscellaneous

The final filter is the Miscellaneous filter which focuses on areas of risk. The Miscellaneous filter supports multi-select capabilities, allowing Users to combine multiple risk areas in a single filter. Below, we define the different Miscellaneous filters available.

Filter	Definition
Failed AutoRec	Identifies Reconciliations that have AutoRec Rules assigned but – for the period – the Reconciliation did not meet the criteria. This filter identifies any additional work required for the given period because the Reconciliation did not meet the expected Auto Reconciliation Rule.
Frequency Changed	Identifies Reconciliations that were created for the period based on the frequency set, but the frequency was subsequently updated and the Reconciliation is no longer required. When this occurs, the Reconciliation that was created for the period will move off the grid. By selecting this filter, Users will be able to retrieve those

Filter	Definition
	Reconciliations. Example: *Reconciliation Houston-1000 Cash* was set to a frequency of 1-12 (Monthly). In February, the balances loaded and the Reconciliation was created for the period. Subsequently, the Administrator changed the frequency to 3,6,9,12 (Quarterly), which deems the Reconciliation not required for the February period. The Reconciliation will be removed from the active grid but can be retrieved through this filter.
High Risk	Filters Reconciliations that have been assigned high risk in the category attribute field. Typically, high risk indicates a Reconciliation that is due sooner in the process and requires more oversight.
Improper Sign	Filters for Reconciliations where the balance is going in the opposite direction than expected. Example: Accounts Receivable is expected to have a positive balance. If, upon trial balance load, the balance is negative, this would be an improper sign and an indication that something may be wrong within the General Ledger, identifying potential risk in the balance.
Past Due	Identifies all Reconciliations that are currently In Process and past due *or* fully through the process, but the full Workflow was completed after the due date.

Figure 4.12

Status Bar

Reconciliation statistics are calculated by the system and are presented in the top-right portion of the grid view in the status bar.

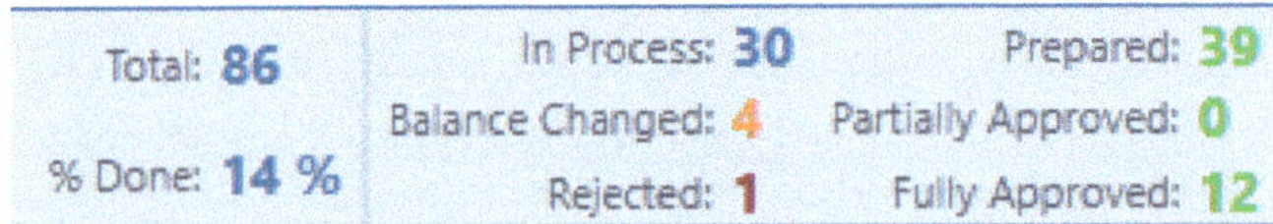

Figure 4.13

Statistics are critical to monitoring the Reconciliation process. Understanding where the Reconciliations are in the Workflow assists management in monitoring the close process as well as the overall financial statement risk. Accounts expected to be reconciled by a specific due date that reside in an unreconciled state introduce risk and exposure to the financial statements.

Statistics are calculated based on the total number of Reconciliations being displayed in the grid view and will update if the top filters are being applied. In the next section, we will define the different statistics and how they are calculated by the system.

Statistic	Definition
Total	Total number of Reconciliations displayed in the grid regardless of state. This value represents the Reconciliations that need to be Fully Approved for the period.
% Done	Percentage is based on the summation of the Fully Approved count divided by the total count defined above.
In Process	Number of Reconciliations to be processed by the Preparer which are not yet in the Prepared state. This number is exclusive of the Reconciliations in

Statistic	Definition
	the Balance Changed and Rejected state. All Reconciliations are in the In Process state upon creation and will remain in this state unless one of the following actions (below) occur.
Balance Changed	Number of Reconciliations that were created from a trial balance load for which a new updated balance has been loaded different from the original balance, creating a change. Regardless of the state, the Reconciliation will be updated to Balance Changed and moved back to the Preparer's Workflow to be reviewed/updated.
Rejected	Number of Reconciliations Rejected by an Approver. Rejection will also move the Reconciliation back into the Preparer's Workflow to be updated.
Prepared	Number of Reconciliations Prepared but not yet Approved by any of the required approval levels. This includes both manual and Auto Reconciliations.
Partially Approved	Number of Reconciliations Prepared and Approved but not yet through all the required approval levels.
Fully Approved	Number of Reconciliations that are Prepared and Approved through all required approval levels, including Auto Approved Reconciliations.

Figure 4.14

Statistics are updated as events occur, such as when you prepare a Reconciliation the state is updated to Prepared. Although the state is updated dynamically by the system, you will need to select the Refresh icon in the header to update the status bar and the Reconciliation grid.

Figure 4.15

Reconciliation Grid

The Reconciliation grid is a powerful tool that is used for multiple purposes. First and foremost, the Reconciliation grid is a listing of all Reconciliations available to you for a specific period. Because the grid contains many of the Reconciliation attributes, you can leverage the grid for reporting purposes. The Reconciliation grid is also used to open and view a specific Reconciliation, or for **mass action Reconciliations**, if this feature is turned on within Global Options.

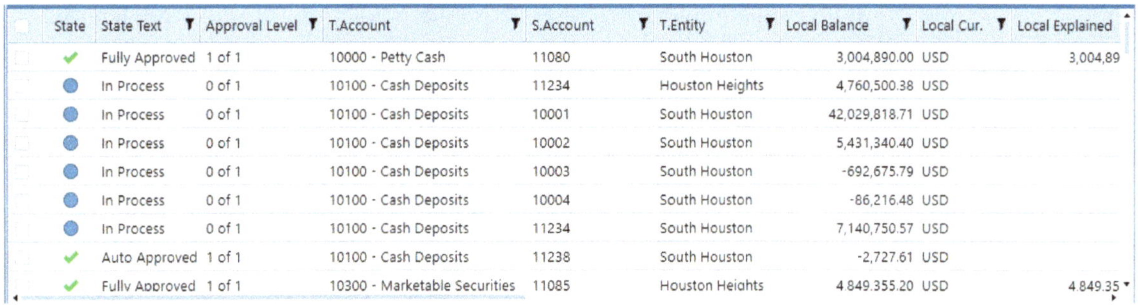

State	State Text	Approval Level	T.Account	S.Account	T.Entity	Local Balance	Local Cur.	Local Explained
	Fully Approved	1 of 1	10000 - Petty Cash	11080	South Houston	3,004,890.00	USD	3,004,89
	In Process	0 of 1	10100 - Cash Deposits	11234	Houston Heights	4,760,500.38	USD	
	In Process	0 of 1	10100 - Cash Deposits	10001	South Houston	42,029,818.71	USD	
	In Process	0 of 1	10100 - Cash Deposits	10002	South Houston	5,431,340.40	USD	
	In Process	0 of 1	10100 - Cash Deposits	10003	South Houston	-692,675.79	USD	
	In Process	0 of 1	10100 - Cash Deposits	10004	South Houston	-86,216.48	USD	
	In Process	0 of 1	10100 - Cash Deposits	11234	South Houston	7,140,750.57	USD	
	Auto Approved	1 of 1	10100 - Cash Deposits	11238	South Houston	-2,727.61	USD	
	Fully Approved	1 of 1	10300 - Marketable Securities	11085	Houston Heights	4,849,355.20	USD	4,849.35

Figure 4.16

Reconciliation Grid Columns

There are many columns displayed within the grid that provide detailed information about a Reconciliation. Each column is defined below.

Column	Definition
☐	Multi-select is part of the grid view and used for the mass action Workflow and audit package creation. It is important to note that you do not need to select the check box to access a Reconciliation.
State / State Text	State image correlates with the State text. The circle is an indication that the Reconciliation is only partially through the process, whereas the check mark is an indication that it is fully signed off. In Process Balance Changed Rejected Prepared Partially Approved Auto Prepared Fully Approved Auto Approved
Approval Level	Number of approvals completed and required for the specific Reconciliation. Example: 1 of 3, which indicates that 1 Approver has completed their sign-off of the 3 Approvals required.
T.Account	T.Account is the OneStream Target Account that the Source Account (S.Account) is mapped to, and typically reflects the financial statement line. It is the link between the two key processes Account Reconciliations and Consolidations, and normalizes the Accounts when there are multiple ERPs.
S.Account	S.Account is the specific ERP Account (Source Account) from the trial balance load and is the level at which the Reconciliation is performed.
T.Entity	T.Entity is the OneStream Target Entity that the Source Entity is mapped to for reporting/Consolidation purposes. It is the link between the two key processes, Account Reconciliations and Consolidations.
S.Entity	S.Entity is the Entity from the ERP associated (Source Entity) with the trial balance.
Tracking Detail	Tracking detail allows the Reconciliation to be performed at a lower level. If you want to reconcile below Entity and Account, the tracking detail allows you to break the balance down using additional dimensionality. We typically see an additional tracking detail for Intercompany, where you may want to reconcile at the Entity-Account-Trading Partner level. However, other breakdowns may include Customer, Vendor, Department, or Accounting Standard (Statutory, GAAP, IFRS). Within this field, the system will display both the Target and Source Dimension breakdown.
Acct. Balance*	Acct. Balance is used for single-currency Reconciliations when the Account within the General Ledger is denominated in a currency other than Local. This is common when the organization has foreign bank accounts or investments where the transactions flowing through the

Column	Definition
	Account are in a different currency. The Acct. Balance can be loaded or calculated by the system.
Acct. Cur.*	Represents the currency code of the Account Balance as defined in the Reconciliation Inventory.
Acct. Explained*	Summation of the detail items translated in Account currency.
Acct. Unexplained*	Calculated difference between the Acct. Balance and the Acct. Explained.
Acct. Activity*	Difference between current period Acct. Balance and the prior period Acct. Balance, based on the Reconciliation frequency. If the frequency is Monthly, it will look to the prior month to calculate activity. If the frequency is Quarterly, month 1 (1,4,7,10 based on a calendar year), and we are in period 4, the system will look to period 1 to calculate activity.
Local Balance	Local Balance represents the amount loaded from the trial balance and is a required field. This balance is used for both the Reconciliation process and the Consolidation process.
Local Cur.	Local Cur. is defaulted to the Local currency code for the T.Entity as defined in Entity Dimension.
Local Explained	Summation of the detail items added to explain the ending balance. If using multi-currency, it is the summation of the detail items translated in Local currency.
Local Unexplained	Calculated difference between the Local Balance and the Local Explained.
Local Activity	Difference between current period Local Balance and the prior period Local Balance, based on the Reconciliation frequency. If the frequency is Monthly, it will look to the prior month to calculate activity. If the frequency is Quarterly, month 1 (1,4,7,10 based on a calendar year), and we are in period 4, the system will look to the period 1 to calculate activity.
Rpt. Balance*	Rpt. Balance reflects the Local Balance translated to the Reporting currency set in Global Options. This balance can be loaded or calculated by the system.
Rpt. Cur.*	Represents the Reporting currency code as defined in the Global Options.
Rpt. Explained*	Summation of the detail items translated to Reporting currency.
Rpt. Unexplained*	Calculated difference between the Rpt. Balance and the Rpt. Explained.
Rpt. Activity*	Difference between current period Rpt. Balance and the prior period Rpt. Balance, based on the Reconciliation frequency. If the frequency is Monthly, it will look to the prior month to calculate activity. If the frequency is Quarterly, Month 1 (1,4,7,10 based on a calendar year), and we are in period 4, the system will look to the period 1 to calculate activity.
Account Group	Displays the Account Group name. Account Groups allow Users to reconcile a set of Accounts in a single Reconciliation. Examples of Account Groups include: Fixed Assets, Equity, Intercompany Accounts, etc.
Preparer	Primary Preparer assigned to the Reconciliation. User responsible for the preparation of the Reconciliation.
Approver 1	Primary Approver 1 assigned to the Reconciliation. User responsible for the first level of approval.

Column	Definition
Approver 2	Primary Approver 2 assigned to the Reconciliation. User responsible for the second level of approval.
Approver 3	Primary Approver 3 assigned to the Reconciliation. User responsible for the third level of approval.
Approver 4	Primary Approver 4 assigned to the Reconciliation. User responsible for the fourth level of approval.
Access Group	Displays the Access Group assigned to the Reconciliation. Access Groups provide the ability to have backup Preparers and Approvers, as well as assign Viewers, Commenters, and Local Admins.
Type	Account Type as defined in the Account Dimension: Asset, Liability, Revenue or Expense.
Risk	Attribute assigned to the Reconciliation indicating the risk ranking: High, Medium, or Low.
Preparer Due Date	Calculates the due date based on the month-end day set for the period, and the Preparer workday due attribute set on the Reconciliation. Although the attribute displays as the number of workdays (e.g., +1, +2, etc.), the system will convert this to an actual date for ease of use.
Approver Due Date	Calculates the due date based on the month-end day set for the period and the Approver workday due attribute set on the Reconciliation. Although the attribute displays as the number of workdays (e.g., +1, +2, etc.), the system will convert this to an actual date for ease of use.
Due-in	Calculation of the due date less the current date. If the value is positive, it will appear in this column. If the Calculation is negative, a zero will appear as the Reconciliation is past due.
Past Due	Calculation of the due date less the current date. If the value is negative, it will appear in this column. If the Calculation is positive, a zero will appear as the Reconciliation is on time.
Proper Sign	Accounts typically have an expected sign of positive or negative, such as assets versus liabilities, respectively. If an Account is a *contra Account*, we would expect it to be contrary to the typical sign. To identify potential risk, an attribute can be set on the Reconciliation to identify the expected sign. If the loaded balance has the expected sign, the Proper Sign field will populate OK. If the balance is contrary to the expected sign, the field will display Warning: Balance Not Proper Sign.
Update User	Field captures the User that last updated the state of the Reconciliation.
Update Time UTC	Field captures the date and time stamp of the last time the Reconciliation state was updated.
Process User	Field captures the User that initiated the process that last updated the Reconciliation.
Process Time UTC	Field captures the date and time stamp of the last time the Reconciliation was processed by the system.
* Only visible if multi-currency is enabled within Global Options, and the field will only populate with information in the grid for the specific Reconciliations where multi-currency is enabled.	

Figure 4.17

Reconciliation Grid Configuration

As mentioned, the Reconciliation grid is often used for reporting. All the columns above will appear in the grid by default, but you can configure the grid by removing or reordering columns as desired. You can also filter the data in the grid using the column filters or pivot the columns for additional analysis. The grid can also be exported from the system in multiple formats. When you think about it, the reporting options using the grid are endless.

Column Filter

Let's start by reviewing the column filter capabilities. Different from the top filters, you can filter any column where the column filter icon appears.

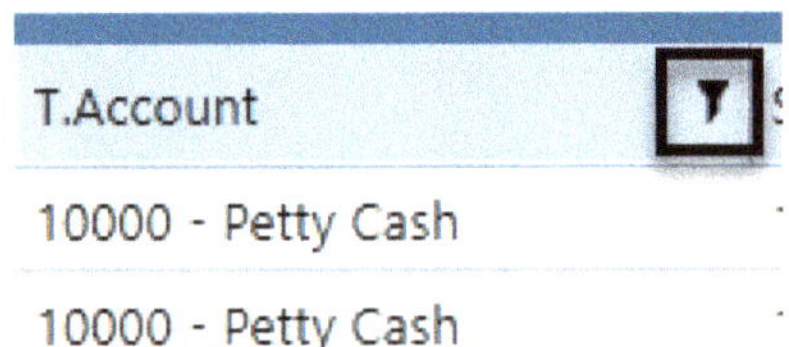

Figure 4.18

Upon selecting the column filter icon, you can select a specific item, multiple items, or you can build out search criteria.

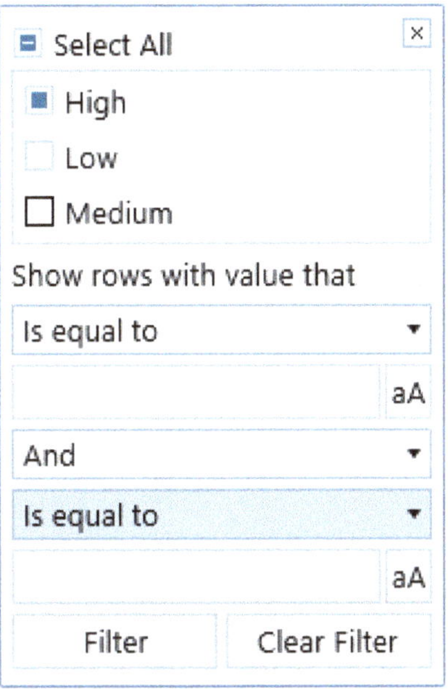

Figure 4.19

The column filter icon will appear orange if a filter is set.

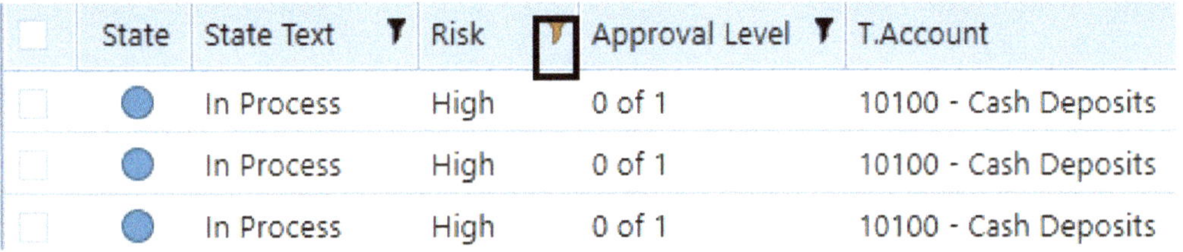

Figure 4.20

> **Note:** If you do not see Reconciliations that you expect within the grid, it is likely you have a column filter set limiting your view. To remove the filter, select the column filter icon and select the Clear Filter button at the bottom right.

Column Settings

As different attributes have different orders of magnitude for different organizations, being able to reorder and/or remove columns is valuable. A column can be reordered by simply dragging and dropping the column to the desired location. Another option for reordering is through the right-click menu by selecting the Column Settings.

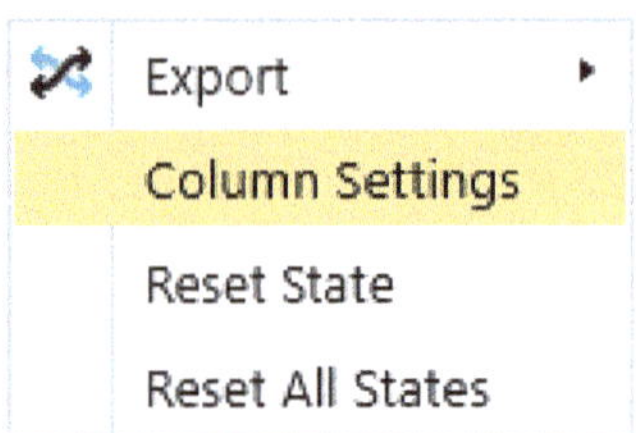

Figure 4.21

From the Column Settings dialog, you can reorder or remove columns as desired.

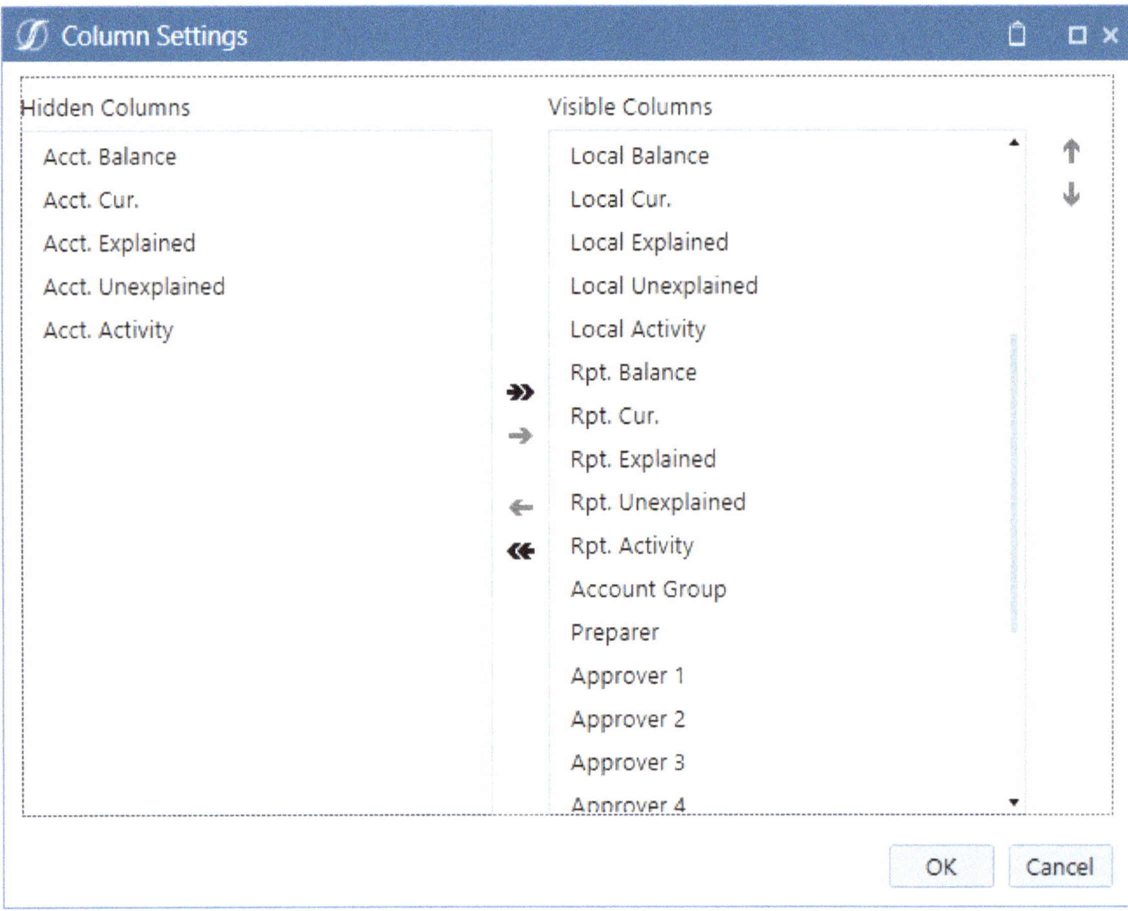

Figure 4.22

Column Pivot

Another configuration option is the ability to pivot the Reconciliation grid. You can pivot on one or multiple columns by dragging the column header into the blue bar at the top of the grid. Reconciliations will pivot, based on the order the column name appears from left to right.

In Figure 4.23, below, we are pivoting on Risk and then State Text. This allows us to quickly see the high-risk Accounts that are in an In Process state, so we can target our work. To remove a column from the pivot, simply select the column name in the blue bar and drag it back into the grid.

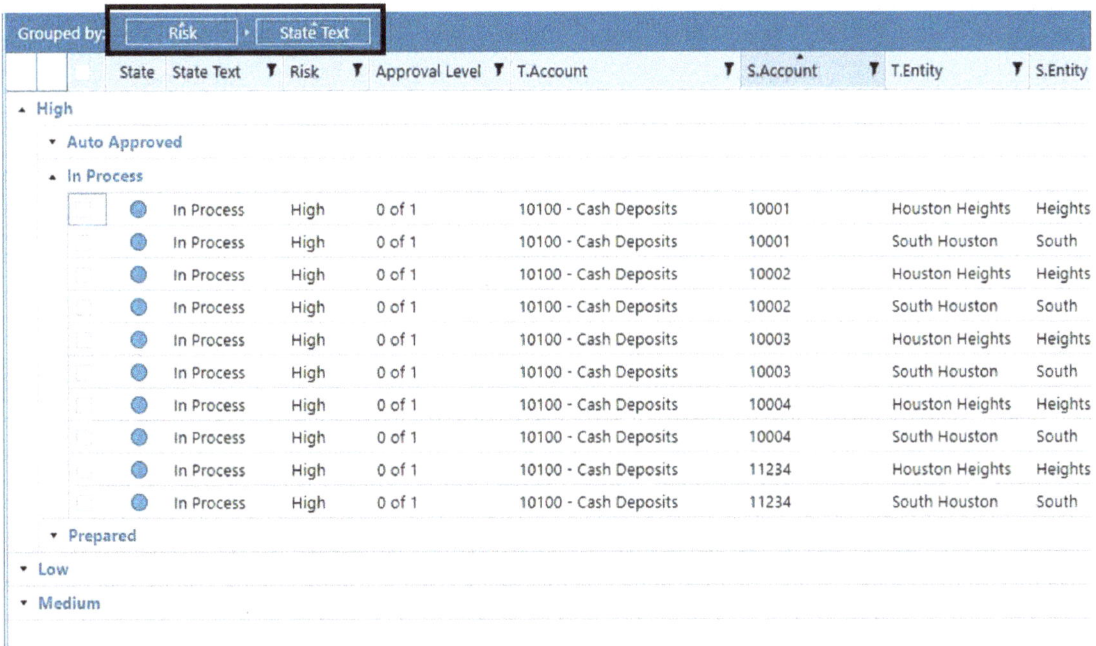

Grouped by: Risk State Text
State State Text Risk Approval Level T.Account S.Account T.Entity S.Entity
High
Auto Approved
In Process
In Process High 0 of 1 10100 - Cash Deposits 10001 Houston Heights Heights
In Process High 0 of 1 10100 - Cash Deposits 10001 South Houston South
In Process High 0 of 1 10100 - Cash Deposits 10002 Houston Heights Heights
In Process High 0 of 1 10100 - Cash Deposits 10002 South Houston South
In Process High 0 of 1 10100 - Cash Deposits 10003 Houston Heights Heights
In Process High 0 of 1 10100 - Cash Deposits 10003 South Houston South
In Process High 0 of 1 10100 - Cash Deposits 10004 Houston Heights Heights
In Process High 0 of 1 10100 - Cash Deposits 10004 South Houston South
In Process High 0 of 1 10100 - Cash Deposits 11234 Houston Heights Heights
In Process High 0 of 1 10100 - Cash Deposits 11234 South Houston South
Prepared
Low
Medium

Figure 4.23

Saved State

All the grid configurations discussed above are specific to the User making the change. These changes will persist as the User logs in and out of the system because it leverages the saved state capability within OneStream. Saved state preserves your changes to your User ID and allows you to customize your interaction without impacting others. Also, if you would like to reset the page to the default columns, you can right-click and select Reset State.

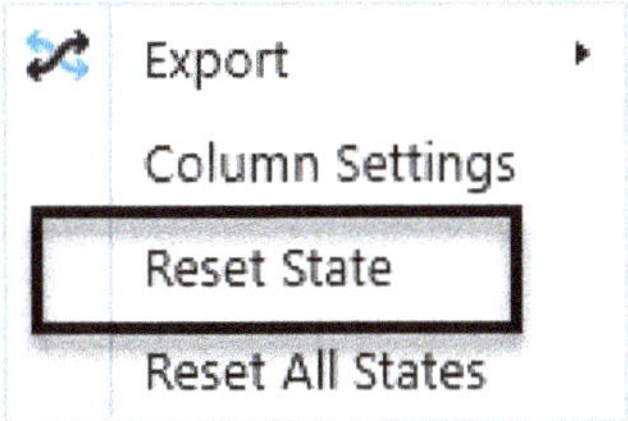

Figure 4.24

However, when selecting Reset State, it not only resets the column filters and the pivot criteria selected, but it also reorders the columns and reinserts any columns previously removed. Therefore, be careful when using Reset State functionality as it could undo all the configuration you have done. From my perspective, I have found that it is easier to manually reset the column filters or the pivot so that I can maintain my column configuration.

Accessing a Reconciliation

Accessing a Reconciliation is done from the Reconciliation grid. You can open or view a Reconciliation by clicking anywhere within the Reconciliation line. Upon selection, the detailed Reconciliation view will appear in the bottom grid. You can navigate from one Reconciliation to the next by simply selecting the respective line.

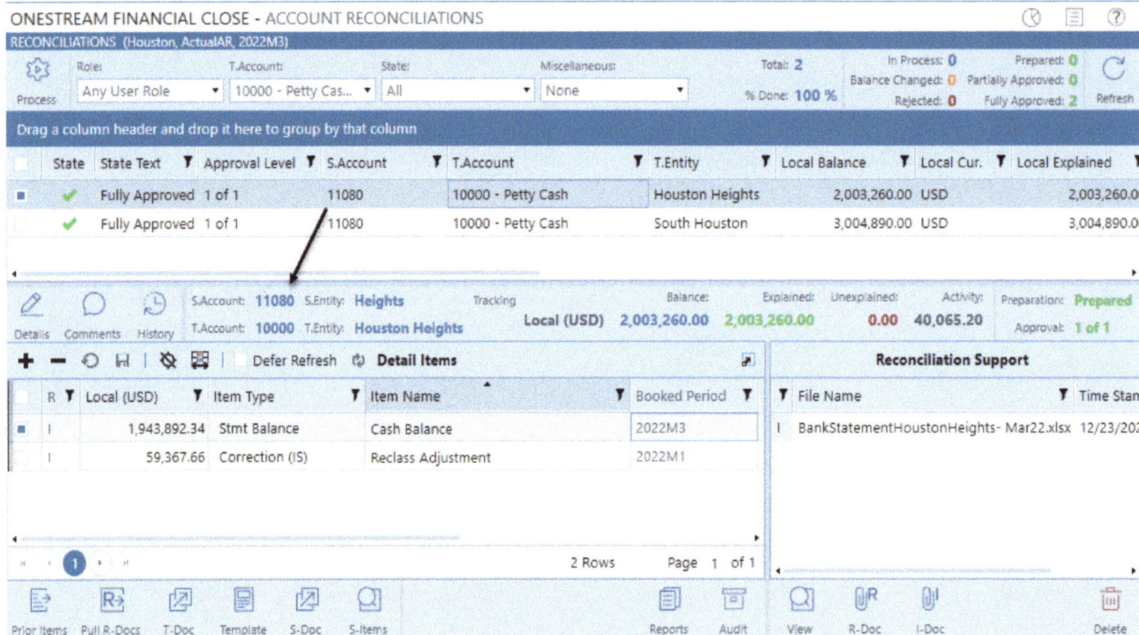

Figure 4.25

You will notice that when you select a Reconciliation line within the grid, the check box to the far left will automatically be selected. Although you can select a Reconciliation using the check box, it is not necessary and not recommended. The check box is required for mass action functionality, but is not needed for navigational purposes. Selecting a Reconciliation by clicking on the line is more efficient.

Mass Actions

Efficiencies are key when trying to optimize the Reconciliation process. Mass action functionality allows you to efficiently perform Workflow functions. Rather than having to action Reconciliations one by one, Preparers and/or Approvers can action multiple Reconciliations with the overall controls still applied – such as thresholds, completion rules, segregation of duties, role security, etc. Also, you can add certification comments (if enabled) that will be applied across the selected Reconciliations.

To utilize mass action, this functionality must be enabled by the Administrator. Depending on which roles are enabled (Preparer, Approver, or Both), the mass action icons may include Recall, Prepare, Reject, Unapprove, and Approve, respectively.

Figure 4.26

To mass action a set of Reconciliations, you will select the check box to the left of the specific Reconciliation. Mass actions will only engage if you have more than one Reconciliation selected.

All selected Reconciliations will appear in the bottom grid, and the mass action icons will appear. Based on the icon selected, the system will update the Reconciliations that meet the requirements. If a Reconciliation is selected that cannot be actioned as requested, you will receive a message indicating what has (or has not) been completed and why.

Let's walk through an example, below. I have selected four In Process Reconciliations to mass action.

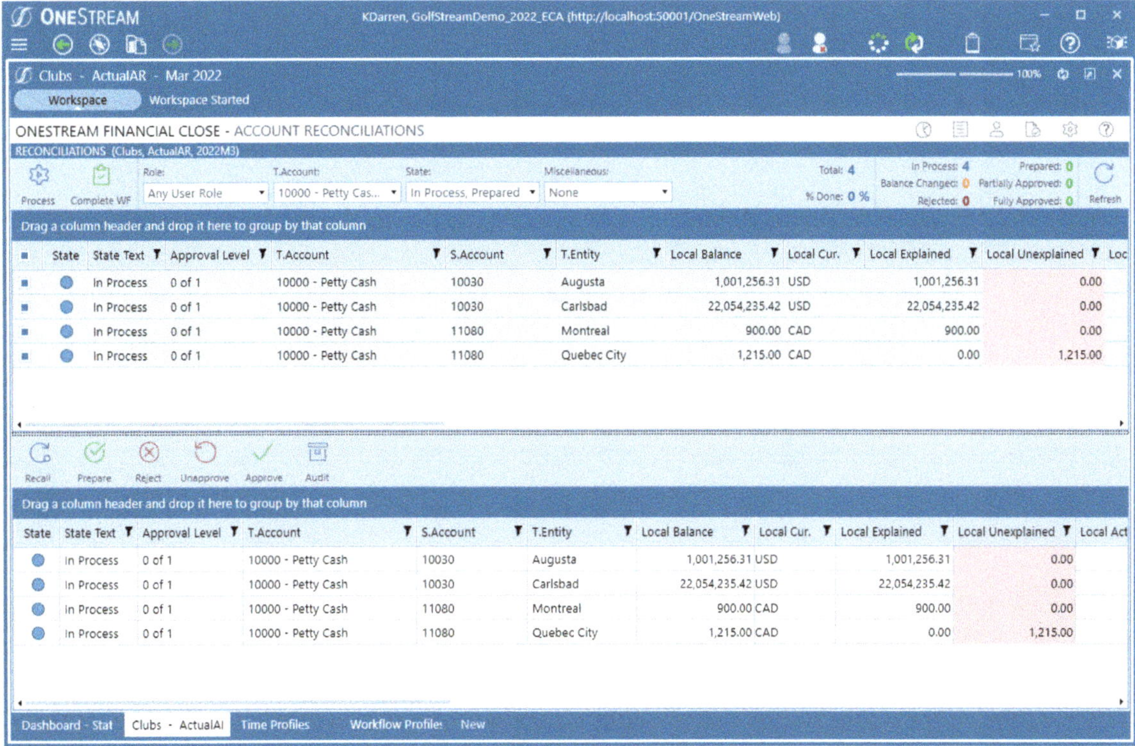

Figure 4.27

When I select the Prepare icon to certify the Reconciliations, I receive a comment box allowing me to add Certification Commentary to all four Reconciliations as this global option is enabled in my solution.

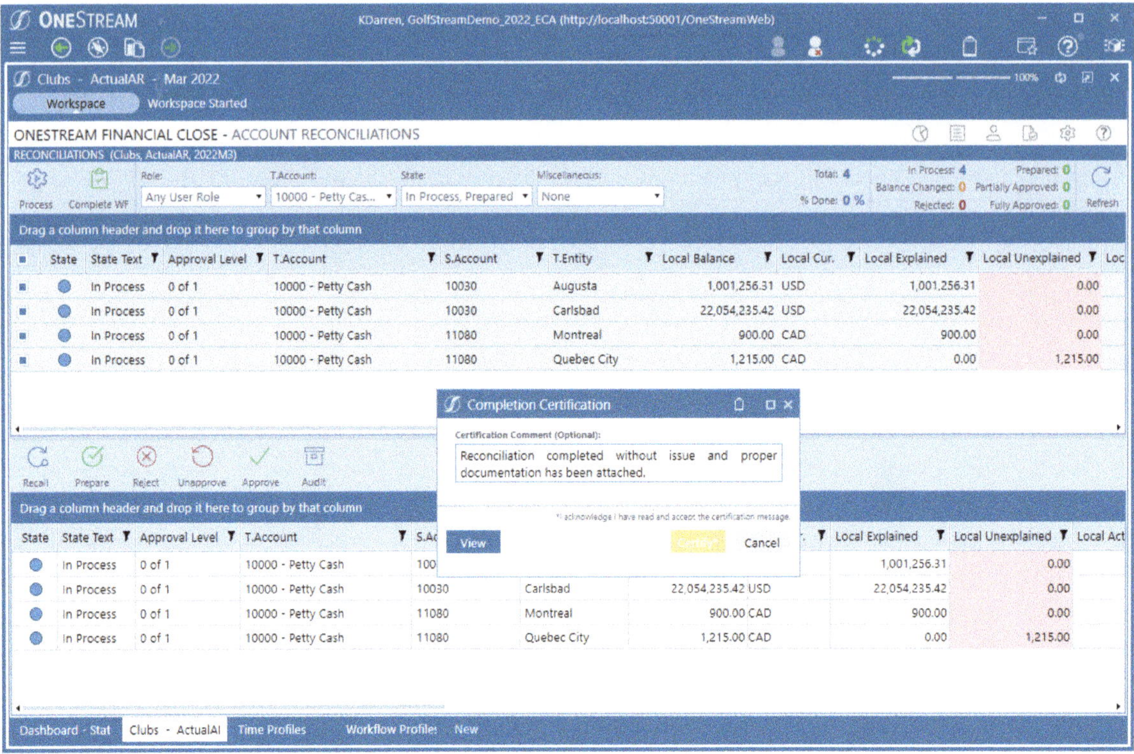

Figure 4.28

Once I input my comments, I can select the Certify button. The system will run through the applicable controls and only action those Reconciliations that meet the criteria.

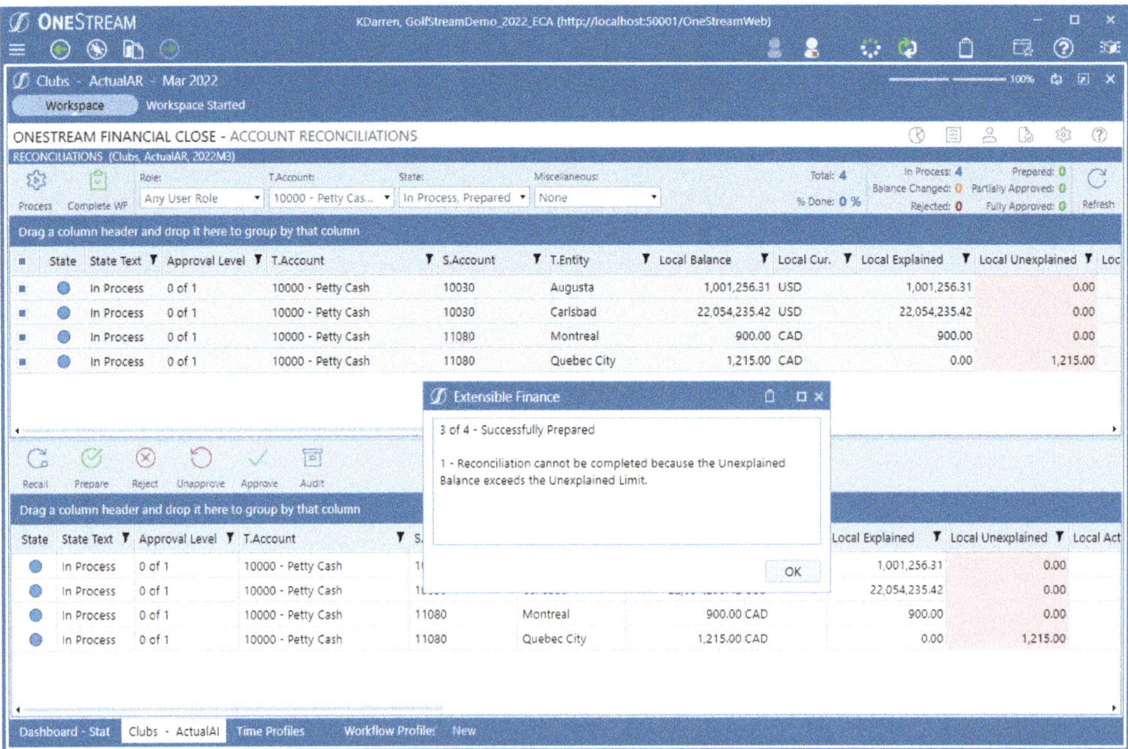

Figure 4.29

As you can see, the system only prepared three of the four Reconciliations. Although I thought that I had prepared the selected Reconciliations, only three of the Reconciliations have an Unexplained balance within the required threshold. The system is preventing the final Reconciliation from moving to the Prepared state because it does not meet the rule.

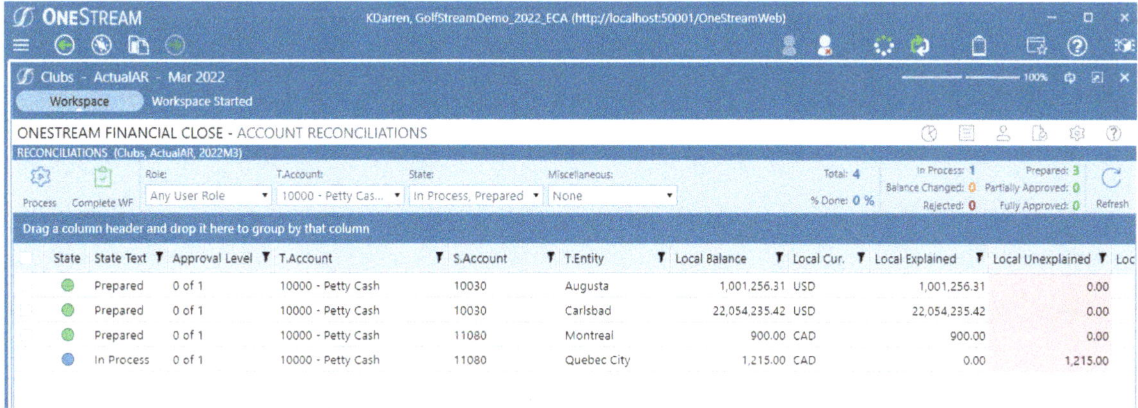

Figure 4.30

As mentioned at the beginning of this section, mass action for the Workflow functions is a setting that is turned on within the Global Options. If not enabled, the multi-select box to the left of the Reconciliation is still available for audit package creation. Audit packages can be created en masse by the Administrators and this icon will only be available for this role. For more information regarding audit, see the audit package section later in this chapter.

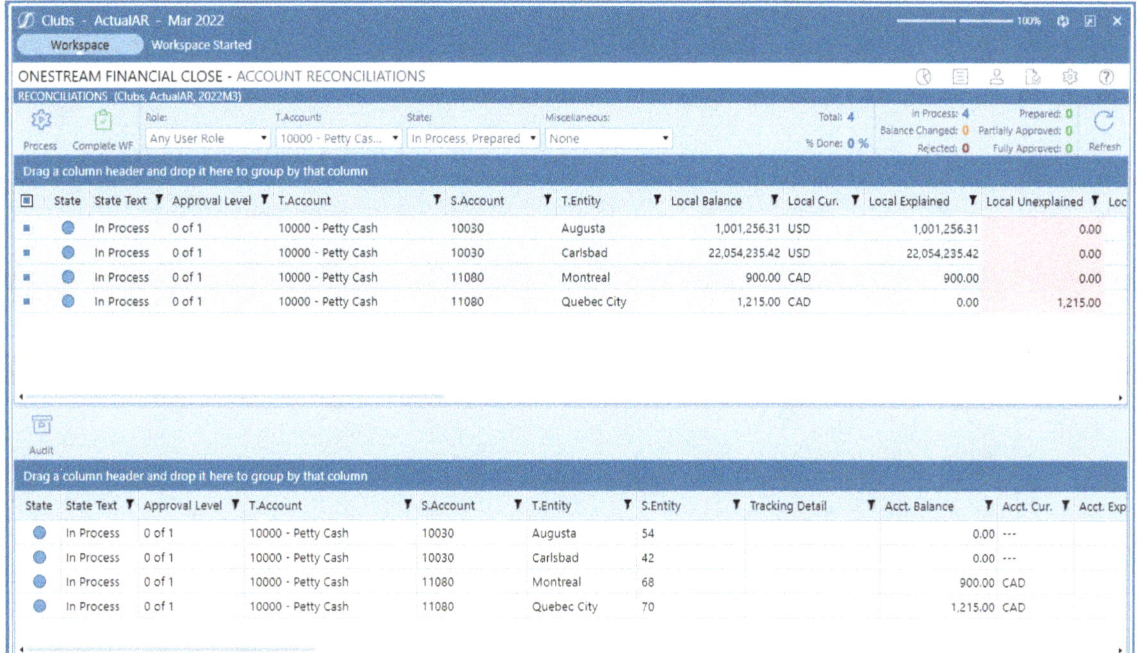

Figure 4.31

Detailed Reconciliation View

The detailed Reconciliation view is where the Reconciliation is performed. When a Reconciliation is selected in the top grid, the detailed Reconciliation view will appear at the bottom of the screen. Preparers use the detailed Reconciliation view to add reconciling items, supporting documentation, and comments to explain the ending balance. Approvers leverage this view to perform their review process and add comments if necessary. In the following section, we will discuss the detailed Reconciliation view and the related functionality. This section is intended to create a foundation for the User. Additional preparation options, along with viewing the Reconciliation from the Preparer and Approver perspective, will be covered in later sections.

The detailed Reconciliation view can be seen in Figure 4.32. The Reconciliation presented is for a Bank Account; however, the User Interface in the solution is the same, regardless of the type of Account you are reconciling. This is intentional.

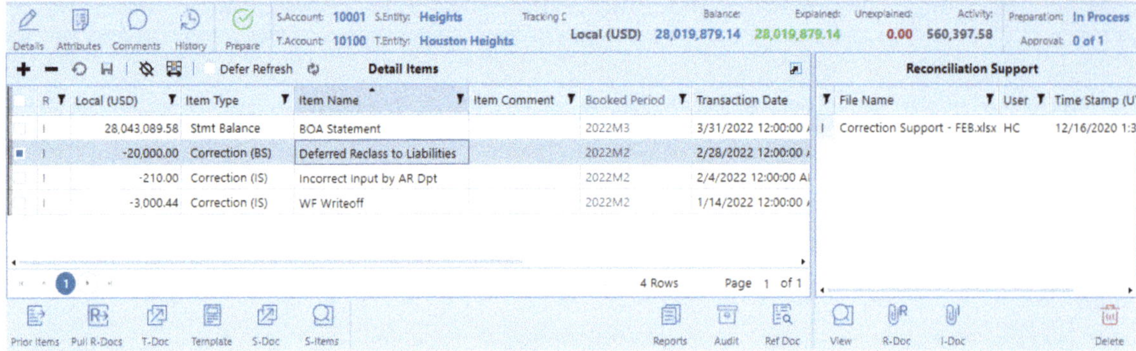

Figure 4.32

Whether I am viewing a Bank Account, Prepaid, Subledger, Accrual, or any other type of Account, the User Interface will be the same for ease of use and review. Like a lead sheet concept, the system captures the key information needed for control purposes and to provide robust reporting.

The next question we are normally asked is whether OneStream supports Reconciliation templates. The answer is: of course! Instead of building varying formats within the system that will not satisfy every organization, our templates are built in Excel. Excel allows full flexibility to create a format that works for you and your Users. You are not limited to the number of templates created and the templates can be linked to specific Reconciliations.

Leveraging Excel for templates creates the best of both worlds: a consistent User Interface within the application with flexible use of a template format in Excel for analysis. Why do organizations like the Excel templates? Templates help guide the User through the analysis portion of the process. Users can perform their work within the template and then upload the template into the system for Automatic Reconciliation creation. We will talk more about using templates later in this chapter. Also, see Section 2 for more information on creating and linking templates to Reconciliations.

Let's get started by walking through the three main sections of the detailed Reconciliation view:

- Detailed Reconciliation header
- Detail items grid
- Reconciliation support

Detailed Reconciliation Header

The detailed Reconciliation header contains multiple key components associated with the specific Reconciliation being viewed. Within the header, you can view the preparation state, approval levels, Reconciliation balances, Reconciliation level, tracking detail, history, Child Accounts (if a grouped Reconciliation), and attributes. You can also perform actions such as adding comments or updating the Workflow if allowed. Below, we will detail the different components of the Reconciliation header.

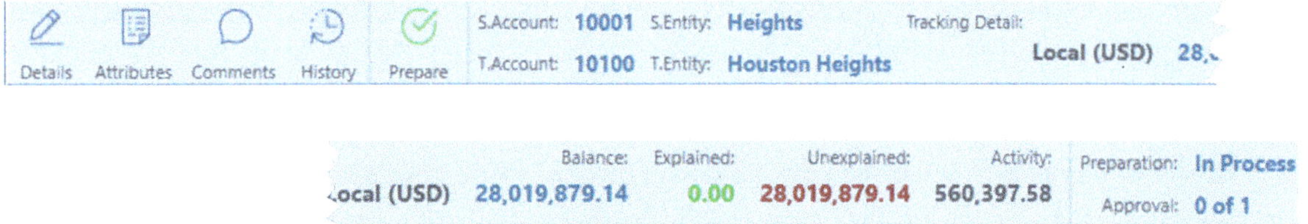

Figure 4.33

Preparation State

The preparation state is shown in the top-right corner of the detailed Reconciliation header and indicates the state of the Reconciliation as it moves through the preparation process. The possible states include: In Process, Balance Changed, Rejected, or Prepared.

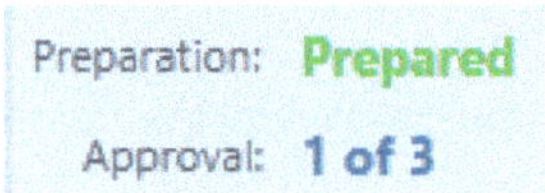

Figure 4.34

Approval Levels

Approval levels indicate the number of Approver sign-offs that are required for the Reconciliation to be in the Fully Approved state. The solution supports up to four levels of approval. Typically, we see organizations use one to two levels; however, four levels are available should the need occur. In the example presented in Figure 4.34, this particular Reconciliation requires three levels of approval, and it has been signed off by the first Approver. At this point, the Reconciliation is in the **Partially Approved** state. To be Fully Approved, the remaining two Approvers will need to sign-off.

Reconciliation Balances

The Reconciliation balances are located in the top-right corner of the detailed Reconciliation header and display different amount fields, which include the Balance, Explained, Unexplained, and Activity amounts. These amounts are populated and/or calculated by the system and cannot be edited. Each amount presents key information about the Reconciliation.

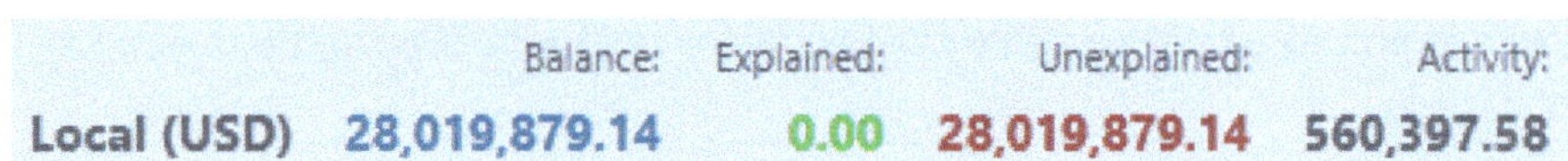

Figure 4.35

The Balance amount field populates from the trial balance (the Stage data) loaded within the Actual Scenario. As trial balances are loaded throughout the period, the Balance amount will be updated when the Reconciliation process function is run. The Reconciliation process can either be run manually from within the Account Reconciliation solution (as noted in the Process icon section above), linked to the trial balance load process in the Actual Scenario, or scheduled via **Task Scheduler**.

If the Balance amount subsequently changes after the Reconciliation has been created, the Reconciliation will move to the Balance Changed state. Also, note that if the Reconciliation is already in the Workflow process (Prepared, Approved, AutoRec, etc.), the system will revert the Reconciliation back to the Preparer to re-reconcile, and email alerts can be sent if desired.

The Balance amount may also represent an Aggregation of Account balances if the Reconciliation is set up as a **Group Reconciliation**. Grouping is common when you want to analyze Accounts together like fixed assets, intangibles, equity, etc. Rather than prepare each Account as a separate Reconciliation, you can group them into a single Reconciliation. In this case, the Balance amount will be the summation of the underlying Child Accounts.

The remaining balances presented – Explained, Unexplained, and Activity – are all calculated values that are populated by the system. The Explained balance is the summation of the detail items. As detail items are saved to the Reconciliation, the Explained balance will be updated automatically.

The Unexplained amount is calculated as the difference between the Balance amount and the Explained amount. It is the Preparer's job to explain the balance to within a threshold set by the organization. Some organizations do not require a threshold and allow for differences to remain unexplained; others require the balance to be explained down to zero or within a set tolerance. It is typically defined in the company's policy whether a threshold is required or not. If there is a threshold, you will not be able to mark the Reconciliation as Prepared, from a certification perspective, until the Unexplained balance is within the threshold set.

Activity is provided for informational purposes. It is calculated as the change in the current balance minus the prior balance based on the frequency set. For example, if the Reconciliation has a Monthly frequency (1-12) and we are in the March 2022 period (2022M3), the activity will be calculated as the March balance minus the February balance. Assuming we are still in March, if the frequency was Quarterly (3,6,9,12), the activity would be calculated as the March balance minus the December 2021 balance. If there is no balance loaded for the prior period, based on the frequency, the prior balance is assumed to be zero.

All balances are presented in Local currency unless the Reconciliation is set for multi-currency. If multi-currency is enabled on the Reconciliation, you will see three sets of balances – one for each currency type: Account, Local, and Reporting. As you add items, Explained and Unexplained will update for all three currency-type balances.

	Balance:	Explained:	Unexplained:	Activity:
Account (GBP)	**260,526.54**	**0.00**	**260,526.54**	**5,601.11**
Local (EUR)	308,543.64	0.00	308,543.64	6,170.87
Reporting (USD)	416,842.46	0.00	416,842.46	46,435.81

Figure 4.36

Also, notice that the currency-type Account in Figure 4.36 is displayed in an enhanced font. This is an indication that the Account balance is the designated Reconciliation balance, and although all three balances are presented, the threshold is being applied to the Account balance for certification purposes.

Reconciliation Level

Reconciliations are typically performed at the Entity and Account levels. However, you do have the ability to reconcile at a lower level, such as Trading Partner, Profit Center, Department, Customer, etc. The more levels associated with an Account, the more granular the balance is defined and the more Reconciliations that are created. The Reconciliation Level always displays the S. Account, S.Entity, T.Account, and T.Entity. If the Reconciliation has additional levels, they are displayed in the Tracking Detail section.

Figure 4.37

Tracking Detail

As described above, if the Reconciliation is being performed at a lower level, the Tracking Detail will display the additional information. In the example below, we are reconciling at the Entity-Account-IC-UD1 level. This means that, in addition to the Entity and Account, the balance is broken down further by the Intercompany Partner (Montreal) and Cost Center (Event Management). Therefore, what used to be a single Reconciliation for Heights-11257 is potentially multiple Reconciliations, one for each unique Trading Partner and Cost Center combination.

Figure 4.38

History

History tracks the audit trail for the Reconciliation. You can navigate to the History page by selecting the History icon.

Figure 4.39

As the Reconciliation moves through the Workflow process, the system will keep track of the actions taken (prepare, approve, reject, recall, etc.), the time stamp, User ID, state, approval level, Reason Code, and any comments added during the certification or rejection process. If the Reconciliation is auto reconciled, the History page will also track the **AutoRec Rule** used to certify the Reconciliation.

In addition, this page will display all the supporting documents, attached in the historical periods, allowing you to view the documents at your discretion.

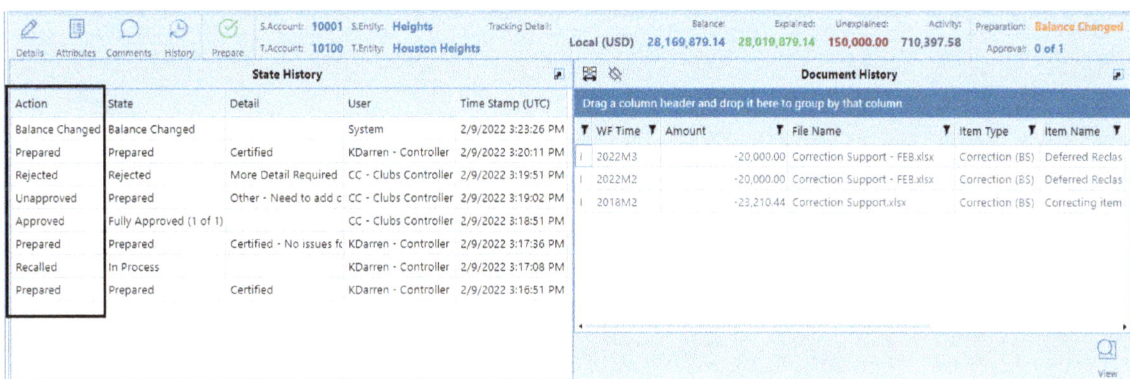

State History

Action	State	Detail	User	Time Stamp (UTC)
Balance Changed	Balance Changed		System	2/9/2022 3:23:26 PM
Prepared	Prepared	Certified	KDarren - Controller	2/9/2022 3:20:11 PM
Rejected	Rejected	More Detail Required	CC - Clubs Controller	2/9/2022 3:19:51 PM
Unapproved	Prepared	Other - Need to add c	CC - Clubs Controller	2/9/2022 3:19:02 PM
Approved	Fully Approved (1 of 1)		CC - Clubs Controller	2/9/2022 3:18:51 PM
Prepared	Prepared	Certified - No issues fc	KDarren - Controller	2/9/2022 3:17:36 PM
Recalled	In Process		KDarren - Controller	2/9/2022 3:17:08 PM
Prepared	Prepared	Certified	KDarren - Controller	2/9/2022 3:16:51 PM

Document History

WF Time	Amount	File Name	Item Type	Item Name
2022M3	-20,000.00	Correction Support - FEB.xlsx	Correction (BS)	Deferred Reclas
2022M2	-20,000.00	Correction Support - FEB.xlsx	Correction (BS)	Deferred Reclas
2018M2	-23,210.44	Correction Support.xlsx	Correction (BS)	Correcting item

Figure 4.40

Attributes

The Attributes page displays the specific attributes associated with the Reconciliation, like Access Group, approval level, risk level, proper sign, etc., and can be accessed from the Attributes icon.

Figure 4.41

This page provides you with visibility to key information about the Reconciliation that is not displayed in the detailed Reconciliation view. Attributes can be edited from this page if you have the proper security, and the Reconciliation is not yet in the Prepared state.

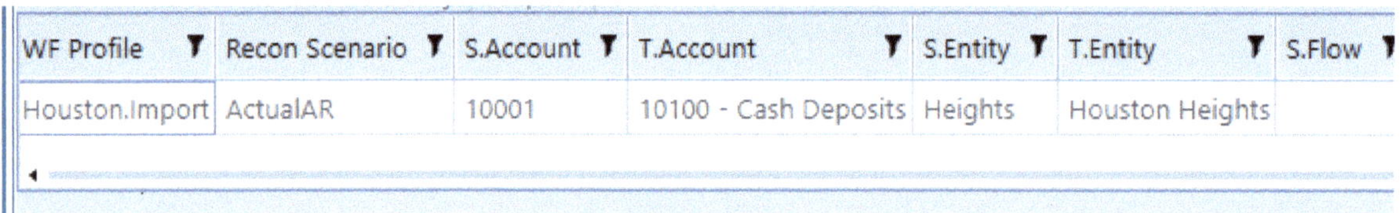

WF Profile	Recon Scenario	S.Account	T.Account	S.Entity	T.Entity	S.Flow
Houston.Import	ActualAR	10001	10100 - Cash Deposits	Heights	Houston Heights	

Figure 4.42

Child Recs

The Child Recs icon only appears if the Reconciliation is a Group Reconciliation.

Figure 4.43

As discussed previously, grouping is the process of combining multiple Accounts together to create a single Reconciliation for you to prepare. The Reconciliation – from a User perspective – will look and act the same regardless of whether it is grouped or not. However, if the Reconciliation is grouped, the underlying detail Accounts can be viewed on the Child Recs page.

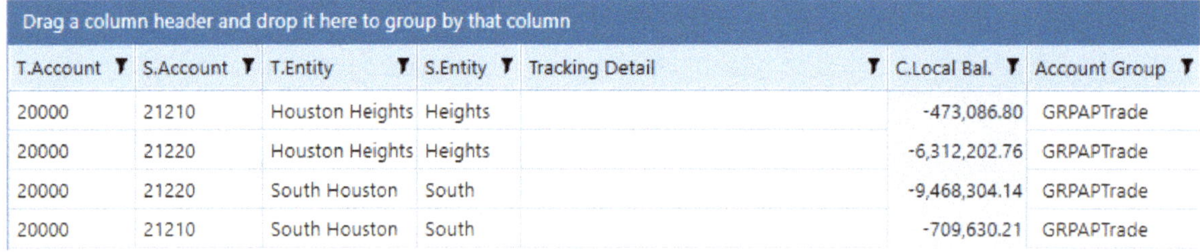

Drag a column header and drop it here to group by that column

T.Account	S.Account	T.Entity	S.Entity	Tracking Detail	C.Local Bal.	Account Group
20000	21210	Houston Heights	Heights		-473,086.80	GRPAPTrade
20000	21220	Houston Heights	Heights		-6,312,202.76	GRPAPTrade
20000	21220	South Houston	South		-9,468,304.14	GRPAPTrade
20000	21210	South Houston	South		-709,630.21	GRPAPTrade

Figure 4.44

Grouping can be done across different Entities, Accounts, or currency codes. If grouping across multiple currency codes, the group Reconciliation will have to be set as a **Multi-Currency Group** and a common currency code will need to be selected for the Account and Local balances. In addition, the Child Accounts will be translated to the common currency codes so that the balances can be aggregated properly. Visibility to the original balances and translated balances are also presented on the Child Recs page.

Drag a column header and drop it here to group by that column

T.Account	S.Account	T.Entity	S.Entity	C.Acct Bal.	C.Acct Cur.	G.Acct Bal.	G.Acct Cur.	C.Local Bal.	C.Local Cur.	G.Local Bal.	G.Local Cur.
11000	11240	Frankfurt	Frankfu	837,622.13	EUR	1,131,627.50	USD	837,622.13	EUR	1,131,627.50	USD
11000	11201	Frankfurt	Frankfu	237,095.44	EUR	320,315.94	USD	237,095.44	EUR	320,315.94	USD
11000	11240	Houston Heights	Heights	8,683,002.80	USD	8,683,002.80	USD	8,683,002.80	USD	8,683,002.80	USD
11000	11201	South Houston	South	2,762,131.26	USD	2,762,131.26	USD	2,762,131.26	USD	2,762,131.26	USD
11000	11240	South Houston	South	13,024,504.21	USD	13,024,504.21	USD	13,024,504.21	USD	13,024,504.21	USD
11000	11201	Houston Heights	Heights	1,841,420.84	USD	1,841,420.84	USD	1,841,420.84	USD	1,841,420.84	USD
11000	11200	Houston Heights	Heights	4,275,081.47	USD	4,275,081.47	USD	4,275,081.47	USD	4,275,081.47	USD
11000	11200	South Houston	South	6,412,622.21	USD	6,412,622.21	USD	6,412,622.21	USD	6,412,622.21	USD
11000	11000	Carlsbad	42	14,436,643.00	USD	14,436,643.00	USD	14,436,643.00	USD	14,436,643.00	USD
11000	11111	Carlsbad	42	-294,578.00	USD	-294,578.00	USD	-294,578.00	USD	-294,578.00	USD

Figure 4.45

Comments

Comments can be added at the Reconciliation level and allow you to provide additional insight or context around the Reconciliation. Preparers and Approvers can add commentary prior to actioning the Workflow. In addition, Users that have the Commenter role can add comments at any time regardless of the state of the Reconciliation. Once added, comments cannot be edited or deleted.

To add a comment, select the Comments icon.

Figure 4.46

The Comments icon navigates you to the Commentary page. You can type the comment in the bottom box and select the Add icon. The comment is added to the Reconciliation with your User ID and date and time stamp for audit purposes.

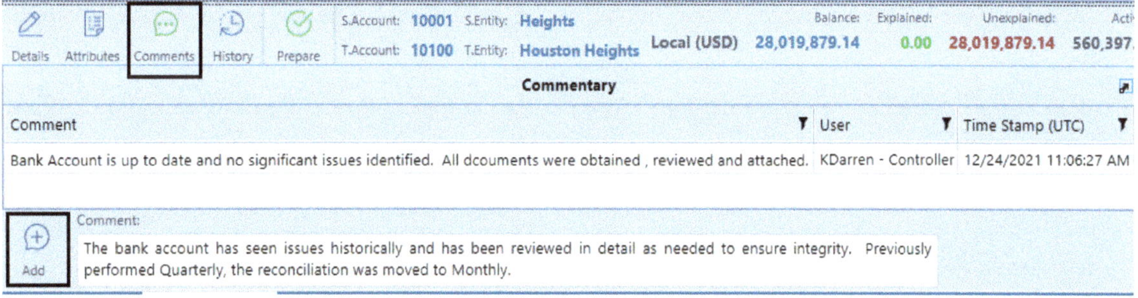

Figure 4.47

Once a comment has been added to the Reconciliation, the Comments icon(s) will move from blue to green as a visual indicator that a comment has been attached. If turned on, email alerts can also be sent when comments are added. Also, note there is no limitation to the number of comments added to a particular Reconciliation.

Workflow Actions

Workflow icons appear in the header and allow you to move the Reconciliation through the sign-off process. There are multiple different Workflow icons available, and what appears to the User depends on their security and the state of the Reconciliation. For example, if I am a Preparer on the Reconciliation and it is in the Prepared state, I will only have the Recall icon available when I view that particular Reconciliation. The different Workflow icons are defined below, alongside the User Role that can perform the action.

Icon	Definition	Preparer	Approver	Admin
Prepare	Preparer sign-off. Available when the Reconciliation is in the In Process, Balance Changed, or Rejected state.	X	X	X
Recall	Recalls the Reconciliation and moves it back to the In Process state. Available when the Reconciliation is in the Prepared state (not yet Approved).	X	X	X
Reject	Rejects the Reconciliation back to the Preparer with a Rejection Reason Code and possible commentary if added.		X	X
Approve	Approver sign-off. Available when the Reconciliation is in the Prepared or Partially Approved state.		X	X
Unapprove	Sends the Reconciliation back to the Prepared state with a Reason Code and possible commentary if added.		X	X

Figure 4.48

Details Icon

The final icon that appears in the far left of the header is the Details icon.

Figure 4.49

If you navigate to another page like History, Attributes, or Comments, the Details icon will return you to the Detail Items page, which is the default when selecting a Reconciliation.

Detail Items Grid

Detail items are also known as reconciling items or transactions that explain the ending balance. The detail items grid is the heart of the Reconciliation and is where the Preparer will spend most of their time adding items and explanations. It is expected the Preparer will add as many items as required to explain the ending balance. As items are saved to the detail items grid, the Explained and Unexplained balances update accordingly. As a reminder, you will not be able to sign-off on the Reconciliation if the Unexplained balance is not within the threshold set on the Reconciliation.

In the following section, we will walk through:

- Detail item fields
- Creating, editing, or deleting detail items (I Items)
- Prior item functionality

- Multi-currency items
- Multi-currency overrides

We will be starting with the basic steps to create items. However, there are multiple different ways you can automate this process through templates, Transaction Matching, and Balance Check functionality. Each of these automation options will be covered later in this section.

Detail Item Fields

Let's start by walking through the fields within the detail items grid. The table below provides a definition of each field and how it is used. The more information provided when creating a detail item, the easier it will be for the Approver to review and the Auditor to audit, as well as offering better overall reporting and analysis.

Field	Definition
☐	Multi-select box is used to select specific items in the grid. Users leverage this for mass deleting.
O*	Override status field. The Override status is for multi-currency Reconciliations and will automatically populate only if the User types over a translated value in any one of the translated detailed amount fields (Account, Local, or Reporting). The override capability is a Reconciliation attribute and must be enabled by the Administrator on the specific Reconciliation. If an override occurs, the field will populate with an A (Account), L (Local), and R (Reporting) depending on the fields overridden.
R	Reconciliation Item Type classifications. This field is a system-generated field and defines how the item was created. The field is very useful for the Approver and Auditor. All of the possible Reconciliation Item Types are defined below, and each will be discussed in detail throughout this section. I = Manually added or prior items carried forward. T = Items imported from the period-specific template (T-Doc). S = Items imported to the current and/or future period from the schedule template (S-Doc). B = Balance item imported from an independent source through data integration. X = Items created from Transaction Matching.
Amount*	Value of the item in transactional currency.
Currency*	Transactional currency code populated from a drop-down list. The drop-down will default to the currency code on the Account but can be updated by the User to any currency code available in the system.
Account*	Calculated value translating the Amount field to Account currency leveraging the currency rates within the system. The calculated amount can be overridden by the User if the *Allow Override* feature is turned on.
Local	Value of the item in Local currency. For single-currency Reconciliations, this value is inputby the User and assumed to be in the Local currency of the Reconciliation. For multi-currency Reconciliations, this field is the calculated value, translating the Amount field to the Local currency, leveraging the currency rates within the system. The calculated amount can be overridden by the User if the *Allow Override* feature is turned on.

Field	Definition
Reporting*	Calculated value translating the Amount field to Reporting currency, leveraging the currency rates within the system. The calculated amount can be overridden by the User if the *Allow Override* feature is turned on.
Item Type	Item Types categorize the detail items added and are used for reporting and analysis purposes. Item Types are assigned to the detail item by the User, upon creation, and are selected from a standard drop-down list. The list is set up by the organization and is used across the solution by all Preparers for consistency.
Item Name	Description of the item. Item name is a required field and the User will not be able to save the detail item if this field is not populated.
Item Comment	Comment field on the detail item to provide additional information.
Booked Period	Automatically populated and represents the Workflow period when the item was created/added. Booked period cannot be altered.
Transaction Date	The specific date of the item, such as check date, invoice date, etc. Transaction date drives the aging Calculation and can be any date prior to, or equal to, the booked period end date. Users can type in the date or use the calendar object to make their selection. If not updated, this field will default to the period end date of the booked period.
Aging	Automatically calculated as the difference between the current Workflow period being viewed minus the transaction date. The field is populated upon save and is read-only.
Ref 1	Optional field used to store additional information about the item.
Ref 2	Optional field used to store additional information about the item.
User	Name of the User that originally created and saved the line item. The field is automatically populated by the system and is read-only.
Time Stamp	Time stamp based on the time the line item was created and saved. The field is automatically populated by the system and is read-only.
* Only visible if multi-currency is enabled within Global Options, and the field will only be visible in the detail items grid for multi-currency Reconciliations.	

Figure 4.50

Manual Items (I Items)

Manual items, also referred to as I-items, are the most used Reconciliation Item Type because they can be generated by the User or created upon pull-forward from prior periods. In the next section, we will discuss the actions that can be performed when preparing the Reconciliation manually. You will only be able to perform actions within the detail items grid if the Reconciliation is in the In Process state.

Next, in Figure 4.51, we will define the action icons:

Icon	Definition
	Insert row icon creates new lines in the detail items grid.
	Delete row icon removes lines in the detail items grid.
	Cancel all changes icon will undo any unsaved changes such as new lines added, updates, or deletions. Once saved, changes cannot be undone.
	Save icon saves changes in the detail items grid.
	Deselect All icon unchecks any line that is selected via the multi-select check box in the grid.
	Column settings icon allows you to rearrange or remove columns. However, it does not maintain your selection and will reset when you navigate away from the Reconciliation. This feature within the detail items grid does not leverage saved state capability and is therefore not recommended.
Defer Refresh	Defer Refresh will allow you to add or delete items without updating the Explained and Unexplained Calculations until you select the refresh. Although available, this functionality is not recommended.

Figure 4.51

You can manually create, edit, and remove items as needed. To create new items, you will select the insert row icon. This action will create new lines in the grid that will appear shaded yellow, indicating that the line has not yet been saved.

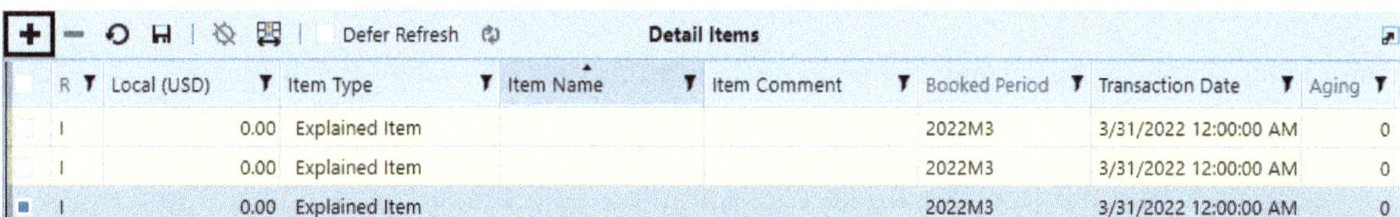

R	Local (USD)	Item Type	Item Name	Item Comment	Booked Period	Transaction Date	Aging
I	0.00	Explained Item			2022M3	3/31/2022 12:00:00 AM	0
I	0.00	Explained Item			2022M3	3/31/2022 12:00:00 AM	0
I	0.00	Explained Item			2022M3	3/31/2022 12:00:00 AM	0

Figure 4.52

When creating the items, you will populate the fields desired and, most importantly, select the save icon once complete. As you add, update, or delete information within the grid, the save icon will become active, indicating that a save action is required. If you fail to select save and navigate away from the detail item grid, your changes will be lost. If the save icon appears shaded, as shown below, it is an indication that the items have been properly saved.

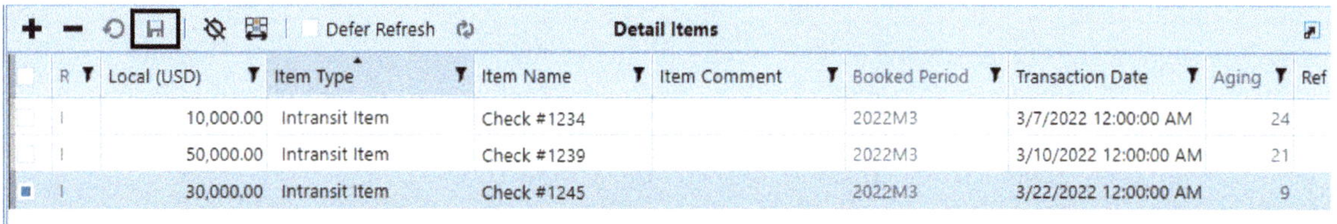

R	Local (USD)	Item Type	Item Name	Item Comment	Booked Period	Transaction Date	Aging	Ref
I	10,000.00	Intransit Item	Check #1234		2022M3	3/7/2022 12:00:00 AM	24	
I	50,000.00	Intransit Item	Check #1239		2022M3	3/10/2022 12:00:00 AM	21	
I	30,000.00	Intransit Item	Check #1245		2022M3	3/22/2022 12:00:00 AM	9	

Figure 4.53

Also, note that the Item Name is a required field, and you will not be able to save the detail item line if this field is not populated. If you attempt to save the item with a blank item name field, the system will provide the following error message.

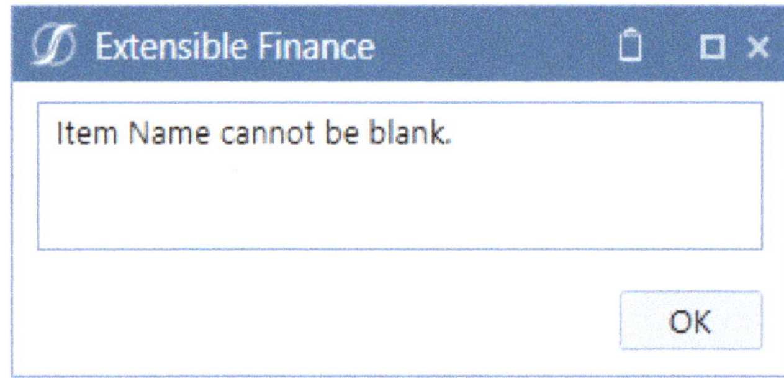

Figure 4.54

All current booked period items can be edited if the Reconciliation is not in the Prepared state. Edits will also need to be saved prior to navigating away from the grid, or updates will be lost.

If you need to delete a detail item, you can select the specific line or use the multi-select box to the left of the items. Once all the items to be deleted are selected, you will need to select the minus icon and then the save icon. This will remove the lines from the grid.

> **Note:** Deleting items only affects the current period and will not impact historical Reconciliations.

Whether you are adding, editing, or deleting, if during the process you make a mistake or change your mind, you can select the cancel changes icon to reset the changes. The cancel changes functionality only works on unsaved changes. Once you save the changes, there is no ability to cancel the change.

Prior Items

Prior items is the ability to bring historical detail items forward into the current period Reconciliation to help explain the ending balance. Prior items allow you to be more efficient in preparing the Reconciliation. There are two options when leveraging prior items functionality. You can either **Pull Items** or **Copy Items** into the current period. Each option is unique in how it functions.

The Pull Items function is used when a transaction from a prior period still belongs to the current ending balance. This function allows you to carry forward the item into the current period, maintaining audit integrity. Pulled items are read-only except for the item comment field. The detail item will carry forward with all existing I-Docs and the system will maintain the original booked period. You will be able to add additional I-Docs if desired, but you cannot remove any previous period documents for control and audit purposes.

Contrary to the Pull Items function, you can copy items, which is the ability to take the historical item and replicate it as a new item in the current period. The new item will have an updated booked period and all fields will be editable. Also, historical I-Docs are not brought forward with the copy item function because it is treated as a new item and requires new documentation. The copy feature is normally used to be more efficient. If you have an item that is similar each month, but which varies in amount, copy items allows the system to create the item with all the information and you will only have to update the amount field and add the proper support.

To initiate either Pull or Copy Items, select the Prior Items icon located in the bottom-left corner of the grid.

Figure 4.55

Once selected, you will receive a dialog box displaying all the items that are available to be pulled or copied. The system will look to the prior Reconciliation based on the frequency; monthly will look to the prior month, quarterly to the prior quarter, etc. Select the check box next to the desired items and then select either Copy Items or Pull Items in the bottom-right corner.

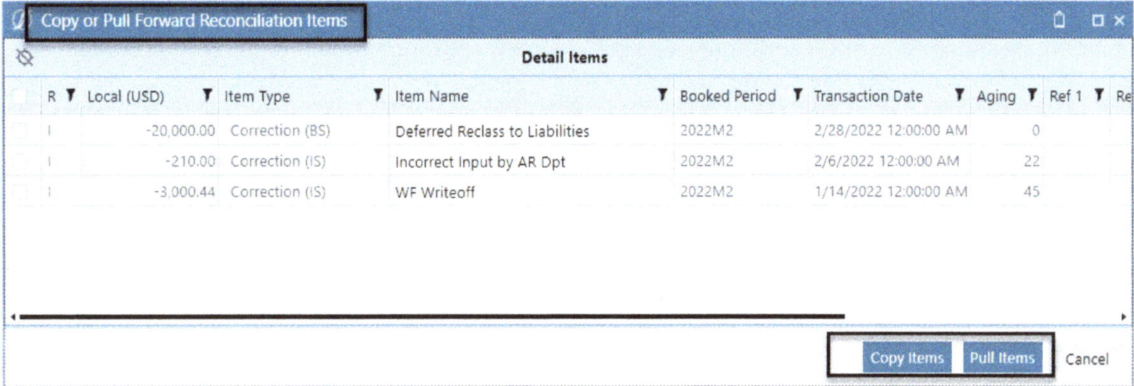

Copy or Pull Forward Reconciliation Items
Detail Items
R
Local (USD)
Item Type
Item Name
Booked Period
Transaction Date
Aging
Ref 1
I -20,000.00 Correction (BS) Deferred Reclass to Liabilities 2022M2 2/28/2022 12:00:00 AM 0
I -210.00 Correction (IS) Incorrect Input by AR Dpt 2022M2 2/6/2022 12:00:00 AM 22
I -3,000.44 Correction (IS) WF Writeoff 2022M2 1/14/2022 12:00:00 AM 45
Copy Items
Pull Items
Cancel

Figure 4.56

> **Note:** Only certain Reconciliation Item Types and Detail Item Types are available to be pulled forward.

For Reconciliation Item Types, only manual items (I-Items) and template items (T-Items) will appear in the dialog box. Schedule items (S-Items), Transaction Matching items (X-Items), and Balance Check items (B-Items) are period-specific and cannot be pulled forward. Also, for audit and control purposes, all template items (T-Items) – pulled or copied – will be converted to manual items (I-Items) because they are no longer associated with a template.

Similarly, only certain Detail Item Types can be pulled forward. If the Item Type was created within the control list (by the Administrator) as a statement type, it will not be available in the Prior Item dialog box as it is assumed to be period-specific. All other Item Type definitions, which include Explained, Correction (BS), and Correction (IS), will be available assuming they meet the Reconciliation type criteria above.

Also, during this process, if you copy or pull items in error, you have the ability to delete the items in the current period. Deletion will remove the item from the current period but not impact historical Reconciliations.

Multi-Currency Functionality

Most organizations typically perform single-currency Reconciliations in the Entity's Local currency. However, there are times when an Entity may have Accounts that are denominated in a currency other than the Local currency or the transactions flowing through the Account are in multiple different currencies. In these situations, we would want to turn on multi-currency functionality.

For single-currency Reconciliations, you will see a single Local amount field in the detail items grid with the Local currency code displayed in the header for presentation purposes.

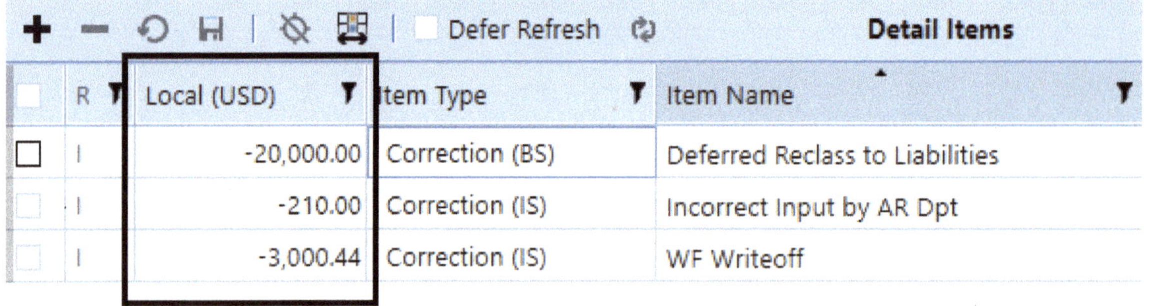

R	Local (USD)	Item Type	Item Name
I	-20,000.00	Correction (BS)	Deferred Reclass to Liabilities
I	-210.00	Correction (IS)	Incorrect Input by AR Dpt
I	-3,000.44	Correction (IS)	WF Writeoff

Figure 4.57

When a Reconciliation is set for multi-currency, the detail items grid will contain four amount fields as follows: Amount representing the value in transaction or document currency (input by the User) and three additional amount fields which represent the translated values for Account, Local, and Reporting based on the currency codes set for the Reconciliation. The currency code associated with each Amount field is visible in the column header, as seen in the screenshot below, indicating that the Account value is in GBP, Local is in EUR, and Reporting is in USD.

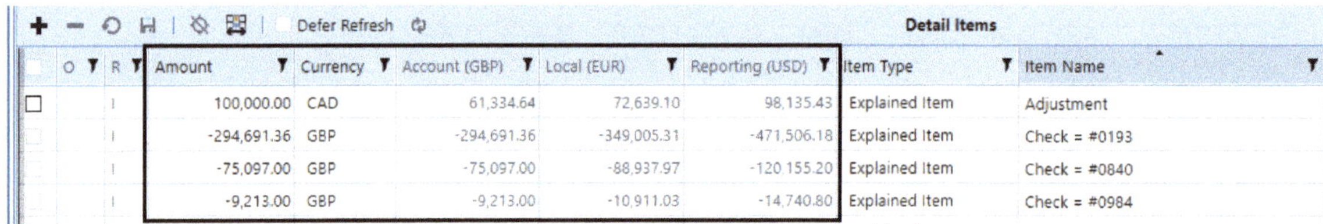

O	R	Amount	Currency	Account (GBP)	Local (EUR)	Reporting (USD)	Item Type	Item Name
	I	100,000.00	CAD	61,334.64	72,639.10	98,135.43	Explained Item	Adjustment
	I	-294,691.36	GBP	-294,691.36	-349,005.31	-471,506.18	Explained Item	Check = #0193
	I	-75,097.00	GBP	-75,097.00	-88,937.97	-120,155.20	Explained Item	Check = #0840
	I	-9,213.00	GBP	-9,213.00	-10,911.03	-14,740.80	Explained Item	Check = #0984

Figure 4.58

When creating an item in a multi-currency Reconciliation, you will input the Amount value and select the currency code of the transaction from the currency drop-down list. The currency drop-down will default to the currency code of the Account balance but can be updated accordingly. The drop-down list is populated by the system and will reflect the currency codes set up in the application. The solution supports all currency codes, so if an expected currency code does not appear, you should contact the organization's OneStream Administrator.

Once you save the newly-created item, the system will automatically translate the Amount value to the Account, Local, and Reporting values. The Translation Calculation is leveraging the FX rates within the application for the specific rate type and period. The **FX Reporting Currency** and the **FX Rate type** (typically the ClosingRate) are defined by the Administrator on the Global Options page. The translated amounts will be read-only to the User if the multi-currency override is not turned on for the Reconciliation.

Multi-Currency Override Values and Support

Multi-currency override is a feature that allows you to override the translated values calculated by the system. Overrides are typically used in situations where the transaction needs to be held at a historical or spot rate, and using the system Translation will not provide an accurate value.

This feature is turned on at the Reconciliation level and is typically only set on specific Accounts. Overrides can be performed on any one of the three translated values: Account, Local, or Reporting. If any of the value fields are overridden, the system will keep track of which fields have been updated and note it in the Override column. The letters in the Override column correlate to the first letter of the value columns, A for Account, L for Local, and R for Reporting. In addition, if any of the three values are overridden on any of the lines, a message will appear in the top-right corner of the Reconciliation, indicating that overrides have occurred.

Figure 4.59

If you override a value in error, and would like the system to calculate the Translation, simply type a zero in the specific value field and select save. You cannot leave the field blank – it must contain a zero which will trigger the system Translation. If you want a zero in any of the translated values because you are adjusting just Reporting or Local values only etc., you will need to add a zero-amount item as shown below.

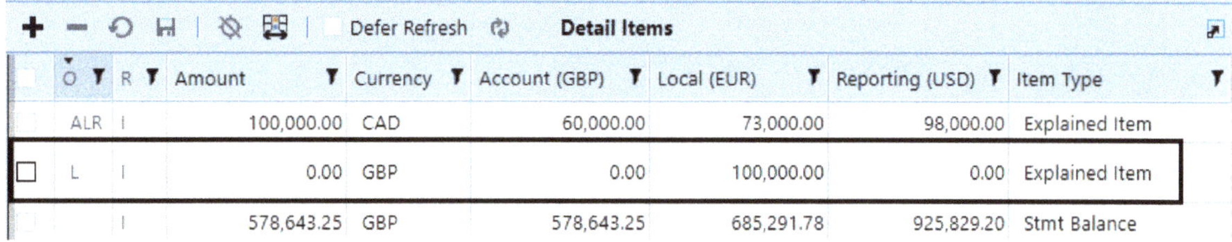

Figure 4.60

In addition to value overrides, you can set the Reconciliation to require that documentation be attached if overrides are performed. Because override values are calculated by the User, it is good practice to require support to explain the translated values. The override support requirement will check for either an I-doc for each item overridden or an overall R-doc at the Reconciliation level. If a document is not attached, you will receive the following error message, and you will not be able to mark the Reconciliation as Prepared.

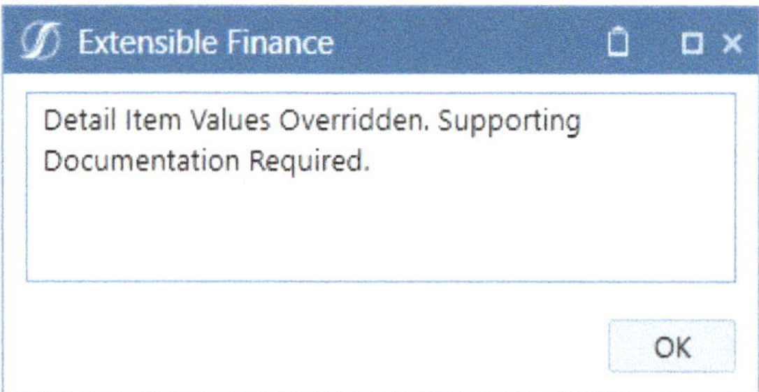

Figure 4.61

Reconciliation Support

Support is critical to the Reconciliation process to validate the item created. Reconciliation support can come in many different forms, such as statements, reports, invoices, Calculations, etc. Within this area, we will discuss the ability to upload, view, and delete documentation. The ability to action a document will depend on your security and the state of the Reconciliation.

The supporting documentation action icons are as follows:

Icon	Definition
View	View the document selected in the Reconciliation support screen.
Delete	Delete the document selected in Reconciliation support screen.
I-Doc	Allows User to upload a document to a detail item. This icon is only visible when a detail item is selected.
R-Doc	Allows User to upload an overall Reconciliation support document.
Pull R-Doc	Allows User to pull overall Reconciliation support documents forward from the prior Reconciliation period.

Figure 4.62

Uploading Documents

Documents can only be uploaded if the Reconciliation is in the In Process state. You can upload as many documents as needed to a detail item or at the Reconciliation level. Documents added at the item level are referred to as I-Docs, and overall Reconciliation documents are referred to as R-Docs.

To upload support, you will select the I-Doc and R-Doc icons, which are located within the Reconciliation support screen at the bottom of the detail items grid. The R-Doc icon is always visible because it supports the overall Reconciliation, whereas the I-Doc icon will only appear when a specific saved detail item is selected.

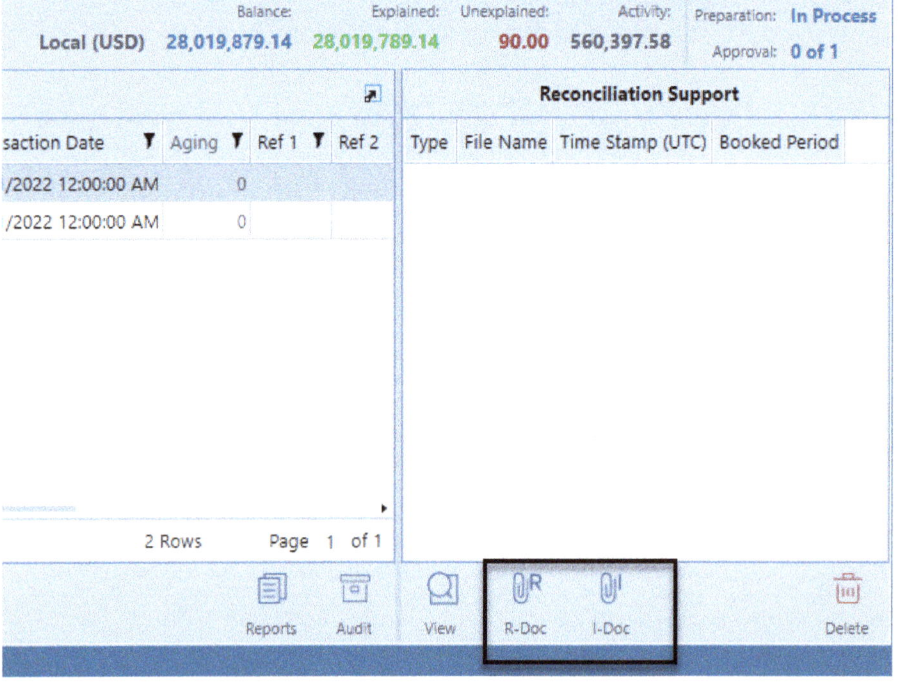

Figure 4.63

When you select the applicable upload icon, a file explorer dialog will appear. You can navigate to your file and select Open.

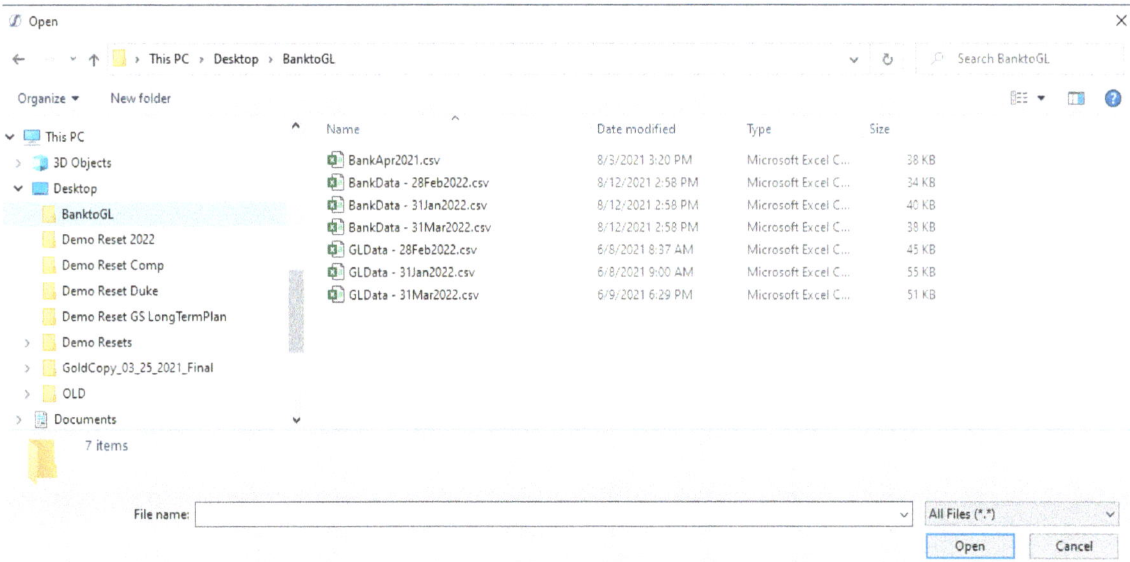

Figure 4.64

This will add the file to the Reconciliation support screen.

> **Note:** You can have multiple documents on a detail item or Reconciliation; however, you can only add one document at a time.

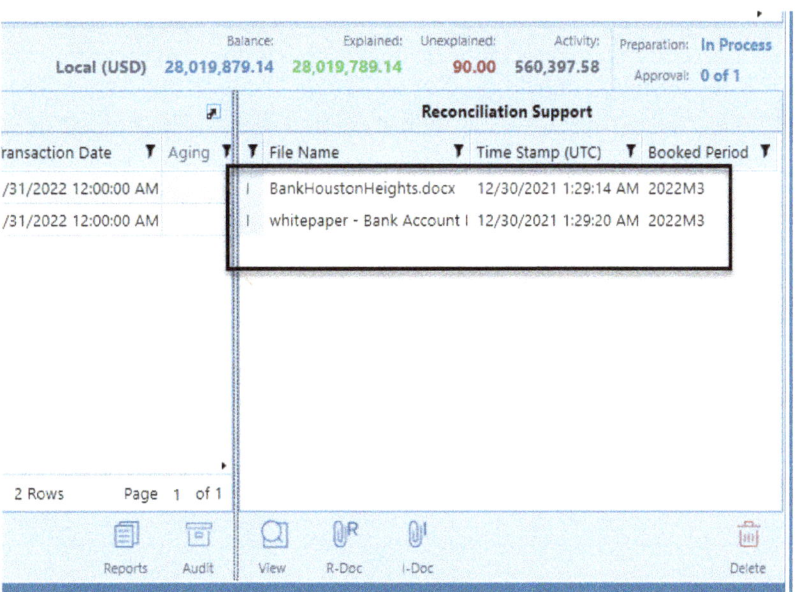

Figure 4.65

From a support perspective, documents are typically in the following formats PDF, HTML, MHT, RTF, DOCX, XLS, XLSX, CSV, Text, Image, and Zip files (to name a few). Outside of XML, the system does not limit the file format but assumes the User viewing the document will have the software necessary to open the specific file. Each file cannot exceed 2 GB.

Viewing Documents

If you have access to the Reconciliation, you will have the ability to view any of the attached supporting documentation. To view the document, highlight the file and select the View icon. The system will open the file in the software required or pop up a dialog asking you what application you would like to open the file with (such as Notepad, Wordpad, etc.). When viewing the document, it is read-only and changes made will not be automatically saved back to the system.

Editing Documents

All documents uploaded to the solution are read-only. You cannot change the document from within the system. To update a document, you will need to open the file using the View icon and save it externally to the solution. Once all the updates are complete, you will need to re-upload the file to the Reconciliation. If the file has the same name, the system will replace the original file and provide the User with a message indicating that the file will be replaced.

Deleting Documents

Current period I-Docs, R-Docs, or pull forward R-Docs can be deleted in the current period if you have Preparer rights and the Reconciliation is in the In Process state. You cannot delete historical I-Docs that are attached to a detail item created from the pull forward process for control and audit purposes. To remove a historical I-Doc, you will need to delete the pull forward item from the current Reconciliation (and any other period the historical item was pulled into) and navigate back to the original period and delete the document within that period's Reconciliation and re-pull the items. If, however, the documentation is accurate for the historical periods but not valid in the current period, you should copy the detail item – versus pull – as noted in the prior items section above. The copy function creates the item in the current period but does not bring forward the documentation.

Pull Forward R-Docs

Similar to prior item functionality, you can pull forward R-Docs from the prior Reconciliation based on the Reconciliation frequency. Pull R-Docs functionality is more efficient because it eliminates the need for you to reattach the historical documents and ensures document integrity. If R-Docs are pulled forward, you have the ability to delete the documents from the current period if you have the proper security rights and the Reconciliation is not in the Prepared state. Deleting pulled forward R-Docs will only impact the current period and will not delete the document from the prior periods.

Document Auditability

When a document is added to a Reconciliation, the system will assign a type, User ID, time stamp, and the booked period. Although tracked, the User ID is only viewable from the History page. Document types are described below and include the S-Doc and T-Doc, which will be covered later in the automation section.

- I – Item document visible when the item is selected.
- R – Reconciliation document visible at the Reconciliation level.
- T – Template document visible at the Reconciliation level.
- S – Schedule document visible at the Reconciliation level.

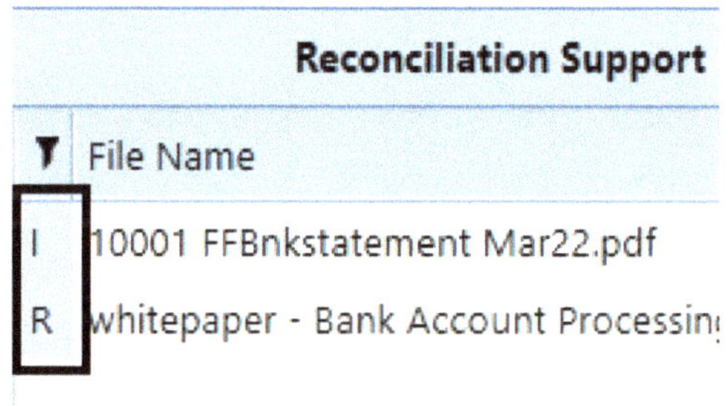

Figure 4.66

Additional Reconciliation Features

There are additional features that are available within the detailed Reconciliation view that help support the process, such as Reports, Audit, and Ref Doc. Each of these is a separate icon located at the bottom-center of the detail items grid and can be accessed by any User that has access to the Reconciliation.

Figure 4.67

Reference Document

The Reference Document is used to provide more information about a particular Reconciliation. Typically, this document will contain the purpose of the Account, the Reconciliation procedures, and detailed work instructions identifying the steps required to prepare the Reconciliation. It is useful to have a Reference Document because it helps a Preparer who may be new to reconciling the particular Account understand what they need to do. It is also useful for management to understand how the Account is being used by the organization. In addition, it can assist the Auditor because they can use the document to answer questions around how the Account is being analyzed.

The Reference Document can be accessed from the Ref Doc icon, which only appears if a Reference Document has been associated with the specific Reconciliation.

Figure 4.68

Like all documents, the Reference Document is read-only. Also, Reference Documents are attached by the Administrator and are set at the T.Account level and cannot be maintained by the Preparer. If you would prefer the Preparer to maintain this type of documentation, you can use the R-Doc functionality in lieu of the Reference Document. The R-Doc can be carried forward, period over period, or referenced from the History page. R-Docs, as discussed previously, are also read-only, but can be replaced by the Preparer as needed without impacting history.

Reports

Reports functionality allows you to view the Reconciliation in a Report format. Reports are valuable because you can provide the Reconciliation to a person external to the process without having to give them access to the Account Reconciliation Solution. The Report contains key information about the Reconciliation, including attributes, balance information, detail items, commentary, and sign-off history. To run the Reconciliation Report, you select the Reports icon.

Figure 4.69

Upon selection, a dialog box will appear requiring you to select the Report Type and Currency Level.

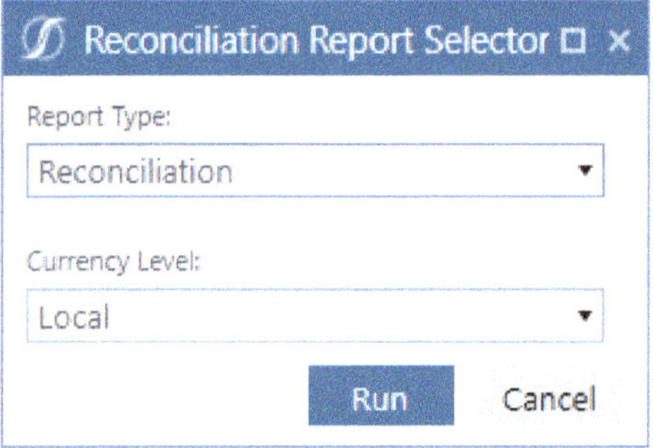

Figure 4.70

The Report Type allows you to select Reconciliation or History. If you select Reconciliation, the system will run the current period Reconciliation Report. If History is selected, the system will create a Report package that contains the Reconciliation for each period the Reconciliation exists in the system.

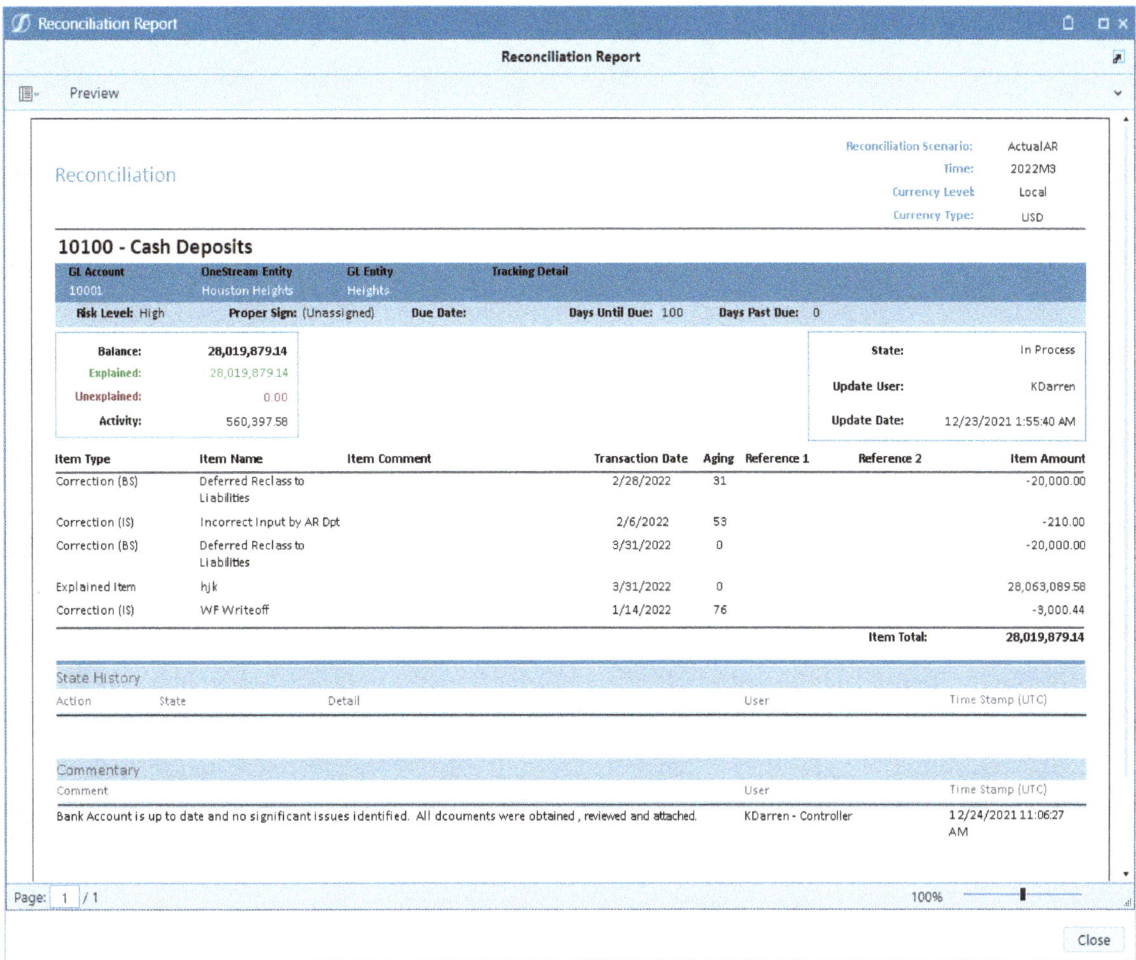

Figure 4.71

The Currency Level selection drop-down is dependent on the type of Reconciliation. If you are viewing a single-currency Reconciliation, the currency type options will be either Local or Translated to Reporting. If you are viewing a multi-currency Reconciliation, you can run the Report in any of the currency values (Account, Local, or Reporting) or All, which will present all three currencies in the Report. The Currency Type selected is visible in the top-right corner of the Report.

Reconciliation Scenario:	ActualAR
Time:	2022M3
Currency Level:	Account
Currency Type:	GBP

Figure 4.72

Reconciliation Reports can be printed, exported, or sent electronically to another User. The Export and Send formats are presented in the screenshot below.

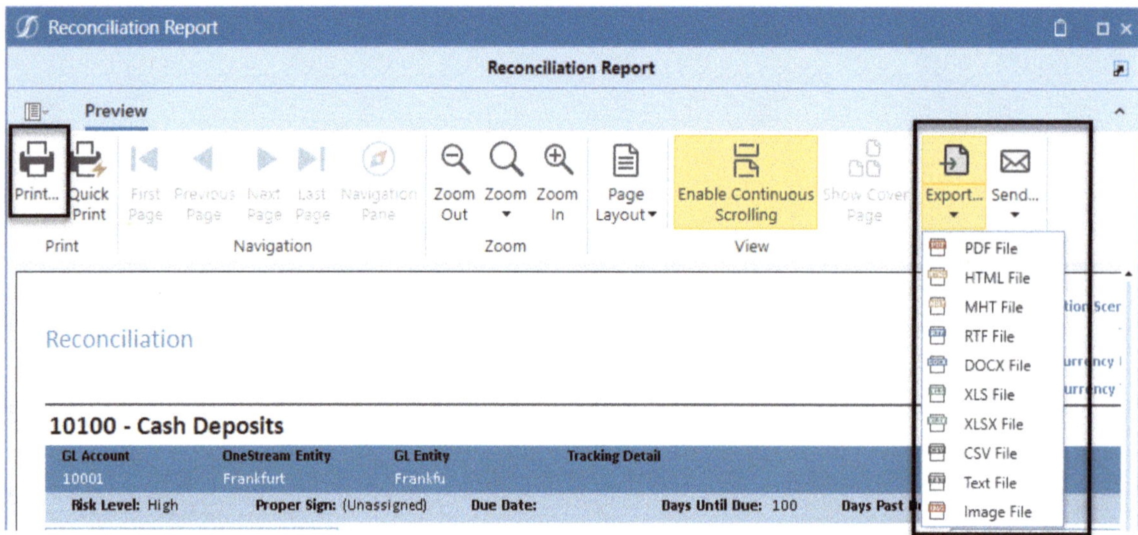

Figure 4.73

Audit Package

Audit functionality allows the ability to create an audit package that contains the Reconciliation Report (discussed above, excluding the Reconciliation-level comments) and all the supporting documentation within the Reconciliation support screen for the specific period. Audit functionality provides the ability to extract the full Reconciliation and provide it to Users outside of the system, like the internal or external Auditor. It is best practice to allow the Auditor within the solution to perform their work; however, if your organization prefers not to allow this access, the Audit function allows you to provide the information with minimal effort.

The audit package is created when you select the Audit icon.

Figure 4.74

For single-currency Reconciliations, the system will immediately create the ZIP file and require you to select the Download button.

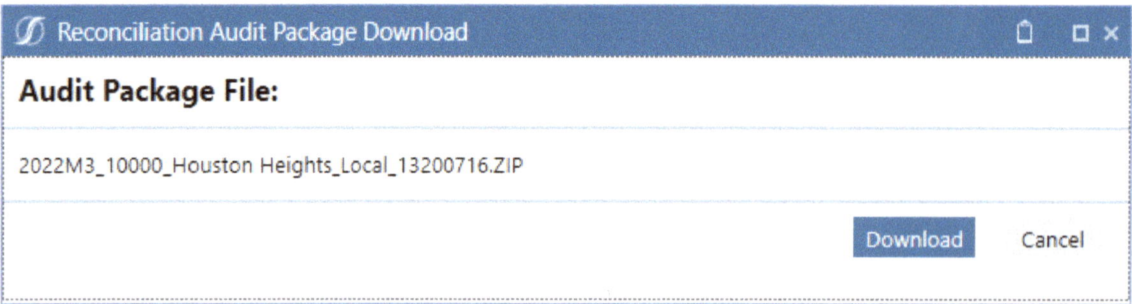

Figure 4.75

For multi-currency Reconciliations, the system will ask which Currency Level you would like to run the audit package in – Account, Local, Reporting, or All – before creating the ZIP file for download.

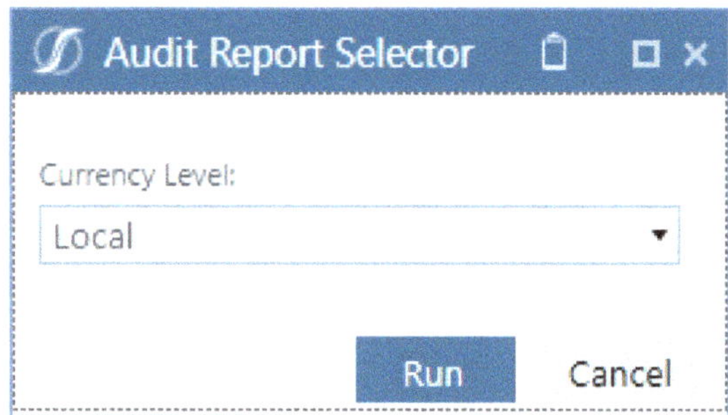

Figure 4.76

All audit packages created are stored in the **OneStream File Share**. You can locate the audit package by navigating to your personal folder and then to the `Recon Audit Packages` subfolder. From here, you can download the file, add a description, or delete it if desired.

Audit Package Folder:

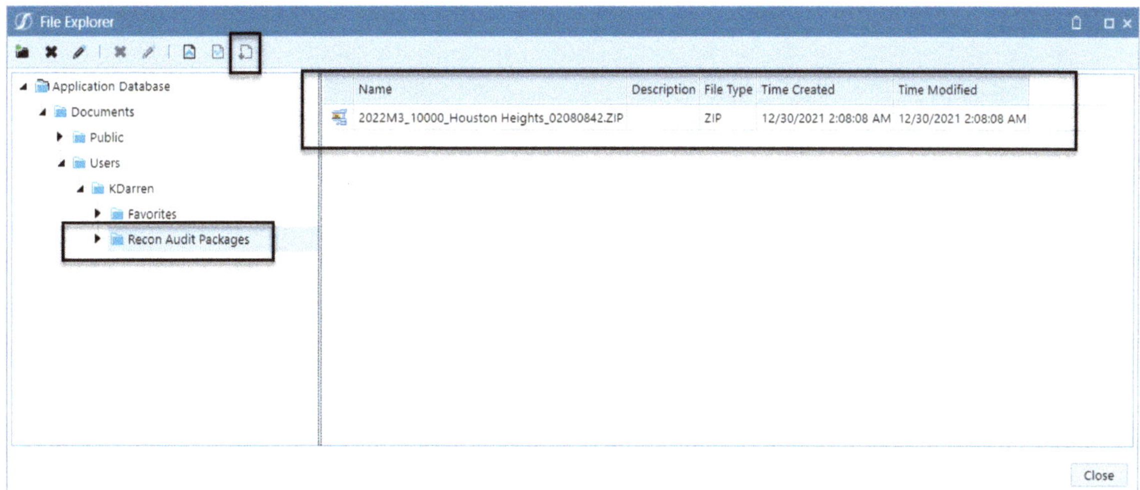

Figure 4.77

> **Note:** The Reconciliation Report included in the audit package does not contain the overall Reconciliation comments. This was by design so that Preparers and Approvers can communicate with each other without the Auditor seeing the comments within the audit package.

Automating Reconciliations

As mentioned earlier, leveraging the Account Reconciliation Solution provides the ability to automate certain steps within the process. In the previous section, we discussed the manual creation of reconciling items which is one of the many ways you can interact with the system. In the next section, we will discuss other ways you can automate item creation and sign-off.

Automation can be gained using the following functionality:

- Period Templates
- Schedule Templates
- Balance Check
- Transaction Matching

We will walk through each of these processes in detail and discuss where they are most used.

Period Templates

As discussed, the User Interface is set up to be the same, regardless of the type of Account you are reconciling; this was done by design. Organizations typically have their own desired templates, layouts, analysis, etc., that they prefer to use for reconciling. Although we could build standard templates in the User Interface, feedback we received from our customers – who have historically used other Reconciliation tools – is that set templates designed in the User Interface are rigid, not intuitive, and would not meet all Users' needs. Therefore, they preferred utilizing Excel.

To address the ability to have consistency and flexibility, the Excel template capability was created. Because OneStream integrates with Excel, it was natural to leverage Excel for item upload purposes. Templates allow you to analyze and explain in Excel, but then provide you with the ability to upload the template. Upon upload, the system automatically creates the detail items and attaches the template to the Reconciliation for support. You are not limited to the number of items you can upload, and the import process can be more efficient than manually creating each detail item, line by line.

Templates are designed and assigned by the Administrator, and an organization can have as many templates as desired. However, minimizing the number of unique templates is key to creating standardization and consistency. The Administrator will link the template to the specific Reconciliations where applicable.

> **Note:** Only one template can be linked to a single Reconciliation for a given period. See the Administration section for more information on template creation and maintenance.

You can access the Reconciliation template by selecting the Template icon at the bottom of the detailed Reconciliation view.

Figure 4.78

By selecting the Template icon, the system will launch Excel and open the specific Reconciliation template for you. Depending on the design, templates will typically show the Account information and current period balance with additional tabs available for you to perform your analysis. The template can contain multiple tabs leveraging formulas, pivot tables, charts, etc., as needed.

In Figures 4.79 and 4.80, there is a sample of the basic template delivered for single-currency Reconciliation, and multi-currency Reconciliation, respectively.

Single-Currency Basic Template:

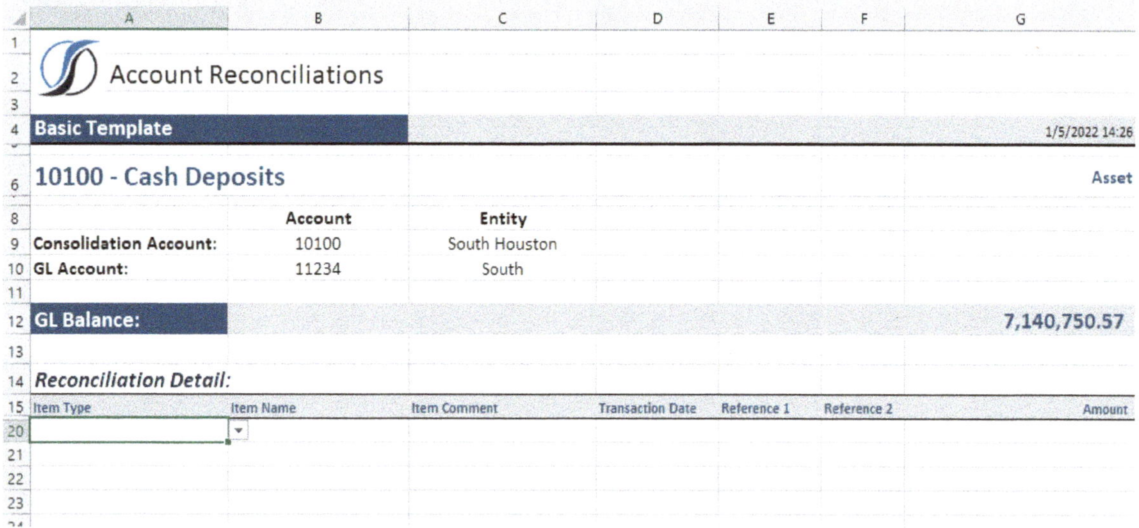

Figure 4.79

Multi-Currency Basic Template:

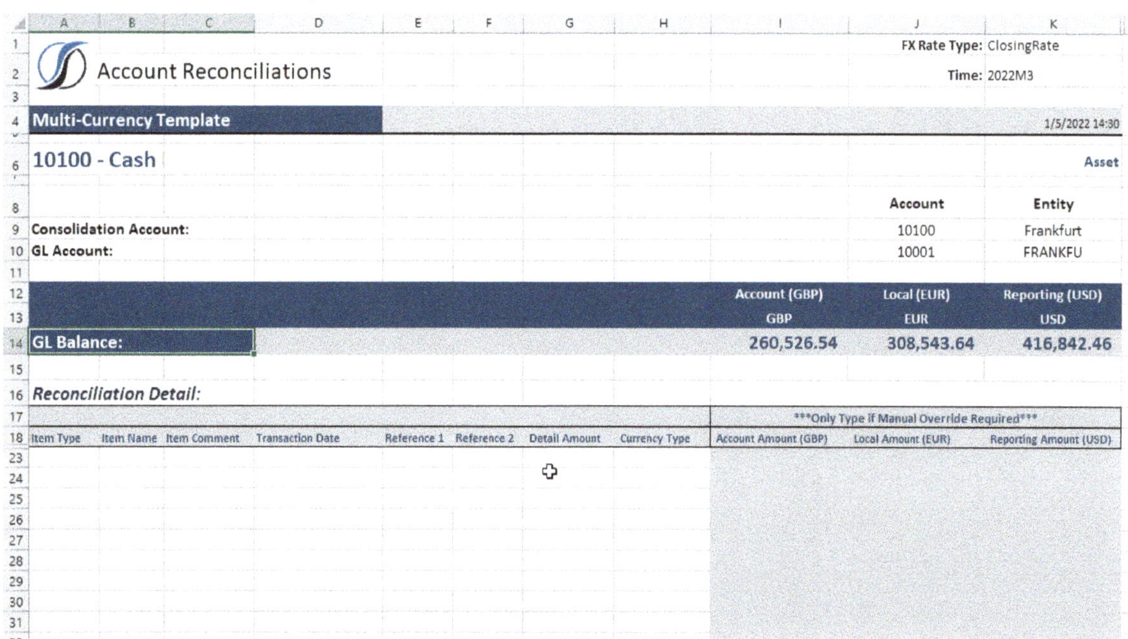

Figure 4.80

Once the template is prepared and ready for upload, you will save the file outside of the application. The file cannot be opened in Excel when you attempt to upload it. The upload process is initiated by selecting the T-Doc icon at the bottom of the detail items grid.

Figure 4.81

Upon selection, a file explorer dialog will appear, and you will navigate to your file and select open.

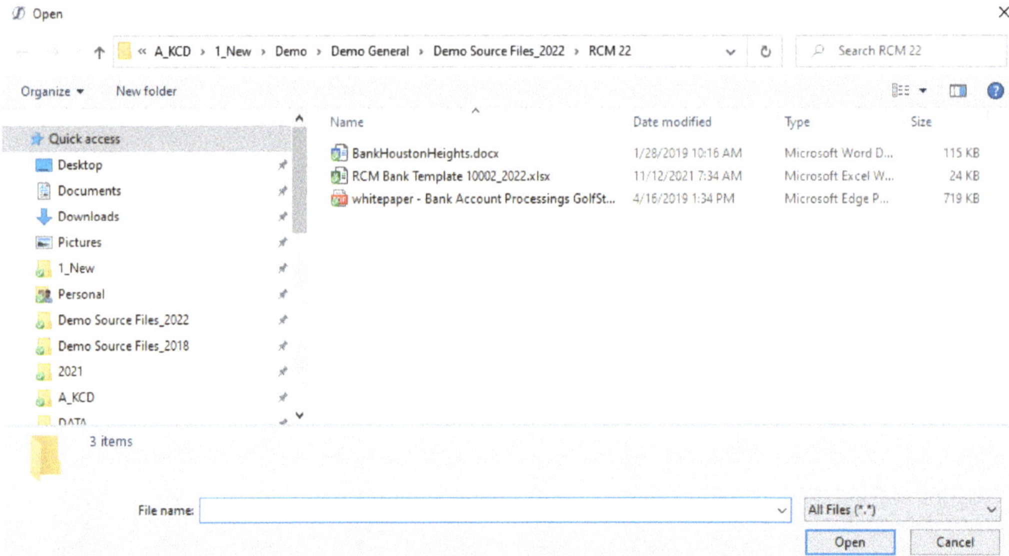

Figure 4.82

The T-Doc functionality will upload the detail items from the Reconciliation-named range within the Excel Workbook and attach the file for support. The items created in the system will be denoted with a Reconciliation Item Type of T, indicating that it was generated from a template upload. Also, the template will automatically be attached in the Reconciliation support screen, and it will be denoted with a T indicating that it came from the T-Doc load. The T-Doc is presented at the Reconciliation level and will appear regardless of the detail item selected. See the screenshot in Figure 4.83 for an example of the Reconciliation following the template upload.

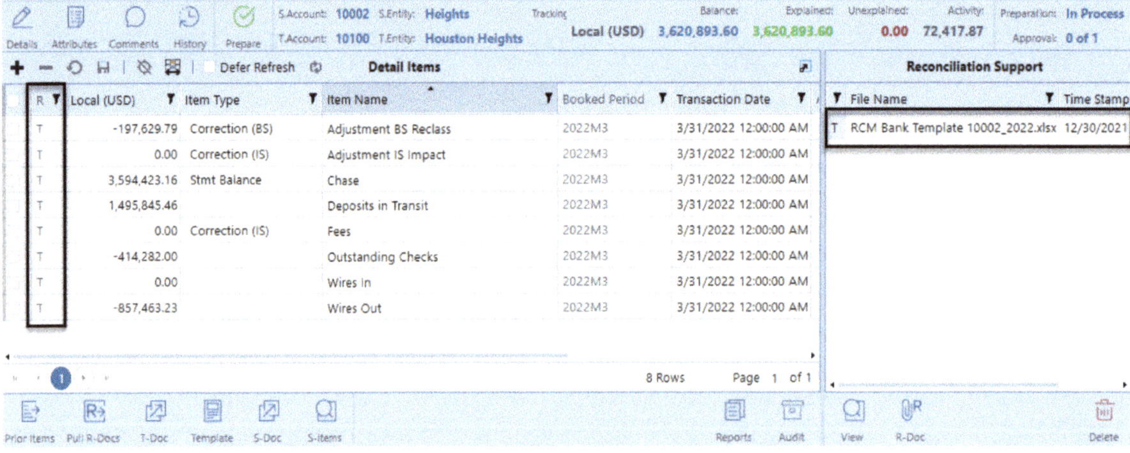

Figure 4.83

Below are a few items to consider when using templates.

- Only one template can be associated with a Reconciliation for a given period. As an example, assume I upload Template A which creates the detail items and attaches the template in the Reconciliation support screen. Subsequently, I upload Template B to the same Reconciliation. At the point I upload Template B, all the detail items created from Template A and the Template A document attached will be removed. The solution will replace the detail items and supporting document with Template B.

- Templates may need to be edited or adjusted after being uploaded into the solution due to new information or Approver comments. Although you cannot update the template directly in the system, changes can be made through the template process. If you have an update to make, open the specific template file (from the system or from where it was saved prior), make the change, save the file and close Excel, and reload the T-Doc. As discussed above, the new load will remove all previous T items and the attached document and replace it with the new file information.
- Template loads will only replace T Reconciliation Item Types. If the Reconciliation for the period contains other Reconciliation Item Types – such as I, B, X, or S – the T-Doc import process will not impact these lines.
- Template items can be brought forward into the next Reconciliation period using the Prior Items icon. When brought forward, the detail items will be updated from a T to an I Reconciliation Item Type.
- T-Docs cannot be pulled forward period over period.
- Templates can be reused month over month. It is not necessary to download a blank template each period if you prefer to use the prior template. The prior template will allow you to have a starting point and the ability to update accordingly. Prior templates can be accessed by navigating to the prior Reconciliation or through the document grid in the History page.
- If, upon upload, not all of your detail items appear in the Reconciliation, it is typically due to the XFT-named range. The import functions are reading the defined named ranges when importing, so if the range is not all-inclusive of your detail items, your upload may be incomplete.
- The template import functions (XF references) can also be added to an existing Reconciliation file if desired. You do not need to create templates or a template library. Existing Reconciliation files that are already in use by an organization can be updated and used to populate the solution.

Schedule Templates/Multi-Period Templates

Schedule templates, also known as multi-period templates, allow for multiple period item creation and Auto Reconciliation. This means that you can create a schedule and prepopulate future periods for expected items that are scheduled to occur. If the detail items loaded to the future periods sum to the value of the General Ledger balance in that future period, the system can auto reconcile the Reconciliation, creating efficiency in preparation and completion. Use cases for the schedule templates include depreciation, accretion, amortization, and standard accruals, to name a few.

A standard multi-period template is included, but your organization can update and configure the template to support different schedule formats. The Administrator will link the template to the specific Reconciliations where a schedule is required. As a reminder, only one template can be linked to a Reconciliation for a given period. To access the multi-period template, you will select the Template icon at the bottom of the detail items grid, which will launch the template in Excel for you to prepare.

Figure 4.84

When viewing the multi-period template, the main difference from the period template is a field for the Amortization period. The Amortization period is required because it indicates the period the balance should be loaded into. Because a Reconciliation is validating the ending General Ledger balance, the amount to be loaded for each period should not be the Expense amount (Accretion, Amortization, or Depreciation, etc.) but the period's ending balance amount after adjusting for the Expense that has been incurred. Schedule templates are available in both single-currency and multi-currency formats.

Single-Currency Multi-Period Template:

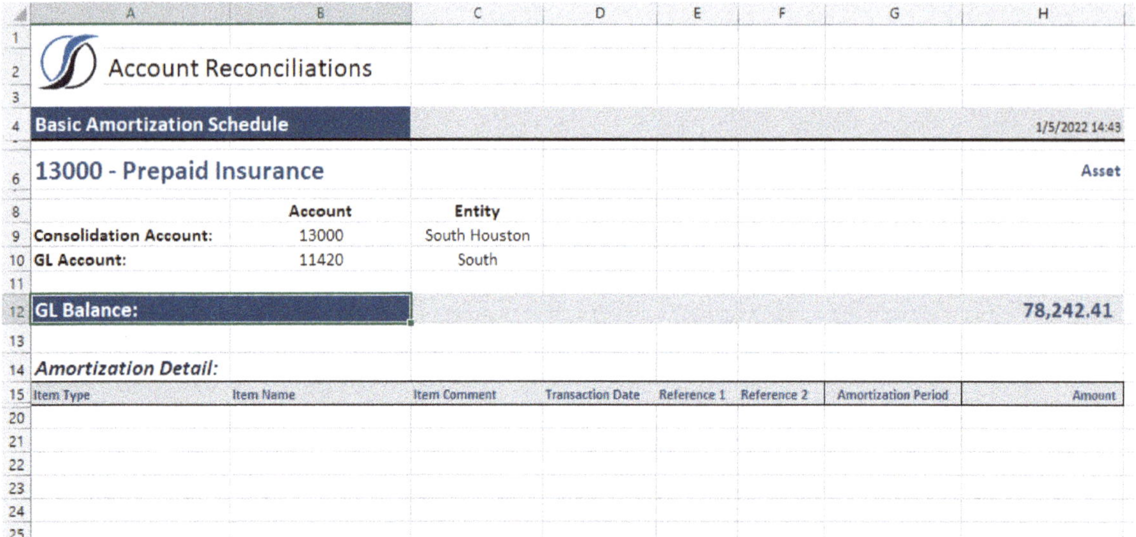

Figure 4.85

Multi-Currency Multi-Period Template:

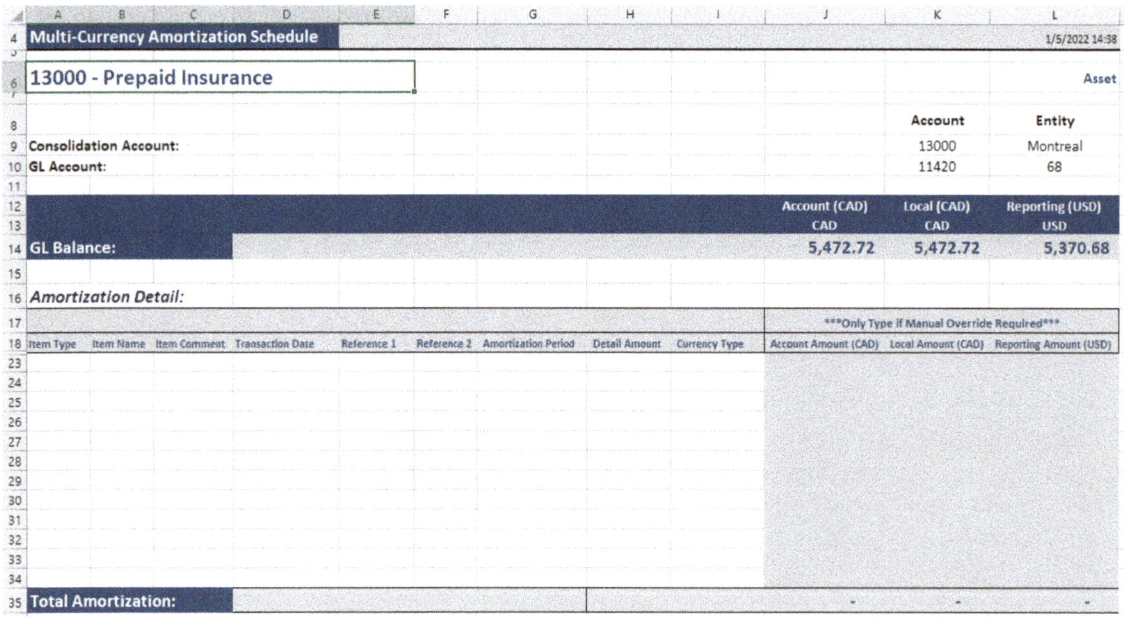

Figure 4.86

Upon downloading the template, you will prepare the schedule, save the file outside of the application, and close the file from Excel. The file cannot be opened in Excel when uploading. To load the schedule template, select the S-Doc icon.

Figure 4.87

The load process for the schedule template is similar to the period template process, in that it will read the detail items and populate the system. However, this template will also read the amortization period and load the items into all periods within the file. Future period Reconciliations must be in the In Process state in order for the upload to be successful. The items created in the system will be denoted with a Reconciliation Item Type of S. All S items will have the same booked period, based on the period the file was uploaded. Also, the template will automatically be attached in the Reconciliation support screen, and it will be denoted with an S, indicating that it came from the S-Doc load. The S-Doc is presented at the Reconciliation level and will appear regardless of the detail item selected. The S-Doc will also be attached to all the future periods where an item was created.

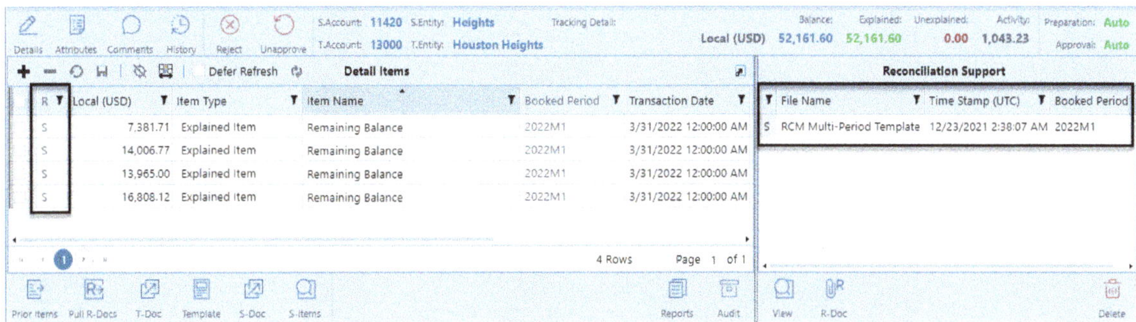

Figure 4.88

Below are a few items to consider when using the schedule template.

- Only one multi-period template can be loaded in a specific Reconciliation for a specific period. If you attempt to import a secondary multi-period template within the same period, the system will delete the existing items and create new items based on the secondary template. In addition, the existing template attached for the period will be replaced with the second template.
- The S-Doc should be loaded into the oldest Reconciliation period defined in the schedule. Example: if your file has items from 2022M1 through 2022M12, you should load the schedule into the 2022M1 Reconciliation. If you are starting the Reconciliation in period 2022M3, then you should only load values for 2022M3 and forward. It is not recommended that you load into historical periods.
- If, in a future period, your schedule should change or need to be updated, you can load an updated file. The file should contain the current period to be updated and any future periods accordingly.
- The amortization period field requires a specific format. The field should reflect the period that you want to load into, along with an exclamation point added to the beginning of the syntax as follows: !2022M3, !2022M4, !2022M5, etc.
- The S-doc will only be added to current and future periods. The document will not attach to historical periods even if historical items are part of the schedule. Again, if you have historical periods, you should load the S-Doc into the oldest period within the schedule.
- S items cannot be loaded into future periods where the Reconciliation is in the Prepared state, the Workflow is marked complete, or where the period is locked.

- Auto Reconciliation for S items will only occur for future periods. This is for control purposes. The first period the schedule is loaded into requires manual review and sign-off. This is to ensure that the schedule is accurate. Once validated, it is assumed that future periods are accurate and can be properly auto reconciled.

Balance Check

Balance Check is the ability to confirm the General Ledger balance using an independent source that has been loaded into the system through the **Data Management Import** process. As part of the Reconciliation, the Balance Check amount will compare to the General Ledger balance and can auto reconcile if the Unexplained balance is within the threshold set automating the Reconciliation preparation and Workflow.

Balance Check can be used for any source (including third-party sources) in which the first step the Preparer takes is to affirm the General Ledger to a Report or set of information. Examples include: Subledgers, Subsystems, Bank Sources, Payroll Processors, Third-Party Service Providers, Investment Statements, etc.

The Balance Check import leverages the application data integration functionality and can be loaded either via a flat file or **Direct Connect**. The level of detail loaded from the independent source is up to the organization. You can load ending balances, transaction-level detail, or anything in between – like customer or vendor level, etc. The import process is typically done independently of the Preparer.

When a Reconciliation is set up as a Balance Check, the T-Doc and S-Doc functionality will no longer be visible at the bottom of the detail items grid and is replaced with the Pull B-Chk and Go To B-Chk icons.

Figure 4.89

When imported, the Balance Check can automatically pull into the Reconciliation or be pulled in manually by the User. To automatically pull the Balance Check into the Reconciliation, the Reconciliation must be linked to an AutoRec Rule and Process must be run for the period. However, you can also manually pull in the Balance Check amount by selecting the Pull B-Chk icon.

> **Note:** The data must be loaded into the system via the import process in order for the Balance Check amount to pull into the Reconciliation. Balance Check items are denoted as a B Reconciliation Item Type. Also, note that the Balance Check can be updated after the initial load. If the Balance Check data changes, and a new pull occurs (either automatically or manually), the existing B items will be removed and the system will create the new Balance Check items accordingly.

Balance Check functionality can be done for single-currency or multi-currency Reconciliations. If the Balance Check is loaded for a single-currency Reconciliation, the balance loaded will be assumed to be in the Local currency of the Reconciliation. For multi-currency Reconciliations, the Balance Check is expected to be loaded in the transactional currency. The data should contain the amount along with the currency code. Upon load, the system will summarize the transactions creating a balance by currency code. The Reconciliation will display a balance for each currency code and translate the respective balance to the Account, Local, and Reporting amounts. Balance Check also supports overrides which means if the organization would like to also load the translated Account, Local, or Reporting balances from the source, the loaded balance will supersede the Translation and the override column will indicate the balances were overridden.

An example of a Balance Check Reconciliation is shown below.

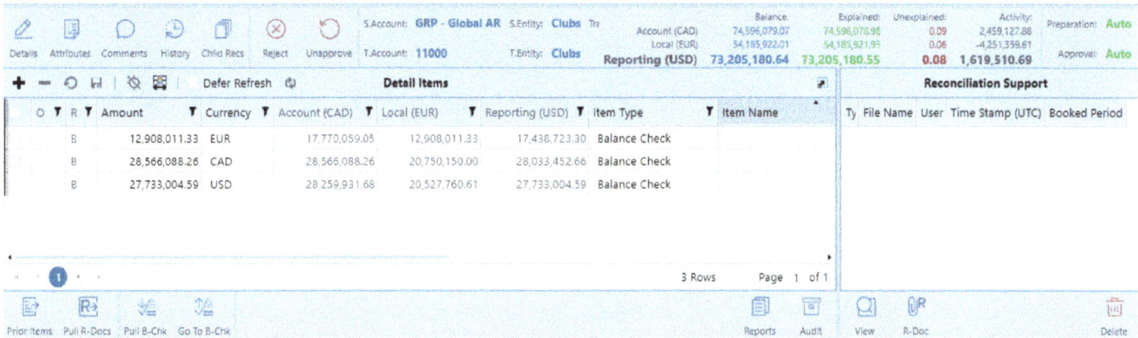

Figure 4.90

Transaction Matching Items

Transaction Matching is another solution within OneStream Financial Close that is available to assist in the preparation of a Reconciliation. There are many different Accounts that lend themselves to the matching process. The most common use cases are Bank to GL, Credit Cards, Subledgers (AR/AP), Suspense, and Intercompany, to name a few. There really is no limitation. Anywhere you are sifting through high volumes of transactions to identify Unmatched items, Transaction Matching can assist.

How I tend to determine if an Account is a good candidate for matching is if there are significant transactions being analyzed, the criteria being used to match or clear items is *consistent* period over period (i.e., the Match Rules), and the Reconciliation is normally derived from the uncleared or open items. In these scenarios, you can set up Transaction Matching to automate the creation of the detail items and AutoRec the Reconciliation if the matching items tie out to the General Ledger balance within the threshold set.

Item creation can occur either through the push process – where transactions are pushed from the Transaction Matching Match Set to the Reconciliation, or through the pull process – which pulls transactions manually from within the Reconciliation. Both options are available to you and are used in different situations. Either way – push or pull – the system automates the creation of items, eliminating a lot of manual work. In this section, we will walk through the pull process, which is done from the Reconciliation point of view. The Transaction Matching process, plus push capabilities, will be discussed in detail within the Transaction Matching Chapters 5-8.

To pull transactions into a Reconciliation, the Reconciliation must be associated or linked to Match Sets. Once a Reconciliation has at least one Match Set associated with it, the Reconciliation view will change to include two new icons: Match Item and Match Set.

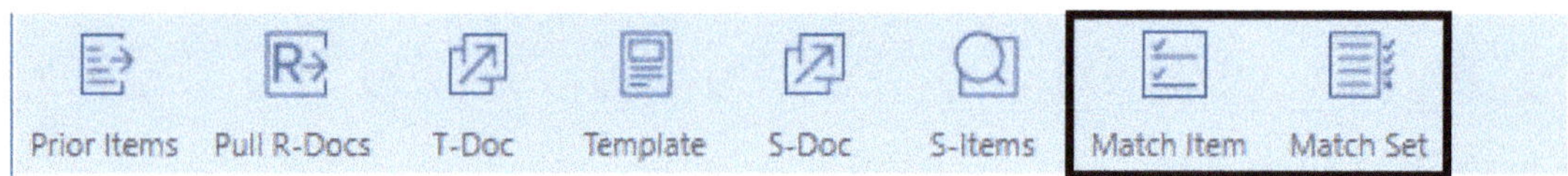

Figure 4.91

In the following example, we will be working with a Bank to General Ledger Match Set. In this scenario, the Unmatched transactions represent timing items (deposits in transit, outstanding checks, wires, bank fees, NSFs, etc.) that support the General Ledger balance. All Unmatched transactions will need to be pulled into the Reconciliation as detail items.

To pull an item from Transaction Matching, select the Match Item icon.

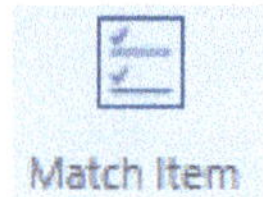

Figure 4.92

The system will launch the Create Detail Items dialog box, which displays the transactions from the data sets associated with the Match Set. In this example, there are two data sets, DS1, which is the General Ledger transactions, and DS2, which represents the bank transactions. In the screenshot below, we are looking at the Unmatched transactions.

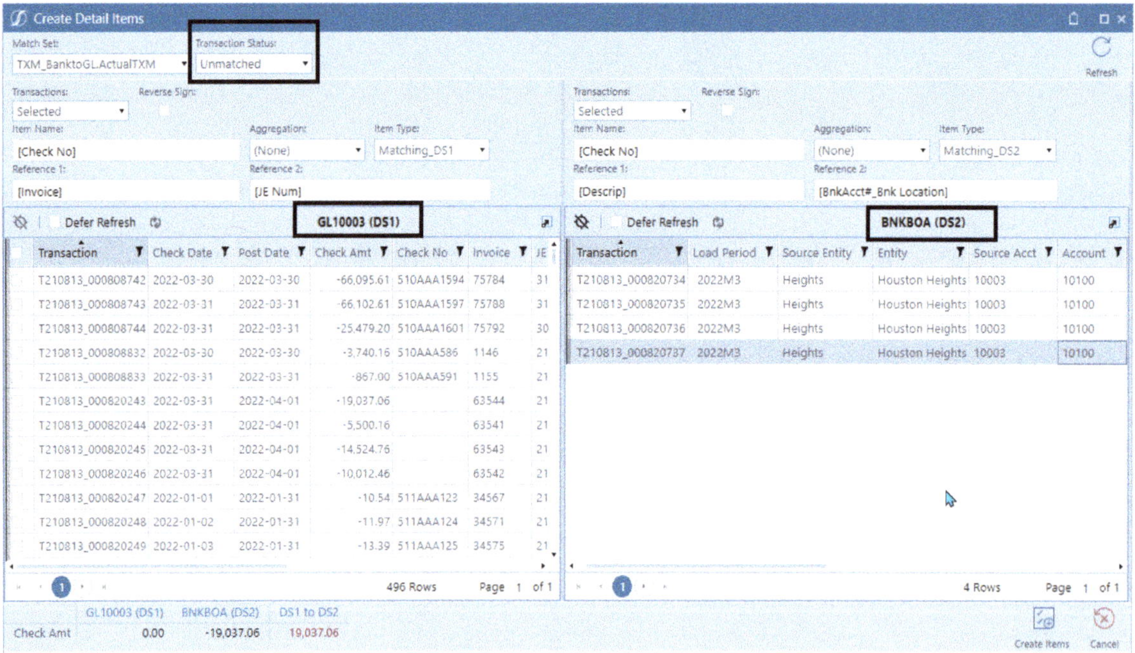

Transaction	Check Date	Post Date	Check Amt	Check No	Invoice	JE
T210813_000808742	2022-03-30	2022-03-30	-66,095.61	510AAA1594	75784	31
T210813_000808743	2022-03-31	2022-03-31	-66,102.61	510AAA1597	75788	31
T210813_000808744	2022-03-31	2022-03-31	-25,479.20	510AAA1601	75792	30
T210813_000808832	2022-03-30	2022-03-30	-3,740.16	510AAA586	1146	21
T210813_000808833	2022-03-31	2022-03-31	-867.00	510AAA591	1155	21
T210813_000820243	2022-03-31	2022-04-01	-19,037.06		63544	21
T210813_000820244	2022-03-31	2022-04-01	-5,500.16		63541	21
T210813_000820245	2022-03-31	2022-04-01	-14,524.76		63543	21
T210813_000820246	2022-03-31	2022-04-01	-10,012.46		63542	21
T210813_000820247	2022-01-01	2022-01-31	-10.54	511AAA123	34567	21
T210813_000820248	2022-01-02	2022-01-31	-11.97	511AAA124	34571	21
T210813_000820249	2022-01-03	2022-01-31	-13.39	511AAA125	34575	21

Transaction	Load Period	Source Entity	Entity	Source Acct	Account
T210813_000820734	2022M3	Heights	Houston Heights	10003	10100
T210813_000820735	2022M3	Heights	Houston Heights	10003	10100
T210813_000820736	2022M3	Heights	Houston Heights	10003	10100
T210813_000820737	2022M3	Heights	Houston Heights	10003	10100

Figure 4.93

The transactions within the Create Detail Items dialog box are specific to the Reconciliation from which the icon was selected. Although the data sets contain transactions that cross many Entities and Accounts, the system is filtering the data sets to only include the transactions associated with this Reconciliation. In addition, the dialog box contains a set of options that can be set by the Preparer prior to creating the detail items. Each option is defined in Figure 4.94.

Field	Definition
Match Set	Main drop-down menu to toggle between Match Sets associated with the Reconciliation. The transactions that appear within each data set grid are dependent on the Match Set selected within the drop-down.
Transaction Status	Identifies the types of transactions being displayed, Unmatched or Matched. By default, the drop-down is set to Unmatched.
Match Reason Code*	Allows Users to filter the transactions in both data sets based on the Reason Code assigned to the match.
Match Period*	Filters the Workflow period of when the match occurred either by the system rules or manually by a User. The selections available are All, Current, or Future. This filter is used for cutoff purposes, to be discussed below.
Import Period*	Filters the Workflow period of when the transactions were loaded into Transaction Matching. This is limited to the current period and any historical periods. This filter is used for cutoff purposes, to be discussed below.
Transactions	Drop-down contains the selection options for the data set: • Selected (Default) – Indicates that the transactions selected via the multi-select box in the grid will be pulled into the Reconciliation. Selections can be made across multiple pages as needed. • (All) – Regardless of the transactions selected in the grid, all transactions – across all pages – will be pulled into the Reconciliation. • (None) – Regardless of the transactions selected in the grid, no transactions will be pulled into the Reconciliation for that data set.
Reverse Sign	Reverse sign is applied to the amount fields mapped (Detail Amount, Account, Local, and Reporting) so that it will display the value in the opposite direction for Reconciliation purposes. If the value is a positive $2,000 and reverse sign is selected, the value will pull into the Reconciliation as a negative -$2,000.
Item Name	Mapped from the Match Set, the item name will populate based on the field identified. The field name is denoted within the brackets, e.g., [Check No]. Users can override the field by typing into the box. If the User overrides, the typed information will populate to all the transactions pulled. If Aggregation is set to the date field or Total (where multiple item names can exist), or if the item name field is left blank, the item name will default to Transaction Matching Item because the item name field must be populated when the item is created. Also, note that if the field is overridden, it cannot be reset by the User by typing in the field name with the brackets. To reset it back to the mapped field, the User will need to close the Create Detail Item dialog and relaunch.
Aggregation	Aggregation is the ability to sum transactions in a meaningful way. This will minimize the number of transactions presented in the detail items grid on the Reconciliation. Transactions will aggregate for each data set independently. If the Reconciliation is a single-currency Reconciliation, the system will aggregate first based on the currency codes prior to performing the Aggregation defined below. Although aggregating, the detail is not lost. From the Reconciliation, the User can drill back to the

Field	Definition
	transaction detail using the Drill Back icon in the Reconciliation Support screen. Aggregation is highly encouraged for high-volume Accounts. Possible Aggregation methods are as follows: • None – Each transaction selected will be pulled into the Reconciliation and create a distinct detail item. Typically, utilized on lower volume Accounts. • Total – Summarizes all transactions selected to a single, detail item aggregated by currency codes. If the Reconciliation is a single-currency Reconciliation, there will be one detail item for each data set from which transactions are pulled. If the Reconciliation is multi-currency, the system will first sum the transactions by currency code and pull the items into the Reconciliation, creating a detail item for each currency code and data set combination. The Total Aggregation option is used when there are a significant number of open items. Although the items will be aggregated, there is still drill down capability. However, if aging on the Reconciliation is important, the User should not use Total because the transaction dates are not considered upon Aggregation. When the item is created, the transaction date for the detail item will default to the month-end date. • Transaction Date – Summarizes the items based on the transaction date field identified in the Match Set mapping. The system will create a detail item for each unique transaction date and currency code combination (if multi-currency is used). This still minimizes the number of items created, but also supports aging on the Reconciliation. • Item Name – Summarizes the items based on the Item Name field identified in the Match Set mapping. The system will create a detail item for all transactions with the same item name and currency code combination. This will minimize the number of items created but also loses the aging as the transaction date on the items will default to the month-end date.
Item Type	Presents the Item Type list created by the organization. By default, the Item Type is set to Matching_DS1, 2, or 3, depending on the data set being referenced. However, the User can select any Item Type from their drop-down prior to pulling the items into the Reconciliation.
Reference 1	Mapped from the Match Set, the Reference 1 field will populate, based on the fields identified (up to two fields can be assigned). The field name is denoted within the brackets, e.g., [Invoice]. Users can override the field by typing into the box. If the User overrides, the typed information will populate to all transactions pulled. If Aggregation is used, the reference field will be replaced with the data set name and transaction status (Matched or Unmatched). If the Reference Field mapping is deleted and the field left blank – regardless as to whether you aggregate or not – the Reference Field will appear blank when pulled into the Reconciliation. Also, note that if the field is overridden, it cannot be reset by the User typing in the field name. To reset it back to the mapped field, the User will need to close the Create Detail Item dialog and relaunch.
Reference 2	Mapped from the Match Set, the Reference 2 field will populate based on the field identified (up to two fields can be assigned). The field name

Field	Definition
	is denoted within the brackets, e.g., [JE Num]. Users can override the field by typing into the box. If the User overrides, the typed information will populate to all transactions pulled. If Aggregation is used, the Reference Field will be replaced with how the transactions were selected (All versus Selected) and the Aggregation method utilized. If the Reference Field mapping is deleted and the field left blank – regardless as to whether you aggregate or not – the Reference Field will appear blank when pulled into the Reconciliation. Also, note that if the field is overridden, it cannot be reset by the User typing in the field name. To reset it back to the mapped field, the User will need to close the Create Detail Item dialog and relaunch.
* Only visible if Matched is selected in the Transaction Status drop-down.	

Figure 4.94

Set your options and select the transactions to be pulled. If you select the transactions directly from the data set grids, the totals at the bottom will update for informational purposes.

	GL10003 (DS1)	BNKBOA (DS2)	DS1 to DS2
Check Amt	-510,858.300	-49,074.440	-461,783.860

Figure 4.95

The data set totals are not necessary and only provide you with information about the selected transactions as you move from page to page. If you do not want to select transactions directly from the data set grid but prefer to use the None or All Transaction option, the totals at the bottom will not update. This is by design.

Once you have all the options and selections made, you will select the Create Item icon in the bottom-right corner of the dialog box. You will then be navigated back to the Reconciliation and the new detail items will appear in the detail items grid. Depending on the Aggregation option selected, you may see one or more lines with a Reconciliation type of X indicating it originated from Transaction Matching. See Figures 4.96-4.99 for the different Aggregation views.

Aggregation: None (created 500 detail items):

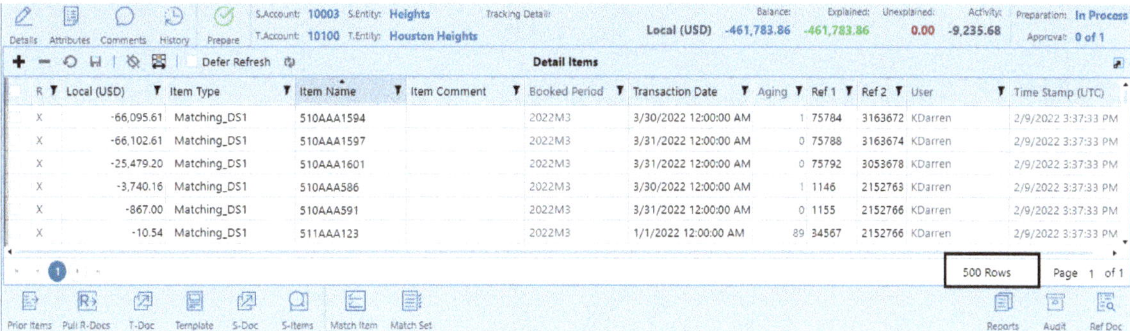

Figure 4.96

Aggregation: Total (created 2 detail items):

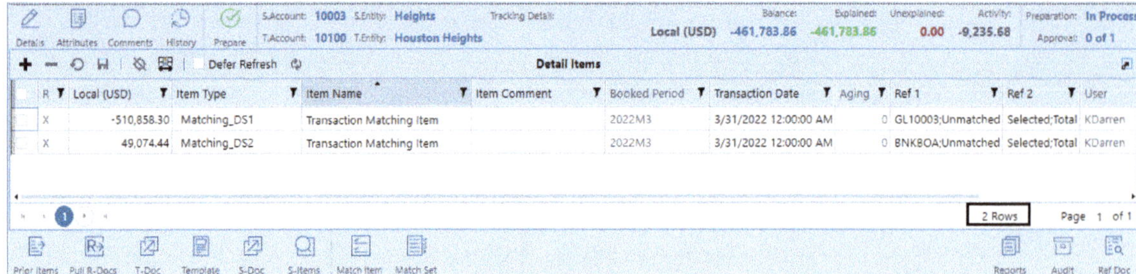

Figure 4.97

Aggregation: Transaction Date (created 94 detail items):

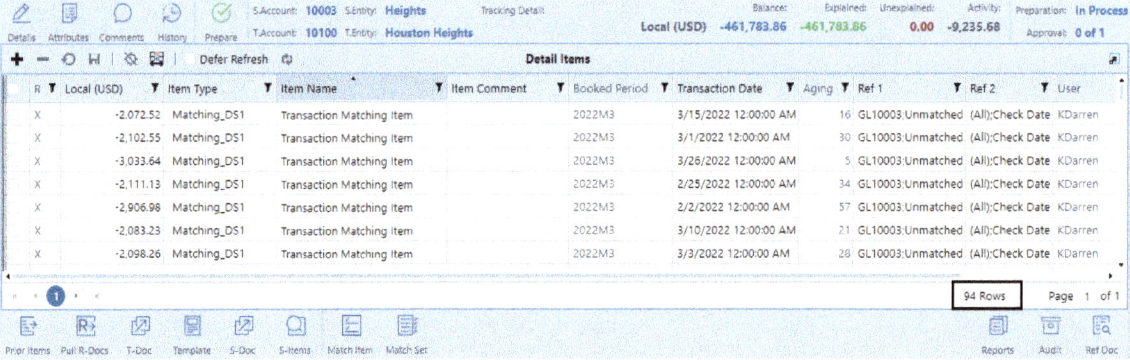

Figure 4.98

Aggregation: Item Name (created 497 detail items)

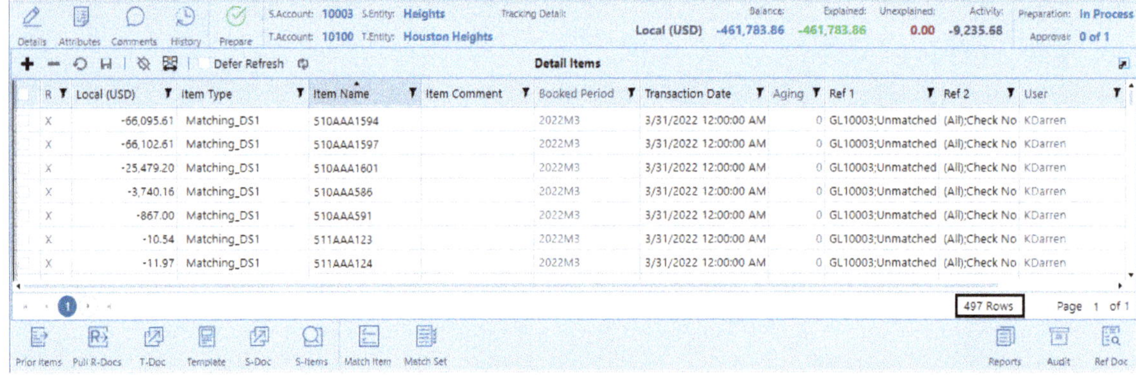

Figure 4.99

Within the Reconciliation, if you select an X-type detail item, the Drill Back icon will appear on the Reconciliation Support screen.

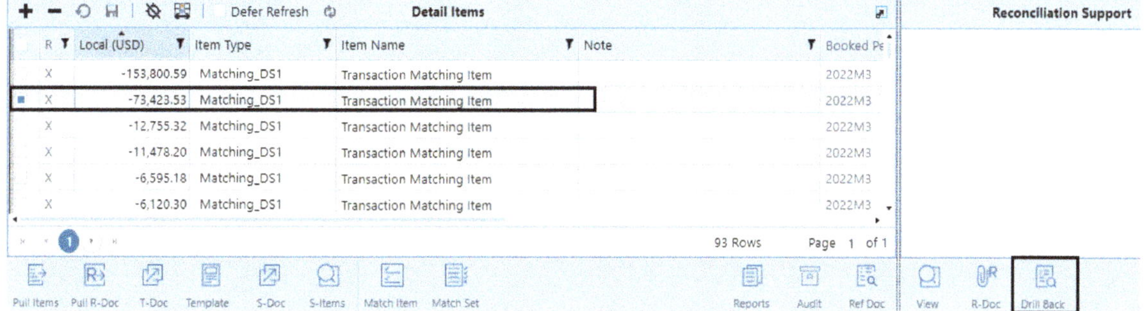

Figure 4.100

If you select the Drill Back icon, you will be taken to the Transaction Drill Back page, which will display the transaction and all the additional Transaction Matching data fields. Also, if the detail item is an Aggregation of transactions, you will see all the underlying transactions and related detail upon drill back, as shown below.

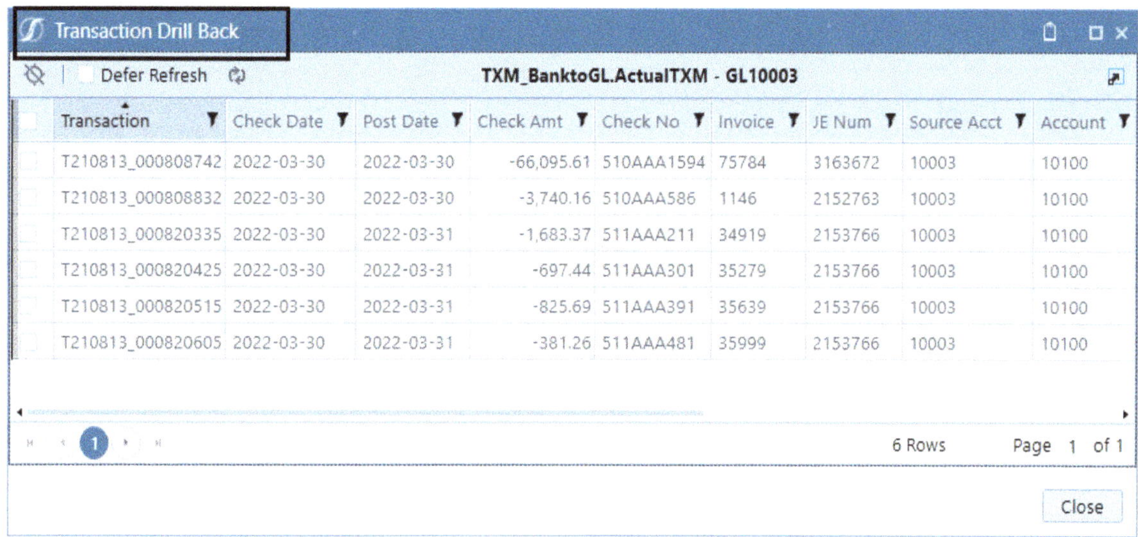

Figure 4.101

There are several things to note when pulling items from Transaction Matching.

1. Transactions from a Match Set can only be pulled into a Reconciliation once in a given period. Once pulled into the Reconciliation (Matched or Unmatched), the transactions will be removed from the Create Item dialog box for that period.
2. Matched transactions can be pulled into the Reconciliation to capture variances. If your rules allow for an amount tolerance, the match variance may need to be pulled into the Reconciliation as a detail item. To capture the variance, all Matched transactions from all data sets must be pulled into the Reconciliation (at whatever Aggregation desired) to properly calculate the variance amount. Note, you may need to reverse the sign on one of the data sets to net to the proper amount.
3. Transaction Matching is a continuous process. Although data is loaded into a specific period, and rules are run, the Unmatched transactions are not time-based. If you have an Unmatched transaction from 2022M2 that was Matched at the beginning of 2022M3, it will no longer appear Unmatched when viewing the 2022M2 transactions. This means – depending on the timing of when the 2022M2 Reconciliation is completed – we need to understand what was Unmatched at a point in time to provide proper cutoff. To determine cutoff, it is a two-step process. First, you will pull in the Unmatched transactions. Second,

you will select Matched in the Transaction Status filter and then select Future Periods from the Match Period filter drop down. This will return all current and historical transactions that were Matched in a future period (i.e., had matching not run in the future, the transactions would appear Unmatched in the current period). For a more detailed explanation of cutoff, and to view an example, please see the Matched View section in Chapter 8.

4. Transactions created from Transaction Matching cannot be pulled or copied, period over period, using the prior items function.
5. Transactions can be Deleted from the current Reconciliation if the Reconciliation is not yet in the Prepared state. To delete, you will select the specific X items, then select the Delete Row icon, and, finally, select Save. Items Deleted from the Reconciliation do not impact Transaction Matching but will be released back into the Create Detail Item dialog box.
6. Transaction Matching items can be set to auto reconcile. This is typically done in conjunction with the push process, but can be used for the pull process as well. If the Reconciliation is set with the appropriate Auto Reconciliation Rule, the transaction items have been created, the Unexplained balance is within the threshold set, and Process is initiated – the Reconciliation can auto certify.
7. I-Docs cannot be added to X items.

Roles and Responsibilities

We have covered a great deal of information thus far regarding how a Reconciliation can be prepared within the system and different ways we can automate the process. In the next section, I would like to focus on the responsibilities of the different roles. We will walk through *who* does what within the system, *when* the step is typically performed, and *why* the User may perform that step. We will be looking at this from the User perspective, covering the Preparer, Approver, Viewer, Commenter, and Auditor roles. The Administrator roles and a more detailed look at Security can be found in the Administration Chapter (2).

Preparer

The Preparer role is key in any Reconciliation process. These Users have ultimate responsibility for analyzing and creating detail items, attaching the appropriate supporting documentation, and adding commentary as needed. These steps were discussed in the previous section and ultimately initiate the Reconciliation process.

However, a Reconciliation is not considered Prepared until the User signs off on their work. The sign-off process attests that the Preparer performed the Reconciliation in compliance with the company's policy and procedures. Preparers are required to sign-off on the Reconciliation within the due date set. If a User misses the Reconciliation due date, the company is at risk, from a control perspective, creating an audit exposure.

The sign-off is tracked in the system for audit purposes, along with the date and time stamp the sign-off occurred. Electronic sign-off is ultimately what moves the Reconciliation from the In Process state to the Prepared state, locking down the Reconciliation so no additional changes can occur. Additional commentary can be added by other roles, but from a Preparer perspective, no additional changes can be made once the Reconciliation is in the Prepared state. The User initiates sign-off by selecting the Prepare icon.

Figure 4.102

When signing off on the Reconciliation, there is the option to acknowledge **Certification Language** and the ability to add comments that are either optional or required. If these features are turned on, the Preparer will receive a dialog box when they select the Prepare icon.

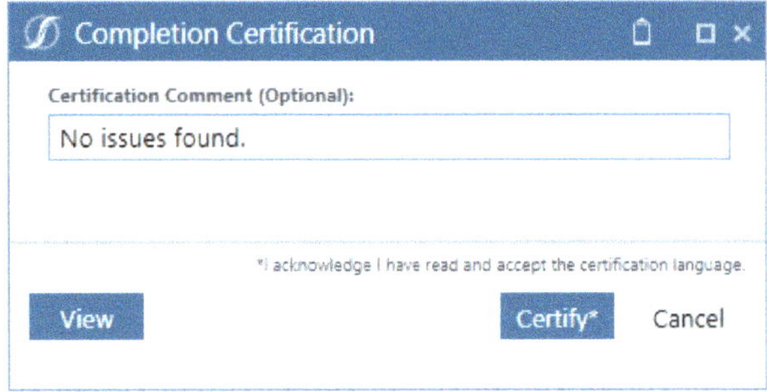

Figure 4.103

Comments can be added by typing into the Certification Comment field. These comments are stored within the audit trail on the History page, as shown below.

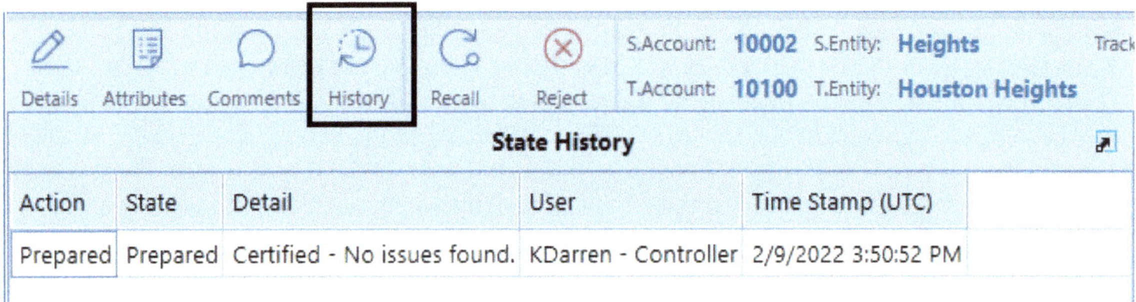

Figure 4.104

To view the certification language, the User will select the View button in the bottom-left corner of the Completion Certification dialog box. This action will display the certification dialog. Once read, the box can be closed and the User will be taken back to the Completion Certification dialog.

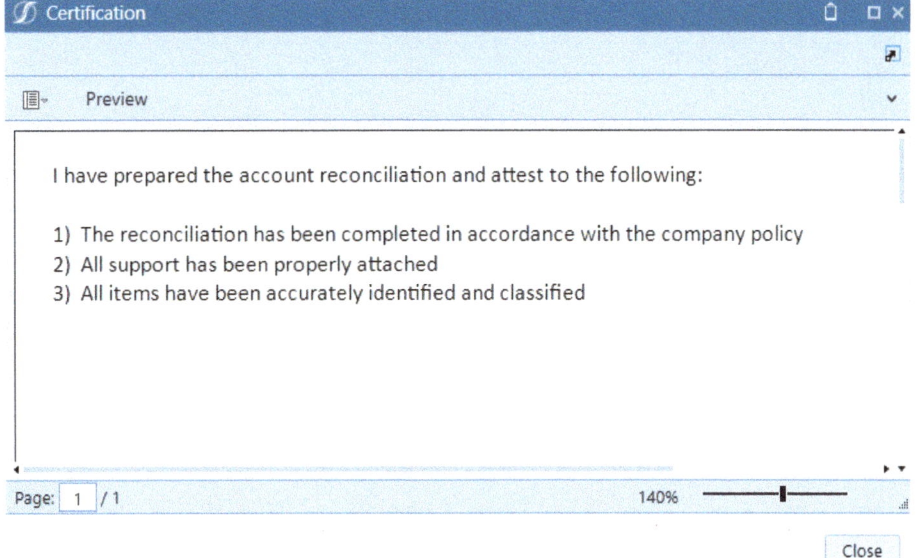

Figure 4.105

Upon sign-off, the Reconciliation moves into the Prepared state and an email alert can be sent to the Approver indicating that the Reconciliation is ready for them to review. At this point, the Preparer will move on to other Reconciliations as no further work will be required unless the Approver finds an issue or the balance changes.

However, there may be a situation requiring a User to update a Reconciliation before it is Approved. If the User needs to add a document, correct a spelling error, or add additional commentary, the Reconciliation will need to be recalled. Preparers can recall a Reconciliation using the Recall icon, as long as the Reconciliation has not yet been Approved. The Recall process will unlock the Reconciliation and move it to the In Process state, allowing the User to update it. The Recall process is also captured in the audit trail.

Figure 4.106

If, however, the Reconciliation is Approved, the User will need to contact the Approver or Administrator so that it can be Rejected or Unapproved and then Recalled.

From a Preparer's perspective, outside of the Recall process there are other situations (as mentioned previously) that may unlock a Reconciliation and put it back into the User to-do list. The Reconciliation might be Rejected by the Approver upon their review. Also, the Reconciliation may be put back into process if a new trial balance is loaded and the balance associated with this Account has subsequently changed. In both scenarios, Rejected or Balance Changed, the state of the Reconciliation will be updated, and the Reconciliation will be routed back to the Preparer. Email alerts can also be sent to the Preparer, notifying them of the change that has occurred. Like the Prepared state, these other state changes are tracked on the History page with the User and date and time stamp.

Details Attributes Comments History Prepare S.Account: 10001 S.Entity: Heights Tracking Detail:
T.Account: 10100 T.Entity: Houston Heights

State History

Action	State	Detail	User	Time Stamp (UTC)
Balance Changed	Balance Changed		System	2/9/2022 3:23:26 PM
Prepared	Prepared	Certified	KDarren - Controller	2/9/2022 3:20:11 PM
Rejected	Rejected	More Detail Required	CC - Clubs Controller	2/9/2022 3:19:51 PM
Unapproved	Prepared	Other - Need to add c	CC - Clubs Controller	2/9/2022 3:19:02 PM
Approved	Fully Approved (1 of 1)		CC - Clubs Controller	2/9/2022 3:18:51 PM
Prepared	Prepared	Certified - No issues fc	KDarren - Controller	2/9/2022 3:17:36 PM
Recalled	In Process		KDarren - Controller	2/9/2022 3:17:08 PM
Prepared	Prepared	Certified	KDarren - Controller	2/9/2022 3:16:51 PM

Figure 4.107

Approver

Reconciliations typically require an approval process which is an independent review of the Reconciliation. The role of the Approver is to validate the work performed by the Preparer within the set due date. Because the Approver is required to be independent, this role cannot change any items, documents, or comments made by the Preparer for control purposes. The Approver can add additional Reconciliation-level commentary, but they cannot add or delete detail items or documents. If something needs to be updated, the Approver will need to Reject the Reconciliation back to the Preparer for updating. See the Comments section, above, for instructions on how to add Reconciliation-level comments.

If the review process is complete without issue, the Approver will need to sign-off. Similar to the Preparer, the sign-off process will move the Reconciliation into the Approved state. The electronic sign-off is done through the Approve icon, and the system stores the User, date, and time stamp on the History page for audit purposes.

Figure 4.108

If using the certification language, the Approver will also receive a dialog box that will allow them to add certification comments and view the Approver certification language. Once the Reconciliation is Approved, email alerts can be sent. We should note here that although you may have multiple roles in the process, a User will only be able to sign-off on a specific Reconciliation once, in a given period, as segregation of duties is enforced.

There are situations when, upon review, the Approver identifies an issue. In this case, it is recommended that the Approver rejects the Reconciliation. To reject, the Approver will select the Reject icon.

Figure 4.109

The Reject icon will prompt a Reject Reconciliation dialog box, requiring a Reason Code to be selected.

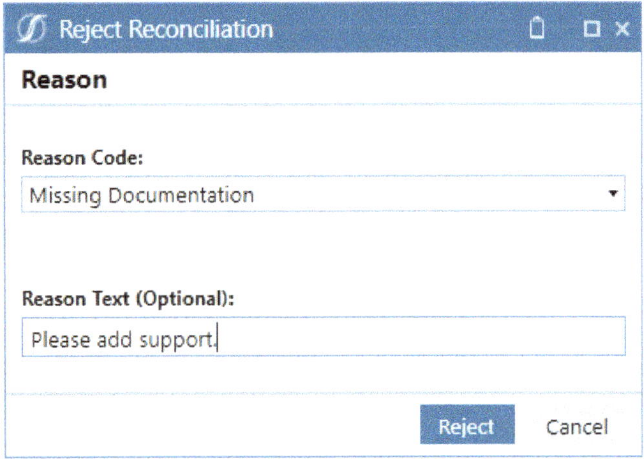

Figure 4.110

The Reason Code drop-down is defined by the organization and is used to create a standard list of rejection reasons from which Approvers can select. Understanding why Reconciliations are being Rejected helps the organization target training or process improvement opportunities. The Approver must select a Reason Code prior to selecting Reject. In addition, they also have the ability to add commentary in the Reason Text field to better communicate the changes or updates being requested. The rejection Reason Code and the Reason Text are included on the History page and in the rejection email if this notification type is enabled.

Another possible scenario for the Approver is the need to unapprove a Reconciliation. The unapprove process will send the Reconciliation to one state below. If multiple levels of approval exist, it will have one less level of approval. If only one level of approval is required, the Reconciliation will revert to the Prepared state. An Approver might want to unapprove a Reconciliation if it was Approved in error or additional commentary needs to be added. To unapprove, select the Unapprove icon.

Figure 4.111

This will prompt the Unapprove Reconciliation dialog box, requiring a Reason Code to be selected.

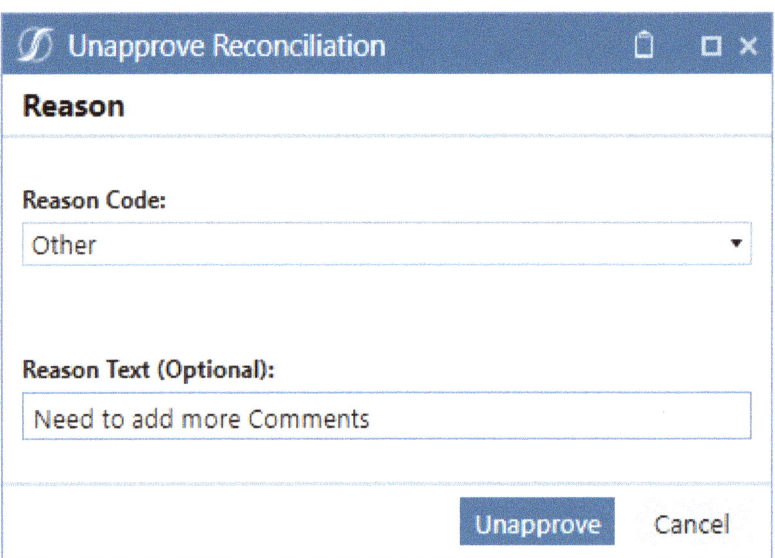

Figure 4.112

The Approver also has the ability to add commentary in the Reason Text field to better communicate why the Reconciliation was Unapproved. The unapprove Reason Code and the Reason Text are included in the History page and in the Unapproved email if this notification type is enabled.

As mentioned, the approval process is necessary to provide an independent review of the work performed by the Preparer. Although typically set to one level of approval, the system supports up to four levels of approval on any Reconciliation. Best practice is to assign additional levels of approval if the Reconciliation contains a critical Account or the activity in the Account is at risk of error or fraud. Levels 3 and 4 are typically utilized in situations where a company outsources the Reconciliation process. This allows the outsourcer to leverage an approval process (Levels 1 and 2) while still allowing the organization to approve the Reconciliations (Levels 3 and 4).

The number of approval levels is assigned by the Administrator on a Reconciliation basis. The Reconciliation must move through all the required levels of approval before it is considered Fully Approved. The number of required approval levels on a Reconciliation can be seen in the Reconciliation grid, the status section of the Reconciliation header, and on the Attributes page. The system will always report back to the User what level of approval the Reconciliation is currently in.

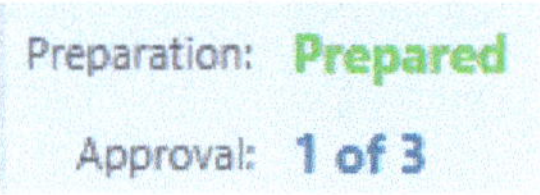

Preparation: **Prepared**
Approval: **1 of 3**

Figure 4.113

Viewer

The Viewer role provides the ability to access the details of Reconciliations without being able to make any changes. View access can be granted at the **Global** level – to access all Reconciliations – or granted at the **Access Group** level to limit the User to view only specific Reconciliations.

There are multiple reasons a User may need access to view Reconciliations. Management typically views Reconciliations to understand risk within the balances. The tax department may need information for tax filing purposes. The Consolidation team may use the Reconciliations to understand changes that impact Cash Flow. The FP&A team may use the Reconciliations to explain period over period variances. Granting access to view Reconciliations is of low risk because, as stated above, the view role cannot make changes but only view the information within.

Commenter

The Commenter role is very similar to the Viewer role but allows the User to add Reconciliation-level comments, regardless of the state of the Reconciliation. This role is normally granted to the Auditor to add comments, based on their review and testing performed. Also, we see this role used internally to evaluate the quality of Reconciliations. Upon review, the evaluator can add comments regarding possible improvements. Comments can then be reported on, as needed.

Auditor

The final role to discuss is the Auditor role. Auditors are a critical part of the Reconciliation process as they test to make sure all controls are properly in place. Allowing Auditors to access the system to perform their testing should improve the efficiency of the audit and reduce the amount of time Users spend gathering audit documentation.

This role is very similar to the Commenter role in that the Auditor can access the details of the Reconciliation and add Reconciliation-level commentary, but they cannot make any other changes. However, Auditors will only have access to Reconciliations in the Fully Approved or auto reconciled Approved state. Limiting their view to only Reconciliations that are fully through the process will ensure they are not evaluating Reconciliations that are not yet ready. This role can only be assigned by the System Administrator in the Global Options, and Users assigned to the Auditor role cannot have multiple roles within the solution for independence purposes. The Auditor role will override all other access except Administrator.

Reconciliation Reporting

Reporting is a critical part of the Reconciliation process. Typically, reporting is done around Reconciliation Status, Timing, Aging, Item Types, etc. The more you utilize the features to build your Reconciliations, the more robust your reporting will be. The solution delivers standard reporting and Dashboards but – in addition – you can leverage reporting functionality within the platform to create your own visualizations. Being able to create your own Reports allows you to create KPIs and risk analysis that is important to you and your organization.

To access reporting, select the Show Analysis and Reporting icon in the top-right corner of the Reconciliation Workspace.

Figure 4.114

You will be taken to the Scorecard page by default; however, you can navigate to any of the Reporting pages by utilizing the icons in the top-left of the header.

> **Note:** The information that you see within any of the delivered reporting will be dependent on the Workflow, period selected, and your security.

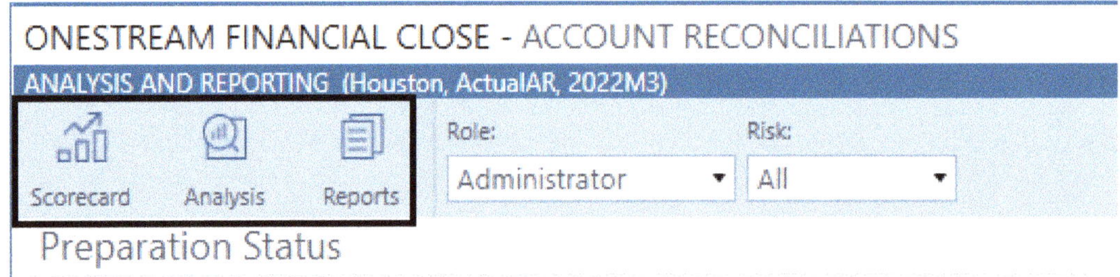

Figure 4.115

Scorecard

The Scorecard is a Dashboard that delivers multiple graphical views of the Reconciliation status with drill down capability to the underlying data.

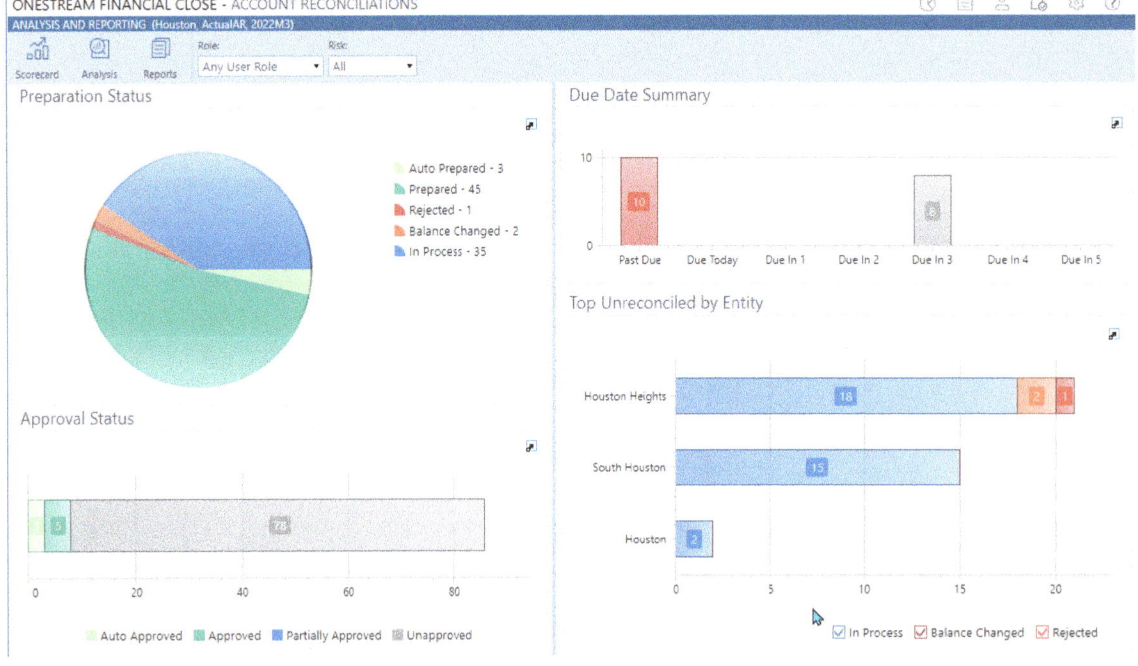

Figure 4.116

The graphs within this page can be filtered based on role and risk. The four graphical views are as follows:

- **Preparation Status** – Detail count of the number of Reconciliations in each state from a Preparer's perspective. The states include In Process, Balance Changed, Rejected, Prepared, and Auto Prepared. For those Reconciliations reported as Prepared, this includes all the Prepared Reconciliations regardless of the approval state.
- **Due Date Summary** – Chart displays a count of all Reconciliations Past Due, Due Today, and Due within the next five days. If you have Reconciliations due more than five days from now, they will not be included in the chart.
- **Approver Status** – Displays the number of Reconciliations in the various approval states, which includes Unapproved, Partially Approved, Auto Approved, and Fully Approved (manual sign-off).
- **Unreconciled by Entity** – Number of Reconciliations by Entity by Unprepared state (In Process, Balance Changed, or Rejected).

Analysis

The Analysis page has two Dashboards that you can toggle between 1. Reconciliation Exposure, or 2. Aging Pivot. Each of these Dashboards is intended to highlight areas of potential risk.

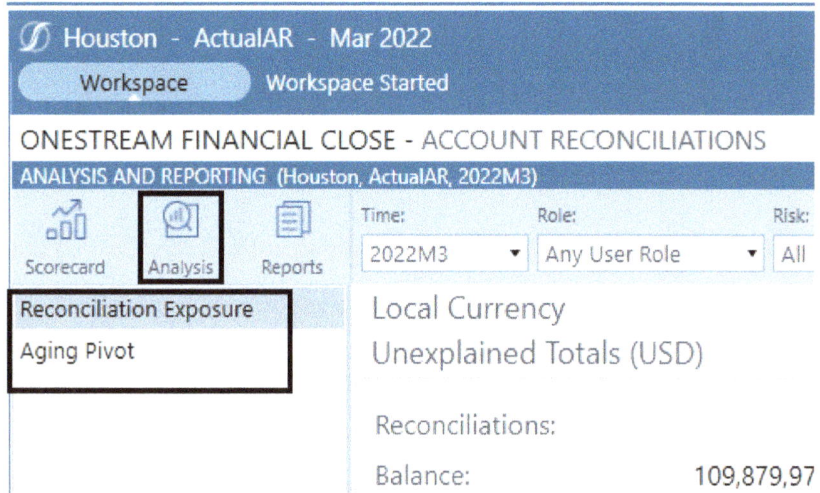

Figure 4.117

Reconciliation Exposure

The Reconciliation Exposure Dashboard displays information related to all unprepared Reconciliations in the past due state. This Dashboard contains calculated values as well as graphs that show the true exposure of incomplete Reconciliations. There are also additional filters at the top of the page to be able to view a specific Time, Role, Risk, Currency Level, and Currency Type.

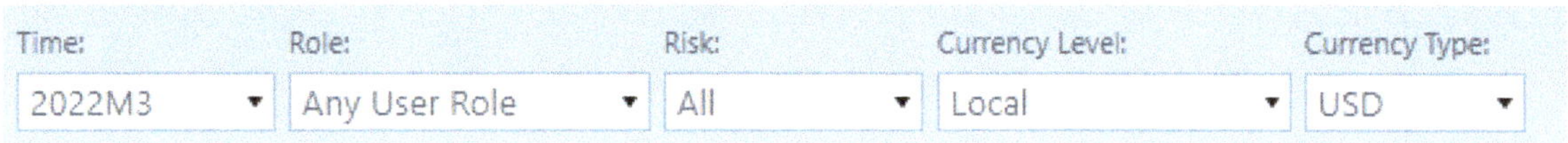

Figure 4.118

To understand what is being reported, we have detailed each visualization from the screenshot below.

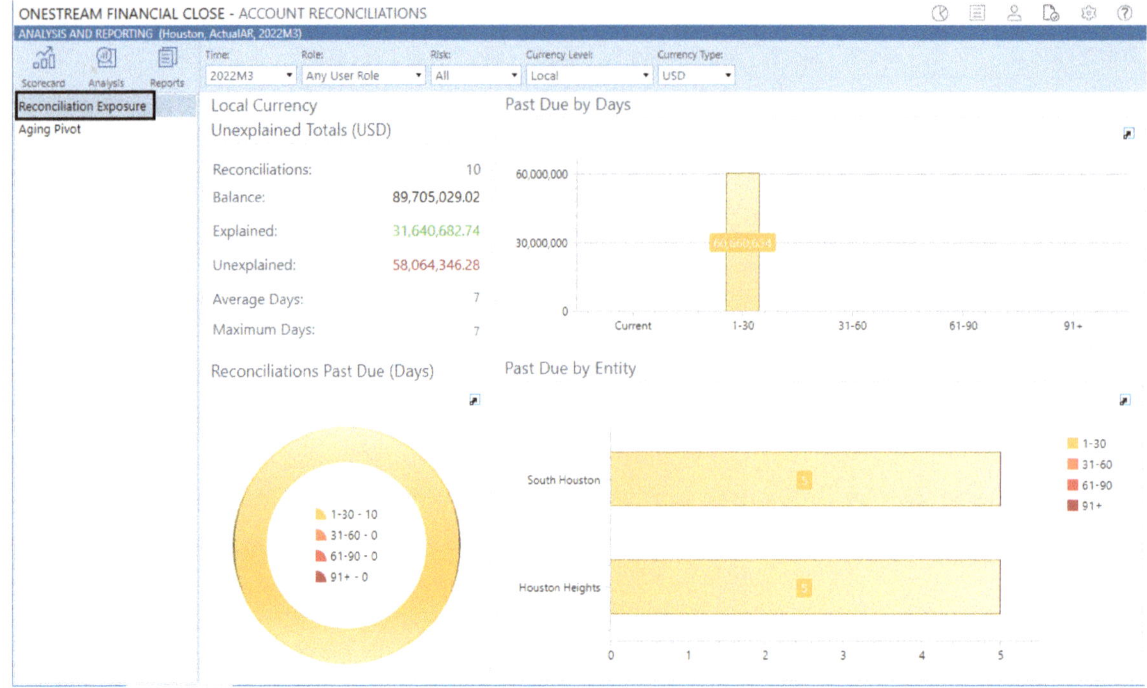

Figure 4.119

- Unexplained Totals Section
    - **Reconciliations** – Total number of past due unprepared Reconciliations
    - **Balance** – Total General Ledger balance for all past due unprepared Reconciliations
    - **Explained** – Represents the total explained balance for all past due unprepared Reconciliations
    - **Unexplained** – Balance minus Explained
    - **Average Days** – Sum of total past due days / total number of past due Reconciliations
    - **Maximum Days** – Number of days for the oldest past due unprepared Reconciliation
- **Past Due by Days** – Absolute value of total unexplained balance amount for unprepared Reconciliations presented in aging buckets based on the number of days past due
- **Reconciliation Past Due (Days)** – Total count of unprepared Reconciliations by aging buckets based on the number of days past due
- **Past Due by Entity** – Total count of unprepared Reconciliations by Entity by aging bucket based on the number of days past due

Aging Pivot

The Aging Pivot is one of my favorite reporting tools because it provides visibility to all of the detail items created for a specific period. By default, the pivot displays the total detail items by Entity, Currency Code, Account, and Aging bucket. You can update the row and column field selections, and all fields associated with an item are available. Also, you can filter on time to navigate to another period if desired.

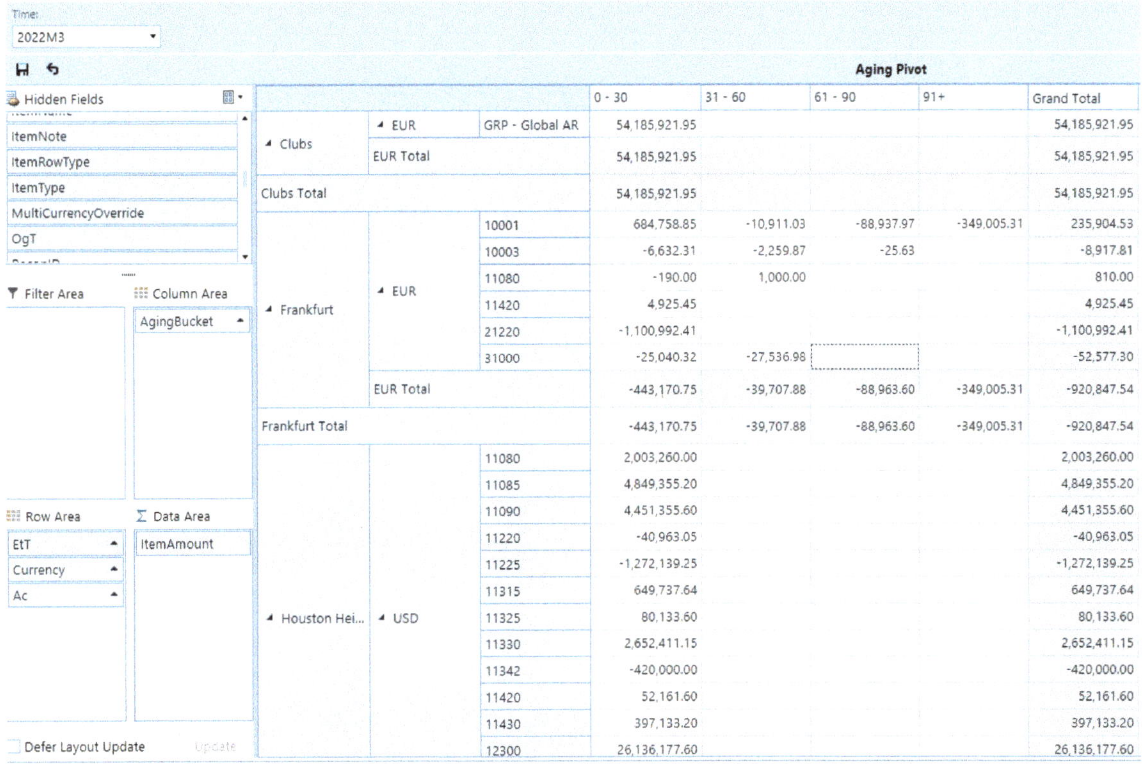

Time:
2022M3
Aging Pivot
Hidden Fields
ItemNote
ItemRowType
ItemType
MultiCurrencyOverride
OgT
Filter Area
Column Area
AgingBucket
Row Area
Data Area
EtT
Currency
Ac
ItemAmount
Defer Layout Update
Update
0 - 30
31 - 60
61 - 90
91+
Grand Total
Clubs
EUR
GRP - Global AR
54,185,921.95
54,185,921.95
EUR Total
54,185,921.95
54,185,921.95
Clubs Total
54,185,921.95
54,185,921.95
Frankfurt
EUR
10001
684,758.85
-10,911.03
-88,937.97
-349,005.31
235,904.53
10003
-6,632.31
-2,259.87
-25.63
-8,917.81
11080
-190.00
1,000.00
810.00
11420
4,925.45
4,925.45
21220
-1,100,992.41
-1,100,992.41
31000
-25,040.32
-27,536.98
-52,577.30
EUR Total
-443,170.75
-39,707.88
-88,963.60
-349,005.31
-920,847.54
Frankfurt Total
-443,170.75
-39,707.88
-88,963.60
-349,005.31
-920,847.54
Houston Hei...
USD
11080
2,003,260.00
2,003,260.00
11085
4,849,355.20
4,849,355.20
11090
4,451,355.60
4,451,355.60
11220
-40,963.05
-40,963.05
11225
-1,272,139.25
-1,272,139.25
11315
649,737.64
649,737.64
11325
80,133.60
80,133.60
11330
2,652,411.15
2,652,411.15
11342
-420,000.00
-420,000.00
11420
52,161.60
52,161.60
11430
397,133.20
397,133.20
12300
26,136,177.60
26,136,177.60

Figure 4.120

Using the drag and drop functionality, fields can be swapped in and out as needed. In addition, you can right-click on the blue bar above the pivot rows to launch the following options menu. You can update how totals are displayed, add Calculations, export, print, etc.

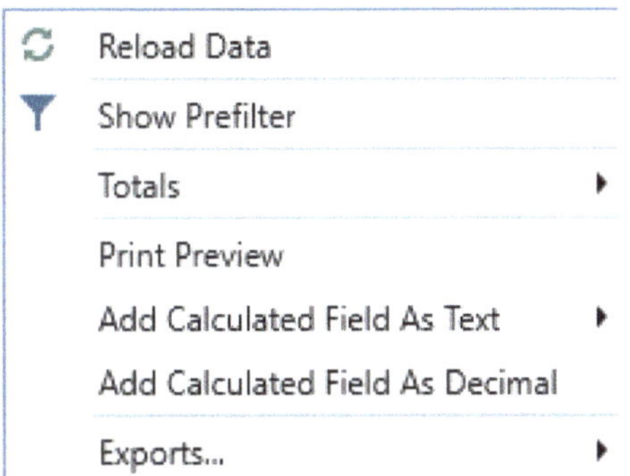

Figure 4.121

Also, if you select a cell within the pivot, you can right-click to add conditional formatting.

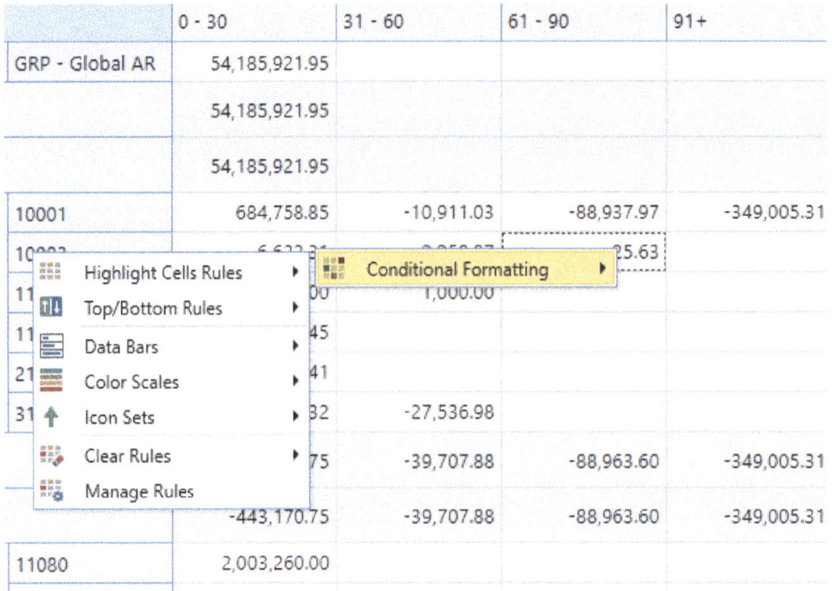

Figure 4.122

Once the Report is in the desired layout, you can select the Save button to make it your default. You can also reset to the default at any time, removing the saved format.

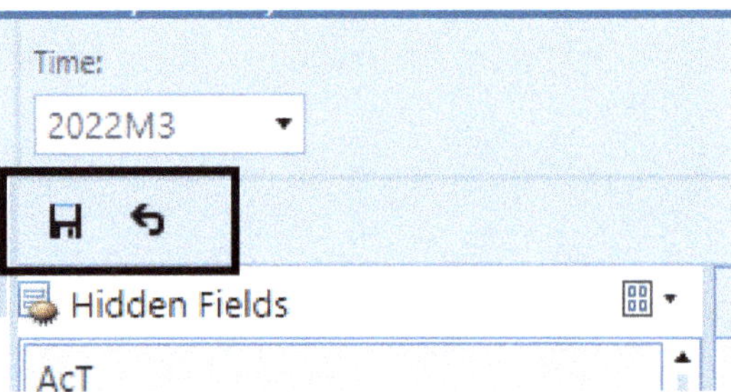

Figure 4.123

Reporting

The Reporting page contains the formatted Reports included with the solution. There are seven different Reports available with the ability to filter the Report information by Time, Role, State, and Currency Level.

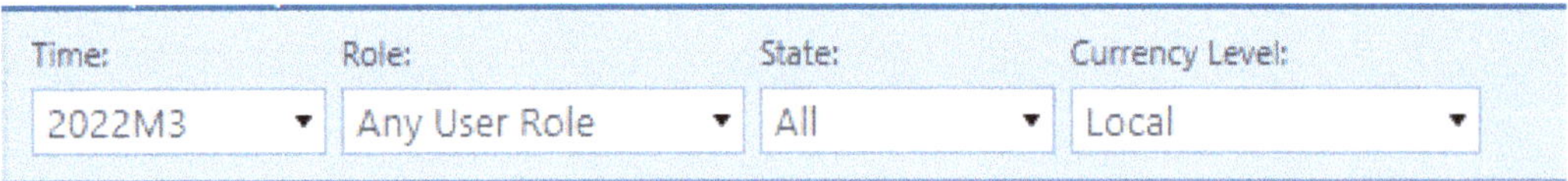

Figure 4.124

Below is a detailed definition for each Report, along with a screenshot.

Reconciliation State – Displays the Reconciliations by the different Workflow states with sign-off and time stamp information. The Report contains the key Reconciliation level, which includes: the OS Account, GL Account, OS Entity, and GL Entity, along with the Balance, Explained, Unexplained, and Activity Totals.

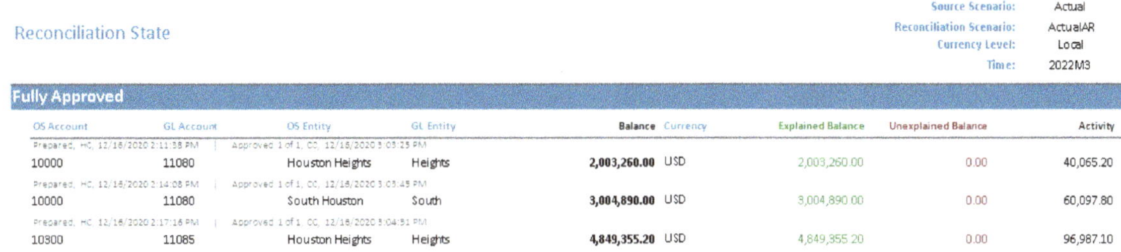

Figure 4.125

Reconciliation Detail – This Report is similar to the Reconciliation State Report, but it includes all Detail Items associated with the Reconciliation.

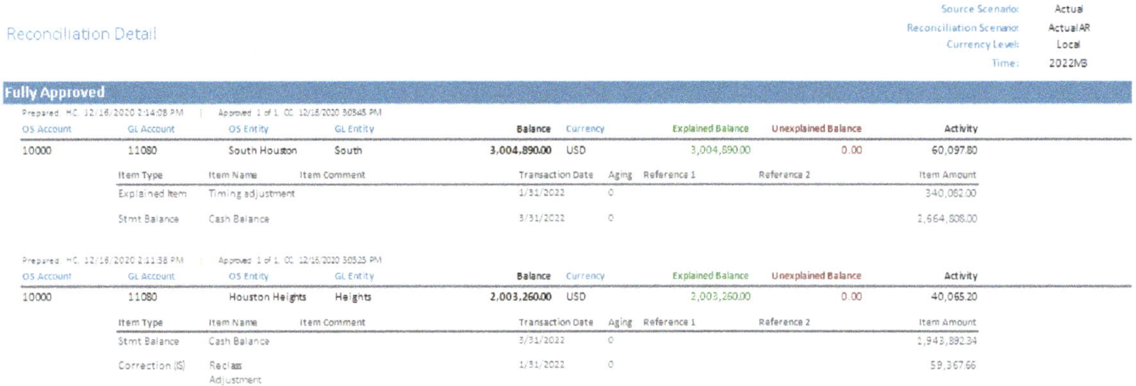

Figure 4.126

Reconciliation by Preparer – This Report is the Reconciliation Detail Report organized by the last User that updated the Preparation State.

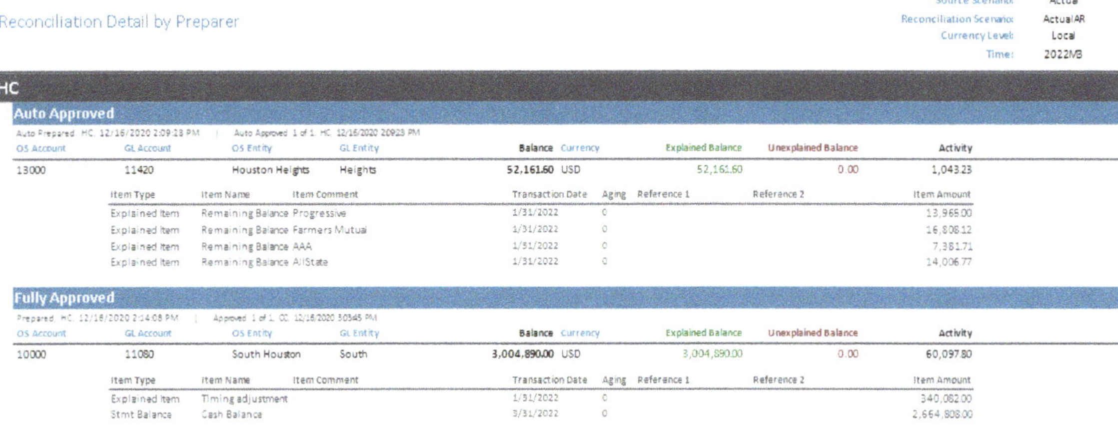

Figure 4.127

Reconciliation Risk Analysis – This Report is the Reconciliation State Report organized by assigned Risk Level and Account Type.

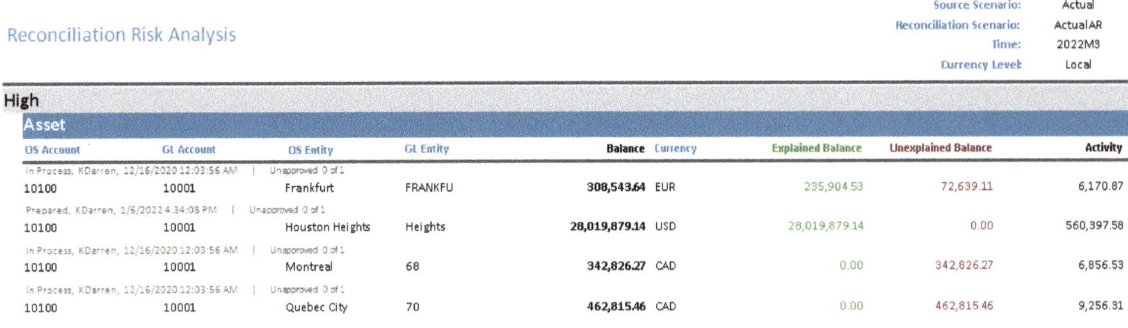

Reconciliation Risk Analysis

Source Scenario: Actual
Reconciliation Scenario: ActualAR
Time: 2022M3
Currency Level: Local

High

Asset

OS Account	GL Account	OS Entity	GL Entity	Balance	Currency	Explained Balance	Unexplained Balance	Activity
In Process, KDarren, 12/16/2020 12:03:56 AM | Unapproved 0 of 1								
10100	10001	Frankfurt	FRANKFU	**308,543.64**	EUR	235,904.53	72,639.11	6,170.87
Prepared, KDarren, 1/6/2022 4:34:08 PM | Unapproved 0 of 1								
10100	10001	Houston Heights	Heights	**28,019,879.14**	USD	28,019,879.14	0.00	560,397.58
In Process, KDarren, 12/16/2020 12:03:56 AM | Unapproved 0 of 1								
10100	10001	Montreal	68	**342,826.27**	CAD	0.00	342,826.27	6,856.53
In Process, KDarren, 12/16/2020 12:03:56 AM | Unapproved 0 of 1								
10100	10001	Quebec City	70	**462,815.46**	CAD	0.00	462,815.46	9,256.31

Figure 4.128

Reconciling Item Analysis – This is the Reconciliation Detail Report organized by Item Types.

Reconciling Item Analysis

Source Scenario: Actual
Reconciliation Scenario: ActualAR
Time: 2022M3
Currency Level: Local

Balance Check

Auto Prepared, Admin, 12/16/2020 1:08:05 AM | Auto Approved 1 of 1, Admin, 12/16/2020 1:08:08 AM

OS Account	GL Account	OS Entity	GL Entity	Balance	Currency	Explained Balance	Unexplained Balance	Activity
11000	GRP - Global AR	Clubs	Clubs	**54,185,922.01**	EUR	54,185,921.95	0.06	-4,251,359.61

Item Type	Item Name	Item Comment	Transaction Date	Aging	Reference 1	Reference 2	Item Amount
Balance Check			3/31/2022	0			12,908,011.33
Balance Check			3/31/2022	0			20,750,150.00
Balance Check			3/31/2022	0			20,527,760.61

Auto Prepared, Frankfurt Controller, 12/16/2020 12:45:31 AM | Auto Approved 1 of 1, Frankfurt Controller, 12/16/2020 12:45:31 AM

OS Account	GL Account	OS Entity	GL Entity	Balance	Currency	Explained Balance	Unexplained Balance	Activity
20000	21220	Frankfurt	FRANKFU	**-1,100,991.99**	EUR	-1,100,992.41	0.42	-22,019.84

Item Type	Item Name	Item Comment	Transaction Date	Aging	Reference 1	Reference 2	Item Amount
Balance Check	21220		3/31/2022	0			-193,216.68

Figure 4.129

Reconciliation Item Aging – Displays the detail items by booked period by OS Account.

Reconciling Item Aging

Source Scenario: Actual
Reconciliation Scenario: ActualAR
Currency Level: Local
Time: 2022M3

3 Months

10000

GL Account	OS Entity	GL Entity	Booked Period	Item Type	Item Name	Item Comment	Transaction Date	Aging	Reference 1	Reference 2	Detail Amount	Currency
11080	Houston Heights	Heights	2022M1	Correction (IS)	Reclass Adjustment		1/31/2022	3			59,367.66	USD
11080	South Houston	South	2022M1	Explained Item	Timing adjustment		1/31/2022	3			340,082.00	USD

2 Months

10100

GL Account	OS Entity	GL Entity	Booked Period	Item Type	Item Name	Item Comment	Transaction Date	Aging	Reference 1	Reference 2	Item Amount	Currency
10001	Houston Heights	Heights	2022M2	Correction (IS)	WF Writeoff		1/14/2022	2			-3,000.44	USD
10001	Houston Heights	Heights	2022M2	Correction (BS)	Deferred Reclass to Liabilities		2/28/2022	2			-20,000.00	USD

Figure 4.130

Reconciliation Access Groups – This Report is only available to Local and System Administrators. The Report is organized by Access Group Names. Within each Access Group, the Report will display the Member's Name, the Role, and whether or not the Member is a Security Group, will receive notifications, or is a designated Local Admin. If the User running this Report is a System Administrator, the Report will display all Reconciliation Access Groups. If the Report is run by a Local Admin, the Report will display only the Access Groups where they are the assigned Local Admin.

Reconciliation Access Groups

All_APTrade — **AP Trade for all entities**

Member Name	Role	Is Group	Notify	Local Admin
CC	Preparers	☐	☐	☐
Finance	Preparers	☑	☐	☐
Admin	Approvers 1	☐	☐	☐
GolfStream Controller	Approvers 1	☐	☐	☐
CEO	Viewers	☐	☐	☐

Eagle — **Eagle**

Member Name	Role	Is Group	Notify	Local Admin
Eagle Controller	Preparers	☐	☐	☐
Admin	Approvers 1	☐	☐	☐
CC	Approvers 1	☐	☐	☐
CEO	Approvers 2	☐	☐	☑

Figure 4.131

The Reports can be run within the solution, printed, exported, or emailed. Reports that are exported or emailed can be done in any of the formats, as shown in the screenshot below.

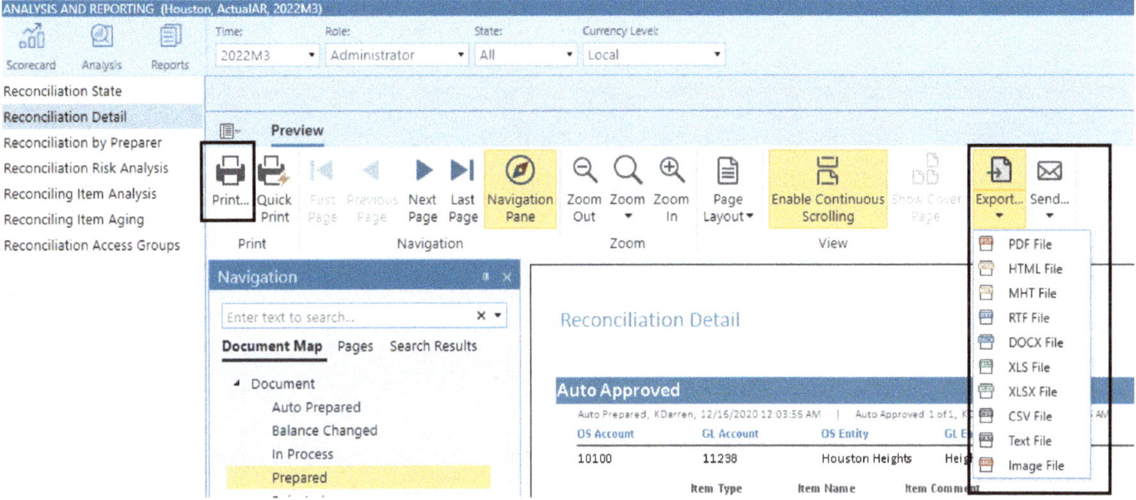

Figure 4.132

Conclusion

As this chapter comes to an end, it also concludes the Account Reconciliation section of this book. We hope that, after reading Chapters 1-4, you have a better understanding of how the Account Reconciliation solution is implemented, administered, and used. Thank you for taking the time to invest in this process, and I am confident that once implemented, you should experience greater visibility, standardization, efficiency, and control – far beyond what you have today.

5
Transaction Matching Overview

At the beginning of this book, our discussion was focused on Account Reconciliations, which is the process of validating Account balances to be accurate and complete. At its core, an Account balance is an accumulation of transactions over time and, therefore, to understand a balance, the User needs to analyze the transactions flowing through it. Transaction Matching is a solution that helps to automate and optimize the analysis process, and in this chapter, we will define what Transaction Matching is, how organizations perform matching today, and the value of using the OneStream Transaction Matching solution. We shall also identify potential use cases where Transaction Matching can be leveraged.

Transaction Matching Process

In today's world, the process of matching transactions to ensure accuracy has become a very important part of daily operations. With the evolution of financial systems, the ability to capture data has become expansive, and managing data to ensure accuracy is difficult. As we use data to make decisions, understanding the risks and exposures at the transactional level are critical, and Transaction Matching is a process that is used to help facilitate analysis and provide the signals needed to make decisions.

At its core, Transaction Matching can be defined as the process of collecting and matching large volumes of data across multiple sources. The process assists in identifying Unmatched transactions and resolving differences to accurately finalize period-end balances and close the books. Although typically used in conjunction with preparing Reconciliations, Transaction Matching can be done on any data where you are trying to ensure the information matches system to system, process to process, or item to item.

Manual Process

Transaction Matching is typically performed manually in organizations today. It is a very time-consuming process that requires each User to set up their own matching files. The files are normally prepared in Excel and must be updated and rolled forward each period.

As soon as the matching files are ready, Users will extract the transactional data from the source systems. Often, Users do not have the proper access required to retrieve all the necessary transactions, or the transaction files are difficult to extract. In addition, external file sources may be received in a format that is not usable, requiring the Users to manipulate the file.

Assuming the match file is prepared, and all the data is received, the User is then ready to perform the matching process. To identify a match, the User creates formulas, performs sorting, and highlights transactions that agree. Because there are multiple different Match Rules, and the process is manual, the User must iteratively pass through their data multiple times trying to identify matches, which is time-consuming and prone to error as items might be Matched incorrectly by the User.

Once matching is completed, the User is left with a list of Unmatched transactions, also referred to as **open items**. The open items have to be manually copied into the Reconciliation or reported to management. These transactions also need to be transferred to next month's matching file so the process can start again.

Although each step is not independently difficult, when combined they create an arduous process that is very prone to errors. In addition to the steps above, the User is also responsible for ensuring that extracts are up to date, files are manipulated consistently month over month, the match formulas are accurately applied each period, and none of the steps get missed. Also, note that this is not simply done by a few Users but by many across an organization where high volumes of transactions need to be reviewed. It is almost impossible to ensure control(!) and – because of these concerns – organizations are looking for solutions that automate the matching process.

Automating with OneStream

The OneStream Financial Close solution offers an automated process for Transaction Matching. The Transaction Matching solution is broken down into five key process steps:

1. Data Sets
2. Match Sets
3. Match Rule Creation
4. Match Processing
5. Unmatched Transactions

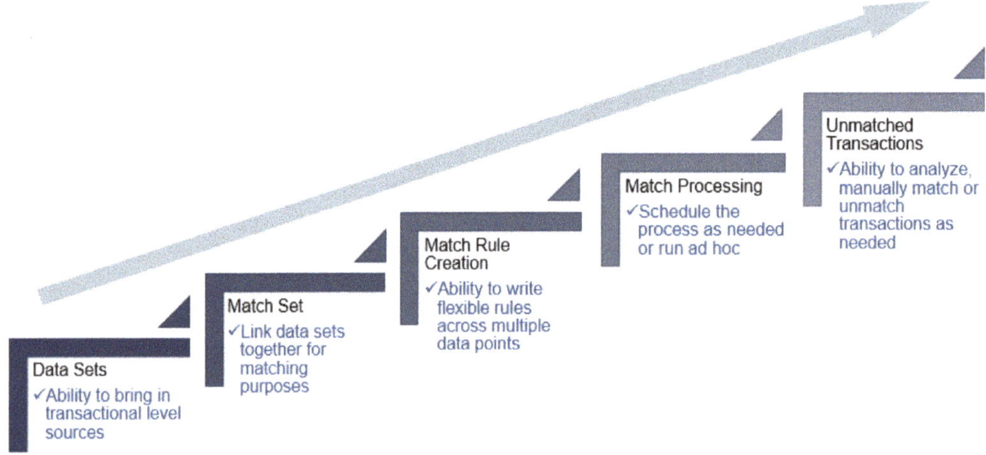

Figure 5.1

Below, we will walk through each of the process steps to better define the value delivered when using the Transaction Matching solution.

Data Sets

Data sets are the first step in the Transaction Matching process, where raw data or transactions are gathered to perform matching. Data also needs to be loaded at the right detail level with the appropriate fields to ensure Match Rules and matches are successful.

The Transaction Matching solution utilizes the data integration capabilities of the OneStream platform. By leveraging this core functionality, data can be imported using the **Direct Connect** process or through flat file loads. Data loads can be set up within the Task Scheduler to automate the process and allow data to be imported more frequently. When performing the work manually, non-OneStream Users tend to only pull the data once, due to the amount of time spent manipulating the files. However, when using our solution, organizations typically load data on a daily or weekly basis allowing the process to stay current and corrections to be performed in a timely manner.

Data can also be aggregated and transformed by the system upon import, eliminating manual manipulation, and the system can enhance data by adding and updating fields as necessary. Data fields can be augmented by parsing, concatenating, calculating, populating from lookup tables, or applying business logic as needed.

In addition, there is the ability to stack or split data files upon import. **Data stacking** is used in situations where you may have multiple General Ledgers or source files that define a specific data set. Rather than requiring *all* the files to be in the same format, the system allows you to map the detail data fields to the OneStream data fields on a file-by-file basis. This provides the flexibility to bring in many different file layouts without the need to standardize the format. Similarly, if you have a single file that contains data for multiple Match Sets, the solution can split the file. **Data splitting**, meanwhile, allows you to leverage a single file to populate multiple Match Sets. Data stacking and data splitting provide efficiency in data loading.

Match Sets

A Match Set links data sets together for processing. Within the system, you can have multiple Match Sets to support your process. Match Sets are typically defined by the type of data required (Bank versus Suspense versus Intercompany, etc.), the rules applied, and the security needed.

Although manual matching is typically done Account by Account, this creates inconsistency on how matching is performed. Being able to have similar Accounts together in a single Match Set provides not only efficiency but also consistency and standardization on how the matching occurs. Also, the solution supports Match Set-level security (as well as transaction-level security) to ensure Users see only what they should see. This allows us to bring data together in a single Match Set but still ensure data is only viewed by those with appropriate security.

Match Rules

The power of the matching process comes from its rule capabilities. Match Rules are the logic that runs against the data, and are created and maintained by the Match Set owner. You can create as many rules as needed to complete your process. Rules can be applied to the entire Match Set or – when utilizing filtering capabilities – they can be applied to a subset of data for more precision.

Within a rule, the system can match single transactions to each other or aggregate transactions prior to matching. Rules can be set up as either automatic or suggested. **Automatic Rules** create the match and move the transactions to the Matched state with no further action needed. **Suggested Rules** also create the match but require the User to accept the match, thus creating a review process. Regardless of the type of rule (automatic or suggested), the system automates the creation of the match and eliminates the formula errors that are prevalent in a manual process.

Rules are also easy to set up and maintain. Within the interface, Users will select the required fields from sets of drop-downs. Users do not have to write any complicated code or know programming logic to create rules. In addition, tolerances can be set up for amount and date fields to allow for variation (as needed). Rules are prioritized in the order that Users desire them to run; the most precise rules run first, and the least precise rules run later in the process. In addition, if data changes, new rules can be created at any time, and they can be reordered or deactivated as necessary.

Processing

Processing is the step of running the rule-based logic against the transactional data to automatically create matches. The process can be initiated on demand, set up on a schedule using the OneStream Task Scheduler, or linked with the data load process to automatically run after the data is imported.

Automating Match Rule processing can result in a completely hands-off approach so that when Users come into the solution, they can spend their time analyzing Unmatched transactions. Also, processing the rules initiates the audit on the matches. Each match creates a Match ID, identifies the rule by which the match was made, captures the date and time stamp of the match, and updates the status of the transaction to ensure that a transaction is not Matched twice. All of these items provide control and auditability in the process.

Unmatched Transactions

Once the matching process is complete, all Unmatched transactions are available for analysis, reporting, or future matching. Users can perform manual matches on transactions, adding Reason

Codes, attaching supporting documentation, or providing commentary (as needed) for enhanced auditability. All Unmatched transactions are also automatically carried forward into future periods and are made available for future matching. In addition, Unmatched transactions can be pushed to a Reconciliation to create detail items with the ability to drill back to the underlying transactional information.

Overall Solution

The steps defined above make up the Transaction Matching solution. When implemented, it creates a controlled, consistent, efficient and automated process where Users can perform matching more frequently, and proactively correct any issues found. In addition, they can surface this data into information and create Dashboards and Reports.

Transaction Matching Use Cases

Matching can be used in many different scenarios. Although most Users think of matching as a financial activity, the process can be used in any situation where you are trying to validate two or three sets of information. Below are some examples of how Transaction Matching is used:

Financial Use Case

- Bank to General Ledger
- Third-Party Processors to General Ledger
- Sub-ledger Matching
- Deferred Revenue
- Clearing/Suspense Accounts
- Intercompany
- Accruals

Non-Financial Use Case

- Physical Inventory counts
- Contract/Employee Hour Tracking
- Project and Quantity Information
- Employee Validation
- System Migrations
- SKU Number Validations
- Invoice/PO Item Counts

Driving Optimization

Implementing Transaction Matching, as discussed, will drive optimization, consistency, visibility, and overall control. In chapters 6-8, we will walk through the administration process, implementation best practices, and the User Experience to start you on the path of matching automation. I am sure many readers will have Accounts or processes already in mind for the solution, but I would encourage people to think beyond the typical. Remember that matching can be used in any situation where we are trying to tie out information, so why not extend the investment even further by using it in scenarios beyond finance? There are lots of opportunities to really make a difference!

6

Transaction Matching Administration

Transaction Matching Administration was designed to require as little maintenance as possible. **Match Sets** are created for two or three data sets, where information is to be compared and – where possible – you should aim to create as few Match Sets as possible and create multiple Match Sets only when different information is being tied out. Case in point, you shouldn't expect to create a separate Match Set for each Intercompany trading partner. Rather, you would create a single Match Set for *all* Intercompany information and set up security on the data to enable Users to only see data that applies to them. Within this chapter, we will dive into Match Set setup, security, and rules, and further explain the 'why' behind the Administration, plus how to set up your Transaction Matching environment.

Settings

The Settings page is the first step you will take in setting up your Transaction Matching application. Within this page, you will do the initial configuration for the entire application. As this page is used to create your application, only OneStream Administrators or Transaction Matching Administrators may access it. This security access is configured in **Global Options**, discussed in this section. There are four different sections within settings, including:

- Global Options
- Access Control
- Match Sets
- Uninstall

> **Note:** Transaction Matching Match Sets relate to Workflow Profiles, meaning each Match Set is assigned to a different Workflow Profile. However, the settings are the same for all Match Sets, and thus, the settings pages persist through all Match Sets.

Global Options

This page contains the key properties that guide the Transaction Matching administration and is used for the initial setup and configuration of Transaction Matching. All settings within this page are retained during solution upgrades.

Security Role (Manage Transaction Matching Setup)

Anyone assigned to this OneStream User Group is considered a Transaction Matching Super User and is also referred to as a Transaction Matching Administrator, meaning they have access to all aspects of the Transaction Matching application.

Once a group is assigned, initially by a OneStream Administrator, anyone within the group will have the ability to configure *all* aspects of the Transaction Matching solution (which does not include the ability to set up Workflows), as well as the ability to match, unmatch, suspend, and delete transactions. The only role that supersedes the Transaction Matching Administrator is the OneStream System Administrator, and as such, any OneStream Administrator can perform all actions within Transaction Matching that a Transaction Matching Administrator can perform. As this group's rights encompass all aspects of Transaction Matching configuration, the default group assigned upon install is Administrators.

To change the group assigned, select a system Security Group from the drop-down, and then click Save at the bottom of the page. To create a group to be used, follow the steps defined as per Chapter 2 – Account Reconciliations Administration.

Data Splitting Workflow Profile

Data splitting provides the ability to divide a single data source between numerous data sets across multiple Match Sets. This flexibility enables a file to be accessed across different areas such as departments or divisions, while controlling access and visibility through the separate Match Sets. This drop-down contains all Workflow Profiles within the OneStream Application. Select the Workflow Profile that is to be used for data splitting. This Workflow Profile will not have the ability to perform any matching activity (as shown in Figure 6.1); rather, this is simply an import profile to be used when a single file contains data that must be split into different Match Sets.

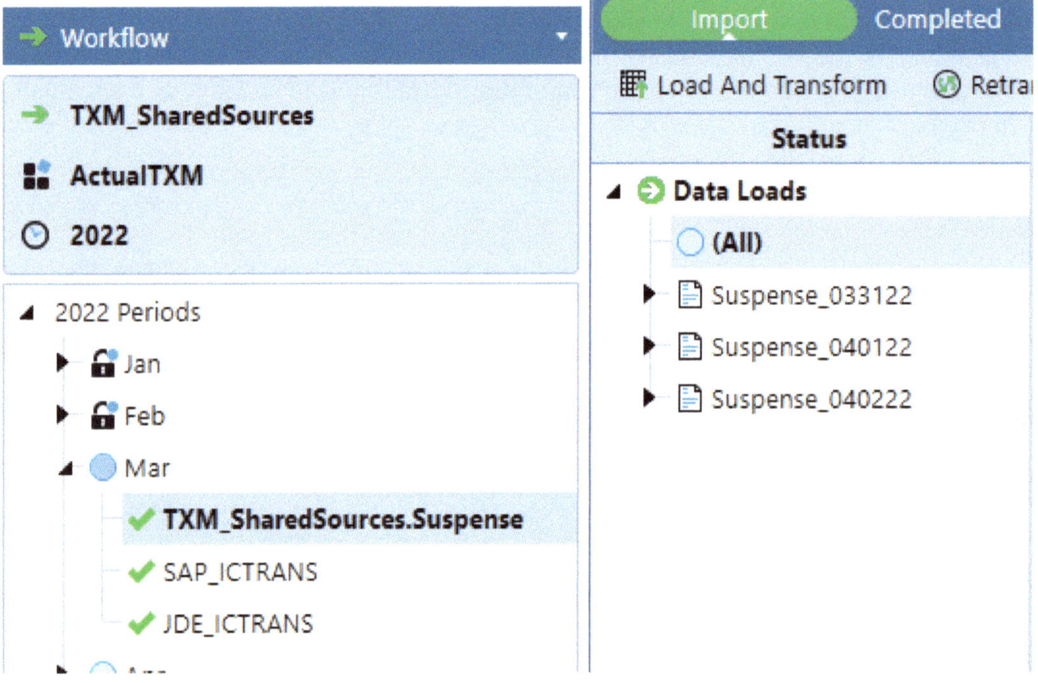

Figure 6.1

Let's walk through a couple of examples as to when data splitting would be necessary.

Within this section, we will show screenshots from within the Administration page, the setup of which will be discussed later. This information is given now to provide a context of when and why you would use data splitting. One instance would be if you have a single file that contains all suspense activity – both debits and credits – and you need to compare the debit activity to the credit activity. Transaction Matching requires at least two data sets, so matching would not be possible unless:

1. Your IT department uses the initial file to create two separate files.
2. Your IT department creates two different data sources for the file, one for debits and one for credits.
3. Or you create a data-splitting Workflow Profile.

Choosing the third option is definitely best from a OneStream Administrator's perspective, as it gives the finance User the ability to administer the file without IT involvement. For this example, you would import the suspense file, and the debit amount (Figure 6.2) would be the amount being compared for the first data set, and the credit (Figure 6.3) would be the amount compared for the second within the Transaction Matching Administration page. Note that both data sets have the same **Import Workflow Profile** but are comparing different columns of values.

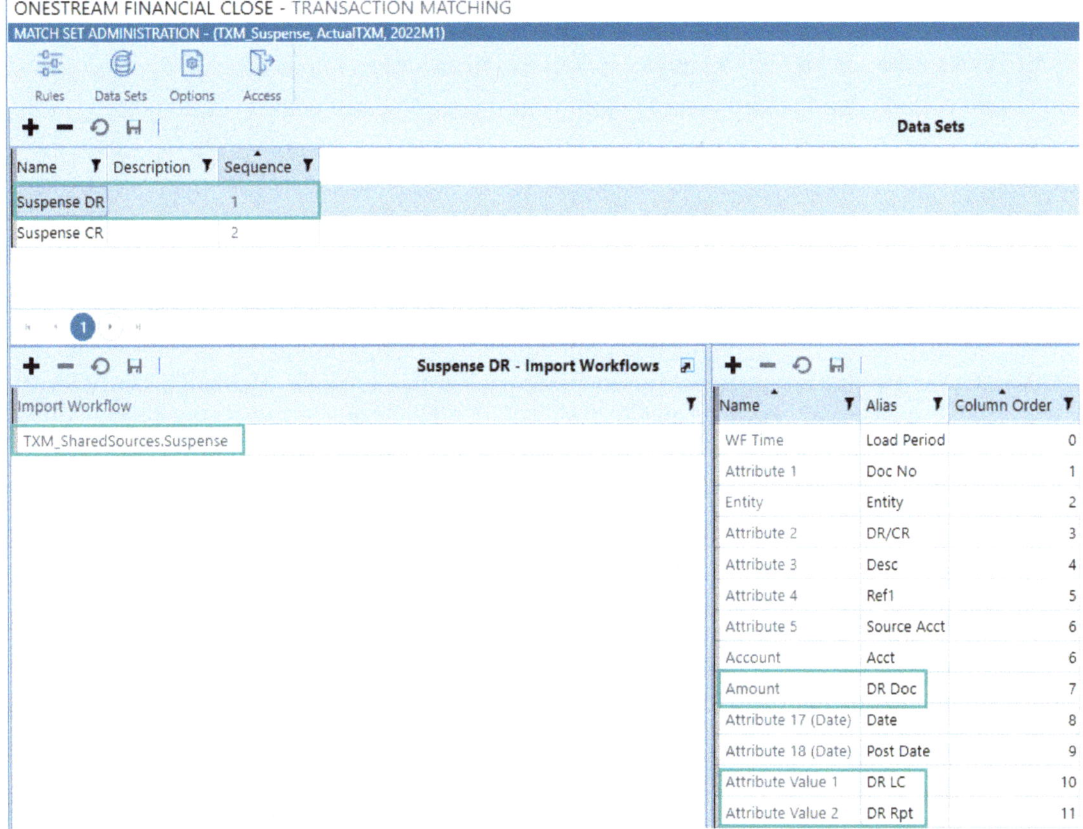

Figure 6.2

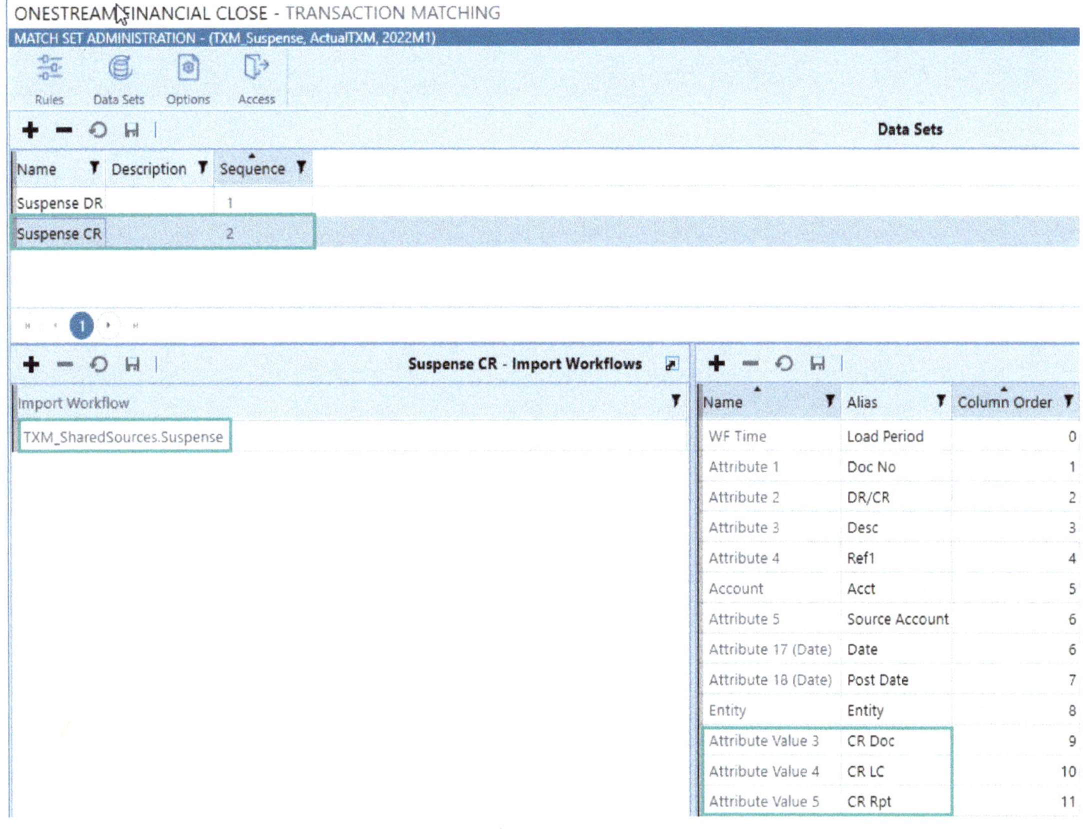

Figure 6.3

Another example of when data splitting would be useful would be for Intercompany matching.

In many instances, all Intercompany balances are held within a single, top-level Account, and the Entity balances are held within that roll-up. Let's assume your company's total Intercompany Payables are held on Account 20XXX, and you use this Account number to pull the total balance, and each Entity's Intercompany Payables balance is input into XXX to pull up their specific balance (e.g., if Houston Heights is Entity number 002, the corresponding Intercompany Payables Account for that Entity is 20002).

As you can imagine, creating different connectors or files for each Entity would be extremely cumbersome for IT, so here is where a reader can come in as a superstar Administrator! Utilize data splitting for your Intercompany payables file and create Match Sets where ownership exists.

What do we mean by this?

Creating Match Sets for each Entity also wouldn't be desirable from a OneStream perspective because you don't want to have to maintain rules and set up for thousands of companies. Instead, split the data up to a level appropriate for your company's maintenance. Maybe you have **Shared Services** in North America, AMEA, and APAC, so – in this instance – three Match Sets would be ideal because you have ownership at each level. Furthermore, you can set security at the Entity level on data, so if Users should only be able to see transactions for specific Entities – for which they have read/write permissions – we can prevent them from seeing data that does not relate to them (discussed in Data Security).

In order to assign a data splitting Workflow Profile, it must first be created within the Application tab. Note that the examples shown throughout this book are within a separate Parent-level Workflow Profile, Transaction Matching. Creating a separate Workflow Profile for Transaction Matching is not necessary. The Profile Properties for the data splitting Workflow Profile should be set as shown in Figure 6.4.

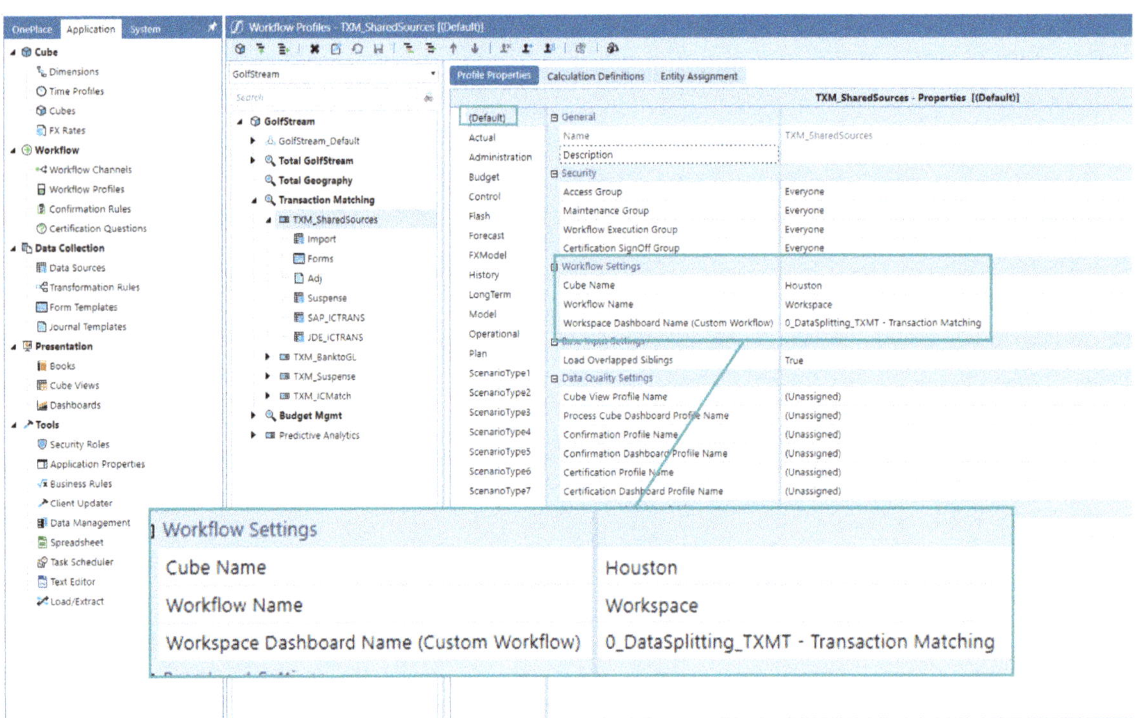

Figure 6.4

For all import steps added (data to be split), follow Figure 6.5.

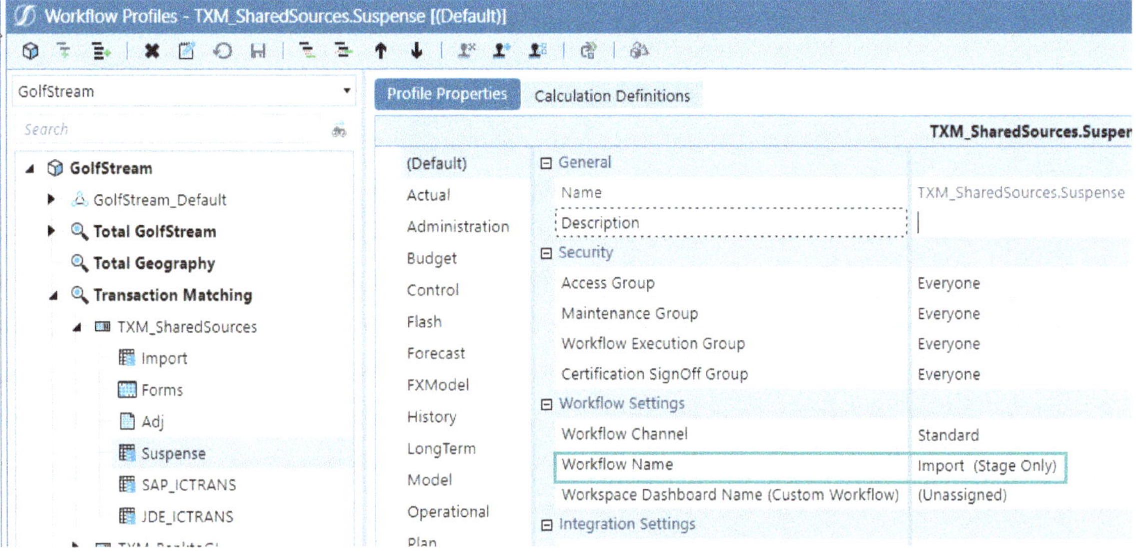

Figure 6.5

Access Control

The Access Control page within Global Options is used to set up Access Groups to be applied to the Match Sets.

An **Access Group** is a list of Users and their respective roles that are created by OneStream Administrators or Transaction Matching Administrators. Unlike Account Reconciliations, Match Sets do not have primary roles. As such, any person assigned to a role within the Access Group may take action on the Match Set for that role level.

For instance, an Access Group may contain more than one User assigned to the Preparer role. In this instance, all Users assigned as Preparer may take Preparer actions. Additionally, like Account Reconciliations, Transaction Matching security utilizes a step-down approach, meaning that a User may take action on a Match at any role equal or below the role they are assigned, as long as they have not already taken action on a Match.

The table in Figure 6.6 outlines the various roles, what Platform System Security Roles may be assigned to the role, where the role is configured, and the actions the role may take.

Role	Assignable System Security Roles	Configuration	Actions
Viewer	Users	Access Control	• View transactions (Unmatched, Matched, Suspended, Pending Delete) • View Matches page • View Scorecard • View comments and attachments • Drill back to transaction details
Commenter	Users	Access Control	• Perform all Viewer actions • Add comments to matches and transactions
Preparer	Users	Access Control	• Perform all Commenter actions • Add attachments to matches and transactions • Create manual matches and match + • Accept suggested matches

Role	Assignable System Security Roles	Configuration	Actions
			• Unmatch suggested and manual matches • Process Match Set Rules • Suspend transactions • Create detail items (used to support Account Reconciliations) • Assign match Reason Codes • Assign suspension Reason Codes • Delete transactions (putting them in a 'Pending Delete' status) • Recall transactions that are Pending Delete • Complete the Workflow
Approver	Users	Access Control	• Perform all Preparer actions • Approve and unapprove suggested and manual matches • Permanently delete transactions that are Pending Delete
Local Admin	Users	Access Control	• Perform all Approver actions • View all pages within Administration (Rules, Data Sets, Options, and Access) • Create and manage rules • Create and edit data sets and data set fields • Create and edit rule sets • Create and edit Reason Codes • Add, remove, and edit User access to Match Sets
Transaction Matching Admin	Group	Global Options	• Perform all Local Admin actions • Navigate to the Transaction Matching Settings page and modify and configure all Matching Settings • View Deleted transactions from the Transactions page • Remove Deleted transactions
OneStream System Admin	Users	System Security	• Perform all Transaction Matching Admin actions • Assign Transaction Matching Admin

Figure 6.6

It is important to note that if your organization is planning to utilize Transaction Matching information to support Account Reconciliations, User security should be in line between both solutions. This means that if Muhammad is a Preparer of the cash Reconciliations, he should also be a Preparer of the Match Set assigned to the cash Reconciliations.

In this way, Muhammad could either push support from Transaction Matching to all of his cash Reconciliations or go into each cash Reconciliation and pull the support from Transaction Matching into the Reconciliation. Creating detail item support using Transaction Matching data is discussed, in detail, in both Chapter 4 and Chapter 8.

To create an Access Group (Figure 6.7):

1. Navigate to the Access Control page within Settings.
2. Select + to create a new group.
3. Name the Access Group. This name is what will appear in the drop-down of available Access Groups on the Match Sets setting page. Note that this name cannot be changed upon Save.
4. Add a description for the Access Group. This description will not appear anywhere else in the solution but is for your reference. Save the Access Group.
5. Once the Access Group is created, you can assign Security Users. To add a User, select +.
6. Select a User from the drop-down.
7. Assign a role to that User.

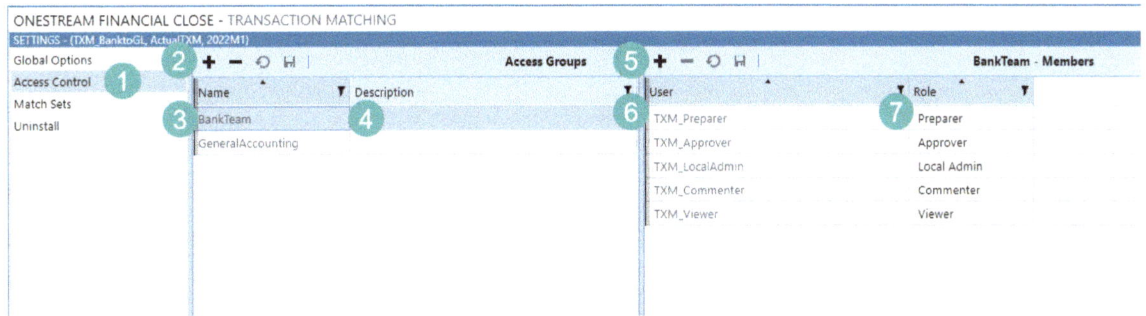

Figure 6.7

Match Sets

The Match Sets page is where you assign a Workflow Profile for a Match Set. In order to set up your Match Sets, you must first create the Workflow Profiles within the application. As such, prior to configuring Transaction Matching, first determine where you will be performing your matching activities. You do not need to create new Workflow Profiles or Scenarios for Transaction Matching, as we show in many of our examples throughout this book. However, for our examples, you will see specific Scenarios and Workflow Profiles created to easily identify the matching activities.

Prior to assigning the Match Sets to the Workflow Profiles, assign the Transaction Matching Workspace Dashboard, `0_Frame_TXM_OnePlace-TransactionMatching`, to at least one Workflow Profile within the Application tab, as shown in Figure 6.8.

Again, for our examples, we have created distinct Workflow Profiles for matching purposes, which is not necessary. The only necessity is that the Dashboard is assigned to a top Workflow Profile (and not a Base Input step within the Profile).

In the example shown, the Dashboard has been assigned to the `TXM_BanktoGL` Profile. However, we could have just as easily assigned this to one of the Workflow Profiles used for Actuals or Forecasting, such as the Houston Workflow Profile. In the past, we have seen customers perform matching activities that support Actual Account balances, such as Intercompany matching. In these instances, customers have chosen to assign the matching Dashboard to the Workflow Profile where the Intercompany Accounts are reported, and in the Actual Scenario.

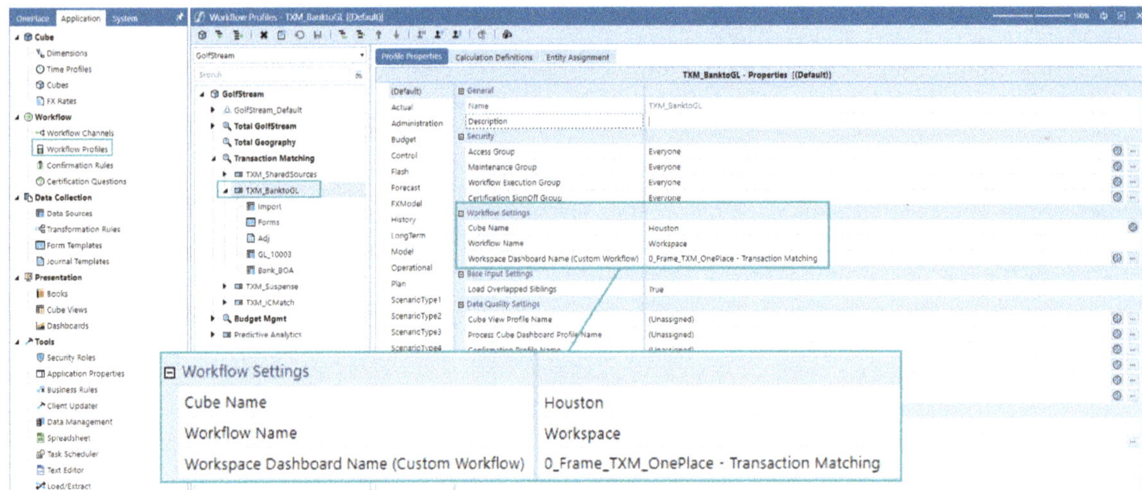

Figure 6.8

Once all Workflow Profiles related to matching have been created, you can assign matching activity to the Workflow Profile. Creation of a Match Set, or identifying the Workflow Profile where the Match Set will be held, doesn't do much in terms of creating the rules, etc., but rather, is setting up the shell to start matching.

Figure 6.9 shows the Match Sets page. Essentially, utilize this page to select the Workflow Profile where the Match Set will live, the Scenario related to the Match Set, and the Access Group for the Match Set.

> **Note:** Workflow Profile Security must also be set up for Users. Simply creating and assigning an Access Group *will not* work if the Users within the Access Group do not also have access to the Workflow Profile.

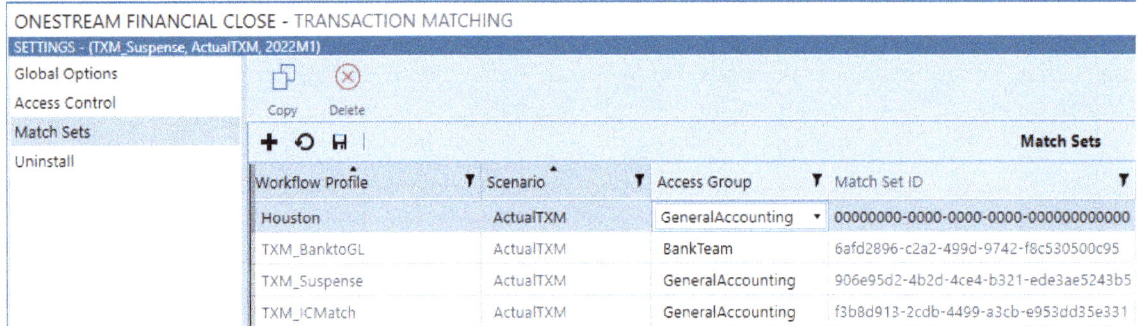

Figure 6.9

Note that once you have gone through the process of creating Match Set Rules and a data set framework, you can copy a Match Set. Utilizing Copy will allow you to replicate all rules configured from the source Match Set. This is a great tool to utilize in instances where rules are similar across Match Sets but have subtle differences that can be easily updated after creation. Let's say I had Intercompany Matching Rules that I set up for Houston, which would be the same for all Workflow Profiles except for the Entity number, I would configure the rules for Houston, and then copy that Match Set to all other Entities. In Figure 6.10, we are copying the Houston Match Set and assigning the same rules to the Quebec Match Set. Configuring rules and data sets will be discussed later in this chapter.

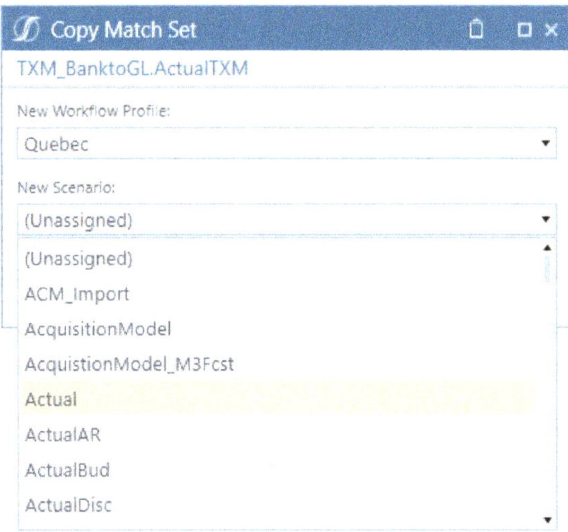

Figure 6.10

Uninstall

The Uninstall page allows you to uninstall all solutions within OneStream Financial Close, which includes Account Reconciliations and Transaction Matching. If uninstall is performed as part of an upgrade, any modifications that were made to standard solution contents are removed.

Uninstall UI – OneStream Financial Close

Removes all solutions within OneStream Financial Close, including all Dashboards and Business Rules but leaves the databases and related tables intact. Performing this step is encouraged for most upgrades as Dashboards are often modified within the solutions. However, it is important to note that when this is done, the Workspace Dashboard Name for every Workflow Profile – including data splitting Workflow Profiles – must be reassigned.

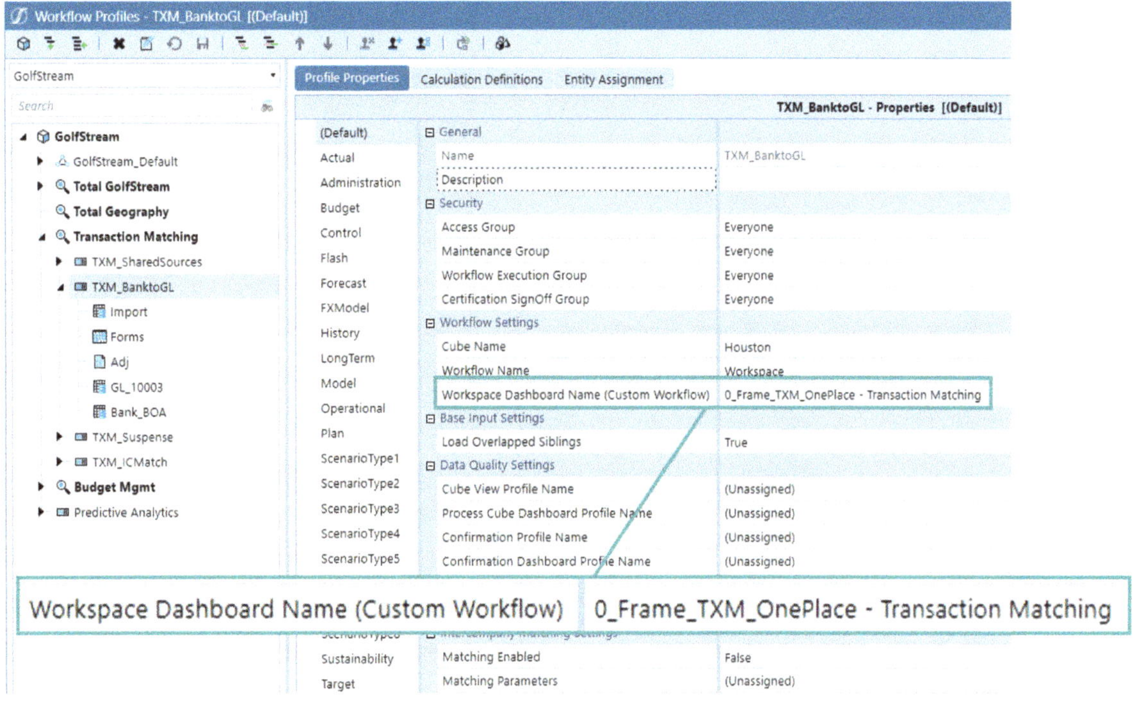

Figure 6.11

Uninstall Full

Removes all related data tables, all data, all solutions' Dashboards, and all Business Rules. Select this option to completely remove the solutions.

> **Note:** This option is irreversible and is therefore not recommended.

This option should only be utilized if your company has determined it will not be using any of the OneStream Financial Close solutions, or if the Release Notes for the version being installed state that the upgrade is so significant in its changes to the data tables that this method is required.

Administration

The Match Set Administration contains pages to design the Match Set Rules, configure data sets, configure Match Set options, and update Access Groups. The Administration relates to the specific configuration of the Match Set that is selected in the Workflow. As such, to configure the rules, data sets, etc., for your Match Sets, first select the Match Set to be configured in the Workflow, and then navigate to the Administration, as shown in Figure 6.12. This area can only be accessed by Transaction Matching Administrators or OneStream Administrators.

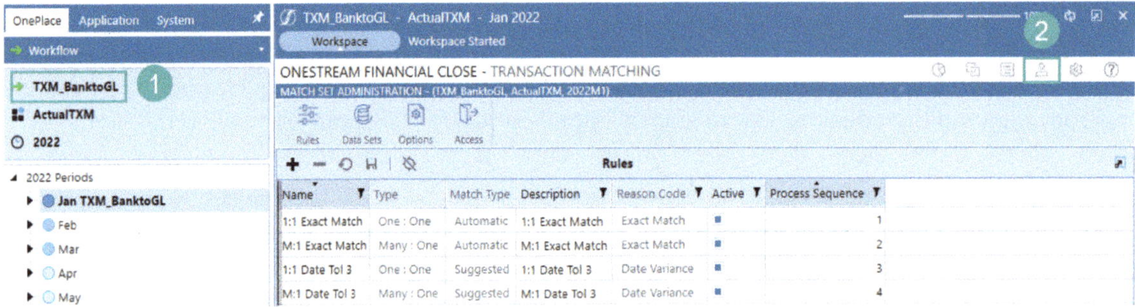

Figure 6.12

Data Sets

While this icon is not the first in order within the header, it should be the first step for Match Set configuration. The Rules icon is at the far left as rules are often updated and/or changed, but the rules should not be created until your data sets are properly configured.

A data set is the transactional data that is imported and used for matching. You must have at least two, and up to three, sources of information for matching purposes. Some examples of data sets for matching purposes would be a bank file Matched against a GL file, a Suspense Account file split between debits and credits (discussed in the data splitting section), and an Intercompany file split between debits and credits.

In these instances, we would be comparing two different data sources to see where matches and variances exist. An example of where three data sets would exist within a single Match Set would be comparing a register of purchase orders created, a register of goods received, and a listing of invoices – and ensuring the three match prior to making payment on invoice.

Add a line item for each type of data that is being Matched. While we have listed a single source of transaction-level information, it is important to also note that data can be compiled from multiple different files to make up a single data set, which is discussed more in the Import Workflows section. Be sure you have created a line item for each data set (up to three), prior to performing any matching activity because data sets may not be added once a match has been made.

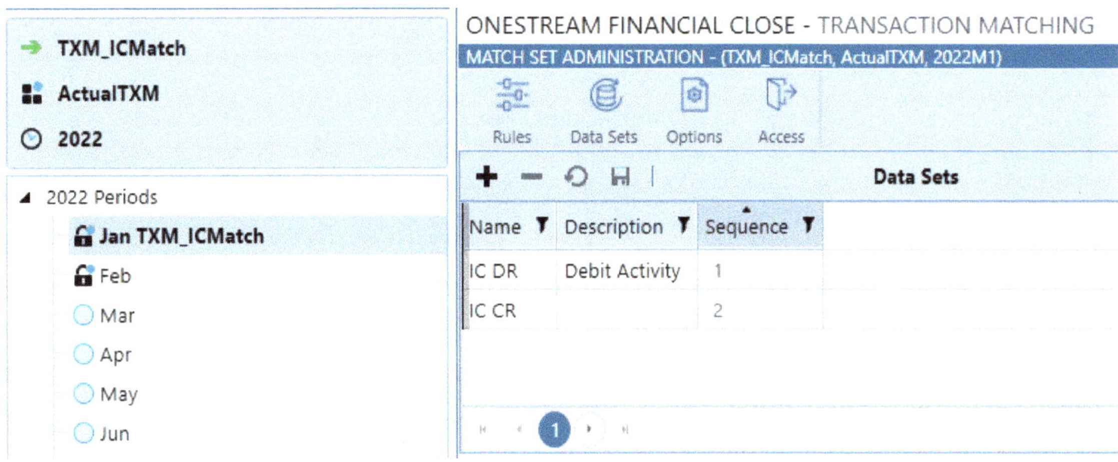

Figure 6.13

Name

The name created here will be the name displayed for the data set throughout the solution, including headers on the Transactions and Matches page and in the Analysis section. The name may be edited at any point.

Description

This is a reference column for the description of the data set. This information is not displayed elsewhere in the solution. The description may be edited at any point.

Sequence

This is a drop-down list utilized to establish the order of the data sets (1, 2, 3) displayed on the Matches and Manual Matches pages. The first data set (DS1) should be your primary data set as it is used to compare against the remaining data sets. This cannot be edited once saved.

Data Security

If a Cube is selected for data security on the Options page, this column will appear, as shown in Figure 6.14. This is to set the security level for the data set, either Entity, IC, Entity OR IC, and Entity AND IC. This setting establishes what is displayed to the User and can therefore be edited at any point.

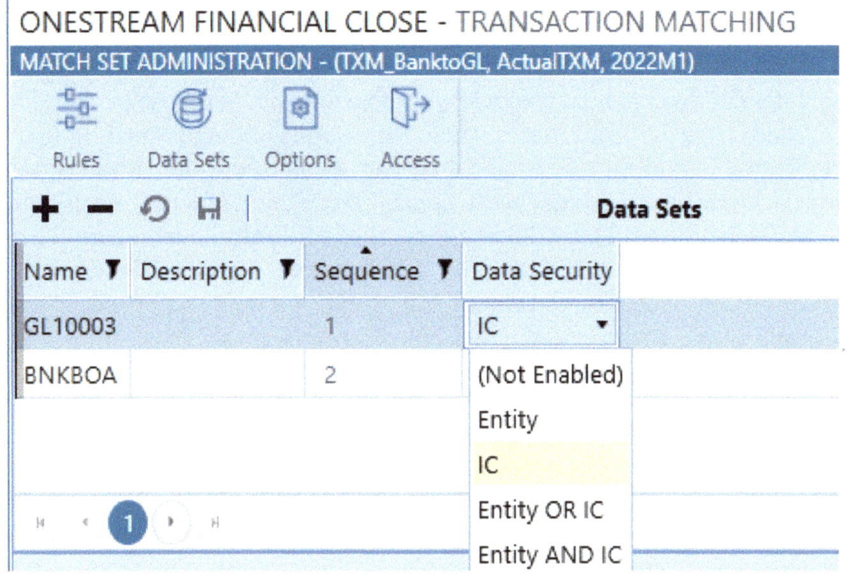

Figure 6.14

For this setting, the system looks to the System Security Groups assigned in the Read and Write Data Group, or the Read and Write Data Group 2, in the security section of the Member Properties on the Entity Dimension.

Although the Transaction Matching Administrators User group has the access necessary to manage the solution, if Data Security is enabled, the ability to view transactions is dependent upon the individual User's Entity-level security. Users are only able to see transactions for the Entities to which they have Read and Write access (including Transaction Matching Administrators). Leaving the default of Not Enabled allows Users with Workflow access to see all transactions in the Match Set.

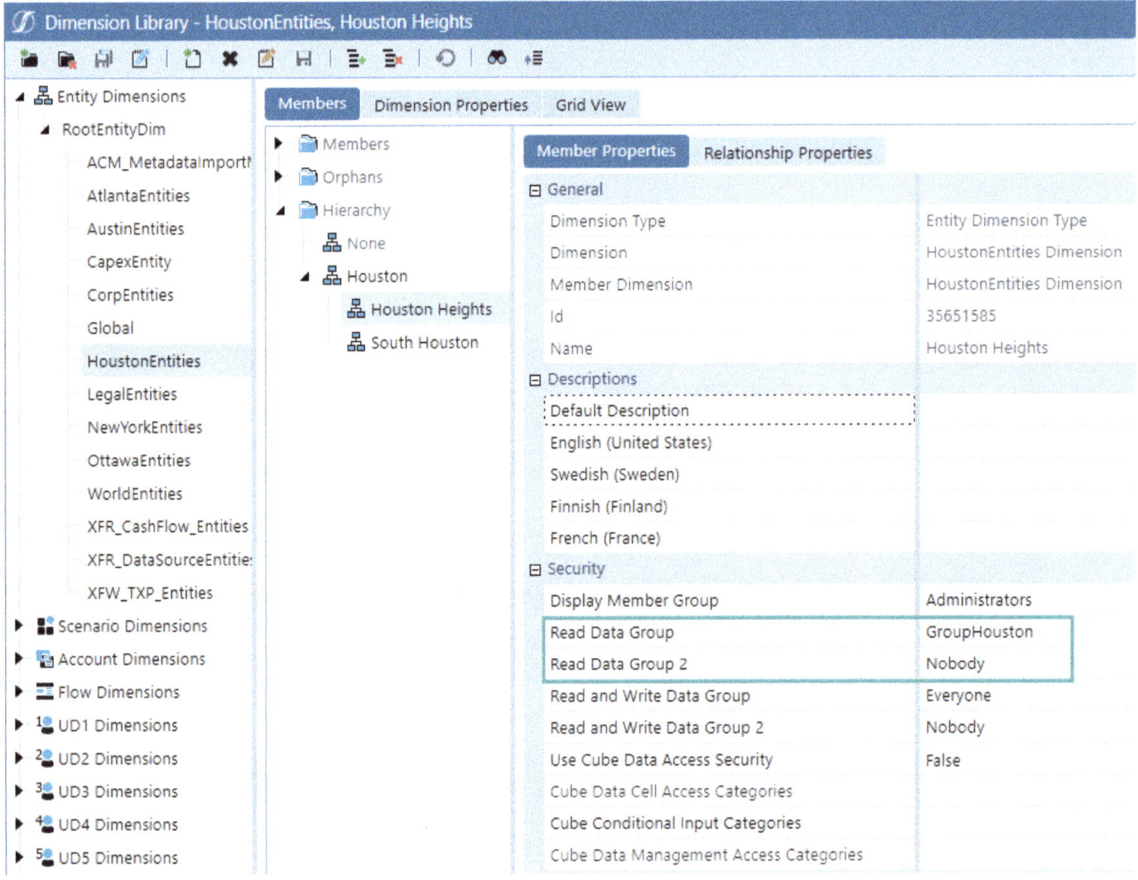

Figure 6.15

This feature was requested by customers utilizing matching for Intercompany purposes. They had a single file containing all Intercompany activity for the company, but those performing matching were only supposed to see data for Entities where they were a trading partner. In this instance, they set the security to show for Entity OR IC and then they would see all transactions where their Entity was involved. For banking, however, you may only want Users to see bank information where their Entity is identified. This would be a use case for Entity-level security. The one item of note is Transaction Matching does not allow for Account-level security. Therefore, if Users should not be able to see certain Accounts, you should utilize data splitting and break out your file by User Account access and create separate Match Sets based on Account security.

Import Workflows

Once you have created the data sets, the next step is establishing where the data will be imported into – for the data set. Each data set may have separate Import Workflow Profiles, or the Profiles may be the same and different fields are referenced.

> **Note:** Prior to adding the Import Workflows on the Data Set page, the Workflow Import step must be added and created in the Workflow Profile.

To set up your Transaction Matching Import Workflows, set the Workflow Name to Import (Stage Only), as shown in Figure 6.16

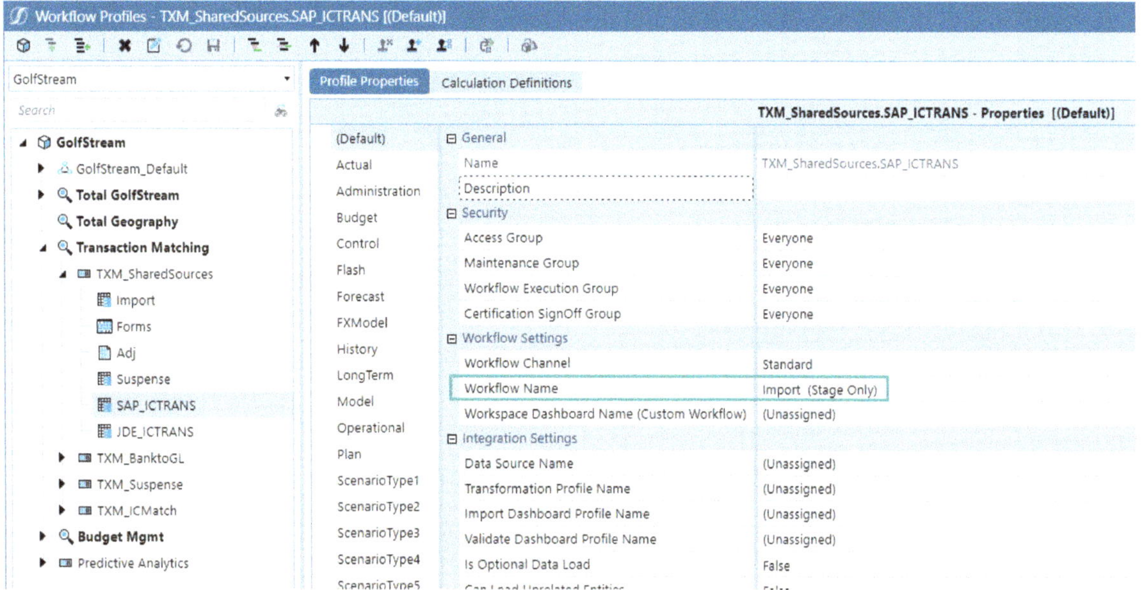

Figure 6.16

Next, select the Profile Property for the Scenario where you will be performing the matching, which is `ScenarioType1` in our example, but can be any Scenario as discussed in Settings. There, select your Data Source Name, as shown in Figure 6.17.

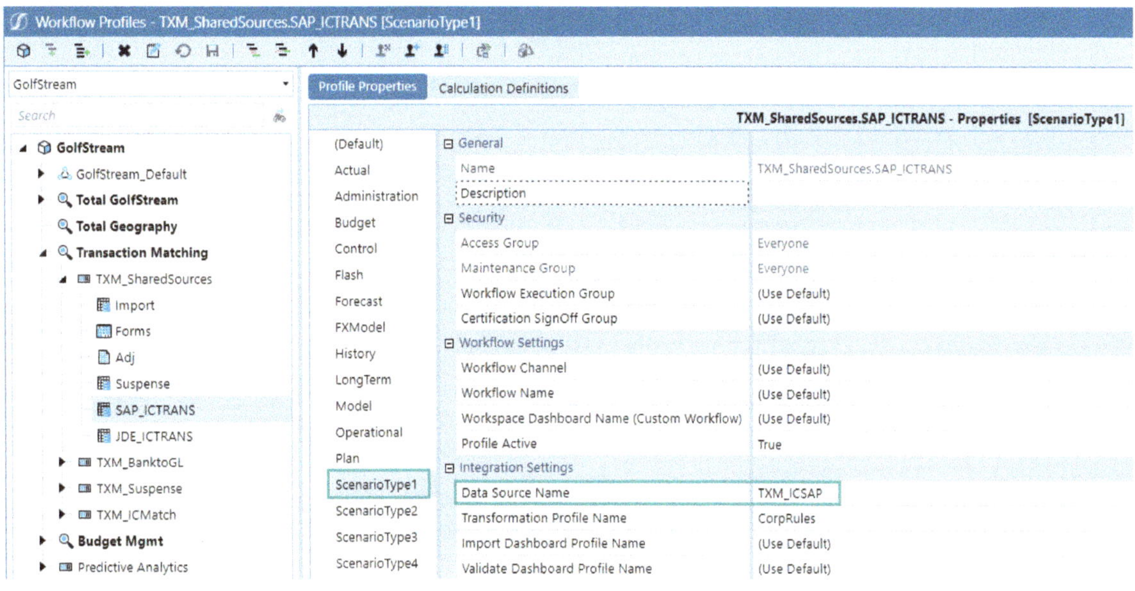

Figure 6.17

After the Workflow Profile Imports have been created for the data set, add them to the data set by selecting the appropriate data set, and then click the + button under Import Workflow Profiles. A drop-down list will appear with all active Import Workflow Profiles for that Workflow Profile, and for the data splitting Workflow Profiles. Select the appropriate Import Profile and save.

> **Note:** In our example, in Figure 6.18, we have included multiple Import Workflow Profiles. If multiple Profiles are added, they will be sequentially stacked together into a single data set.

Import Workflows can be added or removed at any point.

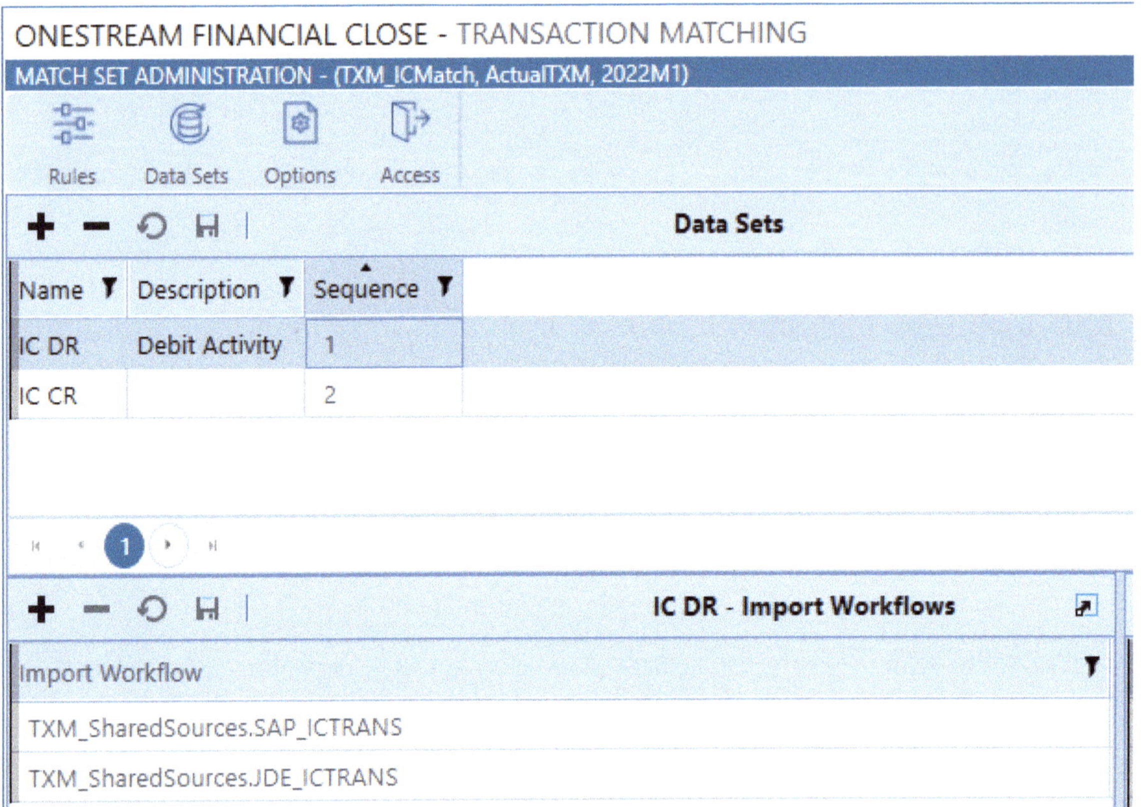

Figure 6.18

Fields

Once you have created the data sets and defined their Import Workflows, you must then define the data fields. In order to complete this step, you must first set up your data source within the Application tab. This is discussed further in Chapter 7.

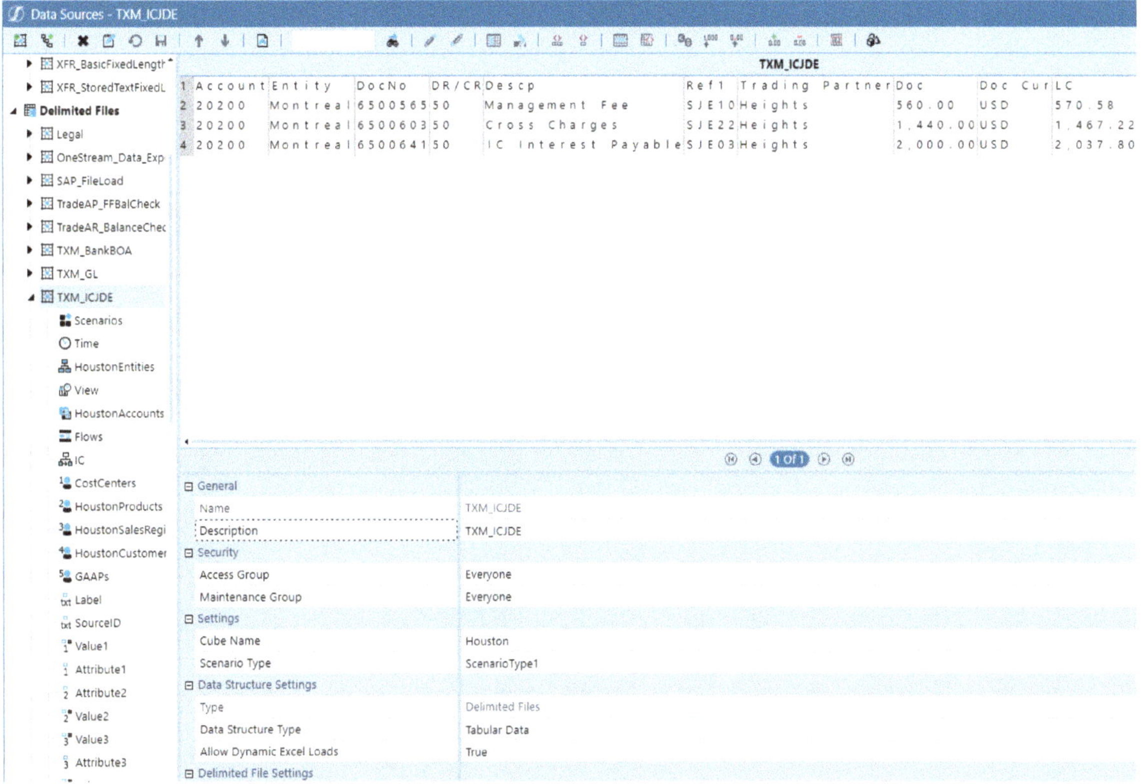

Figure 6.19

The Grid View control can display up to 50 fields at a time. Three of the 50 fields are used to display the Transaction ID, Transaction Number, and Comment/Attachment identification. Therefore, although there are 73 fields available in the Transaction Matching table, only 47 of the fields can be displayed in the Transaction Matching Grid View.

Name

The name column directly correlates to the Stage column headers, which means this drop-down includes all column headers that are included in Stage. Once the name is selected and the row is saved, this field cannot be edited, only deleted. Make sure that all columns of data that are configured for the data source are added to the list here. The available field names and description of each are as follows:

21 Cube Dimensions

Entity, Account, Scenario, Flow, Time, IC, UD1-8, Label, SourceID, TextValue, WF Profile, WF Scenario, WF Time, and Status WF Time are the Cube Dimensions available in the drop-down.

It is very important, when setting up your Match Sets, to first determine if the Match Set will be used to support Account Reconciliations. If the Match Set is used to support Account Reconciliations, you must include all Tracking Levels used for Account Reconciliations in your data set. In many cases, these are S.Entity, S.Account, T.Entity, and T.Account, but could also contain other Tracking Levels such as UDs. This is to allow Administrators to easily utilize existing OneStream dimensionality to configure and set up their Match Sets. While intentional in design, this setup can initially be confusing for Users coming from other point solutions.

Let's walk through an example of how to configure the fields to map to Account Reconciliations.

As a company, you may have a Match Set that matches a bank file to your GL balances. This bank file could be for multiple, different Bank Accounts which relate to multiple, different Entities which may also have their own set of distinct Source Accounts. This bank file would not contain your source, or GL, Bank Account number and would not have your internally-maintained Entity codes. So, how would you map this data set to Account Reconciliations? You will need to preprocess the data to enhance your external files so that, upon import, the transactional line contains the source Dimensions based on a field in the data.

Step 1: Data source creation, map file to the specific fields. In Figure 6.20, we are identifying the location – per the bank file – to be mapped to the S. Entity; and in Figure 6.21, we are identifying the Bank Account number to be mapped to the GL or S. Account.

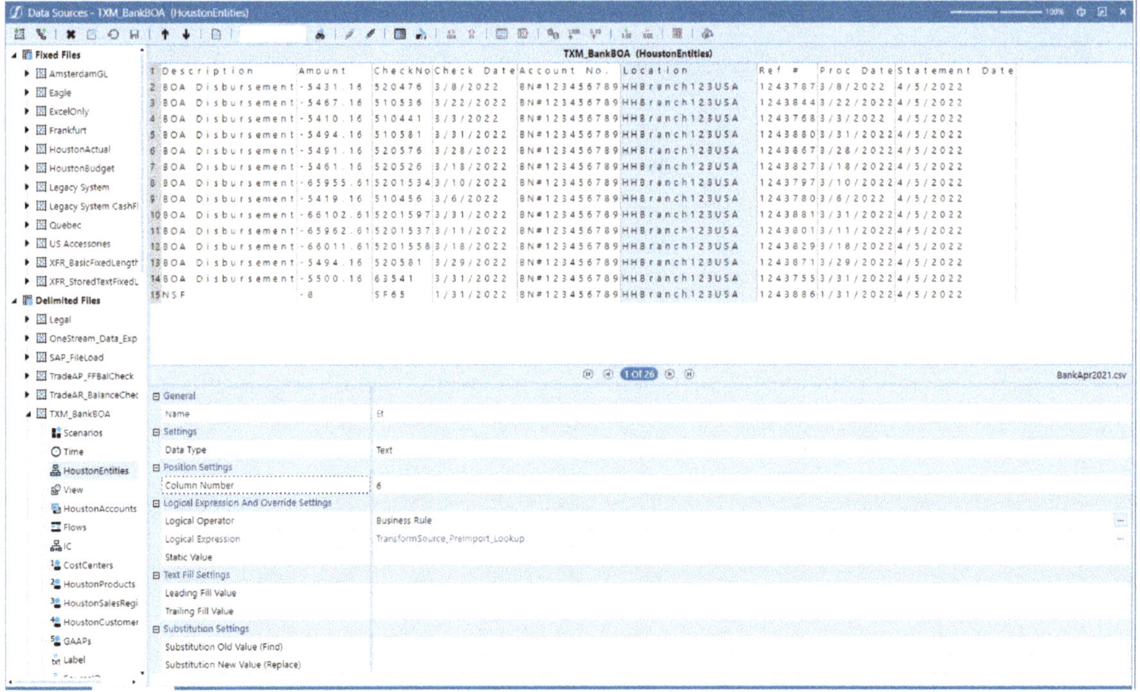

Figure 6.20

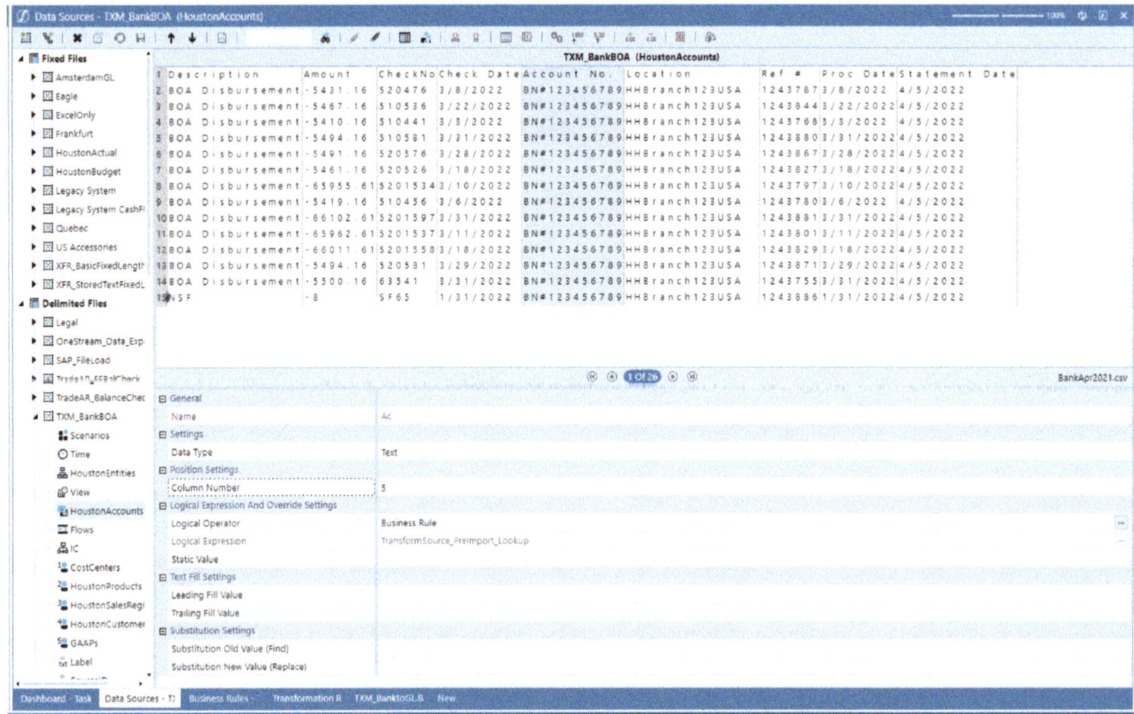

Figure 6.21

Step 2: Create a **Transformation Lookup Rule** to take the source bank information and map it to the Reconciliation Source Account level. For example, you can see on the first line of Figure 6.22 that we are mapping the HHBranch123USA location listed in the bank file to a Target Value of Heights. This is NOT the final T.Account that is held in the Entity Dimension; rather, this will be your S.Account for Reconciliation mapping purposes.

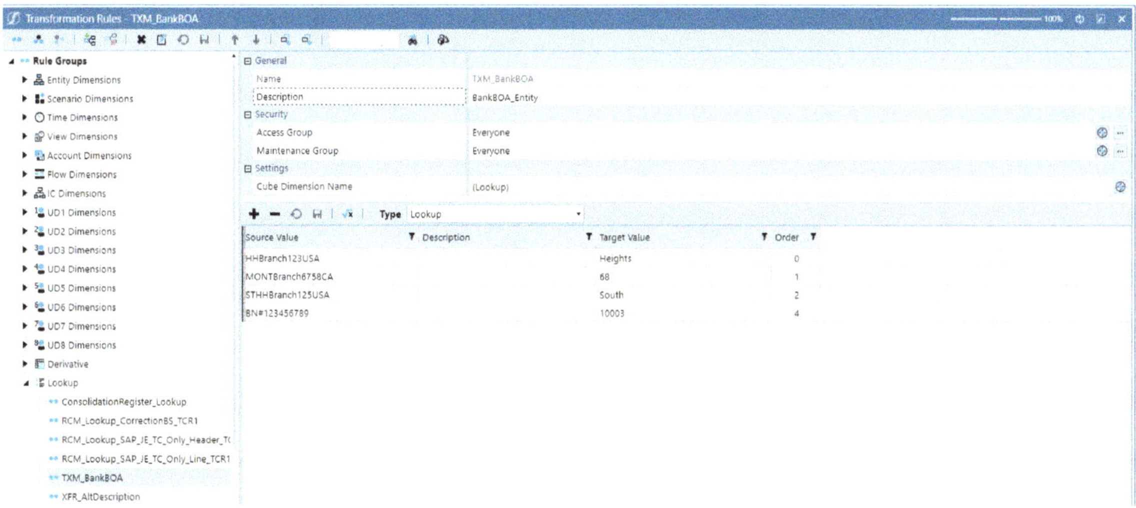

Figure 6.22

Step 3: Create a Parser Rule and update it to call the Lookup Rule created in Step 2.

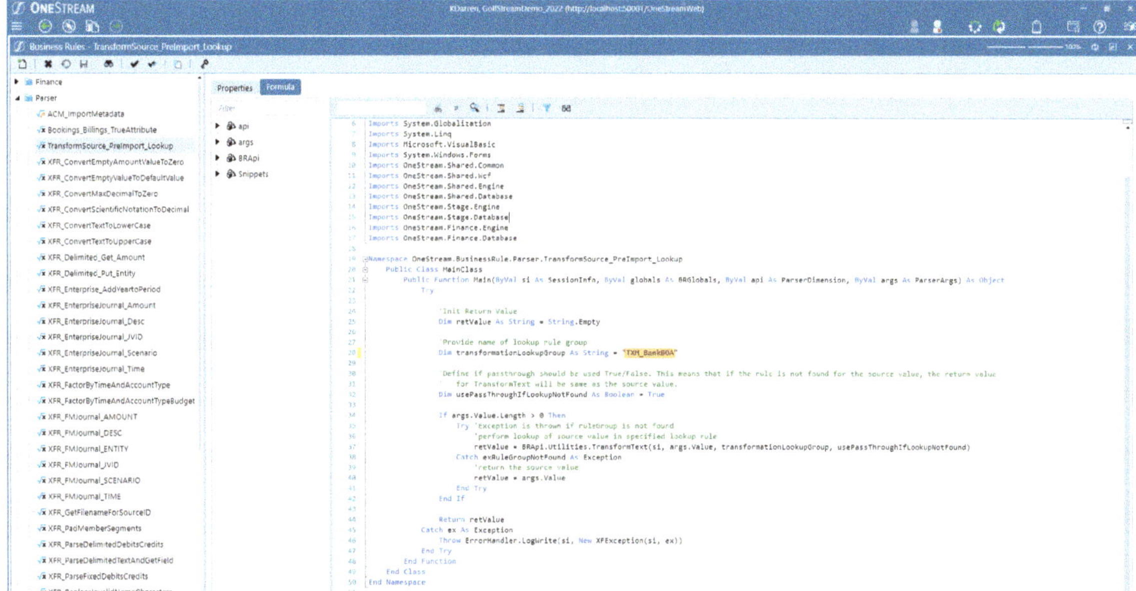

Figure 6.23

Step 4: Update the data source mapping for Entity and Account to call the Parser Rule.

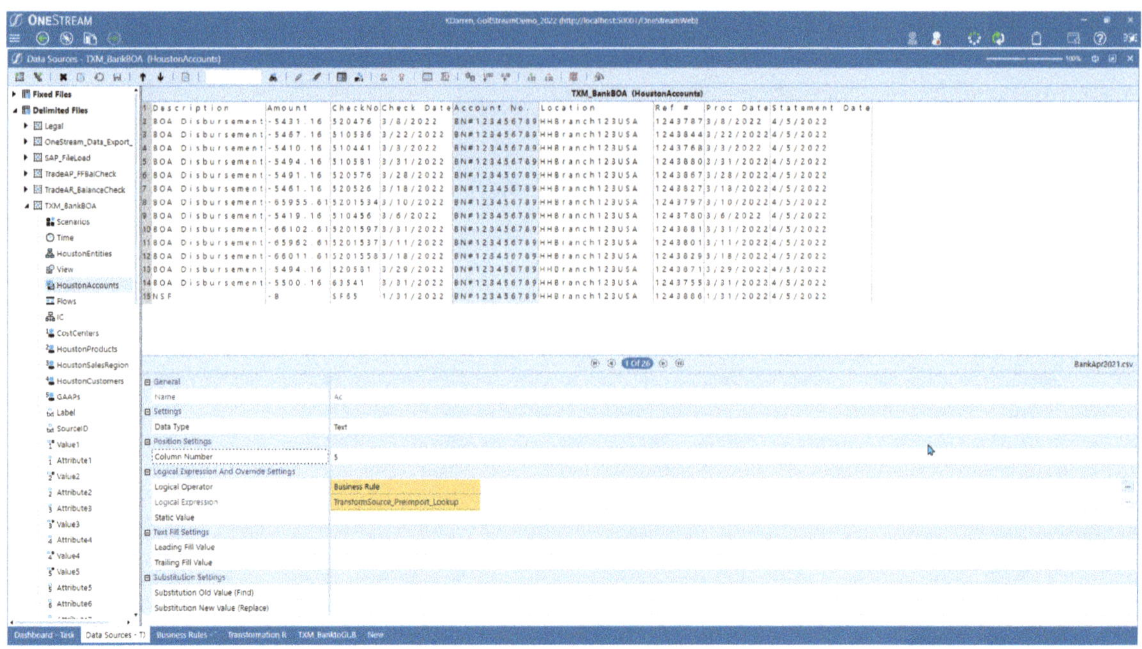

Figure 6.24

Step 5: Load your data file. Note in Figure 6.25 that in our bank CSV file, we see a location of HHBrank123USA and an Account number of BN#123456789.

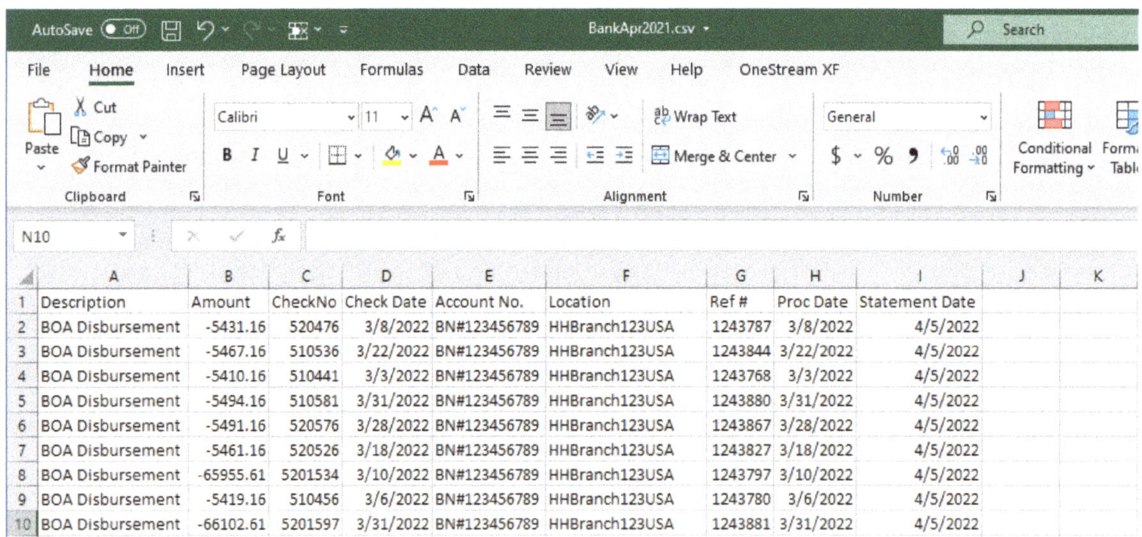

	A	B	C	D	E	F	G	H	I
1	Description	Amount	CheckNo	Check Date	Account No.	Location	Ref #	Proc Date	Statement Date
2	BOA Disbursement	-5431.16	520476	3/8/2022	BN#123456789	HHBranch123USA	1243787	3/8/2022	4/5/2022
3	BOA Disbursement	-5467.16	510536	3/22/2022	BN#123456789	HHBranch123USA	1243844	3/22/2022	4/5/2022
4	BOA Disbursement	-5410.16	510441	3/3/2022	BN#123456789	HHBranch123USA	1243768	3/3/2022	4/5/2022
5	BOA Disbursement	-5494.16	510581	3/31/2022	BN#123456789	HHBranch123USA	1243880	3/31/2022	4/5/2022
6	BOA Disbursement	-5491.16	520576	3/28/2022	BN#123456789	HHBranch123USA	1243867	3/28/2022	4/5/2022
7	BOA Disbursement	-5461.16	520526	3/18/2022	BN#123456789	HHBranch123USA	1243827	3/18/2022	4/5/2022
8	BOA Disbursement	-65955.61	5201534	3/10/2022	BN#123456789	HHBranch123USA	1243797	3/10/2022	4/5/2022
9	BOA Disbursement	-5419.16	510456	3/6/2022	BN#123456789	HHBranch123USA	1243780	3/6/2022	4/5/2022
10	BOA Disbursement	-66102.61	5201597	3/31/2022	BN#123456789	HHBranch123USA	1243881	3/31/2022	4/5/2022

Figure 6.25

Results: The Stage information will now show the data to have source data that aligns with the S.Account, 10003, and S.Entity, Heights, that are used in the Account Reconciliation Tracking Levels.

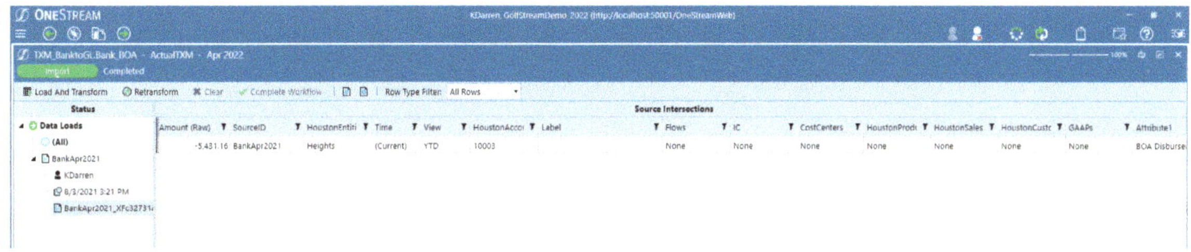

Figure 6.26

By setting this up in this way, once the initial Match Set is set to map to OneStream's core dimensionality, you no longer need to constantly map your Match Set to new Reconciliations. Rather, you would just need to add to the Transformation Lookup Rule from Step 2. For example, if the bank file added a new Bank Account number, simply add the Bank Account Number Source Account here and identify the corresponding Source Account, and then the system will know where to push the transactional-level information for detail item support creation.

16 Text Fields

Utilize Attribute Fields 1-16 for any text columns.

Four Date Fields

Attribute Fields 17-20 are to be used for any dates.

13 Value Fields

Amount and Attribute Value Fields 1-12 are to be used for values. Examples of multiple types of values would be:

1. Account, Local, and Reporting amounts in a file
2. Gross, tax, and net amounts
3. Or, if comparing invoices and POs, maybe you could have quantity and cost per unit

This configuration establishes what is displayed to the User and, therefore, fields can be added or removed at any point.

Alias

Here, you enter free form text, which will be the column header to be displayed to Users on the Transactions page, and on the bottom of the Matches page when a match is selected.

Column Order

Enter the numerical order the column is to be displayed on the Transactions and Matches page. If you have two columns that you would like to always sit next to each other, give them the same numerical order. The column that was added first, S.Entity in Figure 6.27, will be shown to the left of the column with the same numerical value.

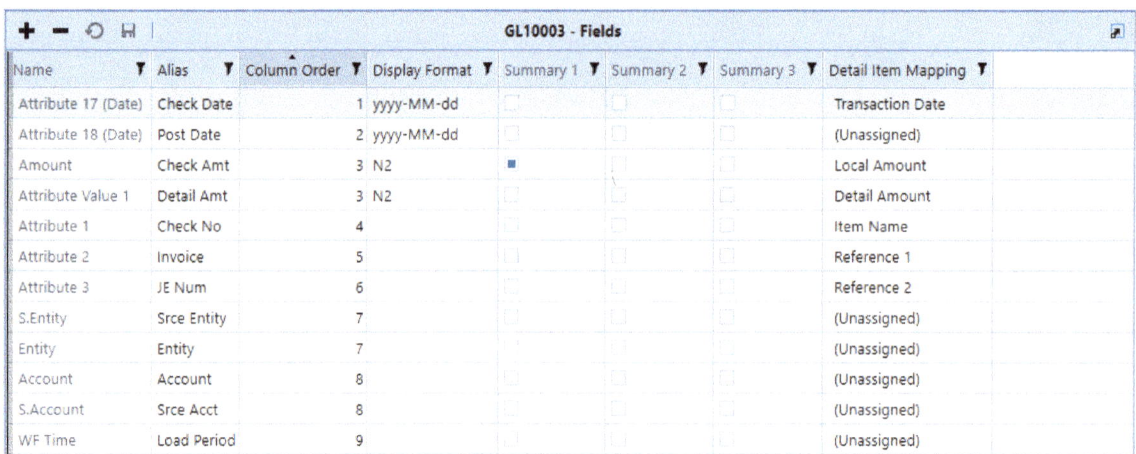

GL10003 - Fields

Name	Alias	Column Order	Display Format	Summary 1	Summary 2	Summary 3	Detail Item Mapping
Attribute 17 (Date)	Check Date	1	yyyy-MM-dd				Transaction Date
Attribute 18 (Date)	Post Date	2	yyyy-MM-dd				(Unassigned)
Amount	Check Amt	3	N2				Local Amount
Attribute Value 1	Detail Amt	3	N2				Detail Amount
Attribute 1	Check No	4					Item Name
Attribute 2	Invoice	5					Reference 1
Attribute 3	JE Num	6					Reference 2
S.Entity	Srce Entity	7					(Unassigned)
Entity	Entity	7					(Unassigned)
Account	Account	8					(Unassigned)
S.Account	Srce Acct	8					(Unassigned)
WF Time	Load Period	9					(Unassigned)

Figure 6.27

Display Format

This is a text field where you configure how numerical values – such as dates, amounts, and decimals – will be displayed throughout the solution. Some commonly used formats are:

- **N0** will not show any decimals or zeroes.
- **N1-N6** shows X number of decimals (N2 shows two decimals, N5 shows five decimals, etc.)
- **#,###,0\%** displays 10,000% and -10,000%
- **#,###,0.00** displays 10,000.00 and -10,000.00
- **yyyy-MM-dd** displays year, month, and date

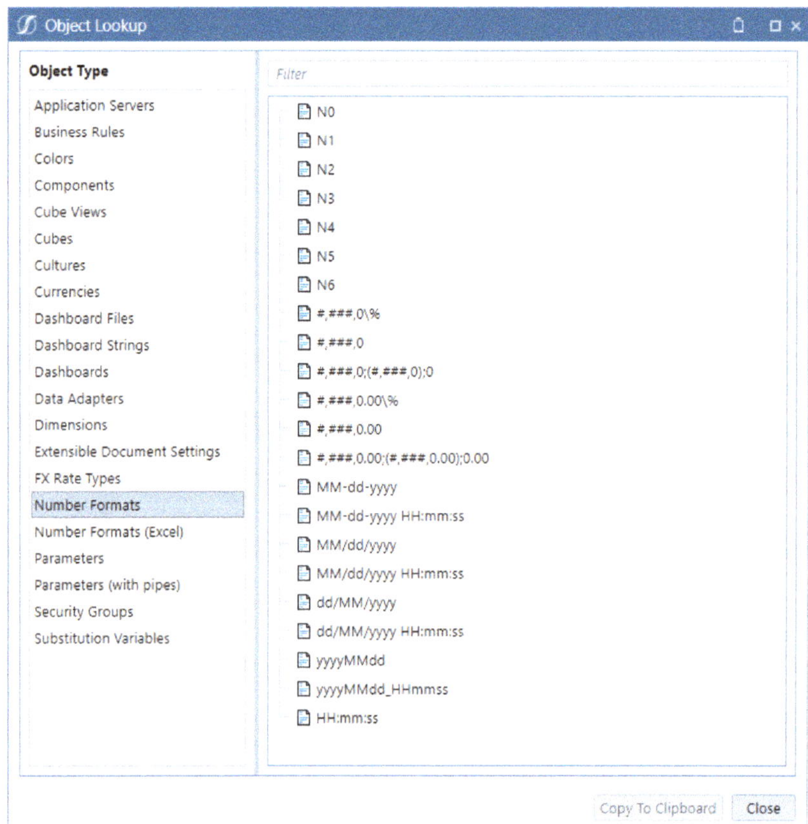

Figure 6.28

Summary 1 – 3

Transaction Matching can summarize and display up to three value columns. Set the check box to True if this field should be used for the comparison of values for matching purposes. For example, we discussed previously that a Suspense Account could be loaded as a single file, and we could utilize data splitting to compare our debits and credits. For this example, we are summarizing the Amount, DR Local Amount, and DR Reporting Amount for the debit data set (Figure 6.29), and the corresponding credit columns, CR Doc, CD Local Amount, and CR Reporting are being summarized for the credit data set (Figure 6.30).

Suspense DR - Fields

Name	Alias	Column Order	Display Format	Summary 1	Summary 2	Summary 3	Detail Item Mapping
WF Time	Load Period	0		☐	☐	☐	(Unassigned)
Attribute 1	Doc No	1		☐	☐	☐	(Unassigned)
Entity	Entity	2		☐	☐	☐	(Unassigned)
Attribute 2	DR/CR	3		☐	☐	☐	(Unassigned)
Attribute 3	Desc	4		☐	☐	☐	(Unassigned)
Attribute 4	Ref1	5		☐	☐	☐	(Unassigned)
Attribute 5	Source Acct	6		☐	☐	☐	(Unassigned)
Account	Acct	6		☐	☐	☐	(Unassigned)
Amount	DR Doc	7	N2	■	☐	☐	(Unassigned)
Attribute 17 (Date)	Date	8	yyyy-MM-dd	☐	☐	☐	(Unassigned)
Attribute 18 (Date)	Post Date	9	yyyy-MM-dd	☐	☐	☐	(Unassigned)
Attribute Value 1	DR LC	10	N2	☐	■	☐	(Unassigned)
Attribute Value 2	DR Rpt	11	N2	☐	☐	■	(Unassigned)

Figure 6.29

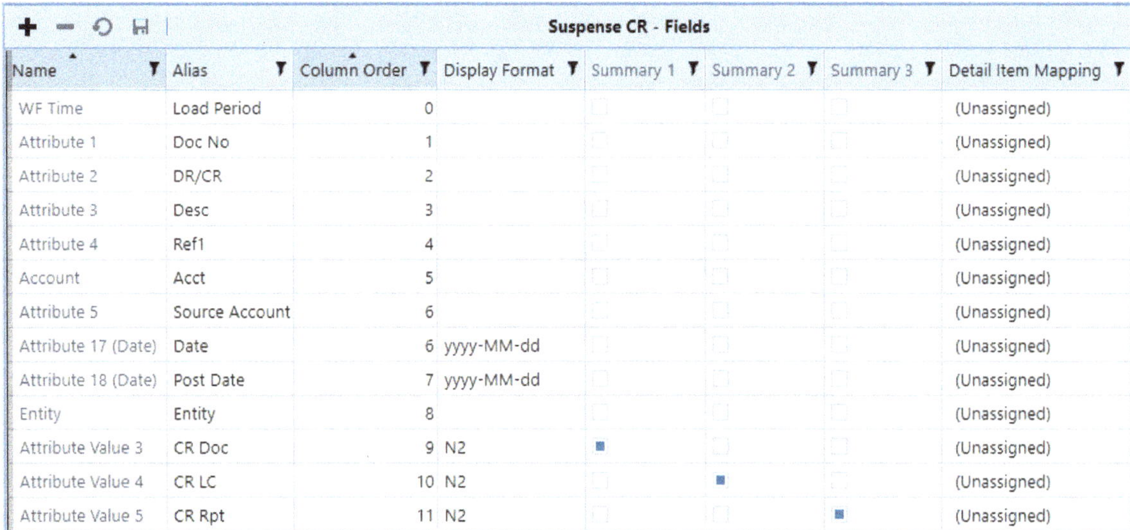

Suspense CR - Fields

Name	Alias	Column Order	Display Format	Summary 1	Summary 2	Summary 3	Detail Item Mapping
WF Time	Load Period	0		☐	☐	☐	(Unassigned)
Attribute 1	Doc No	1		☐	☐	☐	(Unassigned)
Attribute 2	DR/CR	2		☐	☐	☐	(Unassigned)
Attribute 3	Desc	3		☐	☐	☐	(Unassigned)
Attribute 4	Ref1	4		☐	☐	☐	(Unassigned)
Account	Acct	5		☐	☐	☐	(Unassigned)
Attribute 5	Source Account	6		☐	☐	☐	(Unassigned)
Attribute 17 (Date)	Date	6	yyyy-MM-dd	☐	☐	☐	(Unassigned)
Attribute 18 (Date)	Post Date	7	yyyy-MM-dd	☐	☐	☐	(Unassigned)
Entity	Entity	8		☐	☐	☐	(Unassigned)
Attribute Value 3	CR Doc	9	N2	■	☐	☐	(Unassigned)
Attribute Value 4	CR LC	10	N2	☐	■	☐	(Unassigned)
Attribute Value 5	CR Rpt	11	N2	☐	☐	■	(Unassigned)

Figure 6.30

Discussion on the implementation for this example will be discussed in Chapter 7, but for now, it is important to note that these summary amounts are the columns that will be summarized and compared at the bottom of the Transactions and Matches pages, as shown at the bottom left of Figure 6.31, and are utilized for manual matching tolerances. As more transactions are selected within the grid, the summarized information will automatically update so that you can easily determine the variance between the data sets.

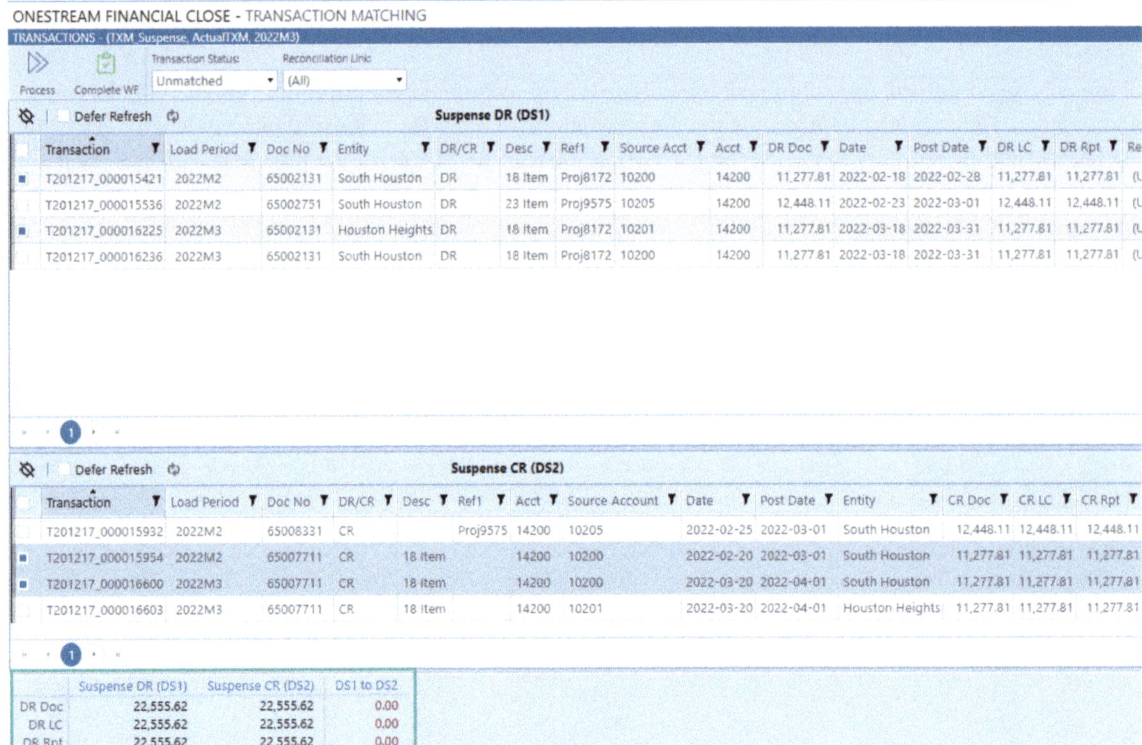
ONESTREAM FINANCIAL CLOSE - TRANSACTION MATCHING

TRANSACTIONS - (TXM_Suspense, ActualTXM, 2022M3)

Transaction Status: Unmatched | Reconciliation Link: (All)

Suspense DR (DS1)

Transaction	Load Period	Doc No	Entity	DR/CR	Desc	Ref1	Source Acct	Acct	DR Doc	Date	Post Date	DR LC	DR Rpt
T201217_000015421	2022M2	65002131	South Houston	DR	18 Item	Proj8172	10200	14200	11,277.81	2022-02-18	2022-02-28	11,277.81	11,277.81
T201217_000015536	2022M2	65002751	South Houston	DR	23 Item	Proj9575	10205	14200	12,448.11	2022-02-23	2022-03-01	12,448.11	12,448.11
T201217_000016225	2022M3	65002131	Houston Heights	DR	18 Item	Proj8172	10201	14200	11,277.81	2022-03-18	2022-03-31	11,277.81	11,277.81
T201217_000016236	2022M3	65002131	South Houston	DR	18 Item	Proj8172	10200	14200	11,277.81	2022-03-18	2022-03-31	11,277.81	11,277.81

Suspense CR (DS2)

Transaction	Load Period	Doc No	DR/CR	Desc	Ref1	Acct	Source Account	Date	Post Date	Entity	CR Doc	CR LC	CR Rpt
T201217_000015932	2022M2	65008331	CR		Proj9575	14200	10205	2022-02-25	2022-03-01	South Houston	12,448.11	12,448.11	12,448.11
T201217_000015954	2022M2	65007711	CR	18 Item		14200	10200	2022-02-20	2022-03-01	South Houston	11,277.81	11,277.81	11,277.81
T201217_000016600	2022M3	65007711	CR	18 Item		14200	10200	2022-03-20	2022-04-01	South Houston	11,277.81	11,277.81	11,277.81
T201217_000016603	2022M3	65007711	CR	18 Item		14200	10201	2022-03-20	2022-04-01	Houston Heights	11,277.81	11,277.81	11,277.81

	Suspense DR (DS1)	Suspense CR (DS2)	DS1 to DS2
DR Doc	22,555.62	22,555.62	0.00
DR LC	22,555.62	22,555.62	0.00
DR Rpt	22,555.62	22,555.62	0.00

Figure 6.31

> **Note:** Once a match exists, the summary fields cannot be edited and new summary fields cannot be added, so make sure you identify these fields during your design process.

Detail Item Mapping

This column will only be present for applications where integration between Transaction Matching and Account Reconciliations has been enabled in Account Reconciliations. To use Transaction Matching transactions to create detail items in Account Reconciliations, the data sets in Transaction Matching must be assigned to the Account Reconciliation fields. Figure 6.32 shows all the columns that are available with the detail item information.

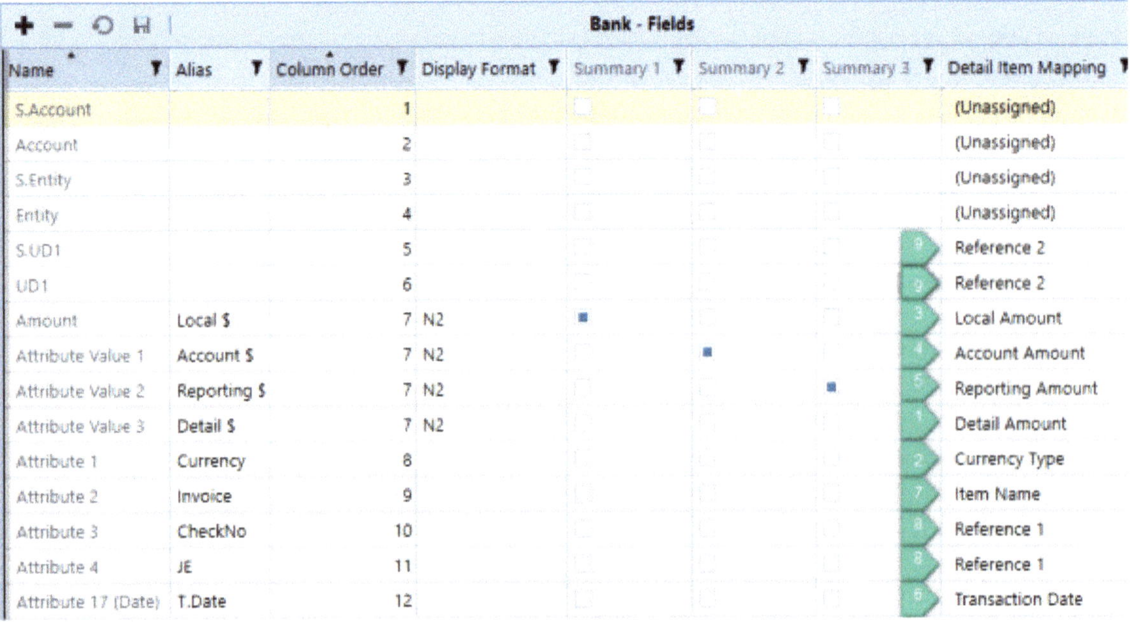
Bank - Fields

Name	Alias	Column Order	Display Format	Summary 1	Summary 2	Summary 3	Detail Item Mapping
S.Account		1					(Unassigned)
Account		2					(Unassigned)
S.Entity		3					(Unassigned)
Entity		4					(Unassigned)
S.UD1		5					Reference 2
UD1		6					Reference 2
Amount	Local $	7	N2	■			Local Amount
Attribute Value 1	Account $	7	N2		■		Account Amount
Attribute Value 2	Reporting $	7	N2			■	Reporting Amount
Attribute Value 3	Detail $	7	N2				Detail Amount
Attribute 1	Currency	8					Currency Type
Attribute 2	Invoice	9					Item Name
Attribute 3	CheckNo	10					Reference 1
Attribute 4	JE	11					Reference 1
Attribute 17 (Date)	T.Date	12					Transaction Date

Figure 6.32

1. **Detail Amount**: This is the transactional-level amount. If multi-currency is enabled, it identifies the amount to be pulled in as the Account Reconciliation detail amount and this value column must be identified. If no other values are identified, system Translation will occur upon item creation, in line with the process of manually creating detail items.
2. **Currency Type**: Detail Amount currency type used when multi-currency is enabled. If a currency type is not mapped, the currency type will default to the Account currency type for the Reconciliation upon creation, which is the same process for manual item creation.
3. **Local Amount**: If multi-currency is not enabled, this column must be mapped as it identifies the detail item amount. If multi-currency is enabled, mapping the column is not required.
4. **Account Amount**: Overrides what would be calculated for the Account amount if multi-currency is enabled. If this column is not mapped, the Account amount will be automatically calculated upon creation.
5. **Reporting Amount**: Overrides what would be calculated for the Reporting amount if multi-currency is enabled. If this column is not mapped, the Reporting amount will be automatically calculated upon creation.
6. **Transaction Date**: Date of the transaction. This date is used to create item aging within Account Reconciliations. It is not required to be mapped.
7. **Item Name**: Default value for item name. This column is required to be mapped for detail item creation purposes. However, once the transactional detail item has been created using the column information, the item name can be edited within Account Reconciliations prior to the Reconciliation moving to a prepared state.
8. **Reference 1**: Concatenates up to two fields and is used to provide additional information. It can be overridden and is dependent on selections made when creating a detail item. Mapping is not required.
9. **Reference 2**: Concatenates up to two fields and is used to provide additional information. It can be overridden and is dependent on selections made when creating a detail item. Mapping is not required.

Rules

After configuring your data sets, navigate to the Rules page to configure the matching rules that will be used to match your transactions. Prior to configuring the rules, make a list of all data fields that your transactions can be Matched across, determine if multiple line items in one data set can make up a single line item in another data set (think multiple invoices paid off with a single check), and establish the thresholds you would like for your rules. The more specific and thought-out you can get with your rules during the design phase, prior to implementation, the smoother your implementation will be.

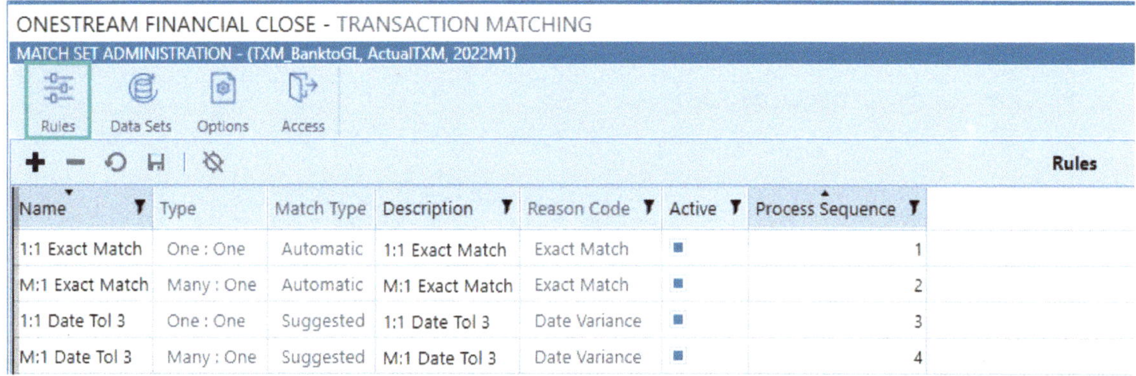

Name	Type	Match Type	Description	Reason Code	Active	Process Sequence
1:1 Exact Match	One : One	Automatic	1:1 Exact Match	Exact Match	■	1
M:1 Exact Match	Many : One	Automatic	M:1 Exact Match	Exact Match	■	2
1:1 Date Tol 3	One : One	Suggested	1:1 Date Tol 3	Date Variance	■	3
M:1 Date Tol 3	Many : One	Suggested	M:1 Date Tol 3	Date Variance	■	4

Figure 6.33

The rules are maintained in a table. Some fields can be edited after creation, while others cannot. A rule cannot be deleted once it has been used to make a match. If you would like to edit the rule definitions after a match was made, you must unmatch all your matches. Alternatively, if you have created definitions, groupings, etc., that are needed, but a part of your rule needs to be altered in a non-editable field, such are changing the Reason Code, copy the rule and create a new rule.

It is recommended, if you have Match Sets with similar rules, to first configure that Match Set, including all the applicable rules, and then copy the Match Set and use it as a starting point for future Match Set configurations. This is because, while you can copy a Match Set, rules cannot be copied from one Match Set to another.

Name

This is a free form text box where you name the rule. The name you enter here is displayed throughout the solution, such as on the Matches page in the "Rule" column indicating the rule used to make the match. It is also the name that appears on the Match Details screen when you drill into the transaction information on the Transactions page. This display text can be edited at any time.

Type

This is a drop-down list containing the rule types. Once the rule is created, the type cannot be changed. The rule types include:

- **One to One (1:1)** – an exact match in which a single transaction in one data set is compared to a single transaction in the other. An example would be comparing a check register to a bank clearing account. All checks written should directly correlate to the checks that have cleared the bank, and you would expect the check numbers to exactly match.
- **One to Many (1:M)** – a single transaction in one data set that can be Matched with one or more transactions (a grouping) in another. An example would be one check that was applied to many invoices.
- **Many to One (M:1)** – one or more transactions (a grouping) in one data set that are condensed into one transaction and then compared to a single transaction in another.
- **Many to Many (M:M)** – one or more transactions (a grouping) in one data set that are collapsed into a single amount and then compared to the same in another.

Additionally, the following rule types are available for three data set matches:

- One to One to One (1:1:1)
- One to One to Many (1:1:M)
- One to Many to One (1:M:1)
- Many to One to One (M:1:1)
- One to Many to Many (1:M:M)
- Many to Many to One (M:M:1)
- Many to One to Many (M:1:M)
- Many to Many to Many (M:M:M)

Match Type

This is a drop-down list of available types, either **Automatic** (default) or **Suggested**. Automatic matches do not require any User intervention to be completed but can be Unmatched if desired. Suggested matches require a Preparer to accept the match before the transactions are moved to a Matched status. Suggested matches can also be configured to require approval, if desired. Use Suggested when you set thresholds, expect variances, etc., and want a User to review the match for accuracy and/or material variance.

Description

This is an optional free form text field that you can utilize to enter additional rule information. This information is not displayed in the solution and is for Administrator reference purposes only. This display text can be edited at any time.

Reason Code

This is a pre-populated drop-down list containing the Reason Codes that are set up on the Options page. This field cannot be edited once the rule is created. As such, make sure you set up the Reason Codes first – prior to making your rules – or this field will be set to the default of Unassigned.

Active

By default, this is set to True, meaning the rule should be run during rule processing. Set this to False if the rule is no longer used but has been used in the past to create matches, as rules used to create matches cannot be deleted for audit purposes.

Process Sequence

The order in which the rules are run. Rules are run in ascending order of the process sequence. Best practice is to have the rules that create the most matches run first. This way, when subsequent rules are processed, the system will have fewer transactions to loop through, thus decreasing the processing time.

Definition

Once you have created the shell for the rule, including its name and what type of rule you would like to make, you must then configure the real intent of the rule. You do this within the bottom section of the Rules page, starting with the Definition. Here, you will configure the detailed information that is to be applied to the rule. To add the Definition, select the rule at the top of the page. By default, the display at the bottom will show the rule Definition. Note that there are two Field Name and Condition columns because we are selecting the Field Name and Condition for each data set, where Data Set 1 (DS1) is selected first. If there were three data sets for the Match Set, these columns would appear three times. You do not need to apply definitions to all data sets; you can apply to only one if necessary.

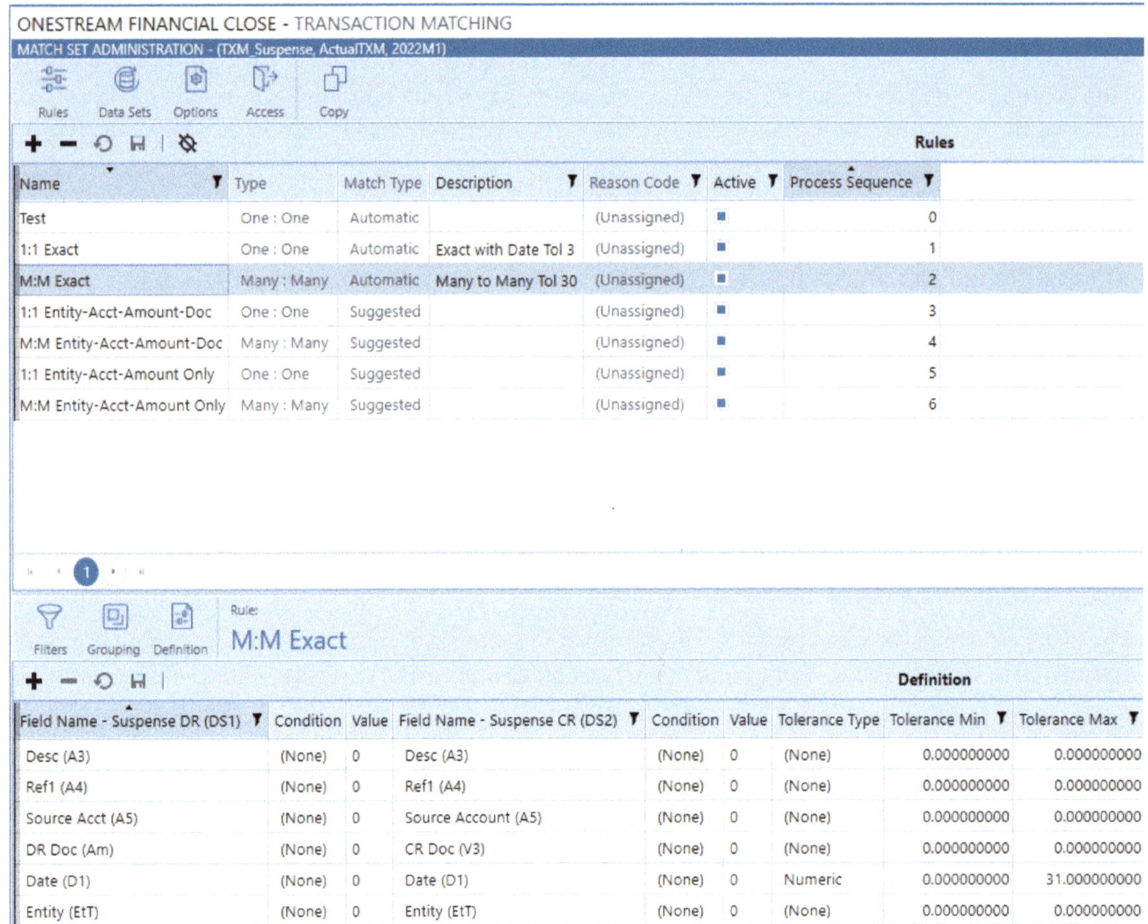

ONESTREAM FINANCIAL CLOSE - TRANSACTION MATCHING

MATCH SET ADMINISTRATION - (TXM_Suspense, ActualTXM, 2022M1)

Rules | Data Sets | Options | Access | Copy

Rules

Name	Type	Match Type	Description	Reason Code	Active	Process Sequence
Test	One : One	Automatic		(Unassigned)	■	0
1:1 Exact	One : One	Automatic	Exact with Date Tol 3	(Unassigned)	■	1
M:M Exact	Many : Many	Automatic	Many to Many Tol 30	(Unassigned)	■	2
1:1 Entity-Acct-Amount-Doc	One : One	Suggested		(Unassigned)	■	3
M:M Entity-Acct-Amount-Doc	Many : Many	Suggested		(Unassigned)	■	4
1:1 Entity-Acct-Amount Only	One : One	Suggested		(Unassigned)	■	5
M:M Entity-Acct-Amount Only	Many : Many	Suggested		(Unassigned)	■	6

Filters | Grouping | Definition

Rule: M:M Exact

Definition

Field Name - Suspense DR (DS1)	Condition	Value	Field Name - Suspense CR (DS2)	Condition	Value	Tolerance Type	Tolerance Min	Tolerance Max
Desc (A3)	(None)	0	Desc (A3)	(None)	0	(None)	0.000000000	0.000000000
Ref1 (A4)	(None)	0	Ref1 (A4)	(None)	0	(None)	0.000000000	0.000000000
Source Acct (A5)	(None)	0	Source Account (A5)	(None)	0	(None)	0.000000000	0.000000000
DR Doc (Am)	(None)	0	CR Doc (V3)	(None)	0	(None)	0.000000000	0.000000000
Date (D1)	(None)	0	Date (D1)	(None)	0	Numeric	0.000000000	31.000000000
Entity (EtT)	(None)	0	Entity (EtT)	(None)	0	(None)	0.000000000	0.000000000

Figure 6.34

Field Names

This is a drop-down list of all fields configured for the data set with the **Alias** shown and the name in parentheses. Note, in Figure 6.34, that for several of the items we are comparing, the same fields are shown, as this example uses rules created for a suspense file where data splitting occurred. But for the value, we are comparing the DR Doc (Amount) in DS1 to the CR Doc (Value 3) in DS2.

Conditions

Select the placement (None, Left, Right) for each data set; this is particularly useful if there will be leading or trailing zeroes in one data set that may not exist in the other data sets. For example, if DS1 had values of N6 (100.123456) and DS2 had values of N2 (100.12), you would not want to do an exact match without excluding the last four digits of DS1 as no match would ever occur. In this instance, you would set the placement to the left and the value would be five, to select the first five numbers. Note that this would only work if you knew the count of numbers that exist before the decimal. A good example would be if you know that all invoice numbers have five digits. If you do not, you should format your data as part of your data integration set up to truncate values as needed (e.g., remove the last four digits, 3456).

> **Note:** Rule conditions help guide the position the rule should be applied to a certain data element. The position can start at the beginning of a string (left) or the end of a string (right). The rule definitions have conditions and value fields for each data set.

Tolerances

Select the type of tolerance to be applied, either percentage or numeric. For example, if you know that check dates might not exactly match the date they clear the bank, but you expect them to clear within the month, you would select the date field for each data set and then set a numeric tolerance of 30.

Or, if you have large currency fluctuations that might cause some values not to exactly match, you could set a percentage tolerance to allow for foreign exchange fluctuations. Only value, amount, and date fields may have tolerances applied to them, and date fields can only have numeric tolerances (not percentages). Dimension fields and attributes cannot have tolerances.

> **Note:** The tolerance type *must* be selected for definitions to be applied. If values, conditions, and minimum and maximum tolerances are set, and the type is not selected, the tolerance will not be applied.

Filters

Filters are used to determine which transactions should have rules run against them. For example, you may have a single bank file that is used for a data set that contains multiple bank Accounts, but different Accounts may require different rules. In this instance, you would filter out specific Accounts for the rule, as shown in Figure 6.35. To do so, select the rule at the top of the page, click the filter icon, and then add a filter. Only the Unmatched transactions returned by the filter are used during rule processing. Filters can be deleted at any time.

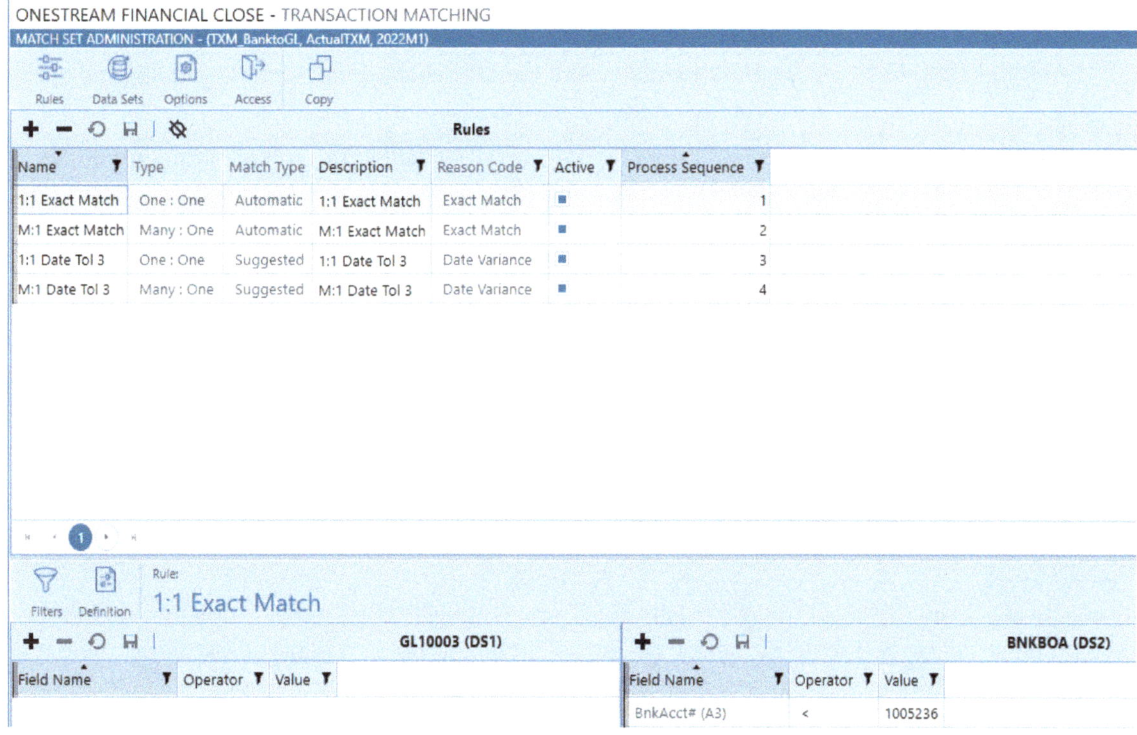

Figure 6.35

Field Name

This is a drop-down list of all fields configured for the data set with the Alias shown and the name in parentheses. In our example, we are using Bank Account #3 (Alias), or Attribute 3 (Name). Once the filter has been saved, the Field Name cannot be changed.

Operator

There is a drop-down list of functions that are used to combine items or determine the parameters to create a filter. Below are the available operators and their functions.

Operator	Actions
=	Is equal to the value specified (exact match). To return fields that are blank, leave Value blank.
>	Is greater than the value specified.
>=	Is greater than, or equal to, the value specified.
<	Is less than the value specified.
<=	Is less than, or equal to, the value specified.
<>	Is not equal to the value specified. To return fields that are not blank, leave Value blank.
In 1;2;3 or 'A'; 'B'; 'C'	Displays values that are the same as what is specified.
Between 1;2 or 'A'; 'Z'	Displays values that fall between the first and second values (including the listed values).
Starts With	Displays results where the data in the column starts with the value in the filter.
Does Not Start With	Displays results where the data in the column starts with anything except the value in the filter.
Ends With	Displays results where the data in the column ends with the value in the filter.
Does Not End With	Displays results where the data in the column ends with anything except the value in the filter.
Contains	Displays only records where the data in the column contains all the values in the filter.
Does Not Contain	Displays only records where the data in the column does not contain any of the values in the filter.

Figure 6.36

Value

This is a free form text field where you define the criteria to be used by the operator.

Grouping

When using many to one, or many to many rules, you will need to establish which transactions should be grouped together to be part of the 'many' to be Matched. When a **Many Rule Type** is selected, the Grouping icon appears, providing the ability to specify how to aggregate (group) the data. Once the grouping is defined, the items in the group become the only items available in the Definition Field Name list for selection, in addition to the Summary fields.

Field Name

This is a drop-down list of all fields configured for the data set with the Alias shown and the name in parentheses. Add all the fields that are to be grouped together for each data set if a Many to Many Rule is used, or for the individual data set if a One to Many or Many to One Rule is used.

Options

The Options page is used to set up approval requirements, data security, Reason Codes, and matching tolerances. All fields within this page can be updated at any point, with the exception of Reason Codes.

Required Approval – Manual

Set this to True to require an Approver to approve every manual match.

Required Approval – Suggested

Set this to True to require an Approver to approve every suggested match.

Require Comment

Set this to True to require a comment to be entered for every manual match. Because this can be burdensome if you have numerous manual matches, this setting is not recommended where a lot of manual interventions occur.

Require Attachment

Set this to True to require an attachment be uploaded for every manual match. Because this can be burdensome if you have multiple manual matches, and because the database storage size would also be affected (and therefore performance), this setting is not recommended where a lot of manual interventions occur.

Data Security

To enable data set security for the Match Set, select the Cube you would like referenced – for the Entity security for the Match Set – from the drop-down list. For example, when we discussed setting data set security on the Data Sets page, we showed the Houston Heights Read Write Access in Figure 6.15. This Entity sits in the Houston Cube, so we would set the Houston Cube here.

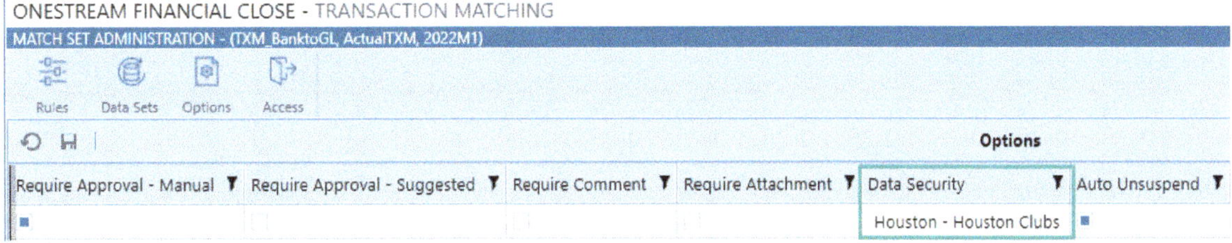

Figure 6.37

Auto Unsuspend

During a period, you will identify transactions that are known to be out of period transactions, which will get Matched in a future period. In this instance, you would suspend the transaction, which is discussed in more detail in Chapter 8.

By default, the transactions will stay in a Suspended state, preventing them from having Match Rules run against them, until a User manually moves the transaction to an Unmatched status. If this option is set to True, the transactions Suspended in a prior Workflow period will be *unsuspended*, moving them to an Unmatched status, upon running Process. This will allow Match Rules to be run against the previously Suspended transactions. If this option is not enabled, Suspended transactions are excluded from rules-based matching.

> **Note:** Auto Unsuspend will only unsuspend transactions Suspended in a prior period; anything that is Suspended in the *current* Workflow period will remain Suspended.

Manual Matching Tolerances

Because manual matching is a transaction-selecting process, you can select transactions that have an amount variance range by defining and applying tolerances. A tolerance allows transactions to be Matched when they do not have exact matching values, which would otherwise trigger User intervention. Defining a tolerance range (upper and lower levels of acceptable variance) tells the system how far outside of the exact amount it can consider an acceptable match.

Tolerance Type options are numeric or a percentage of the total (or none), and different tolerances can be set against each of the summary fields. If a tolerance is not applied to a summary field, the field will not be considered when determining whether a manual match can occur.

Admin Override

Setting this option to True allows Administrators to create manual matches even if the variance is outside the tolerance threshold for any of the summary fields.

Approver Override

Setting this option to True allows Approvers to create manual matches even if the variance is outside the tolerance threshold for any of the summary fields.

Summary 1-3 Type

The threshold types that can be applied to the summary fields are either numeric or percentage. Remember, you can summarize on up to three fields; some fields may be currency or value fields, while some may be a count, such as inventory. Therefore, keep in mind which fields you established as Summary 1-3 when setting your type.

Summary 1-3 Min

This is a free form text field where you enter the absolute value of the lower limit that would be accepted for a manual match. If you were comparing three currency levels – such as Account, Local, and Reporting – it would be expected to use the same type here, but your minimum and maximum thresholds would most likely be different as currency fluctuates. I would care a lot more about a $1,000 USD variance than a $1,000 MXN variance.

Summary 1-3 Max

This is a free form text field where you will enter the absolute value of the upper limit that would be accepted for a manual match.

Figure 6.38 shows an example of entering your minimum and maximum ranges. Note for Summary 1, we have selected a numeric tolerance type, and for Summary 2 we have selected a percentage type. Therefore, if the variance for Summary 1 is between (10) and 10, it would be possible to create a manual match.

Likewise, if the variance for Summary 2 were between (10%) and 10% of the total amount, a manual match could be created. Additionally, if we had elected to summarize a third field on the Data Set page, and a variance existed on this field, it would not be considered when determining if matching is permitted.

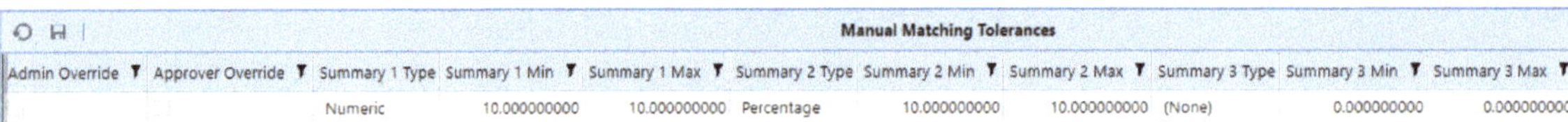

Manual Matching Tolerances

Admin Override	Approver Override	Summary 1 Type	Summary 1 Min	Summary 1 Max	Summary 2 Type	Summary 2 Min	Summary 2 Max	Summary 3 Type	Summary 3 Min	Summary 3 Max
		Numeric	10.000000000	10.000000000	Percentage	10.000000000	10.000000000	(None)	0.000000000	0.000000000

Figure 6.38

Reason Codes

Reason Codes are a custom list created by either a Transaction Matching Administrator or a OneStream Administrator, and are specific to your company. They are not required to be used or configured but are helpful when analyzing information such as *why* manual matches were made and *why* transactions were Suspended. This list is provided in a drop-down format when:

1. A User creates a Match +.

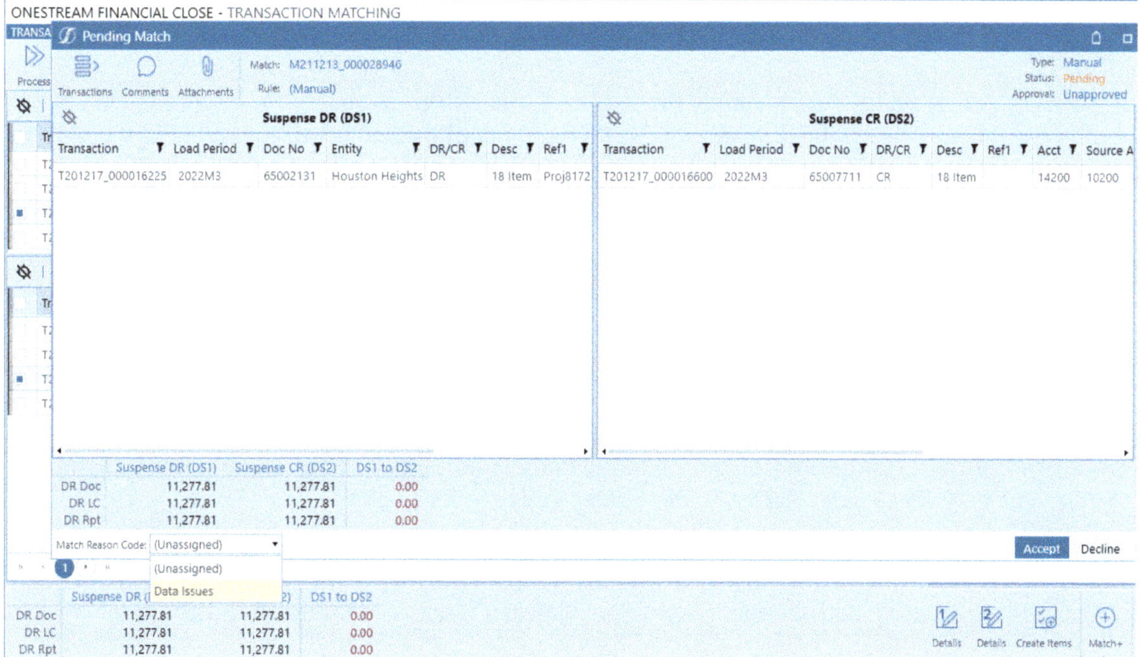

Figure 6.39

2. A User suspends a transaction.

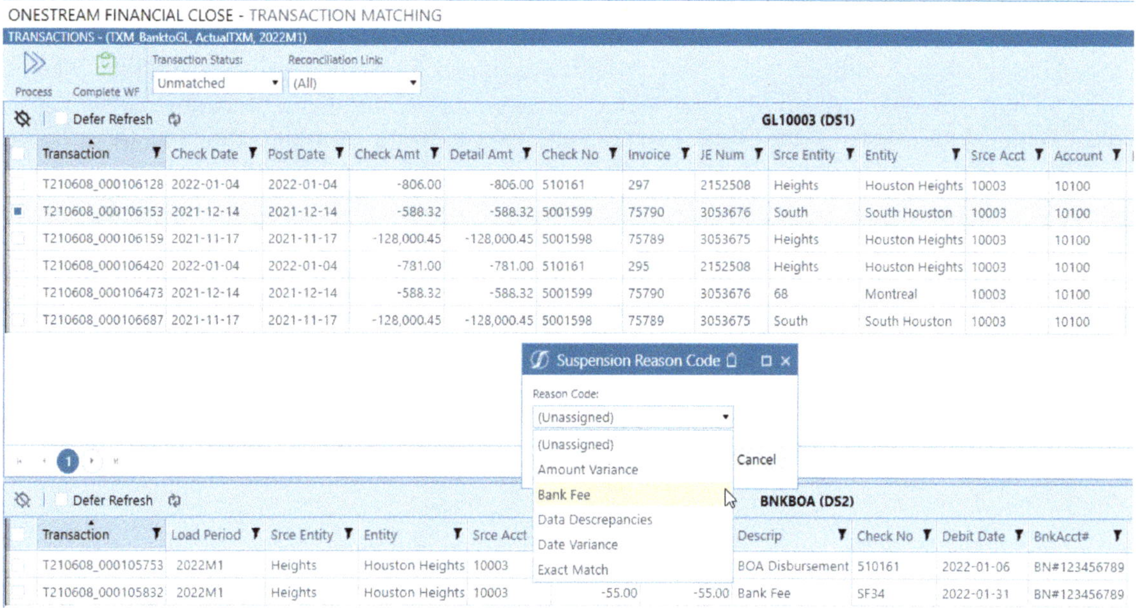

Figure 6.40

Reason Code names cannot be edited once saved. Additionally, a Reason Code cannot be deleted once it is assigned to a match.

Name

The name created here will be the name displayed in the Reason Code drop-down throughout the solution, as shown in Figures 6.39 and 6.40.

Description

This is a reference column for the description of the Reason Code. This information is not displayed elsewhere in the solution. The description may be edited at any point.

Active

By default, this is set to True, meaning the Reason Code will be available for Users to select and apply. Set this to False if the Reason Code is no longer applicable but has been used in the past to create matches or suspend transactions, as Reason Codes used to create matches or suspend transactions cannot be deleted for audit purposes.

Access

Access is configured at the Match Set level. The Access page displays the User's name and role and each User assigned to the current Match Set. Setting up access here will determine what type of actions the User can take on transactions. Note that this setup is in addition to giving Users access to the Workflow Profile. This page is included within the Administration, in addition to the Access Control within Settings, so that Transaction Matching Administrators can make updates to the security, as they do not have access to the Settings page.

User

A drop-down list of all active OneStream Users. Select a User to add them to the group.

Role

Set the security role for the User here (Preparer, Approver, Commenter, Viewer, or Local Admin). For more information on security roles, see the Access Control section in Settings.

Conclusion

In this chapter, we have learned about the components that are used to configure your Transaction Matching solution. Additionally, we have provided examples on when to use data splitting, when to keep all data in a single Match Set, and when to break out information into more granular Match Sets. With the knowledge gained here, you are now ready to move on to implementing the solution in your development environment, which will be discussed in the next chapter.

7

Transaction Matching Implementation

Transaction Matching is one of the newer OneStream Marketplace solutions that is quickly becoming invaluable in the OneStream world.

If you have never worked with a Transaction Matching tool, its concept and use may be foreign. At the simplest level, Transaction Matching is used to compare data sets and help identify missing information. The OneStream Transaction Matching solution facilitates matching by utilizing rules that are set up in a User-friendly interface.

Chapter 6 focused on the administration of Transaction Matching, and Chapter 8 will focus on User Experience. Both chapters cover all of the included functionality that comes with the Transaction Matching solution and how to use the tool. In this chapter, however, the focus will be on the design and build concepts of Transaction Matching, and we will explain *why* we build the solution the way we do. The Design and Build chapter of the OneStream Foundation Handbook covers all the functional ideas of requirements and design, so this chapter will be focused on requirements and design that are specific to Transaction Matching.

Design

As stated in the OneStream Foundation Handbook, "Design is the most important part of the project." I think this becomes even more true when you have never been a part of a Transaction Matching project. My hope is that – after reading this section of the chapter – you will understand all of the different pieces that need to be discussed for a OneStream Transaction Matching project, guiding and enabling you to run a successful project from start to finish.

Scoping

As with any project, it is important to clearly define what is considered *in scope* versus *out of scope*. This is a standard concept that consultants should be familiar with. Scoping has a section in this chapter for two reasons:

1. Transaction Matching projects can be handled very differently than a standard Consolidation or Planning project.
2. To provide you with high-level scoping considerations and questions.

Similar to a Consolidation or Planning project, some customers want the implementation partner to build out the full solution from start to finish. Other customers will ask the implementation partner to build out the more difficult Transaction Matching Match Sets, customizations, and custom Reports. Once the more difficult work is complete, the customer will proceed to finish the rest of the work on their own. This is a common approach that works for Transaction Matching and should be discussed with the customer.

Below is a high-level list of specific Transaction Matching questions that should be asked when scoping a Transaction Matching project:

Data:

- How many data sources will you be loading into Transaction Matching?
- How will the data be loaded to OneStream (e.g., direct connect or file load)?

- Do any of the data imports need to be split during import?
- Will the data files be incremental (every file will only contain net new data)?
- Does any of the source data need Calculations, additional fields, or Business Rule-generated data before being loaded to Transaction Matching?

Security:

- How many Users will need access to Transaction Matching?
- What will the roles be for each User?
- Is security driven by Entity/IC or by other Dimensions?

Workflows:

- Do they want a centralized or decentralized Workflow process?
- How many Match Sets will be needed?

Match Sets:

- What is the data volume for each Match Set?
- How frequently do you perform matching for each Match Set?
- How many rules will each Match Set need?

Reporting:

- Provide examples of Reports you are looking to receive out of the OneStream Transaction Matching system.
- What custom Reports and Dashboards are needed?

Customizations:

- Are there any customizations you are looking to have built out for your Transaction Matching solution? (Note: Due to the solution's Business Rules being encrypted, you are limited to the customizations that you can perform in the solution.)

Training:

- Currently, OneStream does not offer specific training for Transaction Matching, so do you need to include custom training in the scope of the project?

Data

Data Volume

Typically, data volume is not something that is heavily discussed during a standard design session. However, when designing Transaction Matching, there needs to be a discussion around the volume of data. If you are working with a large company and they are implementing Transaction Matching, there is a good chance you may be dealing with millions of lines of data per month.

Similarly, when dealing with large data loads to a Cube, you want to consider how you can break up the data into smaller loads. There are two main performance reasons for breaking up large data loads: the processing time to import data, and Matching Rules will process faster with smaller, more frequent loads. Another benefit to having multiple imports is that they provide you with more flexibility if data needs to be reloaded or reprocessed. If only one of the imports has an issue, you will only need to reprocess that specific load and not the full data set.

It is important, during the design phase, to identify the fields the customer needs (versus wants) in Transaction Matching. It can be helpful to identify the source fields and separate them into groups of how they will be utilized in Transaction Matching. The table below provides the breakout I like to use during design sessions. This approach helps during the build and will also point out to the customer the fields they use for Transaction Matching.

#	Grouping of Data Fields
1	Used for data splitting
2	Used for matching
3	Used for matching and reporting
4	Used for reporting only
5	Used for supporting detail to Account Reconciliation

Figure 7.1

Data Storage

As discussed in chapter 6, OneStream utilizes Workflows to import data into Transaction Matching. It is important to keep in mind – during the design discussions – that the import works differently to how you might be accustomed. When an import for Transaction Matching kicks off, it first loads the data into a Stage table. Next, it moves the data to the Transaction Matching `XFW_TXM_Transaction` table where each record is assigned a unique Transaction ID. Finally, all but one row is deleted from the Stage table as shown in Figure 7.2.

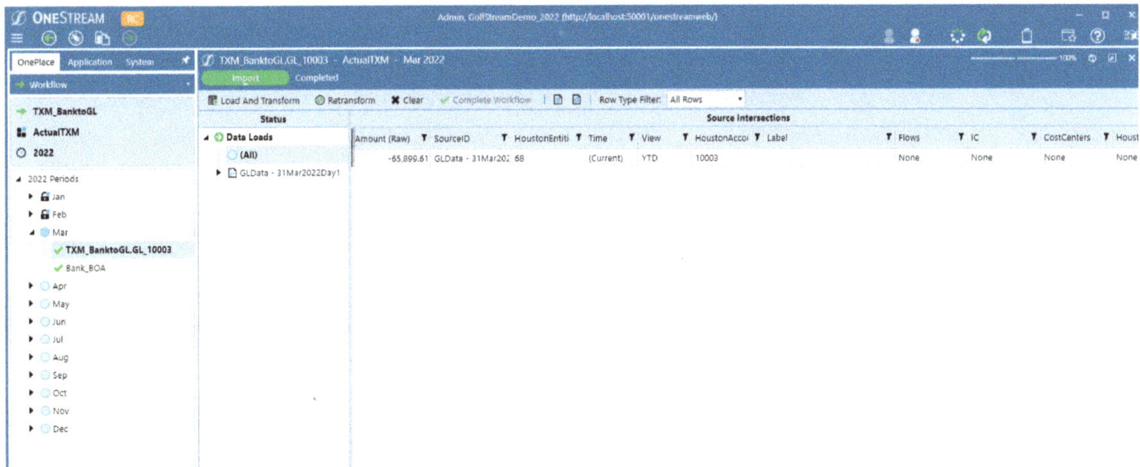

Figure 7.2

The import process was changed for performance reasons since there is no need to hold all the data in the OneStream environment in two different places, especially when you are dealing with the volume of data that comes with Transaction Matching. The one row of data persists per Workflow, Scenario, Time, and data source ID. This allows OneStream to identify where all the data in Transaction Matching was loaded from, and becomes important when clearing data out of Transaction Matching.

Not having the data stored in Stage may seem problematic because we cannot use traditional drill down functionality, but it has no impact on the ability to report off any Member brought in during an import. As shown in Figures 7.3 and 7.4, the Transaction Matching tables that hold the source and target data are almost identical to the Stage tables.

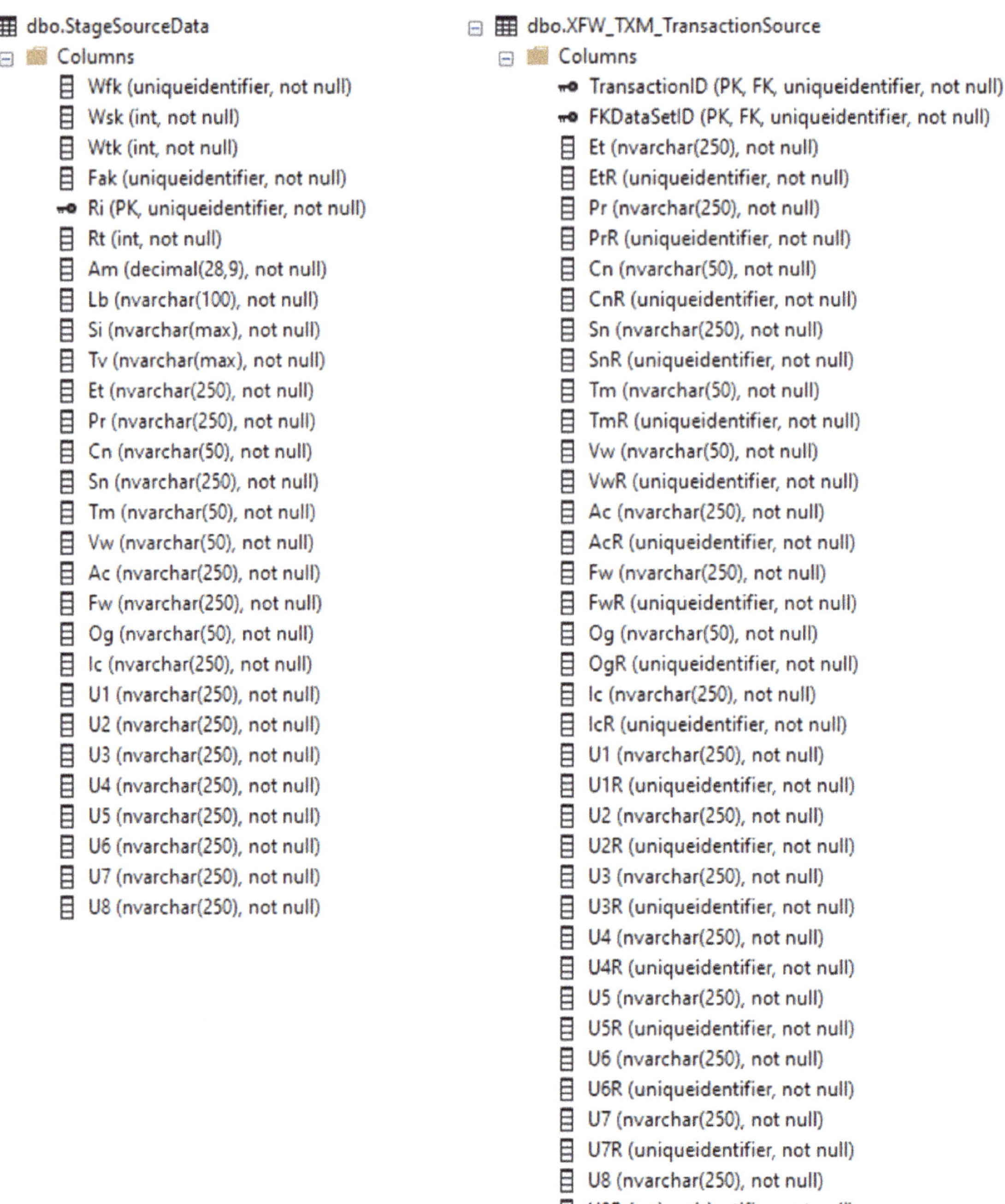
dbo.StageSourceData
Columns
Wfk (uniqueidentifier, not null)
Wsk (int, not null)
Wtk (int, not null)
Fak (uniqueidentifier, not null)
Ri (PK, uniqueidentifier, not null)
Rt (int, not null)
Am (decimal(28,9), not null)
Lb (nvarchar(100), not null)
Si (nvarchar(max), not null)
Tv (nvarchar(max), not null)
Et (nvarchar(250), not null)
Pr (nvarchar(250), not null)
Cn (nvarchar(50), not null)
Sn (nvarchar(250), not null)
Tm (nvarchar(50), not null)
Vw (nvarchar(50), not null)
Ac (nvarchar(250), not null)
Fw (nvarchar(250), not null)
Og (nvarchar(50), not null)
Ic (nvarchar(250), not null)
U1 (nvarchar(250), not null)
U2 (nvarchar(250), not null)
U3 (nvarchar(250), not null)
U4 (nvarchar(250), not null)
U5 (nvarchar(250), not null)
U6 (nvarchar(250), not null)
U7 (nvarchar(250), not null)
U8 (nvarchar(250), not null)
dbo.XFW_TXM_TransactionSource
Columns
TransactionID (PK, FK, uniqueidentifier, not null)
FKDataSetID (PK, FK, uniqueidentifier, not null)
Et (nvarchar(250), not null)
EtR (uniqueidentifier, not null)
Pr (nvarchar(250), not null)
PrR (uniqueidentifier, not null)
Cn (nvarchar(50), not null)
CnR (uniqueidentifier, not null)
Sn (nvarchar(250), not null)
SnR (uniqueidentifier, not null)
Tm (nvarchar(50), not null)
TmR (uniqueidentifier, not null)
Vw (nvarchar(50), not null)
VwR (uniqueidentifier, not null)
Ac (nvarchar(250), not null)
AcR (uniqueidentifier, not null)
Fw (nvarchar(250), not null)
FwR (uniqueidentifier, not null)
Og (nvarchar(50), not null)
OgR (uniqueidentifier, not null)
Ic (nvarchar(250), not null)
IcR (uniqueidentifier, not null)
U1 (nvarchar(250), not null)
U1R (uniqueidentifier, not null)
U2 (nvarchar(250), not null)
U2R (uniqueidentifier, not null)
U3 (nvarchar(250), not null)
U3R (uniqueidentifier, not null)
U4 (nvarchar(250), not null)
U4R (uniqueidentifier, not null)
U5 (nvarchar(250), not null)
U5R (uniqueidentifier, not null)
U6 (nvarchar(250), not null)
U6R (uniqueidentifier, not null)
U7 (nvarchar(250), not null)
U7R (uniqueidentifier, not null)
U8 (nvarchar(250), not null)
U8R (uniqueidentifier, not null)

Figure 7.3

Figure 7.4

There is also a view of the data in Transaction Matching that contains all of the source, target, and attribute Members which is very similar to the `vStageSourceAndTargetDataWithAttributes`; see Figures 7.5 and 7.6.

`vXFW_TXM_TransactionDetailWithSource` becomes extremely useful for reporting purposes as will be discussed in the reporting section of this chapter.

dbo.vStageSourceAndTargetDataWithAttributes
Columns
Wfk (uniqueidentifier, not null)
Wsk (int, not null)
Wtk (int, not null)
Fak (uniqueidentifier, not null)
Ri (uniqueidentifier, not null)
Rt (int, not null)
Si (nvarchar(max), not null)
Lb (nvarchar(100), not null)
Tv (nvarchar(max), not null)
Et (nvarchar(250), not null)
EtT (nvarchar(250), not null)
EtR (uniqueidentifier, not null)
Pr (nvarchar(250), not null)
PrT (nvarchar(250), not null)
PrR (uniqueidentifier, not null)
Cn (nvarchar(50), not null)
CnT (nvarchar(50), not null)
CnR (uniqueidentifier, not null)
Vw (nvarchar(50), not null)
VwT (nvarchar(50), not null)
VwR (uniqueidentifier, not null)
Sn (nvarchar(250), not null)
SnT (nvarchar(250), not null)
SnR (uniqueidentifier, not null)
Tm (nvarchar(50), not null)
TmT (nvarchar(50), not null)
TmR (uniqueidentifier, not null)
Ac (nvarchar(250), not null)
AcT (nvarchar(250), not null)
AcR (uniqueidentifier, not null)
Fw (nvarchar(250), not null)
FwT (nvarchar(250), not null)
FwR (uniqueidentifier, not null)
Og (nvarchar(50), not null)
OgT (nvarchar(50), not null)
OgR (uniqueidentifier, not null)
Ic (nvarchar(250), not null)
IcT (nvarchar(250), not null)
IcR (uniqueidentifier, not null)
U1 (nvarchar(250), not null)
U1T (nvarchar(250), not null)
U1R (uniqueidentifier, not null)
U2 (nvarchar(250), not null)
U2T (nvarchar(250), not null)
U2R (uniqueidentifier, not null)
U3 (nvarchar(250), not null)
U3T (nvarchar(250), not null)
U3R (uniqueidentifier, not null)
U4 (nvarchar(250), not null)
U4T (nvarchar(250), not null)
U4R (uniqueidentifier, not null)
dbo.vXFW_TXM_TransactionDetailWithSource
Columns
TransactionID (uniqueidentifier, not null)
TransactionNumber (varchar(18), not null)
FKMatchSetID (uniqueidentifier, not null)
FKDataSetID (uniqueidentifier, not null)
Wfk (uniqueidentifier, not null)
Wsk (int, not null)
Wtk (int, not null)
Status (tinyint, not null)
StatusWtk (int, not null)
ImportDate (datetime, not null)
CommentOrDoc (bit, not null)
FKReasonCodeID (uniqueidentifier, not null)
Lb (nvarchar(100), not null)
Si (nvarchar(max), not null)
Tv (nvarchar(max), not null)
EtT (nvarchar(250), not null)
Et (nvarchar(250), not null)
PrT (nvarchar(250), not null)
Pr (nvarchar(250), not null)
CnT (nvarchar(50), not null)
Cn (nvarchar(50), not null)
SnT (nvarchar(250), not null)
Sn (nvarchar(250), not null)
TmT (nvarchar(50), not null)
Tm (nvarchar(50), not null)
VwT (nvarchar(50), not null)
Vw (nvarchar(50), not null)
AcT (nvarchar(250), not null)
Ac (nvarchar(250), not null)
FwT (nvarchar(250), not null)
Fw (nvarchar(250), not null)
OgT (nvarchar(50), not null)
Og (nvarchar(50), not null)
IcT (nvarchar(250), not null)
Ic (nvarchar(250), not null)
U1 (nvarchar(250), not null)
U1T (nvarchar(250), not null)
U2 (nvarchar(250), not null)
U2T (nvarchar(250), not null)
U3 (nvarchar(250), not null)
U3T (nvarchar(250), not null)
U4 (nvarchar(250), not null)
U4T (nvarchar(250), not null)
U5 (nvarchar(250), not null)
U5T (nvarchar(250), not null)
U6 (nvarchar(250), not null)
U6T (nvarchar(250), not null)
U7 (nvarchar(250), not null)
U7T (nvarchar(250), not null)
U8 (nvarchar(250), not null)
U8T (nvarchar(250), not null)

Figure 7.5

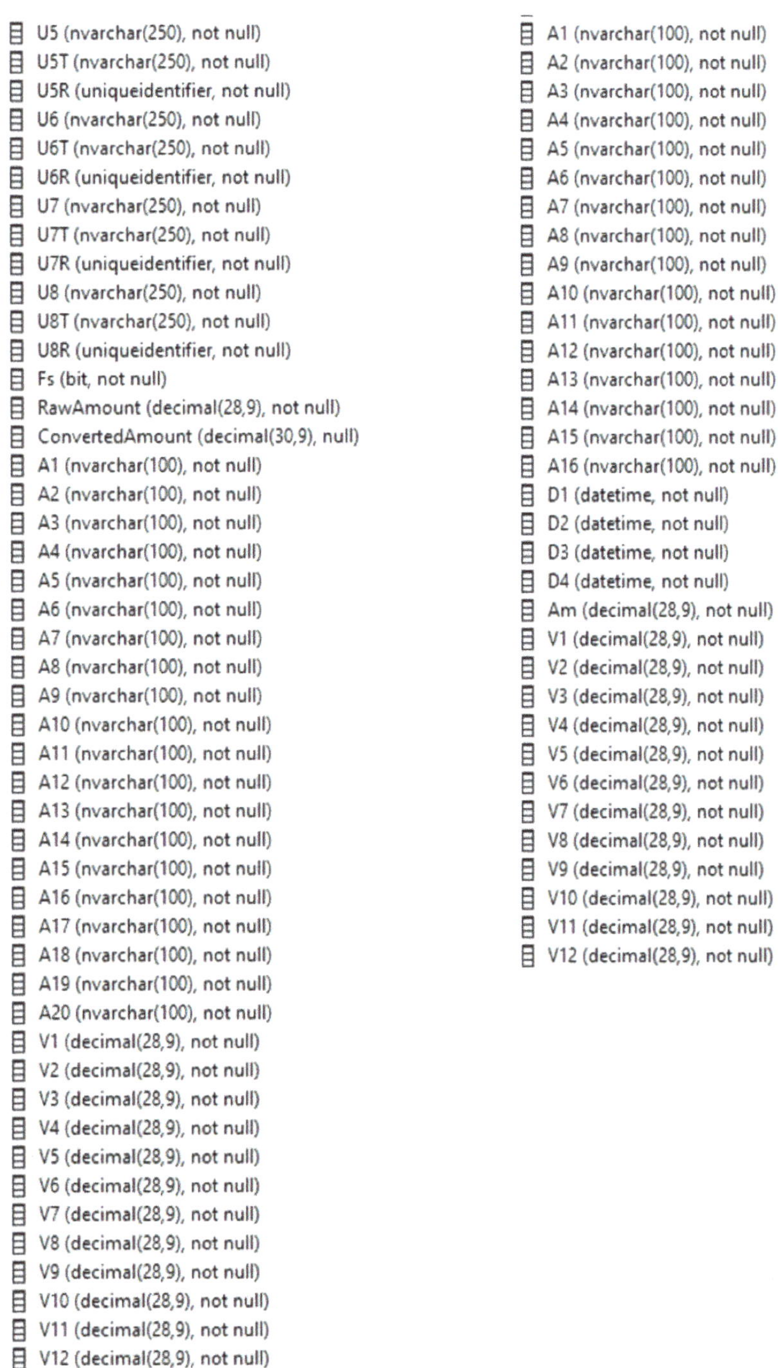

Figure 7.6

Loading Data

Reporting vs. Matching Amounts

It is important to understand how Transaction Matching views the amount fields when running the Matching Rules. The system does not *net the amounts* when trying to find matches, so the numbers need to have the same signage for each data set that gets Matched. When a customer is analyzing the data, they typically want to see the numbers net against each other. This requirement forces you to bring in the same amounts twice and have a matching amount and a reporting amount. This can be achieved by utilizing one of the **12 value fields**. The matching amount will be used in the Matching Rules and the reporting amount will be used for reporting purposes. Depending on the raw data imported, you will need to flip the sign for one of the amount fields to achieve the appropriate signage.

Workflow Time

Understanding how Workflow Time works for Transaction Matching is critical for design discussions. The import period assigned to transactions is based on the Time Dimension, per the data source setup. In the data source, there are two main options used: **Current Data Key Time** and **DataKey Text**.

When using the Current Data Key Time setting, the data load Time period is based on the import Workflow Time. If using this option, all transactions will be associated to the Workflow Time where the data was loaded.

If using the DataKey Text option, you are telling OneStream to read a field from the data load and map each transaction to the appropriate Time period. When applying mapping to the Time Dimension, you can still import data to multiple months from one file. Transaction Matching creates a distinct list of source ID and target Time periods to identify where it needs to hold a single row of data in Stage.

Figures 7.7 to 7.9 show examples of a data file and what the Workflows look like after loading the file to the March Time period. You will notice that March and April both have a green check on the import step and contain a single row of data in Stage.

	A	B	C	D	E	F	G	H	I	J
1	Date	Trans Code	Amount	CC Process	POS Location	POS	Posted Date	Account	Entity	
2	22-Apr	#1345879664123	-65486.61	AMEX	2153559	Atlanta	3/7/2022	10003	South	
3	22-Apr	#1345879664124	-5248.16	AMEX	2153559	Atlanta	3/13/2022	10003	Montreal	
4	22-Apr	#1345879664125	-5233.16	AMEX	2153559	Atlanta	3/6/2022	10003	Heights	
5	22-Apr	#1345879664126	-65485.61	AMEX	2153559	Atlanta	3/7/2022	10003	South	
6	22-Apr	#1345879664127	-5247.16	AMEX	2153559	Atlanta	3/13/2022	10003	Montreal	
7	22-Apr	#1345879664128	-5232.16	AMEX	2153559	Atlanta	3/6/2022	10003	Heights	
8	22-Apr	#1345879664129	-65484.61	AMEX	2153559	Atlanta	3/7/2022	10003	South	
9	22-Apr	#1345879664130	-5246.16	AMEX	2153559	Atlanta	3/13/2022	10003	Montreal	
10	22-Apr	#1345879664131	-5231.16	AMEX	2153559	Atlanta	3/6/2022	10003	Heights	
11	22-Mar	#1345879664132	-65483.61	AMEX	2153559	Atlanta	3/7/2022	10003	South	
12	22-Mar	#1345879664133	-5245.16	AMEX	2153559	Atlanta	3/13/2022	10003	Montreal	
13	22-Mar	#1345879664134	-5230.16	AMEX	2153559	Atlanta	3/6/2022	10003	Heights	
14	22-Mar	#1345879664135	-65482.61	AMEX	2153559	Atlanta	3/7/2022	10003	South	
15	22-Mar	#1345879664136	-5244.16	AMEX	2153559	Atlanta	3/13/2022	10003	Montreal	
16	22-Mar	#1345879664137	-5229.16	AMEX	2153559	Atlanta	3/6/2022	10003	Heights	
17	22-Mar	#1345879664138	-65481.61	AMEX	2153559	Atlanta	3/7/2022	10003	South	
18	22-Mar	#1345879664139	-5243.16	AMEX	2153559	Atlanta	3/13/2022	10003	Montreal	
19	22-Mar	#1345879664140	-5228.16	AMEX	2153559	Atlanta	3/6/2022	10003	Heights	
20	22-Mar	#1345879664141	-65480.61	AMEX	2153559	Atlanta	3/7/2022	10003	South	
21	22-Mar	#1345879664142	-5242.16	AMEX	2153559	Atlanta	3/13/2022	10003	Montreal	
22	22-Mar	#1345879664143	-5227.16	AMEX	2153559	Atlanta	3/6/2022	10003	Heights	
23	22-Mar	#1345879664144	-65479.61	AMEX	2153559	Atlanta	3/7/2022	10003	South	
24	22-Mar	#1345879664145	-5241.16	AMEX	2153559	Atlanta	3/13/2022	10003	Montreal	
25	22-Mar	#1345879664146	-5226.16	AMEX	2153559	Atlanta	3/6/2022	10003	Heights	

Figure 7.7

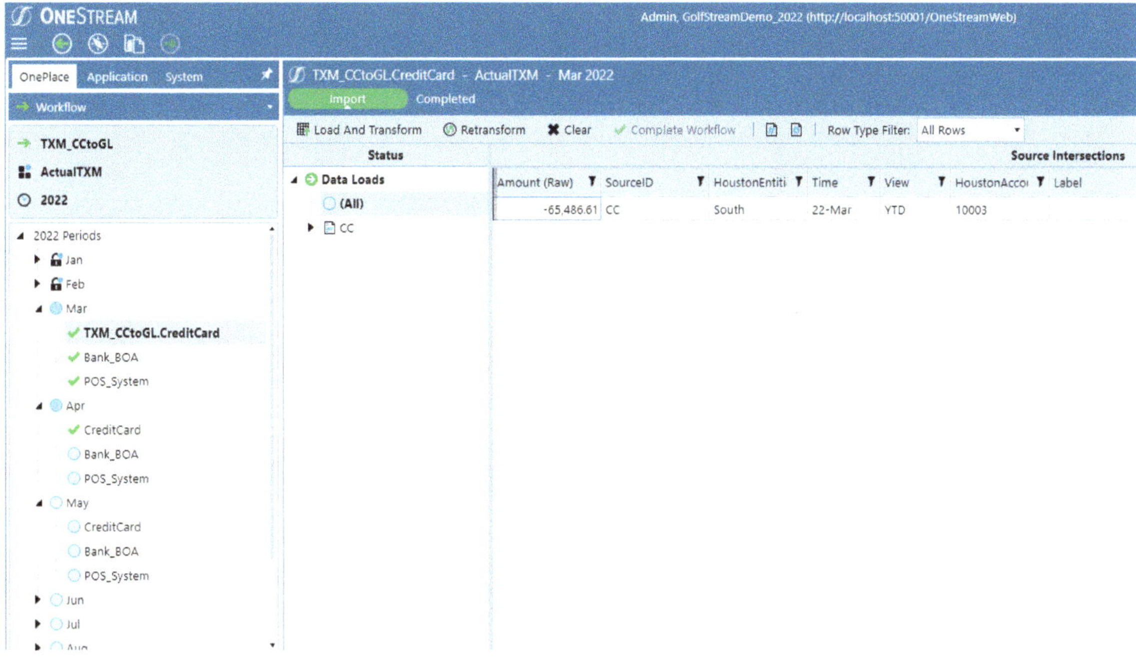

Figure 7.8

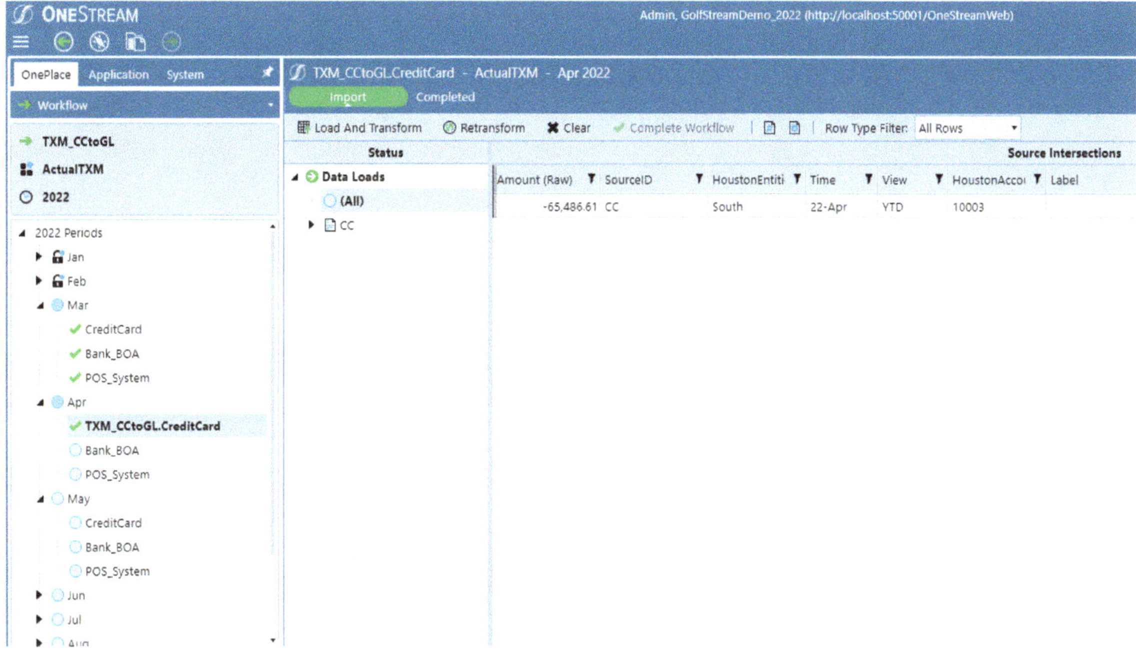

Figure 7.9

Incremental vs. Cumulative Files

The data storage section covered how Transaction Matching holds the data in the solution tables. Even though Transaction Matching utilizes Workflows to import data, it acts very differently, as seen by the data not residing in the Stage tables.

Most data loads to OneStream are performed as a replace, and loading a cumulative file is usually not a problem; however, with Transaction Matching it becomes an issue. Once a transaction is Matched in the system (either via Matching Rules or manually by the User), it becomes locked to ensure the integrity of the match. In order to update or remove a transaction from Transaction Matching, it needs to be Unmatched. That is why Transaction Matching expects incremental data files.

At times, though, incremental data loads may not be possible. When this is the case, the recommended approach is to create a process that checks the data which has already been loaded to Transaction Matching. This will ensure no duplicate data is loaded into the system.

Historical Data

If a customer is currently performing Transaction Matching, you will need to discuss the process of loading historical Unmatched items. Depending on the age of their current Transaction Matching process, they may have a large volume of Unmatched transactions that need to be brought into the system. This process may require its own data source setup, meaning it will also need its own import step. Logistically, this is not a problem because you can have multiple import steps assigned to one data set. I recommend loading all the Unmatched historical data to a prior month with no transactions. For example, if your start month is February, load all of the Unmatched transactions to January. The Transaction Matching solution displays all Unmatched transactions from both the current and prior months, so loading data to the prior month provides a clean load process and still allows you to access the historical Unmatched transactions.

Go Forward Data

Typically, Transaction Matching data is loaded daily and even more frequently during close. The cadence of the loads should be discussed during design as well as when the cutover will take place. With Transaction Matching being a live system, you will need to discuss – in detail – when the cutover will take place.

Match Sets

As explained in Chapter 6, a Match Set in Transaction Matching relates to a specific Workflow Profile. The number of Match Sets that will be needed in a Transaction Matching environment is driven by your matching process and security requirements.

I like to think of a Match Set as its own standalone matching process that is not impacted by any other Match Sets. The Settings page is the only page that will be the same across multiple Match Sets (Figure 7.10). Every other setting – including everything on the Match Set Administration page – are independent and have no impact on other Match Sets.

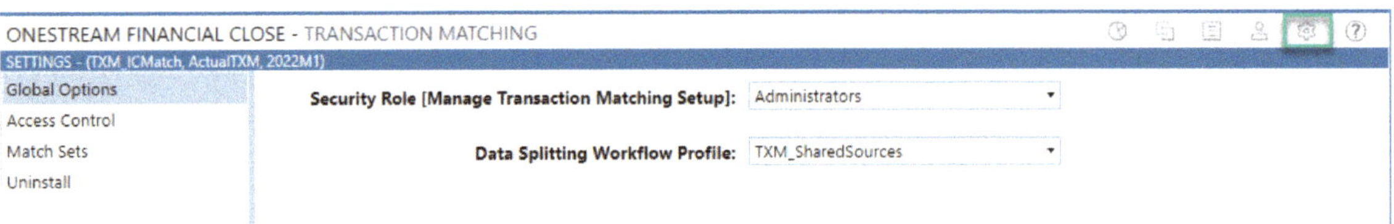

Figure 7.10

It is important to understand that Match Sets are not related to each other for a few reasons. First, and most importantly, this means that every single setting is unique to each Match Set. For example, say there are 10 people who are responsible for matching a certain data set – if you create 10 different Match Sets, one for each person, you just created 10 different Match Sets that all need to be setup and maintained separately. This situation can quickly become a maintenance nightmare, which is what we want to avoid.

When discussing Match Sets during the design phase, I always try to capture the full picture of *who* is responsible for the data. Often, a full data set will be broken up into subsets based on multiple Users being responsible for their own subset. Depending on how the data is broken up, this may call for multiple Match Sets to be created, or all the data can still sit in one Match Set. A common mistake people make is thinking they need to create a Match Set for each Account Reconciliation. This is not necessary and only ends up creating more points of maintenance. Security capabilities are explained in the Security section of this chapter.

Match Set Rules

Match Set Rules are straightforward, but there are a few important things to keep in mind. As noted in the Match Set section, Match Set Rules are specific to a Match Set. This means Match Set Rules cannot be shared across Match Sets and must be manually created as they cannot be uploaded to a Match Set. As shown in Figure 7.11, you have the ability to copy a rule within a Match Set.

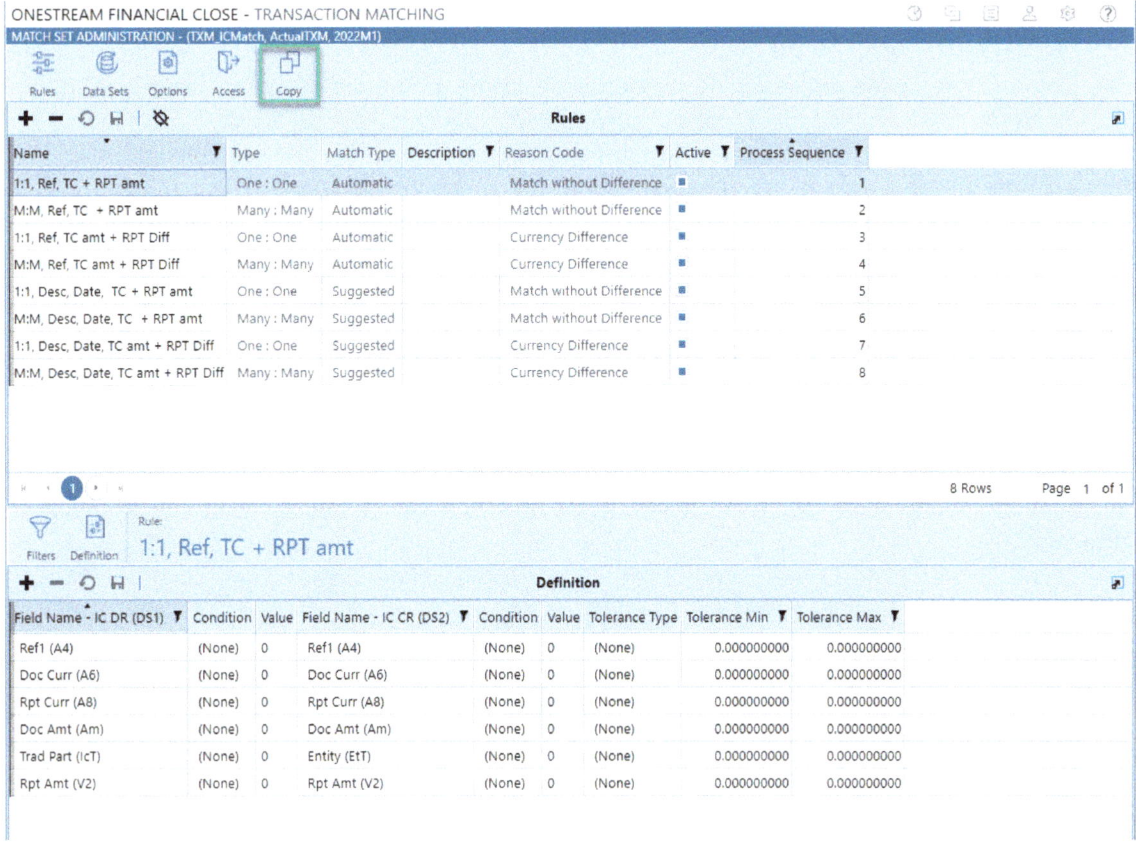

Figure 7.11

Even though we cannot copy rules across Match Sets, we do have the ability to create a copy of a Match Set, as shown in Figure 7.12. This can be very helpful during the build phase, especially if you have multiple Match Sets that have similar settings and Matching Rules. Copy functionality allows you to setup one Match Set and create as many copies as needed.

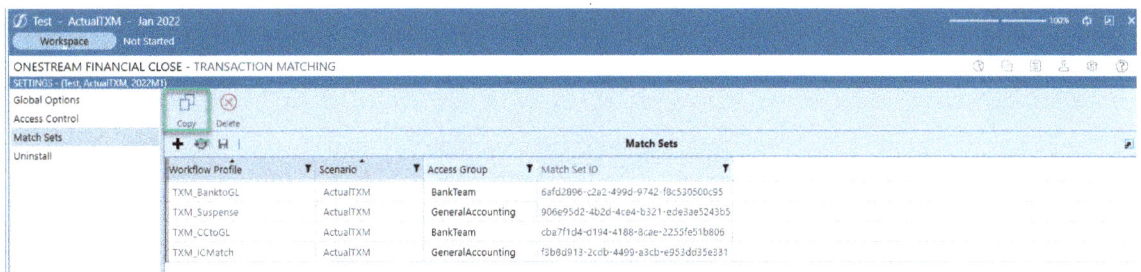

Figure 7.12

Below is a summary of what can and cannot be done with Match Sets and Match Rules.

- Match Set Rules cannot be shared across Match Sets (the concept of a Parent Match Set does not exist).

- Match Set Rules must be created using the OneStream interface; Match Set Rules cannot be uploaded to a Match Set.
- Match Set Rules cannot be exported together.
- Match Set Rules may be copied within the same Match Set.
- Match Sets may be copied.

Data Access Security

While security is always discussed during a design session, the conversation will often be high-level with the more detailed discussions occurring during the build phase. When it comes to security for Transaction Matching, the design should be broken up into two sections: granting access to the data and the actions a User can perform once they have access. The detailed discussions on data access need to take place during design as data access security is one of the main drivers for how many Match Sets need to be created. This section is focused on data access security as the security within Transaction Matching is covered in the Access Control section in Chapter 6.

The data access security discussion should start by asking the customer to identify the people who need access to each group of data. After identifying the people assigned per data group, the discussion needs to be focused on whether the security needs to go down to the next level. Once a User has access to a Match Set, we can limit their data access by Entity, IC, Entity or IC, or Entity and IC. Let's review a few different situations, and how data access security drives the Match Set design.

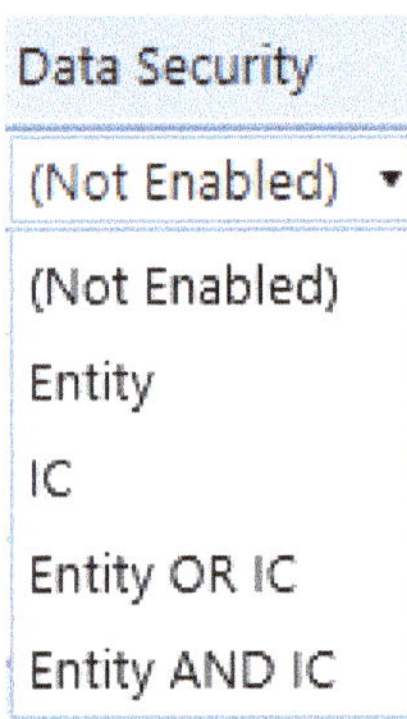

Figure 7.13

In this first example, a customer wants to perform matching against their Bank Accounts to their GL. If one person is responsible for each Account, this would result in five different Match Sets with the data for each Account being loaded to its respective Match Set. Remember, once a User has access to a Match Set, we have no way to limit the data they can view except by the Entity and IC Dimensions.

In the second example, a customer wants to perform matching for their IC Accounts. Multiple people will be involved in this process, but the segregation of data is by Entity and IC. This situation allows you to load all of the data to one Match Set and apply the Entity/IC security within the Match Set. When encountering an example like this, it is important to keep in mind that going with one Match Set just because security allows for it may not be the best design decision. This is where data volume should also be considered alongside security requirements.

The final thing to keep in mind about data access security is how it relates to Account Reconciliations. As mentioned in Chapter 6, if a customer is going to utilize data from Transaction Matching to help support their Account Reconciliation process, User security should align between both solutions.

Transaction Matching to Account Reconciliation

Chapter 6 goes into detail about how to correctly setup the process of linking Transaction Matching with Account Reconciliations. When discussing each Match Set with the customer, it is important to understand if they want to use the data in Transaction Matching to help support their Account Reconciliation process. If the customer is planning on using Transaction Matching with Account Reconciliations, it is crucial to discuss with them that all tracking levels used for Account Reconciliations must also be included in the Transaction Matching data sets. This includes both the source and target Members for each Dimension used in the tracking level.

Reporting and Analysis

Chapter 8 covers in detail the reporting that is included in Transaction Matching. Both the Scorecard and the Analysis pages provide snapshot reporting that is useful for understanding how successful the rules are. While the included reporting is a good starting point, most companies will require custom reporting. Every customer will have different requirements for their reporting but the most important thing to understand is how the Users need to analyze each Match Set. Custom Reports will be used to help identify issues with their data, and it is important to create Reports that enhance the User Experience. Below is a list of common Custom Reports which may be beneficial.

- Customized Aging
- Drill Down Reporting
- Snapshot information in an email
- The ability to analyze subsets of data

Customizations

When implementing a OneStream MarketPlace Solution, it is common for a customer to ask for customizations to the solutions that fit their business needs. In turn, it is important to know that the majority of Transaction Matching Business Rules are encrypted, so you will not be able to accommodate every request from the customer. The encryption of Business Rules for MarketPlace solutions is becoming more common, especially for newer solutions. You will not be able to see the source code in any of the Business Rules that are encrypted so customizing anything within the solution-delivered Business Rules is not possible.

The one area where customizations can be setup is during certain events that occur in Transaction Matching based on a User's actions. The Build Customization section of this chapter goes into detail as to how this customization can be setup along with the different options that are available.

> **Note:** Any customizations from a customer that cannot be accommodated due to encrypted Business Rules should be submitted to OneStream support.

Build

Chapters 6 and 8 both discuss how to setup up all of the artifacts and how they work in Transaction Matching. In this section of the chapter, I will cover the nuances of implementing Transaction Matching and provide some tips and tricks to help guide you during the build phase.

Pre-Configuration

After installing the OneStream Financial Close solution, there are several pre-configuration steps that need to occur before setting up Transaction Matching. The first step is the same as every other OneStream MarketPlace solution which is clicking the Create Tables button.

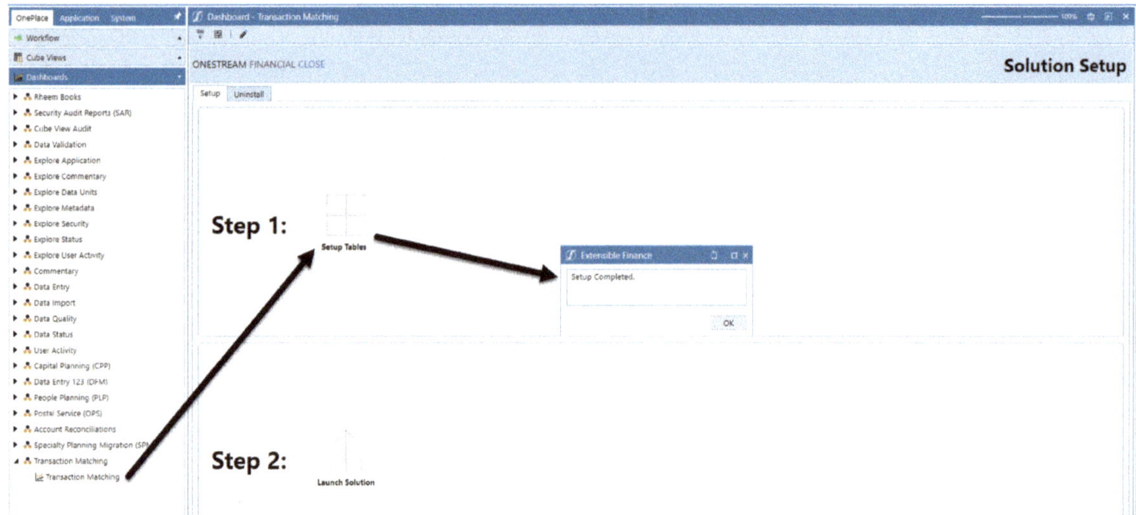

Figure 7.14

The second step is to modify the **Transformation Event Handler** Business Rule. The OneStream application does not come with a Transformation Event Handler so if your application does not have one, you will need to add it to make the required modifications. You can find a standard Transformation Event Handler in the GolfStream application that comes with every OneStream installation. Once the Transformation Event Handler is in the environment, the next step is to update it for Transaction Matching. You need to add the following two lines after the Select Case that checks for the operations name:

```
Dim txmHelper As New DashboardExtender.TXM_SolutionHelper.MainClass
txmHelper.ProcessImportOrClear(si, globals, args)
```

```
        'Evaluate the operation type in order to determine which sub-event is being processed
        Select Case args.OperationName
            Case Is = BREventOperationType.Transformation.ParseAndTrans.InitializeExcelRangeLayout
                'Call template version validation handler
                If processEvents Then Me.XFR_HandleExcelTemplateVersionCheck(si, globals, api, args)
                If processEvents Then Me.XFR_HandleExcelTemplateForceZeroSuppress(si, globals, api, args)

            Case Is = BREventOperationType.Transformation.ParseAndTrans.ParseSourceData
                'Call selective global data key(Scenario & Time) validation
                If processEvents Then Me.XFR_HandleParseSourceData(si, globals, api, args)

            Case Is = BREventOperationType.Transformation.ParseAndTrans.ProcessTransformationRules
                'Call mapping override (Force BalanceSheet accounts to View of YTD)
                If processEvents Then Me.XFR_HandleProcessTransRules_OverrideView(si, globals, api, args)
                If processEvents Then Me.XFR_HandleProcessTransRules_Allocate(si, globals, api, args)

            Case Is = BREventOperationType.Transformation.ValTrans.SetEventRules
                'Call custom validation rules
                If processEvents Then Me.XFR_HandleSetEventRules(si, globals, api, args)

            Case Is = BREventOperationType.Transformation.ValTrans.FinalizeValidateTransform
                'Send custom email message if map errors exist after transformation validation is run
                If processEvents Then Me.XFR_HandleAfterValidateTransform(si, globals, api, args)

            Case Is = BREventOperationType.Transformation.ParseAndTrans.EndPreserveData
                'Call custom cube data preserve
                If processEvents Then Me.XFR_HandleEndPreserveData(si, globals, api, args)

        End Select

        Dim txmHelper As New DashboardExtender.TXM_SolutionHelper.MainClass
        txmHelper.ProcessImportOrClear(si, globals, args)

        Return returnValue

    Catch ex As Exception
        Throw ErrorHandler.LogWrite(si, New XFException(si, ex))
    End Try
End Function
```

Figure 7.15

Next, you need to add `BR\TXM_SoultionHelper` to the Referenced Assemblies of the Transformation Event Handler Properties tab, as shown in Figure 7.16:

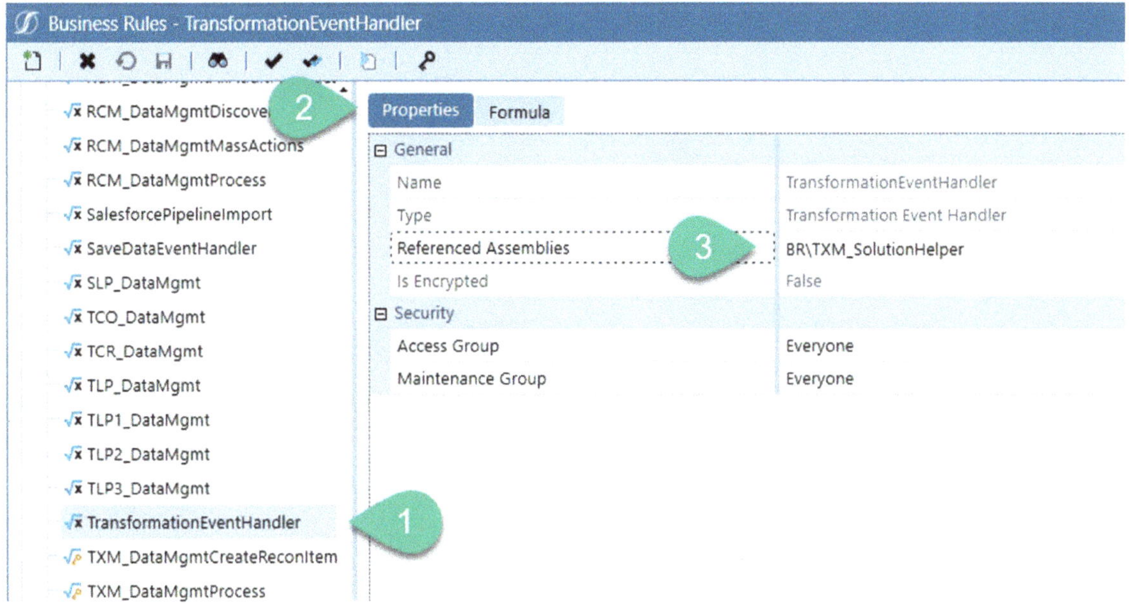

Figure 7.16

Modifying the Transformation Event Handler Business Rule is a vital step that completes setting up Transaction Matching. The modification initiates the process of moving the imported data to the Transaction Matching tables, creating the unique Transaction ID, and deleting the data from the staging tables.

I have received a lot of emails from people implementing Transaction Matching claiming they loaded data to Transaction Matching but are confused as to why they are *not seeing data* in the solution. Assuming the Workflow has been assigned as a Match Set in the Transaction Matching settings page, this is usually a signal that you either missed modifying the Transformation Event Handler or you incorrectly modified it.

Another indicator that this step was missed is if you see multiple lines of data from the same Source ID in the staging table. If more than one record exists, it means there is an issue with the Transformation Event Handler.

Figure 7.17 shows how the Stage data looks when there is an issue with the Transformation Event Handler, and Figure 7.18 shows how the Stage data looks when it is working correctly.

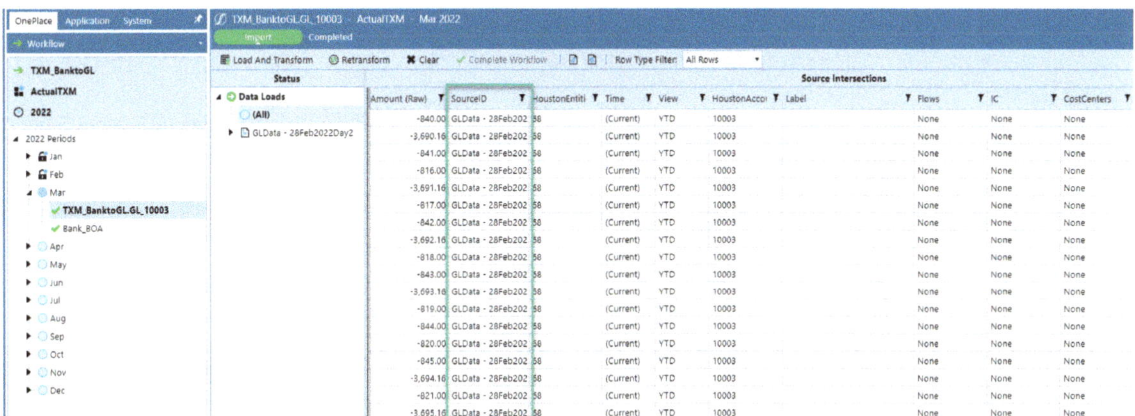

Figure 7.17

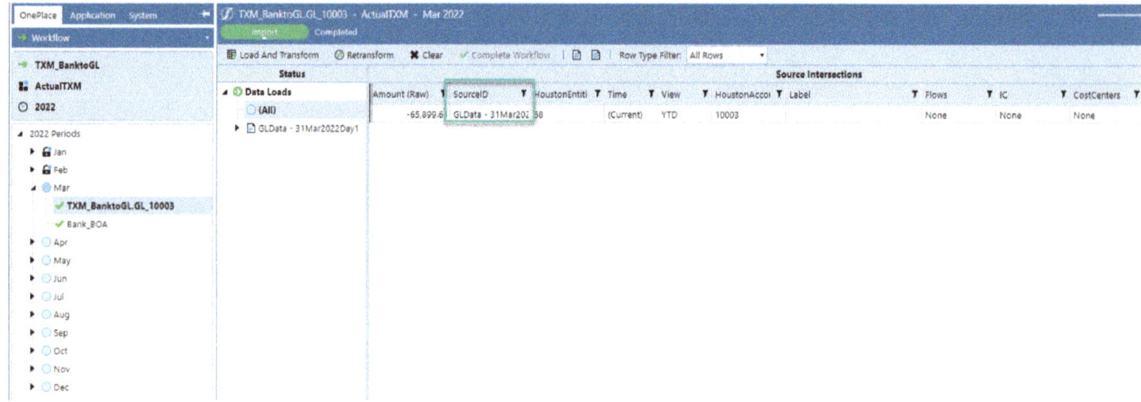

Figure 7.18

Standard Configuration

Data Sources

Source ID

OneStream Workflows allow you to load multiple data files to the same import step if the Source ID is unique. If the Source ID is the same, it will replace the existing data. Due to Transaction Matching expecting incremental data files, the Source ID becomes an important piece of the data load. When building out the Source ID for Transaction Matching loads, everyone's first instinct is to apply a Parser Rule to the data load that captures a time stamp of when the data gets loaded. On the surface, this seems like a great idea, but this approach will cause issues with loading data to Transaction Matching and should not be used.

A Parser Business Rule is processed on a row-by-row basis which becomes a problem when trying to utilize a time stamp. When loading data to Transaction Matching, we are often dealing with a large volume of data which can take time to import. By trying to utilize a time stamp in a Parser Rule with a data file that takes time to import, you can potentially create a disconnect between the Source ID that is shown in the Workflow Status Section and the Source ID that is associated to a specific data row. If a disconnect occurs, it can cause issues when trying to clear data as the system can no longer connect with where the rogue rows were loaded from.

Source ID with Flat File

Creating a unique Source ID with a flat file load is more complicated than a connector import. The ideal solution is to have the customer provide a time stamp in the file name and utilize the file name as the Source ID. This approach provides a unique ID for each load and because the time stamp is in the file name it will be the same for each row loaded to OneStream. If the customer is not able to provide a time stamp in the filename, the recommended approach is to create a process that renames the file with a time stamp included in the file name before importing it to the Workflow.

Source ID with Connector

When loading data to Transaction Matching via a data connector, the recommended approach is to create a new GUID, as per Figure 7.19, which can be passed to the SQL `Select` statement. You can then apply the GUID to the Source ID field in the data source. This approach ensures the Source ID will be unique per import, but every row per import will have the same Source ID.

```
Dim SourceID As String = System.Guid.NewGuid.ToString()
Dim SQLSelect As New Text.StringBuilder

SQLSelect.Append("TmT as Time, " & vbcrlf & " ")
SQLSelect.Append("EtT as Entity, ")
SQLSelect.Append("AcT as Account, ")
SQLSelect.Append("FwT as Flow, ")
SQLSelect.Append("ICT, ")
SQLSelect.Append("U1T, ")
SQLSelect.Append("U2T, ")
SQLSelect.Append("U3T, ")
SQLSelect.Append("U4T, ")
SQLSelect.Append("U5T, ")
SQLSelect.Append("U6T, ")
SQLSelect.Append("U7T, ")
SQLSelect.Append("U8T, ")
SQLSelect.Append("A1, ")
SQLSelect.Append("A2, ")
SQLSelect.Append("A3, ")
SQLSelect.Append("A4, ")
SQLSelect.Append("A5, ")
SQLSelect.Append("A6, ")
SQLSelect.Append("A7, ")
SQLSelect.Append("A8, ")
SQLSelect.Append("A9, ")
SQLSelect.Append("A10, ")
SQLSelect.Append("A11, ")
SQLSelect.Append("A12, ")
SQLSelect.Append("A13, ")
SQLSelect.Append("A14, ")
SQLSelect.Append("A15, ")
SQLSelect.Append("A16, ")
SQLSelect.Append("A17, ")
SQLSelect.Append("A18, ")
SQLSelect.Append("A19, ")
SQLSelect.Append("A20, ")
SQLSelect.Append("V1, ")
SQLSelect.Append("V2, ")
SQLSelect.Append("V3, ")
SQLSelect.Append("V4, ")
SQLSelect.Append("V5, ")
SQLSelect.Append("V6, ")
SQLSelect.Append("V7, ")
SQLSelect.Append("V8, ")
SQLSelect.Append("V9, ")
SQLSelect.Append("V10, ")
SQLSelect.Append("V11, ")
SQLSelect.Append("V12, ")
SQLSelect.Append(" '" & SourceID &"' as SourceID, ")
SQLSelect.Append("RawAmount as Amount ")
SQLSelect.Append("From vStageSourceAndTargetDataWithAttributes ")
SQLSelect.Append("Where 1=1 ")
```

Figure 7.19

Match Sets

The steps for setting up a Match Set are covered in Chapter 6. Once a Match Set has been created, there are other items to setup. Let's start with the Rules page.

Rules

Transaction Matching Rules are like Transformation Rules in Stage, and the same concepts can be applied when building out the rules. Like the Transformation Rules, the Transaction Matching Rules run in a predefined order which is set by the Process Sequence column as shown in Figure 7.20. The more precise rules should be set to run first, and the more generic rules should run last.

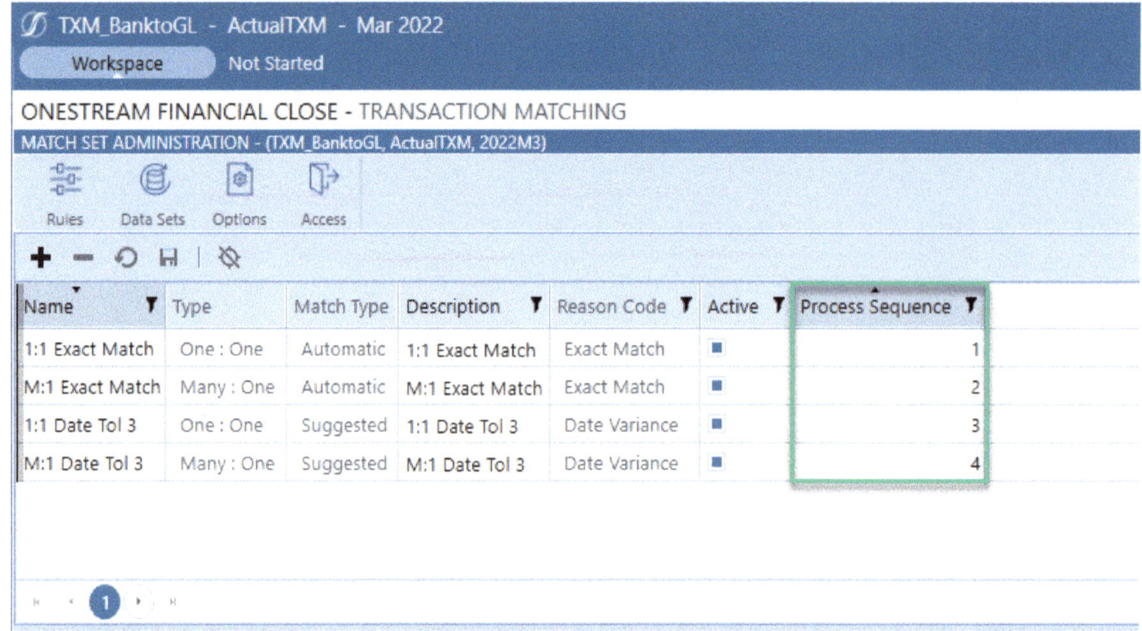

Figure 7.20

Data Sets

Once a data set is created within a Match Set, and the data sources for all of the imports associated to the data set have been created, you need to assign the required fields. The field setup is specific to each data set within a Match Set. You only have one field setup per data set, so if you have multiple imports (as shown in Figure 7.21), you need to make sure the data sources for both imports align for the necessary fields. For example, if the data set field setup is utilizing Attribute 1 for document number, then both imports need to map the document number to Attribute 1 upon import.

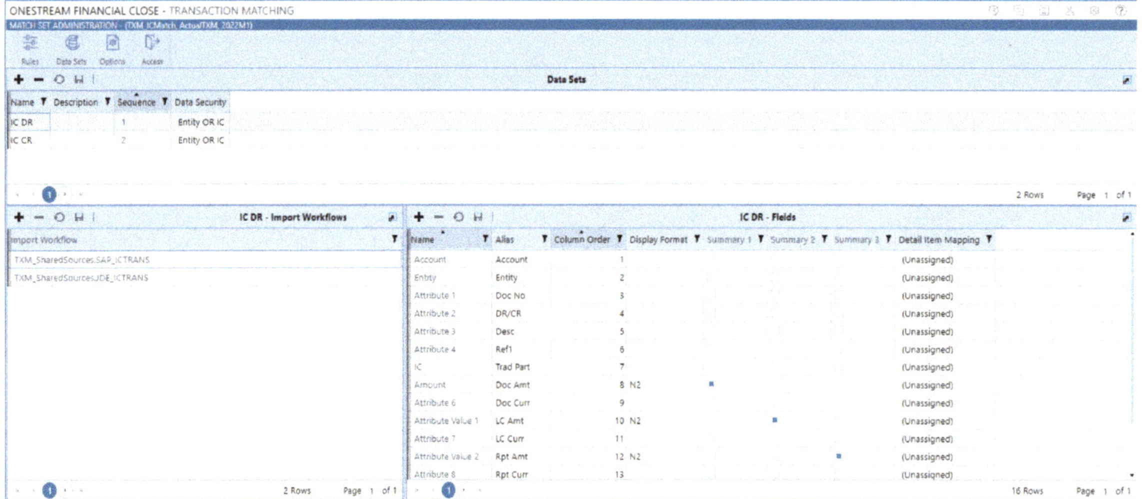

Figure 7.21

The Fields setting controls which Dimensions are displayed on the Transaction page and the detail on the Matches page. The Fields setting drives the available fields that can be utilized for Transaction Matching Rules so any field that needs to be used in a Matching Rule will need to be included.

The Fields setting also controls how the data syncs with Account Reconciliations so you will need to bring in the source and target Dimensions that are used to reconcile the data in Account

Reconciliations. Other fields that are not used in rules can also be brought in, but I would not recommend selecting every field that is available. If too many fields are brought into the Match Set, it can have a negative impact on the End-User Experience. In the design section, I discussed grouping the data fields that will be loaded to Transaction Matching; this is another area where the grouping exercise becomes important. Any field that is only used for reporting can be left out of the Fields setting.

> **Note:** Any field imported to Transaction Matching can be utilized in Custom Reports; even if it is not assigned in the Fields setting of a data set, you can still access the information.

Data Splitting

Data splitting may not be needed by every customer who implements Transaction Matching, but if it is needed it provides a lot of flexibility and requires less intervention with their IT team. You will identify if you need to utilize data splitting during the design phase of the project, but it is still something I recommend setting up even if it is not going to be used.

The steps to set up a data splitting Workflow are described in Chapter 6, but adding a Match Set to utilize the data splitting Workflow is a bit more complicated as the order of operations comes into play. The order and steps to add a Match Set to the data splitting Workflow are listed below.

The first step is to create an import step under the data splitting Workflow, make it active for the Transaction Matching Scenario Type, and apply the appropriate data source and Transformation Rules, as shown in Figure 7.22.

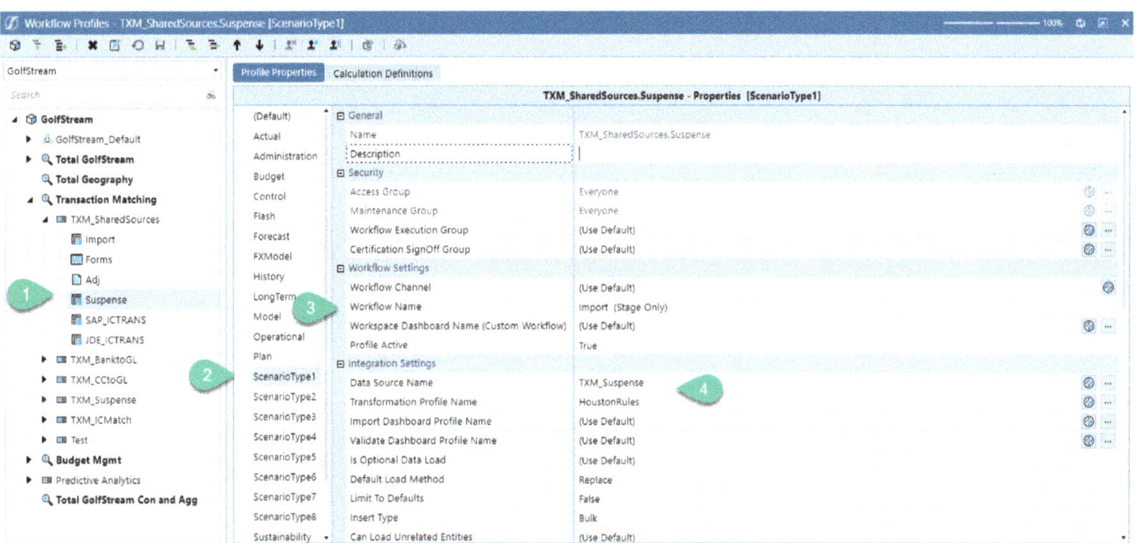

Figure 7.22

The next step is to create the Match Set Workflow where the matching activity will take place. If the Match Set is only using the data splitting Workflow to load data, then the Match Set Workflow should not have an active import step.

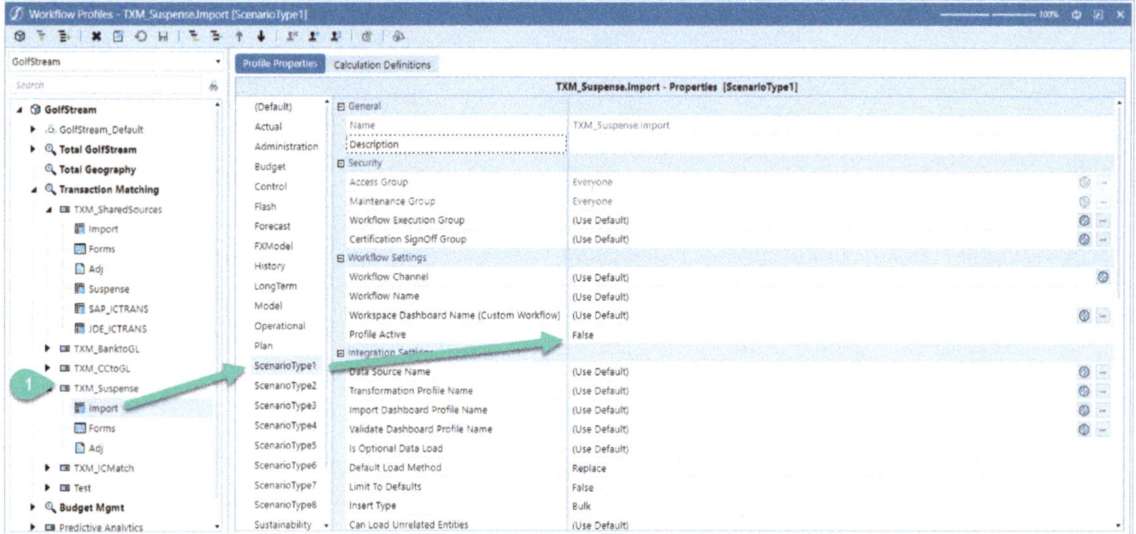

Figure 7.23

Next, you will navigate to the newly-created Match Set Workflow. Select the Match Set Administration page and create the appropriate data sets. Once the data sets are created, you need to assign the import Workflow step you created under the data splitting Workflow, as shown in Figure 7.24.

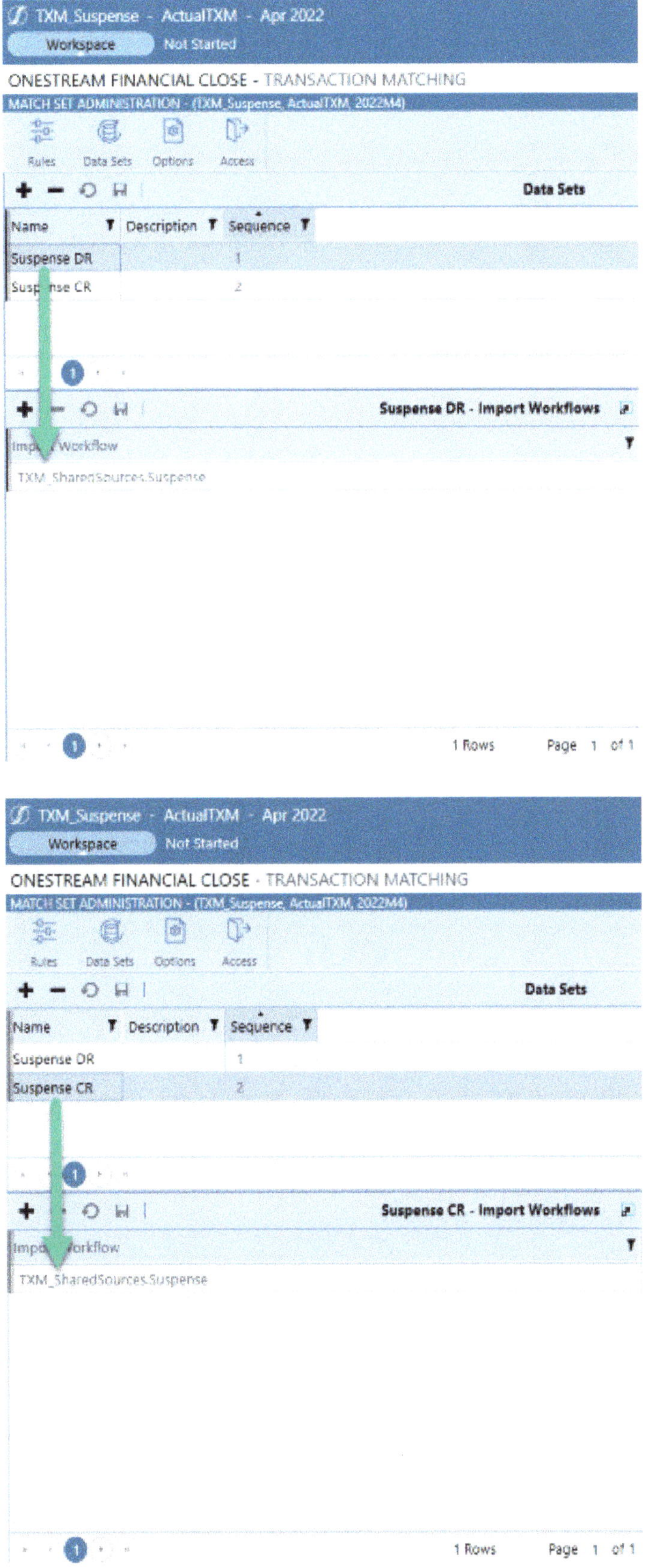

Figure 7.24

Once the import Workflows are assigned to the data set, go to the data splitting Workflow. From the data splitting Workspace, select the import Workflow from the Source Import drop-down, as per Figure 7.25.

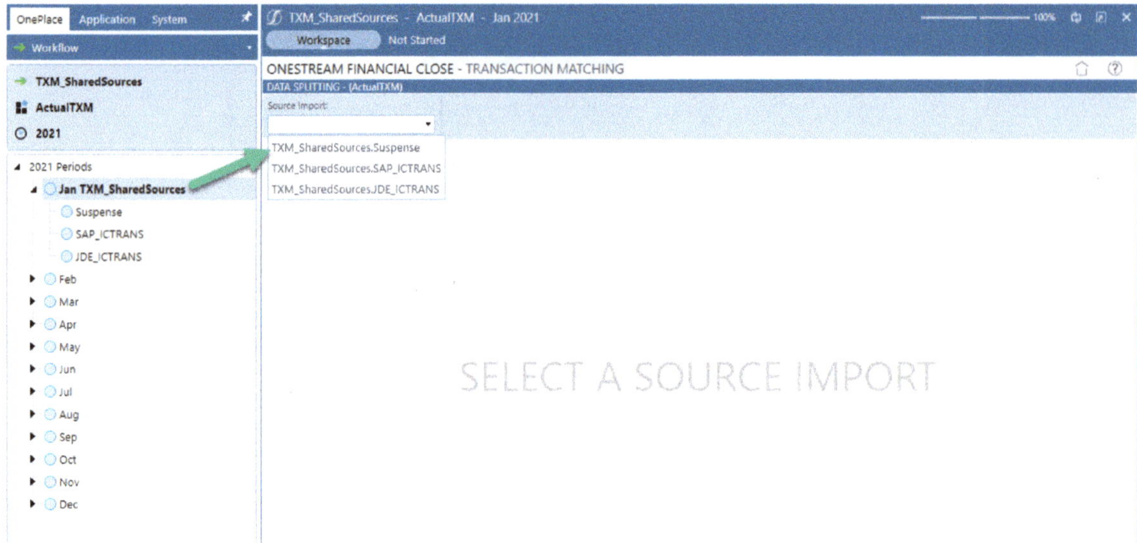

Figure 7.25

After selecting the appropriate import Workflow from the Source Import list, you need to add the data sets to the Target Data Sets screen, Figure 7.26. You should only see the data sets you just created under the Match Set Workflow.

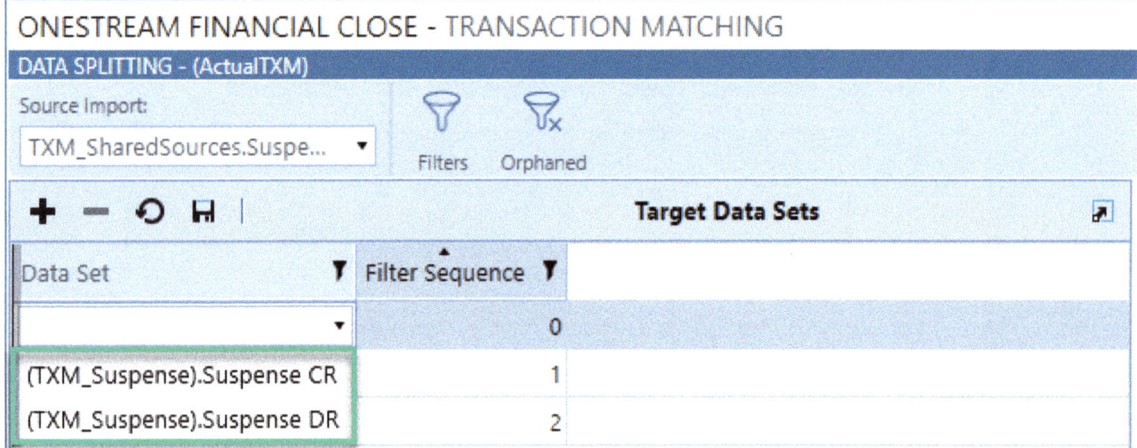

Figure 7.26

The final step is to assign the filter logic for each data set which is done in the Splitting Filters screen, Figure 7.27.

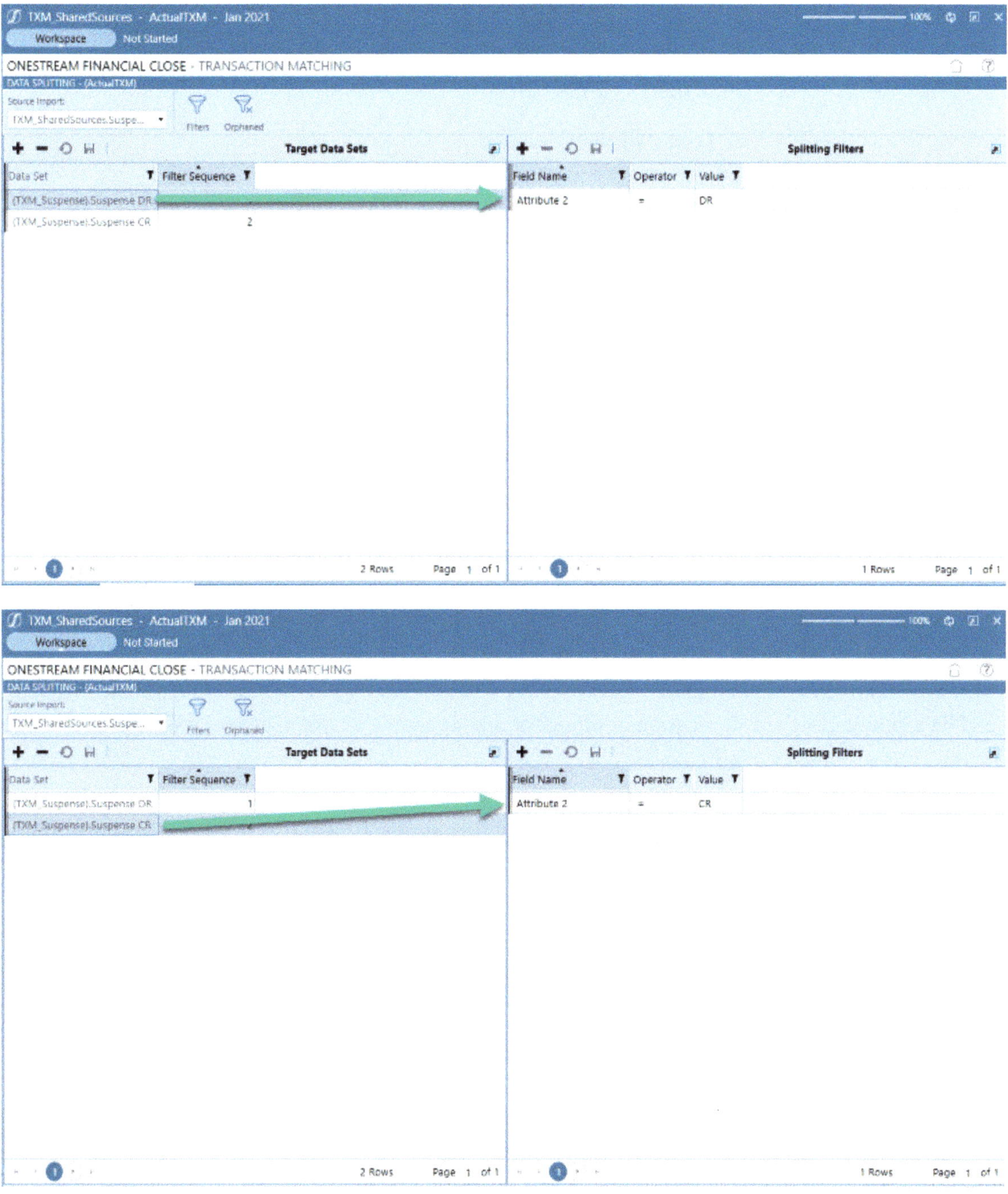

Figure 7.27

As mentioned previously, the order in which these steps are performed is very important and if they are not followed, you will receive errors during the set-up process.

Custom Configuration

Business Rules

As mentioned in the customization design section, you are limited to how much customization can be done within Transaction Matching due to the majority of Business Rules being encrypted. The table below provides a list of all of the Business Rules that come with Transaction Matching, plus their encryption status.

Business Rules	Encrypted
TXM_DataMgmtCreateReconItem	Yes
TXM_DataMgmtProcess	Yes
TXM_EventHandler	No
TXM_HelperQueries	Yes
TXM_ParamHelper	Yes
TXM_SolutionHelper	Yes
TXM_SetupHelper	Yes

Figure 7.28

Notice the one Business Rule that is not encrypted is the `TXM_EventHandler` Rule. This rule was left unencrypted so that customizations can be applied to Transaction Matching. `TXM_EventHandler` allows you to utilize the Business Rule to apply customizations to certain events that occur within Transaction Matching. The Business Rule requires some initial setup steps, which are explained below.

The first step is to download the `CustomEvents_TransactionMatching` Business Rule which can be found under the Files section of the XFW Transaction Matching (TXM) Dashboard Maintenance Unit. See Figure 7.29.

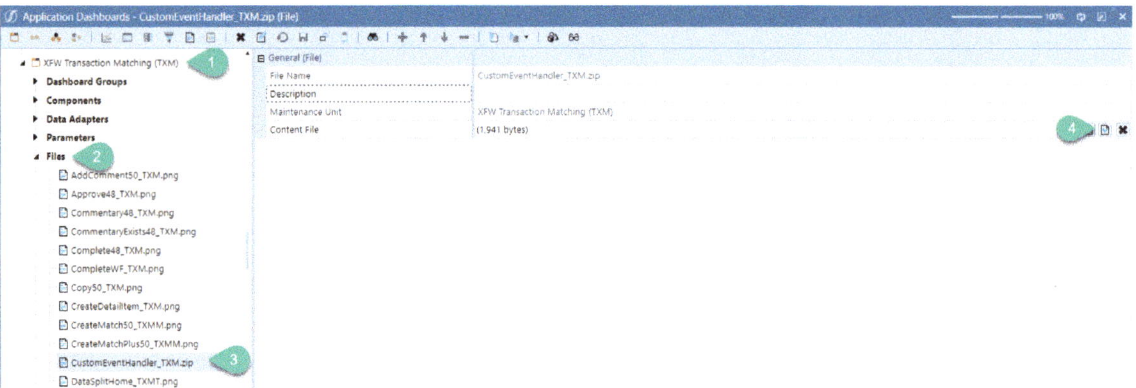

Figure 7.29

After downloading the zip file, it needs to be uploaded to the OneStream environment.

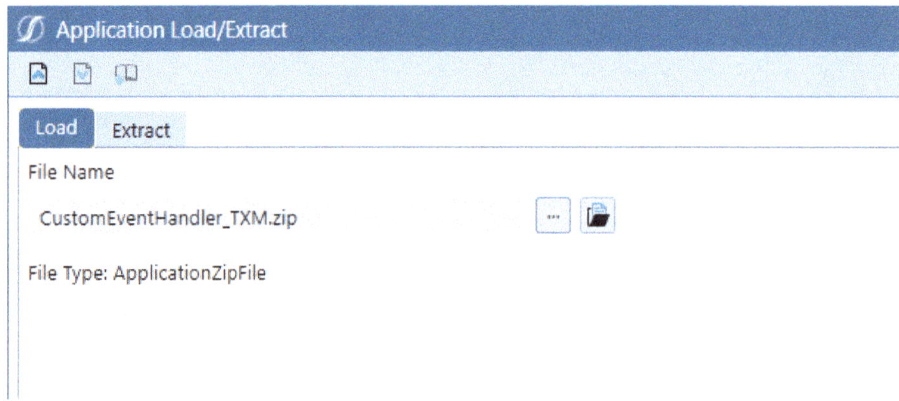

Figure 7.30

Once the file has been imported to the environment, you should see the `CustomEvents_TransactionMatching` Business Rule under the Dashboard Extender section.

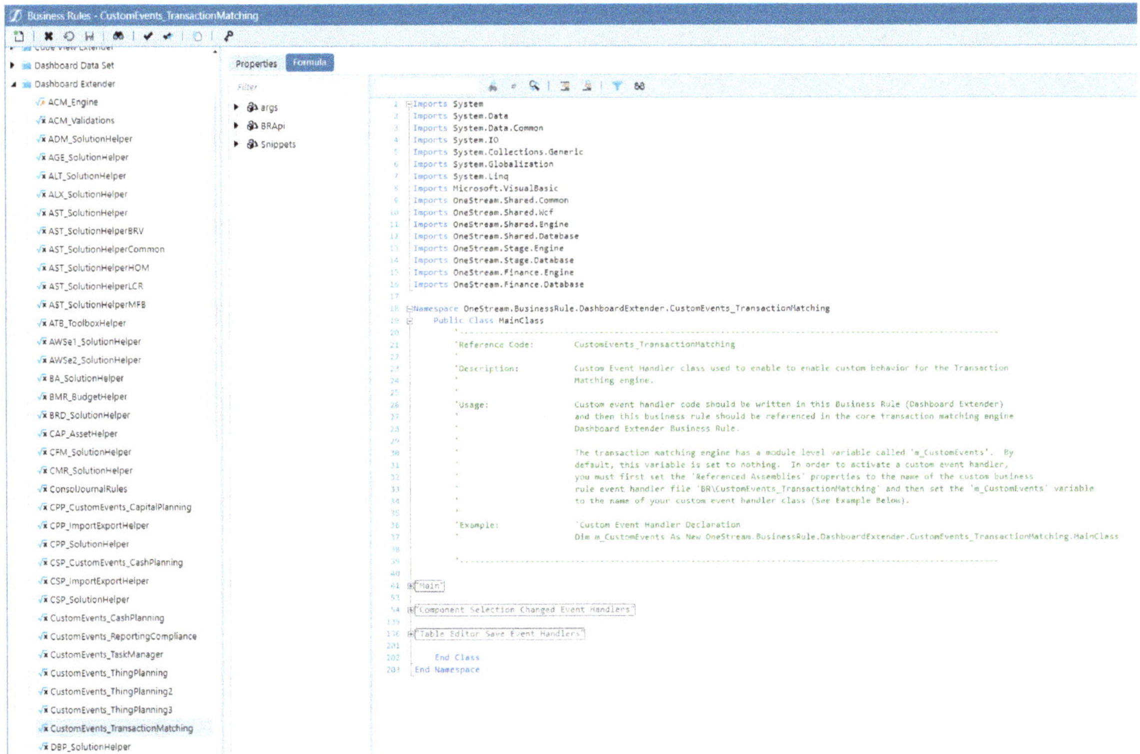

Figure 7.31

Next, the following Business Rules need to be updated to include the `CustomEvents_TransactionMatching` in their Referenced Assemblies, as shown in Figures 7.32 and 7.33.

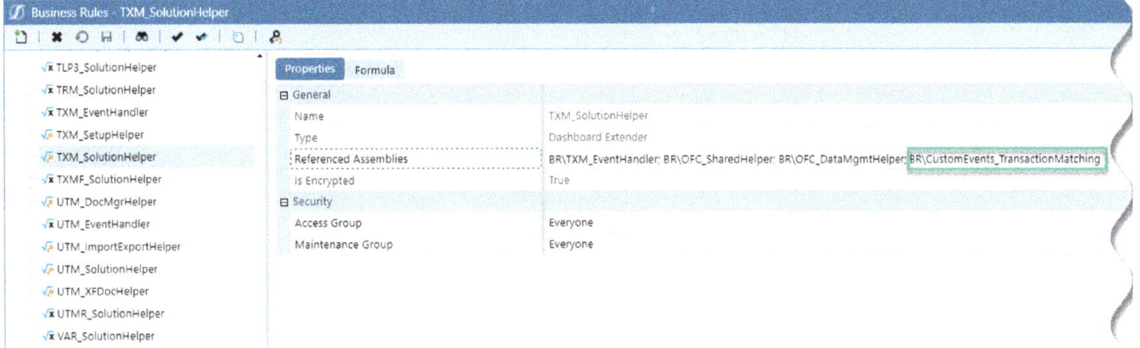

Figure 7.32

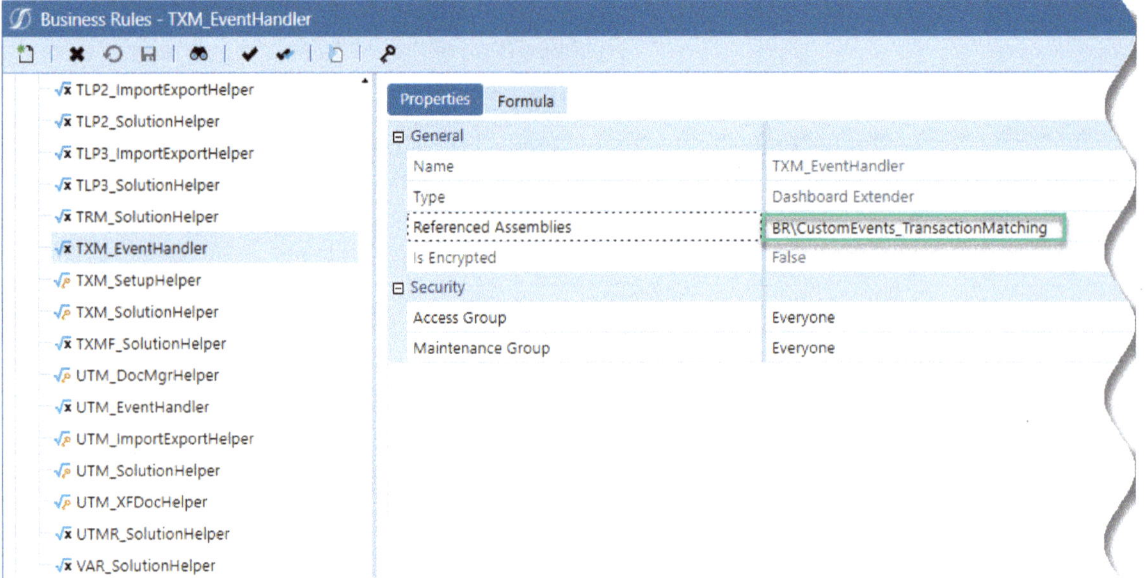

Figure 7.33

Finally, you need to modify the code in the `TXM_EventHandler`.

Line 42 needs to be commented out.

```
8  Imports Microsoft.VisualBasic
9  Imports OneStream.Shared.Common
10 Imports OneStream.Shared.Wcf
11 Imports OneStream.Shared.Engine
12 Imports OneStream.Shared.Database
13 Imports OneStream.Stage.Engine
14 Imports OneStream.Stage.Database
15 Imports OneStream.Finance.Engine
16 Imports OneStream.Finance.Database
17
18 Namespace OneStream.BusinessRule.DashboardExtender.TXM_EventHandler
19     Public Class MainClass
20         '------------------------------------------------------------------------------------------
21         'Reference Code:         TXM_EventHandler
22         '
23         'Description:            Transaction Matching Event Handler For Custom Events (EVENT MODEL).
24         '
25         'Usage:                  This business rule is intended to be called from the TXM_Solution Helper before/after
26         '                        a component selection change and/or save data action.
27         '------------------------------------------------------------------------------------------
28         Public Function Main(ByVal si As SessionInfo, ByVal globals As BRGlobals, ByVal api As Object, ByVal args As DashboardExtenderArgs) As Object
29             Try
30
31                 'Do Nothing
32                 Return Nothing
33
34             Catch ex As Exception
35                 Throw ErrorHandler.LogWrite(si, New XFException(si, ex))
36             End Try
37         End Function
38
39 #Region "Constants and Enumerations"
40
41         'Custom Event Handler Declaration
42         Public Property m_CustomEvents As Object = Nothing
43         'Public Property m_CustomEvents As New DashboardExtender.CustomEvents_TransactionMatching.MainClass
44 #End Region
45     End Class
46 End Namespace
47
```

Figure 7.34

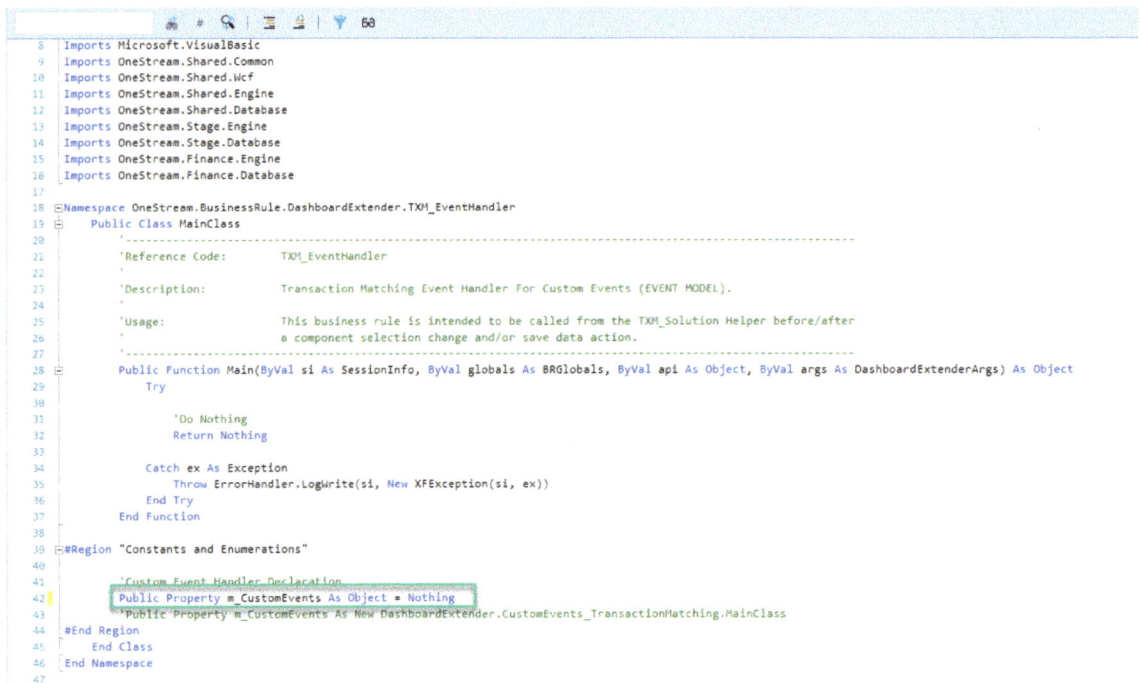

Then, you need to uncomment the line that calls the `CustomEvents_TransactionMatching` Business Rule, which should be on line 43.

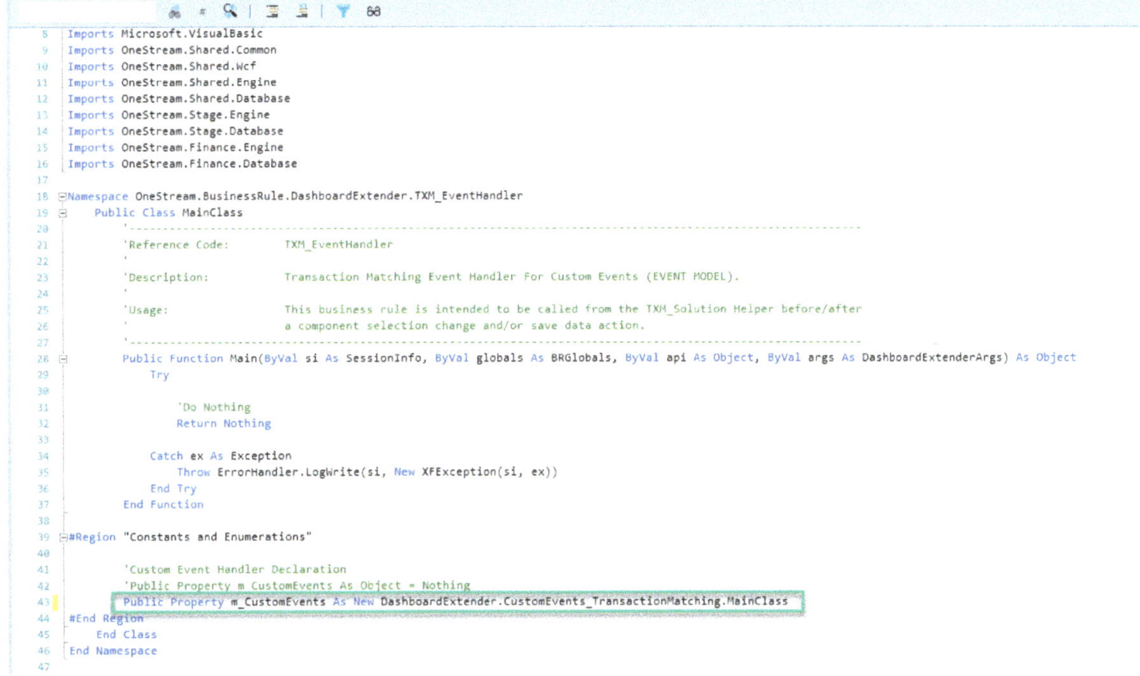

Figure 7.35

Once the setup is complete for the CustomEvents_TransactionMatching Business Rule, you can now apply customizations to Transaction Matching before or after the following events are clicked:

- SaveSettings
- CreateSolutionTables
- ValidateSetupStepsExecuted
- Uninstall
- OnTableEditorOrGridSelection
- OnComboBoxSelection
- OnButtonClick
- OnShowContentPage

You can also apply customizations to Transaction Matching before or after the save event for a Table Editor.

- OnSaveOrUpdateTableEditor

The following code provides examples of the types of customizations that can be setup utilizing the CustomEvents_TransactionMatching Rule.

```
        '-------------------------------------------------------------------------------------------------

"Main"

#Region "Component Selection Changed Event Handlers"

        Public Sub BeforeSelectionChangedEvent(ByVal si As SessionInfo, ByVal globals As BRGlobals, ByVal api As Object, ByVal args As DashboardExtenderArgs,
            Try
                'BEFORE
                '*************************************************************************
                'Transaction Matching Component Selection Changed Events
                Dim componentName As String = args.ComponentInfo.Component.Name
                Select Case True
                    Case args.FunctionName.XFEqualsIgnoreCase("OnTableEditorOrGridSelection")
                        'EXAMPLE
                        'If componentName.XFEqualsIgnoreCase("ted_Matches_TXM") Then
                        '   EXAMPLE - STOP FURTHER PROCESSING SKIP TO AFTER EVENT
                        '   taskResult.IsOK = False

                        '   EXAMPLE - LOG TO ERROR LOG
                        '   If taskResult.IsOK = False Then
                        '       taskResult.ShowMessageBox = True
                        '       taskResult.Message = "My Error Message"
                        '       BRApi.ErrorLog.LogMessage(si, taskResult.Message)
                        '   End If
                        'End If

                    Case args.FunctionName.XFEqualsIgnoreCase("OnComboBoxSelection")

                    Case args.FunctionName.XFEqualsIgnoreCase("OnButtonClick")

                    Case args.FunctionName.XFEqualsIgnoreCase("OnShowContentPage")

                    Case args.FunctionName.XFEqualsIgnoreCase("SaveSettings")

                    Case Else
                        BRApi.ErrorLog.LogMessage(si, "Unknown Function Name: " & args.FunctionName)
                        Exit Select
                End Select
```

Figure 7.36

When upgrading Transaction Matching, the `CustomEvents_TransactionMatching` Business Rule will not be deleted but the Referenced Assemblies and modifying the `TXM_EventHandler` will need to be setup again.

Automation

Due to the frequency of data loads to Transaction Matching, most companies want to automate them. The automation for loading data to Transaction Matching works exactly the same as for any other job that is automated to import data to a Workflow. Where Transaction Matching becomes unique is that after the data is loaded, you want to automatically run the Matching Rules. As part of the Transaction Matching install, a Data Management job is installed that processes the Matching Rules. The out-of-the-box **Data Management job** runs the rules based on the Match Set the User is on.

When setting up the process to automate the rules running after a data load, the first step is to create a new Data Management Group. I typically like to call it `TXM_Custom`. By creating a new Data Management Group, you are ensuring that this customization piece will not be deleted during an upgrade. After creating a new group, you need to create a step that calls the `TXM_DataMgmt_Process` Business Rule. As shown in Figure 7.37, this is what the Data Management job calls.

⊟ General (Step)	
Name	ProcessRules_TXM
Description	
Data Management Group	Transaction Matching (TXM)
Step Type	Execute Business Rule
Use Detailed Logging	False
⊟ Business Rule	
Business Rule	TXM_DataMgmtProcess
Parameters	

Figure 7.37

Your new custom step will need one modification, as shown in Figure 7.38, where you need to pass in the correct `Match Set ID` to inform Transaction Matching which rules need to be processed.

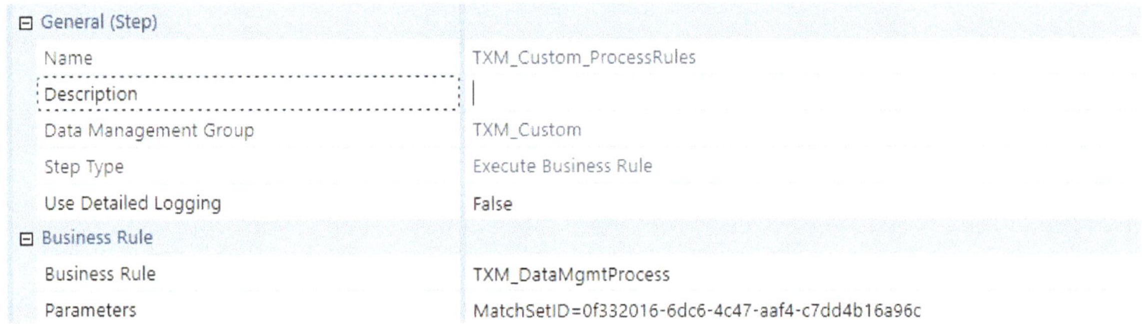

Figure 7.38

You can find the `Match Set ID` for each Match Set on the Settings page under the Match Sets section, Figure 7.39.

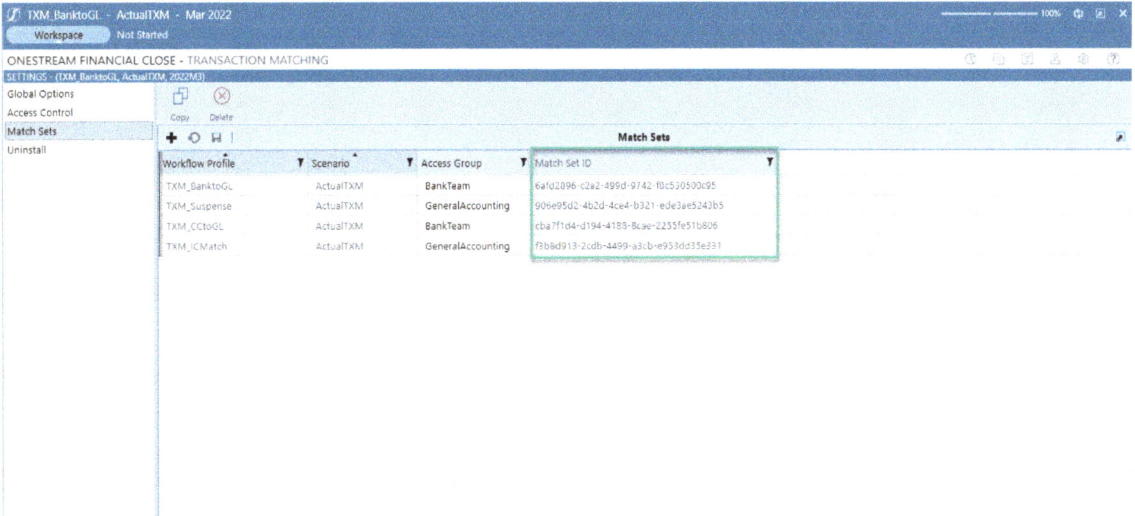

Figure 7.39

Custom Reports

As I have mentioned a few times, when working with Transaction Matching, you will be dealing with a large volume of data. The volume of data can become a big issue with Custom Reports as it will have a significant impact on Report performance. The best approach to dealing with the volume is to break up data sets into a more manageable size. This section of the chapter will provide you with vital information from the backend tables that will help you in breaking up the data sets.

Transaction Matching Tables

All of the data in Transaction Matching sits in tables that are specific to the solution and are outside OneStream Cubes. Because the data does not sit in the Cubes, you cannot utilize a Cube View to pull data out of Transaction Matching. Instead, you need to utilize data adaptors and write SQL `Select` statements to create Custom Reports.

Understanding the Transaction Matching tables is the first step to creating Custom Reports. Figure 7.40 shows all the tables, and Figure 7.41 shows all the views that hold all the data in Transaction Matching.

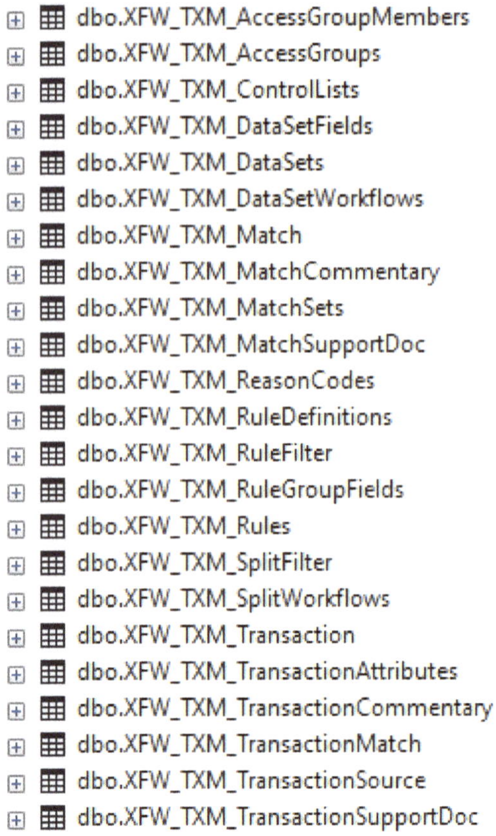

dbo.XFW_TXM_AccessGroupMembers
dbo.XFW_TXM_AccessGroups
dbo.XFW_TXM_ControlLists
dbo.XFW_TXM_DataSetFields
dbo.XFW_TXM_DataSets
dbo.XFW_TXM_DataSetWorkflows
dbo.XFW_TXM_Match
dbo.XFW_TXM_MatchCommentary
dbo.XFW_TXM_MatchSets
dbo.XFW_TXM_MatchSupportDoc
dbo.XFW_TXM_ReasonCodes
dbo.XFW_TXM_RuleDefinitions
dbo.XFW_TXM_RuleFilter
dbo.XFW_TXM_RuleGroupFields
dbo.XFW_TXM_Rules
dbo.XFW_TXM_SplitFilter
dbo.XFW_TXM_SplitWorkflows
dbo.XFW_TXM_Transaction
dbo.XFW_TXM_TransactionAttributes
dbo.XFW_TXM_TransactionCommentary
dbo.XFW_TXM_TransactionMatch
dbo.XFW_TXM_TransactionSource
dbo.XFW_TXM_TransactionSupportDoc

Figure 7.40

dbo.vXFW_TXM_TransactionDetail
dbo.vXFW_TXM_TransactionDetailMatched
dbo.vXFW_TXM_TransactionDetailWithSource

Figure 7.41

The name of each table and view provides a hint as to what each table contains, but to see all the detail you will need to look at all the columns in each table. The query shown in Figure 7.42 can be run – using a data adaptor – against any table or view and will allow you to see all the columns for each table. You will need to replace the table or view name depending on what table or view you want to see. Notice, the query is only grabbing the top 10 rows from each table. This is done on purpose as some of the tables will contain millions of rows of data.

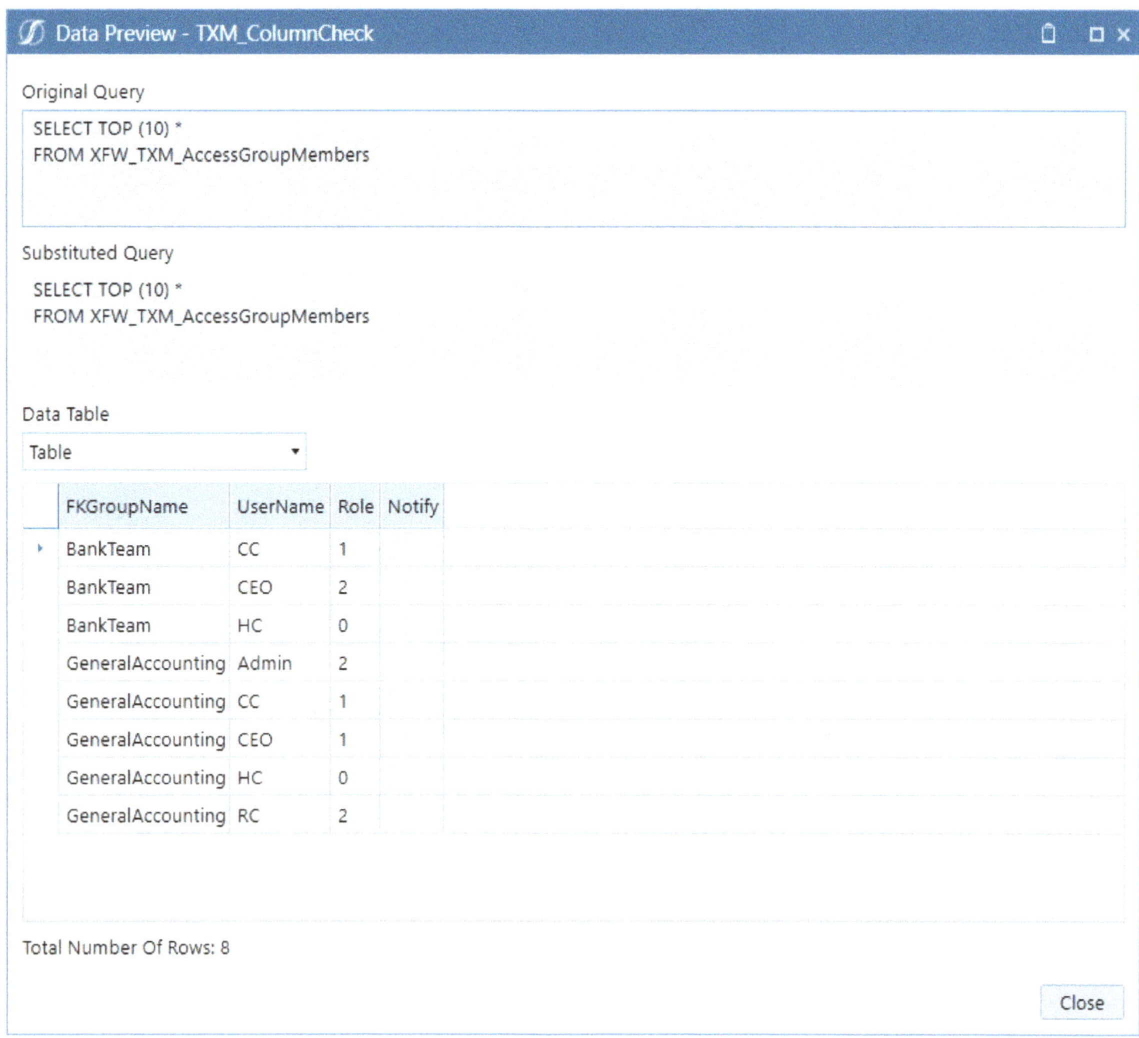

FKGroupName	UserName	Role	Notify
BankTeam	CC	1	
BankTeam	CEO	2	
BankTeam	HC	0	
GeneralAccounting	Admin	2	
GeneralAccounting	CC	1	
GeneralAccounting	CEO	1	
GeneralAccounting	HC	0	
GeneralAccounting	RC	2	

Figure 7.42

Tips and Tricks

Below are helpful tips and tricks that will assist you with creating Custom Reports for Transaction Matching.

Status table code for the following:

- `XFW_TXM_Transaction`
- `vXFW_TXM_TransactionDetail`
- `vXFW_TXM_TransactionDetailWithSource`

Status Code	Definition
0	Unmatched State
1	Suspended State
2	Matched State
3	Pending Delete State
4	Deleted State

Figure 7.43

Status table code for the following:

- `XFW_TXM_Match`
- `vXFW_TXM_TransactionDetailMatched`

Status Code	Definition
0	Pending Approval Status
1	Approved Match Status

Figure 7.44

The query in Figure 7.45 captures all the data sets that have Matched transactions in Transaction Matching.

Figure 7.45

The query in Figure 7.46 captures all the Workflows and data sets associated with Transaction Matching.

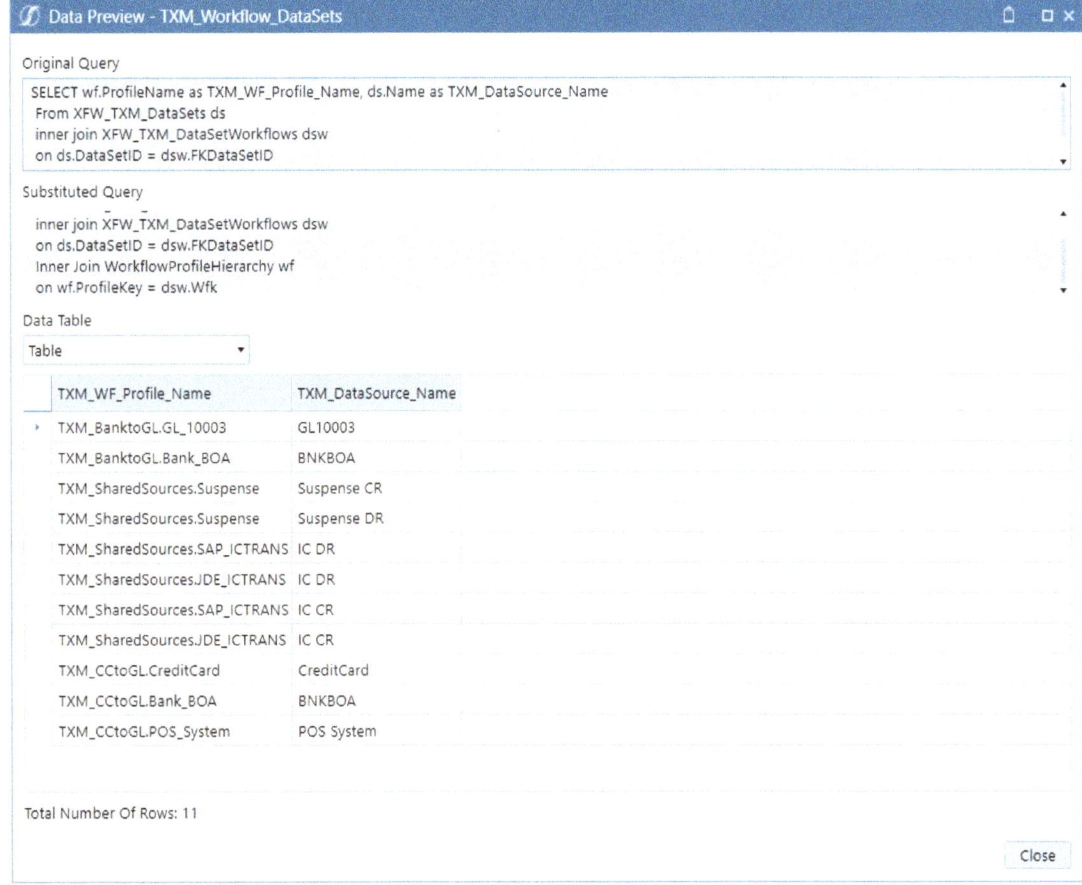

Figure 7.46

The query in Figure 7.47 captures all the Workflow imports, Transaction Matching data sources, and splitting information associated with the data splitting Workflow.

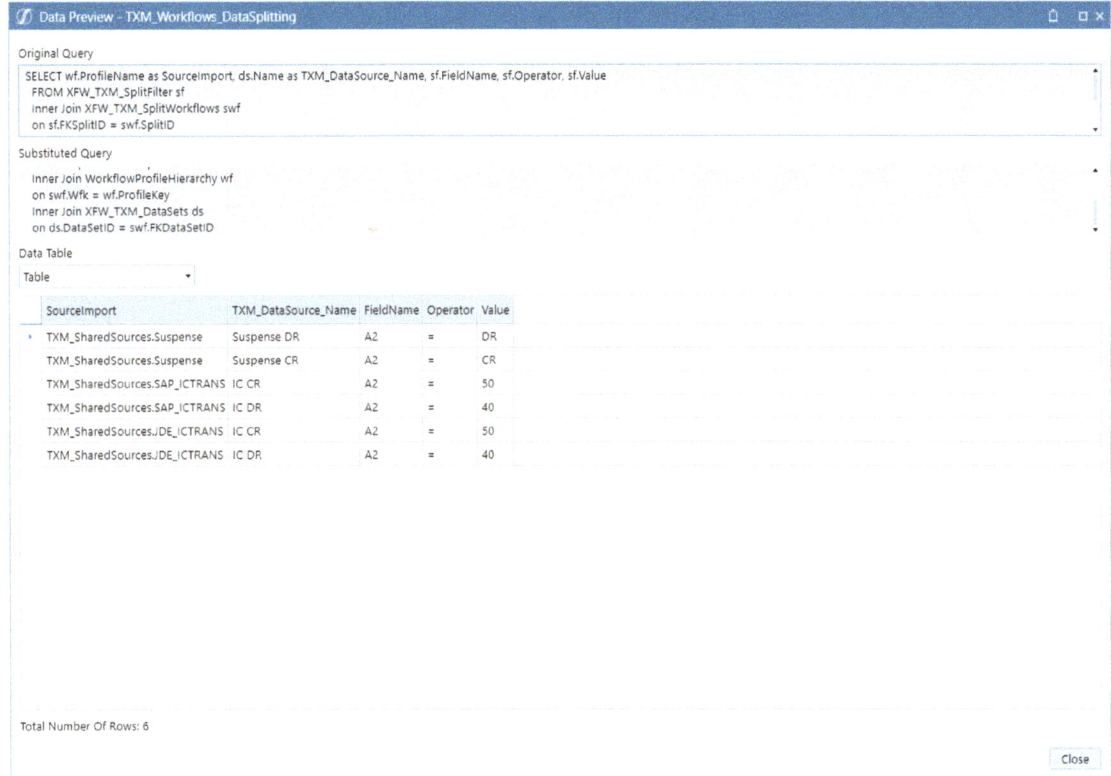

Figure 7.47

I recommend providing a **Large Data Pivot Grid** to every Transaction Matching customer because it provides each User with the ability to manipulate the data and save their unique changes. The large data pivot is also made to handle large data sets with its **Grid's Paging** feature and server-based processing.

Figures 7.48 to 7.50 show how you can utilize a large data pivot grid and make it fully dynamic by pulling the data associated with the Match Set the User is on when they run the Custom Report. This will work for all Match Sets in the Transaction Matching system.

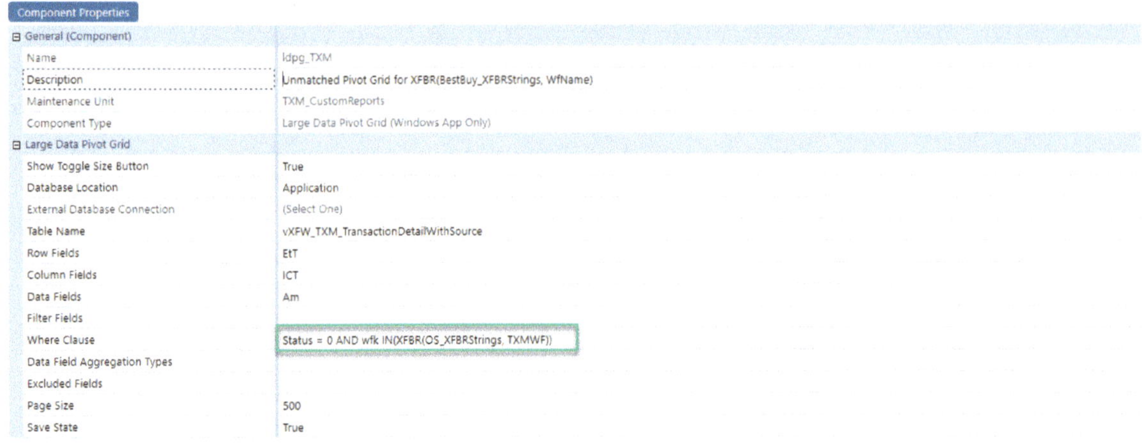

Figure 7.48

```
Imports OneStream.Stage.Database
Imports OneStream.Finance.Engine
Imports OneStream.Finance.Database

Namespace OneStream.BusinessRule.DashboardStringFunction.OS_XFBRStrings
    Public Class MainClass
        Public Function Main(ByVal si As SessionInfo, ByVal globals As BRGlobals, ByVal api As Object, ByVal args As DashboardStringFunctionArgs) As Object
            Try
                If args.FunctionName.XFEqualsIgnoreCase("TXMWF") Then

                    Dim wfUnitInfo As WorkflowUnitInfo = args.SubstVarSourceInfo.WorkflowUnitInfo
                    Dim wfPfKey As String = wfUnitInfo.WfUnitPk.ProfileKey.ToString
                    Dim sqlQuery As New Text.StringBuilder

                    sqlQuery.Append("Select Distinct b.wfk as WF" & vbcrlf)
                    sqlQuery.Append("From XFW_TXM_MatchSets a " & vbcrlf)
                    sqlQuery.Append("left Join vXFW_TXM_TransactionDetailWithSource b " & vbcrlf)
                    sqlQuery.Append("On a.MatchSetID = b.FKMatchSetID " & vbcrlf)
                    sqlQuery.Append("Left Join WorkflowProfileHierarchy c " & vbcrlf)
                    sqlQuery.Append("on b.wfk = c.ProfileKey " & vbcrlf)
                    sqlQuery.Append("Where 1=1 " & vbcrlf)
                    sqlQuery.Append("And a.Wfk = '" & wfPfKey & "' " & vbcrlf)

                    Dim dt As DataTable
                    Using dbConn As DbConnInfo = BRApi.Database.CreateApplicationDbConnInfo(si)
                        dt = BRApi.Database.ExecuteSql(dbConn, sqlQuery.ToString, True)
                    End Using

                    Dim wfkList As String = Nothing
                    Dim firstRow As Boolean = True

                    For Each Row As DataRow In dt.Rows
                        If firstRow = True Then
                            wfkList += "'" & Row.Item("WF").ToString &
                                firstRow = False
                            Else
                                wfkList += ",'" & Row.Item("WF").ToString & "'"
                        End If
                    Next

                    Return wfkList
                End If
```

Figure 7.49

> **Note:** The above code demonstrates how to dynamically grab all of the Workflow imports that are associated to the Match Set the User is viewing.

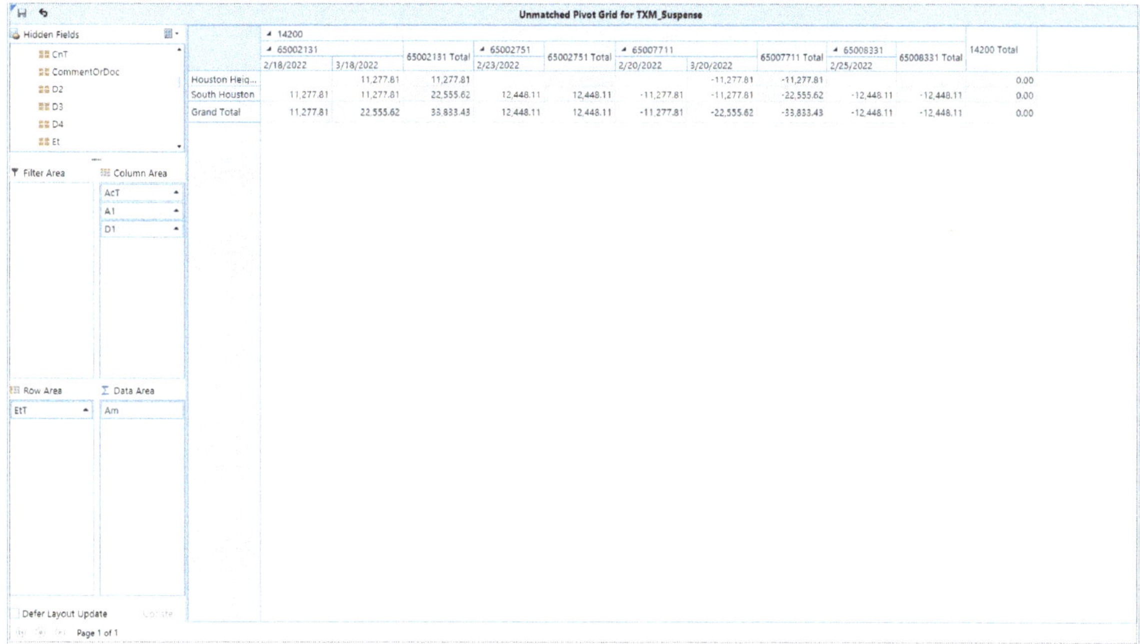

Figure 7.50

Testing and Training

If a customer is just starting out with Transaction Matching, or if they perform their current matching in Excel, testing and data validation should be easy to perform. However, if they are coming from an existing Transaction Matching solution, the data validation and parallels will be more complex to coordinate and perform.

Data Validation

Data volume can impact data validation for Transaction Matching. It is unrealistic for a customer to validate millions of lines of data each month. Instead, most customers are comfortable with high-level checks like a row count check for each import, or a sum of all the data loaded to each Workflow. Figures 7.51 and 7.52 provide some sample queries that can be used for some high-level validation checks.

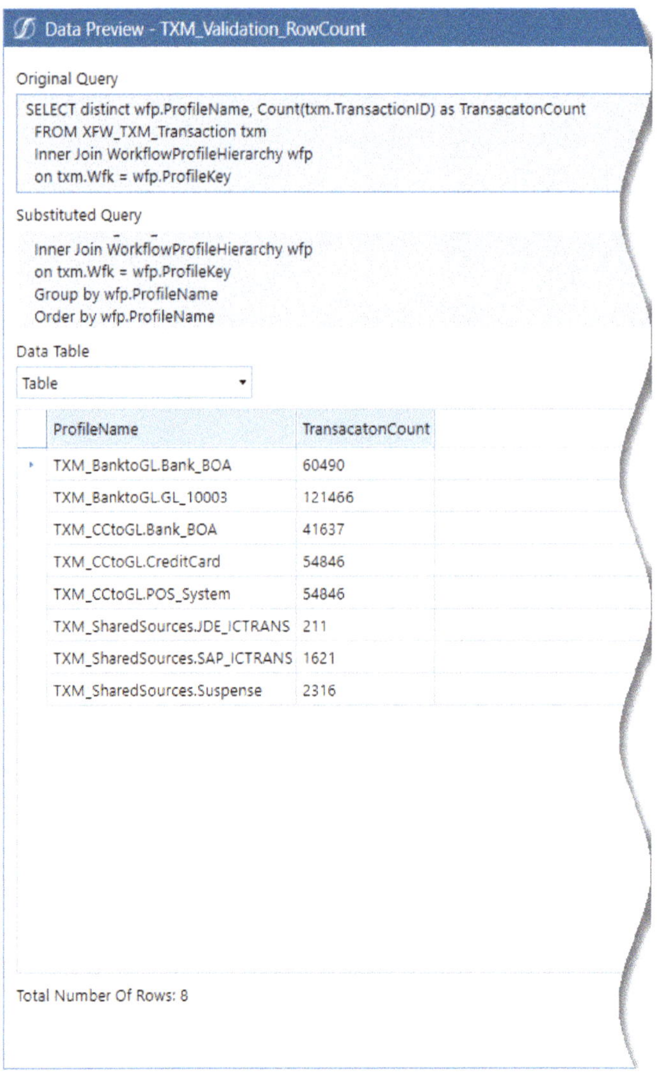

Data Preview - TXM_Validation_RowCount

Original Query

```
SELECT distinct wfp.ProfileName, Count(txm.TransactionID) as TransacatonCount
  FROM XFW_TXM_Transaction txm
  Inner Join WorkflowProfileHierarchy wfp
  on txm.Wfk = wfp.ProfileKey
```

Substituted Query

```
  Inner Join WorkflowProfileHierarchy wfp
  on txm.Wfk = wfp.ProfileKey
  Group by wfp.ProfileName
  Order by wfp.ProfileName
```

Data Table

Table

ProfileName	TransacatonCount
TXM_BanktoGL.Bank_BOA	60490
TXM_BanktoGL.GL_10003	121466
TXM_CCtoGL.Bank_BOA	41637
TXM_CCtoGL.CreditCard	54846
TXM_CCtoGL.POS_System	54846
TXM_SharedSources.JDE_ICTRANS	211
TXM_SharedSources.SAP_ICTRANS	1621
TXM_SharedSources.Suspense	2316

Total Number Of Rows: 8

Figure 7.51

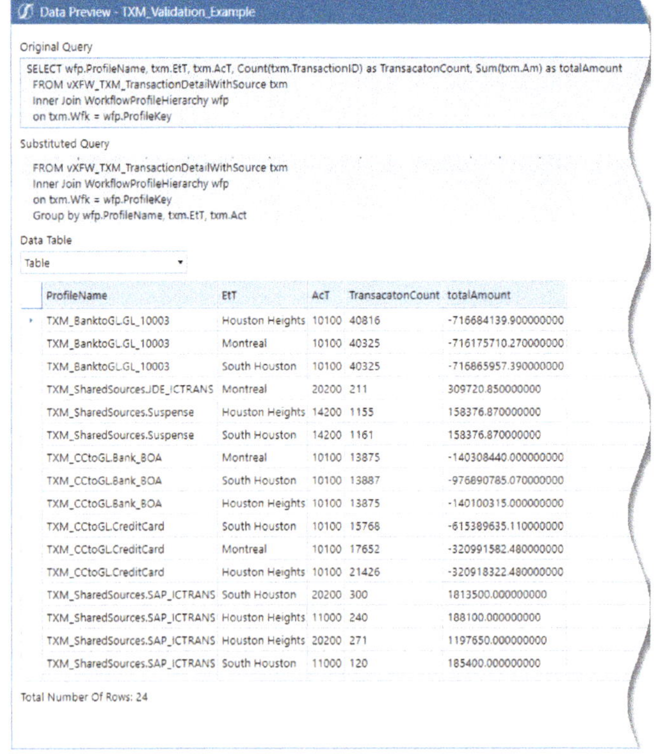

Data Preview - TXM_Validation_Example

Original Query

```
SELECT wfp.ProfileName, txm.EtT, txm.AcT, Count(txm.TransactionID) as TransacatonCount, Sum(txm.Am) as totalAmount
  FROM vXFW_TXM_TransactionDetailWithSource txm
  Inner Join WorkflowProfileHierarchy wfp
  on txm.Wfk = wfp.ProfileKey
```

Substituted Query

```
  FROM vXFW_TXM_TransactionDetailWithSource txm
  Inner Join WorkflowProfileHierarchy wfp
  on txm.Wfk = wfp.ProfileKey
  Group by wfp.ProfileName, txm.EtT, txm.Act
```

Data Table

Table

ProfileName	EtT	AcT	TransacatonCount	totalAmount
TXM_BanktoGL.GL_10003	Houston Heights	10100	40816	-716684139.900000000
TXM_BanktoGL.GL_10003	Montreal	10100	40325	-716175710.270000000
TXM_BanktoGL.GL_10003	South Houston	10100	40325	-716865957.390000000
TXM_SharedSources.JDE_ICTRANS	Montreal	20200	211	309720.850000000
TXM_SharedSources.Suspense	Houston Heights	14200	1155	158376.870000000
TXM_SharedSources.Suspense	South Houston	14200	1161	158376.870000000
TXM_CCtoGL.Bank_BOA	Montreal	10100	13875	-140308440.000000000
TXM_CCtoGL.Bank_BOA	South Houston	10100	13887	-976890785.070000000
TXM_CCtoGL.Bank_BOA	Houston Heights	10100	13875	-140100315.000000000
TXM_CCtoGL.CreditCard	South Houston	10100	15768	-615389635.110000000
TXM_CCtoGL.CreditCard	Montreal	10100	17652	-320991582.480000000
TXM_CCtoGL.CreditCard	Houston Heights	10100	21426	-320918322.480000000
TXM_SharedSources.SAP_ICTRANS	South Houston	20200	300	1813500.000000000
TXM_SharedSources.SAP_ICTRANS	Houston Heights	11000	240	188100.000000000
TXM_SharedSources.SAP_ICTRANS	Houston Heights	20200	271	1197650.000000000
TXM_SharedSources.SAP_ICTRANS	South Houston	11000	120	185400.000000000

Total Number Of Rows: 24

Figure 7.52

End User Training

OneStream does not currently offer specific training for Transaction Matching which means that End Users will need custom training. I personally prefer the *train the trainer* approach as I think it helps Power Users/Admin(s) become stronger in understanding their Transaction Matching solution. End User training for Transaction Matching should not take more than a full day.

Parallels

After a parallel is complete, you need to keep in mind whether the customer continues to load with the same frequency post-parallel. If they do not, this may cause you to clear the data out of Transaction Matching and reload the history before the next parallel or go-live.

Conclusion

I hope this chapter provided you with enough knowledge to feel confident in leading a Transaction Matching project. Hopefully, you can now utilize this information to create an ideal User experience that will have them excited about working with the OneStream Transaction Matching solution.

8

Using Transaction Matching

In this chapter, we will discuss one of my favorite OneStream MarketPlace solutions – Transaction Matching.

As part of the OneStream Financial Close, this solution is beneficial because it takes a very manual, tedious process and transforms it into an automated approach. Leveraging rules, the solution will automatically match transactions while identifying Unmatched items that need to be addressed.

In my previous life, I would perform these tasks in Excel using formulas and color coding. I would spend significant time concatenating fields, performing look up formulas, Variance Calculations, highlighting, etc., to try to determine what was relevant in my data. My process was time-consuming, error prone, and inconsistent. Moving out of the manual process to a solution allowed me to focus on transactional issues or open items versus data cleansing and clearing.

Matching is typically done for Financial Reconciliations such as Bank, Intercompany, Subledgers, Suspense, or Clearing Accounts, to name few. However, matching can also be performed on non-financial data like inventory counts, hours, SKUs, GL migrations, system to system tie outs, etc. Matching is unlimited in its possibilities. Anywhere you perform a manual review of one data set to another – to ensure both sources contain the same information – matching can be leveraged.

In Chapter 6, we discussed the setup of the Match Set and the Administrator's functions and responsibilities. Now, we will focus on the User and walk through the Match Set interface and the actions that can be performed around the different types of transactions, along with various roles and responsibilities. Let's start with the Workflow.

Matching Workflow

The Matching Workflow represents a Match Set, and each Match Set is defined as its own unique Workflow. The number of Match Sets is dependent on your matching process and security requirements which are defined during implementation (Chapter 7).

To access the Matched and Unmatched transactions, you will navigate to the specific Workflow to complete your responsibilities. Transactions should be loaded into the Workflow period they relate to in order to ensure proper cutoff. The system tracks both the period in which the transactions are loaded, as well as what period the transaction is Matched. Unmatched transactions automatically persist into future periods with no additional action needed by the User.

When leveraging the Workflow period, it is important to understand that the state of a transaction – Unmatched or Matched – is not captured period over period. This means that if I have a transaction Unmatched in 2022M3 that is subsequently Matched in 2022M4, the transaction will no longer appear Unmatched in the system regardless of the period I view. If I navigate back to 2022M3, the transaction will appear Matched.

Also, transactions are only viewable in the period they are loaded or future periods. Therefore, the 2022M3 transaction, previously discussed, is only viewable from the 2022M3 period forwards. You will not see this transaction in 2022M2 or prior because it did not exist at that time. This prevents you from accidently referring to the transaction in M2 – when it didn't exist – and also supports proper cutoff, which will be discussed later in this section.

Workspace

The Transaction Matching Workspace is where you will perform your matching responsibilities.

The Workspace is made up of key pages which include the Scorecard, Matches, Transactions, Administration, Settings, and Help. The Workspace will default to the Transactions page as this is where most of the work occurs. You can move between the pages by utilizing the navigation icons in the top-right corner. The icons that are visible to a User will depend on the User's security level. Within this chapter, we will walk through the Scorecard, Matches, and Transactions pages.

Navigation Icons

As mentioned, to navigate to different areas of the Transaction Matching solution, you will utilize the navigation icons located in the top-right portion of the Workspace. The icons are consistent with those found within the Account Reconciliation solution, with the exception of two new icons for the Matches page and the Transactions page. All Users have access to the Scorecard, Matches, Transactions, and Help pages. In addition to these pages, Local, Transaction Matching (TXM) and System Administrators will have access to the Administration page, while TXM and System Administrators will have access to the Settings page. The navigation icons are described in Figure 8.1.

Icon	Description	Roles	Definition
	Scorecard Page	All Roles	Navigates Users to solution-delivered Dashboards and reporting. (Only available in the windows application.)
	Matches Page	All Roles	Navigates Users to the Matches page to review all matches made: Automatic, Suggested, and Manual.
	Transactions Page	All Roles	Set as the default page. Navigates the User to the Transactions page to view Matched, Unmatched, Suspended, Pending Delete, and Deleted Transactions (TXM and System Administrators only) by data set.
	Match Set Administration Page	Local and System Admins	Navigates Local, TXM and System Administrators to the Data Sets, Rules, Options and Match Set Access pages for the Match Set.
	Settings Page	System Admins	Navigates TXM and System Administrators to Global Settings and Security Access.
	Help Page	All Roles	Navigates to the Help Menu.

Figure 8.1

Matches Page

The Matches page is where you can view the details associated with specific matches made in the period, and perform actions like accepting, approving, or unmatching matches if security permits. The Matches page can be broken up into three key areas:

- Header
- Matches Grid View
- Detail Match Pane

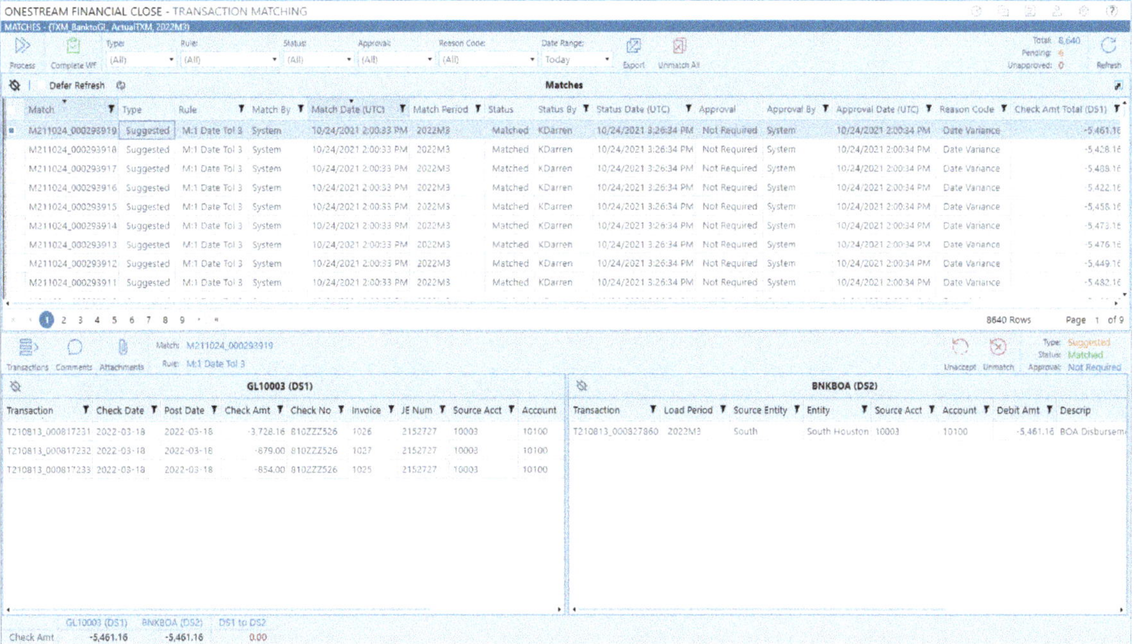

Figure 8.2

Matches Header

The header section, as shown below, contains the following key action icons: Process, Complete Workflow, Export, and Unmatch All. In addition, the header contains the match statistics and predefined filter capabilities. In the following paragraphs, we will walk through all these components in detail.

Figure 8.3

Process

The Process icon is used to run the active Match Rules for the given period.

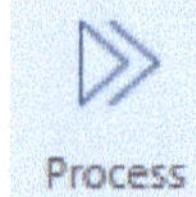

Figure 8.4

Match Rules will run against all Unmatched transactions based on the Workflow period (i.e., all Unmatched transactions from the current and prior Workflow periods).

Although typically scheduled to run automatically with the data load, any role that has access to the Match Set – with the exception of the Viewer and Commenter roles – can manually run the process if the Workflow is not yet marked complete. The results of the process run are stored in the **Task Activity log**.

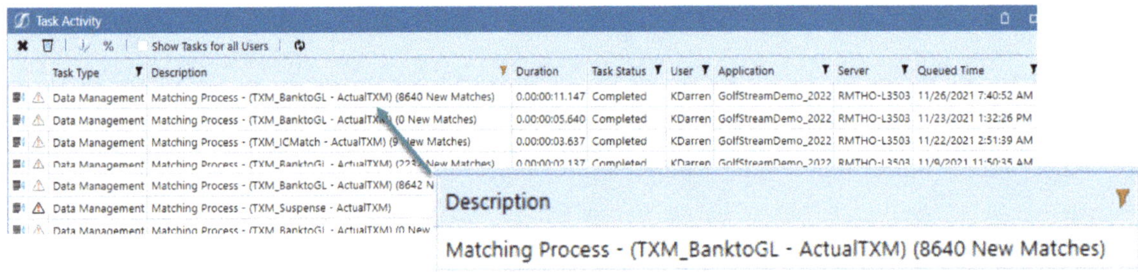

Figure 8.5

> **Note:** while the match process is running, you will not be able to perform manual matching within the Transactions page because the transactions are being used by the process. Also note, that only one active job per Match Set can run at a time.

Complete Workflow

Completing the Workflow allows an organization to accurately reflect that the matching process is done for the period. Users with access to the Match Set will have access to this icon. The Complete WF icon will appear until you select it.

Figure 8.6

Once selected, the icon will update to show the Revert WF icon at which time the Scorecard, Matches, and Transactions pages will be unavailable. No additional actions can be taken in that Workflow period as the Workspace will appear as shown below.

If you need to perform actions on the transactions for that period, the Workflow will need to be reverted. The Revert WF icon allows you to reopen the Workflow for update purposes.

Figure 8.7

Also, note that the Workflow can be locked for a specific period. Locking (an example is in Figure 8.8) is used to prevent you from importing data. You will also not be able to complete or revert the Workflow if the period is locked. However, locking does not prevent you from actioning transactions. If the period is locked and the Complete WF has not been set, you can still match, unmatch, accept, suspend, request deletion, etc.

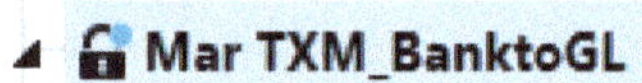

Figure 8.8

Filters

There are multiple filters available within the header section. These top filters (Figure 8.9) are applied to the grid and narrow down the matches presented, based on the filters selected. Filtering is valuable in being able to quickly get to specific matches so you can accept or approve the match, unmatch transactions if a manual match was done incorrectly, or simply to find matches that were made for a particular reason based on a Reason Code. Matches are just as important as Unmatched transactions in that they tell a story. Filters allow you to slice the matches into a view that is important to you and provide efficiency. The top filters include six key areas that Users tend to search: Type, Rule, Status, Approval, Reason Code and Date Range.

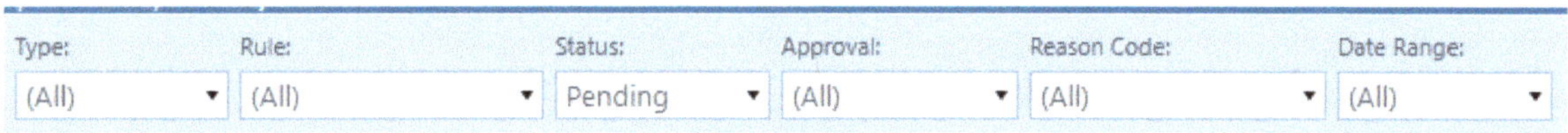

Figure 8.9

Type

The Type filter retrieves the matches based on how the match was made. Matches are made either through rules that are set as Automatic or Suggested, or through the User manually matching the transactions. With this filter, you can either view All matches or by the specific type: Automatic, Suggested, or Manual.

Pulling back suggested matches is important because all suggested matches must be accepted by a User for the match to be considered complete and may require approval if this option is turned on. Manual matches are also important because they too can require an approval process but – more importantly – Approvers and auditors prefer seeing all the manual matches made in a given period to understand why manual intervention was required.

Rule

The **Rule Filter** allows you to view matches by the rule that was used to create the match. As an example, if a rule allows for tolerances, you may want to pull all the matches with tolerances to generate a Journal correction. Or, if during implementation you determine a rule needs to be corrected or changed, you can filter for the matches made from the specific rule and unmatch the transactions associated, so the rule can be updated.

Status

Filtering for status will navigate you to all the matches that need to be Accepted. Within this filter you can choose All, Pending, or Matched. Users will filter for Pending matches to identify all matches awaiting acceptance. Users can also filter for the status of Matched which will remove those that have not yet been reviewed.

Approval

Most matches do not require an approval process, however; approval is an option that can be enabled for either suggested or manual matches. Typically, we see Workflow used around the manual match process on higher risk Match Sets. If utilizing Workflow, the approval process is performed on this page. This filter assists in getting to the matches in the different approval states. The filter includes All, Unapproved, Approved, or Not Required.

Reason Codes

Reason Codes are used to provide additional information regarding the match. Reason Codes can be assigned to the Match Rules and are associated to the matches that were created by the rule. An example would be a Reason Code of 'Fees'. I may have several rules that match fee-type transactions, and if I assign the Fees Reason Code to each of these rules, I can pull all the matches related to fees by leveraging the Reason Code filter (versus pulling the matches rule by rule). Reason Codes are also used in the manual matching process to identify reasons around why the manual match occurred.

Reason Codes are not required to be used or set up. The Reason Code filter will contain a list of all active Reason Codes set up by the Administrator. If Reason Codes are not set up or active, the filter will be set to All, and the drop-down will only contain an option for Unassigned.

Date Range

Filtering by date range minimizes the data being viewed. The filter allows you to view matches made Today, in the last 7 Days, or All. The default is set to Today so you can review the most recent matches made. If you change the filter to All, it will pull back all the matches made in the current Workflow period. If you want to see a match made in a previous period, you will need to navigate to that period in the Workflow.

Export

At times, you may need to export the Matched data to prepare Journal entries, provide additional reporting, or send information to Users outside the match process. The Export icon allows you to export the matches in the grid, based on the applied filters.

Figure 8.10

When selecting the Export icon, you will receive a dialog box allowing you to select the Export Type.

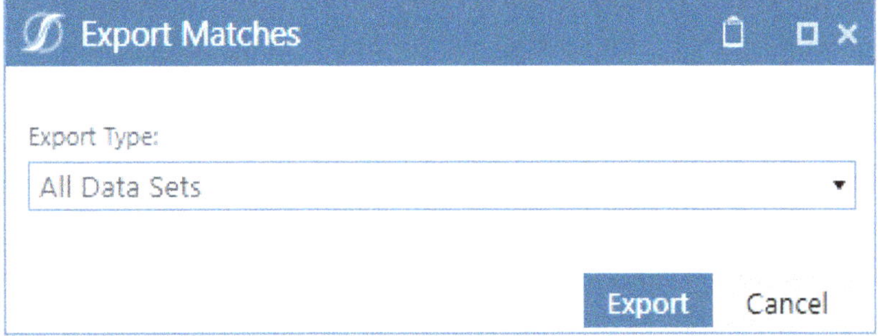

Figure 8.11

Data can be exported by all data sets, or for each data set individually. All data sets would be exported to provide the tolerance amount related to the matches, whereas you may only export a specific side of the match if a correction needs to be made or a Journal posted. Once the export type is chosen from the drop-down, you select the Export button. The system will prepare a .CSV file, open Excel, and present the data for you to save. An example of an export file is shown in Figure 8.12.

Export Type: All Data Sets:

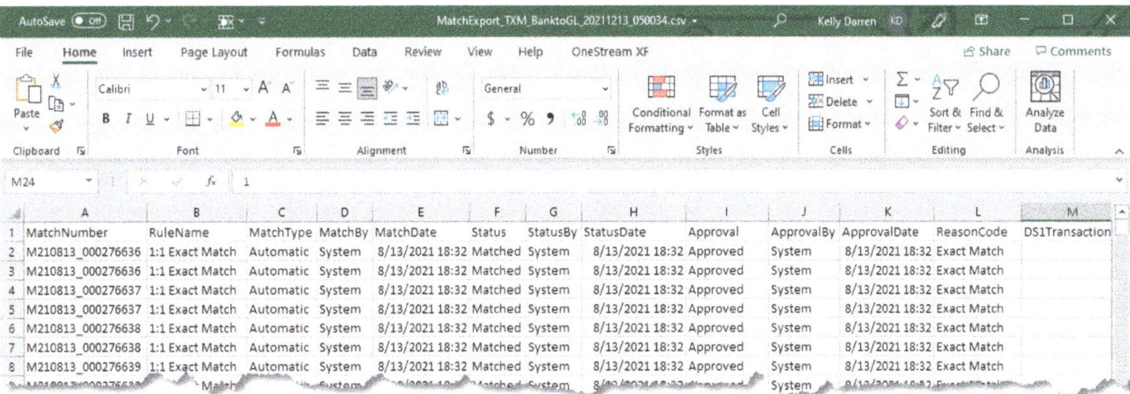

MatchNumber	RuleName	MatchType	MatchBy	MatchDate	Status	StatusBy	StatusDate	Approval	ApprovalBy	ApprovalDate	ReasonCode	DS1Transaction
M210813_000276636	1:1 Exact Match	Automatic	System	8/13/2021 18:32	Matched	System	8/13/2021 18:32	Approved	System	8/13/2021 18:32	Exact Match	
M210813_000276636	1:1 Exact Match	Automatic	System	8/13/2021 18:32	Matched	System	8/13/2021 18:32	Approved	System	8/13/2021 18:32	Exact Match	
M210813_000276637	1:1 Exact Match	Automatic	System	8/13/2021 18:32	Matched	System	8/13/2021 18:32	Approved	System	8/13/2021 18:32	Exact Match	
M210813_000276637	1:1 Exact Match	Automatic	System	8/13/2021 18:32	Matched	System	8/13/2021 18:32	Approved	System	8/13/2021 18:32	Exact Match	
M210813_000276638	1:1 Exact Match	Automatic	System	8/13/2021 18:32	Matched	System	8/13/2021 18:32	Approved	System	8/13/2021 18:32	Exact Match	
M210813_000276638	1:1 Exact Match	Automatic	System	8/13/2021 18:32	Matched	System	8/13/2021 18:32	Approved	System	8/13/2021 18:32	Exact Match	
M210813_000276639	1:1 Exact Match	Automatic	System	8/13/2021 18:32	Matched	System	8/13/2021 18:32	Approved	System	8/13/2021 18:32	Exact Match	

Figure 8.12

Note: There are a couple of nuances when using the exporting feature in matching. First, if the data security option is enabled, the Export icon will only be visible for the Transaction Matching Administrator. This is to ensure that data security is enforced, and you are not exporting matches that do not belong to you. Next, the export feature is only available in the Windows application. If you are running OneStream in the browser, and you attempt to export, you will receive an error message. Keep these things in mind when leveraging this functionality.

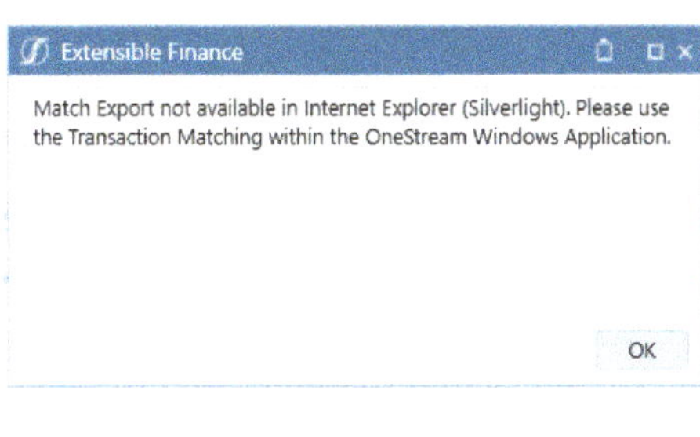

Figure 8.13

Unmatch All

Match Sets can have a significant number of matches in a given period. The Unmatch All icon allows you to quickly unmatch all the transactions in the grid (Manual, Automatic, and Suggested matches), based on the filters applied (versus selecting matches one by one). This may be necessary if you need to update rules or reload a data file. This icon is only available to the Approver and Administrator roles.

Statistics

Statistics are critical for monitoring the matching process. Understanding where the matches are in the Workflow assists management in monitoring the process, as well as the overall risk in the data.

Match statistics are calculated by the system and are presented in a status bar located in the top-right portion of the Matches page.

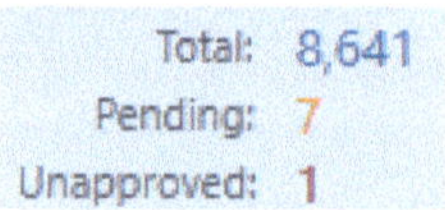

Figure 8.14

The statistics include: the total number of matches in the current grid view, a count of the suggested matches in the Pending state, and a count of the matches (either manual or suggested, depending on the options enabled) awaiting approval. The Calculations are based on the specific period selected and the top filters being applied.

The statuses are updated as events occur, such as when a Pending match is Accepted or matches Approved. Although the status is updated dynamically by the system, you may need to select the Refresh icon to update the status bar and grid information.

Figure 8.15

Matches Grid

The Matches Grid is a listing of all matches for a specified period. The grid is used to view a specific match, or to mass action matches if necessary.

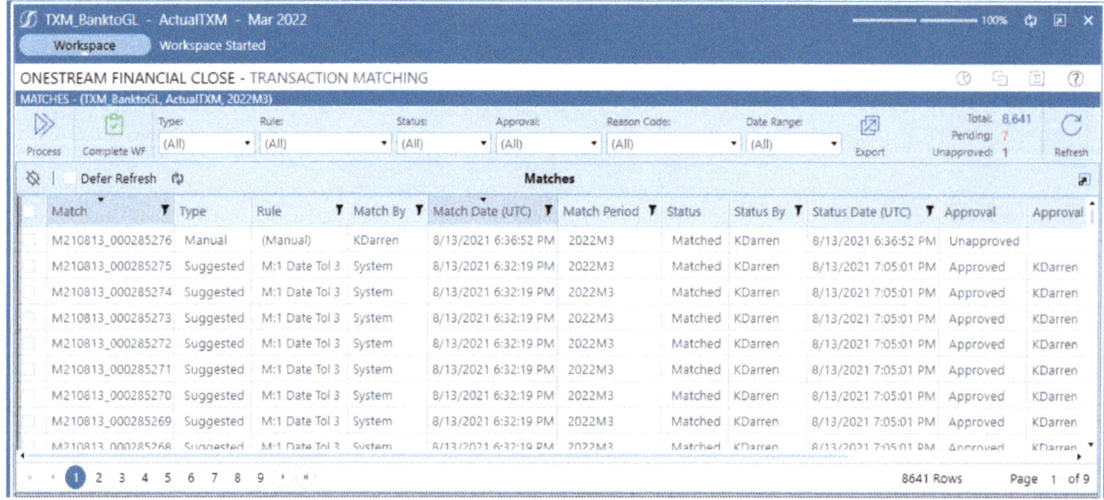

Figure 8.16

Although referred to as a grid, the display is a SQL Table Editor which limits the number of items viewable per page for faster performance. When selecting matches, you may need to cross pages to find a specific match. If you move from page to page, the matches selected via the check box will be retained. Also, if you select the check box at the top of the page in the first column, it will select all the matches on the current page only. If you want all matches across all pages, you will need to navigate page to page and select the top check box on each of the pages accordingly.

The number of items viewable on a page is based on the User's platform security settings. By default, the attribute for the User is set to 50 grid rows per page and applies to any SQL Table Editor in the application. However, it is recommended that if the User will be working heavily in Transaction Matching that this be updated to 1,000 grid rows per page, limiting the number of pages the User needs to navigate.

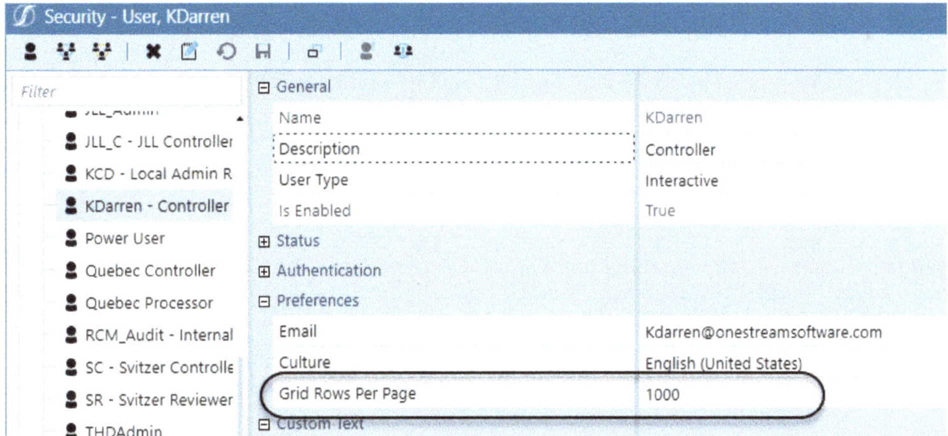

Figure 8.17

As noted earlier, the Matches Grid will display the matches made for the period. If the grid is empty, this should be an indication that data needs to be loaded for the period, the rule process needs to be run, or the filters set are too narrow in scope.

Filters can be set in the header, as previously discussed, or in a specific column using the filter icon in the column header. When using column filters, the filter icon will be orange, indicating that the column is being filtered. Unlike the Reconciliation Grid, column filters do not participate in saved state and will reset if you select a new header filter, action a match, or navigate away from the page. Therefore, you should leverage the header filters, when at all possible, for efficiency.

Matches Grid Columns

There are many columns displayed within the grid that provide detailed information about the match. Each of the attributes are defined below.

Column	Definition
☐	The multi-select check box is used for mass actions, or to select multiple matches.
Match	The Field represents the match number assigned by the system. The match number is a smart number which contains the Year, Month, and Day along with a unique ID. The color coding used in this example is to help break down the smart number into its pieces. The number will appear in the system as follows: M220116_000002206 Example: M220116_000002206 M = Match

Column	Definition
	22 = Year 01 = Month 16 = Day 000002206 = Unique ID
Type	The Type field displays the match type which includes Automatic, Suggested, or Manual.
Rule	The Rule field will display the name of the Match Rule used to create that specific match. If the match was manually created, the field will display (Manual).
Match By	This field indicates the User ID associated with who created the match. If created by a rule, the User ID will be System. If manually Matched, this will indicate the User ID of the specific User.
Match Date (UTC)	Match date is the date and time stamp of when the match occurred, either through the processing of the rules or through manual matching. If Matched, Unmatched, and reMatched, the system only reflects the most recent date and time, based on Coordinated Universal Time (UTC).
Match Period	Represents the Workflow period in which the match occurred.
Status	Indicates whether the match is in a Matched or Pending state. Pending is the initial state of a match that was made from a suggested Match Rule. All suggested matches need to be Accepted or Approved in order to move to the Matched state. If Accepted or Approved, these matches can be reset to Pending – if needed – by unaccepting, or unapproving then unaccepting, at any point by a User with the appropriate security.
Status By	This field indicates the User ID of the last User to update the match status. This field will automatically populate upon match with the User ID of System if Matched by a rule, or the specfic User ID if manually Matched. As noted above, the status will only be updated if the match is actioned to Accept, Approve, Unaccept, or Unapprove. As it moves through these states, the User ID of the last person to action will be captured in this field.
Status Date (UTC)	Status date captures the date and time stamp the status was updated. The system only reflects the most recent date and time stamp, based on the latest update.
Approval	Identifies the approval state of the match from a Workflow perspective, which includes Not Required, Unapproved, or Approved. Matches created by Automatic Rules will be Approved upon match by the system. Suggested or Manual match approval requirements will depend on the options set by the Administrator at the Match Set level. If Workflow is turned on for a particular match type (Suggested or Manual), the match will be in the Unapproved state until Approved. If Workflow is not turned on for a particular match type, the Approval field will display Not Required upon match. If approval is required, matches can be Approved and Unapproved as needed.
Approval by	This field indicates the User ID associated with the approval process based on the last User to approve or unapprove the match. This field will automatically populate upon match with the User ID of System if Matched by an Automatic Rule or if the approval status is Not Required. If approval is required, this field will remain empty until it is Approved, at which time the system will track the User ID. The match

Column	Definition
	can be Approved and Unapproved as needed with the system tracking the User ID of the last person to action.
Approval Date (UTC)	Approval date captures the date and time stamp of when the approval or unapproval was performed. The system only reflects the most recent date and time stamp, based on the latest update. (If a match is not yet Approved, the Approval Date will display as 1/1/1900 12:00:00 AM.)
Reason Code	This field reflects the Reason Code associated with the Match Rule that created the match, or the Reason Code selected by the User when creating the manual match. Reason Codes are not required. If not used on the rule, or in the manual matching process, this field will populate with (Unassigned).
DS1 Total (Summary 1-3)	Aggregated amount of the Summary 1 value field, based on the transactions in Dataset 1 (DS1) of the match. The column header will display the alias name for the value field selected. There is a DS1 Total column for each summary level utilized. Each data set can have up to three summary fields selected.
DS2 Total (Summary 1-3)	Aggregated amount of the Summary 1 value field based on the transactions in Dataset 2 (DS2) of the match. The column header will display the alias name for the value field selected. There is a DS2 Total column for each summary level utilized. Each data set can have up to three summary fields selected.
DS2 Variance (Summary 1-3)	Calculated difference between DS1 Total minus DS2 Total for each summary level. The column header will display the alias name for the DS2 value field selected for Summary 1. Because a Match Set can have up to three summary fields, there is the possibility to have three calculated variance columns.
DS3* Total (Summary 1-3)	Aggregated amount of the Summary 1 value field, based on the transactions in Dataset 3 (DS3) of the match. The column header will display the alias name for the value field selected. There is a DS3 Total column for each summary level utilized. Each data set can have up to three summary fields selected.
DS3* Variance (Summary 1-3)	Calculated difference between DS1 Total minus DS3 Total for each summary level. The column header will display the alias name for the DS3 value field selected for Summary 1. Because a Match Set can up to three summary fields, there is the possibility to have three calculated variance columns.
Transactions (DS1)	Total number of transactions in DS1 that are part of the specific match.
Transactions (DS2)	Total number of transactions in DS2 that are part of the specific match.
Transactions (DS3*)	Total number of transactions in DS3 that are part of the specific match.
*DS3 is only visible if the Match Set is a three-way match.	

Figure 8.18

Something to consider… if you do not see values in DS1, DS2, or DS3 Total columns or the value that appears is not what you would expect – it is an indication that the Summary levels (1-3) have not been set up properly. You will need to contact the Administrator of the Match Set to make the appropriate updates.

Accessing a Match

Accessing a match is done from the Matches Grid. You can view a detailed match by clicking anywhere within the line associated with the specific match. Upon selection, the detailed match will appear in the bottom view. You can navigate from one match to the next by simply selecting the respective line in the Matches Grid.

You will notice that when you select a line, the check box to the far left will automatically be selected. Although you can select a match using the check box, it is not necessary and not recommended. The check box is required for mass action functionality, but ultimately is not needed for navigation purposes. Selecting a match by clicking on the line is much more efficient.

Match Security

Match Sets can also have transaction-level security. Because the matching process may be similar across Users and Entities, leveraging a single Match Set is more efficient from an administrative perspective. Being able to restrict the transactions allows Users to move through their process without impacting others.

Security can be set up to restrict transactions based on Entity, IC, Entity or IC, or Entity and IC Dimension combinations. This feature is set by the Administrator. Security will limit the transactions that you can view and, in turn, will limit the matches you have access to. If you navigate to a match in the Matches Grid that does not contain any transactions within your security rights, the Detail Match pane will display a security message, as shown in Figure 8.19. However, if within the match there is at least one transaction (regardless of the data set), the full match is visible.

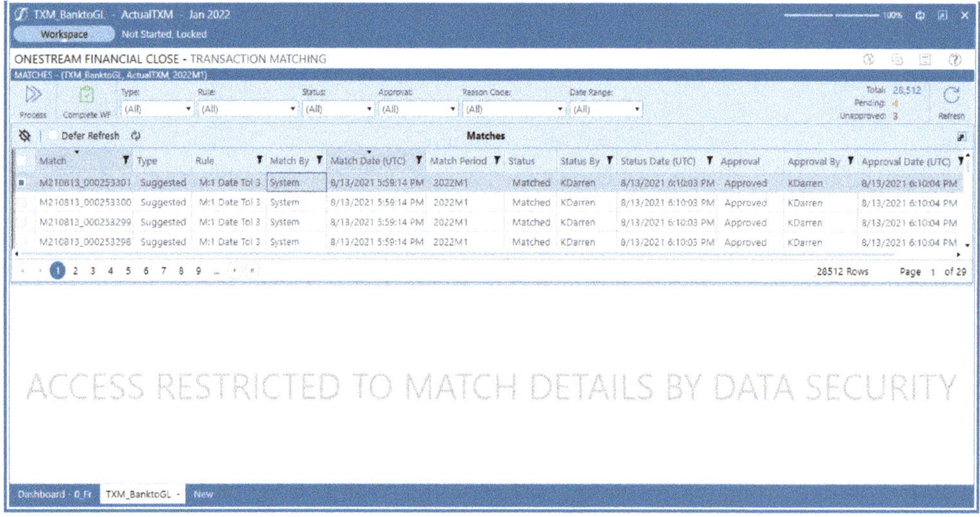

Figure 8.19

Mass Actions

Mass action functionality allows you to efficiently perform your responsibilities. Rather than performing actions one by one, Preparers, Approvers, and/or Administrators can execute across multiple matches when ready. When utilizing mass actions, you can Accept, Approve, Unapprove, or Unmatch matches if you have the proper security.

To mass action a set of matches, you select the check box to the left of the specific match one by one, or select the line and use the *ctrl* or *shift* keys to quickly select multiple matches. Mass actions will only engage if you have more than one match selected.

All selected matches will appear in the bottom view and the mass action icons will appear as shown in Figure 8.20.

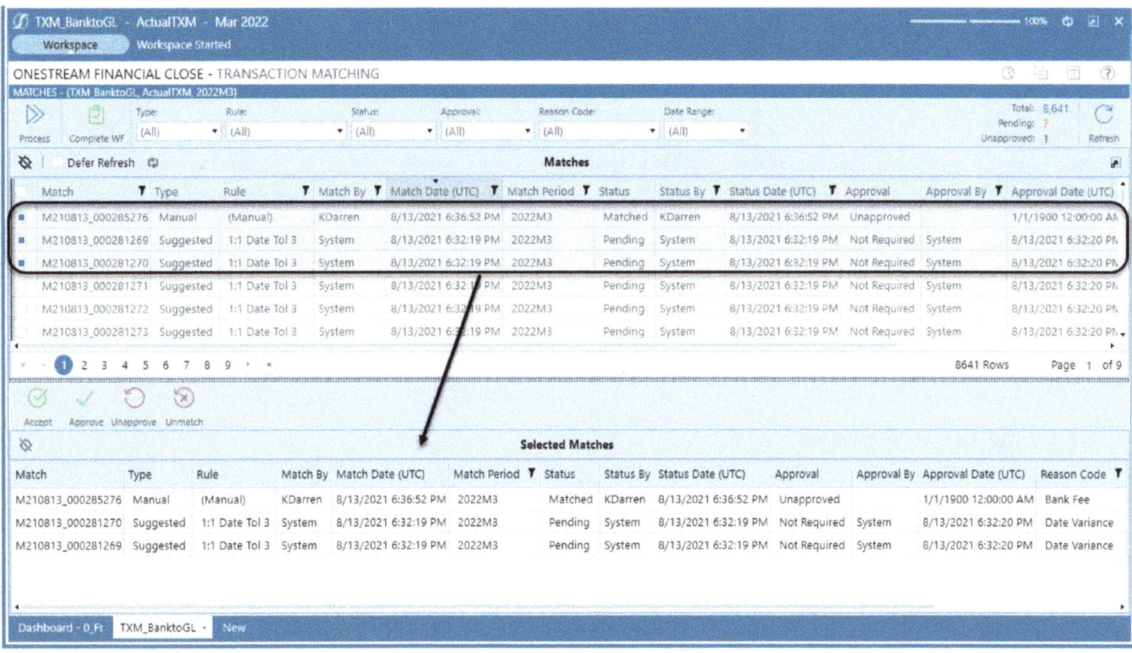

Figure 8.20

Based on the action icon selected, the system will update the matches that meet the requirements. If a match is selected that cannot be actioned as requested, you will receive a message indicating what actions were taken and why. See Figure 8.21 for a system message, and Figure 8.22 for updated matches. As a reminder, depending on the number of matches, the Matches Grid might contain multiple pages requiring you to navigate from page to page to find the specific matches you want to action.

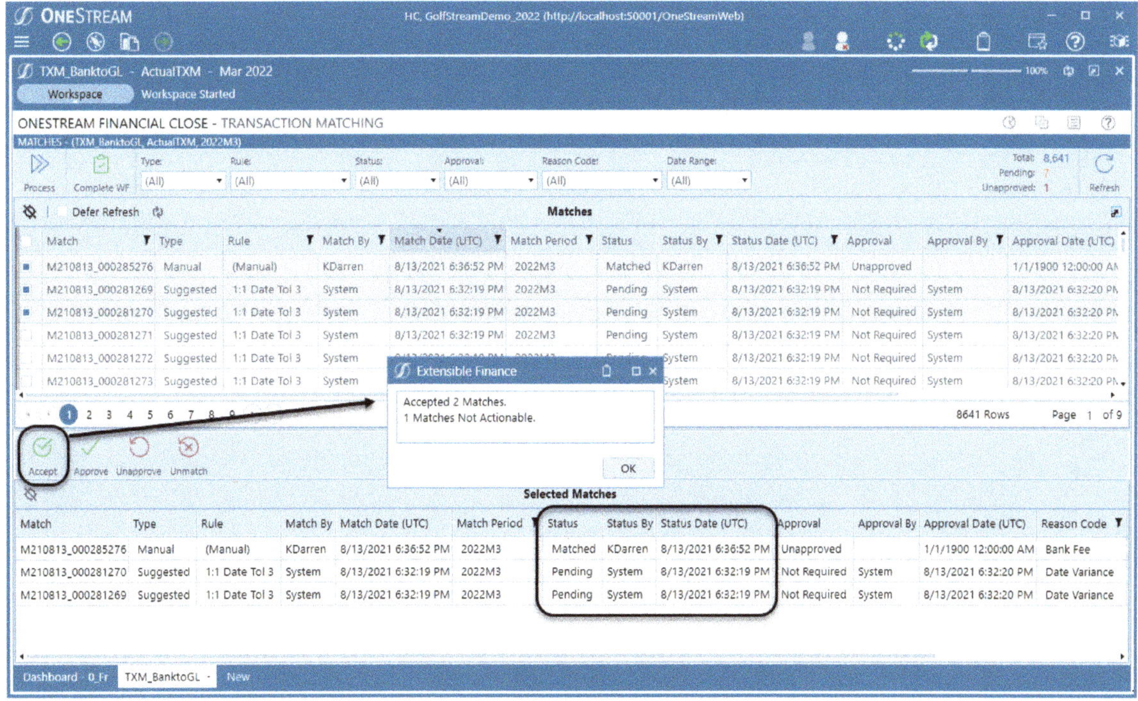

Figure 8.21

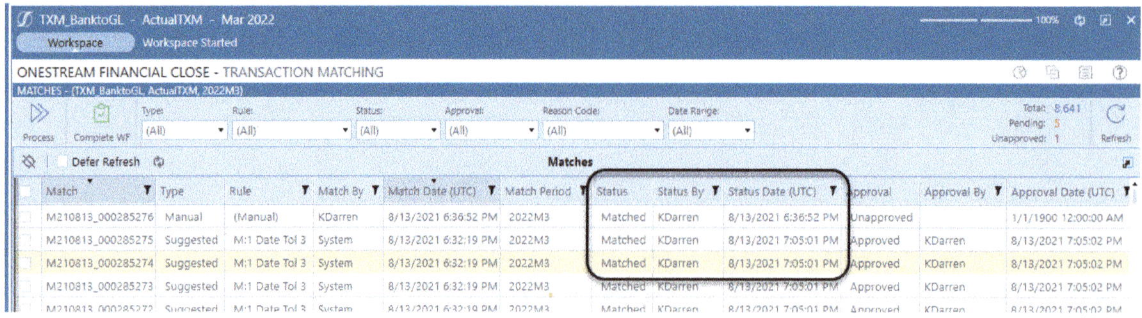

Figure 8.22

Detail Match Pane

The Detail Match pane is used to view the details of a selected match. You can review the transactions by data set, add or view comments and attachments, or action the match as needed. We will walk through the three main areas of the Detail Match pane which include:

- Detail Match Header
- Data Set Grids
- Match Summary

Detail Match Header

The header section contains the key attributes for the selected match. These are the same attributes that are displayed in the Match Grid and include the Match number and Rule which are visible in the center section of the header, as well as the Type, Status, and Approval located to the right. These attributes were previously defined in Figure 8.18.

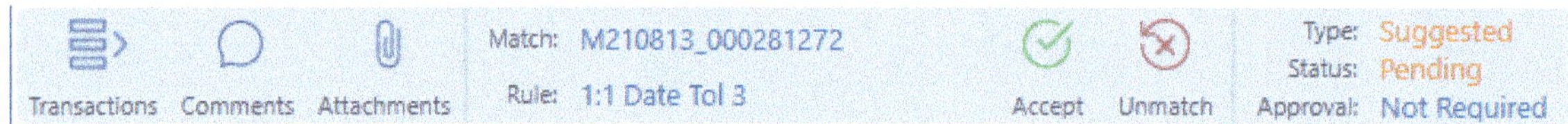

Figure 8.23

There are also action icons that appear in the header, which allow you to move the match through the process. There are multiple different actions available and what appears for you will depend on the match type, your role, and the state of the match.

We will walk through each match type and the actions available for the different roles, defining when and why a User may perform the specific actions. The action icons for each role, based on the match type, are also summarized below.

Icon	Match Type	Preparer	Approver	Admin
Unmatch	Automatic		X	X
Accept	Suggested	X	X	X
Unaccept	Suggested	X	X	X

Icon	Match Type	Preparer	Approver	Admin
Unmatch	Suggested/Manual	X	X	X
Approve	Suggested/Manual (If enabled)		X	X
Unapprove	Suggested/Manual (If enabled)		X	X

Figure 8.24

Automatic Matches

Automatic Matches are transactions that get Matched, based on an Automatic Rule. Automatic Rules are precise rules that – when met – should move the transactions off with no further actions needed. Preparers have visibility to these matches but cannot perform any actions on them. Only higher-level roles – Administrator and Approver – can update an automatic match by selecting the Unmatch icon, moving the transactions to the Unmatched state.

Unmatching automatic matches is not common in everyday operations. This function is typically used during implementations or with new rule creation. If the rule is not running as expected, it may need to be updated. Only rules without existing matches can be changed. Therefore, to update an existing rule, the existing matches need to be Unmatched. This process can only be performed by an Administrator or Approver for control purposes because, as we start changing rules within the Match Set, we are altering the process and the overall results. See Figure 8.25 for role-specific views related to an automatic match.

Automatic Match

Preparer:

Approver/Administrator:

Figure 8.25

Suggested Matches

Suggested Matches are transactions that get Matched based on a rule that is less precise and could result in invalid matches. We use suggested matches to ease the manual process. These types of rules will apply logic and create a match. However, because not all the matches may be valid, suggested matches have a Pending status. Upon review, the suggested match can either be Accepted or Unmatched. In addition, there is an option to require an approval process on suggested matches. If this option is enabled, the match will need to be both Accepted and Approved.

All roles, except for the Viewer and Commenter, can accept, unaccept, or unmatch a suggested match. If the match is reviewed and determined valid, you will accept the match which moves the status from Pending to Matched. The system also keeps track of who accepted the match with the date and time stamp. Once accepted, you will then have the ability to unaccept the match should you choose to move it back to the Pending state. This allows you to revert the status of the match if acceptance was performed in error.

If – upon review – a match is determined not to be valid, you can unmatch. If Unmatched, the Pending match will be deleted, and the transactions will be moved to the Unmatched state and will be available for future matching. If you unmatch in error, you can navigate to the Transactions page and manually rematch the transactions. It is not recommended to run the rule process at this point to recreate the match. Although this would rematch the transactions, the rules are applied to all Unmatched items. This means, if you have properly Unmatched other matches, they will rematch as a result of running the rules again, creating more work for you.

Also, note that the match does not need to be unaccepted to be Unmatched. You can unmatch matches *at any time*, as long as the match has not yet been Approved. Preparers cannot unaccept or unmatch if the approval process has occurred. However, Approvers and Administrators can unmatch a match at any time – even if Approved – as they have full authority.

The approval process is an additional review that can be tracked in the system. Approvers or Administrators can approve matches using the Approve icon. The approval action can be performed on matches in either the Pending or Matched state. If the match is Pending, the match will move from Pending to Matched and Approved. For audit purposes, the system will track who Approved the match with the date and time stamp. If the match needs to go back to the Preparer to action, the match will need to be Unapproved.

Below are detailed screenshots of the action icons available for suggested matches, based on User role, match status, and match approval.

Suggested Match

Preparer (Approval required):

Pending

Match: M211105_000285282 Rule: 1:1 Date Tol 3 Accept Unmatch Type: Suggested Status: Pending Approval: Unapproved

Accepted

Match: M211105_000285282 Rule: 1:1 Date Tol 3 Unaccept Unmatch Type: Suggested Status: Matched Approval: Unapproved

Approved

Match: M211105_000285282 Rule: 1:1 Date Tol 3 Type: Suggested Status: Matched Approval: Approved

Figure 8.26

Approver/Administrator (Approval required):

Figure 8.26 (cont.)

Manual Matches

Manual matches are transactions Matched by a User from the Transactions page. Manual matching can be performed by the Preparer, Approver, or Administrator. Upon match, the system will update the match type and the status, identifying the User ID and time and date stamp when the match occurred.

The User actions allowed for a manual match include the ability to unmatch, approve, or unapprove (if utilizing this option) depending on security and match state. If the manual match needs to be Unmatched, the Preparer can perform this action if it is *not* in the Approved state. If Approved, no additional action can be taken by the Preparer. This differs for the Approver and Administrator roles; these roles can unmatch at any time, even if the match is in the Approved state. Also, the system will keep track of the User ID and the date and time stamp of the User who Approved the match. Below are detailed screenshots of the action icons available for manual matches based on the User role, match status, and match approval.

Manual Match

Preparer (Approval required):

Matched

Match: M211106_000285286
Rule: (Manual)
Unmatch
Type: Manual
Status: Matched
Approval: Unapproved

Approved

Match: M211106_000285286
Rule: (Manual)
Type: Manual
Status: Matched
Approval: Approved

Figure 8.27

Approver/Administrator (Approval required):

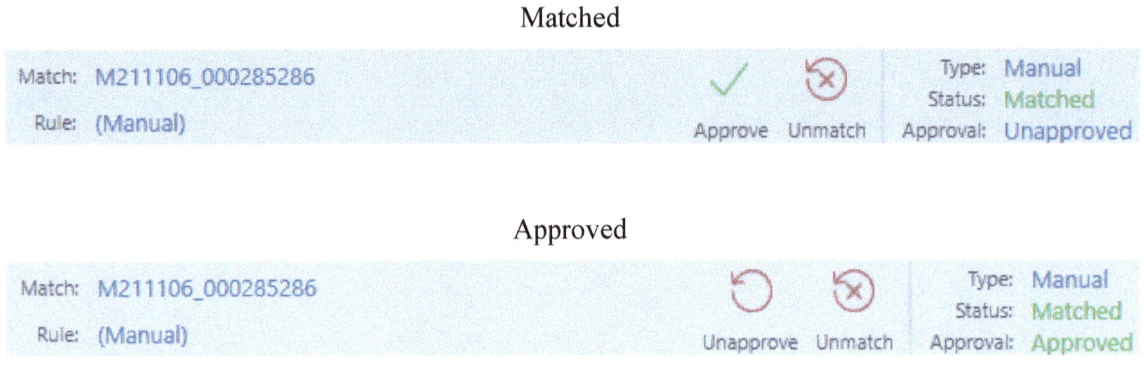

Figure 8.27 (cont.)

Comments

Comments can be added to a match at any time, regardless of the status. All roles, except for the Viewer role, can add commentary. Once added, comments cannot be edited or deleted within the match. If comments are added to the match and the match is subsequently Unmatched, all comments made on the match will be deleted. To add a comment, you will select the Comments icon, as shown in Figure 8.28, which will navigate to the Commentary page as seen in Figure 8.29.

Figure 8.28

You can type a comment in the bottom box and select the Add icon. The comment is added to the match with the User's ID and date and time stamp for audit purposes. Once a comment has been added to the match, the Comments icon will move from blue to green as a visual indicator that a comment has been added.

There is no limitation to the number of comments added to a particular match. Also, note that commentary added at the transaction level can be viewed in the right portion of this screen. Commentary cannot be added to a transaction from the Match pane. Adding commentary to a transaction is done from the Transactions page and will be discussed in detail later in the chapter.

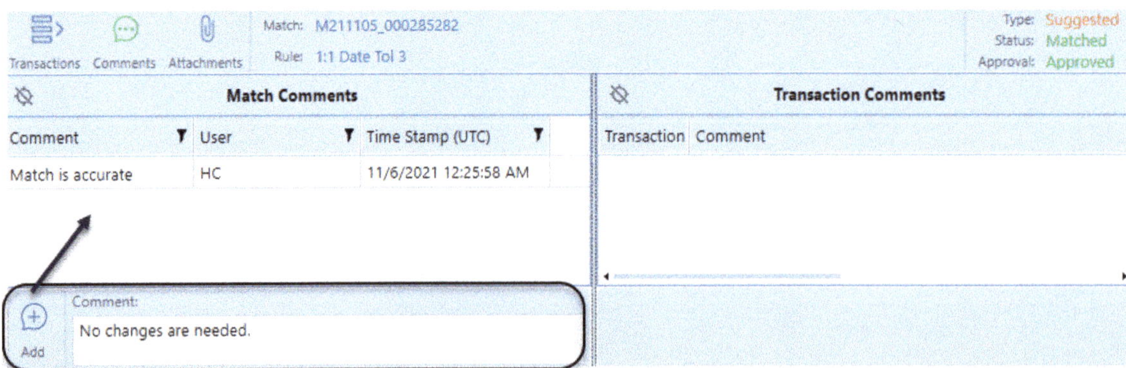

Figure 8.29

Attachments

Similar to comments, attachments can also be added to a match at any time in the process, regardless of the match status or approval. Only the Preparer, Approver, or Administrator roles can upload, or delete documentation, whereas all roles can view supporting documentation if they have access to the match. You can upload as many files as needed to support a specific match. Select the Attachments icon to navigate to the Match Attachments pane.

Figure 8.30

To upload a file, select the Upload icon in the bottom-left corner of the Attachments pane to initiate a file explorer dialog.

Figure 8.31

Then, navigate to your file and select Open, which will add it to the match. The system will keep track of who added the attachment with the date and time stamp.

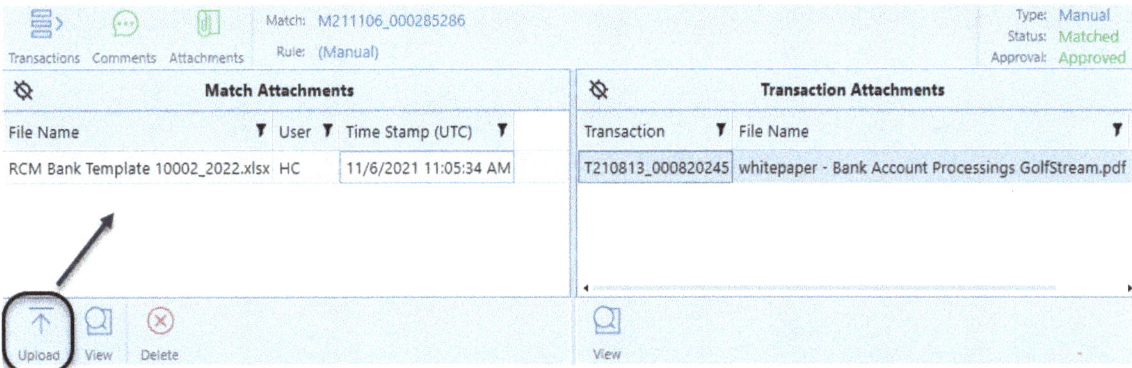

Figure 8.32

> **Note:** you can have multiple files on a match; however, you can only add one file at a time.

Once a file has been added to the match – like with the Comments icon – the Attachments icon will also move from blue to green as a visual indicator that an attachment is associated with the match.

From a support perspective, files are typically in the following formats: PDF, HTML, MHT, RTF, DOCX, XLS, XLSX, CSV, Text, Image, and Zip files (to name but a few). Outside of XML, the system does not limit the file format but assumes the User viewing the document will have the software necessary to open the specific file. Each file cannot exceed 2 GB. Also, each file must have a unique name. If the User uploads a file with the same name, the system will overwrite the existing file accordingly.

If you have access to the match, you will have the ability to view any of the supporting documentation attached. In the Match Attachment pane, displayed in Figure 8.32, Users can view documentation that has been added on the match, or on a transaction within the match. To view the support, highlight the file and select the View icon.

> **Note:** the View icon on the match will only appear after a document has been selected. Also, you can only view one document at a time.

When viewing, the system will open the file in the software required, or pop up a dialog asking you what application you would like to open the file (e.g., Notepad, Wordpad, etc.). The file being reviewed is read-only and changes made will not automatically be saved back to the system.

Files can also be deleted at any time, regardless of the status or approval state. Deletion can be performed by any of the roles that can add attachments (Preparer, Approver, or Administrator) and attachments can be deleted by any User even if they were not the User that uploaded the file. In addition, if the file is added to the match and the match is subsequently Unmatched, all files added during matching will be deleted.

> **Note:** Transaction-level documents can be viewed from the match but cannot be added or deleted from the Match Attachment Pane. This action must be performed from the Transactions page.

Transactions Icon

The Transactions icon appears in the far left of the header. If you navigate to Comments or Documents, this icon will return you to the Detail Match pane, which is the default when selecting a match.

Figure 8.33

Data Set Grids

Data set grids display the transactions that are included in the match. Each data grid will display all the fields associated with the transaction in the display order defined during setup. The columns have filter and sorting capabilities if needed.

The number of grids visible will depend on the Match Set. If set up as a two-way match, the User will see two data set grids in the order of succession, i.e., DS1 and DS2. If the Match Set is a three-way match, the User will see three grids. The name of the data set will also display for the User for ease of use. Figure 8.34 offers examples of two-way and three-way Match Sets.

Two-Way Match

Transactions Comments Attachments
Match: M210813_000285275
Rule: M:1 Date Tol 3
Type: Suggested
Status: Matched
Approval: Approved

GL10003 (DS1)

Transaction	Check Date	Post Date	Check Amt	Check No	Invoice	JE Num
T210813_000817231	2022-03-18	2022-03-18	-3,728.16	810ZZZ526	1026	2152727
T210813_000817232	2022-03-18	2022-03-18	-879.00	810ZZZ526	1027	2152727
T210813_000817233	2022-03-18	2022-03-18	-854.00	810ZZZ526	1025	2152727

BNKBOA (DS2)

Transaction	Load Period	Source Entity	Entity	Source Acct	Account	De
T210813_000827860	2022M3	South	South Houston	10003	10100	

	GL10003 (DS1)	BNKBOA (DS2)	DS1 to DS2
Check Amt	-5,461.16	-5,461.16	0.00

Figure 8.34

Three-Way Match

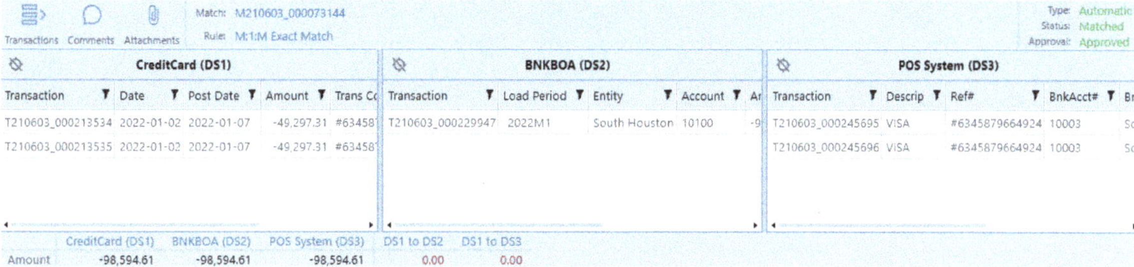

Figure 8.34 (cont.)

When viewing transactions in the grid, you may notice that the first column displays a transaction number. This is a system-generated **Transaction ID**. All transactions loaded into a Match Set will be assigned a Transaction ID as a unique identifier. Similar to the Match ID, the Transaction ID is a smart number which contains the Year, Month, and Day along with a unique ID. Below is a color-coded example to help break down the smart number into its pieces. Although the system is tracking when the data is loaded, the smart number provides more visibility to the End User related to the transaction.

Example: T220603_000331921
T = Transaction
22 = Year
06 = Month
03 = Day
000331921 = Unique ID

Figure 8.35

Match Summary

The match summary will appear in the bottom-left corner and displays the Aggregation of the designated value field for each of the data sets. The system also automatically creates a Variance Calculation between the summary values for each data set for greater visibility.

Note: The name of the summary line that appears will take on the field name from DS1.

There are up to three summary levels available for each data set and the number of summaries selected is determined during implementation. Most Match Sets will be set with one summary level to tie out an invoice amount, check value, hours, counts, etc. However, multiple summary levels are nice to have for situations where you want to tie out multiple value fields and have visibility to the Aggregation.

Examples of where multiple summaries are used are in global Intercompany matching where you may want to see transaction amount, local amount, and reporting amount; or in Inventory where you may want to check part counts, price, or full calculated value; or in payable situations where you may want to tie out invoice gross, tax, and net amounts. Regardless of how you choose to use summary levels, at least one summary level should be selected for each data set. Examples of the different summary views are below.

Single Summary

	GL10003 (DS1)	BNKBOA (DS2)	DS1 to DS2
Check Amt	-5,461.16	-5,461.16	0.00

Two Summaries

	Suspense DR (DS1)	Suspense CR (DS2)	DS1 to DS2
DR LC	38,982.75	38,982.75	0.00
DR Rpt	38,982.75	38,982.75	0.00

Three Summaries

	IC DR (DS1)	IC CR (DS2)	DS1 to DS2
Doc Amt	880.00	880.00	0.00
LC Amt	880.00	895.20	-15.20
Rpt Amt	880.00	880.00	0.00

Figure 8.36

Transactions Page

The Transactions page is the most utilized page in the Transaction Matching solution and is the default when navigating to the Match Set. This is where Preparers will spend most of their time viewing transactions, performing manual matches, and creating Reconciliation detail items as needed.

The Transactions page displays transactions in the different statuses, allowing Users to view the Unmatched, Matched, Suspended, Pending Delete, or Deleted transactions if security permits. Being able to search the data sets to find specific transactions – regardless of their status – provides full transparency into the process.

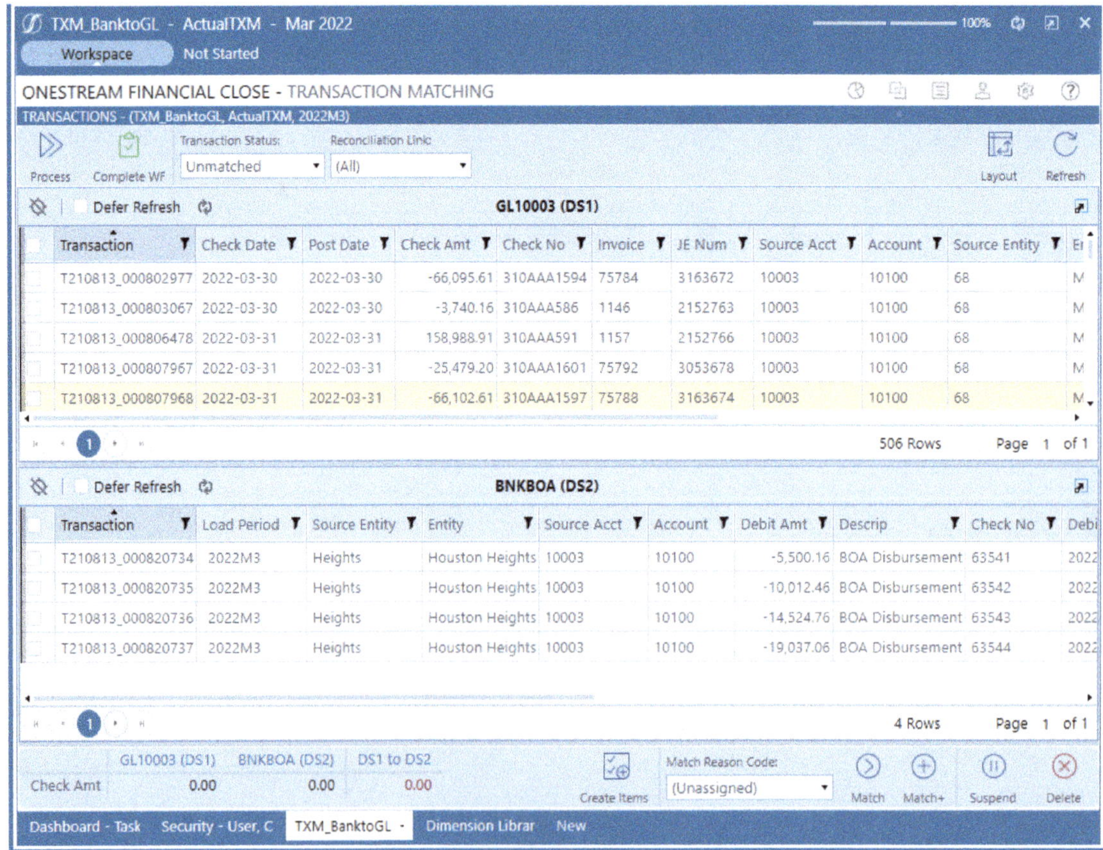

Figure 8.37

Transaction Page Layout

In the next section, we will walk through the general layout of the Transactions page. There are three main areas which include: the header, the data set grids, and the action bar.

Header

The header section of the Transactions page is where you will perform actions and filtering. You will notice that there are several icons available for you to action which include: Process, Complete WF, Layout and Refresh. The Process and the Complete WF icons at the top-left are identical to those on the Matches page. These icons are repeated for ease of use so that Users do not have to navigate from page to page to perform key functions like processing Match Rules or completing the Workflow. See the Matches page header section for a detailed explanation of the Process and Complete WF icons.

Figure 8.38

To the top-right, you will notice the Layout and Refresh icons. The Layout icon is a User-set preference and allows you to customize how you view the data set grids.

Figure 8.39

You can either view the grids horizontally (which stacks the grids one on top of the other) or vertically (which displays the data set grids side by side). Both layout options are shown in Figure 8.40. By default, the data set grids are presented horizontally. However, you can select the Layout icon to switch the current state. The layout selected will be saved for your User ID and will persist as you navigate the system.

Horizontal View

TXM_BanktoGL - ActualTXM - Mar 2022

Workspace Not Started

ONESTREAM FINANCIAL CLOSE - TRANSACTION MATCHING

TRANSACTIONS - (TXM_BanktoGL, ActualTXM, 2022M3)

Process | Complete WF | Transaction Status: Unmatched | Reconciliation Link: (All) | Layout | Refresh

Defer Refresh — GL10003 (DS1)

Transaction	Check Date	Post Date	Check Amt	Check No	Invoice	JE Num	Source Acct	Account	Source Entity	Entity	Load Perio
T210813_000802977	2022-03-30	2022-03-30	-66,095.61	310AAA1594	75784	3163672	10003	10100	68	Montreal	2022M3
T210813_000803067	2022-03-30	2022-03-30	-3,740.16	310AAA586	1146	2152763	10003	10100	68	Montreal	2022M3
T210813_000806478	2022-03-31	2022-03-31	158,988.91	310AAA591	1157	2152766	10003	10100	68	Montreal	2022M3
T210813_000807967	2022-03-31	2022-03-31	-25,479.20	310AAA1601	75792	3053678	10003	10100	68	Montreal	2022M3
T210813_000807968	2022-03-31	2022-03-31	-66,102.61	310AAA1597	75788	3163674	10003	10100	68	Montreal	2022M3

506 Rows Page 1 of 1

Defer Refresh — BNKBOA (DS2)

Transaction	Load Period	Source Entity	Entity	Source Acct	Account	Debit Amt	Descrip	Check No	Debit Date	BnkAcct#
T210813_000820734	2022M3	Heights	Houston Heights	10003	10100	-5,500.16	BOA Disbursement	63541	2022-03-31	BN#123456789
T210813_000820735	2022M3	Heights	Houston Heights	10003	10100	-10,012.46	BOA Disbursement	63542	2022-03-31	BN#123456789
T210813_000820736	2022M3	Heights	Houston Heights	10003	10100	-14,524.76	BOA Disbursement	63543	2022-03-31	BN#123456789
T210813_000820737	2022M3	Heights	Houston Heights	10003	10100	-19,037.06	BOA Disbursement	63544	2022-03-31	BN#123456789

4 Rows Page 1 of 1

	GL10003 (DS1)	BNKBOA (DS2)	DS1 to DS2
Check Amt	0.00	0.00	0.00

Create Items | Match Reason Code: (Unassigned) | Match | Match+ | Suspend | Delete

Figure 8.40

Vertical View

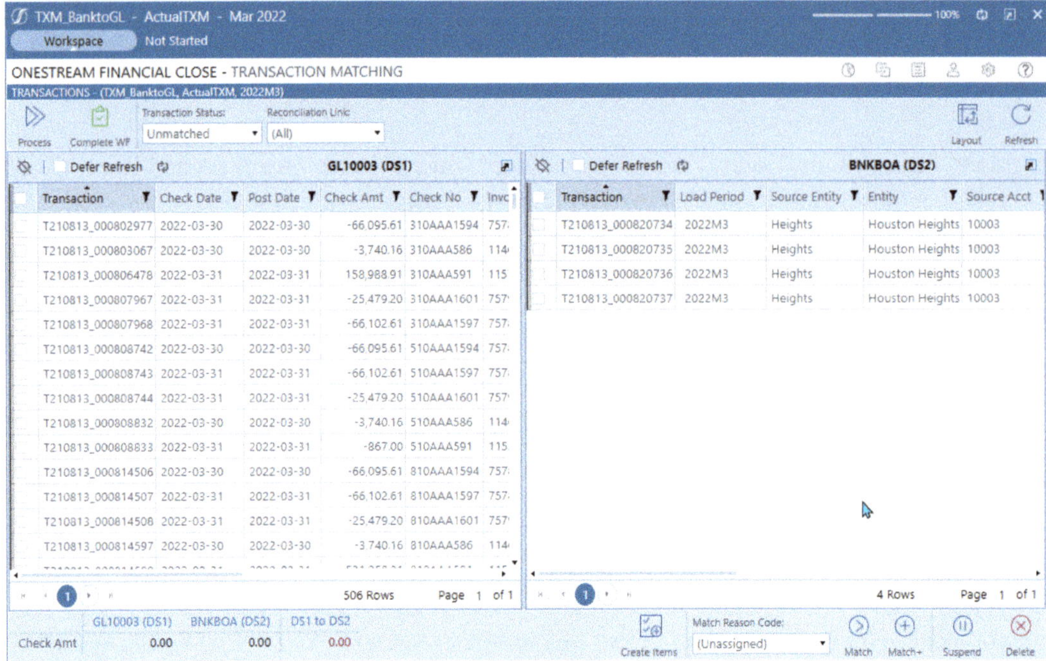

Figure 8.40 (cont.)

The Refresh icon is used to update the page for changes that have been made. Because multiple Users can be in a single Match Set – actioning matches or transactions at the same time – it is necessary to refresh the page periodically to ensure that you are viewing the most up-to-date information.

Figure 8.41

There are also predefined filters in the header to narrow the transactions being viewed. You can filter by **Transaction Status** and **Reconciliation Link**. By default, the Transaction Status filter is set to the Unmatched transactions because this is the view that is most used and where most of the work is performed. However, you can navigate to the other status views which include Matched, Suspended, Pending Delete, or Deleted if security permits. We will discuss each of the Transaction Status views in more detail later in this section. Also, note that these two filters appear across all the different status views. Additional filters are available if the Transaction Status is set to Matched. We will define the additional filters in the Matched View section below.

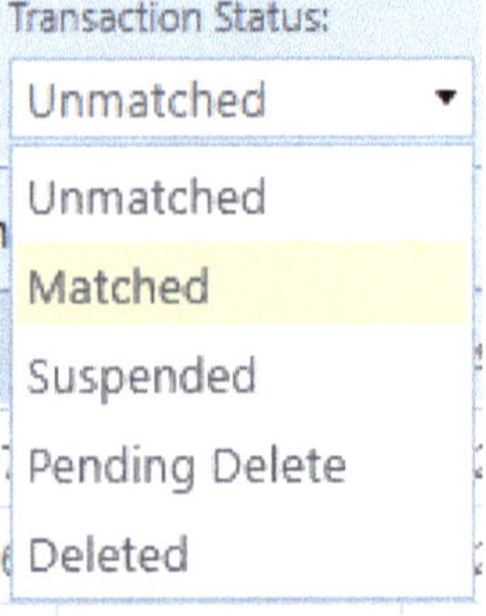

Figure 8.42

The second filter available in the transaction screen is the Reconciliation Link. With the integration between Transaction Matching and Account Reconciliations, you can push transactions from a Match Set to a Reconciliation to automate the creation of detail items.

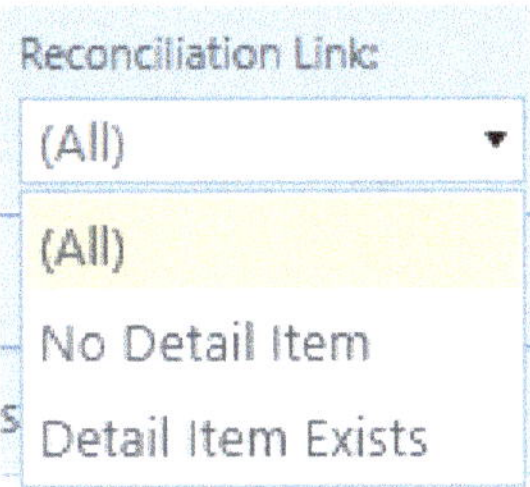

Figure 8.43

> **Note:** Transactions can only be linked to a detail item once in a period.

This filter provides visibility to what has already been pushed from the Match Set versus transactions that are not yet linked. Because this filter is only used when creating items, by default it is set to All to show all transactions. However, you can select the other options to show the state of the transaction as it relates to the Reconciliations when you are ready to create detail items. We will discuss linking transactions to Reconciliations in the Create Item section below.

Data Set Grids

The main section of the Transactions page contains the data set grids, where all the detailed transactions will be presented. Leveraging the data set grids, you can select transactions to either view or action. Data set grids will display the detailed transaction fields defined during set up, and the fields provide you with the ability to search, sort, or filter.

Once you locate specific transactions, you can utilize **multi-select functionality** to select transactions across the different data set grids for actioning. The number of grids visible will depend on whether the Match Set is a two-way or three-way match. Also, as previously mentioned, depending on the number of transactions in the data set, the grids may contain multiple pages. If you are searching for certain transactions, you may have to navigate to the different pages to make selections prior to actioning. See Figure 8.44 for an example of the data set grids.

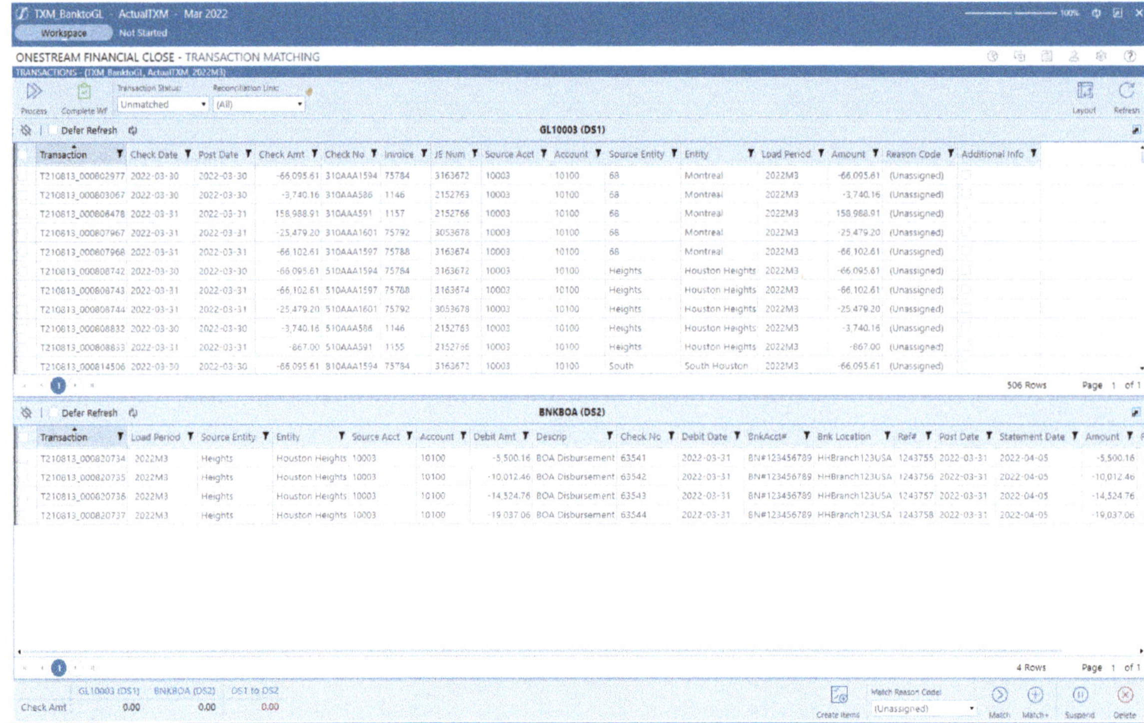

Figure 8.44

Action Bar

The action bar is where you can view the transaction summary, as well as act on the transaction.

The summary is used to display the Aggregation of the designated value fields for each of the data sets. As you select transactions in the respective grids, the summaries will update to provide visibility to the total value. The system will automatically create a Variance Calculation between the summary values for each of the data sets to determine if the transactions selected are in balance. Users leverage the summary information to help determine if the selected transactions should be Matched.

There are up to three summary levels available for each data set and the number of summaries selected is determined during implementation. Most Match Sets will be set with one summary level; however, multiple summary levels are nice to have for situations where we want to tie out multiple value fields prior to matching. As touched upon in the Match Summary section, some examples include Intercompany where we want to tie out the invoice amount in the Transaction currency and Reporting currency to ensure proper eliminations, or in a contractor situation where we may want to tie out hours and amounts on the contractor's invoice.

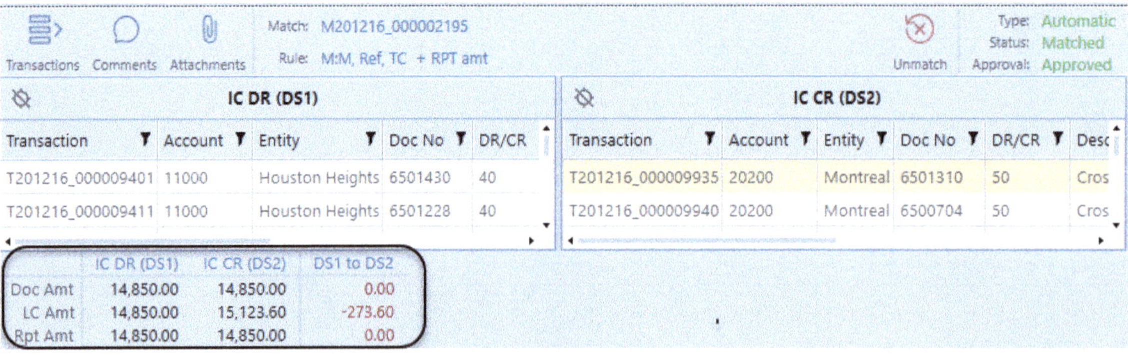

Figure 8.45

Tolerances can be set on any of the summary levels which will prevent Users from creating a match if the variance is outside the tolerance set. Regardless of how you choose to use summary levels, at least one summary level should be selected for each data set.

> **Note:** The name of the summary line that appears will take on the field name from DS1.

See the Match Summary section above for more information on Summary Calculations and to review specific examples.

As implied by its name, the Action Bar is where you will also find the action icons related to transactions. There are multiple actions that can be performed and the icons available will depend on the status of the transaction. We will walk through the different transaction statuses in detail and define what actions can be performed and – more specifically – why you may action the transaction in that way. Let's begin, however, by simply viewing a single transaction and the transaction details where you can add comments and documents or drill back to transformations.

Transactions

Within the Match Set, Users will only have access to transactions based on their security. You can view transactions and all their related fields from the data set grid. If you want more information about a transaction – like Transformation Rules used, comments added, or documents attached – you can open the transaction details.

Viewing Transaction Detail

The Details icon provides additional information about a transaction. From this page, you can add or view transaction-level comments and attachments. By default, the Details icon is hidden and only activates when you select a transaction in the data set grid. Upon selecting the transaction, the Details icon will appear in the action bar.

There is a Details icon for each data set respectively; however, the icon will only appear based on the transaction selected. If you select a transaction in each grid, you will see three icons – one for each data set (Figure 8.46). However, if you only select a single transaction in DS2, you will only see a single icon for Details 2. Also, note that if you select more than one transaction in a specific data set grid, the Details icon will disappear as details can only be viewed one transaction at a time.

Figure 8.46

When selecting the Details icon, you will receive a dialog box. The dialog displayed will depend on the transaction status. Transactions in the Unmatched, Suspended, Pending Delete, or Deleted status will have a single Transaction Detail view as shown below. The dialog will display the Transaction ID and the Transaction Status. Based on the status, certain action icons will appear in the top-right corner. These icons are the same icons that are visible in the Action Bar on the Transactions page. Presenting the action icons in the dialog box allows the User to be more efficient when adding information to a transaction.

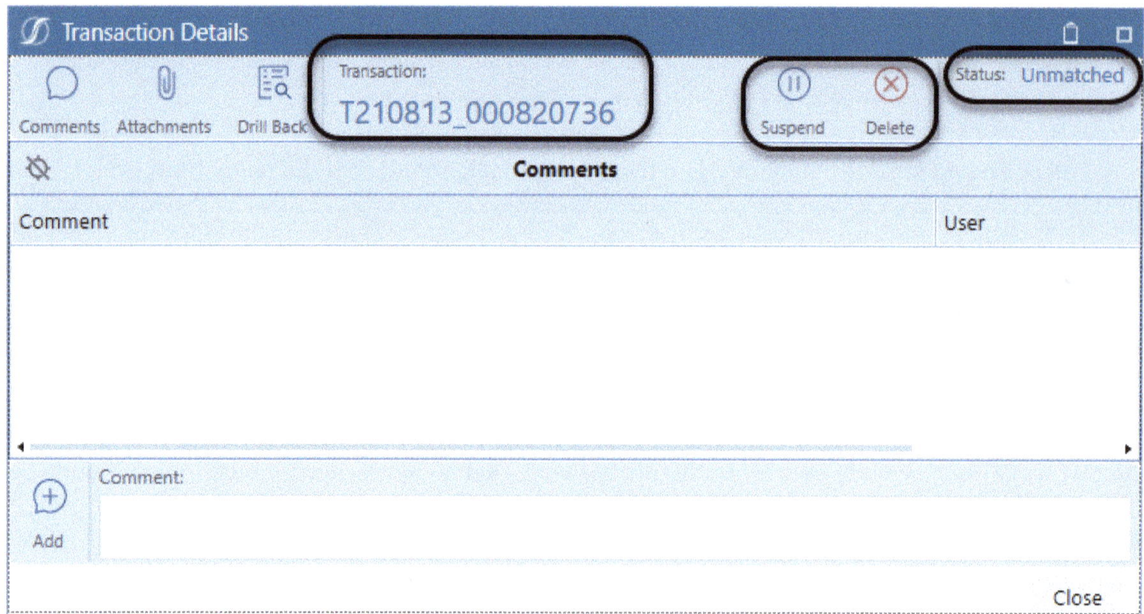

Figure 8.47

For those transactions in the Matched state, the dialog will have two tabs: Transaction Details and Match Details, as shown in Figure 8.48. Users can still interact with the transaction as defined above but will also have visibility into the match information for which this transaction belongs. Match Details will present the Matches Pane (as previously defined in the Matches page section) and display the match-related action icons available based on the User's security.

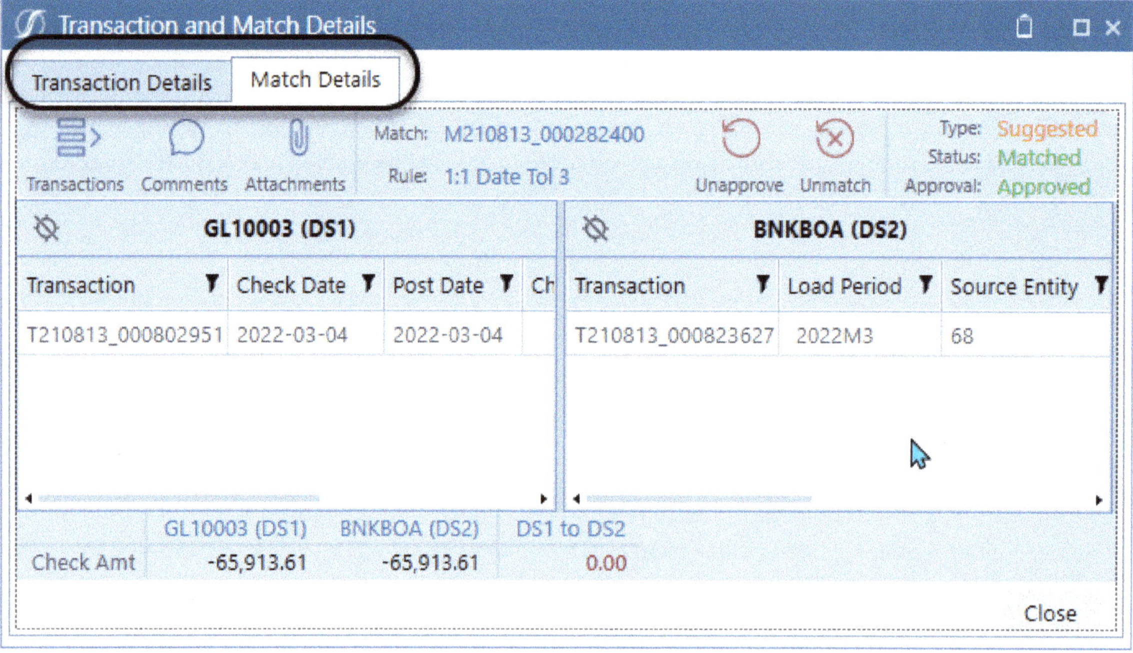

Figure 8.48

Transactional Comments and Attachments

Comments can be added to a transaction at any time, regardless of the transaction status, from the Transaction Details dialog. All roles, except for the Viewer role, can add commentary. Once added, comments cannot be edited or deleted.

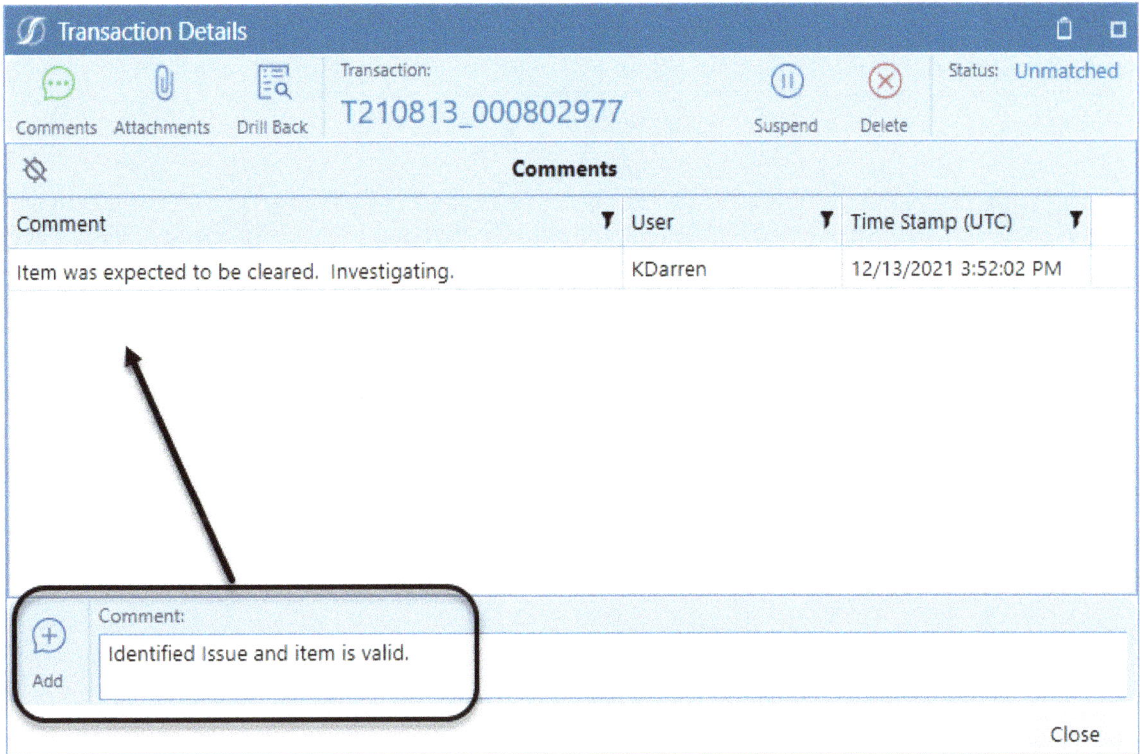

Figure 8.49

The Transaction Details page defaults to the Comment view but can also be accessed by selecting the Comments icon.

Figure 8.50

To add a comment, type into the comment box at the bottom of the page and select the Add icon. The comment will be added to the transaction with the User's ID and date and time stamp for audit purposes. Once a comment has been added to the transaction, the Comments icon will move from blue to green as a visual indicator that a comment has been added. There is no limitation on the number of comments added to a transaction.

Similar to comments, attachments can also be added to a transaction at any time in the process, regardless of the transaction status. Only the Preparer, Approver, or Administrator roles can upload or delete attachments, whereas any role can view them. You can upload as many files as needed. Select the Attachments icon to navigate to the Attachments pane to add documentation.

Figure 8.51

To upload a file, select the Upload icon to initiate a file explorer dialog, then navigate to your file and select open. This will add the document to the transaction.

Figure 8.52

The system will keep track of who added the file with the date and time stamp. Once a file has been added to the transaction – as per the Comments icon – the Attachments icon will also move from blue to green as a visual indicator that a file is associated with the match.

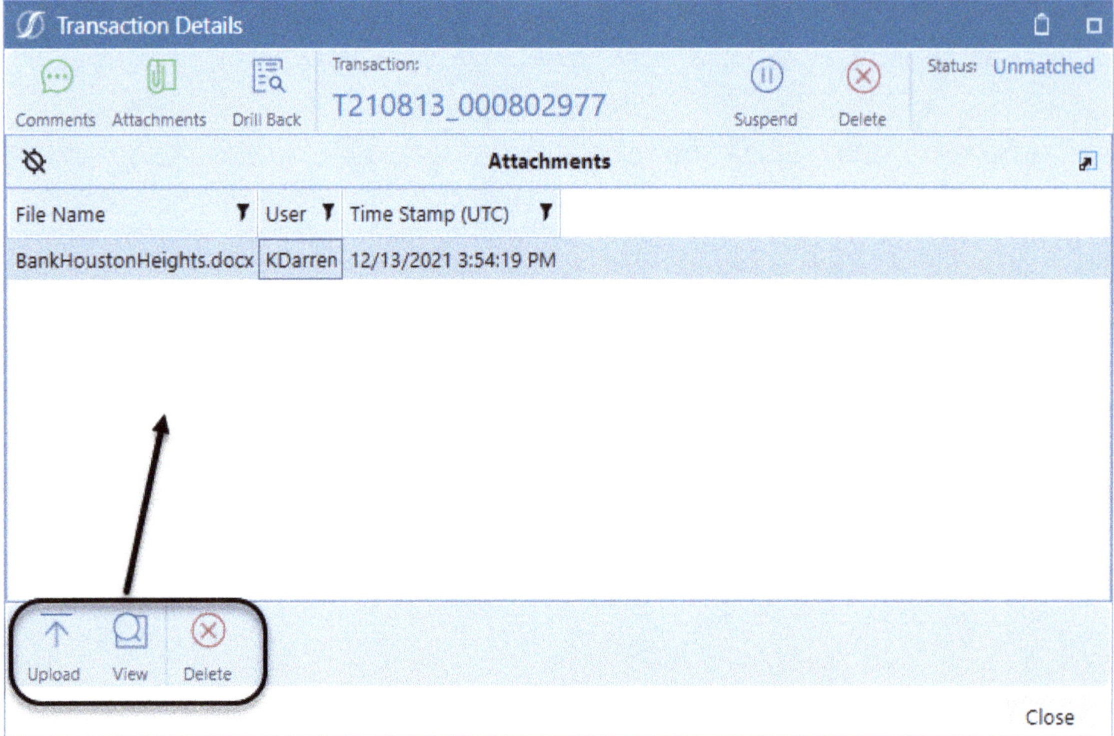

Figure 8.53

From the data set grid, you will be able to see if comments or attachments have been added to a transaction. By default, each data set grid has a system column titled Additional Info. If a comment or attachment has been added to a transaction, the check box will be active, to provide a visual indicator for the User.

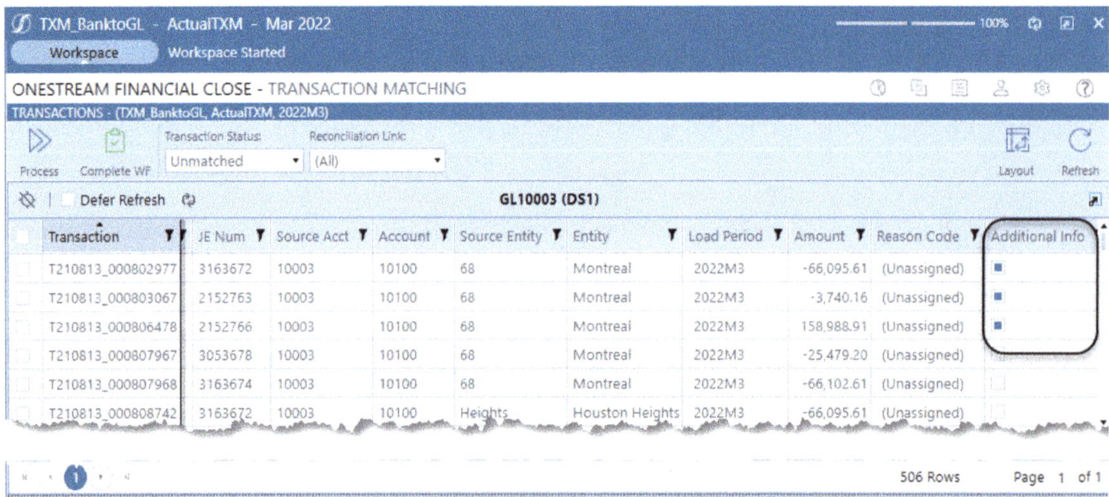

Figure 8.54

Drill Back

Drill back provides you with visibility into the transformations performed on transactional data. As noted in the administration section, above, aligning transactional data is critical when integrating with Reconciliations. Being able to leverage Transformation Rules to map Source Dimension fields to the Target is critical to ensure integration is successful. However, because transaction data is not stored in Stage, the User does not have the native drill down capabilities to be able to view the transformations that have been performed. Being able to view transformations helps to resolve issues when viewing transaction details.

To navigate to the drill back, you first navigate to the Transaction Details pane as defined above. From this page, select the Drill Back icon in the top-left corner.

Figure 8.55

This will update the page to the transformation details where you will see the Dimensions, Source Values, Target Values, and Rule information. Although no changes can be made from this screen, it is useful to understand if anything was not properly transformed. See Figure 8.56 for a transformation view.

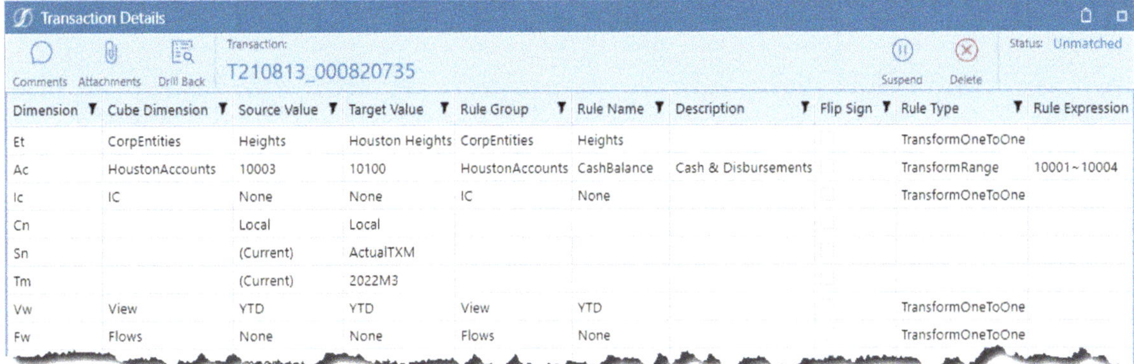

Dimension	Cube Dimension	Source Value	Target Value	Rule Group	Rule Name	Description	Flip Sign	Rule Type	Rule Expression
Et	CorpEntities	Heights	Houston Heights	CorpEntities	Heights			TransformOneToOne	
Ac	HoustonAccounts	10003	10100	HoustonAccounts	CashBalance	Cash & Disbursements		TransformRange	10001~10004
Ic	IC	None	None	IC	None			TransformOneToOne	
Cn		Local	Local						
Sn		(Current)	ActualTXM						
Tm		(Current)	2022M3						
Vw	View	YTD	YTD	View	YTD			TransformOneToOne	
Fw	Flows	None	None	Flows	None			TransformOneToOne	

Figure 8.56

Transaction Status Views

Next, we will move into the different Transaction Status views available to the User. You can set your current view by updating the Transaction Status Filter. Each view provides different actions that can be performed, and the actions will vary based on the User's security.

The views available include:

- Unmatched
- Suspended
- Pending Delete
- Deleted
- Matched

Unmatched View

The Unmatched view is the default view for the Transaction page, and this is where you will perform the majority of your work. Select the transactions desired, review the Summary Calculations, and then select the appropriate action.

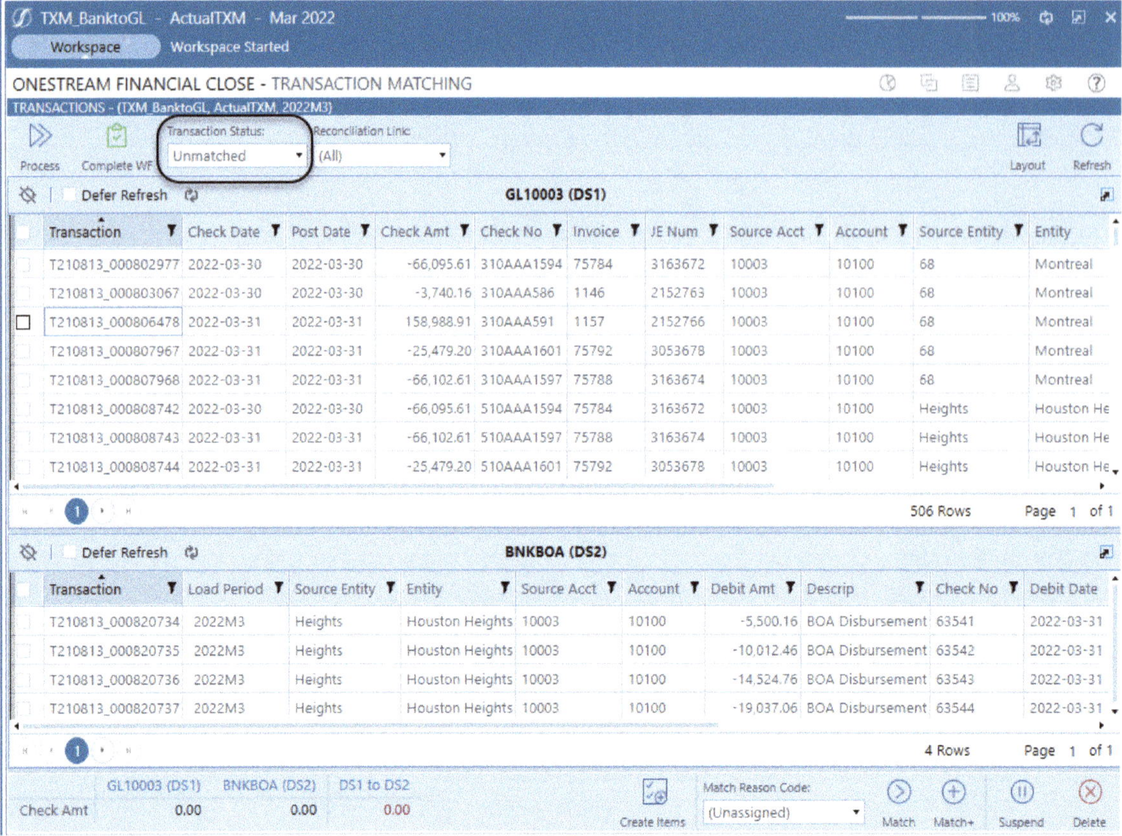

Figure 8.57

The different action icons available in the Unmatched view include the ability to create Reconciliation detail items, as well as match, suspend, or delete transactions as needed. Users can also assign Reason Codes if desired. Each of the icons are shown in Figure 8.58 and will be defined in more detail below.

Figure 8.58

Match Reason Codes

Reason Codes are created by the Administrator and are specific to a Match Set. Reason Codes are used to tag transactions for additional reporting. You can select a Reason Code from the drop-down prior to creating a match or suspending a transaction.

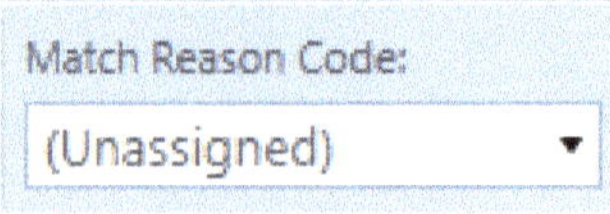

Figure 8.59

Quick Match

A quick match is the ability to select Unmatched transactions and move them to the manual match state with no additional action needed. The Quick Match icon (Figure 8.60) is used when you do not need to add comments or attachments. When creating a quick match, you have the ability to select a Reason Code prior to selecting the Match icon. Once Matched, the transactions are moved to the Matched status and are viewable in either the Matches page or through the Matched view.

Figure 8.60

Match +

Match + is similar to the quick match process in that it creates a manual match. However, Match + allows you to add comments and attachments prior to accepting the match.

Figure 8.61

When you select the Match + icon, the system will launch a Pending Match dialog box. From within this page, you can add comments and attachments as required. You can also assign a Reason Code from the Match + dialog box.

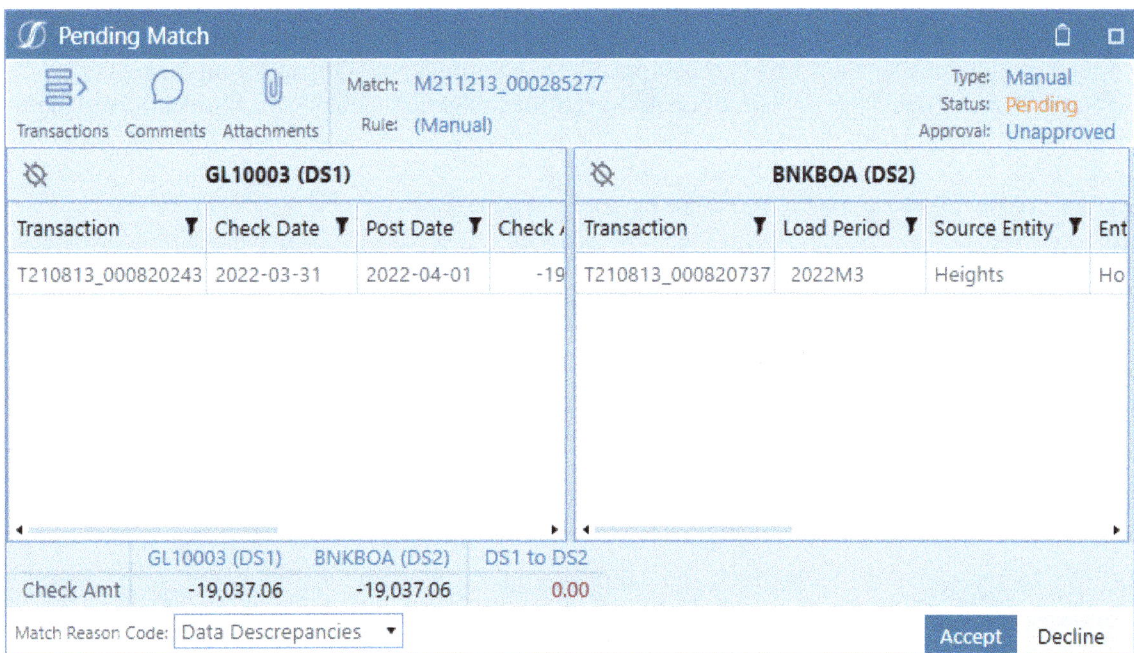

Figure 8.62

Adding comments and attachments is common in the manual match process. A Match Set can be enabled to require either a comment or attachment, or both, prior to matching. If either of these options is turned on, you will no longer see the Quick Match icon and will only have the Match +

icon available. If you fail to action appropriately, you will receive an error message, as shown below, and the match will not be complete.

Document Required

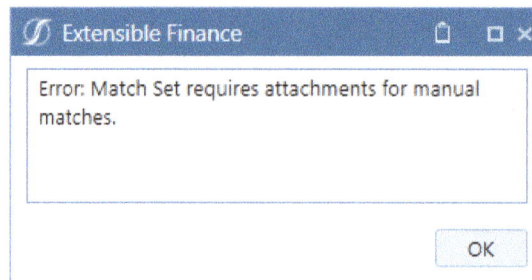

Extensible Finance

Error: Match Set requires attachments for manual matches.

OK

Comment Required

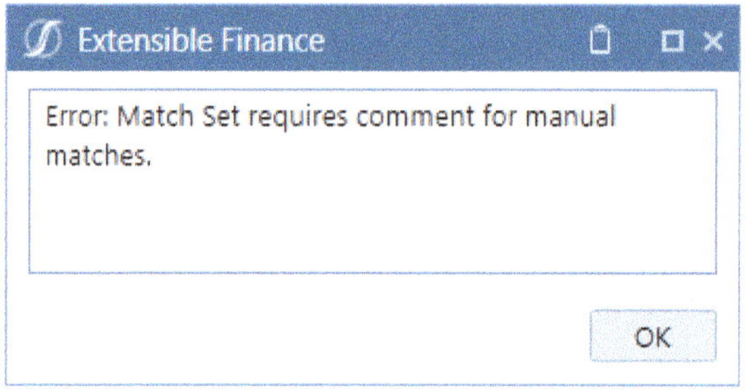
Extensible Finance
Error: Match Set requires comment for manual matches.
OK

Figure 8.63

Adding comments and attachments was covered in the Detail Match Header section, above. If you need more information, please reference this section.

Manual Match Tolerance

As part of the manual match process, Administrators can set a match tolerance on the manual matches made. Tolerances prevent Users from creating manual matches with significant variances. The match tolerance can be set on any (or all) of the summary levels. When set, you will not be able to create a match if the variance is not within the tolerance. If you attempt to create a match outside of the tolerance, you will receive an error message.

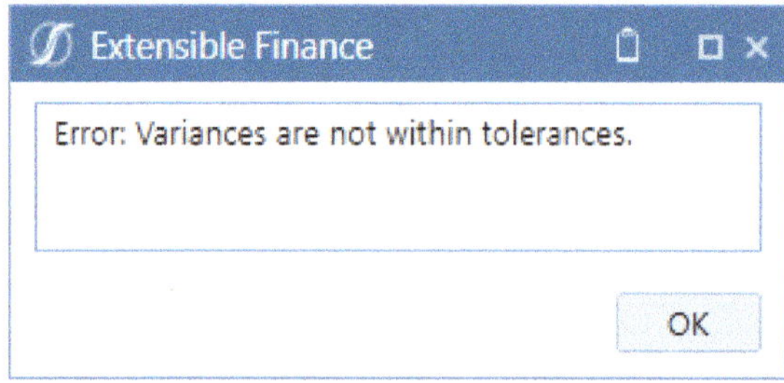
Extensible Finance
Error: Variances are not within tolerances.
OK

Figure 8.64

Although tolerances can be set, there are options within the Match Set to allow the Approver or the Administrator to bypass the tolerance restriction. This will prevent Preparers from creating matches with significant variances but provides flexibility for higher-level roles.

One-Sided Match

One-sided matching allows you to create a manual match without selecting transactions within all data sets. This is utilized when Users need to clear or net transactions within a given data set, or if there are transactions that will never be received by the other sources, like fees or charges.

To create a one-sided manual match, select the transactions within the data set and then select either the Quick Match or Match + icon. You must select at least two transactions to create a one-sided match. If you try to move a single transaction, you will receive an error message (Figure 8.65). Figure 8.66 is an example of a one-sided match.

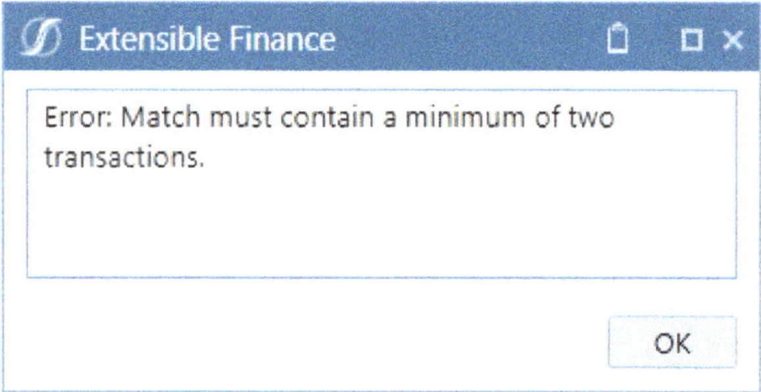

Figure 8.65

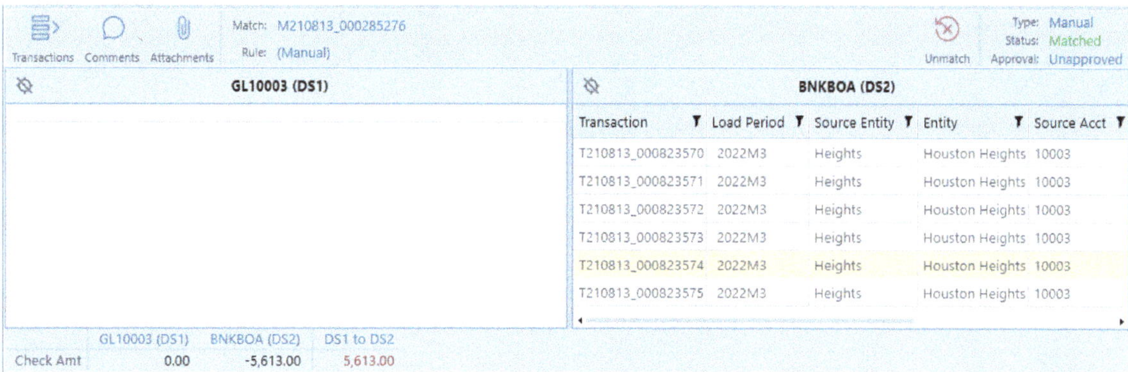

Figure 8.66

Suspending a Transaction

Suspending transactions is the ability to set Unmatched transactions aside. You may want to do this to reduce Unmatched transactions in the data set grids for better visibility while manually matching, or to remove Unmatched transactions that you have already reviewed and analyzed.

Suspended transactions are just that – 'suspended' – which means not only are the transactions no longer available to be manually Matched, but they do not participate in the Match Rules process. These transactions will remain Suspended in the current and all future periods until a User recalls them back into the Unmatched grid. There is also a Match Set option available to automatically unsuspend. If this is turned on, Suspended transactions will be released back into the Unmatched state once the Process is initiated – either manually or through the Task Scheduler in a future period.

Preparers, Approvers, and Administrators have the ability to suspend transactions. To suspend, select the transactions within the data set grids and select the Suspend icon in the bottom-right corner.

Figure 8.67

Upon selection, you will receive a dialog box to assign Reason Codes if desired.

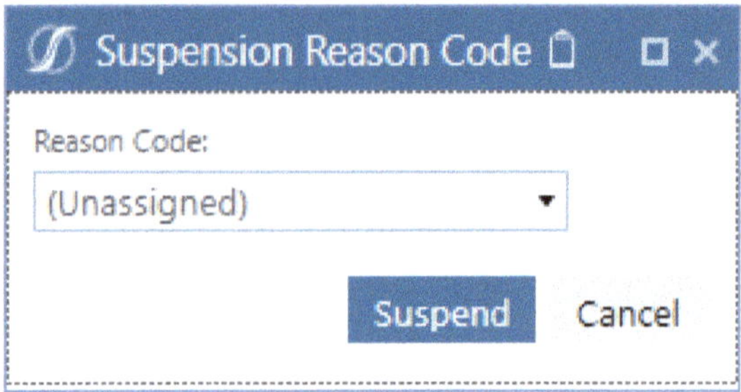

Figure 8.68

Once Suspended, you will see a warning message in the top-right portion of the solution which appears on the screen regardless of the page you navigate to. Because these transactions are set aside and are not being actioned, Suspended transactions are reported on the scorecard to ensure Users are aware that there are transactions not participating in the process.

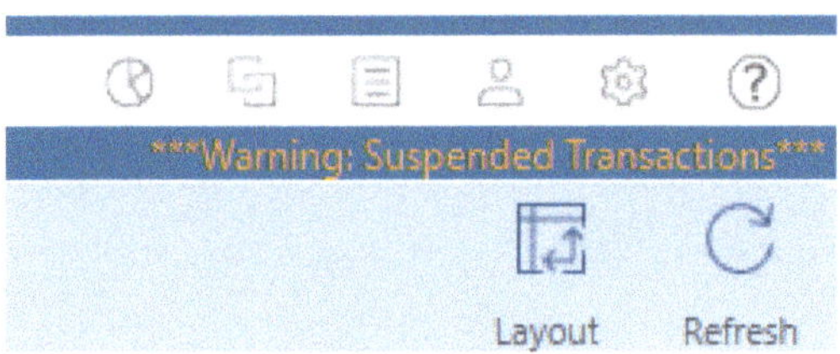

Figure 8.69

Deleting a Transaction

When working in Transaction Matching, there are times when data may get loaded into the system which is not valid or which needs to be removed and reloaded. Bad data will sit in an Unmatched state if not corrected, and will create noise for the User. Although you can suspend the transactions, if the data is never going to be used, it may be best for you to request deletion.

The process of deletion will depend on the amount of bad data. If the issue resides with a specific file load, it is best practice to have the Administrator unmatch all the transactions for the specific data load, then clear the file and reload the corrected data. However, if the issue is not found until late in the process, or there are only a few transactions that need to be removed, the unmatching, clearing, and reloading process may create a lot of work for Users. Therefore, the ability to delete helps facilitate removing small amounts of data from the system.

Deletion functionality is available for Unmatched and Suspended transactions and is a rigorous multi-step process. To truly remove a transaction from the system, the transaction must move from the Unmatched or Suspended state to Pending Delete then from Pending Delete to Deleted and then from Deleted to the final step of Removed. This is purposeful to ensure that transactions are not arbitrarily being deleted from the system.

At any time prior to selecting the Remove icon, Users with the appropriate security will have the ability to recall the transactions. The Recall icon will move the transactions from the current state (Pending Delete or Deleted) back to the Unmatched state. Preparers, Approvers, and Administrators have the ability to request deletion and also have access to the Pending Delete view. However, only Administrators have access to the Deleted view. Also, there is segregation of duties to remove a transaction, which means that I cannot approve a Pending Delete and also remove the transaction.

To delete a transaction, select the applicable transactions and then select the Delete icon.

Figure 8.70

The transactions status will update to Pending Delete and will only be viewable from the Pending Delete view as discussed below.

Creating an Item

From the Unmatched or Matched view, Users have the ability to automatically create detail Reconciliation items. This is referred to as the **push process** because it pushes the transactions from the Match Set into the respective Reconciliations. The push process can update multiple Reconciliations in a single push, and this process can also utilize the Task Scheduler. In the following section, we will discuss the manual push process. See the Implementation section for instructions on how to set up the Push Process via the Task Scheduler.

The first step in creating detail items is to filter the transaction view by updating the Reconciliation Link filter in the header. You should select the No Detail Item from the drop-down as shown.

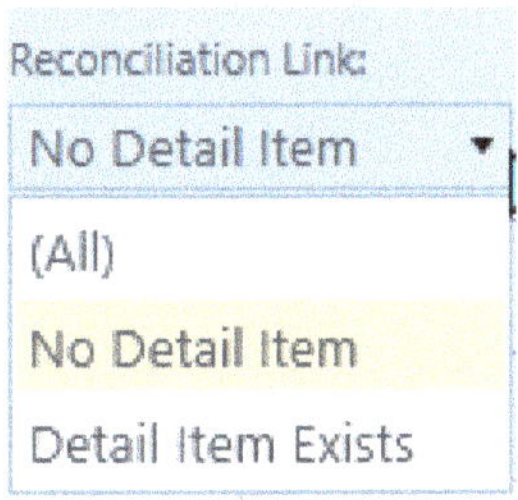

Figure 8.71

This will filter for all transactions that are not currently associated with a Reconciliation. Transactions can only be linked to a Reconciliation once in a given Workflow period. If you attempt to push a transaction that is already linked, you will receive a task activity error; therefore, it is important to perform this filter process *first*, to ensure you are only working with available transactions.

To create items, you can either select specific transactions or push all transactions from the grids. If you prefer to push specific items, you will need to select the transactions from the grids prior to selecting the Create Items icon.

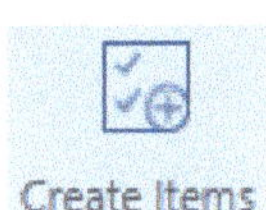

Figure 8.72

If you choose to push all transactions, this will be done from the Create Detail Items dialog.

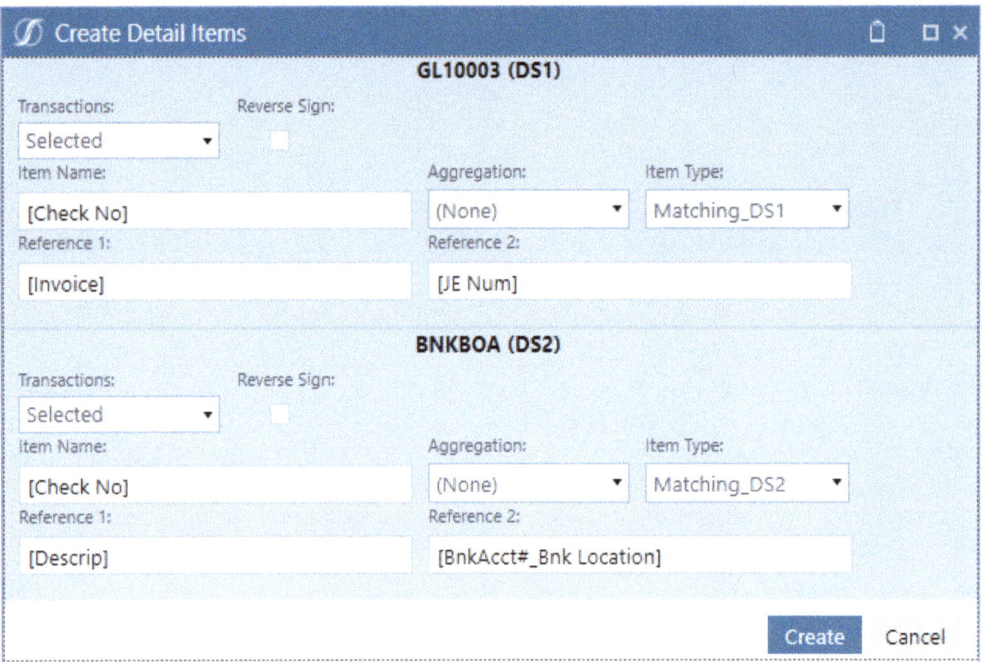

Figure 8.73

Within the Create Detail Items dialog, there are many different options the User can select. The options are the same as what was defined in Chapter 4 regarding the pull process. We will review them again here, for your convenience.

Field	Definition
Transactions	Drop-down contains the selection options for the data set: • Selected (Default) – Indicates that the transactions selected via the multi-select box in the grid will be pulled into the Reconciliation. Selections can be made across multiple pages as needed. • (All) – Regardless of the transactions selected in the grid, all transactions across all pages will be pulled into the Reconciliation. • (None) – Regardless of the transactions selected in the grid, no transactions will be pulled into the Reconciliation for that data set.
Reverse Sign	Reverse sign is applied to the amount fields mapped (Detail Amount (if multi-currency), Account, Local, and Reporting) so that it will display the value in the opposite direction for Reconciliation purposes. If the value is a positive $2,000 and reverse sign is selected, the value will pull into the Reconciliation as a negative $2,000.
Item Name	Mapped from the Match Set, the item name will populate based on the field identified. The field name is denoted within the brackets e.g., [Check No]. Users can override the field by typing into the box. If the User overrides, the typed information will populate to all the transactions pulled. If Aggregation is set to the date field or Total (where multiple item names can exist), or if the item name field is left blank, the item name will default to "Transaction Matching Item" because the item name field must be populated when the item is created. Also, note that if the field is overridden, it cannot be reset by the User by typing in the

Field	Definition
	field name with the brackets. To reset it back to the mapped field, the User will need to close the Create Detail Item dialog and relaunch.
Aggregation	Aggregation is the ability to sum transactions in a meaningful way. This will minimize the number of transactions presented in the detail items grid on the Reconciliation. Transactions will aggregate for each data set independently. If the Reconciliation is a multi-currency Reconciliation, the system will aggregate first, based on the currency codes prior to performing the Aggregation defined below. Although aggregating, the detail is not lost. From the Reconciliation, the User can drill back to the transaction detail using the Drill Back icon in the Reconciliation Support screen. Aggregation is highly encouraged for high-volume Accounts. Possible Aggregation methods are as follows: • None – Each transaction selected will be pulled into the Reconciliation and create a distinct detail item. Typically, utilized on lower-volume Accounts. • Total – Summarizes all transactions selected to a single detail item based on currency codes. If the Reconciliation is a single-currency Reconciliation, there will be one detail item for each data set from which transactions are pulled. If the Reconciliation is multi-currency, the system will first sum the transactions by currency code and pull the items into the Reconciliation, creating a detail item for each currency code and data set combination. The Total Aggregation option is used when there are a significant number of open items. Although the items will be aggregated, there is still drill down capability. However, if aging on the Reconciliation is important, the User should not use Total because the transaction dates are not considered upon Aggregation. When the item is created, the transaction date for the detail item will default to the month-end date. • Transaction Date – Summarizes the items based on the transaction date field identified in the Match Set mapping. The system will create a detail item for each unique transaction date and currency code combination (if multi-currency is used). This still minimizes the number of items created but also supports aging on the Reconciliation. • Item Name – Summarizes the items based on the Item Name field identified in the Match Set mapping. The system will create a detail item for all transactions with the same item name and currency code combination. This will minimize the number of items created but also loses the aging as the transaction date on the items will default to the month-end date.
Item Type	Presents the Item Type list created by the organization. By default, the Item Type is set to Matching_DS1, 2 or 3 depending on the dataset being referenced. However, the User can select any Item Type from their drop-down prior to pushing the items into the Reconciliation.
Reference 1	Mapped from the Match Set, the Reference 1 field will populate based on the fields identified (up to two fields can be assigned). The field name is denoted within the brackets, e.g., [Invoice]. Users can override the field by typing into the box. If the User overrides, the typed information will populate to all transactions pulled. If Aggregation is used, the reference field will be replaced with data set name and transaction status (Matched or Unmatched). If the reference field mapping is deleted, and

Field	Definition
	the field left blank – regardless as to whether you aggregate or not – the reference field will appear blank when pulled into the Reconciliation. Also, note that if the field is overridden, it cannot be reset by the User typing in the field name. To reset it back to the mapped field, the User will need to close the Create Detail Item dialog and relaunch.
Reference 2	Mapped from the Match Set, the Reference 2 field will populate based on the field identified (up to two fields can be assigned). The field name is denoted within the brackets, e.g., [JE Num]. Users can override the field by typing into the box. If the User overrides, the typed information will populate to all transactions pulled. If Aggregation is used, the reference field will be replaced with how the transactions were selected (All versus Selected) and Aggregation utilized. If the reference field mapping is deleted and the field left blank – regardless as to whether you aggregate or not – the reference field will appear blank when pulled into the Reconciliation. Also, note that if the field is overridden, it cannot be reset by the User typing in the field name. To reset it back to the mapped field, the User will need to close the Create Detail Item dialog and relaunch.

Figure 8.74

Once you have the options in place for each of the data sets, select the Create icon in the bottom-right corner of the dialog box. This will initiate a data management job that will run in the background. The status of the job will be reported in the Task Activity page. If the task job fails, the User can review the error message to determine why items were not created. Also, if you select the Refresh icon in the header, the No Detail Item grid will update, removing the items that were successfully pushed.

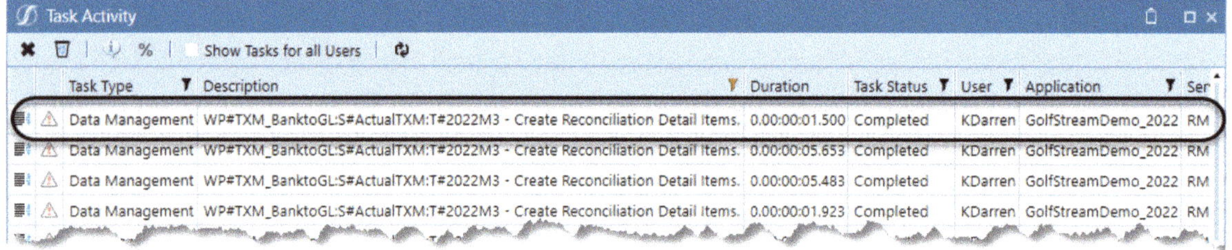

Figure 8.75

Suspended View

The Suspended view presents all the transactions in a Suspended state. As discussed above, these transactions have been set aside and do not participate in either automated or manual matching. Typically, Suspended transactions are only set aside for a short period of time while you work in the Unmatched grid. Once ready, the Suspended transactions are normally released back into the process as they are still required to be Matched.

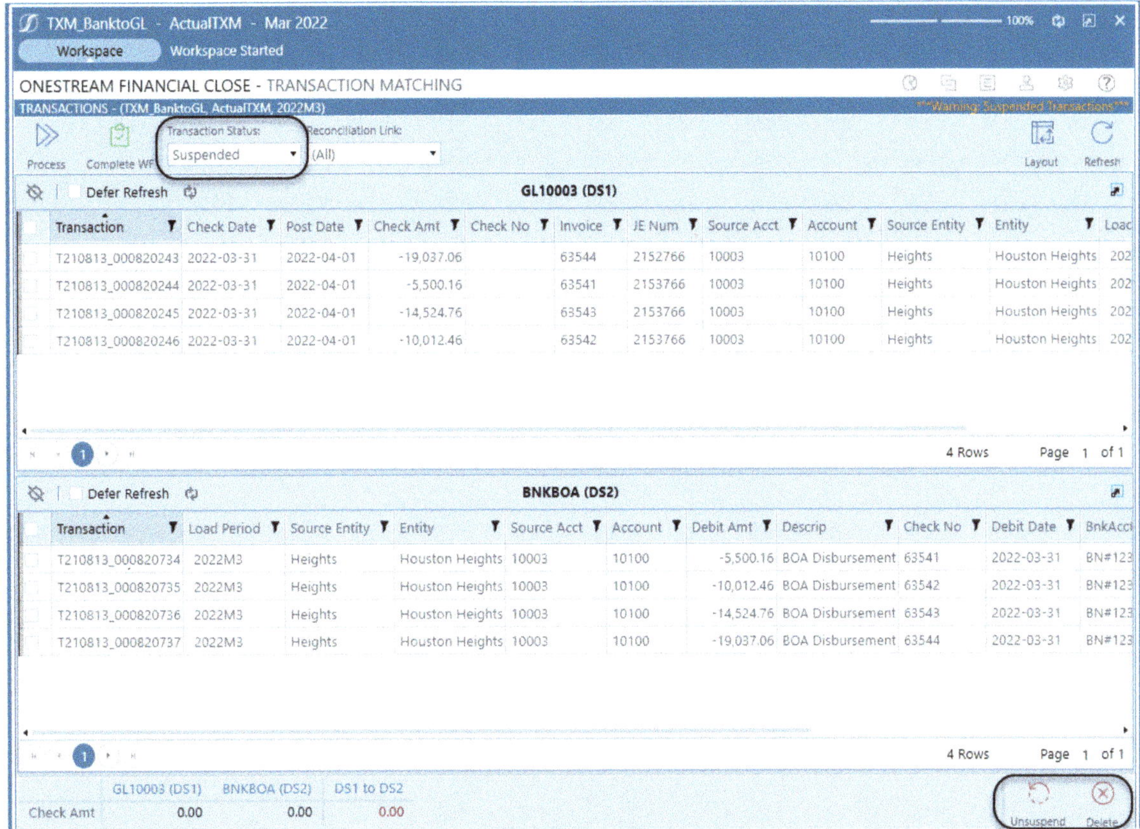

Figure 8.76

To release the transactions, Users select the specific items from the grid and then select the Unsuspend icon. This process will update the status of the transactions from Suspended to Unmatched and the transactions will now be visible in the Unmatched view.

Figure 8.77

If the Suspended transactions are determined to be invalid transactions, and need to be removed from the system, you can also delete them. To delete, select the applicable transactions and then select the Delete icon. Transactions selected for deletion will update to the Pending Delete status. See the Pending Delete View for additional actions that can be performed.

Figure 8.78

Pending Delete View

The Pending Delete view presents all the transactions that have been selected for deletion but which are still awaiting approval. Deletion can be requested for transactions in either the Unmatched or Suspended state. Once moved to the Pending Delete state, these transactions are no longer available for the matching process.

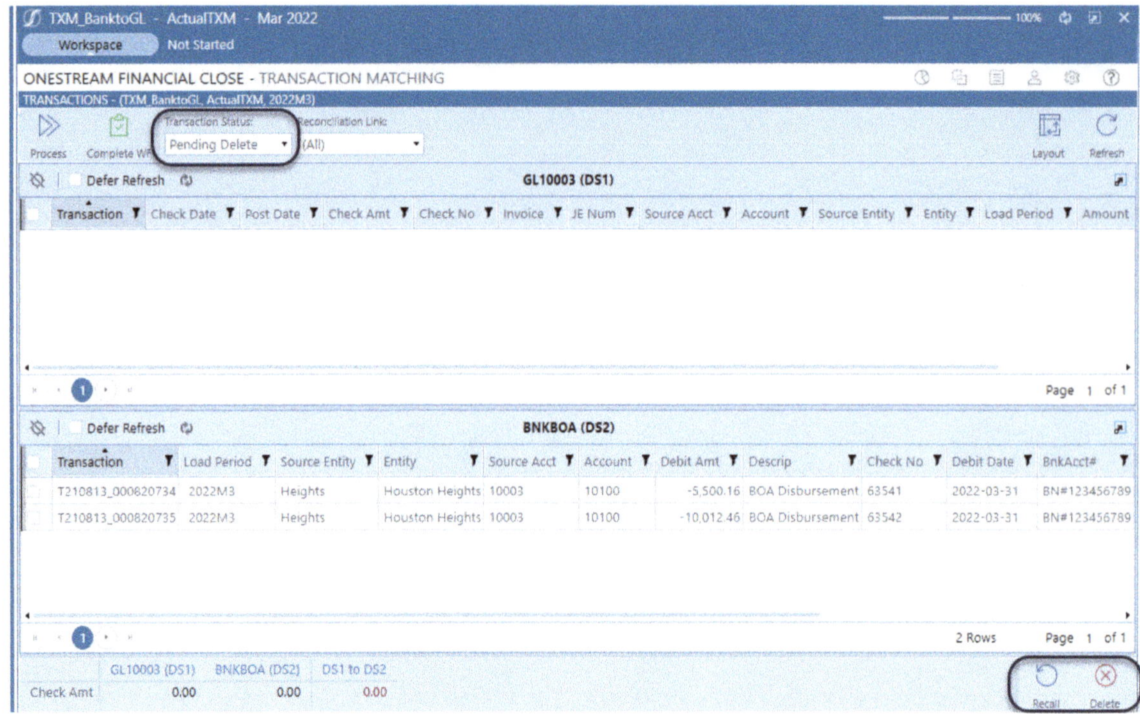

Figure 8.79

Transactions in the Pending Delete state require approval to move them to the Deleted state. Only the Approver and Administrator roles can approve transactions for deletion.

To approve, select the transactions within the data set grid and then select the Delete icon, in the bottom-right corner of the page.

Figure 8.80

The system will display a message asking you to confirm that you would like to permanently delete the transactions. If you select OK, the state of the transactions will be updated from Pending Delete to Deleted. The transactions will still reside in the system, but are only viewable by the Administrator in the Deleted View. See the Deleted View section below to permanently remove the transactions from the system.

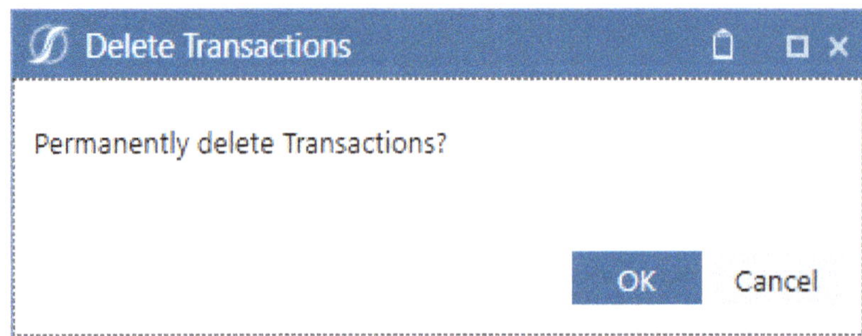

Figure 8.81

If the request for deletion was done in error and the transaction is still pending deletion, the User can recall the transaction at any time. To recall, select the applicable transactions and then select the Recall icon in the bottom-right corner. Recalling a transaction will move the item from Pending Delete to the Unmatched state regardless of where it originated from (Unmatched or Suspended). The recall function can be done by the Preparer, Approver, or Administrator role.

Figure 8.82

Deleted View

Transactions that have been Approved for deletion are moved to Deleted state and are only visible by Administrators in the Deleted view (Figure 8.83). Although the transactions are in the Deleted state, they still reside in the system until they are fully removed. This multi-step process (Pending Delete to Deleted to Removed) was created for control purposes to ensure that Administrators are confident in their decisions to purge transactions from the system. For further control around this process, the system also enforces segregation of duties between the Deletion and Removal process. The User authorizing the deletion cannot also remove the transaction from the system, thus ensuring a secondary review is performed. Once removed, the transactions are no longer available within the application and cannot be recalled.

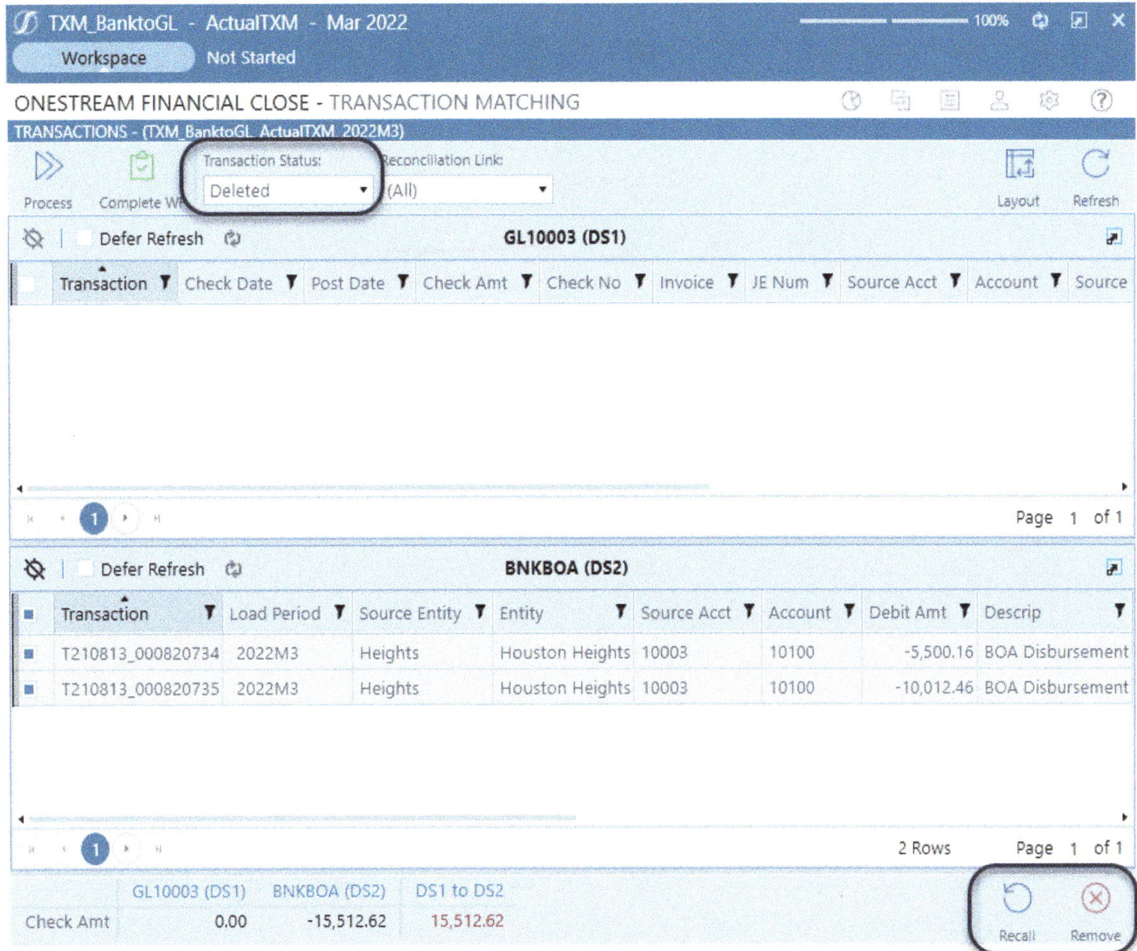

Figure 8.83

To fully delete the transactions from the system, the Administrator will select the specific transactions from the data set grids and then select the Remove icon.

Figure 8.84

The remove process will permanently delete the transaction and you will receive a system message indicating the number of transactions that have been Deleted.

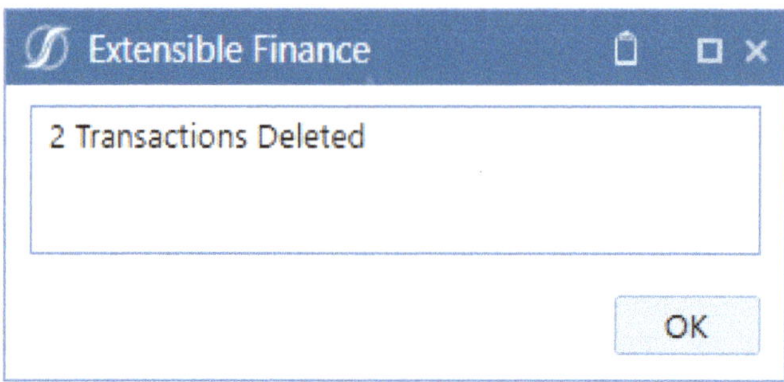

Figure 8.85

As mentioned above, because this is a permanent removal, the system enforces a segregation of duties between the deletion and removal. If you try to perform both actions, you will receive an error message and the transactions will not be removed.

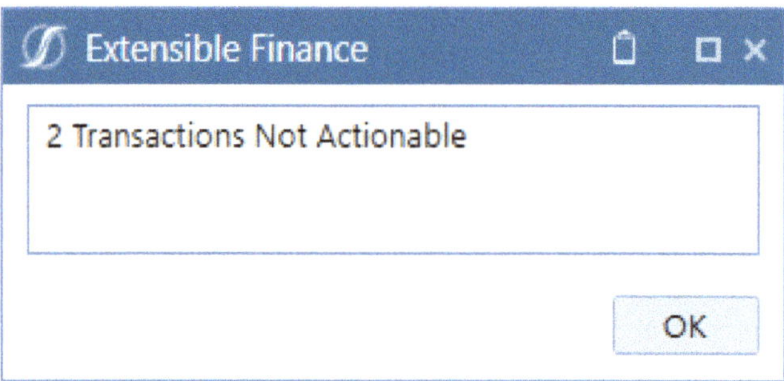

Figure 8.86

As with the other views, if at any time (prior to removal) the deletion was determined to be performed in error, the Administrator can select the transactions and then select the Recall icon to move the transactions back to the Unmatched state.

Matched View

The final view available for Users is the Matched View. Opposite to the Matches page – that starts with the match and displays the transactions – the Matched View starts with the transactions and allows you to drill to the match. Having visibility into transactions that are Matched allows Users to search for transactions that may have been Matched in error.

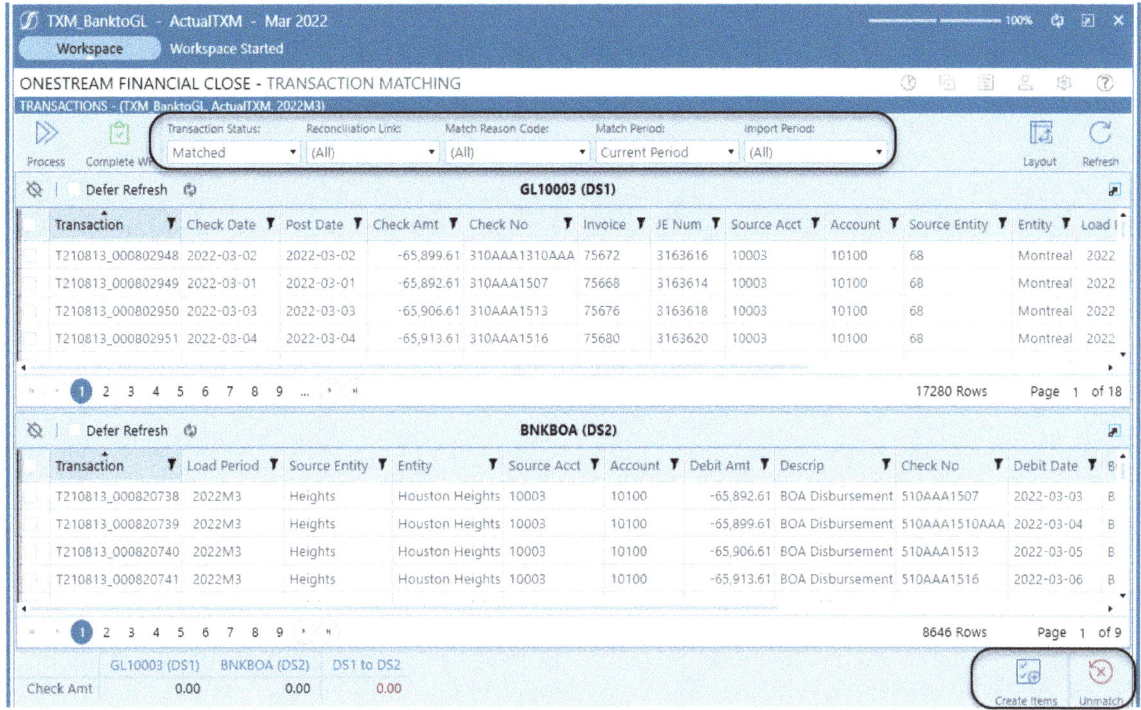

Figure 8.87

When in the Matched View, you may notice additional columns are presented in the data set grids. The grid updates to include the match Reason Code, the Match ID, and the match period to assist Users in sorting and searching. In addition to searching the new match columns, you can also view the match information on the transaction through the Details icon, as described previously.

In addition, depending on your security and the match type associated with the transaction (see Figure 8.24), you may also have the ability to Unmatch from this view. If while reviewing the transaction you determine it needs to be Unmatched, you can select the transaction and then the Unmatch icon at the bottom-right corner of the page. This will unmatch all transactions in the match – even if not physically selected in the grid.

Figure 8.88

Also, you may have noticed that the Matched View has additional filter capabilities in the header.

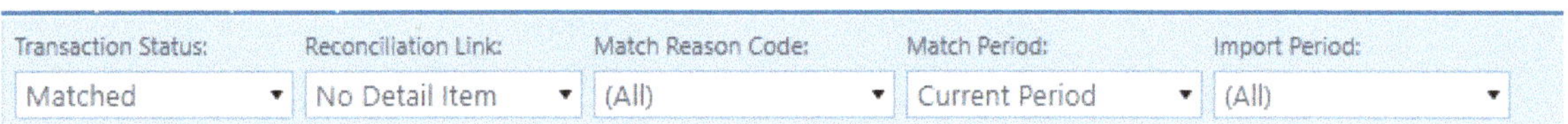

Figure 8.89

The additional filters are defined in Figure 8.90:

Field	Definition
Match Reason Code	Allows Users to filter the transactions in all data sets based on the Reason Code assigned to the match.
Match Period	Filters the Workflow period of when the match occurred. The Match Period is used for cutoff purposes (to be discussed below). The selections available are All, Current, or Future.
Import Period	Filters the Workflow period of when transactions were loaded into the solution. This is limited to the current period and any historical periods. This filter is also used for cutoff purposes.

Figure 8.90

The new filters are used to define cutoff. Cutoff is critical when creating Reconciliation detail items. As mentioned at the beginning of this chapter, matching is a continuous process; transactions continually match as new data is loaded and Match Rules are run. Although leveraging the Workflow period, it is important to understand that the state of a transaction, Unmatched or Matched, is not time-based. This means that if I have a transaction Unmatched in 2022M3 that is subsequently Matched in 2022M4, the transaction will no longer appear Unmatched in the system regardless of the period I view.

Let's walk through an example. Assume you are preparing your M3 Reconciliation which has a balance of $100. The Reconciliation is normally supported with the Unmatched transactions at the end of the period. If no new data is loaded, and Match Rules run for M4, you can simply push the Unmatched transactions from M3 which total $100 and your Reconciliation is complete. See the example in Figure 8.91.

Reconciliation: General Ledger Balance for 2022M3 = $100

Transaction Matching: 2022M3 Transaction Statuses

Invoice #	Unmatched
AB123	$10
BD231	$30
DC321	$60
Total	$100

Create Item through Single Push: Unmatched Transactions only

Figure 8.91

However, if you are loading data into future periods while in the process of reconciling the current period, 2022M3, you may need to include transactions Matched in the next period, 2022M4. As transactions are not Workflow time-based, they would show as Matched in M3 but were actually Unmatched for the period of Reconciliation. This is where the filters can assist. If you navigate to the Matched view and set the Matched Period filter to Future Period, the system will identify historical transactions that were Matched in the period of M4 (or later) but which would be considered Unmatched for the current period. See the example in Figure 8.92.

Reconciliation: General Ledger Balance for 2022M3 = $100

Transaction Matching: 2022M3 Transaction Statuses

Invoice #	Unmatched	Matched	Matched Period
AB123		$10	2022M4
BD231		$30	2022M4
DC321	$60		
Total	$60	$40	

Create Item through Two Push Processes: Unmatched Transactions and Matched Transactions filtered for Match Period=Future Period

Figure 8.92

Therefore, if you are loading data daily, and you need to ensure proper cutoff, you cannot simply use Unmatched transactions for 2022M3. You will need to push Unmatched transactions of $60 from the Unmatched view as well as $40 of Matched transactions from the Matched View, filtering the Match Period for Future Periods. Here is a filter example.

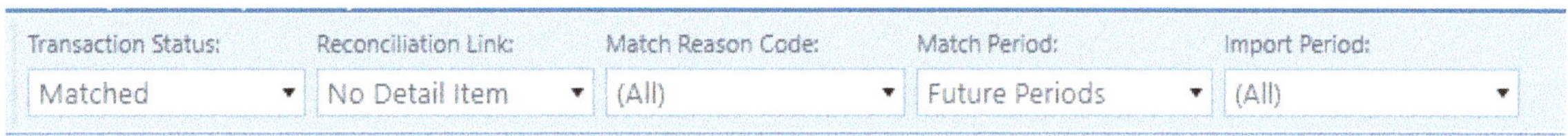

Figure 8.93

Roles and Responsibilities

The roles available in Transaction Matching are similar to the Account Reconciliation solution. The system supports Preparers, Approvers, Administrators, Viewers, or Commenters. However, *unlike* Reconciliations, matching does not require a Preparer and Approver on every Match Set, nor does the Match Set support multiple levels of approval.

Matching is more of a process to assist in preparing Reconciliations, and the controls typically reside through the Reconciliation process. For those Match Sets that are critical and require more structure, the different roles are available along with Workflow and the segregation of duties. However, in situations where one person owns the process end to end, you may only assign the Administrator role. As an Administrator, the User will have the ability to manage the Match Set, update rules, unmatch matches, etc.

There really is no specific ‘right way’ to set up matching security. It really is processed-based, which is why role assignment is very flexible and set on a Match Set by Match Set basis.

Common across all Match Sets is the assignment of the Viewer and Commenter roles. The Viewer role provides the ability to access the matches and transactions without being able to make any changes. Similarly, the Commenter role allows the User to view but also add comments at the match or transaction level. These roles are granted in situations where you want to provide visibility to upper management or other departments. Also, you would typically assign one of these roles to the auditor so they can perform their review and testing.

Reporting

Reporting is important in monitoring the matching process. The solution delivers standard Reports and Dashboards, giving Users important insights into transactions and matches. In addition, Users can leverage reporting capabilities within OneStream. Being able to create your own visualizations allows you to analyze the information in a way that is meaningful.

Solution reporting can be accessed by navigating to the Scorecard page. By default, you will land on the Scorecard but can subsequently navigate to the Analysis page utilizing the icons in the top-left corner of the header. The information presented to the User will be dependent on the User's security, and you can limit the data retrieved based on the Time Period filter. This filter will default to Periodic, but can be updated to show Year to Date (YTD) or Trailing 12 months.

The header also contains a Refresh icon in the top-right corner. Reports and Dashboards will update to the current information the first time you navigate to this page for the specific period. Once the data is retrieved, the page will not update automatically unless you change the Time Period filter or navigate to another Workflow period. Therefore, if the Dashboard is populated, and additional matching or processing occurs within the period being viewed, the reporting will not update until you select the Refresh icon. This is by design for performance purposes. Rather than updating the data dynamically, we cache the information and update on demand. The time stamp of the last refresh is displayed underneath the Refresh icon for your reference.

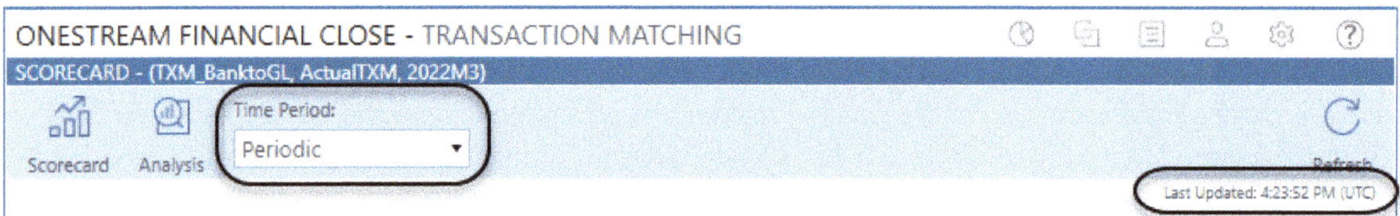

Figure 8.94

Note: Reporting is only viewable in the Windows application. If you try to view a Report through the browser, you will receive the following message on the Scorecard and Analysis pages:

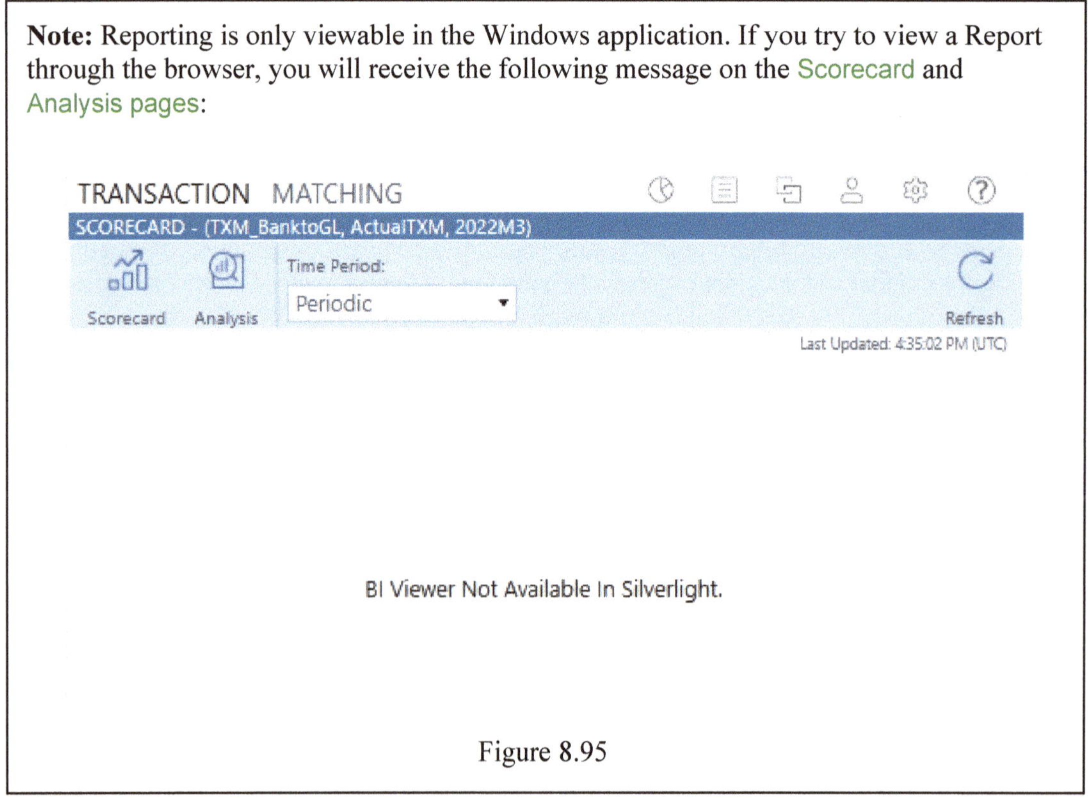

Figure 8.95

Scorecard Page

The Scorecard is a Dashboard that delivers detailed information and graphical views of the matching process. The User will have visibility into important information about the transactions and the matches within the Match Set, based on their security.

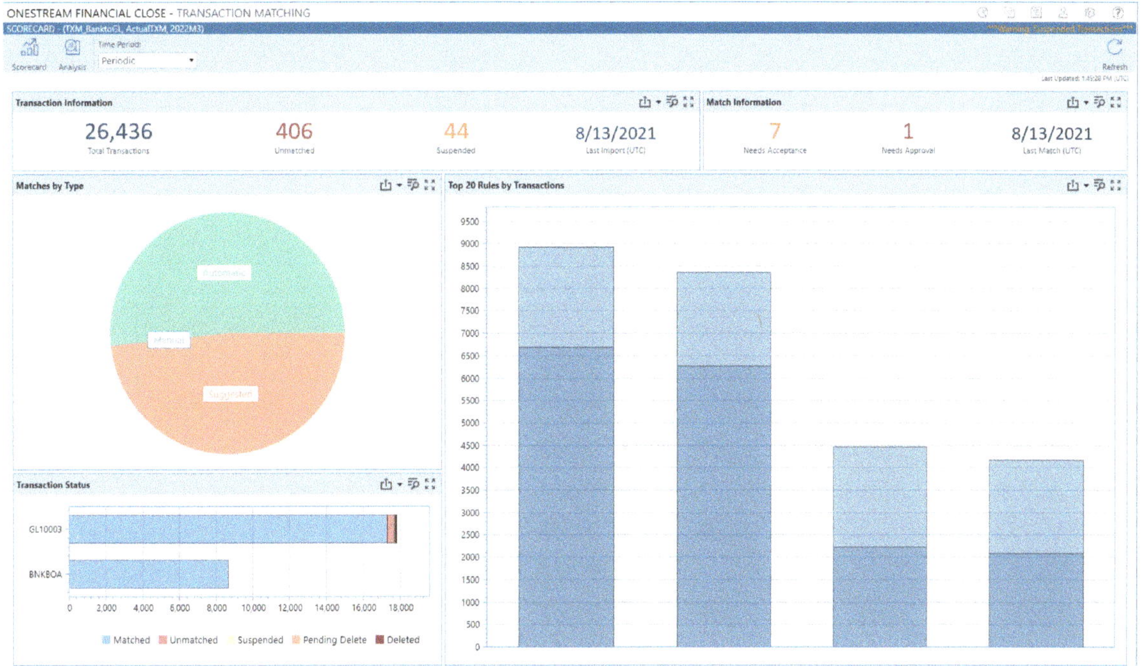

Figure 8.96

The values displayed will depend on the Time Period filter set in the header. We will define the five key sections of the Dashboard below. Within each section, you can print or export the information, inspect the underlying data, or expand the screen leveraging the icons shown below.

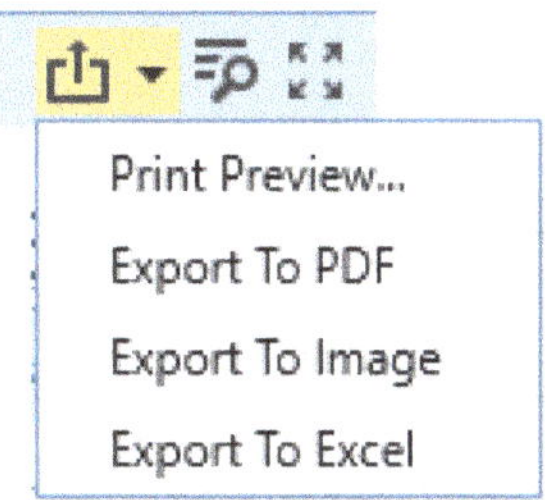

Figure 8.97

Transaction Information

The Transaction Information section (Figure 8.98) presents four key transactional metrics which include:

- Total number of transactions
- Total number of transactions in the Unmatched state
- Total number of transactions that have been Suspended
- Last date transactions were imported

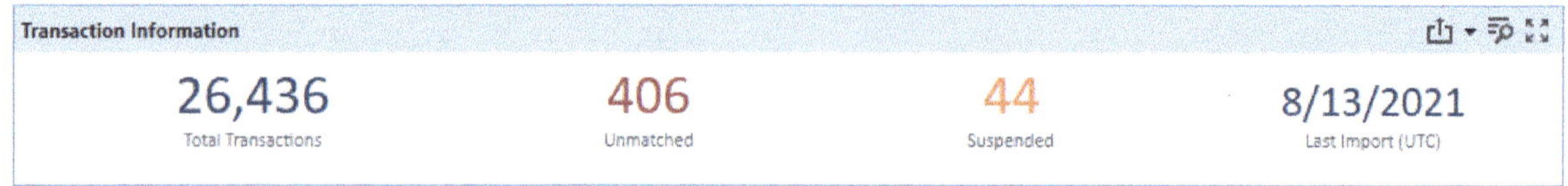

Figure 8.98

Match Information

The Match Information section presents key information about the matches. This section will display three key match metrics:

- Total number of suggested matches awaiting acceptance
- Total number of matches awaiting approval
- Last date the Match Rule process ran

Figure 8.99

Matches by Type

Matches by Type is a pie chart that displays the total number of matches by the three match types: Automatic, Suggested, and Manual. If you hover over any portion of the graph, the system will display the total number of matches for that specific type, as well as the specific type as a percentage of total matches.

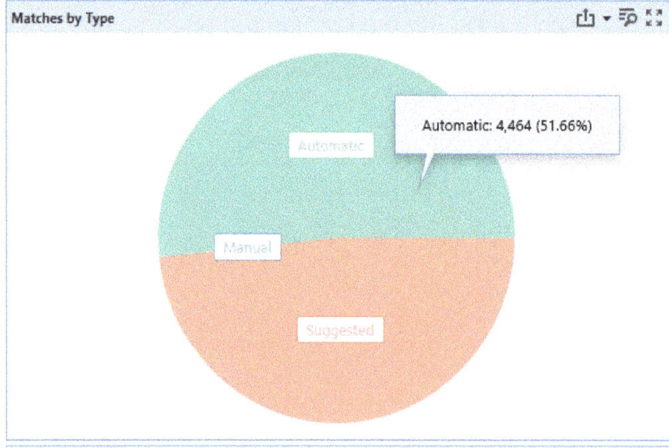

Figure 8.100

Top 20 Rules

The Top 20 Rules by Transactions section displays the top relevant Match Rules from highest to lowest. The chart is a stacked column chart with each column displaying the total number of transactions Matched by the specific rule, detailed by specific data set.

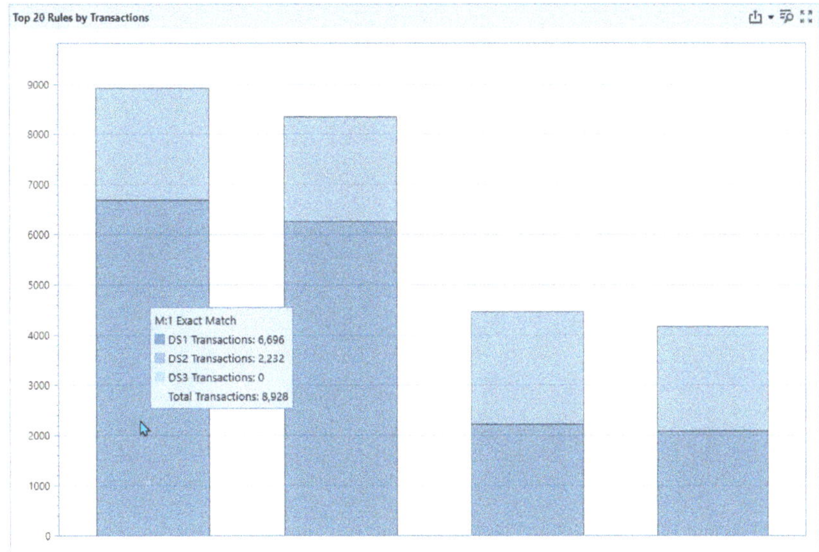

Figure 8.101

Transaction Status

The Transaction Status section presents a stacked bar chart for each data set, displaying the number of transactions by status Unmatched, Matched, Suspended, Pending Delete, and Deleted.

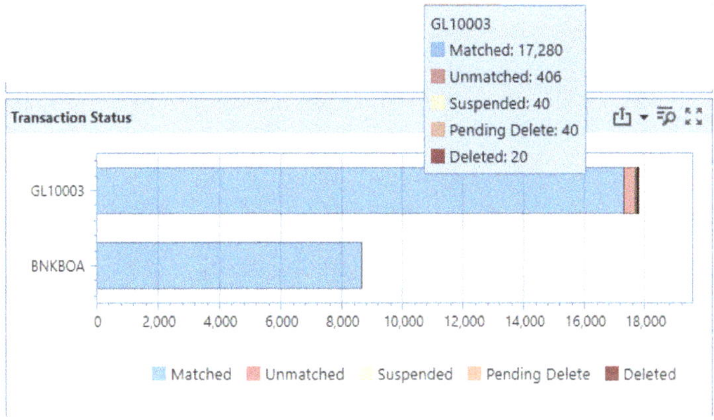

Figure 8.102

Analysis

The Analysis page has a list of delivered Reports in the solution. Each of these Reports is intended to highlight more detailed operational information regarding the Match Set. There are four different Reports that cover analysis around the transactions, matches, Match Rules, variances, etc. Each of the Reports is defined in detail below.

Transactions by Data Set

Transactions by Data Set displays total transaction counts broken down by period, by data set, and by the specific data loads that have occurred. This Report assists in determining if there are any issues with the data or data files. If you have a specific load, and 100% of the transactions are Unmatched, it may be an indication that a data issue exists.

Within the Report, you will see the number of transactions by status which include Unmatched, Suspended, Manual, Suggested, and Automatic, as well as in Total. In addition, you can see the total transactions Matched as a percentage of total transactions.

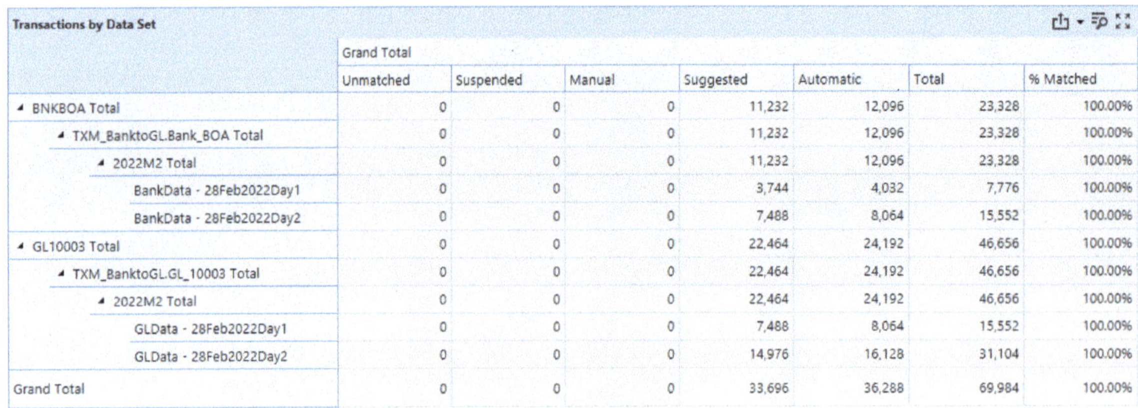

Transactions by Data Set

	Grand Total						
	Unmatched	Suspended	Manual	Suggested	Automatic	Total	% Matched
◢ BNKBOA Total	0	0	0	11,232	12,096	23,328	100.00%
◢ TXM_BanktoGL.Bank_BOA Total	0	0	0	11,232	12,096	23,328	100.00%
◢ 2022M2 Total	0	0	0	11,232	12,096	23,328	100.00%
BankData - 28Feb2022Day1	0	0	0	3,744	4,032	7,776	100.00%
BankData - 28Feb2022Day2	0	0	0	7,488	8,064	15,552	100.00%
◢ GL10003 Total	0	0	0	22,464	24,192	46,656	100.00%
◢ TXM_BanktoGL.GL_10003 Total	0	0	0	22,464	24,192	46,656	100.00%
◢ 2022M2 Total	0	0	0	22,464	24,192	46,656	100.00%
GLData - 28Feb2022Day1	0	0	0	7,488	8,064	15,552	100.00%
GLData - 28Feb2022Day2	0	0	0	14,976	16,128	31,104	100.00%
Grand Total	0	0	0	33,696	36,288	69,984	100.00%

Figure 8.103

Matches by Rule

Matches by Rule displays total matches, transactions, Pending matches, and matches in the Unapproved state. This information is presented for each rule included in the Workflow. The Report will also display the percentage of Accepted and Approved, as well as the Last Match Date.

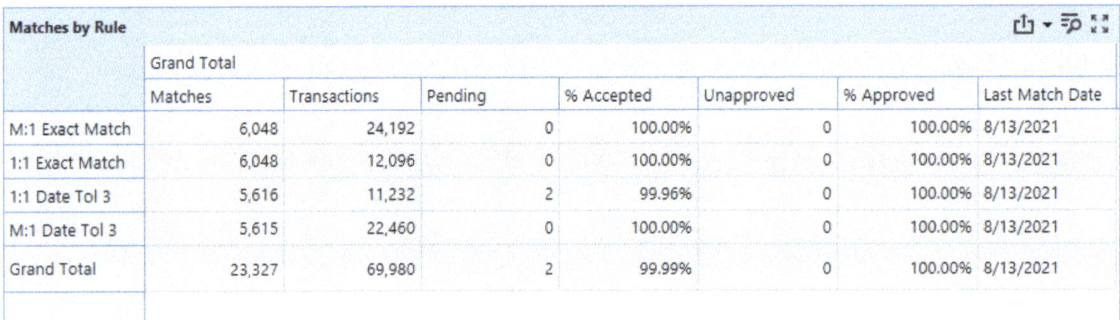

Matches by Rule

	Grand Total						
	Matches	Transactions	Pending	% Accepted	Unapproved	% Approved	Last Match Date
M:1 Exact Match	6,048	24,192	0	100.00%	0	100.00%	8/13/2021
1:1 Exact Match	6,048	12,096	0	100.00%	0	100.00%	8/13/2021
1:1 Date Tol 3	5,616	11,232	2	99.96%	0	100.00%	8/13/2021
M:1 Date Tol 3	5,615	22,460	0	100.00%	0	100.00%	8/13/2021
Grand Total	23,327	69,980	2	99.99%	0	100.00%	8/13/2021

Figure 8.104

Matches with Variance

The Matches with Variance Report lists all matches containing a variance in amounts.

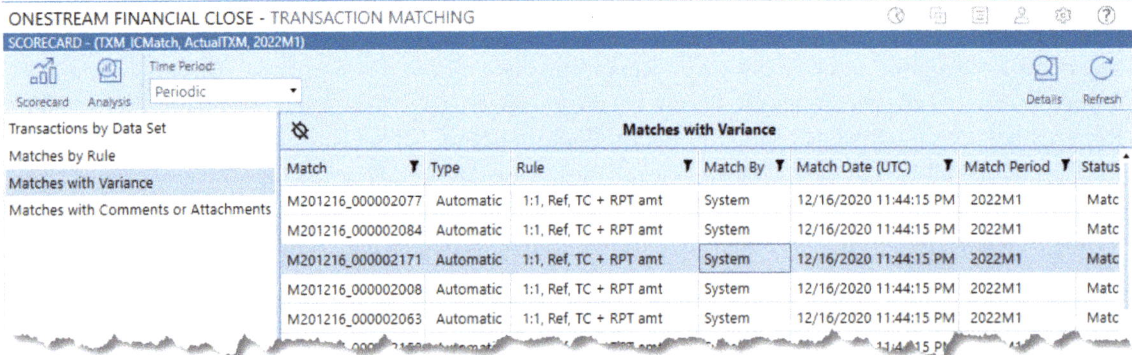

ONESTREAM FINANCIAL CLOSE - TRANSACTION MATCHING
SCORECARD - (TXM_ICMatch, ActualTXM, 2022M1)
Scorecard
Analysis
Time Period:
Periodic
Details
Refresh
Transactions by Data Set
Matches by Rule
Matches with Variance
Matches with Comments or Attachments
Matches with Variance
Match | Type | Rule | Match By | Match Date (UTC) | Match Period | Status
M201216_000002077 | Automatic | 1:1, Ref, TC + RPT amt | System | 12/16/2020 11:44:15 PM | 2022M1 | Matc
M201216_000002084 | Automatic | 1:1, Ref, TC + RPT amt | System | 12/16/2020 11:44:15 PM | 2022M1 | Matc
M201216_000002171 | Automatic | 1:1, Ref, TC + RPT amt | System | 12/16/2020 11:44:15 PM | 2022M1 | Matc
M201216_000002008 | Automatic | 1:1, Ref, TC + RPT amt | System | 12/16/2020 11:44:15 PM | 2022M1 | Matc
M201216_000002063 | Automatic | 1:1, Ref, TC + RPT amt | System | 12/16/2020 11:44:15 PM | 2022M1 | Matc

Figure 8.105

This Report can be filtered, sorted, and/or exported, and is used to generate adjustments or Journal Entries. You can also select a match from the grid with the ability to display the details by selecting the Details icon in the top-right corner.

Figure 8.106

Matches with Comments or Attachments

This Report is exactly as titled; it lists matches that contain comments or attachments. Similar to above, Users can select a match and – utilizing the Details icon – drill to the specific match to be able to view the comments and attachments.

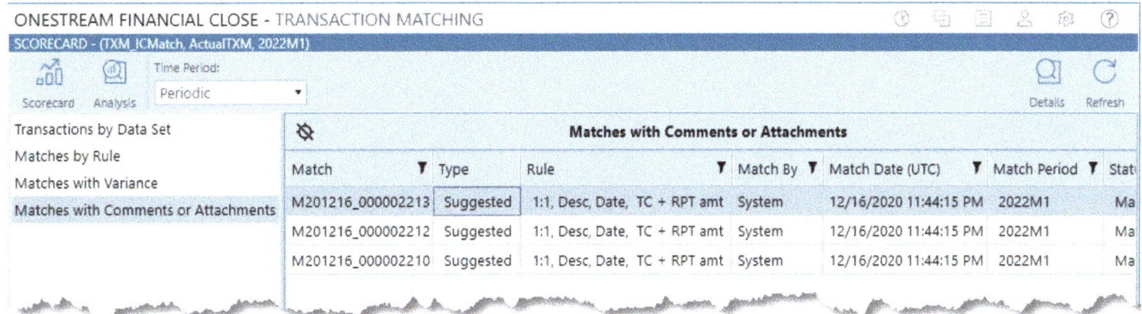

Figure 8.107

Conclusion

As this book comes to an end, hopefully we were able to provide you with insight into all the key areas of the OneStream Financial Close (OFC) solutions. Our intent was for you to walk away with the knowledge to set up and administer the solutions, implement best practices, and understand how Users will utilize the system on a regular basis. We covered the two key processes – Account Reconciliations and Transaction Matching – but we anticipate future growth around OFC. The intent for this suite of solutions is to grow into a full Record-to-Report process to drive the full Financial Close process. Thank you for taking the time to read this book, and we wish you well in your Close endeavors!

Index

OneStream Foundation Handbook

The Definitive Reference to Design, Configure and Support Your OneStream Platform.

OneStream is a modern, unified platform that is revolutionizing Corporate Performance Management. This proven alternative to fragmented legacy applications is designed to simplify processes for the most sophisticated, global enterprises. Hundreds of the world's leading companies are turning to OneStream to help with reporting and understanding financial data.

In this practical guide, The Architect Factory team at OneStream Software explains each part of an implementation, and the design of solutions. Readers will learn the core guiding principles for implementing OneStream from the company's top team of experts. Beyond offering a training guide, the focus of this book is on the 'why' of design and building an application.

- Manage your Implementation with the OneStream methodology
- Understand Design and Build concepts
- Build solutions for the Consolidation of financial data, and develop Planning models
- Create Data Integration solutions that will feed your models
- Develop Workflows to guide and manage your End-Users
- Advance your solutions with Rules and Security
- Take advantage of detailed Data Reporting using tools such as Analytic Blend, Advanced Excel reporting, and Dashboarding
- Tune Performance, and optimize your application

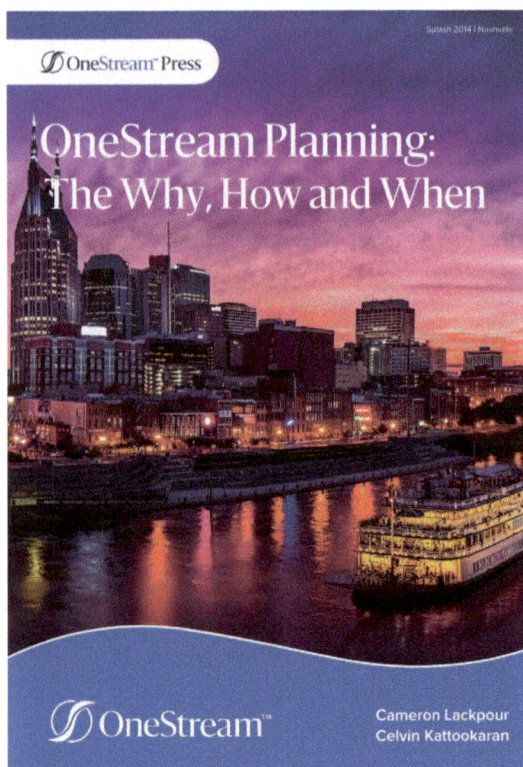

OneStream Finance Rules and Calculations Handbook

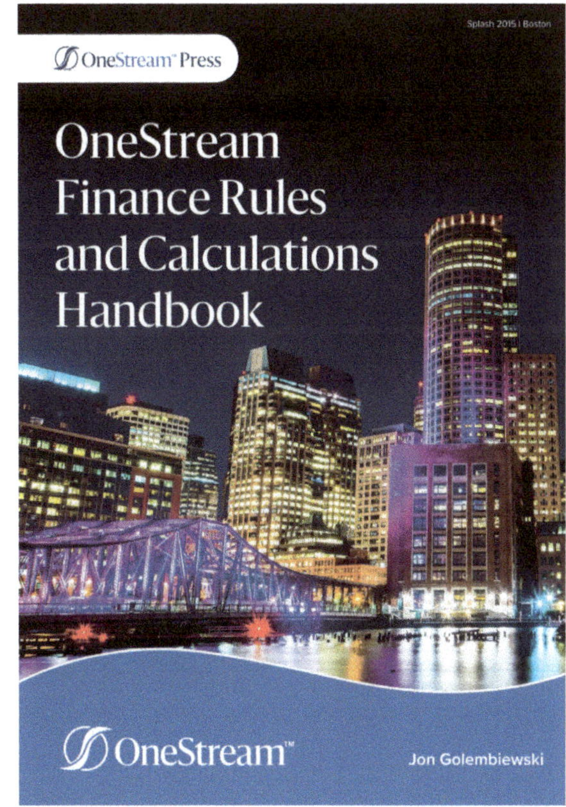

Hundreds of companies have turned to OneStream to solve complex planning, consolidation and operational reporting needs. OneStream's unique ability to provide a multitude of solutions across dozens of industries is largely due to its dynamic Finance Engine which provides the capability to add industry- and company-specific business intelligence to data. Employing the full power of the Finance Engine allows companies to extend the platform and fully exploit the power of their investment.

Aimed at everyone from novices to seasoned veterans, this handbook—by OneStream Distinguished Architect Jon Golembiewski—will break down the Finance Engine and outline how to write Finance Business Rules and Calculations. Its insights will help propel OneStream applications to the next level.

- Fundamentals of the Finance Engine
- Detailed breakdown of the Cube and Data
- A look under the hood of the api.Data.Calculate function
- Techniques for tackling complex calculation requirements
- How to use the Custom Calculate function to make calculations dynamic
- How to write calculations for optimal performance
- How to troubleshoot calculations
- How to solve and avoid common errors and pitfalls
- Real-world calculation examples with detailed explanations
- A full application with all referenced code examples is available to download

www.ingramcontent.com/pod-product-compliance
Lightning Source LLC
Chambersburg PA
CBHW041621220326
41598CB00046BA/7430
* 9 7 8 1 8 3 8 2 5 2 8 4 7 *